Emmert's

FAVORITE RECIPES *of American Home Economics Teachers*

MEATS

EDITION
including SEAFOOD • POULTRY

Table of Contents

Edited by...

RUTH STOVALL—Managing Editor

Ruth Stovall is Managing Editor of the Meats Edition of Favorite Recipes of American Home Economics Teachers. She is presently State Supervisor of Home Economics for Alabama. She received her B. S. in Home Economics from Alabama College and her M. S. in Education from Cornell University. She is a former teacher of Vocational Home Economics; past Secretary and past president, National Association of State Supervisors of Home Economics; National Treasurer, American Home Economics Association; member of Advisory Boards of Forecast Magazine; past member of Advisory Board of Seventeen Magazine; author of many articles in her field; member of Omicron Nu, Pi Lambda Theta, Kappa Delta Pi and Delta Kappa Gamma; and listed in "Who's Who in American Education", 1959-1961.

The Supervisory Editor is Ruth McRae Carlson, past Supervising Director of Home Economics Curriculum for the District of Columbia. Her home economics background includes: B. S. and M. S. in Education, University of Maryland; advanced graduate work, University of Maryland, Columbia University and Pennsylvania State University; former home economics teacher, past president of the District of Columbia Home Economics Association; past Chairman of the Elementary, Secondary and Adult Section of the American Home Economics Association; member, Home Economics Advisory Board for the Wool Bureau, New York City; member of Advisory Board of Seventeen Magazine; author of booklet, "Meals Using Low Cost Foods"; and member of Phi Kappa Phi, Omicron Nu, Delta Kappa Gamma and Zonta International Service Club for Women.

RUTH McRAE CARLSON—Supervisory Editor

BOARD OF ADVISORY EDITORS

MARTHA ARTIST
Supervisor of Homemaking Education
Omaha Board of Education

DOROTHY E. BREVOORT
State Supervisor
Home Economics Education
State of New Jersey

ANNE G. EIFLER
Supervisor, School Lunch
and Nutrition
Pennsylvania Department
of Public Instruction

GENEVEVE K. JOHNSTON
Consultant, Home Economics
Minneapolis Board of Education

CLIO S. REINWALD
Coordinator, Home Education
State of Pennsylvania

DOROTHY M. SCHNELL
Chief, Bureau of Homemaking Education
State of California

ANORMALLEE WAY
Supervisor, School Lunch
Washington County
Past State F.H.A., N.H.A. Supervisor
State of Maryland

MARY LOIS WILLIAMSON
State Director, Home Economics
State of Kentucky

Foreword

"May I have your recipe?" is the usual request of the homemaker who wants to try a recipe someone else has used successfully.

The recipes in this collection have been used by high school home economics teachers and found to be good enough to label "a favorite recipe." These recipes were obtained as a service to homemakers who are seeking varied, but reliable ways of preparing meat, fish, and poultry.

These recipes have not been processed through a test kitchen but have been tried in the home economics teacher's own kitchen. If you have questions or comments about a recipe, you may write to the teacher who submitted it.

One of the joys of the homemaker is preparing appetizing and nutritious food for her family. Good food contributes to the health, happiness, and stability of families. You will be pleased to find in this cookbook sufficient variety to meet the needs of American families everywhere. Both conventional and convenience foods have been used and the methods range from the simple to the gourmet type. There are recipes to interest both the beginner and the expert with recipes that are quickly prepared and those that take longer. Among this collection of recipes are the well-liked traditional ones of the regions, together with many foreign recipes.

Study these recipes, try them, and share them. This unique collection will become one of your prized possessions.

Appreciation is extended to the U. S. Department of Agriculture and the National Livestock and Meat Board for some of the educational materials used in this book.

Ruth McRae Carlson

Ruth Stovall

Meat - An Important Food!

Meat is the food around which meals are usually planned, prepared and served. Meat occupies a central place in the meal since it contains many of the nutrients essential to health and is a food well-liked by most people.

Meat is a relatively expensive item in the food budget. The homemaker, therefore, recognizes the need to buy meat wisely, care for it properly and prepare it so as to conserve the nutrients and develop the flavor. The wise homemaker will plan her meat budget carefully, shop with understanding and prepare the meats in a variety of nutritious and appetizing ways to please her family.

Guides to Meat Buying

In buying meat, look for the *Meat Inspection Stamp,* the *Meat Grade and Brand names stamp,* and observe the appearance of the meat.

The round purple stamp used for marking meat to show that it has passed federal inspection. The number appearing on the stamp indicates the establishment.

The round purple stamp on meat shows it has passed federal inspection. This *Meat Inspection Stamp* is the consumer's guarantee that the meat is from healthy animals and has been processed under sanitary conditions. The marking fluid used for this stamp is a vegetable color and is harmless. It need not be trimmed from the meat.

The *meat Grade and Brand name* stamp indicates the grade and the brand name of the packer and retailer and the Grade name of the U.S. Department of Agriculture. Information on the grades and brand names of the packers and retailers may be obtained from the particular company. Information on the Government grades of meat may be obtained from the meat Grading Branch, Livestock Division, Agricultural Marketing Service, United States Department of Agriculture, Washington 25, D.C.

The quality of meat may be judged to some extent by appearance. The best quality meat has well-marbilized lean, (intermingling of fat with lean) fine grained texture and has a color typical of the particular meat. (See Beef, Veal, Lamb and Pork sections.)

Aging of Meat

The purpose of aging meat is to develop certain factors of palatability, particularly tenderness and flavor. The two meats most frequently aged are high quality beef and mutton. Aging does not improve veal and pork. Lamb of high quality is sometimes aged. To be suitable for aging the meat must have a fairly thick covering of fat to prevent discoloration of the lean and to keep evaporation to a minimum. This means that only the higher grades of beef, mutton and lamb have a sufficiently thick fat covering to stand aging for the necessary period of from three to six weeks at temperatures of from 34°F. to 38°F. Those who like aged meat usually prefer to buy it already aged at their retail markets.

Usually only the ribs and loins of beef, lamb and mutton are aged. After aging, they are carefully trimmed, then cut into roasts or steaks, or in the case of lamb, into chops.

Guides to Meat Care

FRESH MEAT

Place fresh meat in the coldest part of the refrigerator or in the meat compartment. The temperature should be as low as possible without actually freezing the meat.

Unless meat is to be used on the same day it is purchased, it should be removed from the market wrapping paper and stored unwrapped or loosely wrapped in waxed paper or aluminum foil.

If fresh meat is to be kept for three or more days, it should be frozen. To freeze fresh meat, wrap it in special freezing wrap or bags but not in ordinary waxed paper. To insure easy separation before thawing, separate individual cuts of meat such as chops, steaks and ground patties. Two pieces of freezer paper make a satisfactory separation. Wrap together the desired number of servings into larger packages.

Remember that fresh meat that is frozen for longer storage should be frozen and stored at 0°F. or lower. The frozen food storage or ice cube section of most household refrigerators is not designed for rapid freezing and will not substitute for a home freezer when the meat is to be frozen and stored for longer than one week.

PROCESSED MEAT

Store cured and ready-to-serve meats in the coldest part of the refrigerator. Store in the original wrapper. Keep ready-to-serve meats not longer than one week. Keep cured meats not longer than one to two weeks (hams, picnics, loin).

It is not advisable to freeze cured meats and ready-to-serve meats because the salt in the meat favors the development of rancidity when the meat is frozen. The texture of some cured meats, such as frankfurters, is affected by freezing. When freezing is absolutely necessary, wrap properly and limit the storage time to not more than sixty days.

Canned hams should not be frozen. Store unopened in the refrigerator until ready to use.

FROZEN MEAT

Meats which have been properly wrapped and promptly frozen under recommended freezing conditions should be stored at 0°F. or lower for periods not to exceed those in the following table:

Meat	Maximum Storage Time*
	Months
Beef	6 to 12
Lamb and Veal	6 to 9
Fresh Pork	3 to 6
Ground Beef and Lamb	3 to 4
Ground Pork	1 to 3

*This range in maximum storage time reflects differences in recommendations of various authorities using meat from different sources.

COOKED MEAT

Cooked meat should be chilled rapidly, then covered and stored in the coldest part of the refrigerator.

Guides to Meat Cookery

The tenderness of a meat cut determines the method or methods of cooking to insure satisfaction. Tender cuts of meat are best when cooked by dry heat method, such as roasting, broiling, panbroiling and frying. Less tender cuts are made tender by cooking with moist heat such as braising and stewing.

In general, it is advisable to cook meat slowly. Cooking meat at a low temperature results in a more tender, juicy and more flavorful product.

A meat thermometer is the most accurate guide to doneness and insures against overcooking or undercooking roasts, thick steaks, chops and poultry. In order to register the internal temperature accurately, the thermometer should be inserted into the thick portion of the meat at the beginning of the cooking period and allowed to remain until the cooking has been completed.

How to Roast

Any tender cut of beef, veal, pork, or lamb may be roasted. The steps in this method of cooking are as follows: *(1) Season with salt and pepper, if desired.* It matters little whether a roast is salted before or during cooking because when it is done, the salt has penetrated only to a depth of about half an inch. *(2) Place meat, fat side up, on rack in open shallow roasting pan.* The rack holds the roast out of the drippings; with the fat on top, the roast will do its own basting. *(3) Insert a meat thermometer so that its bulb is in the center of the largest muscle.* The bulb should not touch bone or rest in fat. *(4) Add no water and do not cover.* Roasting is a dry heat method of cooking, and if the pan is covered or water added, the meat will become a pot-roast. *(5) Roast in a slow oven— 300° to 350° F.* The oven may be started just as the roast is put in it. *(6) Roast to the desired degree of doneness.* There will be no overcooking nor undercooking if a meat thermometer is used.

How to Broil

Tender beef steaks, lamb or mutton chops, sliced ham or bacon, and ground beef or lamb are suitable for broiling. Fresh pork and veal are seldom broiled. Steaks and chops should be cut at least an inch thick for best broiling and a slice of ham at least half an inch. These steps show how to broil: *(1) Turn the oven regulator to "broil."* The broiler may be preheated or not, as desired. With some broilers thick steaks or chops may be cooked without preheating the broiler. *(2) Place meat on rack of broiler pan, two to three inches from the heat.* Steaks or chops one and a half to two inches thick should be at least three inches from the heat; those one inch or less in thickness, about two inches. *(3) Broil until top side is brown.* The meat should be approximately half done by the time it is browned on top. *(4) Season the top side with salt and pepper.* For a slice of ham or bacon this step would be omitted. Steaks and chops brown better if browned before salting. *(5) Turn and brown the other side.* For determining accurately the degree of doneness of a thick steak, a meat thermometer may be used; for thick chops or patties, it may be used in one of them. *(6) Season and serve at once.* To keep broiled meats hot, the platter should be heated.

How to Panbroil

The same tender cuts suitable for broiling may be panbroiled or griddle-broiled. When cuts are very thin, panbroiling or griddle-broiling may even be preferred. Panbroiling is also a convenient method for a small steak or a few chops. Follow these steps, whether panbroiling or griddle-broiling: *(1) Place meat in heavy frying-pan or on griddle. Cook slowly.* The pan or griddle need not be sizzling hot nor is it necessary to preheat it. The meat merely starts cooking more quickly if it is warm or hot at the beginning. *(2) Do not add fat or water. Do not cover.* Most meat cuts have enough fat to prevent their sticking; if fat is added they will be fried. *(3) Turn occasionally.* Since the meat is in contact with the hot metal of the pan or griddle, turning more than once is essential for even cooking. *(4) Pour off or remove fat as it accumulates.* If fat is permitted to collect, the meat will fry instead of panbroil or griddle-broil. *(5) Brown meat on both sides.* It does not need to be seared or browned quickly at the beginning—searing does not hold in meat juices—a gradual browning is better. *(6) Do not overcook. Season and serve at once.*

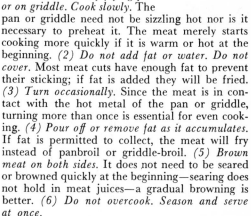

How to Fry

Comparatively thin pieces of tender meat, or that made tender by pounding, scoring, cubing, or grinding, and left over meat may be fried. When a small amount of fat is added or allowed to accumulate during cooking, the method is called *frying, panfrying* or *sauteing.* When the meat is immersed in fat, it is called *deep-fat frying.*

TO PANFRY: *(1) Use a heavy frying-pan.* The fat will heat more evenly and the meat cook more uniformly if a heavy pan is used. *(2) Brown meat on both sides in a small amount of fat.* Any meat that has a coating of flour, meal or egg and crumbs will need fat added; also, meats that are very low in fat, such as liver or cubed steak, will need additional fat. On the other hand, it will not be necessary to add fat for a slice of ham or for a pork chop unless the chop is breaded. *(3) Season with salt and pepper.* If the meat is cooked with a coating, the seasoning may be added to the coating ingredients, otherwise the meat is seasoned after browning. *(4) Do not cover the meat.* If covered, the meat is braised, and its crispness, which is one object in frying, is lost. It is true that the meat will be less tender than if a cover is used; but in frying, there is some sacrifice of tenderness in order to obtain crispness and a desired flavor. *(5) Cook at moderate temperature until done, turning occasionally.* When fat smokes it is burning or breaking down. Such a temperature is not only too high for the fat but also for the meat. A frying thermometer is helpful in determining the temperature of the fat. The object in all frying is to cook the meat through while it is browning. Turning is necessary in panfrying, as it is in panbroiling, to insure even cooking.

TO DEEP-FAT FRY: *(1) Use a deep kettle and a frying basket.* There should be enough fat to completely cover the meat; a wire basket is needed to lower the meat into the fat and to remove it from the fat when done. *(2) Heat fat to frying temperature.* Suitable temperatures for deep-fat frying meat range from 300° to 350° F., depending upon the size of the pieces and whether it is uncooked or leftover meat. A frying thermometer is essential to successful deep-fat frying, unless an automatically controlled fryer is used. *(3) Using the frying basket, lower a few uniform pieces of meat at a time, gradually, into the hot fat.* Before placing in the basket, the meat may be coated with egg and crumbs or a batter, or dredged with flour or corn meal. This increases the browning and adds to the crispness and flavor. *(4) Brown meat and cook it through.* When the meat is covered with fat, no turning is necessary and both sides are cooked at once. The cooking time, therefore, is less than in panfrying. *(5) When done, drain fat from meat into kettle before removing meat from basket. (6) Strain fat through cloth and cool. Cover and store in refrigerator.*

Braising is a method for cooking less-tender meat cuts. Some tender cuts also are best if braised. These include: Pork chops, steaks and cutlets; veal chops, steaks and cutlets; and pork liver. *(1) Brown meat slowly on all sides in heavy utensil.* The browning develops flavor and color. To intensify the browning, the meat may be dredged with flour—then it is necessary to add fat to the pan. A slow brown stays on the meat better than a quick brown at high temperature. *(2) Season with salt, pepper, herbs, spices and vegetables.* In moist heat cookery, the seasoning penetrates the meat to a greater extent than in roasting. The less-demanded cuts and lower grades of meat are the ones adapted to this method of cooking, and seasoning is important with these cuts. *(3) Add a small amount of liquid to less-tender cuts.* The liquid may be water, soup stock, vegetable juice, sour cream, or marinade. Liquid is not essential in braising tender cuts. *(4) Cover closely.* A tight-fitting lid holds in the steam needed for softening the connective tissue and making the meat tender.

(5) Cook at low temperature until tender. This means simmering—not boiling. It may be done on top of the range or in a slow oven—not above 300° F. *(6) Make sauce or gravy from the liquid in the pan.* The gravy is an essential part of any braised meat dish. It contains meat flavors and soluble food nutrients, and should be used to accompany the meat.

Both large cuts and stews are prepared by cooking in liquid. This is another method adapted to the less-tender cuts.

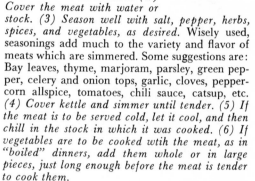

LARGE CUTS: *(1) Brown meat on all sides, if desired.* The browning develops flavor and increases color. Corned beef and cured pork, however, need not be browned. *(2) Cover the meat with water or stock. (3) Season well with salt, pepper, herbs, spices, and vegetables, as desired.* Wisely used, seasonings add much to the variety and flavor of meats which are simmered. Some suggestions are: Bay leaves, thyme, marjoram, parsley, green pepper, celery and onion tops, garlic, cloves, peppercorn allspice, tomatoes, chili sauce, catsup, etc. *(4) Cover kettle and simmer until tender. (5) If the meat is to be served cold, let it cool, and then chill in the stock in which it was cooked. (6) If vegetables are to be cooked wtih the meat, as in "boiled" dinners, add them whole or in large pieces, just long enough before the meat is tender to cook them.*

STEWS: *(1) Cut meat in uniform pieces, usually one- to two-inch cubes.* If desired, the meat may be cut into rectangular pieces or into long narrow strips. *(2) If a brown stew is desired, brown meat cubes on all sides.* Dredging in flour intensifies the browning. If meat is floured, fat must be added before browning. If a light stew is preferred, browning is omitted. *(3) Add just enough water, vegetable juices or soup stock to cover the meat. (4) Season with salt, pepper, herbs, and spices. (5) Cover kettle closely and simmer until meat is tender. Do not boil.* It will require from one to three hours to cook the stew, depending upon the kind, quality and cut of meat. *(6) Add vegetables to the meat at the proper time so as not to overcook them.* The vegetables may be left whole, quartered or cut in small uniform pieces. Carrots, onions, potatoes, and peas are standard, though no better than many other combinations which have variety in color, texture and flavor. *(7) When done, remove meat and vegetables to a pan, platter or casserole and keep hot.* The peas or other bright green vegetables may be cooked separately for garnishing the stew. When cooked separately, boil quickly to protect the green color. *(8) Thicken the stock with flour made into a paste, using a small amount of cold water or stock.* Use two tablespoons of flour for each cup of stock in the pot. Bring to a hard boil. *(9) Pour hot gravy over the meat and vegetables or serve separately in a sauce boat. (10) If desired, make meat pie from the stew.* A meat pie is merely a stew with a top on it. The top may be made of pastry, shortcake, biscuits, mashed potatoes, or cereal.

MEAT CALORIE CHART

(Meat, cooked, without bone)

BEEF:

Pot roast or braised:

Lean and fat .... 3 ounces (1 thick or 2 thin slices, 4 by 2½   245
inches).

Lean only .... 2½ ounces (1 thick or 2 thin slices, 4 by 2   140
inches).

Oven roast:

Cut having relatively large proportion of fat
to lean:

Lean and fat .... 3 ounces (1 thick or 2 thin slices, 4 by 2½   390
inches).

Lean only.. 2 ounces (1 thick or 2 thin slices, 4 by 1½   120
inches).

Cut having relatively low proportion of fat
to lean:

Lean and fat.. 3 ounces (1 thick or 2 thin slices, 4 by 2½   220
inches).

Lean only.. 2½ ounces (1 thick or 2 thin slices, 4 by 2   130
inches).

Steak, broiled:

Lean and fat.. 3 ounces (1 piece, 4 by 2½ inches by ½ inch)   330
Lean only.. 2 ounces (1 piece, 4 by 1½ inches by ½ inch)   115

Hamburger patty:

Regular ground beef .... 3-ounce patty (about 4 patties per pound of   245
raw meat).

Lean ground round.............................. 3-ounce patty (about 4 patties per pound of   185
raw meat).

Corned beef, canned........................... 3 ounces (1 piece, 4 by 2½ inches by ½   180
inch).

Corned beef hash, canned............................... 3 ounces (scant half cup).................................   120
Dried beef, chipped............................. 2 ounces (about ⅓ cup).................................   115
Meat loaf... 2 ounces (1 piece, 4 by 2½ inches by ½   115
inch).

Beef and vegetable stew.......................... ½ cup   90
Beef potpie, baked............................ 1 pie, 4¼ inch diameter, about 8 ounces be-   460
fore baking.

Chili con carne, canned:

Without beans... ½ cup   255
With beans.. ½ cup   170

VEAL:

Cutlet, broiled, meat only.................... 3 ounces (1 piece, 4 by 2½ inches by ½   185
inch).

LAMB:

Chop (about 2½ chops to a pound, as purchased):

Lean and fat .... 4 ounces   405
Lean only.. 2⅝ ounces   140

Roast, leg:

Lean and fat.. 3 ounces (1 thick or 2 thin slices, 3½ by 3   235
inches).

Lean only.. 2½ ounces (1 thick or 2 thin slices, 3½ by   130
2½ inches).

PORK, FRESH:

Chop (about 3 chops to a pound, as purchased):

Lean and fat.. 2⅓ ounces   260
Lean only.. 2 ounces   130

MEAT CALORIE CHART (Continued)

		Number of calories
Roast, loin:		
Lean and fat	3 ounces (1 thick or 2 thin slices, 4 by 2½ inches).	310
Lean only	2⅖ ounces (1 thick or 2 thin slices, 3 by 2½ inches).	175
PORK, CURED:		
Ham:		
Lean and fat	3 ounces (1 thick or 2 thin slices, 4 by 2 inches).	290
Lean only	2⅕ ounces (1 thick or 2 thin slices, 3½ by 2 inches).	125
Bacon, broiled or fried	2 very thin slices	95
Sausage and variety and luncheon meats:		
Bologna sausage	2 ounces (2 very thin slices, 4 inches in diameter).	170
Liver sausage (liverwurst)	2 ounces (4 very thin slices, 3 inches in diameter).	175
Vienna sausage, canned	2 ounces (4 to 5 sausages)	135
Pork sausage, bulk	2 ounces (1 patty, 2 inches in diameter), 4 to 5 patties per pound, raw).	170
Liver, beef, fried (includes fat for frying)	2 ounces (1 thick piece, 3 by 2½ inches)	120
Heart, beef, braised, trimmed of fat	3 ounces (1 thick piece, 4 by 2½ inches)	160
Tongue, beef, boiled	3 ounces (1 thick piece, 4 by 2½ inches)	205
Frankfurter	1 frankfurter	155
Boiled ham (luncheon meat)	2 ounces (2 very thin slices, 3½ by 3½ inches).	170
Spiced ham, canned	2 ounces (2 thin slices, 3 by 2½ inches)	165
POULTRY, COOKED, WITHOUT BONE:		
Chicken:		
Broiled	3 ounces (about ¼ of a small broiler)	185
Fried	½ breast, 2⅘ ounces	215
	1 leg (thigh and drumstick), 3 ounces	245
Canned	3½ ounces (½ cup)	190
Poultry pie (with potatoes, peas, and gravy)	1 small pie, 4¼ inches in diameter (about 8 ounces before cooking).	485
FISH AND SHELLFISH:		
Bluefish, baked	3 ounces (1 piece, 3½ by 2 inches by ½ inch)	135
Clams, shelled:		
Raw meat, only	3 ounces (about 4 medium clams)	70
Canned, clams and juice	3 ounces (1 scant half cup, 3 medium clams and juice).	45
Crab meat, canned or cooked	3 ounces, ½ cup	90
Fish sticks, breaded, cooked, frozen (including breading and fat for frying)	4 ounces (5 fish sticks)	200
Haddock, fried (including fat for frying)	3 ounces (1 fillet, 4 by 2½ inches by ½ inch)	135
Mackerel:		
Broiled	3 ounces (1 piece, 4 by 3 inches by ½ inch	200
Canned	3 ounces, solids and liquid (about ⅗ cup)	155
Ocean perch, fried (including egg, breadcrumbs, and fat for frying)	3 ounces (1 piece, 4 by 2½ inches by ½ inch)	195
Oysters, shucked: Raw meat only	½ cup (6 to 10 medium-size oysters, selects)	80
Salmon:		
Broiled or baked	4 ounces (1 steak, 4½ by 2½ inches by ½ inch).	205
Canned (pink)	3 ounces, solids and liquid, about ⅗ cup)	120
Sardines, canned in oil	3 ounces, drained solids (5 to 7 medium sardines).	180
Shrimp, canned, meat only	3 ounces (about 17 medium shrimp)	110
Tunafish, canned in oil, meat only	3 ounces (about ⅖ cup)	170

(Courtesy of U. S. Dept. of Agriculture)

FAVORITE HERBS, SPICES, AND SEASONINGS
FOR USE WITH MEATS — SEAFOOD — POULTRY

DIRECTIONS: Herbs, spices, and seasonings, must be used sparingly to enhance, not overpow the flavor of meats, seafood, or poultry. The general rule as to quantity is one-fourth teaspo per pound for meats, seafood, and poultry or according to individual taste. Herbs and spic should be stored in tightly covered containers when not in use.

USE IN

HERB OR SPICE	APPETIZERS AND SAUCES	SOUPS	MEATS	SEAFOOD	POULTRY	SALAD
Allspice	Meat ball appetizers	Beef Oyster Stew	Pot Roasts Beef Stew Ham, Lamb	Oyster		
Basil	Crab spread	Turtle	Liver, Lamb Meat Loaf Heart Venison	Bluefish Halibut Mackerel	Goose Duck Turkey	
Barbecue spice seasoning	Barbecue sauces	Beef-vegetable	Broiled Steaks Chops Hamburgers	Fish	Chicken	
Bay Leaf		Beef Fish Chowders	Liver, Veal Spareribs Beef Stew Lamb, Goulash	Pickled Fish Shrimp Crab	Boiled Chicken	Seafood
Caraway Seed			Roast Pork Kidneys Sauerbraten	Tuna Casseroles	Roast Goose	
Cayenne	Gravies	Chowders	Pork Chops	Oysters Shell Fish	Creamed Chicken	Chicken Tuna
Celery (Salt, Flakes, Seeds)	Ham Spread	Oyster Stew Bouillon	Meat Loaf Meat Stews Pot Roasts	Codfish	Chicken Croquettes Chicken Pie	Tuna
Chili		Chowders	Chili Con Carne		Chicken with Rice Casserole	
Cloves		Beef	Ham Pork Roasts Boiled Tongue	Baked Fish	Chicken a la King Roasted Chicken	
Curry Powder		Clam Chowder Chicken Soup	Lamb Veal	Shrimp Baked Fish	Chicken Hash	
Dill	Topping for Meat Canapes		Lamb Chops Lamb Steaks	Shell Fish		
Fennel Seed				Boiled Fish		
Garlic (Liquid, Powder, Salt)	Clam Dip Barbecue Sauce	Use Sparingly	Steaks, Stews Italian and French Meat Dishes	Any Fish	Chicken	

(Continued on Next Pag

USE IN

HERB OR SPICE	APPETIZERS AND SAUCES	SOUPS	MEATS	SEAFOOD	POULTRY	SALAD
Ginger			Boiled Beef Lamb Veal		Sauted or Baked Chicken Cornish Hen, Squab	
Marjoram		Oyster Stew	Pot Roasts Stews Lamb	Creamed Crab Scallops Broiled Fish		Chicken Seafood
Mint	Lamb and Fish Sauces	Beef				
Mustard	Meat Dips Sauces for Ham	Beef-Onion	Pickled Meat Ham Kidney	Casseroles Boiled Fish Oysters, Shrimp		Garnish for Lobster Shrimp
Nutmeg	Chopped Oysters	Cream of Chicken	Salisbury Steak Meat Loaf		Chicken	
Onion—(Flakes, Minced, Powder, Salt)	When onion flavor is desired		Steaks Stews Hamburgers	Fried Shrimp		
Oregano	Meat sauces	Beef	Pork, Veal Lamb Swiss Steak	Seafood Stuffing	Fried Chicken	Seafood
Paprika	Seafood Dip Smoked Salmon	Chicken soup Chowders	Hungarian Goulash	Shellfish	Poultry	
Parsley Flakes	Fish Canapes		Stews Meat Patties		Wild Fowl Poultry	Poultry
Pepper	Adds flavor to most foods					
Poultry Seasonings	Gravies and Stuffings		Meat Patties			
Rosemary		Turtle Chicken Meat	Kidneys Veal, Stews Lamb	Creamed Shellfish	Chicken Fricassee	
Saffron	Poultry Stuffing	Chicken Soup Stock	Lamb, Veal Sausage	Halibut Sole	Chicken	Seafood
Sage	Meat Sauces and Gravies Baked Fish Stuffing	Consomme Chowders	Cold Roast Beef Stews Pork Dishes	Baked Fish	Duck	
Savory	Chicken and Fish Sauces Liver Pastes	Fish Chowders	Hamburgers Lamb Roasts Veal, Pork	Baked or Broiled Fish		
Tarragon	Sauces for meats Canape mixture		Veal Sweetbreads	Creamed Seafood dishes	Turkey Game Chicken	Chicken
Thyme	Sauces for meats	Chowders Oyster Stew				

WE gratefully acknowledge our indebtedness to the Durkee Famous Foods, House of Herbs, Inc., McCormick and Company, and John Wagner and Sons, Inc. for literature on the use of herbs, spices, and seasonings.

Abbreviations Used in This Book

Cup .... c.   Gallon .... gal.

Tablespoon .... T.   Large .... lge.

Teaspoon .... t.   Package .... pkg.

Pound .... lb.   Square .... sq.

Ounce .... oz.   Dozen .... doz.

Degrees Fahrenheit .... °F.   Slice .... sl.

Minutes .... min.   Pint .... pt.

Seconds .... sec.   Quart .... qt.

In measuring, remember . . .

3 t. = 1 T.   2 c. sugar = 1 lb.

2 T. = 1/8 c.   5/8 c. = 1/2 c. + 2 T.

4 T. = 1/4 c.   7/8 c. = 3/4 c. + 2 T.

8 T. = 1/2 c.   2 2/3 c. powdered sugar = 1 lb.

16 T. = 1 c.   2 2/3 c. brown sugar = 1 lb.

5 T. + 1 t. = 1/3 c.   4 c. sifted flour = 1 lb.

12 T. = 3/4 c.   1 lb. butter = 2 c . or 4 sticks

4 oz. = 1/2 c.   2 pts = 1 qt.

8 oz. = 1 c.   1 qt. = 4 c.

16 oz. = 1 lb.   A Few Grains = Less than 1/8 t.

1 oz. = 2 T. fat or liquid   Pinch is as much as can be taken

2 c. fat = 1 lb.   between tip of finger and thumb.

2 c. = 1 pt.   Speck = Less than 1/8 t.

Substitutions

1 tablespoon *cornstarch* (for thickening) = 2 tablespoons flour (approximately).

1 cup sifted *all-purpose flour* = 1 cup plus 2 tablespoons sifted cake flour.

1 cup sifted *cake flour* = 1 cup minus 2 tablespoons sifted all-purpose flour.

1 teaspoon *baking powder* = 1/4 teaspoon baking soda plus 1/2 teaspoon cream of tartar.

1 cup *bottled milk* = 1/2 cup evaporated milk plus 1/2 cup water.

1 cup *sour milk* = a cup sweet milk into which 1 tablespoon vinegar or lemon juice
                has been stirred; or 1 cup buttermilk.

1 cup *sweet milk* = 1 cup sour milk or buttermilk plus 1/2 teaspoon baking soda.

1 cup *canned tomatoes* = about 1 1/3 cups cut up fresh tomatoes, simmered 10 minutes.

3/4 cup *cracker crumbs* = 1 cup bread crumbs.

1 cup *cream, sour, heavy* = 1/3 cup butter and 2/3 cup milk in any sour-milk recipe.

1 cup *cream, sour, thin* = 3 tablespoons butter and 3/4 cup milk in sour-milk recipe.

Order Blanks For Additional Books
on Page 384

Beef and Variety Meats

BEEF CHART
Beef Cuts and How to Cook Them

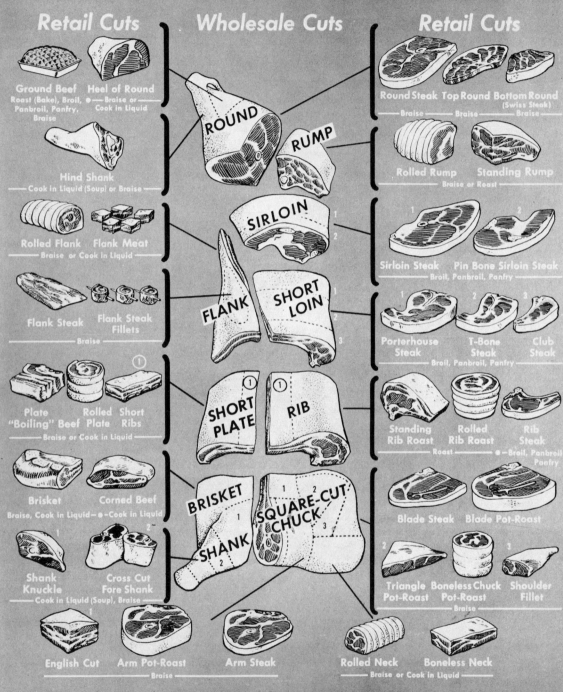

Retail Cuts   **Wholesale Cuts**   **Retail Cuts**

Ground Beef — Roast (Bake), Broil, Panbroil, Pantry, Braise

Heel of Round — Braise or Cook in Liquid

ROUND

RUMP

Round Steak — Braise

Top Round — Braise

Bottom Round (Swiss Steak) — Braise

Hind Shank — Cook in Liquid (Soup) or Braise

Rolled Rump   Standing Rump — Braise or Roast

SIRLOIN

Rolled Flank   Flank Meat — Braise or Cook in Liquid

Sirloin Steak   Pin Bone Sirloin Steak — Broil, Panbroil, Panfry

FLANK   SHORT LOIN

Flank Steak   Flank Steak Fillets — Braise

Porterhouse Steak   T-Bone Steak   Club Steak — Broil, Panbroil, Panfry

SHORT PLATE   RIB

Plate "Boiling" Beef   Rolled Plate   Short Ribs — Braise or Cook in Liquid

Standing Rib Roast   Rolled Rib Roast   Rib Steak — Roast — Broil, Panbroil, Panfry

BRISKET   SQUARE-CUT CHUCK

Brisket   Corned Beef — Braise, Cook in Liquid — Cook in Liquid

SHANK

Blade Steak   Blade Pot-Roast

Shank Knuckle   Cross Cut Fore Shank — Cook in Liquid (Soup), Braise

Triangle Pot-Roast   Boneless Chuck Pot-Roast   Shoulder Fillet — Braise

English Cut   Arm Pot-Roast   Arm Steak — Braise

Rolled Neck   Boneless Neck — Braise or Cook in Liquid

NATIONAL LIVE STOCK AND MEAT BOARD

Selection of BEEF Cuts

WHOLESALE CUTS	RETAIL CUTS	CHARACTERISTICS	COOKING METHODS
Round (and Rump)	Round Steak (full cut)	Round or oval in shape with small round bone. One large muscle, three smaller ones.	Braise
	Top Round Steak or Pot Roast	Most tender portion of round. Is one large muscle.	Braise; roast; panfry
	Bottom Round Steak or Pot Roast	Not so tender as top round. Distinguished from top round by having two muscles.	Braise
	Tip Roast or Steak	Triangular cut; roast may contain kneecap. Steaks are boneless.	Braise; roast; broil; panbroil; panfry
	Standing Rump	Triangular in shape; contains portions of aitch (rump) bone and tail bone. Knuckle end of leg (round) bone usually removed.	Braise; roast (high quality)
	Rolled Rump	Boneless roll.	Braise; roast (high quality)
	Heel of Round	Boneless wedge-shaped cut from lower part of round. Weighs 4 to 8 pounds. Has very little fat and is least tender cut of round.	Braise; cook in liquid
	Hind Shank	Bony, considerable connective tissue, rich in extractives.	Cook in liquid (soup)
Sirloin	Sirloin Steak	Contains portions of back bone and hip bone. Wide variation in bone and muscle structure of the various steaks.	Broil; panbroil; panfry
	Pinbone Sirloin Steak	Lies next to the porterhouse. Contains pin bone which is the forward end of hip bone.	Broil; panbroil; panfry
	Boneless Sirloin Steak	Any boneless steak from the sirloin.	Broil; panbroil; panfry
Short Loin	Porterhouse Steak	Largest steak in short loin. Loin strip and tenderloin muscles. T-shaped bone. Tenderloin larger in porterhouse than in other short loin steaks.	Broil; panbroil; panfry
	T-Bone Steak	Same as porterhouse except tenderloin is smaller (porterhouse and T-bone used more or less interchangeably).	Broil; panbroil; panfry
	Club (Delmonico) Steak	Triangular-shaped; smallest steak in short loin. Tenderloin has practically disappeared.	Broil; panbroil; panfry
	Tenderloin Roast or Steak	Boneless tapering muscle. Most tender cut beef.	Roast; broil; panbroil; panfry
Flank	Flank Steak	Oval-shaped boneless steak weighing ¾ to 1½ pounds. Muscles run lengthwise; usually scored to shorten muscle fibers. Less tender cut.	Braise
	Flank Steak Fillets	Sections of flank steak rolled and fastened with skewers.	Braise
	Flank Meat	Boneless. Coarse fibers. May be rolled, cut into stew or ground.	Braise; cook in liquid
Rib	Standing Rib Roast (Short Cut)	Contains two or more ribs from which short ribs and chine bone have been removed. Comparable to rib roast served in restaurants.	Roast
	Rolled Rib Roast	Boneless roll. Outer cover of roll consists largely of thin plate meat wrapped around rib eye.	Roast
	Rib Steak	Contains rib eye and may contain rib bone.	Broil; panbroil; panfry
	Short Ribs	Cut from ends of ribs; layers of lean and fat.	Braise; cook in liquid
Short Plate	Plate "Boiling" Beef	Cut across plate parallel with ribs.	Braise; cook in liquid
	Rolled Plate	When rolled the absence of the rib eye distinguishes this cut from the rolled rib.	Braise; cook in liquid
	Short Ribs	Cut from ends of ribs; layers of lean and fat.	Braise; cook in liquid
Square-Cut Chuck	Arm Pot-Roast or Steak	Has a round bone and cross sections of 3-5 ribs. A small round muscle near the round bone is surrounded by connective tissue.	Braise
	Blade Pot-Roast or Steak	Pot-roast contains portions of rib and blade bones. Steaks cut between ribs will not contain rib bone.	Braise
	Boneless Chuck	Any part of the square-cut chuck (except the neck) from which the bones have been removed.	Braise
	Boneless Neck	Any part of the neck without the neck bone.	Braise; cook in liquid
	English (Boston) Cut	A rectangular piece cut across 2 or 3 chuck ribs.	Braise
Brisket	Brisket	Layers of lean and fat. Presence of breast bone sure indication that cut is from the brisket.	Braise; cook in liquid
	Boneless Brisket	Same as above with ribs and breast bone removed.	Braise; cook in liquid
Fore Shank	Shank Knuckle	Knuckle or upper end of fore shank.	Cook in liquid; braise
	Shank Cross-Cuts	Small pieces cut across shank bone.	Braise; cook in liquid
Ground Beef	Loaf and Patties	Usually made from flank, shank, plate and chuck.	Roast (bake); broil; panbroil; panfry; braise

BEEF CUTS—Their Appearance and

Blade Pot-Roast (Chuck)

Braise

Standing Rib

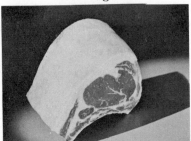

Roast

Porterhouse Steak

Broil, Panbroil, Panfry

Arm Pot-Roast (Chuck)

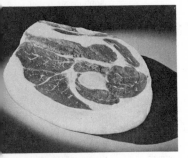

Braise

Rib Steak

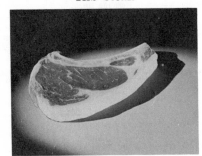

Broil, Panbroil, Panfry

T-Bone Steak

Broil, Panbroil, Panfry

Boneless Chuck

Braise

Rolled Rib

Roast

Club Steak

Broil, Panbroil, Panfry

Shank Cross Cuts

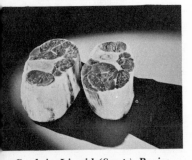

Cook in Liquid (Soup), Braise

Brisket (Bone In)

Braise, Cook in Liquid

Corned Beef (Brisket)

Cook in Liquid

the Best Methods for Cooking Them

Sirloin Steak

Broil, Panbroil, Panfry

Round Steak (Full Cut)

Braise

Standing Rump

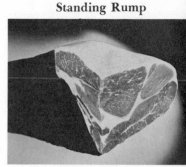

Braise, Roast (high quality)

Pinbone Sirloin Steak

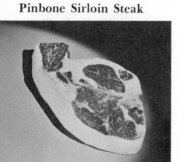

Broil, Panbroil, Panfry

Top Round Steak

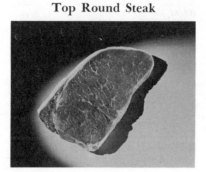

Panfry, Braise

Rolled Rump

Braise, Roast (high quality)

English Cut (Chuck)

Braise

Bottom Round Steak

Braise

Heel of Round

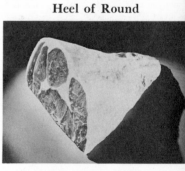

Braise, Cook in Liquid

Plate Beef

Braise, Cook in Liquid

Short Ribs

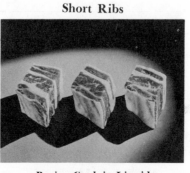

Braise, Cook in Liquid

Flank Steak

Braise

BEEF—Methods of Cooking

HIGH QUALITY BEEF has a smooth covering of firm creamy white fat evenly distributed over the exterior. The lean of this beef should be uniform and bright. The color may range from pale red to deep blood red. It is well marbled with creamy white fat. The texture of the lean is firm, velvety in appearance and fine in grain. The bones in young beef are reddish and porous; in older animals, white and flinty.

Different grades and cuts of beef vary greatly in tenderness. This is why it is necessary to select beef cuts with the cooking methods in mind, or adapt the cooking method to the cut selected.

All of the thick cuts of Prime and Choice grades of beef, excepting the outside round, the outside chuck and the neck, are tender enough to be cooked by dry heat, especially if low temperatures are used. Beef that has been properly aged is particularly tender, palatable and flavorful. Only the higher grades of beef are aged for the market. On the other hand, the cuts of Utility grade beef are best if cooked by moist heat. With Commercial beef, the grade next to Good, the tender cuts—rib, short loin and sirloin—are cooked by dry heat methods, as roasting, broiling, panbroiling and frying; while the less-tender cuts are cooked by moist heat methods, as braising and cooking in liquid.

Less-tender meat may be ground and then cooked by the same methods as the tender cuts—roasting, broiling, panbroiling or frying. Less-tender steaks may be made tender by pounding, scoring, cubing, etc. Beef is cooked rare, medium and well done, depending on your preference.

TIME-TABLE FOR COOKING BEEF [1]

CUT	ROASTED AT 300° F. OVEN TEMPERATURE		BROILED [2]		BRAISED	COOKED IN LIQUID
	Meat Thermometer Reading	Time	Meat Thermometer Reading	Total Time	Total Time	Total Time
Standing Ribs	Degrees F. 140 (rare)	Minutes per lb. 18 to 20	Degrees F.	Minutes	Hours	Hours
Standing Ribs	160 (medium)	22 to 25				
Standing Ribs	170 (well)	27 to 30				
Rolled Ribs	Same as above	Add 10 to 15				
Blade, 3rd to 5th Rib (high quality only)	150-170	25 to 30				
Rump (high quality only)	150-170	25 to 30				
Tenderloin	140-170	20 to 25				
Beef Loaf	160-170	25 to 30				
Steaks (1 inch)			140 (rare) 160 (medium)	15 to 20 20 to 30		
Steaks (1½ inch)			140 (rare) 160 (medium)	25 to 35 35 to 50		
Steaks (2 inch)			140 (rare) 160 (medium)	30 to 40 50 to 70		
Beef Patties (1 inch)			140 (rare) 160 (medium)	12 to 15 18 to 20		
Pot-Roasts						
Arm or Blade					3 to 4	
Rump					3 to 4	
Swiss Steak					2 to 3	
Corned Beef						3½ to 5
Fresh Beef					3 to 4	3 to 4
Stew						2 to 3

[1] *For frying see discussion page 6.*

[2] *Panbroiling or griddle-broiling requires approximately one-half the time for broiling.*

VARIETY MEATS—Methods of Cooking

VARIETY MEATS is the term used to designate the following edible portions of meat animals: Liver, heart, kidney, tongue, tripe, brains, and sweetbreads. Liver, heart, kidney and tongue are very flavorful while brains, sweetbreads and tripe are very delicate in flavor.

Most of the variety meats are slightly more perishable than other meats and should not be purchased far ahead unless given special care. Liver, heart, kidney, brains, and sweetbreads are always purchased fresh. Tongue may be purchased fresh, pickled, corned or smoked. Tripe may be purchased fresh, pickled or canned. Fresh tripe is partly cooked before selling.

Variety meats, like all meats, are cooked according to their tenderness. Liver and kidney from young animals, brains and sweetbreads are tender. Tongue, heart, tripe, beef kidneys and beef liver are less tender and need long, slow cooking in moisture. Pork liver also is at its best when braised.

Variety meats are usually cooked well done, with the possible exception of veal liver which may be served medium. Variety meats from pork are always cooked well done.

TIME-TABLE FOR COOKING VARIETY MEATS[1]

KIND	BROILED Total Time	BRAISED[2] Total Time		COOKED IN LIQUID Total Time	
	Minutes	Minutes	Hours	Hours	Minutes
Liver Beef 3- to 4-pound piece			2 to 2½		
Sliced		20 to 25			
Veal (Calf)—sliced	8 to 10				
Pork (Whole (3 to 3½ pounds)			1½ to 2		
Sliced		20 to 25			
Lamb—sliced	8 to 10				
Kidney Beef				1 to 1½	
Veal (Calf)	10 to 12			¾ to 1	
Pork	10 to 12			¾ to 1	
Lamb	10 to 12			¾ to 1	
Heart Beef					
Whole			3 to 4	3 to 4	
Sliced			1½ to 2		
Veal (Calf) Whole			2½ to 3	2½ to 3	
Pork			2½ to 3	2½ to 3	
Lamb			2½ to 3	2½ to 3	
Tongue Beef				3 to 4	
Veal (Calf)				2 to 3	
Pork } usually sold Lamb } ready-to-serve					
Tripe Beef	10 to 15[3]			1 to 1½	
Sweetbreads Beef	10 to 15[3]	20 to 25			15 to 20
Veal (Calf)	10 to 15[3]	20 to 25			15 to 20
Lamb	10 to 15[3]	20 to 25			15 to 20
Brains Beef	10 to 15[3]	20 to 25			15 to 20
Veal (Calf)	10 to 15[3]	20 to 25			15 to 20
Pork	10 to 15[3]	20 to 25			15 to 20
Lamb	10 to 15[3]	20 to 25			15 to 20

[1] *For frying see discussion page 6.*

[2] *On top of range or in a 300° F. oven.*

[3] *Time required after precooking in water.*

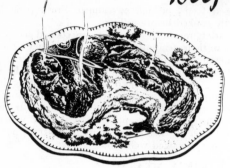

Meanwhile, place the steak on the broiler pan. Remove the sauce from heat as it reaches the boiling point and brush top of steak well, being sure that it is covered with sauce. Place 3 inches below heat and cook 5 minutes, turn and cover other side with sauce and cook 5 minutes.

Edna S. Denby, Seventy-First H. S.
Fayetteville, North Carolina

FILLET MIGNON A LA STANLEY
Number of Servings — 4

4 one inch fillets
4 slices of bacon
2 medium bananas—sectioned
4 T. butter
4 T. boiling water
1 t. beef extract

Trim each fillet into neat circle and wrap a strip of bacon around, fasten securely with toothpick. Let stand twenty minutes before broiling. Serve rare. In two tablespoons of butter sautee both bananas (sectioned). To fat remaining in pan, add four tablespoons of boiling water, one teaspoon of beef extract and two tablespoons butter. Pour around beef.

Sylvia Ann Freeman, Zeb Vance H. S.
Kittrell, North Carolina

PAN-BROILED STEAK
Number of Servings — 2

1 or 2 sirloin steak
Juice of 1 lemon
4 T. margarine
1 T. garlic salt

Use thick skillet. Place on high temperature until butter or margarine is melted and steak is seared on both sides. Add lemon juice and garlic salt while cooking. The desired doneness determines the length of time required in cooking. 10 to 15 minutes is well done.

Mrs. Jean Fite Moore, Clarksdale H. S.
Clarksdale, Mississippi

BROILED SIRLOIN STEAK WITH GARLIC SAUCE
Number of Servings — 4

2½ lbs. choice sirloin steak
1 t. garlic powder
3 T. butter
3 T. Worcestershire sauce
½ c. of A-1 steak sauce

Melt butter in a saucepan over low heat, add garlic powder, Worcestershire sauce, and A-1 sauce. Stir until well mixed and heat to a boiling point.

PEPPER STEAK
Number of Servings — 4

1 lb., ¼ inch Sirloin Tips (cut in serving pieces)
2 T. fat
¼ c. chopped onion
1 clove garlic
1 t. salt
1 beef bouillon cube
1 c. hot water
2 c. cooked tomatoes
1 large green pepper, sliced in rings
2 T. cornstarch
¼ c. cold water
2 T. soy sauce

Brown meat. Add onion and garlic last minutes. Season. Dissolve bouillon cube in hot water and add to meat. Cover and simmer 20 to 25 minutes. Add tomatoes and green pepper. Cook 10 minutes longer. Combine remaining ingredients and stir into meat. Bring to boil. Cook, stirring constantly, 5 minutes longer. Serve with hot chinese noodles or rice.

Thelma J. Jones, Eastern H. S.
Detroit, Michigan

BROILED CHUCK STEAK
Number of Servings — 4

3 lbs. chuck steak cut 1″ thick
¼ c. olive oil
1 t. soy sauce
2 cloves garlic, crushed
¼ t. dry mustard
½ t. sage
¼ c. sauterne wine (or pineapple juice)
2 T. wine vinegar
2 t. Worcestershire sauce
2 T. catsup

For sauce, place olive oil, soy sauce, garlic, mustard and sage in a small pan. Bring to simmer and cook for five minutes. Remove from heat and mix in sauterne and vinegar. Pour sauce over steak, cover and marinate 24 hrs., turning meat often during the 24 hrs. (Refrigerate during marinating.) Broil about 25 min. (10-12 min. on a side) in broiler—or barbecue over barbecue fire. Baste meat often during cooking with remaining sauce.

Mrs. LaVera Kraig, Monroe Jr. H. S.
Aberdeen, South Dakota

LEMON BAKED BEEFSTEAK
Number of Servings — 6

3 lbs. chuck steak
2 T. soft butter
2 t. salt
¼ t. pepper
1 large lemon sliced
2 medium onions, sliced
¼ c. water
1½ c. ketchup
2 T. Worcestershire sauce

Rub steak with softened butter; place in large baking dish. Season, cover with lemon and onion slices. Combine ketchup, Worcestershire sauce and water, pour over steak. Cover tightly so meat will steam tender. Bake in moderate oven (350°) 2 hours, or until tender.

Mrs. Jo-Ann Dawson, Valley H. S.
Lonaconing, Maryland

MINUTE STEAK SCRAMBLE
Number of Servings — 4

4 cube steaks cut in strips
¼ t. garlic salt
¼ t. ginger
¼ c. salad oil
2 green peppers cut in strips
1 c. bias cut celery slices
1 T. cornstarch
¼ c. cold water
3 T. soy sauce
2 tomatoes, peeled and cut in eighths

Season meat with garlic salt and ginger. Heat half the oil in skillet; add meat and brown quickly on all sides. Remove meat. Add remaining oil; heat. Add peppers and celery. Cook just till slightly tender (about 3 minutes). Mix cornstarch, water and soy sauce. Add to skillet; cook and stir till mixture thickens. Add meat and tomatoes; heat. Serve with hot rice and soy sauce.

Mrs. Mildred Doss, Campbellsport H. S.
Campbellsport, Wisconsin

STUFFED CUBE STEAKS
Number of Servings — 4

4 cubed steaks (1 lb.)
¼ t. salt
Pepper, dash
2 T. flour
1 c. soft bread crumbs
¼ t. poultry seasoning
2 T. butter
1 t. minced onion
2 T. margarine, melted
2 T. water
⅓ c. rice, cooked
2½ c. canned tomatoes
¼ t. salt

Wipe steaks with a damp cloth; roll in mixture of salt, pepper and flour. Combine crumbs, poultry

seasoning, onion, margarine, and water to make a stuffing. Place steaks with cut side up, and cover each with a fourth of stuffing. Fold steaks over stuffing, fasten with skewers or toothpicks and place in greased shallow baking dish. Place rice around meat rolls, add tomatoes, salt and butter. Cover dish and bake in moderate oven—350 degrees—about one hour or until steaks are tender.

Elizabeth H. Davis, Fort Le Boeuf H. S.
Waterford, Pennsylvania

STUFFED CUBE STEAKS
Number of Servings — 6

6 cube or minute steaks
2 c. soft bread crumbs
2 T. butter, melted
1 t. salt
¼ t. pepper
2 T. flour
¾ c. minute rice or 2 c. cooked rice
2½ c. tomatoes
½ t. salt
2 T. butter
¼ c. shortening or cooking oil

Roll steaks in flour, 1 teaspoon salt and pepper. Brown in shortening on medium high heat. Remove from heat. Combine bread crumbs, melted butter, ½ teaspoon salt. Stuff centers of steaks with bread crumbs, roll up and secure with toothpicks. Place in baking dish. Place rice around sides. Add tomatoes poured over rice. Dot with butter. Cover. Bake at 350°F. 45-50 minutes.

Freida May Hamlet, Stony Creek H. S.
Stony Creek, Virginia

MINUTE STEAK
Number of Servings — 6

6 minute steaks
Salt and pepper
Butter
½ can cream mushroom soup
½ can cream of celery soup
1 medium chopped onion

Place minute steaks in casserole, cover with cream of mushroom and cream of celery soup and 1 can of water. Add chopped onion and dot with butter. Place in oven and cook 30 minutes at 300 degrees.

Mrs. Herman Stavely, Nashville H. S.
Nashville, Arkansas

ROUND STEAK BAKE
Number of Servings — 4

2 lbs. boneless round steak
1½ oz. package onion soup mix

Spread onion soup over one-half of round steak. Fold over. Wrap securely in foil. Bake at 350° for 2 hours.

Mrs. Evangeline Cox, La Puente H. S.
La Puente, California

ROUND STEAK
Number of Servings — 6-8

2 lb. round steak
2 T. fat
2 T. flour
1 t. salt
½ t. pepper
½ t. paprika
1 can onions
2 cans cream of chicken soup
1 can mushroom soup
1 c. evaporated milk
Topping:
    1½ c. flour
    ½ t. salt
1½ t. baking powder
¾ c. milk
3 T. salad oil
1 c. potato chips—crushed

Score meat with flour, salt, pepper and paprika; fry in fat, place in casserole. Place onions on top. Heat one can cream of chicken soup and liquid of onions in meat skillet. Heat, pour over meat. Bake in oven about 45 minutes at 325°F. Mix up topping. Roll in salad oil and crumbs. Drop on casserole and bake about 20 minutes at 350°F. Serve with mushroom, cream of chicken and milk sauce over it.

Mrs. Harriett Swanke, Scobey H. S.
Scobey, Montana

STUFFED ROUND STEAK
Number of Servings — 4-6

Pound until thin, 2 round steaks totaling 3 lbs. Rub in salt, pepper and plenty of paprika. Overlap steaks on meat board, making one large steak. Spread steaks with ¼ pound of sliced mushrooms arranged in a layer. Blanket with a layer of thinly sliced onions. Add pimento, cover with finely rolled bread crumbs. With beater, combine ½ cup melted butter, 1 tablespoon boiling water and a whole raw egg. Immediately dribble this mixture over bread crumbs. Arrange stuffed olives in a row on long side of steak. Begin the roll of meat around the olives. Tie roll firmly. Flour the outside and brown in ¼ cup butter or bacon drippings, in a roaster or deep earthenware baker. Place 6 whole mushrooms, 3 small onions into roaster and sprinkle lightly with salt, pepper and paprika. Add 1 cup red wine. Roast at 350°F. for at least two hours.

Mrs. Bettie Lou Snapp, Valley H. S.
Albuquerque, New Mexico

BAKED STEAK & DRESSING
Number of Servings — 6

2½ lb. round steak
Salt and pepper
1 qt. dry bread
½ t. poultry seasonings
¼ t. sage
4 pepper slices
6 onion rings
6 tomato slices

Sear meat; salt and pepper it. Combine bread and seasonings. Moisten with meat drippings. Place on top of steak to fit. Decorate with pepper, onion and tomato slices. Keep basted with drippings or water during baking so meat is moist. Bake one hour and a half at 250°.

Mrs. Effie G. Hoyle, Warwick H. S.
Newport News, Virginia

MEAT BIRDS
Number of Servings — 5-6

1 slice round steak about ½" thick
½ c. flour
2 c. bread crumbs
½ c. finely chopped onion
1 egg
Salt and pepper
½ t. sage
½ c. instant milk
3 T. butter

Pound the steak, season and dredge with flour. Combine the other ingredients as for a dressing. Add hot milk or water, just enough for it to hold its shape. Place the dressing down the center of the steak, lengthwise. Fold the edges of the meat over the dressing to form a roll with the meat edges overlapping. Secure these edges with toothpicks. Wrap lightly in foil and bake at 350°F. for 1 hour and 15 minutes (or until tender). Baste with butter about 3 times during the baking. Brown under broiler if necessary. Serves 5 or 6 depending upon the size of the round steak.

Lola S. Pevehouse, Tascosa H. S.
Amarillo, Texas

BEEF PLUS
Number of Servings — 4

½ lb. tender beef (in strips)
2 T. cooking oil
1 medium onion, chopped
1 package frozen green beans
1 green pepper, sliced
1 c. sliced celery
4 t. cornstarch
1 T. soy sauce
¾ c. liquid (juice from mushrooms and water)
1 can (4-oz.) mushrooms

Brown meat in oil in heavy skillet. Add next 4 ingredients and cook 3 to 5 minutes. Vegetables should be crisp. Combine cornstarch, soy sauce, liquid and seasonings; add to skillet, stirring to mix thoroughly. Add mushrooms. Stir, cooking until liquid is clear and shiny. Garnish with pimentos. Serve with hot fluffy rice.

Mrs. Archie Strand, Chester H. S.
Chester, South Dakota

BARBECUED STEAK
Number of Servings — 4-5

1½ lb. round steak (cut in serving pieces)
2 T. lard
¾ c. seasoned flour (1 t. salt and ¼ t. pepper)
2 T. vinegar
2 T. brown sugar
2 T. Worcestershire sauce
¾ c. chili sauce
¼ c. water
¼ t. chili powder

Pound flour into meat. Brown slowly in shortening. Put in baking dish. Pour other ingredients over meat. Cover, bake in 325° oven for 1 hour (or until tender). Uncover last 15 min. of baking.

Mrs. Norma Dubbe, Sturgis H. S.
Sturgis, South Dakota

MOCK DUCK
Number of Servings — 6-8

1 large slice round steak cut 1½-2″
½ c. salad oil
½ t. garlic salt
Dash of pepper
2 t. accent
2 T. Worcestershire sauce
1 clove garlic, chopped
Dressing: 2½ c. bread cubes
½ c. chopped celery (stalk and leaves)
¼ c. chopped onion
⅓ c. melted butter
1 t. thyme
1 t. sage
½ t. garlic salt
2 t. accent
1 T. Worcestershire sauce

Mix salad oil, garlic salt, pepper, accent, Worcestershire sauce and garlic together; pour into shallow pan. Soak steak in this mixture for 5 hours, turning frequently. For dressing, mix all ingredients except bread in a bowl. Then add bread cubes with enough water to give the dressing body. Sprinkle one side of steak with flour. Spread dressing on other side and roll up like a jelly roll. Fasten with skewers. Bake in lightly greased shallow pan for 1½ hour at 325°F. Slice and serve.

Pauline J. Morris, Casselton H. S.
Casselton, North Dakota

MOCK BIRDS
Number of Servings — 6

1 lb. round steak, ½″ thick
Salt and pepper
6 strips bacon
6 small sour pickles
1 c. water
3 T. Worcestershire sauce

Cut steak in six lengthwise strips. Salt and pepper. Place one strip of bacon on each strip of beef. Place one sour pickle on each beef strip. Roll beef strips and anchor with toothpick. Saute. Add 1

cup water and 3 tablespoons Worcestershire sauce. Cover and bake in 300°F. oven for 1 hour.

LaDelle Norris, Menard H. S.
Menard, Texas

OVEN STEAK SUPPER
Number of Servings — 4

1½ lbs. round or chuck steak, 1″ thick
1 envelope onion-soup mix
4 small carrots, quartered
2 stalks celery, cut in sticks
3-4 medium potatoes, halved
2 T. butter
½ t. salt
Aluminum foil

Place meat in center of 3 foot length of foil. Sprinkle meat with soup mix, cover with vegetables, dot with butter, and sprinkle with salt. Fold foil and seal securely to hold in juices. Place on baking sheet; bake in hot (450°) oven 1 to 1½ hours or till done.

Mrs. Gracia Willis, Monona Grove H. S.
Madison, Wisconsin

BAKED ROUND STEAK
Number of Servings — 6-8

2 lbs. round steak (cut 1-in. thick)
¼ lb. butter
1 can mushrooms
1 envelope Lipton's dry onion soup

Spread butter on round steak. Sprinkle soup over the buttered round steak, then sliced mushrooms. Wrap in 2 thicknesses of foil, place in covered roaster and bake at least 2 hours at 325°F. (Be sure rack is in roaster).

Mrs. Dewey Huber, Sr. H. S.
Chippewa Falls, Wisconsin

DEVILED ROUND STEAK
Number of Servings — 4-6

1½ lbs. round steak
Flour for dredging
3 T. lard
3 T. flour
3 T. diced onion
1 t. prepared mustard
1 c. canned tomatoes
1 c. water
1 T. vinegar
1 T. sugar
½ t. salt
¼ t. paprika

Cut steak into individual servings. Dredge with flour and brown on both sides in lard. Mix the 3 tablespoons flour and mustard and combine with remaining ingredients. Cover and cook slowly on top of range or in a slow oven (300°F.) for 1½ hours or until tender.

Elberta Martin, Irma Marsh Jr. H. S.
Fort Worth, Texas

23

MARINATED STEAK BROIL
Number of Servings — 6

3 lbs. beef round steak, cut 1″ thick
½ c. soy sauce
2½ T. brown sugar
1 T. tarragon vinegar
1 clove garlic, crushed (onion may be substituted)
1 T. ground ginger

Using a sharp knife, cut through outside fat covering at 1-inch intervals to prevent curling of steak while broiling. Put remaining ingredients in bowl or screw-top jar and beat or shake until blended. Pour this marinade over the meat and allow to stand at least 30 min., turning once or twice if steak is not covered with the marinade. Drain, reserving marinade for basting. Broil at 500°F., 2 inches from heat, for 9-12 minutes on each side. Baste occasionally with marinade. Serve immediately.

Mrs. Doris Gruber, Walsh H. S.
Walsh, Colorado

PEPPER STEAK
Number of Servings — 6

2 T. shortening
1 T. flour
½ c. water
½ c. catchup
3 T. soy sauce
⅛ t. pepper
1 bouillon cube (beef)
1 clove minced garlic
½ c. finely chopped onion
1 lb. round steak cut into small bite-size cubes
1 box fresh mushrooms
2 large peppers cut into rings
2 med. onions cut into rings

Brown meat in shortening, remove. Blend flour into the shortening from which the meat was removed. Add catchup, water, soy sauce, pepper, bouillon cube, minced garlic and chopped onion. Bring to boil, lower heat to simmer for twenty minutes. Drop meat into sauce and cook only until tender. (This much can be done even two or three days before serving and stored in refrigerator). Ten minutes before serving add fresh mushrooms cut up, pepper and onion rings. Cook until crisply tender, about ten minutes. (CAUTION: Do not add additional salt or accent, or MSG). Serve on hot fluffy rice.

Estelle Delgado, Banning Union H. S.
Banning, California

PEPPER STEAK
Number of Servings — 4

1 lb. beef chuck, cut in very thin strips
¼ c. cooking (salad) oil
1 clove garlic, minced
1 T. soy sauce
1 t. salt

¼ c. water
1 c. green pepper, cut in 1-in. pieces
1 c. onion, chopped
½ c. celery, chopped
1 T. cornstarch
1 c. water
2 tomatoes, cut in eighths

Brown beef in hot oil; add garlic and cook until yellow. Add soy sauce, salt and ¼ cup water; cook 45 minutes. Add vegetables. Cook 10 minutes. Stir in cornstarch blended with 1 cup water. Add tomatoes and cook 5 minutes. Serve over hot fluffy rice.

Mrs. Irene Lentz, Conneaut Lake Area Joint H. S.
Conneaut Lake, Pennsylvania

PEPPER STEAK (ROUND STEAK)
Number of Servings — 4-6

1 thick round steak

Freeze until firm. Slice into thin slices. Oil skillet; put in steak; brown, add 2 or 3 garlic buttons, according to taste. Add one tablespoon soy sauce, ¾ cup water, salt and pepper to taste. Cover and cook for 30 minutes. Add 1 cup chopped onions and one cup chopped green pepper. Add ½ cup more water. Cook slowly until vegetables are tender. Add 3 tablespoons cornstarch, mixed with cold water and one tablespoon soy sauce to thicken. Serve with boiled rice. Add button mushrooms to make this dish fancy.

Mrs. Lena W. Pendergrass, A. L. Miller Sr. H. S.
Macon, Georgia

PEPPER STEAK

1 lb. beef—round or sirloin
2 T. shortening
¼ c. soy sauce
1½ c. water
2 medium onions
2 bell peppers
2 T. cornstarch
Fluffy rice

Cut steak into small cubes. Brown in shortening about 5 minutes, or until tender. Add soy sauce and water. Simmer for 10 minutes. Add onions which have been cut in strips lengthwise. Simmer for 5 minutes. Add bell peppers which have been cut in strips lengthwise. Cook until tender, thicken with cornstarch and serve over steamed rice or in a garnished rice ring.

Mrs. Jane G. Jackson, Mantachie H. S.
Mantachie, Mississippi

ROLLED STEAK
Number of Servings — 3-4

1 lb. round steak
1 clove garlic
¼ c. chopped onions
Salt
Pepper

(Continued on Next Page)

Salt and pepper round steak to taste. Spread chopped onions and garlic over the flat surface of the steak. Roll steak in jelly roll fashion and tie securely with clean string. Brown in small amount of fat on all sides, add desired amount of water, cover and cook slowly on top of stove until done.

Mrs. L. A. Trahan, Jr., Westlake H. S.
Westlake, Louisiana

STEAK ROLL-UPS
Number of Servings — 4

2 lbs. thinly sliced round steak
2 c. bread stuffing
2 T. shortening
1 can (10½ Ounces) condensed cream of
  mushroom soup
½ c. water
½ c. sour cream

Pound steak with meat hammer or edge of heavy saucer. Cut steak into 8 pieces long enough to roll. Place about ¼ cup of stuffing near center of each piece of steak; roll, pinwheel fashion; fasten with toothpick or skewer. In large skillet, brown roll-ups in shortening. Add soup and water. Cover and cook over low heat about 1½ hours or until tender. Spoon sauce over meat during cooking. Remove meat from pan and add sour cream to sauce; heat and serve over roll-ups.

Zedith Ogilbee, Tomlinson Jr. H. S.
Lawton, Oklahoma

ROLLED STEAK
Number of Servings — 4

1 lb. round steak
¼ c. flour
¾ c. dry bread crumbs
3 T. butter, melted
2 T. chopped onion
1 T. parsley flakes
1 t. salt
1 small can button mushrooms

Wipe steak and sprinkle with flour. Pound extra flour into steak. Mix other ingredients and spread on steak, keeping mixture 1 inch from edge to prevent squeezing out. Roll steak, tie securely, and roast in a slow oven (300°-350° F.) about 2 and one-half hours.

Becky Barganier, Talladega H. S.
Talladega, Alabama

ROUND STEAK SMOTHERED IN ONIONS
Number of Servings — 6

2 lbs. round steak
About ⅓ c. flour seasoned with small amount
  of salt and pepper
2 large onions
1 small can of tomato paste
Salt, pepper, and perhaps a little brown sugar
  and chili powder, if desired

Slice into edges of steak every ¾ inches so it won't

curl. Pound flour into steak. In skillet brown steak in hot fat. When nearly done remove and place in another skillet. In original skillet brown onions, which have been sliced crosswise. Place on top of steak in second skillet. In original skillet make a gravy of flour, a small amount of water, tomato paste and seasonings. Pour over steak and onions. Simmer over direct heat or place in 325°-350°F. oven for 45 minutes.

Margaret Nowatzki, Hazen H. S.
Hazen, North Dakota

STUFFED ROUND STEAK
Number of Servings — 6-8

1 round steak ½ inch thick
1½ c. of soft bread crumbs
2 T. grated onion
1 T. chopped parsley
1 t. salt
¼ t. pepper
1 teaspoon of poultry seasoning
¼ c. of water

Combine stuffing. Moisten lightly with meat stock or water. Then spread the stuffing over the surface of the steak. The same as for a jelly roll, the steak if rolled up with the stuffing inside. To hold its shape during cooking, the roll is tied with a heavy string. Skewers may be used if you wish. Next, brown the round steak roll on all sides in 2 or 3 tablespoons of lard or drippings. Do this slowly and thoroughly for that golden brown appearance. Add ¼ cup of water, cover, and simmer until tender or 1½ hours.

Mrs. U. A. Smith, Linn H. S.
Doddsville, Mississippi

SAVORY BEEF ROLL-UPS
Number of Servings — 6

2 lbs. round steak; cut in 6 portions
1 large can mushrooms (drained)
1 c. chopped parsley
¾ c. chopped onion
1 c. grated Parmesan cheese
Salt and pepper
1 can condensed beef consomme
2 T. cornstarch
½ c. water

Combine mushrooms, parsley, onion, cheese. Sprinkle meat sections with salt and pepper. Divide mushroom mixture and place on each meat section. Roll up, fasten with toothpicks. Lace with #8 thread. Brown all sides in skillet. Add consomme, 1 tablespoon Worcestershire sauce, 4 bay leaves, ½ teaspoon Savory Salt. Cover; simmer 1 hour 15 minutes, or bake in oven at 350 degrees. Remove rolls. Add cornstarch to water and then stir into gravy until it thickens. Remove strings and toothpicks.

Mrs. Glenda S. Ballinger, Kirkman Tech. H. S.
Chattanooga, Tennessee

STEAK ROLLS
Number of Servings — 4

1½ lbs. thinly cut steak (round)
Sliced onion
Sliced dill pickles
Salt and pepper to taste

Cut steak into oblong strips. Roll a slice of pickle and a slice of onion into each piece of round steak and secure with a toothpick. Flour steak. Brown steak on all sides in hot grease. Remove steak rolls and make gravy. Pour steak rolls and gravy in pressure cooker and cook at 15 pounds pressure for 30 minutes. Serve hot.

Mrs. Lera H. Manley, Beatrice H. S.
Beatrice, Alabama

ROUND STEAK ROLL-UPS
Number of Servings — 4

1½ lbs. round steak, ½-in. thick
6 T. fat
¼ c. onion, finely chopped
2 c. day-old bread crumbs
½ c. celery, chopped
½ t. salt
¼ t. sage
Dash of pepper
Dash of poultry seasoning
1 T. water
1 can (10½-oz.) mushroom soup

Remove bone from steak. Pound steak to flatten with a meat pounder or edge of heavy saucer. Lightly brown onion in 3 tablespoons hot fat. Add bread crumbs, celery, seasonings and water. Cut steak into four pieces. Place ¼ of the bread crumb dressing on each piece. Roll up and fasten with small skewers or toothpicks. Flour and brown in remaining fat. Dilute soup with soup-can of water and pour over meat. Sprinkle with salt and pepper, cover and simmer over low heat 1½ to 2 hours or until tender.

Mrs. Mary Barringer, Trico H. S.
Campbell Hill, Illinois

CHICKEN FRIED STEAK
Number of Servings — 4

1 lb. round steak, cut in 4 pieces
1 egg
2 T. water
1 t. salt, ¼ t. pepper, ¼ t. paprika mixed with
   1 c. flour

Dip steak pieces in seasoned flour, then in one egg and 2 tablespoons water, beaten together. Dip again in flour. Brown on both sides in hot fat. Cover; cook slowly 20 to 30 minutes.
Gravy: Remove meat—add rest of seasoned flour mixed with 2 cups milk. Stir until gravy comes to a boil. Boil one minute.

Mrs. Lynn J. Fite, Mount Holly H. S.
Mount Holly, Arkansas

BEEF ROUND STEAK STRIPS
Number of Servings — 4-6

1-1½ lbs. round steak
Salt and pepper
Garlic salt
Flour
6 T. fat
Meat tenderizer (optional)

Cut steak into strips about 1 by 3 inches. Season with salt and pepper. Sprinkle lightly with garlic salt. Dredge in flour. Saute in fat until browned on both sides. Serve immediately.

Mrs. Ruby Maynard, Angleton H. S.
Angleton, Texas

BEEF STEAK IN TOMATO SAUCE
Number of Servings — 8

4 lbs. round steak, cut ¾-in. thick
2 cloves garlic
2 chicken bouillon cubes
⅔ c. water
½ t. salt
¼ t. dried basil
¼ t. dried thyme
⅛ t. pepper
8 whole onions (1-in.)
2 (1-lb.) cans seasoned stewed tomatoes

Trim excess fat from meat; rub surface with garlic; cut into 8 equal pieces. Rub heated skillet with piece of fat; brown steak on both sides. Mix bouillon cubes, water, and seasonings; add to skillet; cover and simmer 30 minutes. Add onions (add more water if needed). Cook 30 minutes. Add tomatoes and cook 15 minutes.

Mrs. Adele Logue
Northern Bedford County H. S.
Hopewell, Pennsylvania

BEEF WITH SOUR CREAM GRAVY
Number of Servings — 6

1½ lbs. ¾-in. thick round steak cut in
   serving pieces
1 large onion, diced
5 slices bacon, cut in half
2 T. butter
1 t. salt
Sprinkle of pepper
½ t. paprika
½ pt. sour cream

Melt shortening (butter), add slices of meat and brown them. Remove meat. Cook onions in butter until light golden. Remove onions from pan; then arrange meat in pan. Add salt, pepper, and paprika. Add onions and bacon, placing bacon on top of meat slices. Add about ½ cup water. Cover pan and cook slowly until meat is done. Make gravy, using 3 tablespoons flour to thicken. Add sour cream and heat.

Mrs. Mabel Grooms, Richland Center H. S.
Richland Center, Wisconsin

STEAK WITH SOUR CREAM SAUCE
Number of Servings — 6-8

1½" thick slice of round steak
1 large onion
1 t. brown sugar
1 t. curry powder
¼ t. pepper
½ t. ginger
1 t. salt
1 T. Worcestershire sauce
½ c. water
¼ c. chopped parsley
¾ c. sour cream
1 T. horseradish

Cut round steak into cubes, flour if desired, not necessary, brown in heavy skillet or dutch oven with small amount of fat. Add 1 large onion sliced thin, curry powder, ground ginger, sugar, salt, pepper, worcestershire sauce and water. Cook 2-2½ hours at 300° F. or until tender. Just before serving add chopped parsley, sour cream and horseradish, simmer five (5) minutes and serve on hot plate.

Mrs. Ruth Fishburn, Adair H. S.
Adair, Oklahoma

BEEF WITH SOUR CREAM SAUCE
Number of Servings — 12

3½ lbs. round steak, cut in 1-in. cubes
½ c. flour
¼ c. fat
½ c. onions, thinly sliced
2½ c. sour cream
¼ t. marjoram
¼ t. thyme
¼ t. salt
Pinch parika
½ clove garlic, finely chopped

Roll round steak in flour. Pan-brown steak and onions in hot fat in heavy skillet. Combine all ingredients in large pan. Cover with foil. Bake in a moderate oven (350°F.) for 2 hours. Remove during last hour of baking time. Stir occasionally. For best results, use commercially soured cream.

Jimmie McGuire, Davis H. S.
Davis, Oklahoma

CREOLE STEAK
Number of Servings — 4

2 lbs. round steak, 1-in. thick
1 large onion
1 green pepper
½ c. celery, chopped
Salt and pepper
3 T. green onion tops
3 T. parsley, chopped
1 can tomato sauce
4 T. flour
3 T. fat
2 c. boiling water
1 T. Kitchen Bouquet sauce

1½ T. Worcestershire sauce

Sear steak on both sides. Add hot water and turn on low heat. In a skillet melt fat. Add flour stirring constantly until flour turns a rich golden brown, add chopped onions and cook until wilted. Add this mixture to meat. Add remaining ingredients except green onions and parsley. Simmer gently until meat is tender. Add green onion tops and parsley. Simmer gently 15 minutes. Serve with rice or mashed potatoes.

Mrs. Odessa N. Smith, Area Sup. of Home Ec.,
State Dept. of Education, Baton Rouge, Louisiana

DICED ROUND STEAK WITH ONIONS AND SOUR CREAM
Number of Servings — 4

Melt in a skillet 4 tablespoons butter. Saute in the butter until light brown ½ cup finely minced onions. Cut into ½ inch dice: 1½ pounds round steak. Sear it in the hot butter on all sides. Simmer these ingredients covered for 20 minutes. Add ½ cup minced sauteed mushrooms. Combine 1 cup sour cream and 2 tablespoons flour. Pour these ingredients into the skillet. Stir and simmer them for 5 minutes and add ¾ teaspoon salt and ¼ teaspoon pepper.

Mrs. Eloise M. Speed, Aliceville H. S.
Aliceville, Alabama

ROUND STEAK WITH MUSHROOMS
Number of Servings — 8

6 T. flour
1½ t. salt
¼ t. pepper
3 lbs. round steak
¼ c. fat
2 c. mushrooms (drained)
1½ c. onions (sliced)
1 c. celery (diced)
2 cloves garlic (minced)
1 t. salt
1 c. water

Combine flour, salt and pepper. Cut steak into serving pieces. Pound as much of the dry ingredients as possible into the meat. Brown the steak in the pressure pan. Combine the remaining ingredients and pour over the meat. Cover and set control at 10. Cook for 30 minutes after correct pressure is reached.

Corinne Stene, Lake Benton H. S.
Lake Benton, Minnesota

MEAT PIE WITH BISCUIT TOPPING
Number of Servings — 6

2 lbs. round or rump beef, 1½-in. thick
½ c. flour
1 t. salt
¼ t. pepper
½ t. celery salt
½ c. bacon fat

(Continued on Next Page)

2¼ c. boiling water
½ t. bottled condiment sauce
3 large carrots, pared and cut in large pieces
12 small white onions, peeled
Baking powder biscuit dough

Cut meat into 1½ inch cubes, and dredge with ¼ cup of the flour, to which the salt, pepper, and celery salt have been added. Brown quickly in a large skillet in 4 tablespoons of the bacon fat, heated. Melt remaining 4 tablespoons bacon fat in a deep well cooker, large kettle, or Dutch oven; add 2 tablespoons of the flour, and blend. Dissolve the bouillon cubes in the boiling water, and add gradually to the bacon fat and flour mixture; stir until well blended; add condiment sauce. Add browned meat and drippings to gravy; reduce heat to low, and simmer, covered, for 2 hours. Add vegetables and continue cooking, covered, 1 to 1½ hours longer, or until vegetables and meat are tender. Then thicken gravy with remaining 2 tablespoons of flour blended with 3 tablespoons of water. Turn meat mixture into a greased casserole, and top with baking powder biscuits cut with a doughnut cutter. Bake at 450°F. for 15 minutes. Packaged biscuits may be used. Peas may be added.

Mrs. Viola Lee Roy, Eubank H. S.
Eubank, Kentucky

GEORGE RECTOR'S HUNGARIAN GOULASH
Number of Servings — 6

3 lbs. chuck or round of beef
3 pts. stock
2 cloves garlic
1 bay leaf
1 t. salt
Few grains cayenne pepper
6 medium sized potatoes
3 T. butter
3 T. flour
3 T. paprika
1 c. tomato puree

Cut meat into 1½ inch cubes. Fry out a little of the fat and brown meat in it. Add stock, garlic, bay leaf, salt, and cayenne. Simmer for 2½ hours over low heat, then add potatoes and simmer for 35 to 40 minutes longer. Cream butter, flour and paprika together. Combine with a little of the liquid from the goulash and add tomato puree. Serve on a hot platter and garnish each end with cooked noodles. (1 pkg. for 6)

Mrs. Eleanor Brunski, Olney H. S.
Philadelphia, Pennsylvania

SWISS STEAK (with green beans)
Number of Servings — 4

2 lbs. round steak
1 medium can of French cut beans
1 small can mushrooms
2 t. salt
½ t. pepper
½ c. flour

Pound round steak with flour and brown in frying pan. Salt and pepper and put beans and mushrooms over steak and cook slowly until tender. Approximately two hours at 350°F. in oven.

Mary Jane Fuhlbrugge, Hinckley H. S.
Hinckley, Minnesota

SWISS ONION STEAK
Number of Servings — 6

1½ lbs. round steak
½ c. dehydrated onion soup
1 c. hot water

Brown steak quickly under broiler. Add onion soup and water. Lower heat to 350°F. and cook one hour.

Mrs. Marion Self, Goldsboro Sr. H. S.
Goldsboro, North Carolina

SWISS STEAK
Number of Servings — 10

2 lbs. thick round steak
⅓ c. flour
1½ t. salt
⅛ t. pepper
2 T. onion, chopped
¼ c. fat
1 c. hot water, or tomato juice or sour cream

Wipe meat. Place on meat board and beat flour into the meat with the edge of a saucer until the meat will hold no more flour. Sear well in a heavy iron frying pan into which fat has been added. (An electric skillet may be used—use high heat for searing—then cut down to simmer). The onion may be browned with the meat or added the last ½ hour of cooking. Add ½ cup of liquid. Cover pan and simmer 1 hour, adding more liquid when necessary. Add seasonings and continue cooking ½ hour or longer. Serve with gravy. Arrange on platter with baked potatoes.

Leila Cullison, Lakeview H. S.
Decatur, Illinois

SWISS STEAK (cook by braising)
Number of Servings — 8-10

Pound ½ cup seasoned flour, 1 teaspoon salt, ¼ teaspoon pepper, ¼ teaspoon paprika mixed with 1 cup enriched flour into both sides of 3 pounds of round steak (2 inches thick). Brown in hot fat in a heavy skillet 2 sliced onions. Remove onions and brown meat well on both sides. Top with onions. Add 2 cups tomatoes (No. 303 can). Cover tightly and cook slowly until tender (2½ to 3 hours). *Note:* After Swiss steak has cooked for 1½ hours add 5-6 sliced carrots, 4-5 quartered potatoes and 4-5 stalks of cut up celery.

Mrs. Janet Patton, Cliff Consolidated H. S.
Cliff, New Mexico

SWISS STEAK
Number of Servings — 8-10

½ c. seasoned flour
3 lbs. round steak (2″ thick)
Fat for browning
2 onions, sliced
2 c. cooked tomatoes

Pound ½ cup seasoned flour into both sides of 3 pounds round steak. Brown in hot fat in heavy skillet 2 onions, sliced. Remove onions and brown meat well on both sides. Top with onions. Add 2 cups cooked tomatoes. Cover tightly and cook slowly until tender (2½ to 3 hours).

Mrs. Anne Menefee, David Crockett H. S.
Conroe, Texas

SWISS STEAK
Number of Servings — 8-10

½ c. flour
½ t. salt
Few grains pepper
3 lbs. round steak (2″ thick)
2 sliced onions, browned in ¼ c. fat
2 c. cooked tomatoes

Pound seasoned flour into both sides of steak. Brown onions in fat. Remove onions; brown meat well on both sides. Top with onions. Add tomatoes. Cover tightly and cook slowly for about 3 hrs. Garnish with parsley.

Rita M. Servidea, Youngsville H. S.
Youngsville, Pennsylvania

SWISS STEAK
Number of Servings — 6

1½ lbs. beef, round cut 1-1¼ inches thick
1 medium-sized onion, sliced
3 T. fat
1 c. water
½ c. flour
3 T. chopped green pepper
1 small can tomato sauce
1½ t. salt
¼ t. pepper
1 t. Worcestershire sauce

Beat flour, salt and pepper into steak. Seer on both sides in hot fat. Then cook slowly for 1-1½ hours. After seering, put onion and pepper and Worcestershire sauce on top of steak. Add water. When half done add tomato sauce.

Mrs. Ralph Shipman, Paris H. S.
Paris, Texas

SWISS STEAK
Number of Servings — 6

2 lbs. round steak
1 c. flour
6 T. fat
Salt and pepper
½ c. chopped onion
½ c. chopped celery
¼ c. chopped green pepper
1 No. 2 can tomatoes
1 c. water

Salt and pepper steak (cut for serving, if desired), roll in flour. Brown in hot fat. Brown remaining flour in fat. Add chopped onion, celery, pepper, tomatoes, and water. Cover closely. Cook either in oven or on top of stove. Allow to simmer—do not boil—2 hours or until meat is tender. Add more water, if necessary.

Syble R. Taylor, Elba H. S.
Elba, Alabama

SWISS STEAK
Number of Servings — 4

1½ lbs. round steak
2 T. flour
1 t. salt
⅛ t. pepper
2 T. salad oil
1½ c. canned tomatoes
3 thinly sliced onions
1 minced clove garlic
1 diced stalk celery
1 T. bottled meat sauce
¼ c. light or dark raisins

Combine flour, salt, pepper. Sprinkle on meat, distributing evenly on both sides of meat. Brown meat well on both sides in skillet or Dutch Oven. Add rest of the ingredients. Stir well. Simmer, covered, about 2 to 2½ hours.

Esther Udell, Pomeroy H. S.
Pomeroy, Washington

SWISS STEAK
Number of Servings — 6-8

2 lbs. top round steak, 1 inch thick
½ c. flour
1 t. salt
⅛ t. pepper
2 T. cooking oil
1 can condensed tomato soup
½ c. sliced stuffed green olives
1 large onion thinly sliced
2 T. chopped green pepper
1 can mushroom slices

Rub salt, pepper, and flour on meat and brown in oil using a heavy skillet. Add remaining ingredients and simmer (220°) for about two hours, or until tender.

Ann Uecker, South San Antonio H. S.
San Antonio, Texas

SWISS STEAK
Number of Servings — 6

1 large round steak, 2 in. thick
1 onion (medium) chopped
1 green pepper (small) chopped
½ c. chopped celery

(Continued on Next Page)

1 large can tomato sauce
2 T. Worcestershire sauce
Salt and pepper to season
Flour for dredging steak

Season steak with salt and pepper; dredge in flour then brown quickly on each side in a small amount of fat. Saute onions, pepper and celery in a small amount of fat. Place steak in covered pan (Dutch Oven); Add tomato sauce, Worcestershire sauce, onion, pepper and celery. Cover the pan and cook in 350 degree oven for 2 to 2½ hours.

Opal Wood, Navasota H. S.
Navasota, Texas

SWISS STEAK IN A PACKAGE
Number of Servings — 5-6

1 c. catsup
¼ c. enriched flour
2 lbs. 1-inch round steak
1 large onion, sliced
2 T. lemon juice
Salt and pepper

Tear off 5-foot length of foil; fold double. Combine catsup and flour; spoon half of it in center of foil. Place steak atop; season. Cover meat with onion slices and remaining catsup mixture. Sprinkle with lemon juice. Fold foil and seal. Place in shallow baking pan and bake 1½ hours at 450°.

Joan Loyer Farley, Morenci Area H. S.
Morenci, Michigan

SWISS STEAK SUPREME
Number of Servings — 4

1½ lbs. round steak
½ c. flour
1½ t. salt
¼ t. garlic salt
3 T. fat
1½ c. stewed or canned tomatoes

Steak should be cut 1½ inches thick. Mix all dry ingredients and rub or pound into the steak. Pan-fry the steak on both sides in hot fat; add tomatoes and simmer until tender or bake in a moderate oven (350 degrees F.) 1½ hours. (Multiply all amounts by 4 to serve a group of 100.)

Mrs. Linnie Mae Sharkey, Woodland H. S.
Amite, Louisiana

SWISS STEAK DELUXE
Number of Servings — 4

2 lb. round or flank steak
2½ c. cooked tomatoes
1 medium sliced onion
1 T. Worcestershire sauce
⅛ t. pepper
1 t. vinegar
1 clove garlic
2 T. catsup
2 T. brown sugar
1 t. salt

Pound 6 tablespoons flour into sides of steak. Brown in hot fat in skillet. Add all of above ingredients. Cover. Cook over low heat or in oven (275°-300°) until tender (2-2½ hours). Uncover last 15 min. to cook down to thick sauce.

Rosemary Kuhl, Scottsbluff Sr. H. S.
Scottsbluff, Nebraska

SWISS STEAK
Number of Servings — 4-6

2 lbs. round or flank steak (1½ inches thick)
2 c. cooked tomatoes (No. 1 tall can)
1 small onion (sliced)
1 stalk celery, diced
6 T. seasoned flour

Pound seasoned flour into steak. Brown in hot fat in heavy skillet. Add tomatoes, onion, and celery. Cover. Cook over low heat at simmering temperature or in moderate oven at 300° F. until tender (2 to 2½ hours), uncovering last ½ hour to cook down sauce to a rich thickness. Serve hot.

Mrs. Ethelyn Richman, Wawaka H. S.
Wawaka, Indiana

SWISS STEAK
Number of Servings — 8-10

½ c. flour
¼ t. pepper
3 lbs. round steak (2-in steak)
2 c. cooked tomatoes (No. 303 can)
½ t. salt
¼ t. paprika
2 onions, sliced

Mix flour, salt, pepper, and paprika. Pound mixture of flour, salt, pepper and paprika into both sides of round steak. Brown steak well on all sides in heavy skillet. Add onions and cook for 2-3 minutes. Add tomatoes. Cover tightly and cook slowly until tender for 2½ to 3 hours.

Mrs. Walter Holden, Albany H. S.
Albany, Louisiana

STEAK WITH MUSHROOM SAUCE
Number of Servings — 4

2 lb. round steak
1 t. salt
¼ to ½ c. flour
1 can cream of mushroom soup
1 can water
3 T. fat

Mix salt and flour. Pound into steak, using edge of plate. Cut into serving size pieces. Brown in hot fat. Mix soup and water; heat to boiling. Pour over meat. Let simmer till tender (about 1½ hours). Liquid should cook down to make gravy of nice consistency.

Mrs. Jeanine Williams, Meade Memorial H. S.
Williamsport, Kentucky

SWISS STEAK (USING PIZZA SAUCE)
Number of Servings — 6

⅓ c. enriched flour
2 t. salt
¼ t. pepper
2 lbs. round or chuck steak, 1 inch thick
3 T. fat
1 8-ounce can (1 cup) seasoned tomato sauce
2 5½-ounce cans (1⅓ cups) pizza sauce
1 medium onion, sliced

Combine flour, salt, and pepper; pound into steak. Brown slowly on both sides in hot fat. Pour tomato sauce and pizza sauce over meat. Top with onion slices. Simmer uncovered 10 minutes. Cover and bake in oven-going skillet or large casserole in moderate oven (350°) 1 hour or a little longer, until the steak is fork-tender.

Mrs. Martha Thomas, Franklin-Simpson Sr. H. S.
Franklin, Kentucky

SWISS STEAK
Number of Servings — 6-8

2 lbs. round or chuck steak (1½ or 2 inches thick)
½ c. sifted flour
2 t. salt
½ t. pepper
¼ c. fat
2 c. canned tomatoes
1 small onion, chopped

Combine flour, salt, and pepper; pound into steak. Brown steak in hot fat in Dutch oven or deep skillet. Let one side brown; turn; brown second side. Keep the meat sizzling slowly—don't rush it. Combine tomatoes and chopped onion in a small boiler; heat to a boil; pour over steak. Cover; cook in a moderate oven (350°) 1½ hours.

Mrs. Beth Pittman, Whitehouse H. S.
Whitehouse, Texas

SWISS STEAK
Number of Servings — 8-10

3 lbs. round steak, 2-in. thick
1 t. salt
¼ t. pepper
¼ t. paprika
2 stalks celery, chopped
1 c. flour
2 small onions, chopped
2 c. cooked tomatoes
1 medium sized green pepper

Pound the salt, pepper, paprika and flour mixture into both sides of the round steak. Brown the meat on both sides in hot fat. Then brown the chopped celery, onions and green pepper. Place these on top of the meat. Add the tomatoes and cover tightly. Cook until tender (2½ to 3 hours) over low heat.

Shirley M. Wright, York H. S.
Yorktown, Virginia

SWISS STEAK
Number of Servings — 8

8 T. flour
2 t. salt
¼ t. pepper
3 lbs. round steak, cut in 2-in. pieces
4 T. drippings or oleo
4 c. tomato juice
6 medium onions, sliced
2 c. celery, chopped
2 T. Worcestershire sauce
Few drops Tabasco sauce
2 T. sugar
2 T. salt

Combine salt, pepper and flour. Sprinkle half over steak. Pound. Turn steak and repeat. In a heavy skillet heat fat over low heat. Brown meat and put in roaster. Add remaining ingredients, let come to a boil. Pour over steak. Cover. Bake slowly (325°F.) 1½ to 2 hours.

Mrs. George Raboin, Carney H. S.
Carney, Michigan

SWISS STEAK QUICKIE
Number of Servings — 5

1½ lbs. chuck or round steak, 1-in. thick
1 envelope onion soup mix
2 T. butter or margarine
½ lb. fresh mushrooms or 2 4-oz. cans

Dot the center of 2½ feet of heavy, wide aluminum foil with 1 tablespoon of the butter. Shake ½ of the onion soup mix on the foil (be sure the soup is evenly mixed). Over this place the steak, top with remaining soup mix, 1 tablespoon butter and mushrooms. Bring foil up and seal tightly. Place in shallow baking pan and bake at 375°F. for 1 to 1½ hours.

Sandra Stinebring, Cissna Park H. S.
Cissna Park, Illinois

SUNDAY ROUND ROAST
Number of Servings — 12

4 lbs. round beef (cut 2 to 3 in. thick)
1 c. flour
1 t. salt
½ t. pepper
1 c. tomatoes
2 medium onions
½ c. fat
2 c. hot water

Salt and pepper roast on both sides. Mix remainder of salt and pepper with flour. Dredge roast on both sides. Melt fat in roaster or iron skillet. Sear roast to a medium brown on both sides to hold juices. Turn heat down. Add water. Add onions, and cook 1 hour with cover. Add tomatoes and salt. Simmer 1 hour. Slice and serve.

Ivy Cliff Weldon, B. B. Comer H. S.
Sylacauga, Alabama

SWISS STEAK WITH TOMATOES
Number of Servings — 6

1½-2 lbs. round or chuck steak, ½-in. thick
¼ c. flour
1 t. salt
¼ t. pepper
1 c. canned tomatoes or 1 c. tomato soup
1 chopped onion

Pound flour, salt, and pepper into steak. Brown both sides of steak in a little hot fat in Dutch oven or fry pan. Add chopped onion and tomatoes. Cover; cook in 350°F. oven 1½ hours, in Dutch oven, or on top of range in fry pan slowly for 45 minutes or until tender.

Marilyn Dahlheimer, Montgomery H. S.
Montgomery, Minnesota

SWISS STEAK SUPREME
Number of Servings — 6

1 round or chuck steak
½ c. flour
2 t. salt
½ t. pepper
¼ t. powdered garlic
2 bay leaves
1 c. canned mushroom pieces
½ c. slivered almonds
1 medium onion, chopped
2 10½-oz. cans tomato soup
1½ t. basil
1½ t. celery seed
1½ t. parsley flakes
1½ t. oregano
1½ t. pepper flakes
2 T. Worcestershire sauce
1 T. soy sauce

Mix flour, salt, pepper; pound into steak. Brown steak in a little hot fat in Dutch oven or deep skillet. Brown one side, turn and brown other side. Mix tomato soup, spices, onion, Worcestershire sauce, soy sauce, mushrooms and almonds. Pour over steak. Cover. Cook in moderate oven (350°F.) for 1½ hours.

Mrs. Phyllis Braun, Hagerstown H. S.
Hagerstown, Indiana

FLAVORFUL BEEF ROAST
Number of Servings — 6

4-4½ lbs. chuck or English cut roast
1 can condensed mushroom soup
1 package dry onion soup mix
3 T. steak sauce
Salt and pepper

Place the roast on a large sheet of aluminum foil. Spread the steak sauce on it. Sprinkle the onion soup, salt and pepper over the roast. Pour the mushroom soup on and cover with the foil. Bake in 325° oven for 3½ hours.

Carole Pinover, Vanlue H. S.
Vanlue, Ohio

STEAK STRIPS IN ZESTY SAUCE
Number of Servings — 6

1½ lbs. round steak
1 t. salt
½ t. pepper
4 T. salad oil
5 T. flour
1 medium sized onion
1 T. Worcestershire sauce
1 can tomato paste
1 can tomato soup
1 can tomato sauce

Cut steak into strips. Brown onions in salad oil then remove from pan. Roll steak strips into flour and seasonings and add to pan from which onions have been removed. Brown. Then add tomato paste, soup, sauce, Worcestershire sauce and onions to pan. Cover and simmer for 1 hour. Serve over rice or mashed potatoes.

Frances M. Hallett, Southington H. S.
Southington, Connecticut

CREOLE STEAK

¼ c. flour
2 t. salt
2 t. paprika
½ t. pepper
1 lb. round steak
1 c. onions, chopped
⅓ c. green peppers, chopped
½ c. raw rice
2½ c. canned tomatoes
2 c. hot water

Mix flour, salt, paprika, pepper, and then dredge meat in mixture. Save flour that remains. Brown onion and green peppers in shortening in skillet. Remove them and brown meat in remaining shortening. Cover meat with onions, sprinkle rice over this and top with tomatoes. Sprinkle remaining flour over this and cover tightly. Simmer 1 hour.

Carolyn M. Holley, Heflin H. S.
Heflin, Louisiana

PARTIFIED SWISS STEAK
Number of Servings — 6

2 lbs. round steak, 1½-in. thick
Flour
1 T. fat
1 large onion, thinly sliced
1 c. tomato juice
1 c. tomato sauce
¼ c. vinegar
1 T. sugar
½ t. dry mustard
¼ t. chili powder
2 t. salt
½ c. sliced pimento olives (optional)

Cut steak into 6 pieces. Pound flour into steak with edge of heavy saucer or meat hammer. Pan-

(Continued on Next Page)

brown steak in heavy skillet in hot fat. Add onion. Stir together the tomato juice, tomato sauce, vinegar, dry mustard, chili powder and salt and add to the browned meat. Stir together. Cover, Simmer 2½ hours, or until tender. Stir in olives during last 15 minutes of cooking time.

Ruth Baumback, Harrisburg Union H. S.
Harrisburg, Oregon

SWISS STEAK
Number of Servings — 6-7

2 or 3 stalks celery
1 onion
1 can tomato paste
1 t. Worcestershire sauce
1 small can mushroom pieces
½ bottle catsup
Enough V-8 to thin paste
6 or 7 pieces steak

Pound steak with flour. Braise in small amount of fat. Season to taste. Cook celery and onion until tender. Place steak in greased casserole. Add all ingredients to steak dripping and bring to boil; pour over steak. Bake at 325°F. for 30 to 45 minutes.

Mrs. Meril T. Kenyon, Holyoke H. S.
Holyoke, Colorado

SWISS STEAK ROLL
Number of Servings — 4

½ in. thick round steak
4 c. bread moistened with cream
4 cleaned green onions and stalk
4 long celery heart stalks
4 hard cooked eggs
1 T. parsley, chopped
½ c. flour
1 T. salt
½ t. pepper

Pound round steak slightly. Dip both sides in flour with two teaspoons salt. Spread moistened bread on one side, placing onions, celery and hard cooked eggs down center. Sprinkle with parsley, pepper and salt. Roll like jelly roll and tie with cord or fasten with tooth picks. Roll once more in remaining flour. Sear in frying pan with two tablespoons cooking oil. Add remaining flour and brown. Add 1½ cups water and spread remaining bread. Cook 1½ hours slowly.

Sarah M. Culotta, Northside H. S.
Lafayette, Louisiana

SWISS STEAK
Number of Servings — 6

2 lbs. steak
Salt and pepper
1 can tomato soup
2½ cans water
1 t. sugar
2 T. flour
Fat and flour for frying

Flour steak, fry in fat until brown. Place in roaster, or casserole dish, or pyrex dish. Add 2 tablespoons flour in pan where steak was browned. Then add tomato soup, water and sugar. Salt may be needed. Pour over steak and bake 2 hours, or until tender. Potatoes may be added if desired.

Mrs. Mary Carr Cain, Tygarts Valley H. S.
Mill Creek, West Virginia

SWISS STEAK WITH ONION RINGS
Number of Servings — 6

⅓ c. flour
2 t. salt
¼ t. pepper
2 lbs. round or chuck steak, 1-in. thick
3 T. fat
1 8-oz. can seasoned tomato sauce
2 5½-oz. cans pizza sauce
1 medium onion, sliced

Combine flour, salt, and pepper, pound into steak. Brown slowly on both sides in hot fat. Pour tomato sauce and pizza sauce over meat. Top with onion slices. Simmer uncovered 10 minutes. Now cover and bake in oven-going skillet or large casserole in moderate oven (350°F.) for 1 hour or a little longer, until the steak is fork-tender.

Diane M. Brown, Grayville H. S.
Grayville, Illinois

SWISS STEAK
Number of Servings — 4

1 round steak ¾" thick
1 can condensed cream of mushroom soup
1 can condensed cream of celery soup
1 pkg. dehydrated onions

Cut steak into serving-size pieces. Brown on both sides. Pour soups over meat, sprinkle onion over mixture. Cover skillet and bake at 350° for one hour.

Dianne Knutson, Onomia H. S.
Onomia, Minnesota

ROUND STEAK CASSEROLE
Number of Servings — 3

1 lb. round steak
1 or 2 onions, sliced
Salt and pepper

Cut meat in serving size pieces. Brown in skillet or fry pan. Put in casserole, placing the slices of onion between the layers of meat. Make water gravy out of the brownings of the meat, seasoning with salt and pepper. Pour over meat—put in oven one and one-half hours at 350°.

Mrs. Layne Storment, Post Falls H. S.
Post Falls, Idaho

BEEF STROGANOFF
Number of Servings — 6

1½ lbs. round steak, cut in ½ inch wide strips
MIX TOGETHER:
1 can onion soup
1 can tomato paste
1 T. Worcestershire sauce
1 can mushrooms and juice (3 or 4 ounces)
1 c. sour cream, served separately

Flour the meat by shaking in a paper sack. Brown the meat. Remove from frying pan to a casserole or baking pan, cover with the sauce. (This much can be done a day ahead.) Bake in covered casserole at 300° F. for 1¾ hours. Serve over about ½ pound buttered noodles.

Judy Betlach, Orosi Union H. S.
Orosi, California

BEEF STROGANOFF
Number of Servings — 10

⅓ c. flour
2 lbs. top round steak, ½" thick
¼ c. butter
¾ c. water
4 oz. can mushrooms and juice (optional)
½ c. onion, sliced
½ t. Worcestershire sauce
2 c. sour cream (may use evaporated milk and 2 T. lemon juice)
2 t. salt
¼ t. black pepper

Pound flour into beef until steak is ¼" thick. Cut into strips ½" wide and 2" long. Brown in butter in skillet. Add remaining ingredients, except sour cream. Cook over low heat with tight fitting cover for 25 minutes, stirring occasionally. Stir in sour cream and serve over rice or noodles. May be frozen.

Mrs. May Campbell, Orangefield H. S.
Orangefield, Texas

BEEF STROGANOFF
Number of Servings — 6-8

1 lb. round steak cut thin
¼ c. all-purpose flour
½ t. salt
⅛ t. pepper
2 T. shortening
½ c. chopped onions
1 6-oz. can mushrooms
½ c. diced green pepper
1 clove garlic, minced
1 c. thick sour cream
1 can tomato soup
1 T. Worcestershire sauce
¼ t. tabasco sauce (optional)

Cut meat into ¾ inch cubes and dredge with flour, which has been seasoned with salt and pepper. Brown in hot fat. When meat is browned, add onions, mushrooms and garlic. Combine cream, tomato soup, green pepper and Worcestershire sauce. Pour over meat. Stir so all ingredients are well blended. Cover skillet. Cook on "medium high" until steaming, then reduce heat to "low" and cook 35 to 40 minutes. This is excellent served over spaghetti or Chinese Omelet or steamed rice.

Hazel R. Freeman, West Valley H. S.
Yakima, Washington

BEEF STROGANOFF
Number of Servings — 4-6

3 T. flour
1½ t. salt
¼ t. pepper
1 lb. beef tenderloin, ¼-in thick
1 clove garlic, cut
¼ c. butter
½ c. onions, minced
¼ c. water
1 can condensed chicken soup (undiluted)
1 lb. mushrooms, sliced
1 c. commercial sour cream
Snipped parsley

Combine flour, salt and pepper. Trim fat from meat. Rub both sides of meat with garlic. Pound flour mixture into sides of meat. Cut meat into 1½" x 1' strips. Brown meat strips in hot butter. Add onion. Saute till golden. Add water and stir. Add soup, mushrooms; cook uncovered over low heat, stirring occasionally, until meat is tender—about 20 minutes. Just before serving, stir in sour cream, heat, do not boil. Sprinkle with parsley.

Mrs. Rose Mary Diedrich, Edgar H. S.
Edgar, Wisconsin

BEEF STROGANOFF
Number of Servings — 4-6

3 T. flour
1½ t. salt
¼ t. pepper
1 lb. beef tenderloin
1 cut clove garlic
½ c. minced onion
¼ c. water
1 c. undiluted condensed chicken soup
1 4-ounce can mushrooms
1 c. sour cream

Combine flour, salt and pepper. Trim fat from meat. Rub both sides with garlic. Pound flour mixture into both sides of meat. Cut meat into 1½" x 1" strips. Brown meat. Add onions. Saute until golden. Add water, stir. Add soup, mushrooms. Cook uncovered over low heat, stirring occasionally, until mixture is thick and meat is tender, about 20 minutes. Just before serving, stir in cream, heat, but do not boil. Serve with rice, mashed or riced potatoes.

Joyce Thorson, Union H. S.
Shiocton, Wisconsin

STEAK STROGANOFF
Number of Servings — 4-6

1½ lb. Sirloin or round steak cut in ¾" cubes
Flour
2 T. shortening
½ onion, minced
1 clove garlic, minced
1 6-oz. can mushrooms
1½ c. sour cream
1 can tomato soup
6 drops tabasco sauce
1 T. Worcestershire sauce
½ t. salt

Dip meat in flour and brown in hot shortening. Add onion, garlic and drained mushrooms to meat. Combine tomato soup, liquor from mushrooms and seasonings and pour over meat. Simmer in frying pan about 1 hour. Serve over rice or mashed potatoes.

Deanna Christenson, Cambridge H. S.
Cambridge, Minnesota

BEEF STROGANOFF
Number of Servings — 4

1½ lbs. round steak
¼ c. flour
¼ c. butter or margarine
1 4-oz. can sliced mushrooms
½ c. chopped onion
1 small clove garlic (minced)
1 can beef broth soup
1 c. sour cream
3 c. cooked noodles

Cut round steak into thin strips. Dust with flour. In large skillet, brown meat in fat. Add mushrooms, onion, garlic. Brown lightly. Stir in beef broth. Cover: cook 1 hour or until meat is tender; stir now and then. Gradually stir in sour cream; cook over low heat 5 minutes. Serve over cooked noodles.

Eleanor E. Barnes, General McLane Joint H. S.
Edinboro, Pennsylvania

BEEF STROGANOFF
Number of Servings — 6

3 lbs. round steak, cut in 1-in. strips (less expensive cuts or left over roast may be used)
1 large onion cut fine (diced)
1 cube butter or oleo
1 can mushroom pieces or slices
1 can tomato soup
1 carton commercial sour cream

Brown meat and onions in the cube of butter. Add salt and pepper to taste. Add the tomato soup and simmer until the meat is tender. Add the mushrooms and the sour cream. Continue to simmer, but do not boil. Serve hot over minute rice. Serve a tossed green salad with this meal.

Mrs. Howard M. McBee, Frederick H. S.
Frederick, Oklahoma

BEEF STROGANOFF
Number of Servings — 8

3 lbs. lean beef (sirloin tip or loin tip)
3 T. butter
1 large onion, thinly sliced
4 T. flour
1 can condensed consomme
1 can condensed tomato soup
1 8-oz. can mushroom stems and pieces, drained
1 t. Worcestershire sauce
1 can sour cream
½ t. paprika
Salt and pepper to taste

Remove the skin and fat from the meat. Cut the meat across the grain in narrow strips 2 inches long. Heat butter in a large, heavy utensil. Add meat and cook stirring with a fork, until nicely browned. Add onion and continue cooking 2 or 3 minutes. Sprinkle flour over the meat and stir well. Add consomme and soup, cook stirring constantly, until sauce boils and thickens. Add drained mushrooms and seasonings. Cover and simmer for 1 to 1½ hours, stirring occasionally. Stir in sour cream and paprika. Add additional salt and pepper if needed. Serve over noodles or fluffy rice.

Mrs. Margaret Hollingsworth, Montevallo H. S.
Montevallo, Alabama

BEEF STROGANOFF
Number of Servings — 4

1½ lbs. round steak
¼ c. butter
4 ozs. mushrooms, sliced
½ c. chopped onion
1 small clove garlic (minced)
1 can beef broth
1 c. dairy sour cream
¼ c. flour
Dash of pepper

Cut one and one-half pound round steak into thin strips; dust with flour, dash pepper. In large skillet, brown meat in butter. Add mushrooms, drained, onion, clove garlic (minced); brown lightly. Stir in beef broth. Cover; cook about one hour; stir now and then. Gradually stir in sour cream; cook over low heat five minutes. Serve over three cups noodles.

Revia C. Munch, Branford H. S.
Branford, Florida

BEEF STROGANOFF
Number of Servings — 6-8
2 lbs. beef, round steak
8 T. flour
1½ t. salt
½ t. pepper
Fat or bacon drippings
2 c. water
1 4-ounce can mushrooms
1 onion, sliced
1 c. sour cream

(Continued on Next Page)

Cut beef in long narrow strips. Toss in mixture of 6 tablespoons flour, 1½ teaspoon salt, and ¼ teaspoon pepper. Brown in small amount of fat and add water, ¼ teaspoon pepper, mushrooms and onion. Cover and simmer until tender. Add paste of 2 tablespoons flour and 2 tablespoons water. Add slowly to meat. Simmer until thick. Add sour cream. Do not boil. Serve over rice or Chinese noodles.

Mrs. Imogene D. Spring, Seymour H. S.
Seymour, Texas

STEAK AND POTATO KABOBS
Number of Servings — 8

1½ lbs. round steak, 1 inch thick
2 large potatoes, peeled
Salt and pepper
Flour
12 wooden skewers
About 3 T. shortening

Cut steak and potatoes into one inch cubes. Alternate steak and potato cubes on skewers, beginning and ending with steak. Season and roll in flour. Brown in skillet with shortening over medium heat. Place in casserole or baking pan. Pour 1-2 tablespoons of fat drippings from skillet over kabobs. Add ¼ cup water. Cover well and bake in moderate oven one hour.

Mrs. Francis Garrison, Santa Fe H. S.
Santa Fe, New Mexico

KABOBS (Beef on Skewers)
Number of Servings — 4

½ c. olive oil
¾ t. salt
½ t. pepper
½ t. dried oregano or rosemary
1 lb. lean beef cut in 1½ inch cubes
8 ripe olives pitted
2 onions cut in wedges
2 tomatoes cut in wedges

Mix olive oil, salt, pepper, and herbs. Sprinkle this mixture over meat and let stand in a cool place for at least one hour. Put skewer through meat, olives, and vegetables alternately using ¼ of each for each kabob. Broil until meat is well browned. Turn skewers to brown meat evenly. Loosen and push from skewer directly onto the serving plate.

Georgamy K. Campbell, Western H. S.
Las Vegas, Nevada

BROILED RIB STEAK

Salt and pepper according to desire. Use juice of one lemon to two steaks. Grill on charcoal grill or in oven to desired doneness. Delicious served with tossed green salad, browned rice, and French bread.

Wanda C. Hightower, Limestone County H. S.
Elkmont, Alabama

GOURMET POT ROAST BROILED
Number of Servings — 8

4 lb. roast (2-in. thick), roast should have
   fat on it
1 t. salt
Freshly ground black pepper
1 t. "Fines Herbes" (Spice Island)
1 t. oregano
1 c. cooking wine, it may be red or light

Rub salt, pepper, and herbs into both sides of meat; place in bowl, add wine. Refrigerate overnight, turning once. To broil: remove from wine, brush with oil; place on preheated broiler pan, 4 inches from heat. Broil 15 minutes on each side. This medium well done time may be adjusted to taste. (This may be pot roasted in the wine).

Mrs. Charles Harper, White Cloud H. S.
White Cloud, Michigan

INDIVIDUAL OVEN POT ROAST
Number of Servings — 6

3 lbs. boneless chuck beef (2-in. thick)
1 large clove garlic
Dried herb mix (for meat)
1 envelope (1½-ozs.) onion soup mix
1 can (10½-ozs.) condensed mushroom soup
1 T. red wine vinegar
1 t. sugar

Cut meat into 6 servings; place each on a strip of foil wide and long enough to enclose it generously. Sliver garlic and insert in slits in pieces of meat; sprinkle meat with herb mix. Mix the onion soup mix (in dry form just as it comes from envelope) with the undiluted condensed mushroom soup, vinegar and sugar; spoon over pieces of meat. Wrap foil loosely around meat, making drugstore fold at top and turning up ends several times so packages won't leak. Place on jelly roll pan or cookie sheet. Bake in moderate (350°F.) oven about 2 hours or until beef is very tender; gravy will not be thick. (Test beef by opening one package). MENU NOTE: Serve with mashed potatoes and buttered green peas and celery.

Evelyn Cotney, Northeast District Supvr.
Home Economics Education
Montevallo, Alabama

TENDER CHUCK ROAST & BROWN TASTY GRAVY
Number of Servings — 6

1 beef roast, approx. 3-lbs.
1 can cream of mushroom soup
1 package dried onion soup

Sprinkle onion soup (half the package) on the foil, then spoon half the can of creamed soup over the soup. Lay the raw beef on top of the mixture, then sprinkle the remaining dried onion soup on the meat, and spoon the rest of the creamed soup on top of all. Rinse out the can with 2 tablespoons of water, sprinkle over mixture. Fold foil up and over, air tight and so liquid won't leak out. Bake at 325°F. for approximately 2 hours or until tender. Very juicy and tender.

Mrs. Marjorie Stewart, Fordsville H. S.
Fordsville, Kentucky

ROAST BEEF
Number of Servings — 6

3 lbs. chuck roast
1 can cream of mushroom soup
1 package dry onion soup mix

Line a shallow roasting pan with heavy aluminum foil. Spread dry onion soup mix on bottom of the foil. Place roast on top of mix and spread cream of mushroom soup over the surface. Bring aluminum foil up around sides of roast and fold to seal. Bake in moderate oven (325°F.) for 3 hours.

Mrs. Betty S. Turner, Chicod H. S.
Greenville, North Carolina

BEEF POT ROAST WITH VEGETABLES
Number of Servings — 6-8

¼ c. salad oil
3 lb. beef pot roast (chuck or round)
½ t. pepper
4 t. salt
3½ c. hot water
6 medium onions, peeled
6 medium carrots, scraped and cut in half
    lengthwise
6 medium potatoes, peeled and halved
¼ c. flour

Heat salad oil in large skillet or Dutch oven. Wipe meat with damp cloth, sprinkle with pepper and 2 teaspoons of the salt; slowly brown in hot fat, about 15 minutes on each side. Reduce heat; add ½ cup of water. Cover; simmer for 1½ hours. Add water in small quantities as needed. Add onions; continue to cook, covered, about 30 minutes longer. Add carrots and potatoes, and sprinkle with remaining salt. Cover, simmer for 30 minutes until meat and vegetables are tender; turn occasionally. Remove to serving platter; keep hot. Make a paste of flour and remaining water and add to hot juices. Heat to boiling; stir to keep smooth. Serve in gravy boat immediately.

Mrs. Robert C. Powell, Atkinson Com. H. S.
Atkinson, Illinois

CHUCK ROAST IN FOIL
Number of Servings — 6

3 lbs. beef chuck
1 envelope onion soup mix
1 can cream of mushroom soup (undiluted)

In a dripping pan place a piece of aluminum foil (heavy weight) large enough to wrap your roast in. Place roast on foil, sprinkle with onion soup mix and spread mushroom soup over the top of all. Wrap in the foil and seal well. Place in pre-heated oven of 375 degrees and bake for about 2½ hours. When tender, remove meat onto serving plate, and you will find wonderful brown gravy of the right consistency and flavor, just scrape off the foil and serve.

Mrs. Warren Eiseth, Suring H. S.
Suring, Wisconsin

HARVEST ROAST (CHUCK ROUND)
Number of Servings — 6-8

3-5 lb. beef roast
Salt and pepper
Flour
2 T. melted fat
½ c. wine vinegar
½ c. catsup
1 clove garlic
Bay leaf

Salt, pepper and flour should be rubbed into meat. Brown slowly in hot fat. Simmer in wine vinegar for ½ hour with lid on. Insert garlic in meat; pour catsup on top of meat—then turn meat over. Add bay leaf. Roast in oven at 325°F. until done.

Mrs. Eleanor Roberts, Thompsonville H. S.
Thompsonville, Illinois

DAUBE ROAST
Number of Servings — 12

4-5 lbs. solid beef at least 5″ thick
1½ lbs. fat rib meat
2 onions sliced
Salt and pepper to taste
Garlic if desired
Vinegar

Cut fat meat into strips about ¾ in. square and long enough to go through roast and stick out about an inch on each side. Cut holes in roast about 2 in. apart and put fat meat through holes after being rolled in salt and pepper. Pour vinegar almost to top, but do not cover. Place onions on top. Cover and place in refrigerator overnight. Turn after removing onions then replace onions and let stand about 12 hours longer. Pour off half of vinegar when ready to cook. Add it again as it cooks. Cook at 325 degrees until tender. Baste often. Gravy made with flour as for any roast. I have never eaten this anywhere else but it is delicious. I dilute the vinegar with a little water, about ¾ cup vinegar to ⅓ cup water.

Dionetta K. Talley, Demopolis H. S.
Demopolis, Alabama

COUNTRY STYLE BEEF ROAST
Number of Servings — 6-8

Select a 4-5 pound beef roast. Rub well with seasoned flour. Place in a roaster (on a rack to prevent sticking). Add water to a depth of about 2 inches. Cook uncovered in a moderate oven (350°) until roast is tender. (May need to add more water during cooking time). An onion may be added the last hour of cooking. Remove meat from roaster. Use juice for gravy. May need a little thickening added.

Bernice M. Baker, Cobb Memorial
Ruffin, North Carolina

ROAST BEEF DELIGHT
Number of Servings — 6

3 lbs. boneless chuck beef
1 large clove garlic
Dried herb mix (for meat)
1 envelope onion soup mix
1 can condensed mushroom soup
1 T. red wine vinegar
1 t. sugar

Cut meat into 6 serving pieces; place each on a strip of foil wide enough and long enough to enclose it generously. Sliver garlic and insert in slits in each piece of meat; sprinkle meat with herb mix. Mix onion soup (just as it comes from envelope) with the undiluted mushroom soup, vinegar and sugar. Spoon over meat, wrap foil loosely around meat. Bake at 350° for 2 hours.

Mrs. Margaret Helton, Harrodsburg H. S.
Harrodsburg, Kentucky

MARINATED CHUCK ROAST
Number of Servings — 12

5 lbs. of chuck roast (not over 3″ thick)
Meat tenderizer (optional)
½ c. salad oil
½ c. tomato catsup
½ c. wine vinegar
1½ t. salt
1 t. black pepper
1 clove garlic (optional)

With fork or ice pick pierce roast about one inch apart on both sides. Place in casserole. Combine all other ingredients and pour over roast, cover and let marinate in the refrigerator for 12 to 18 hours. Broil over charcoal for 45 minutes and turn and broil for 30 minutes. Brush with remaining marinade. Left overs very good served cold or warmed over in remaining marinade.

Dorothy E. Perryman, Alpine H. S.
Alpine, Texas

BEEF POT ROAST
Number of Servings — 16

4 lbs. chuck, arm, round bone or rump roast
3 large onions
Salt, pepper, garlic salt and celery salt
2 T. fat

Heat fat in Dutch oven and sear meat on both sides. Add ¼ cup water and cook meat down in it. Turn meat and repeat on other side. Now season each side and add 1 cup water. Add onions, cut in quarters. Cover and cook slowly for 2 hours, turning occasionally, and adding more water if needed. If very brown gravy is desired, tilt the lid and allow it to cook down twice at the end of the cooking time.

Amy D. Thompson, Dolores H. S.
Dolores, Colorado

SAVORY BEEF AU JUS
Number of Servings — 8

4-5 lb. roast (blade or pot may be used)
1 package dry onion soup mix
2 cans condensed cream mushroom soup
⅛ t. pepper
1½ c. water

Place roast in center on two sheets of foil wrap, 1 length straight and one crosswise in order to make a double covering. Sprinkle contents of one package onion soup mix over meat. Empty contents of two cans of mushroom soup in center of roast. Spread evenly over surface. Seal foil with drug-store fold leaving space on top of meat to allow soups to combine. Place in open pan and roast in moderate oven, 300 degrees approximately 25-30 minutes per pound. When meat is thoroughly done open foil and fold back. Brown quickly on top using broiler, then pour 1½ cups water over browned surface. Allow meat to simmer approximately 15 minutes more to make its own gravy.

Betty T. Moran, Pleasant Hill H. S.
Shanghai, Virginia

ROAST BEEF
Number of Servings — 6

2-3 lb. roast
1 can cream of mushroom soup
1 package concentrated onion soup
1 can water
5 small whole potatoes
4 whole carrots

Place concentrated onion soup in bottom of Dutch oven or large skillet, then place roast on top and pour mushroom soup and water over the top. Cook at very low heat 2 hours with cover or lid on pan. Add potatoes and carrots and let all cook for 30-45 minutes more. When finished you have gravy and vegetables cooked right along with meat.

Mrs. Katie B. Harrison, Forrest City Jr. H. S.
Forrest City, Arkansas

SPICED ROAST BEEF
Number of Servings — 15

½ loin of beef (5 lbs.)
¼ box pickling spices
Water—(½ meat covered)

(Continued on Next Page)

Salt and pepper
1 T. bay leaves
1 medium onion (slices to cover and in water)

Combine pickling spice and bay leaves in a small cloth bag. Place meat in roasting pan. Cover ½ of meat with water. (Drop bag of spices in water). Place several onion slices on top of meat, and put remaining slices in water. Salt and pepper to taste. Bake at 325°F. until tender—about 3 or 4 hours. Use drippings to make gravy.

Sondra Singhurse, Speedway H. S.
Speedway, Indiana

ROAST WITH COCA COLA

2-3 lb. beef roast
Salt (for season)
Pepper (for season)
2-4 T. flour
4 T. fat
1 Coca Cola

Salt and pepper roast. Flour on all sides and brown in hot fat. When browned on both sides drain fat off. Open Coca Cola and pour over roast. Place in 325°F. oven and allow to cook until desired doneness. (Cook in covered container approximately 2½-3½ hours.

Mrs. Edna G. Whitley, Lanesville H. S.
Lanesville, Texas

BEEF ROAST
Number of Servings — 10

3 lbs. beef roast
1½ c. water
1 bay leaf
2 T. brown sugar
¼ c. vinegar

Cook under pressure (15 pounds) for 30 minutes.

Alice Neel Eidson, Sans Souci Jr. H. S.
Greenville, South Carolina

QUICK ROAST BEEF DINNER
Number of Servings — 6

4 lbs. beef roast
1 T. Fat
Salt and pepper
1 medium minced onion
½ c. water
4 medium potatoes
6 medium carrots

Heat pressure cooker and add fat. Brown roast well on all sides. Season with salt, pepper, and onions; add water. Close cover securely. Place pressure regulator on vent pipe and cook 25 minutes at 15 pounds pressure. Let pressure drop and add potatoes and carrots. Reclose and cook 10 minutes more at 15 pounds pressure. Let pressure drop of its own accord. If desired, gravy may be made from the liquid in the cooker.

Mrs. Glendine Crider, West Oso H. S.
Corpus Christi, Texas

ONION POT ROAST
Number of Servings —

1 chuck, arm or rump roast
1 can mushroom soup
1 envelope dehydrated onion soup

Sear roast in hot fat. Spoon over roast 1 can undiluted cream of mushroom soup. Sprinkle 1 envelope dehydrated onion soup over all. Cover and cook slowly until meat is tender. If gravy is not thick enough, thicken with cornstarch, diluted in cold water.

Mrs. Billie J. McCarroll, Slidell H. S.
Slidell, Texas

BEEF ROAST ROLLS (From left over roast)
Number of Servings — 10

1½ c. left-over roast
1 c. medium white sauce or 1 c. left-over gravy
1 recipe rich biscuit dough

Heat white sauce or gravy, add ground left-over roast and let stand while dough is being prepared. Prepare biscuit dough, pat and roll into an oblong shape about ¼ inch thick. Spread with meat mixture. Roll like a jelly roll and slice rounds about 1½ inches thick. Place on a greased cooky sheet and bake in a preheated oven, 375°F. about 30 minutes or until brown.

Mrs. Celeste T. Prugel, Sonora H. S.
Sonora, Texas

HOT MUSTARD RUMP ROAST
Number of Servings — 6

4 or 5 lbs. rump roast
2 t. hot mustard
1 t. horseradish
½ t. oregano
½ t. black pepper
Salt to taste
1 c. water

Salt roast and then mix with the other seasoning and rub this over the roast. Wrap securely in aluminum foil. Place on broiler rack. Put 1 cup water in broiler pan. Cook 2½ hours. Oven temperature 325°F.

Mattie Finney, Vashon H. S.
Burton, Washington

HIGHLAND POT ROAST
Number of Servings — 8

2 lbs. rump beef (1 piece)
2 T. shortening
8 small potatoes, peeled
2 stalks celery (cut in 2-in. pieces)
4 medium carrots (quartered lengthwise)
1 T. salt
¼ t. pepper
16 dried apricots (washed)
1 c. sliced mushrooms
1 c. catsup

(Continued on Next Page)

Heat oven to 325°F. Brown beef in shortening in Dutch oven at medium heat. Arrange vegetables around meat. Sprinkle with salt and pepper. Top meat with apricots and mushrooms. Pour catsup over all, cover. Bake two hours or until meat and vegetables are tender. Baste occasionally. Add a little water if thinner gravy is desired.

Mrs. Wendell Bachmann, Colo Com. H. S.
Colo, Iowa

BEEF ESTOUFFADE
Number of Servings — 5-7

2 lbs. boneless beef
½ c. cooking oil
3 lbs. small onions
1 lb. onions, diced
2 T. vinegar
½ c. claret wine
5 cloves garlic
1 c. tomato juice
3 bay leaves
1 t. pickling spices, tied in cheese cloth
Salt and pepper, to taste

Cut meat in pieces the size of walnuts and brown slightly in oil. Peel small onions and add with diced onions to meat in a Dutch oven. Add remaining ingredients and cover oven. Cook in 350°F. oven for two hours, or until meat and onions are done. Remove bay leaves and pickling spices immediately and serve.

Mrs. Bettie Ware Moore, R. E. Lee Institute
Thomaston, Georgia

POT ROAST MEAL
Number of Servings — 6

4-lb. chuck or shoulder cut of beef
¼ c. all-purpose flour
1¼ T. salt
¼ t. pepper
3 T. fat
1 c. water
1 onion, whole
6 medium or small potatoes cut lengthwise
6 carrots cut lengthwise

Dredge meat with flour seasoned with the pepper and half the salt. Place skillet on unit. Add the fat. Turn control to medium-high. When hot, place meat in skillet and brown both sides. Add water, place onion on top of meat and cover skillet. When steam escapes, turn control to "simmer" and continue cooking for 1 hour. Add potatoes and carrots and other half of salt. Cover skillet and continue cooking for 1 hour.

Myrtle Little, Hattiesburg H. S.
Hattiesburg, Mississippi

POT ROAST
Number of Servings — 6-8

4 lb. piece of rump beef
1 t. salt

2 to 3 T. fat dripping or piece of fat cut from meat
½ to 1 c. water
1 onion

Wipe meat with damp cloth. Place fat or drippings in heavy kettle and heat. Place the meat in the kettle and brown on all sides, seasoning meat as it is browned. Add small amount of water if desired. Peel and add onion. Simmer slowly over low heat 3 or 4 hours. Make gravy from liquid.

Mrs. Sam M. Brown, McAdoo H. S.
McAdoo, Texas

POT ROAST AND SPAGHETTI
Number of Servings — 6

1 2-lb. chuck pot roast
1 clove garlic, quartered
2 T. olive oil
2 T. butter
1 clove garlic, minced
1 small onion, chopped
2 t. oregano
1 t. thyme
½ t. basil
⅛ t. cinnamon
1 t. salt
¼ t. pepper
2 cans tomato paste
3½ c. water
1 lb. spaghetti
Grated Parmesan or Romano cheese

Make 4 slits in roast and insert quarters of garlic. Heat oil and butter in large kettle. Brown meat slowly on all sides. Remove meat and lower heat. Add minced garlic and next 7 seasonings. Cook gently about 5 minutes, being careful not to burn. Return meat. Mix tomato paste with water and pour over meat. Bring to full boil. Lower heat and cover loosely. Simmer slowly about 2 hours, turning meat occasionally. When meat is tender and sauce thickened, cook spaghetti. Serve spaghetti and sauce in large shallow dish, sprinkle well with cheese. Arrange sliced meat alongside.

Camille K. Crossley, Conestoga Valley Sr. H. S.
Lancaster, Pennsylvania

SPICY POT ROAST
Number of Servings — 6-8

3 to 5 lbs. beef pot roast
2 T. fat
½ c. brown sugar, firmly packed
¼ t. salt
½ c. vinegar
¼ c. soy sauce
½ bay leaf crumbled
4 stalks celery
2 medium size onions

Brown roast in hot fat in heavy skillet. Mix brown sugar, salt, vinegar, soy sauce and bay leaf. Pour over roast. Cover tightly and cook in 300° oven for 2 hours or fork tender. Remove roast to warm

(Continued on Next Page)

platter. Thicken liquid for gravy if desired. Use 1½ tablespoons flour for every cup of broth.

Mrs. Bert Johnson, Bruce H. S.
Bruce, Mississippi

BROILED FLANK STEAK
Number of Servings — 6

4 T. salad oil
2 T. catsup
2 t. soy sauce
2 T. water
1 small onion, chopped fine
1 clove garlic, minced; or
¼ t. garlic powder
1 flank steak

Place the flank steak in a flat pyrex pan. Put the remaining ingredients into a jar and shake well. Pour over the flank steak. Let stand overnight, but turn occasionally. Broil as you would for any other steak. Don't cut until ready to serve. When serving, cut slantwise across the grain.

Pauline Gist, North Salinas H. S.
Salinas, California

BAKED FLANK STEAK
Number of Servings — 6

1 flank steak, floured
2 T. shortening
1 can (No. 303) tomatoes
1 medium onion, sliced
¼ c. green peppers, chopped
½ t. chili powder
½ t. salt
¼ t. garlic salt
¼ t. pepper
1 t. sugar

Brown the floured flank steak in a skillet with melted shortening. Cover browned meat with onion slices, green pepper and tomatoes. Then sprinkle the remaining seasonings over the meat and vegetables. Place uncovered skillet in a 325°F. oven and bake for 1 hour.

Beryl Sue Boyle Coulson, Mascoutah Com. H. S.
Mascoutah, Illinois

BAKED FLANK STEAK
Number of Servings — 2

1 lb. flank steak (scored)
½ bottle catsup
1½ T. Worcestershire sauce
1 medium onion, diced
Salt and pepper
1 t. dry mustard
2 T. brown sugar
2 T. butter

Preheat skillet in 375° oven. Add butter. Add meat and sauce. Dot with butter. Bake 20 minutes. Cut on bias to serve.

Sherry Hirsch, Colerain H. S.
Cincinnati, Ohio

BAKED STUFFED FLANK STEAK
Number of Servings — 6-8

2 lb. steak, flank, scored
1½ c. bread crumbs, soft
½ c. water or stock
1 t. salt
⅛ t. pepper
¼ c. turnip, ground or diced
¼ c. carrot, ground or diced
¼ c. celery, ground or diced
¼ c. onion, ground or diced
¼ c. flour
¼ c. drippings

Dice the vegetables. Mix all ingredients except steak, flour and drippings. Place mixture on steak and roll it so that slices may be cut across the grain. Fasten roll with toothpicks. Roll in flour and brown in drippings. Place in roasting pan with small amount of water. Cover tightly. Bake for 1½ hours at 325 to 350°F.

Gloria Ann Page, Dodge City Sr. H. S.
Dodge City, Kansas

STUFFED FLANK STEAK
Number of Servings — 3

1 scored flank steak
½ c. salad oil
¼ c. sweet pickle relish
2 slices bread
1 can onion soup
½ c. cooking sherry (optional)

Break bread into pieces and mix with pickle relish and one-half of the salad oil. Spread this mixture on the flank steak and roll into a loaf shape. Fasten ends with skewers or toothpicks. Brown in remaining salad oil; cover with onion soup and sherry and cook at 350° for approximately 1½ hours.

Mrs. William Delaney, Williams H. S.
Williams, Arizona

STUFFED FLANK STEAK
Number of Servings — 4

1 flank steak (about 1 lb.)
4 c. dry bread crumbs
3 T. finely chopped onion
Hot water or stock to moisten
1 t. salt
¼ t. pepper
¼ t. poultry seasoning
Thyme or sage to taste

Combine bread, onion, seasonings; add butter and sufficient liquid to moisten. Toss gently to mix. Spread scored flank steak with dressing. Fold edges together, fasten with toothpicks or skewers and lace with string. Brown steak on all sides in hot fat; add ½ cup water; cover tightly and simmer slowly for one-and-one-half hours.

Sybil Widvey, Medford H. S.
Medford, Wisconsin

STUFFED FLANK STEAK
Number of Servings — 8

1 flank steak
½ lb. pork sausage
1 c. soft bread crumbs
½ c. apple
1 t. chopped onion
1 T. minced parsley
¼ t. baking powder
½ t. sage
2 slightly beaten eggs
¼ t. salt
2 T. fat
1 c. tomato catsup

Combine sausage which has been fried slightly, bread crumbs, onion, apple, parsley and baking powder. Sprinkle sage over. Moisten stuffing with eggs. Score steak and sprinkle with salt and pepper. Spoon stuffing on steak and sew edges together. Brown in hot fat. Place sewn side down in baking dish. Spread with catsup. Cover and bake in moderate oven (350°) 1 hour. Uncover and bake 30 minutes longer or till tender.

Mrs. Katherine Hoar, South Jr. H. S.
Rapid City, South Dakota

GINGER BEEF
Number of Servings — 4-5

2 onions
3 cloves garlic
1½ t. turmeric
¼ t. dried chili peppers (Optional)
5 t. powdered ginger or 2-inch piece fresh
    ginger, chopped
1½ t. salt
pickled watermelon
1¼ lbs. flank steak, cut diagonally, across grain,
    into thin slices or 2-inch by ½-inch strips
3 T. peanut or salad oil
1 1-lb. 3-oz. can tomatoes
1 10½-oz. can condensed onion soup, undiluted
4 to 6 c. hot cooked rice

In chopping bowl, combine onions, garlic, turmeric, chili peppers, ginger and salt; chop fine. Add flank steak slices or strips and toss together. Let stand to season, refrigerator, from 15 minutes to 3 hours, depending on your schedule. Then, in Dutch oven, heat oil. Add flank steak and onion mixture; brown lightly. Add tomatoes; then cook, uncovered, over high heat, 10 minutes. Add soup; cover and simmer 1 hour, if steak is sliced, or 1½ to 2 hours if it's in strips, or until steak is tender.

To serve, measure hot rice into oval vegetable dish; place cookie sheet on top of it; press down well, then remove cookie sheet and unmold rice in center of oval platter. Over rice, spoon a few pieces of the steak, then spoon rest of mixture around it. Garnish at either end with pickled watermelon.

Linda Powell, West Fannin H. S.
Blue Ridge, Georgia

STUFFED FLANK STEAK
Number of Servings — 6-8

2 T. butter or margarine
1 medium onion, chopped
3 c. soft bread crumbs
½ t. poultry seasoning
2 T. fat or salad oil
½ t. salt
Dash of pepper
3 T. hot water
1 egg, well beaten
1 flank steak (about 2 lbs.)
½ c. boiling water

Set oven for slow 325°F. Melt butter in a 10 inch skillet. Add onion. Cook until golden brown. Add next 6 ingredients and mix well. Spread on steak. Roll up like jelly roll; tie securely with string. Heat fat in the skillet. Brown meat roll on all sides. Sprinkle with additional salt and pepper; add the ½ cup boiling water. Cover; bake 1½ hours or until meat is tender.

Mrs. Mary Kay S. Bisignani,
Hempfield Area Sr. H. S.
Greensburg, Pennsylvania

STUFFED BEEF TENDERLOIN
Number of Servings — 6-8

1 3-lb. beef tenderloin
½ small onion, chopped
1 4-oz. can mushrooms
¼ c. butter or margarine
1½ cups soft bread crumbs
½ c. diced celery
Hot water
Salt and pepper
4 slices bacon

Have tenderloin split and flattened. Brown onion and mushrooms in butter. Add bread crumbs, celery, and hot water to moisten. Season; spread over half the meat. Fold over second half; fasten edges. Season; place bacon slices over top. Roast uncovered in moderate oven (350°) 1 hour.

Faye Ruble, Claskeemas H. S.
Milwaukie, Oregon

FLANK STEAK SURPRISE
Number of Servings — 6-8

2 lbs. flank steak, seasoned with ½ t. salt
Cover with dressing by combining the following:
¼ c. celery, ground
⅓ c. carrots, ground
¼ c. onions, minced
1 c. bread crumbs
½ t. salt
¼ t. pepper

Roll and tie. Brown in ¼ cup hot fat. Add 1 cup water. Cover, and bake in 350°F. oven for 1½ hours or until tender. Serve with diced carrots.

Vola May Miller, Sparta Township H. S.
Sparta, Illinois

ROLLED SAUSAGE (Christmas delicacy)
Number of Servings — 12-15

1 t. celery salt
1 t. allspice
1 t. nutmeg
1 t. ginger
Flank from ¼ of beef
1 t. black pepper
1 t. thyme
½ t. cloves
Small amount of salt peter

Mix all spices together. Cut strips of meat, pork and beef. Make sacks of flanks by filling with meat in this manner. Place spices on the flank. Take strips of pork and beef until you have enough meat to fill flanks. Roll together and sew. Place in brine for 2-3 days, made by putting meat in crock and putting salt on. Also cook a brine of salt and water. Wrap with cord and cook slow. Place in press, and cool 1-2 hours.

Juliann Gronbeck, Rugby H. S.
Rugby, North Dakota

BARBECUED SHORT RIBS
Number of Servings — 4-5

3 lbs. beef short ribs
1 onion, chopped
2 T. fat or salad oil
¼ c. vinegar
2 T. sugar
1 c. catsup
½ c. water
3 T. Worcestershire sauce
1 t. prepared mustard
½ c. celery, sliced
2 t. salt

Brown short ribs with onion in hot fat or oil. Combine remaining ingredients and add to ribs. Cover and cook slowly for 1½ to 2 hours, or until tender.

Mrs. Jean Axelson, West Anchorage H. S.
Anchorage, Alaska

BARBECUED SHORT RIBS
Number of Servings — 4

2½ lbs. short ribs of beef
1 large onion, sliced
1 c. catsup
½ c. vinegar
1 t. paprika
1 t. chili powder
2 t. salt

Brown short ribs in fat in heavy utensil. Arrange in a deep baking dish and cover with onion slices. Blend remaining ingredients and pour over the onions. Cover and bake in a moderately slow oven (325°F.) until the meat is tender, and the sauce is thick—about 1½ hours. Baste occasionally with the sauce.

Beatrice Campbell
Leland Consolidated—Dean Center
Leland, Mississippi

BEEF SHORT RIBS — RAISIN SAUCE
Number of Servings — 6-8

3 lbs. beef short ribs
3 T. lard or drippings
Salt and pepper
1 onion, quartered
½ c. brown sugar
1 t. dry mustard
½ c. raisins
1 T. flour
2 T. vinegar
2 T. lemon juice
¼ t. grated lemon rind
1 bay leaf
1½ c. water

Cut short ribs into serving pieces and brown in small amount of fat. Pour off drippings. Season ribs with salt and pepper. Add quartered onion. Combine remaining ingredients and bring to a boil. Pour over short ribs. Cover tightly and cook slowly about 2 hours or until meat is tender. Thicken sauce, if desired.

Evelyn Hardman, Wallowa H. S.
Wallowa, Oregon

SIMMERED SHORT RIBS
Number of Servings — 6

2 lbs. beef short ribs
¾ c. flour
2 t. salt
¼ t. pepper
3 c. water
1 medium onion
1 T. Worcestershire sauce
2 T. vinegar
2 T. tallow or other fat

Roll beef ribs in flour, salt and pepper. Brown in fat in a heavy roaster. Add onion, water, vinegar and Worcestershire sauce. Simmer just at boiling temperature for 4 hours. May need to skim off fat. Watch it and add water if necessary.

Mrs. Grace Montgomery, Twisp H. S.
Twisp, Washington

OVEN BARBECUED BEEF RIBS
Number of Servings — 8

5 lbs. beef short ribs cut in serving pieces
1 bottle Italian type salad dressing
1 t. salt
Pepper to taste
1 8 oz. bottle smoky-flavor barbecue sauce

Marinate ribs in salad dressing 1 hour at room temperature or in refrigerator over night. Drain. Brown under broiler on all sides; cover and cook for 1 hour at 325°. Pour over barbecue sauce and cook uncovered until tender, about one hour. Serve with brown beans, seasoned with chili powder, onion rings or tossed salad and a beverage.

Mrs. Marjorie Vickery, Holland H. S.
Holland, Texas

BARBECUED RIBS
Number of Servings — 2

1½ lbs. beef short ribs
1 c. catsup
1 t. lemon juice
2 T. Worcestershire sauce
1 medium onion, chopped
1 T. brown sugar
1 t. mustard
Salt and pepper to taste

Place all ingredients in casserole and add water to cover. Bake at 350° for 4 hours.

Mrs. Kay Walker, Sequoia Jr. H. S.
Reseda, California

OLD-FASHIONED BEEF STEW
Number of Servings — 6-8

3 T. shortening
2 lbs. stewing beef, cut in 1½″ cubes
¼ c. flour
½ clove garlic, minced
2½ t. salt
½ t. marjoram
½ t. thyme
¼ t. pepper
1 can (15-oz.) tomato sauce
2½ c. water
5 medium onions, sliced
4 medium carrots, cut in strips

Melt shortening in large, heavy frying pan. Dredge meat in flour, add to hot fat and brown. Add garlic, seasonings, tomato sauce and water. Cover; simmer 2 hours. Add vegetables, cover and simmer 30 minutes or until crisp tender. Serve plain or over hot rice.

Mrs. Doris F. Cullop, Marion Sr. H. S.
Marion, Virginia

SOUTHERN STYLE BROWN STEW
Number of Servings — 6

2 lbs. boneless beef chuck cut in 1½″ cubes
2 T. fat
4 c. boiling water
1 t. lemon juice
1 t. Worcestershire sauce
2 small bay leaves
2 t. salt
½ t. pepper
1 clove garlic, minced
6 carrots, cut in quarters
8 small onions
3 potatoes, cut in quarters

Flour meat and brown well on all sides in hot fat. Add the rest of the ingredients, except carrots, onions, and potatoes. Simmer 2 hours, stirring as necessary. Add the vegetables and cook about 30 minutes longer or until vegetables are tender. Thicken with flour, if you wish, for gravy.

Mrs. Frydis M. Hansbrough, Magee H. S.
Magee, Mississippi

BEEF STEW
Number of Servings — 6

1 lb. boneless stew meat
1 c. chopped onions
1 c. chopped celery
2 c. sliced potatoes
2 T. melted fat
2 cans (small) tomato juice
1 package mixed vegetables
Salt, pepper to taste.

Serve with crackers or baking powder dumplings. Brown meat in melted fat (slowly). Add 1 cup boiling water. Let cook slowly until meat is partly done. Add onions and celery. Add extra water if necessary. When meat is almost tender, add potatoes, 1 package frozen mixed vegetables and 2 small cans tomato juice. Salt and pepper to taste. Cook until flavors blend.

Mrs. Milo Hill, Blum H. S.
Blum, Texas

BEEF STEW
Number of Servings — 4

2 T. salad oil
1½ lbs. stew beef
2 t. salt
Pepper
2 c. tomatoes, cooked, canned or raw
1 T. Worcestershire sauce
4 medium potatoes, halved
4 carrots, cut in chunks
4 onions, whole
½ t. mixed spice
2 pieces celery, cut fine

Brown beef in salad oil. Add salt, pepper, tomatoes, spice and Worcestershire sauce and cook until tender in tightly covered pot. Add vegetables and cook until tender.

Helen Mullikin, Wade Hampton H. S.
Hampton, South Carolina

BROWN BEEF STEW
Number of Servings — 4

1 lb. boneless stew beef
Salt and pepper
Flour
Drippings
1½ c. water
3 potatoes, diced
2 onions, sliced
3 carrots, diced
1 c. green beans

Cut meat into inch cubes. Sprinkle with salt and pepper, roll in flour, and brown in drippings. Add water, cover, and simmer until almost tender —2-3 hours. Add vegetables, season with salt and pepper, and continue to simmer, covered, until vegetables are done. Stir occasionally .

Mary B. Lewis, Gilbert H. S.
Gilbert, South Carolina

BEEF STEW OR POT LUCK PIE
Number of Servings — 25

3 lbs. cubed tender beef
2-3 carrots diced and cooked till tender
2 onions, sliced and cooked
Small head cabbage, cut very fine
2 c. green beans, pre-cooked
2 c. tomatoes
1 #2½ can tomato paste
2 c. water
2 green peppers, cut small and cooked in
   shortening till tender
3-4 potatoes, diced and cooked
2 c. peas, frozen or canned
2 c. corn
Seasonings: garlic salt, onion salt, chili powder,
   salt, tiny bit of sugar, salt and pepper

Prepare meat by stewing on low heat for one hour. (2 cups water) Add all the vegetables and allow to simmer slowly. Season to taste. If too dry add the juice from the peas and corn you drained from vegetables. Allow to cook till all are very tender. Place in casserole dishes or in roaster. Just about fifteen minutes before serving, place baking powder biscuits on top and allow to bake. Make biscuits very small, about the size of the center of the doughnut cutter. When brown, remove from oven and serve.

This seems to be a great favorite of my home economics students as they ask for it very frequently.

Sister Mary Louise, Notre Dame H. S.
Clarksburg, West Virginia

BEEF TARRAGON STEW

Olive oil
Garlic clove
Flour
Salt
Pepper
2 t. dried tarragon
3 lbs. boneless beef for stew, cubed
½ c. tarragon wine vinegar
1 c. beef bouillon
2 t. sugar
2 2½-oz. cans mushrooms (whole or stems
   and pieces)
¼ c. chopped green onion

Heat olive oil in heavy skillet. Split garlic clove and brown. Remove garlic. Dredge beef cubes in seasoned flour in which tarragon has been crumbled. Brown in hot olive oil. Add vinegar, bouillon and sugar. Stir. Cover. Simmer 2½ hours or until beef is tender. Add mushrooms and liquid and green onion. Cook with cover off for 10 minutes to' reduce mushroom liquid. Serve hot with cooked spaghetti, rice or noodles. Broiled whole tomatoes, tossed green salad, buttery French bread complete the meal.

Mrs. Paul E. Compton, Custer County H. S.
Miles City, Montana

SAVORY BEEF STEW
Number of Servings — 6

6 slices bacon, diced
3 lbs. lean beef stew meat
12 small whole onions
12 small carrots
12 small potatoes
1 bay leaf
1 pinch thyme
Salt and pepper to taste
2 oz. brandy
1½ c. claret wine
8 oz. can button mushrooms
1 can bouillon

Fry bacon crisp and remove to casserole. Flour meat and brown; remove to casserole. To frying pan add seasonings, bouillon, mushrooms with their liquid; simmer 5 minutes. Add carrots, wine, brandy and contents of frying pan to casserole. Cover and bake 3 hours at 225°F. Add onions and potatoes and bake another hour.

Mrs. Mary Westfall, Colusa H. S.
Colusa, California

BEEF STEW WITH DUMPLINGS
Number of Servings — 4-5

1 lb. beef cubed
2 c. hot water
½ c. diced carrots
½ c. diced potatoes
¼ c. chopped onions
½ t. Worcestershire sauce
½ t. salt
dash pepper

Roll meat in flour; brown in hot fat. Add hot water; cook slowly 1½ hours. Add vegetables and seasonings, cook for 30 min., drop dumplings from spoon; cover tightly and steam without lifting cover 12-15 min. DUMPLINGS: Sift 1 cup flour, ½ teaspoon salt, and 1½ teaspoons baking powder; add ½ cup milk, and 2 tablespoons melted fat or salad oil to make soft dough.

June S. Haddock, Grimesland H. S.
Grimesland, North Carolina

COLD WINTER'S NIGHT STEW
Number of Servings — 4-6

1 lb. stewing beef
4 potatoes, peeled and diced
2 carrots (any left over vegetables may be used)
3 c. stewed tomatoes
Season with the following to taste: salt, onion,
   garlic salt, pepper, Worcestershire sauce

Brown beef in small amount of fat. Add vegetables and seasonings. Pressure in a sauce pan at 10 pounds pressure for 20 minutes or cover and cook for an hour over low heat. Serve hot over biscuits or bread.

Betty Deadman, Sand Creek H. S.
Sand Creek, Michigan

OLD-FASHIONED BEEF STEW
Number of Servings — 6-8

2 lbs. beef chuck
5 medium potatoes, diced
2 carrots, diced
1 #2 can tomatoes
1 medium onion
1 clove garlic
2 t. salt

Cover meat with cold water; bring to boil. Reduce heat; cover—simmer 4 hours. Add potatoes, carrots, onion, garlic. Continue cooking—covered—about 30 minutes or until vegetables are tender. Add tomatoes and simmer fifteen minutes.

Carolyn Sellers, Wallace H. S.
Wallace, South Carolina

OLD TIME BEEF STEW
Number of Servings — 6-8

2 lbs. beef chuck, cut in 1½-in. cubes
2 T. fat
4 c. boiling water
1 T. lemon juice (optional)
1 t. Worcestershire sauce
1 clove garlic
1 medium onion, sliced
1-2 bay leaves
1 T. salt
1 t. sugar
1 t. pepper
1 t. paprika
Dash of allspice or cloves
6 carrots
1 lb. (18-24) small white onions

Thoroughly brown meat in hot fat. Add water, lemon juice, Worcestershire sauce, garlic, sliced onion, bay leaves and seasonings. Cover. Simmer 2 hours, stirring occasionally to prevent sticking. Remove bay leaves and garlic. Add vegetables (may also add cubed potatoes if desired). Cover and cook 30 minutes more or until vegetables are done. Remove meat and vegetables. Thicken liquid for gravy.
Gravy: Skim most of fat from stew liquid. For 3 cups liquid, put ½ cup water in shaker or screw top jar. Add ¼ cup enriched flour. Shake to mix. Add flour mixture slowly to meat stock, stirring constantly till gravy bubbles all over. Cook about 5 minutes more, stirring often. Pour over meat and vegetables.

Mrs. Phyllis Price, Fox Lake H. S.
Fox Lake, Wisconsin

BEEF STEW
Number of Servings — 4

1¾ lbs. beef (chuck or round)
⅓ c. flour
¼ t. pepper
½ t. salt
3 T. fat or drippings

¼ c. onion, diced
1 minced clove garlic
¼ t. celery salt
2¾ c. boiling water
1 c. canned or fresh tomatoes
Approx. 12 small carrots, peeled and cut into 2-in. pieces
3-4 medium potatoes, pared, quartered
½ package frozen peas

Trim excess fat from meat; cut into 1½ inch cubes. Combine flour, pepper and salts in paper bag; add meat; shake until pieces are coated. In Dutch oven with melted fat add meat; brown on all sides. Add onion, garlic, tomatoes (if canned) and boiling water. Cover; reduce heat to low; simmer 2 hours or until meat is tender. Add potatoes and carrots; cook 20 minutes. Add peas and cook 15 minutes longer. Add fresh tomatoes (if any) just before removing from heat. Potatoes may be served separately, or stew may be served over cooked noodles in which case the potatoes are omitted.

Jeannette Vasquez, Los Lunas H. S.
Los Lunas, New Mexico

BEEF STEW TO SERVE FOR INDOOR PARTY ON HIBACCI STOVE

2 lbs. stew meat
1 T. salad oil
½ t. garlic salt
1 t. salt
Dash pepper
¼ t. ginger
¼ c. soy sauce
3 drops noncaloric liquid sweetener
Strips of green pepper
½ c. flour

Saute beef with garlic salt, pepper, salt, ginger sifted into flour. Roll pieces in flour, then brown thoroughly all over about 5 minutes (350°F.) Then add about 1½ cups water and simmer at 215°F. for about ¾ of an hour or until tender. Remove chunks (Kabob style on metal skewers). Gril over Hibacci fire. May be dipped in barbecue sauce if desired.
Note: We served this in Japanese atmosphere—guests take off shoes—sit on floor at low tables. Japanese floral centerpiece, candlelight, Japanese records, (try Geisha Bowl)—bowl of chipped ice with fruit juices, drink through long straws, shared with partner. Float carnation in bowl of iced drink. Nicely festive.

Jane Mosbacher, Dupo H. S.
Dupo, Illinois

BEEF CHUNKS IN SOUR CREAM
Number of Servings — 6-8

3 lbs. lean stewing beef
3 T. fat
2 medium onions, thinly sliced
1½ c. sour cream

(Continued on Next Page)

1 c. mushrooms, sliced
½ t. oregano
¼ t. sweet basil
1 T. salt
1½ t. paprika

Cut 3 pounds of lean stewing beef into 1 inch cubes. Roll in flour and brown in 3 tablespoons fat. Add thinly sliced onions and brown. Add sour cream, sliced mushrooms, oregano, basil, salt and paprika. Cover and simmer over low heat about 2 hours, or until meat is tender. Stir occasionally during cooking.

Mary Stockslager,
Jackson Twp. Farmersville H. S.
Farmersville, Ohio

MEAT ROLL
Number of Servings — 6

1 recipe standard biscuit
2 c. cooked meat or chicken
2 T. onion, chopped
2 T. pimento, chopped
1 t. Worcestershire sauce
½ t. salt
⅛ t. pepper

Roll biscuit dough to ⅛ inch thickness. Spread with meat and seasonings mixture. Roll as for jelly roll. Place on greased baking sheet and bake in hot oven (475°F.) for 20 minutes. Serve with any desired sauce.

Mary Anne Power, Comanche H. S.
Comanche, Texas

BEEF OR LAMB CURRY
(an original recipe from Kuwiat, on the Persian Gulf)
Number of Servings — 6

3 c. raw beef or lamb
1 onion
½ c. butter
1 t. salt
½ t. pepper
½ t. ginger
1½ t. curry powder
½ can tomato paste
1 small can tomato sauce
Juice of lemon or lime

Cut meat into 1½ inch cubes. Brown onion in ½ cup butter. Brown the meat and add the curry powder. Stir until all is mixed. Add the salt, pepper and ginger. Again stir well. Add boiling water to cover meat. Add tomato paste and sauce and lemon or lime juice. Simmer for at least 2 hours. Thicken slightly with flour and water. Serve over plain cooked rice. Sprinkle any or all of the following over the curry and rice: Dry coconut, chopped nuts, chopped eggs, chopped onions, mango, chutney, crisp bacon or tomatoes.

Kirsten G. Giving, Climax Sr. H. S.
Climax, Minnesota

BEEF PIE
Number of Servings — 4

½ recipe baking powder biscuits
1 c. cooked meat, diced (beef)
½ c. celery, diced
½ c. meat stock or 1 beef bouillon cube in ½ c. water
¼ t. onion salt
1 c. grated cheese

Place dough on lightly floured board and roll to ⅜ inch thickness. Put into an 8 to 9 inch baking dish, covering the bottom and sides as for pie. Add meat, celery, meat stock, and seasonings to dough lined dish. Bake pie at 425°F. for 15 minutes. Reduce heat to 350°F. Add grated cheese to pie; bake 5 minutes.

Era H. Sanders, North Clayton H. S.
College Park, Georgia

MEAT PIE WITH BISCUITS
Number of Servings — 4

1 c. diced, cooked beef
½ c. celery, diced
½ c. carrots, diced
½ c. meat stock
¼ t. powdered onion
1 c. grated cheese

Cook diced celery and carrots in the meat stock, until almost tender. Mix the diced meat and vegetables. Put in a 2 inch deep baking pan. Top with baking powder biscuits. Bake at 425°F. for 12 minutes. Remove from the oven, sprinkle the pie mixture and tops of biscuits with grated cheese. Return to the oven at 350°F. for 5 minutes.

Mrs. Bernice Wadlow, Mullen H. S.
Mullen, Nebraska

MEAT PIE
Number of Servings — 8

2 c. left-over meat (chicken, turkey or beef)
2 T. butter
1 t. salt
1 T. dehydrated vegetable flakes
1 small onion, chopped
1½ c. milk

Put 2 tablespoons butter in saucepan, 2 tablespoons flour, add onions stirring until light brown. Add milk and stir until thick. Add meat, salt, and vegetable seasoning. Cut meat into small chunks; add to white sauce and cook for 10 minutes, stirring constantly. Pour into pie crust and top with small biscuits. Makes one 10 inch pie.

Sister Adrienne Marie, CDP, Bishop Forest H. S.
Schulenburg, Texas

BEEF PIE
Number of Servings — 6

1 lb. ground beef
1 medium onion
2 T. chili powder
1¼ c. or 1 can condensed mushroom soup
⅔ c. grated cheese
1 c. tomatoes

Combine meat, onion and chili powder; fry slowly in slightly greased pan. Add mushroom soup and pour into pastry lined pie pan. Top with cheese and tomatoes. Bake in hot oven (450°F.) about 25 minutes.

Myrtle Stevens, Gracemont H. S.
Gracemont, Oklahoma

BEEF PIE SUPREME
Number of Servings — 6-8

1½ lbs. beef for stew (boneless shoulder or
  chuck)
¼ c. flour
1 t. salt
⅛ t. pepper
3 T. fat
1 c. water
1 c. canned tomatoes
2 t. Worcestershire sauce
6 carrots
12 small onions, peeled
3 c. mashed potatoes
⅓ c. process cheese spread
Melted butter or margarine

Cut meat into 1½″ cubes. Mix flour, salt and pepper; roll meat in mixture to coat all sides. Brown meat well in hot fat; add water, tomatoes and Worcestershire sauce. Peel carrots; cut into 1″ crosswise slices. Peel onions; add to meat. Cover tightly. Simmer 2 hours. Stir occasionally to avoid sticking. Pour into greased 2 quart casserole. With mixer blend together mashed potatoes and cheese spread. Drop by spoonfuls around rim of casserole. Brush with melted butter. Bake until bubbly hot in moderate oven (375° F.), about 30 minutes. Makes 6 to 8 servings.

Hilma R. Davis, Kansas State College
College High Lab. School
Pittsburg, Kansas

TEXAS TAMALE PIE
Number of Servings — 4

1½ lbs. ground round
Salt and pepper
½ c. shortening
½ c. grated American cheese
1 chopped onion
2 T. cornmeal
1 clove garlic
1 T. chili powder
1 chopped sweet green pepper
1½ c. chopped fresh tomatoes
1 c. cornmeal
½ c. ripe olives (pitted)

3 c. boiling water
2 chili peppers cut fine
1 t. salt

Cook onion, garlic and green pepper in hot fat until tender; add ground round and brown. Add tomatoes, ripe olives, chili peppers, salt and pepper and simmer 1 hour. Stir in grated cheese, 2 tablespoons cornmeal, chili powder and cook 5 minutes. Gradually add 1 cup cornmeal to 3 cups boiling salted water, stirring constantly until mixture thickens. Pour cornmeal mush over beef mixture. Bake at 400 degrees for 30 minutes and garnish with more ripe olives.

Mrs. Tina O. Cooper, Jourdanton H. S.
Jourdanton, Texas

BEEF BARBECUE
Number of Servings — 12

2 lbs. beef
1 can tomato soup
1 c. water
½ c. vinegar
½ c. Worcestershire sauce
¼ c. sugar
1 onion, cut fine
Clove of garlic
Salt and pepper to taste

Remove fat from beef and cut in cubes. Combine with remainder of ingredients in heavy saucepan and simmer for 2 or more hours until meat cooks up and little juice remains. Stir occasionally.

Mrs. Annette C. Dowdy, Webberville H. S.
Webberville, Michigan

MONGOLIA BARBECUE
Number of Servings — 4

1 lb. beef
4 or 5 scallions (green onions)
1 egg white
1 T. cornstarch
1 T. soy sauce
Salt to taste
4 or 5 T. vegetable oil

Cut beef into strips (about ¼ by 1¼ inches). Cut scallions into pieces ½ inch long. Add soy sauce, salt, egg white, cornstarch to beef and scallions. Mix thoroughly. Heat the vegetable oil in heavy skillet to very hot. Add mixture to hot fat and heat 30 to 40 seconds (not over 1 minute), stirring constantly.

Mrs. Loretta C. Thomas, Mineral Wells H. S.
Mineral Wells, Texas

CANTON SKILLET BEEF
Number of Servings — 4

¼ c. salad oil
1 c. onions, sliced
2 green peppers, cut in strips
1 lb. chuck, cut in 1-in. cubes

(Continued on Next Page)

1 t. vinegar
1½ t. salt
¼ t. pepper
½ t. monosodium glutamate
1 No. 2 can apple slices with ¼ c. their liquid
1 c. water
1 T. Worcestershire sauce
1 T. soy sauce
1⅓ c. packaged pre-cooked rice
¼ c. seedless raisins

About 2 hours before supper: In hot oil in large skillet, saute onions and green peppers until tender. Add meat; cook until it loses red color. Stir in apples, water, Worcestershire sauce, soy sauce, vinegar, salt, pepper, monosodium glutamate; stirring occasionally, simmer, covered for 1½ hour, or until meat is tender. Meanwhile, cook rice as label directs. To serve: Toss raisins with rice; arrange meat mixture and rice in twin serving dishes.

Marjorie Mouser, Grant H. S.
Grant, Michigan

KABOBS
Number of Servings — 4

3 pound shank beef; cut meat off bones and cube it. (Save bones for soup stock). Cover with the following marinade and let stand two hours: 1 tablespoon lemon juice, 3 tablespoons salad oil, 1 clove crushed garlic, ¼ teaspoon salt, 1 teaspoon water, dash pepper, dash Accent. Drain off marinade and save it. String meat alternately on skewers with some or all of the following: mushroom caps, raw apple slices (peel on), pineapple cubes, parboiled carrot chunks, celery and green pepper. Place on broiler pan. To the drained marinade add: ¼ cup honey, ¼ cup pineapple juice and ¼ teaspoon ground ginger. Brush this mixture over skewers. Place 4 inches from heat. Broil 15 to 20 minutes, brushing with sauce, turning often. Serve on fluffy white rice.

Mrs. Berniece Gorsuch, Bellingham H. S.
Bellingham, Washington

MEAT CROQUETTES
Number of Servings — 6

1 c. thick white sauce
1 t. onion, minced
1 t. parsley
2 c. chopped meat

Mix and shape to desired size. (Use ½ cup measure or a funnel for appropriate shape). Roll in fine crumbs. Let dry 2 to 3 hours. Dip in crumbs and then in mixture of 1 egg and 2 Tablespoons water. Roll again. Fry in deep fat at 400°F. and drain.

Mrs. Jacob O. Cozard, Indianola H. S.
Indianola, Iowa

BEEF BRISKET AND ONION SAUCE
Number of Servings — 6-8

4 lbs. beef brisket
1 carrot, diced
1 small onion, diced
2 t. salt
4 whole black peppers
4 whole cloves
1 slightly beaten egg
½ c. dry bread crumbs

Cover meat with boiling water; add vegetables and seasonings. Simmer until tender, about 3 hours. Remove from liquid and place in shallow baking dish. Reserve 1 cup stock for Onion Sauce. (Save remaining stock for soup base). Spread egg over meat and sprinkle with crumbs; brown in hot oven (400°) 20 minutes. Serve with Onion Sauce. **Onion Sauce**—Brown 2 tablespoons sugar in 1 tablespoon fat; add 2 medium-sized onions, sliced; cook until almost tender. Add 1 tablespoon flour; brown slightly. Add 1 cup Brown Stock, 1 tablespoon vinegar, and salt; cook until smooth.

Eleanor Milner, Knox H. S.
Knox, Indiana

CORNED BEEF
Number of Servings — 6

3 lbs. beef (good boneless brisket)
4 T. brown sugar
3 T. salt
½ t. salt peter

Dissolve the brown sugar, salt, and salt peter in water and pour over the brisket which has been placed in a refrigerator bowl of sufficient size. Add additional water to cover the meat. Place in refrigerator and let stand four days—turning the meat once a day. Put meat in a cooking pot of sufficient size and cook in the same water that the meat has been in for the past four days. Simmer for five minutes and take scum off the top. Continue cooking very slowly allowing at least an hour per pound.

Mrs. Edna A. Bouland, Lee Jr. H. S.
Lee, Florida

CORNED BEEF DINNER
Number of Servings — 6-8

1 6-oz. pkg. macaroni
1 12-oz. can corned beef, chopped
¼ lb. American cheese, cubed
1 11-oz. can condensed cream of chicken soup
1 c. milk
½ c. chopped onion
¾ c. buttered crumbs

Cook macaroni in boiling, salted water; drain and rinse. Combine remaining ingredients except crumbs and alternate with layers of macaroni in greased 2 quart casserole. Top with buttered crumbs. Bake in moderate oven 1 hour.

Arlene Holyoak, Valley H. S.
Orderville, Utah

CORNED BEEF SOUFFLE
Number of Servings — 6

2 T. butter
1 slice garlic
1 large onion, chopped with 10 sprigs parsley
2 T. flour
1 T. lemon juice
1 can corned beef
⅛ t. cayenne
¼ t. nutmeg
½ c. milk
3 egg yolks
3 egg whites stiffly beaten

Melt butter, add garlic, onion, parsley, flour, lemon juice and seasonings. When well blended add milk. Cook together until thick and smooth. Shred the corned beef and mix with the egg yolks. Combine corned beef mixture with white sauce mixture. Fold in the stiffly beaten egg whites. Bake in an earthenware casserole. Temperature: 350° F. Time: 30 minutes.

Mrs. Pauline Baskett, Blue Rapids H. S.
Blue Rapids, Kansas

CORNED BEEF BARBECUE
Number of Servings — 8

1 small can corned beef
½ c. chopped onion
½ c. chopped celery
1 c. water
1 c. catsup
¼ c. Worcestershire sauce
2 t. vinegar
2 t. sugar

Combine all of the above ingredients and cook slowly on a low temperature until the liquid cooks down. Cooking time is approximately 1 hour. Serve on a hamburger bun.

Doris G. Kelly, Andrew Lewis H. S.
Salem, Virginia

CORNED BEEF BAR-B-QUE
Number of Servings — 6

1 can corned beef
1 medium onion
½ c. catsup
1 t. sugar
1 T. vinegar
1 t. prepared mustard
1 T. Worcestershire sauce

Chop and saute onion. Add corned beef and mash with fork. Mix the last five ingredients together and pour over the meat mixture. Simmer 1 hour.

Dorothy Kitko, Union City Area H. S.
Union City, Pennsylvania

LIVER & ONIONS
Number of Servings — 4

1 lb. young beef liver
2 sweet onions
3 T. bacon fat

Peel and slice sweet onions. Cook in bacon fat until golden. Cover and cook slowly until tender. Pan fry liver in another skillet. Serve topped with onions.

Karolyn Sisk, Lynnvale H. S.
White Mills, Kentucky

BROILED LIVER STRIPS
Number of Servings — 4

1 lb. beef liver
½ lb. bacon
1 c. French dressing
1½ t. salt
1 t. pepper
Several toothpicks

Slice liver into ½ inch slices. Cut into 1 inch strips. Marinate in French dressing for one hour. Wrap each strip in bacon secured at ends with toothpicks. Broil 10 minutes.

Margaret Henry, Grange Hall H. S.
Mosely, Virginia

LIVER WITH GRAVY
Number of Servings — 4

3 T. fat
½ medium onion, sliced
1 lb. beef liver, sliced
½ c. flour
Salt and pepper
¾ c. water

Put fat into heavy skillet over moderate heat. When fat is hot, add onion. Dip liver slices into seasoned flour, and brown lightly in hot fat. Add water, cover tightly, lower heat and cook 10-15 minutes until liver is well done and gravy has thickened.

Leasle H. Maze, Eva H. S.
Eva, Alabama

GRILLED BEEF LIVER

Have liver sliced thin and as many slices as needed for group. 1 slice bacon for each slice liver. Grill liver on top of bacon at low temperature and increase temperature when nearly done to brown. Takes around 25 to 30 minutes, depending on thickness. This is one of my family's favorite ways of eating liver. Even my small boys say this is one of their favorite meats.

Mrs. Joan Davis, Waskom H. S.
Waskom, Texas

FRENCH-FRIED LIVER

Remove membrane from liver and snip out veins with kitchen scissors. Cut liver in ½-inch strips. Marinate in French dressing ½ hour; drain. Dip in beaten egg, roll in cracker crumbs. (Tongs make the job easy). Fry liver in deep fat (360°F.) till browned. Drain on paper towels. Serve hot.

Nila M. Fuller, Webster H. S.
Webster, South Dakota

TASTY LIVER AND BACON
Number of Servings — 4

1 lb. liver
1 c. French dressing
½ c. flour
8 slices bacon

Remove skin and heavy blood vessels from liver and scald liver. Marinate liver for about 30 minutes in French dressing. Cook bacon over low heat. Drain—keep hot. Roll liver in flour. Cook in bacon fat at moderate heat until golden brown. ½ inch slices take about 5 minutes. Do not overcook.

Martha R. Phillips, Kennett H. S.
Conway, New Hampshire

LIVER PATTIES
Number of Servings — 4

1 lb. beef liver
2 T. fat
¼ c. bread crumbs
1 t. grated onion
1 t. salt
1 egg, beaten
¼ t. pepper
2 T. all purpose flour

Wipe liver with cloth. Remove blood vessels and outer skin. Melt 2 tablespoons fat in skillet and fry liver on both sides until nicely browned. Cool liver, put through food grinder, and mix with other ingredients. Shape into patties, roll in flour, and brown slowly in skillet on both sides. Serve hot.

Mrs. Estelle Beard Cravey, Ellisville H. S.
Ellisville, Mississippi

BAKED BEEF LIVER AND BACON
Number of Servings — 4

1 egg, slightly beaten
¼ c. milk
Flour
Bread crumbs
8 bacon strips
4 slices liver
Shortening
Salt and pepper

Grease a shallow pan generously with cold shortening. Mix egg and milk. Dip liver in flour, then in egg mixture, then in bread crumbs. Lay breaded liver in greased pan so that the pieces are close together. Sprinkle with a little salt and pepper. Cover with slices of raw bacon. Bake at 350°F. until bacon is cooked—about 20 minutes. The liver will be cooked when the bacon is brown.

Mrs. Carolyn Fredrick, Pinckney H. S.
Pinckney, Michigan

BARBECUED LIVER AND ONIONS
Number of Servings — 4

1 lb. liver
1 medium onion
¼ t. pepper
½ t. salt
1 c. tomato juice
1 c. water
2 T. grease

Brown liver and onions in grease. Add seasonings, tomato juice and water. Simmer 30 to 40 minutes.

Joan Nesladek, North Bend Public H. S.
North Bend, Nebraska

SWEDISH LIVER LOAF
Number of Servings — 6

1 lb. ground liver
¼ lb. ground fresh pork
2 eggs
2 t. salt
¼ t. cinnamon
1 c. dry bread crumbs
1 t. sugar
¼ t. cloves
¼ t. nutmeg
¼ lb. ground beef
4 T. onion, chopped
2 c. milk
½ t. pepper
¼ t. allspice

Saute onion in 2 tablespoons fat until tender and add to ground meat. Add eggs beaten slightly. Add remaining ingredients and mix thoroughly. Bake in well greased ring mold or pan. Set in pan of hot water. Cover pan and bake in 350°F. oven for 1 hour. Remove cover and bake 1 hour more.

Ann L. Benson, Senior H. S.
Stillwater, Minnesota

LIVER LOAF
Number of Servings — 6

1 lb. liver
½ lb. sausage
1 c. dry bread crumbs
1 onion, medium
¼ c. liver stock
1 t. Worcestershire sauce
1 T. lemon juice
1 t. salt
⅛ t. pepper
1 t. salt
2 eggs, beaten

Cover with hot water and simmer 5 minutes one pound liver. Drain and reserve liquid for stock. Grind liver and 1 medium onion. To this mixture add sausage, bread crumbs, Worcestershire sauce, lemon juice, salt, pepper, celery salt, beaten eggs, liver stock and mix well. In bottom of loaf pan alternate in rows—2 slices bacon, halved and 6 stuffed olives, halved. Place loaf mixture on top. Bake in a moderate oven (350°F.) 45 minutes.

Mrs. Roberta Brooks, Dimple H. S.
Clarksville, Texas

LIVER LOAF
Number of Servings — 8

1 lb. beef liver
1 medium-sized onion, chopped
½ lb. pork sausage
1 c. dry bread crumbs
1 t. Worcestershire sauce
½ c. stock
1 T. lemon juice
1 t. salt
⅛ t. pepper
1 t. celery salt
2 eggs, beaten
4 slices bacon

Cover liver with hot water; simmer 5 minutes. Drain liquid and reserve for stock. Force liver and onion through food chopper, using medium blade. Add remaining ingredients, except bacon. Form in loaf in 5½ by 10½ inch pan. Top with bacon slices. Bake in moderate oven (350°F.) 45 minutes.

Mildred Timm Paxson, Brawley Union H S.
Brawley, California

LIVER LOAF
Number of Servings — 8-10

1 lb. beef liver
½ lb. sausage
½ c. chopped onion
2 large size shredded wheat biscuits
1 c. milk
2 beaten eggs
⅔ c. cornmeal
1½ t. salt
½ t. pepper
1 t. sage (omit if sausage is sage-flavored)

Pan fry liver only until firm, put through food grinder with sausage and onion. Crumble biscuits into milk and add, along with all remaining ingredients except the bacon, to the ground mixture. Mix thoroughly and let stand a few minutes. Pack lightly into a greased bread pan and lay strips of bacon over top of loaf. Bake for one hour in pre-heated oven at 350° F. Serve hot or cold.

Mrs. Anne Teter, Pike H. S.
New Augusta, Indiana

BRAISED LIVER WITH ONIONS
Number of Servings — 4

¾ lbs. liver (beef)
¼ c. flour
½ t. salt
¼ t. pepper
3 T. shortening
1 medium onion, diced
¾ c. water

Slice liver into ½ inch slices. Mix flour and seasonings together. Dip liver into flour mixture, coating each piece. Heat shortening and brown liver. Pour off excess shortening. Add onion and water, cover and simmer for 30 minutes or until tender.

Lenda Boozer, Bennettsville H. S.
Bennettsville, South Carolina

MARINATED LIVER
Number of Servings — 4

1 lb. baby beef liver
½ c. vinegar
½ c. French dressing (Russian)
1 or 2 t. Italian seasonings

Combine vinegar, dressing and seasonings. Place pieces of liver in the mixture for a minimum of 20 minutes. Be sure all of the meat is covered with the liquid. (It may be necessary to turn the liver once). At the end of 20 minutes or so, remove liver, drain on paper towelling, cover liver with flour. Fry in small amount of shortening at low temperature (300°F.) until done.

Elizabeth L. Stephenson, Brighton Sr. H. S.
Brighton, Colorado

CREOLE LIVER
Number of Servings — 6

1 lb. liver, sliced
½ c. fat
1 medium onion, minced
1 bell pepper, minced
½ c. water
1 No. 2 can tomatoes
1 t. salt
½ t. pepper
⅛ t. garlic salt

Brown flour dredged liver slowly in fat. Remove. Saute onion and bell pepper in remaining fat

(Continued on Next Page)

until tender. Pour off any excess fat. Add liver, tomatoes, water, and seasonings to onion and pepper. Simmer, covered, 30 minutes. Add extra water if needed while simmering.

Mrs. Florence Neason
Anderson H. S., Anderson, Texas
Richards H. S., Richards, Texas

CREOLE LIVER
Number of Servings — 4

1 lb. beef liver
2 onions, chopped
2 cloves garlic, chopped
3 T. bacon fat
¼ t. red and black pepper
1 t. salt
1 t. Worcestershire sauce
½ c. water

Remove thin outer skin, slice liver rather thin. Flour liver, brown in hot bacon fat, remove from pot, season. Saute onion and garlic in same fat. Combine liver with onion, add water and Worcestershire sauce. Simmer for approximately 30 minutes. Serve on hot steamed rice.

Mrs. A. J. Foret, Bayou Chicot H. S.
Ville Platte, Louisiana

CREOLE LIVER
Number of Servings — 4

1¼ lbs. beef liver
¼ c. chopped onion
¼ c. chopped green pepper
½ c. chopped celery
No. 2½ can tomatoes
2 t. salt
½ t. sugar
¼ c. catsup

Skin liver and cut in ½-inch cubes. Salt, dredge with flour. Brown in fat. Add chopped vegetables, cover and simmer for 20 minutes. Stir in seasonings, tomatoes, and catsup. Simmer 20 minutes. Remove cover and cook 10 minutes longer, stirring occasionally.

Mrs. Jean Shwadlenak, Knox City H. S.
Knox City, Texas

BOILED BEEF TONGUE
Number of Servings — 4

3 qts. water (or enough to cover beef tongue)
1 T. salt
¼ c. brown sugar
1 orange, cut in half
1 onion, cut in fourths
1 T. whole allspice
1 red hot pepper

Simmer beef tongue and other ingredients until beef tongue is tender.

Kay Staheli, Palmer H. S.
Palmer, Alaska

TONGUE WITH CHERRY SAUCE
Number of Servings — 8-10

1 beef tongue
½ c. brown sugar
1 T. cornstarch
1 c. stock
½ t. whole cloves
½ bay leaf
1 c. drained, canned pitted sour cherries
1 T. lemon juice
2 T. margarine or butter

Simmer tongue in salted water until tender, about 1 hour for each pound. Trim and remove skin. Cut in ¼" slices; place in a baking dish. Mix brown sugar and cornstarch; combine with stock. Add cloves and bay leaf; cook till thick. Add cherries, lemon juice and butter; bring to a boil. Pour over tongue and bake in a 350°F. oven for 20 minutes. Each pound makes three servings.

Marquita K. Christensen, Marshall H. S.
Marshall, Minnesota

TONGUE WITH CHERRY SAUCE
Number of Servings — 6-8

1 beef tongue
½ c. brown sugar
1 T. cornstarch
½ t. whole cloves
1 cup stock
½ bay leaf
1 c. drained, pitted sour cherries
1 T. lemon juice
2 T. butter

Simmer tongue in salted water until tender, about 1 hour per pound. Trim and remove skin. Cut in ¼ inch slices; place in 8" x 12" x 2" baking pan. Mix brown sugar and cornstarch; combine with stock. Add cloves and bay leaf; cook until thick. Add cherries, lemon juice, and butter. Bring to a boil. Pour mixture over tongue and bake in moderate oven for 20 minutes.

Lydia Dietrich, Bradford H. S.
Bradford, Illinois

BAKED HEARTS WITH PINEAPPLE
Number of Servings — 6-8

2 calves' hearts (about 3 lb.)
½ c. chopped onion
3 T. melted butter
¼ c. chopped celery leaves
2 c. soft bread crumbs
½ t. salt
¼ t. thyme
Dash pepper
2 T. flour
2 t. salt
¼ t. pepper
4 slices bacon
6 pineapple slices

(Continued on Next Page)

Clean hearts, removing arteries and veins; make pocket for stuffing. Sprinkle with salt and pepper. Cook onion in butter till golden; mix with celery leaves, bread crumbs, ½ teaspoon salt, thyme, and dash pepper. Stuff hearts. Combine 2 tablespoons flour, 2 teaspoons salt and ¼ teaspoon pepper; dredge stuffed hearts in the seasoned flour. Place in baking pan and lay bacon strips on top. Bake covered in moderate oven (350°) 2½ hours. Uncover and add pineapple; bake 30 minutes more.

Leanna Boline, Osborne Rural H. S.
Osborne, Kansas

CREAMED BRAINS IN POTATO CASES
Number of Servings — 6

2 pairs calves' brains
2 c. medium white sauce
1 t. celery salt
1 t. paprika
1 t. salt
Few drops Worcestershire sauce
3 c. mashed potatoes

Wash brains, remove skin and veins and soak in cold salted water for twenty minutes. Drain, cover with boiling water and simmer for 20 minutes. Drain and cool, then cut into cubes. Mix with white sauce, add seasoning and heat to boiling point. Make nests of mashed potatoes on large buttered platter, fill with brains and garnish with parsley.

Mrs. Flora May Miller, Elkhart H. S.
Elkhart, Texas

BEEF AND KIDNEY PIE
Number of Servings — 8-10

2 large beef or veal kidneys
4 lb. chuck roast cut into cubes or 3 lb. round steak cubed or stew meat
2-3 large onions, sliced thin
2 t. salt
1 t. garlic powder or 1-2 cloves of fresh garlic minced
Flour for dredging cubed meat
Enough cooking oil to brown meat
1 recipe standard pie pastry

Slice kidneys in half lengthwise. Soak in salted water 2-3 hours. Omit this step if you can get your family to eat them without soaking. Drain, cut into 1" cubes removing all fat and tubes as you cut. Cube beef, removing fat. Dredge kidney and beef cubes in flour separately. Brown each slowly to a deep rich brown in skillet using as little cooking oil as possible. Put browned beef and browned kidney into large cooking pot, add thinly sliced onion, and minced garlic. Add enough water to cover, and simmer two hours, stirring occasionally. A rich gravy will form. (May add meat stock if you have any). Line *sides* (not bottom) of 2 qt. casserole or 2 8x8x2 baking pans with strips of your favorite pie crust. Fill pans with meat mixture and cover with pie crust. Bake at 425°F. for 25 minutes or until golden brown. (If meat has been prepared ahead and is cold, heat well before putting into crust lined pans—otherwise it has to bake too long to be hot).

Mrs. Elizabeth Hayton, Huntington Jr. H. S.
Kelso, Washington

FOR ADDITIONAL BEEF RECIPES SEE MEAT CASSEROLES, MEAT SALADS, FOREIGN DISHES AND SANDWICH SECTIONS

Ground Beef and Hamburger Favorites

MEAT BALLS

1 lb. ground beef
3 pork-link sausage
2 slices dry bread soaked in water 'till completely soaked
1 t. minced onion
⅛ teaspoon garlic salt
¼ t. salt
⅛ t. pepper

Mix thoroughly with hands 'till soft, form small meat balls and fry. (The link sausage gives this the best flavor.)

Mrs. Dorothy Anderson, Montrose H. S.
Montrose, South Dakota

MEAT BALLS IN BUTTERMILK SAUCE
Number of Servings — 6

1½ lbs. ground beef
1 small onion, finely chopped
3 T. chopped green pepper
⅓ c. sliced celery
1 c. cooked rice
1 t. salt
½ t. pepper
1 egg
1 can (10½ oz.) mushroom soup
1 soup can of buttermilk
1 can mushroom stems and pieces (2 oz.)

Put the ground beef, onion, green pepper, celery, rice, salt, pepper, and egg into a large bowl; work together with hands till well mixed. Divide into 12 portions and roll each into a ball. Place in a greased 2 quart casserole. Place the soup, buttermilk, and liquid from the mushrooms in a bowl; beat until smooth. Pour over the meat balls, along with the mushrooms. Bake in a moderate oven (350° F.) for 1 hour. The extra gravy is good to spoon over baked potatoes.

Mrs. M. Judelle Jones, Turlock H. S.
Turlock, California

APPLE BEEF BALLS
Number of Servings — 4

1 lb. ground beef
1 c. dry bread or cracker crumbs
1 c. fresh grated apples
2 eggs, beaten
1½ t. salt
½ t. pepper
1 c. tomato juice

Mix all of the ingredients together thoroughly and form into balls. Place in casserole or electric frying pan and cover with tomato juice. Cook 45 minutes to 1 hour in a 375°F. oven or frying pan. For variation: Use 1 can of cream of mushroom soup or 1 cup dairy sour cream.

Mrs. Berniece Gorsuch, Bellingham H. S.
Bellingham, Washington

CORNMEAL MEAT BALLS
Number of Servings — 6

1 lb. ground beef
2 T. chopped onion
2 T. chopped green pepper
¼ c. cornmeal
1 t. chili powder
1½ t. dry mustard
1½ t. salt
Pepper
½ c. evaporated milk
1 egg
2 c. V-8 cocktail juice

Combine all the ingredients except the cocktail juice; mix well and form into patties. Roll meat ball patties in flour and brown quickly on both sides in a little fat. Add the cocktail juice, cover and simmer for 45 minutes.

Jane Baker, Kopperl H. S.
Kopperl, Texas

BARBECUED MEAT BALLS WITH BEANS
Number of Servings — 4

1 lb. ground beef
1 egg
½ c. fine dry bread crumbs
⅔ c. milk
1 t. salt
⅛ t. pepper
1 can Boston style beans with molasses
2 T. brown sugar
1 T. Worcestershire sauce
¾ c. chopped onion

Mix beef with egg, crumbs, milk, salt and pepper. Shape mixture into 12 balls. Brown on all sides in hot fat. Place beans in greased casserole and top with meat balls, pushing balls into the beans. Mix remaining ingredients and pour over balls and beans. Cover and bake in a 350° F. oven for 20 minutes. Then uncover and bake 20 minutes longer.

Mrs. Jessie Chambers, East H. S.
Cheyenne, Wyoming

JUICY CHICKEN BALLS
Number of Servings — 5

1 lb. hamburger
1 c. water
1 t. salt
1 c. quick oatmeal
1 can cream of chicken soup, undiluted

Mix together hamburger, water, salt, and oatmeal. Chill 30 minutes. Form into balls, roll in flour, and brown on all sides in a small amount of shortening in a skillet. Add the chicken soup and simmer for 20 minutes uncovered.

Mrs. Lucy Jo Tormey, Butte Co. H. S.
Arco, Idaho

MEAT BALLS WITH A COLLEGE EDUCATION
Number of Servings — 6

1 lb. ground round
1 egg
2 T. flour
1 t. salt
1½ T. onion, chopped fine
3 green peppers, cut in large pieces
Salt and pepper to taste
4 slices of pineapple, cut into cubes
1 c. chicken stock or canned chicken soup
3 T. cornstarch
2 t. soy sauce
½ c. vinegar
½ c. sugar

Mix the meat, egg, salt and pepper, onions. Shape into balls. Roll in flour and fry until a light brown. After meat is browned add ⅓ cup chicken stock. 1 tablespoon oil, cubed pineapple, green peppers. Simmer over low flame for a few minutes. Make a sauce of cornstarch, soy sauce, vinegar, sugar and ⅔ cup chicken stock. Stir well. Add to the meat balls. Heat thoroughly. Serve over rice.

Priscilla Horning, Silverton Union H. S.
Silverton, Oregon

LEMON-OLIVE MEAT BALLS
Number of Servings — 4

1 lb. ground beef
3 T. lemon juice
1 t. salt
4 ozs. grated sharp cheese
12 olives, finely chopped
¼ green pepper, finely chopped
1 c. soft bread crumbs
½ c. milk
1 egg, beaten
12 slices bacon partially cooked

Mix all ingredients lightly together except the bacon. Gently shape into 12 balls. Wrap a bacon slice around each ball and fasten with a tooth pick. Arrange in a baking dish and bake at 350° F. about 40 minutes.

LaVelle McCain, Mount Hope H. S.
Mount Hope, Alabama

HAMBURGER BALLS
Number of Servings — 6

1 lb. hamburger
2 T. onion, finely chopped
2 T. green pepper, chopped
¼ cup corn meal
1 t. chili powder
1½ t. dry mustard
1 t. salt
⅛ t. pepper
½ c. milk
1 egg
¼ c. flour
¼ c. shortening
1½ c. canned or cooked tomatoes

Combine hamburger, onion, green pepper, corn meal, seasonings, milk, and egg. Blend thoroughly. Form into 12 balls. Roll in flour and brown in hot fat in skillet. Add remaining flour and tomatoes. Cover and bake in a hot oven (450° F.) 35-45 minutes.

Mrs. Mary Dickey Gill, West Lincoln H. S.
Brookhaven, Mississippi

GRANDMOTHER'S MEAT BALLS
Number of Servings — 25

1 lb. fresh meat, ground
1 lb. ground beef
2 eggs
2½ c. bread crumbs, squeezed out of water
1 medium onion
1 T. salt
1 t. chili powder

Mix together and form into balls the size of an egg. Drop into the following sauce, while it is hot:
2 c. water
1 t. chili powder
1 t. salt
1 can tomato soup
1 onion
½ green pepper, chopped fine

Bake 1 hour in a moderate oven (350° F.) Serve with plain macaroni.

Mrs. Dixie Hester, Scott County H. S.
Georgetown, Kentucky

SWEET AND SOUR MEAT BALLS
Number of Servings — 6

1½ lbs. ground beef
2 eggs
3 T. flour
¾ c. oil
3 large green peppers, diced
1½ c. chicken bouillon
6 slices canned pineapple, diced
2 T. cornstarch
2 T. soy sauce
1 T. Accent
¾ c. vinegar
¾ c. pineapple juice
¾ c. sugar
½ t. each salt and pepper

Shape beef into 18 balls—combine eggs, flour, salt and pepper. Dip meat balls in batter and fry in oil until brown. Remove meat balls and keep hot. Pour out all but 1 tablespoon oil from skillet. Add ½ cup bouillon, green peppers, and pineapple. Cover and cook over medium heat for 10 minutes. Mix remaining ingredients and add. Cook, stirring constantly until mixture comes to a boil and thickens. Add meat balls and simmer 15 minutes.

Ann L. Walsh, Fairbanks H. S.
Fairbanks, Alaska

SWEET SOUR MEAT BALLS
Number of Servings — 4

1 lb. ground round beef
2 T. cornstarch
1 c. water or beef broth
½ c. cider vinegar
½ c. brown sugar
2 T. vegetable oil
1 T. ground ginger
1 t. Accent
1 T. soy sauce
½ t. salt
Vegetables: as desired, celery, green tomatoes, green peppers, ripe tomatoes. 1 to ½ c. each.

Shape beef into small balls, about one inch in diameter. Dust with flour and brown lightly in the vegetable oil, at moderate high heat. Turn to low, and steam with lid on, five minutes. Remove from skillet. Brown, quickly each of the vegetables, one at a time, except the ripe tomatoes. Remove each vegetable as browned. Place them with the meat balls on a warm serving dish. When the last vegetable is completed, add all the other ingredients, mixed together. When this sauce thickens slightly, return the meat balls to the skillet. Turn off the heat. Steam for three minutes, covered. Take up on serving dish, pouring remaining sauce over the vegetables, including the ripe tomatoes. Keeping the vegetables separated, makes for a normal attractive appearance.

Christine E. Faris, Lincoln H. S.
Ypsilanti, Michigan

SURPRISE MEAT BALLS
Number of Servinngs — 8

1 lb. ground steak
½ c. grated sharp cheese
Juice of 1 lemon
½ c. chopped green pepper
2 T. chopped green olives
1 T. chopped pimento
1 c. cubed bread crumbs
1 egg, slightly beaten
½ c. sweet milk

Mix well, shape into 8 equal servings or balls. Flatten balls and roll a slice of bacon around outer edge of patty. Secure or hold with toothpick. Bake at 375° F. for 45 minutes.

Mrs. W. E. McLain, Daingerfield H. S.
Daingerfield, Texas

PENNYWISE STEAK
Number of Servings — 6

½ c. fine bread crumbs
¾ c. evaporated milk
1½ lbs. ground beef
1½ t. salt
¼ t. pepper
1 t. onion juice

Combine all ingredients. Shape meat in the form of a T-bone steak. Rub the surface with butter or margarine. Place steak on broiler rack. Broil steak on one side until well browned (6 to 10 minutes). Turn and brown on the other side. Remove steak to hot platter and serve with French fried potatoes.

Leah W. Little, Johnstown H. S.
Johnstown, Colorado

MEAT BALL SKILLET MEAL
Number of Servings — 10

1 egg
½ c. milk
1 c. soft bread crumbs
1 t. salt
½ teaspoon dry mustard
½ t. celery salt
¼ t. pepper
¼ t. nutmeg
3 T. grated onion
1 lb. ground beef
¼ c. flour
2 T. cooking fat
⅓ c. milk
1 can cream of mushroom soup
½ t. salt
1 No. 2 can mixed vegetables

Combine egg, milk and bread crumbs. Add seasonings, onion and ground beef. Shape into small balls (approximately 40) using 1 tablespoon mixture for each ball, and roll lightly in flour. Heat fat in large skillet on high heat; turn to a low heat and brown meat balls. Push to sides of skillet. Combine milk and soup in bowl, and pour in skillet. Place vegetables in center, add ½ teaspoon salt. Cover skillet and turn switch to high position. When it steams freely, turn switch to Low or Simmer and cook for 10 minutes.

Mrs. Maude C. Pruett, Dadeville H. S.
Dadeville, Alabama

SWEDISH MEAT BALLS
Number of Servings — 6-8

1 lb. ground beef
½ lb. ground pork
½ c. minced onions
¾ c. fine dry bread crumbs
1 T. minced parsley
1½ t. salt
⅛ t. pepper
1 t. Worcestershire sauce
1 egg
½ c. milk

Shape into balls the size of a walnut. Brown in ¼ cup hot fat or salad oil. Remove meat and stir into fat: ¼ cup flour, 1 teaspoon paprika, ½ teaspoon salt and ⅛ teaspoon pepper. Stir in 2 cups boiling water ¾ cup sweet or cultured sour cream. Return meat to gravy; cook 15-20 minutes.

Carolyn Nordlund Arthur, Mayville H. S.
Mayville, Wisconsin

MEAT BALLS IN SOUR CREAM
Number of Servings — 6

MEAT BALLS

1½ lbs. ground beef
½ c. commercial sour cream
2 t. salt
¼ t. pepper
½ t. garlic powder
1 T. butter

GRAVY

1 c. commercial sour cream
¼ t. garlic powder
½ t. sugar
2 t. dried dill

Mix thoroughly the ingredients for the meat balls. Shape into small balls and let chill for 15 minutes. Brown the meat balls in the tablespoon of butter. Pour off any accumulated fat. Place the meat balls in a baking dish and transfer to oven heated to 275°F. for 10 minutes. To the skillet in which meat was cooked add 1 cup sour cream. Season with garlic, dill and sugar. Heat until bubbly. Pour over meat balls.

Mrs. Byrle J. Daugherty, Bessemer H. S.
Bessemer, Alabama

HAMBURGER TOMATO BALLS
Number of Servings — 4-6

1½ lbs. hamburger
1 egg, slightly beaten
2-4 T. minced onion
2 t. salt
2 T. butter or oleo
3 T. flour
¼-⅛ t. pepper
½ t. prepared mustard
½ c. grated cheese
¼ t. Worcestershire sauce
1 T. sugar
2 c. strained tomatoes

Form hamburger, egg, onion, 1½ teaspoons salt and ¼ teaspoon pepper into balls one inch in diameter, and brown in hot fat. Set aside. Melt butter, stir in flour, add tomatoes and stir until thickened. Add ⅛ teaspoon pepper, ½ teaspoon salt, mustard, cheese, Worcestershire sauce, and sugar. Stir until cheese melts. Pour over meat balls. Cover and simmer for 20 minutes.

Mrs. Mary Baxter, Ramona Union H. S.
Ramona, California

CHEESEBURGER MEAT BALLS
Number of Servings — 8

1 egg, beaten
½ lb. lean ground beef or hamburger
¼ c. bread crumbs
½ t. salt
½ t. Worcestershire sauce

Combine above ingredients. Form into 8 balls,

putting a 1 x 1 x 1¼ inch slice of American cheese in each. Brown in 2 tablespoons shortening. Sift together 2¼ cups all purpose flour and 4 teaspoons double-acting baking powder. Cut in ½ cup shortening until almost fine. Add 1 (10½ ounce) can condensed cream of mushroom soup; (or you may use celery soup instead) stir until dough clings together. Knead on a floured surface for a few minutes. Roll out to a 12 inch square. Cut into 3 inch squares. Place meat balls in center of half the squares. Top with remaining squares. Seal the edges; prick tops. Place on ungreased baking sheet. Bake at 450°F. 15 to 20 minutes. Serve hot with catsup or tomato sauce.

Mrs. Joyce Montgomery, College H. S.
Bartlesville, Oklahoma

HAMBURGER HAWAIIAN MEAT BALLS
Number of Servings — 4

1 lb. ground beef
½ t. salt
¼ t. ginger
1 egg
1 teaspoon water
¼ c. flour
2 green peppers (or other vegetable)
3 T. salad oil
1 can pineapple chunks and syrup
¼ c. vinegar
1 T. soy sauce

Season ground beef with salt and ginger. Form into small balls, dip in egg, slightly beaten with water, then in flour, fry in salad oil, browning all sides. Take out meatballs while making sauce in same pan. Drain syrup from pineapple, add water to make one cup. Stir into drippings until sauce thickens. Arrange meatballs, pineapple and peppers in pan, stir to coat with sauce. Cook and simmer 10 minutes.

Sara Lu Greeley, Mountain Iron H. S.
Mountain Iron, Minnesota

MEAT BALL PANCAKES
Number of Servings — 6

3 egg yolks, lightly beaten
½ lb. ground beef
¼ t. baking powder
½ t. salt
Dash of pepper
1 t. lemon juice
1 T. minced parsley
1 T. grated onion
3 egg whites, stiffly beaten

Blend together first 8 ingredients and fold in 3 egg whites, stiffly beaten. Drop by spoonfuls onto greased hot griddle. When puffed and brown turn and brown other side. Serve at once with mushroom sauce or a creamed vegetable.

Mrs. Jo Belton, Robert L. Osborne H. S.
Marietta, Georgia

PORCUPINE MEAT BALLS
Number of Servings — 4-6

½ c. uncooked rice
½ lb. hamburger
1 t. salt
½ t. pepper
1 small onion chopped fine
2 T. cooking oil
1 qt. stewed tomatoes

Mix uncooked rice with hamburger, salt, pepper, and onion. Shape into balls the size of walnuts. Brown on all sides in cooking oil in a covered pan. Add tomatoes, and cook slowly in covered pan for 30 minutes or until the rice is tender and the meatball is doubled. Meatball will look like a porcupine with bristles sticking out.

Virginia Bert, Havana H. S.
Havana, Florida

PORCUPINE MEAT BALLS
Number of Servings — 6

½ c. rice
1 lb. ground beef
1 T. onion, minced
1 t. salt
½ t. pepper
1 (10½ oz.) can tomato soup
¾ c. water

Wash rice. Combine rice, meat, onion, salt and pepper. Form into balls. Mix soup and water in pressure sauce pan. Drop meat balls in pan. Cover, set control at 10 and cook 10 minutes after the control jiggles. Cool normally for 5 minutes, then place under faucet.

Mrs. Lillian W. Lemons, Dublin H. S.
Dublin, Virginia

PORCUPINE MEAT BALLS
Number of Servings — 8

1½ lbs. hamburger
½ c. bread crumbs
¼ c. minced onion
2 T. chopped green pepper
1¼ c. uncooked rice
1½ t. salt
½ t. pepper
1 egg
¼ cup uncooked rice
1 can tomato soup

Step 1. Combine all of the ingredients together except the tomato soup and the 1¼ cup uncooked rice. Shape into meatballs. Step 2. Place 1¼ cups rice into a pan, roll each ball in rice, pressing rice into the meatball. Place the meatballs in a pan. Combine the can of soup with a cup of water and mix well. Pour the tomato soup and water over the meatballs. Cover and simmer 30 to 35 minutes.

Delores Hickenbottom, Sargent H. S.
Sargent, Nebraska

PORCUPINE MEAT BALLS
Number of Servings — 12

2 lbs. ground beef
¾ c. uncooked rice
¼ t. pepper
4 t. celery salt
2 T. onions
1 can tomato soup (10½-oz.)
1 can tomato sauce (8-oz.)
1 c. hot water (add more if necessary)

Blend meat, rice, pepper, celery salt, onions. Form into 24 balls. Place in baking dish; add soup, tomato sauce, and water. Cover and bake in slow oven (325°F.) for 1¼ hours.

Lessie P. Carothers, Frayser H. S.
Memphis, Tennessee

RICE PORCUPINE BALLS
Number of Servings — 6

1 lb. ground beef
½ t. Cumin seed
½ t. dry mustard
½ teaspoon salt
1 t. horseradish
¼ t. pepper
½ c. rice
¼ green pepper (sliced)
1 small onion, chopped fine
2 cans tomato soup

Mix meat, onion, seasoning and rice thoroughly; shape into balls. Put mixture into a heavy aluminum skillet, cover with tomato soup. Put skillet lid on and cook slowly 1 hour. Chopped mushrooms may be added to the sauce if desired.

Mrs. Ruth Sorrells, Stuttgart H. S.
Stuttgart, Arkansas

"LITTLE PORCUPINES"
Number of Servings — 5-6

1 lb. hamburger
½ c. raw rice
1 T. finely chopped onion
2 T. chopped green pepper
1 t. salt
¼ t. celery salt
1 clove garlic, finely chopped
4 whole cloves
2 T. sugar
2 c. tomato juice
1 T. Worcestershire sauce
½ t. cinnamon

Wash rice. Drain. Combine rice, hamburger, onion, green pepper, salt, celery salt, and garlic. Form into balls about 1½ inches in diameter. Heat tomato juice, cloves, cinnamon, sugar, and Worcestershire sauce in a heavy skillet. Drop in meat balls. Cover tightly. Simmer 50 minutes.

Harlene J. Sexton, Clarion H. S.
Clarion, Iowa

PORCUPINE BALLS
Number of Servings — 6

3 T. shortening
1 lb. ground beef
¼ lb. ground pork
1 c. rice
Dash of pepper
1 onion, chopped
2 t. salt
2 c. tomatoes

Wash and drain rice. Add to meat along with onion, salt and pepper. Form into balls. Brown in skillet. When browned, add tomatoes and cover. When steaming, turn switch to low heat for 30 minutes.

Mrs. Geraldine M. Beveridge, Beaufort H. S.
Beaufort, North Carolina

PORCUPINE MEAT BALLS
Number of Servings — 6

1 lb. ground lean beef
1 lb. ground lean pork
1 egg, beaten
½ c. milk
⅔ c. uncooked rice
1 t. chili powder
2 t. salt
2½ c. canned tomatoes
2½ c. water
2 T. chopped onions
1 t. salt
1 t. chili powder

Mix meats; add egg, milk, rice, 1 teaspoon chili powder, and 2 teaspoons salt. Form into 1½ inch balls and brown in hot fat. Combine tomatoes, water, onion, and remaining seasonings; bring to boiling; drop in meat balls. Cover; cook slowly 1½ hours. Makes 24 balls.

Mrs. Lloyd Saxe, Edwards Sr. H. S.
Albion, Illinois

PORCUPINE BALLS
Number of Servings — 5-6

1 lb. ground beef
½ c. uncooked rice
1 T. minced onion
1 t. salt
1 can tomato soup
1 c. water (1 can water)
1 T. Worcestershire sauce

Combine meat, rice, onion, and salt. Mix well and form into balls. Place in a deep baking dish. Combine tomato soup, water, and Worcestershire sauce. Pour over meat balls. Cover dish. Bake at 350°F. for 1 hour. Serve hot and pour the tomato sauce over the balls.

Bessie Jackson, Woodstock Union H. S.
Woodstock, Vermont

PORCUPINE MEAT BALLS
Number of Servings — 6-8

2 eggs, beaten
½ c. uncooked rice
2 t. salt
1 teaspoon pepper
1 medium onion, chopped
1 lb. ground beef

Mix ingredients and shape into medum meatballs. Brown meatballs in a small amount of fat. When browned top each ball with catsup. Cover with water. Cook in a covered container over low heat for 1½ to 2 hours. Serve hot.

Sarah Pfeifer, Narphlet H. S.
Narphlet, Arkansas

PORCUPINE MEAT BALLS
Number of Servings — 6

1½ lbs. ground beef
½ t. pepper
1 T. minced onion
½ c. rice
1 t. salt

Mix well and shape into small balls. Put into kettle: 1 can tomato soup and ½ can water. Let boil, put meat balls into soup, cover and let simmer for 1 hour.

Marjorie Huber, New England Public H. S.
New England, North Dakota

SPAGHETTI AND MEAT BALLS
Number of Servings — 12

3 medium-sized onions
4 stalks celery
½ green pepper
1 can sieved tomatoes
½ t. salt
½ t. pepper
3 t. chili powder
Few drops of Italian seasoning
1 can mushrooms
1 T. sugar
1 t. cinnamon
½ c. catsup
3 T. Tabasco sauce
1 clove garlic

Cut and cook the onions, celery, and pepper for a few minutes. Mix the rest of the ingredients which forms a sauce with the vegetables.

MEAT BALLS (30 small)
2 lbs. hamburger
¼ t. pepper
1 egg
½ t. onion powder
2 t. salt
3 slices bread (1½ c. crumbs)
Milk (to mix)

(Continued on Next Page)

Combine above ingredients. Form into balls and fry until brown. Then put in a pan and cover with the sauce. Simmer for 3-4 hours, stirring occasionally. Cook spaghetti in boiling salted (2 tablespoons) water. Cook until done and pour cold water over to cool and then drain. Put meat balls on a platter and mix spaghetti and sauce and serve with grated Parmesan cheese.

Carolyn Kohntopp, Palouse H. S.
Palouse, Washington

SPAGHETTI AND MEAT BALLS
Number of Servings — 6-8
MEATBALLS
1½ lbs. ground beef (some pork adds flavor)
2 eggs
1 t. salt
½ t. pepper
1 clove minced garlic
1 c. bread crumbs
¼ to ⅓ c. grated romano cheese
Sprig of parsley, chopped

Blend all ingredients together, mixing with hands, and shape into balls. Roll in cracker crumbs. Fry in oil that has been heated, with garlic clove, until browned.

SPAGHETTI SAUCE
2 large cans tomatoes
2 cans tomato paste
2 t. salt
¼ t. black pepper
2 t. sugar
1 clove garlic
Pinch or oregano
Pinch of rosemary
Sprig of parsley

Combine the above ingredients into a large kettle, add the browned meatballs and simmer slowly over low heat for 2 hours. Cook spaghetti according to directions on the box. Combine sauce, spaghetti and serve with meatballs.

Laura Pernice, Turner Jr. H. S.
Warren, Ohio

MEAT BALLS & SPAGHETTI SAUCE
Number of Servings — 6
MEAT BALLS
1 lb. ground beef
1 egg
½ c. bread crumbs
¼ t. pepper
2 T. chopped parsley
1½ t. salt
½ t. garlic powder
SPAGHETTI SAUCE
Cook together—1 stalk celery, 1 green pepper; 2 medium sized onions. Puree. Add 1 t. salt. Add 1 qt. pureed tomatoes.
4 cans tomato paste
2 cans water (use tomato paste can)

3 beef boullion cubes
Simmer 1½ hours. Then add
¼ t. baking soda
2 t. sugar
½ t. garlic salt
1 t. chili powder

Combine all ingredients for meat balls and work thoroughly together. Form into meat balls (small size) and fry in 2 tablespoons olive oil. After the meat balls are browned take them out and add the sauce to the pan and simmer together. Then add the meat balls and let simmer ½ hour. Serve on *vermicelli thin* spaghetti.

Mrs. Arlene Block, Prairie du Sac H. S.
Prairie du Sac, Wisconsin

ITALIAN SPAGHETTI
Number of Servings — 6

1½ lbs. ground beef
½ lb. ground veal
¼ c. olive oil
1 t. salt
⅛ t. pepper
Dash cayenne pepper
1 t. chili powder
½ t. garlic salt
1 c. onion, chopped
½ c. mushrooms
½ c. ripe olives
1 c. carrots, grated
1 c. celery, chopped
2 c. tomato juice
2 cans tomato paste

Brown meat in skillet with olive oil. Add all the spices, slice olives, mushrooms; chop onions and celery; and add grated carrots. Mix vegetables to meat and seasonings. Add liquid, simmer for a half hour. Serve over long cooked spaghetti, garnish with parsley. Delicious served with French garlic bread or hot rolls.

Mary Ann Spangler, Johnson Creek H. S.
Johnson Creek, Wisconsin

SPAGHETTI SAUCE
Number of Servings — 6

1 lb. ground beef
1 large green pepper
1 onion
1 qt. canned drained tomatoes
3 T. catsup
½ t. Worcestershire sauce
Few drops Tabasco sauce
1 bay leaf

Brown meat, pepper, and onion in fat. Bring to a boil tomatoes, catsup, Worcestershire sauce, Tabasco sauce and bay leaf; add to meat. Simmer 3-4 hours. Serve over cooked spaghetti.

Lois O. Crabtree, Ceres H. S.
Ceres, Virginia

SPAGHETTI WITH MEAT SAUCE
Number of Servings — 6

2 T. fat
2 T. chopped onion
1 lb. ground beef
1 T. Worcestershire sauce
1 t. salt
¼ t. black pepper
½ t. garlic salt
2 c. tomato juice
¼ c. tomato catsup

Saute finely chopped onion in melted fat. Add ground meat and seasonings.Stir until meat is slightly browned and add tomato juice and tomato catsup. Simmer for 30 minutes. Serve over hot drained boiled spaghetti (1 lb. uncooked) on a hot platter. Sprinkle with grated Parmesan cheese.

Mrs. Jolene Hartman, Lancaster H. S.
Lancaster, Texas

SPAGHETTI SAUCE
Number of Servings — 10

2 onions
1 bell pepper
1 lb. ground beef
Salt and pepper to taste
Water added to consistency desired
2 T. Worcestershire sauce
1 No. 2 can of tomatoes
1 small can of tomato paste
1 small can of mushroom sauce
1 small can of tomato sauce

Brown in fat 2 onions, 1 bell pepper. Add ground beef and let brown with salt and pepper. Add remainder of ingredients. Cook slowly for 1½ to 2 hours.

Kay W. Nicholson, Lexington H. S.
Lexington, South Carolina

SPAGHETTI WITH MEAT BALLS
Number of Servings — 8

Tomato Sauce:
½ c. chopped onion
3 T. shortening
2 No. 2 cans tomatoes
1 8-oz. can tomato sauce
1 6-oz. can tomato paste
½ c. catsup
1 10½-oz. can tomato soup
1 c. water
½ t. basil
2 T. minced parsley
2 t. salt
½ t. pepper
⅛ t. oregano

Saute onion in shortening in deep skillet. Sieve tomatoes. Add sieved tomatoes and rest of ingredients. Simmer over low heat for 1½ to 2 hours.

Meat Balls:
1½ lbs. ground beef
¼ lb. ground pork
1 c. fine dry bread crumbs
1 T. minced parsley
½ c. milk
2 eggs, beaten
1½ t. salt
⅛ t. pepper

Mix above ingredients together lightly. Shape into balls of 1 inch diameter. Brown meat balls on all sides in hot fat. Pour off excess fat as it collects. Add browned meat balls to tomato sauce 20 minutes before sauce is done. Simmer together until done. Serve meat balls and sauce over hot spaghetti. Sprinkle grated Parmesan or cheddar cheese over it, if desired.

Elda Pinnow, Union Grove H. S.
Union Grove, Wisconsin

"SPECIAL REQUEST" SPAGHETTI SAUCE WITH MEAT BALLS
Number of Servings — 6-8

Sauce:
1 pork chop
2 cans tomatoes
1 can tomato paste
1 can Venice Maid mushroom sauce
Salt and pepper
Small clove garlic, minced
½ green pepper (optional)

Brown pork in large heavy pan. Add the rest of the ingredients and simmer at least an hour.

Meat Balls:
1 lb. ground beef
1 t. baking powder
2 slices bread, soaked in milk
Salt and pepper

Make balls from the meat mixture. Brown in hot oil. Add meat balls to the sauce and simmer for 20 minutes before serving.

Wilma B. Russell, Sterling H. S.
Somerdale, New Jersey

HILDY'S SPAGHETTI
Number of Servings — 6

½ lb. ground beef
2 T. fat
½ c. chopped onion
1 t. salt
½ t. chili powder
3 c. tomato juice
½ box spaghetti (7-oz. size)

Brown meat in skillet in hot fat using low heat. Add onion and cook until tender. Stir in seasonings and tomato juice. When mixture reaches a boil, stir in uncooked spaghetti. Cover skillet. Simmer 30 minutes. Serve with buttered garlic toast or bread.

Thelma Vogel, McAlester H. S.
McAlester, Oklahoma

SPAGHETTI
Number of Servings — 6

1½ lbs. ground meat
3 large onions
1 green pepper
1 t. salt
2½ T. fat
1 (10½-oz. can) condensed tomato soup
1 (10½-oz. can) condensed cream of mushroom soup
2 (8-oz. cans) tomato paste
1 (No. 2 can) yellow kernel corn
1 (No. 2 can) ripe olives

Combine meat, onions, pepper, salt and fat in skillet. Cook until the meat is brown. Mix tomato soup, mushroom soup, tomato paste, corn and ripe olives with meat. Cook one-half 8-ounce package of spaghetti, drain and mix with the sauce. Place in a 2 quart baking dish. Bake in 300°F. oven for 1 hour. Cover with grated cheese. Bake until cheese is melted.

Mrs. Betty Rainwater, Lynn H. S.
Lynn, Arkansas

SPAGHETTI WITH ITALIAN MEAT SAUCE
Number of Servings — 8

½ c. minced onion
¼ c. salad oil
1 lb. ground beef
2 peeled cloves garlic, minced
1 6-oz. can mushrooms
¼ c. minced parsley
1 No. 2 can tomatoes
1 8-oz. can tomato sauce
2½ t. salt
½ t. pepper
¼ t. sugar
Thyme
1 lb. spaghetti
5-6 qts. boiling water
1 T. salt
1 c. diced cheese
½-1 c. grated Parmesan cheese

Simmer onion in oil for 5 minutes. Add beef and garlic; cook until crumbly and slightly brown. Add chopped mushrooms with liquid; parsley, tomato sauce, tomatoes, salt, pepper, sugar, and herbs. Cover and simmer 1-1½ hours. About 20 minutes before serving, cook spaghetti according to directions on package. Mix with meat sauce and let simmer about 10 minutes. Sprinkle with cheese and serve.

Mrs. Dan L. Stoldt, Scurry-Rosser H. S.
Scurry, Texas

ITALIAN SPAGHETTI
Number of Servings — 6

2 lbs. ground beef
1 small bunch celery
2 large bell peppers, chopped
2 large onions, chopped
1 No. 2 can whole tomatoes
Salt, pepper, garlic, thyme, mace, bay leaves, as desired
1 small can tomato paste
2 heaping t. chili powder
½ t. Tabasco sauce
2 T. Worcestershire sauce

In 3 tablespoons fat, brown onion, celery and bell pepper. Remove. Add more fat, and brown meat which has been seasoned, and shaped into balls. Remove. Add flour to make brown gravy. Add water (or meat stock, if available). Add meat, onion mixture, and remaining ingredients. Cook 2-3 hours over low heat. Add garlic. Cook 15 minutes more. Serve over boiled spaghetti with grated Parmesan cheese.

Mrs. Rosabelle G. Mitchell, Chataignier H. S.
Chataignier, Louisiana

IRISH-ITALIAN SPAGHETTI
Number of Servings — 6

1 onion, chopped
2 T. salad oil
1 lb. ground beef
½ t. chili powder
1 t. salt
½ t. Tabasco sauce
¼ t. black pepper
Dash red pepper
1 10½-oz. can condensed cream of mushroom soup
1 10½-oz. can condensed tomato soup
1 small can tomato paste
1 8-oz. package long spaghetti

Cook onion in hot oil till golden; add meat and seasonings; brown lightly. Cover; simmer 10 minutes. Add soups; cover and simmer 45 minutes. Cook spaghetti in boiling, salted water until tender. Drain and rinse with hot water. Arrange on hot platter. Pour sauce over spaghetti.

Lois Winkler, Dieterich H. S.
Dieterich, Illinois

ADDITIONAL SPAGHETTI SAUCE RECIPES ARE CONTAINED IN THE FOREIGN MEAT DISH SECTION.

MEAT LOAF

Number of Servings — 8

1 can (10½ ozs.) condensed tomato soup
½ c. fine dry bread crumbs
½ c. chopped onion
1 T. Worcestershire sauce
1 t. salt
Dash black pepper
1½ lbs. ground beef
½ lb. ground pork
¼ c. chopped bell peppers
1 egg, slightly beaten
1 t. sage

Combine all ingredients; mix well. Shape into a loaf or place in a casserole. If shaped in loaf, place in a shallow baking pan. Bake in a moderate oven (350° F.) about 1¼ hours. If desired, additional tomato soup may be spread on top of the loaf and baked the last ten minutes.

Mrs. Pauline R. Cook, Vernon H. S.
Vernon, Florida

MEAT LOAF

Number of Servings — 8-10

1½ lbs. hamburger
1 c. oat meal (uncooked)
2 eggs
1 c. tomato juice
4 T. minced onion
2 t. salt
½ t. pepper
1 T. catsup
1 T. prepared mustard

Combine ingredients and mix well. Turn into greased baking pan (preferably a loaf pan). Place in preheated oven and bake for 1 hour at 350° F. Let stand 5 minutes. Remove from pan, cut and serve.

Mrs. Jo-Ann Jensen, Eleva-Strum Cent. H. S.
Strum, Wisconsin

ITALIAN MEAT LOAF

Number of Servings — 4

2 slices rye bread
2 slices white bread
1 lb. ground beef
1 medium onion
4 sprigs parsley
3 T. Parmesan cheese
1 egg
1 t. salt
½ t. pepper
2 T. butter
1 can (8 oz.) tomato sauce
1 t. oregano

Let the bread soak in 1 cup water for several minutes. Mash the bread with a fork. Add meat, chopped onions, parsley, grated cheese, egg, salt and pepper. Put into baking pan. Put butter on top and bake 30 minutes. Pour tomato sauce over the meat. Sprinkle with oregano and bake 20 minutes longer.

Mary J. Riehart, Pierce H. S.
Pierce, Nebraska

MEAT LOAF

Number of Servings — 6

1 lb. chuck, ground
5 slices bread
½ c. catsup
1 egg, 1 t. salt
Few grains of pepper
1 small onion
½ c. tomato juice
1 c. milk

Mix beaten egg and milk. Soften crumbs in mixture. Add meat, salt, chopped (fine) onion and pepper. Shape into roll and pour on juice and catsup (mixed). Bake 1½ hours, uncovered, in oven at 350° F. Baste 2-3 times. May put 2-3 strips bacon on top loaf.

Gladys McConkey, Lost Creek H. S.
Jane Lew, West Virginia

MEAT LOAF

Number of Servings — 6

½ c. hot milk
1 c. bread crumbs
1 lb. ground beef
½ lb. ground pork
½ t. salt
1 t. onion juice
1 egg
4 T. catsup
½ t. Worcestershire sauce
⅛ t. pepper

Collect necessary ingredients needed. Pour hot milk over bread crumbs. Combine ground meat, onion juice, and slightly beaten egg. Add moistened bread crumbs. Add catsup, Worcestershire, salt, and pepper. Shape into loaf. Pack in loaf pan. Bake 1 hour at 350° F.

Sarah D. Musgrave, Rattan H. S.
Rattan, Oklahoma

MEAT LOAF

Number of Servings — 8

⅔ c. dry bread crumbs
1 c. milk
1½ lb. ground beef
2 beaten eggs
¼ c. grated onion
1 t. salt
⅛ t. pepper
½ t. sage

Soak bread crumbs in milk; add meat, eggs, onion, and seasonings; mix well. Form into a single loaf in 4¾ x 8¾-inch loaf pan. Spread Piquant Sauce over loaf and bake for 1 hour at 350° F. Piquant Sauce: Combine 3 tablespoons brown sugar, ¼ cup catsup, ¼ teaspoon nutmeg, and 1 teaspoon dry mustard.

Melba Quattlebaum Price, Hanceville H. S.
Hanceville, Alabama

MEAT LOAF
Number of Servings — 8

2 c. fresh bread crumbs
¾ c. minced onions
¼ c. minced green pepper
2 eggs
2 lbs. chuck, ground
½ T. horseradish
2½ t. salt
1 t. dry mustard
¼ c. milk
½ c. catsup

Prepare bread crumbs, minced onions, green pepper. About 1 hour before serving start heating oven to 400°F. With fork, beat eggs slightly. Lightly mix in meat, then crumbs, onions, pepper. Add horseradish, salt, mustard, milk, ¼ cup catsup; combine lightly but well. In bowl, shape meat into oval loaf; transfer to shallow baking dish or broil-and-serve platter; smooth into shapely loaf. Spread top with ½ cup catsup. Bake 50 minutes.

Sue R. Breeze, Winchester Local H. S.
Winchester, Ohio

MEAT LOAF
Number of Servings — 8

1½ lbs. ground beef
2 beaten eggs
2 t. salt
1 c. tomato juice
¾ c. uncooked oats
¼ c. chopped onion
¼ t. pepper

Combine all ingredients thoroughly and pack firmly into a loaf pan. Bake in a moderate oven (350° F.) about one hour. Let stand 5 minutes before slicing.

Mrs. Bobbie Jean Sharpe, Irving College H. S.
McMinnville, Tennessee

MEAT LOAF
Number of Servings — 4

1 lb. ground chuck
¼ c. fine bread crumbs
3 T. minced onion
1 t. salt
Dash of pepper
⅔ c. evaporated milk
2 T. catsup

Mix gently all ingredients except catsup. Shape into a loaf in baking dish. Bake 45 minutes. Remove from oven. Spoon catsup on top. Bake 15 minutes longer. Variation: Omit catsup and cook meat loaf 1 hour. Using a can of cream of celery soup. Open can; stir contents well. Slowly mix in ⅓ to ½ cup milk. Heat to boiling and simmer 2 minutes. Serve over meat loaf.

Mrs. Shirley Pierce, Beedeville P. S.
Beedeville, Arkansas

TOUCHDOWN MEAT LOAF
Number of Servings — 6

1 package (9-oz.) condensed mince meat
½ c. water
1 lb. lean ground beef
½ lb. processed American cheese, finely shredded
⅓ c. water
1 egg, slightly beaten
1 T. chopped onion
1 t. salt
¼ t. pepper
1 c. dry bread crumbs

Break mince meat in small pieces into small saucepan; add ½ cup water. Place over low heat; stir until lumps are broken. Increase heat and bring mince meat to a boil; boil briskly, stirring often, until almost dry. Cool. Put with remaining ingredients into mixing bowl; blend until well mixed. Put meat mixture into well-buttered bomb mold. Bake in 450°F. oven 1 hour.

Helen E. Pyle, Christian Co. H. S.
Hopkinsville, Kentucky

MEAT LOAF
Number of Servings — 6

1½ lbs. beef, ground
½ lb. pork, ground
1 large onion, chopped fine
1 t. salt
½ c. cracker crumbs
1 egg, beaten
½ c. milk
1 can condensed tomato soup
Parsley

Mix all ingredients, except soup, together well; place in a greased loaf pan. Bake at 350° for ½ hour. Remove from oven and pour soup over it. Bake ½ hour longer (basting occasionally with drippings). Garnish with parsley

Mrs. Emily Daniel, Talbot Co. H. S.
Woodland, Georgia

MEAT LOAF
Number of Servings — 6

1 lb. ground beef
1 egg
1¼ c. Franco-American spaghetti sauce with meat
¼ c. chopped onion
¼ c. chopped green pepper
½ c. chopped celery
2 slices toasted bread crumbs
1 t. salt

Beat egg in large bowl. Add all ingredients and stir until well mixed. Pour into a well greased baking dish. Bake at 375°F. until brown. About 1 hour.

Martha Alice S. Cowan, Maplesville H. S.
Maplesville, Alabama

MEAT LOAF
Number of Servings — 4-6

1½ lbs. ground beef
2 c. cereal flakes (corn flakes, 40% bran or
  Wheaties
2 eggs
1 c. milk
3 T. minced green onion
2 t. salt
Pepper
⅛ t. dry mustard
⅛ t. sage

Put eggs, milk, onion, salt, pepper, dry mustard and sage in bowl; mix thoroughly. Add ground meat; mix. Put in greased 9 x 5 x 3 inch loaf pan. If you want to turn out the loaf, line pan with aluminum foil. Bake at 350°F. for 1½ hours. After loaf is in the oven, mix: 3 tablespoons brown sugar, ¼ cup catsup, 1 teaspoon dry mustard and ¼ teaspoon nutmeg. One half hour before meat loaf is done, put sauce mixture on top of loaf.

Alice Fetterman
Punxsutawney Area Joint Jr. H. S.
Punxsutawney, Pennsylvania

MEAT LOAF
Number of Servings — 6-8

2 eggs
⅓ c. catsup
¾ c. warm water
1 package onion soup mix
1½ c. soft bread crumbs
2 lbs. ground beef

Beat eggs lightly in large bowl. Stir in catsup, water, soup mix, bread crumbs and ground beef. Mix well and bake in a loaf pan at 350°F. for 1 hour.

Mrs. Marjorie Browning, Pensacola H. S.
Pensacola, Florida

MEAT LOAF
Number of Servings — 6

1 lb. ground beef
½ c. evaporated milk
⅓ c. rolled oats (uncooked)
¼ c. finely chopped onion
1 t. salt
⅛ t. pepper

Cook 1 cup tomato sauce, 2 tablespoons brown sugar, 1 tablespoon vinegar, 1 teaspoon Worcestershire sauce, ¼ teaspoon dry mustard, ½ teaspoon chili powder, and ½ teaspoon salt for 5 minutes. Stir one half of this mixture into the meat loaf and place in loaf pan. Pour rest of sauce over the top and bake at 350°F. for 50 minutes.

Deeanne Enders, Hebron H. S.
Hebron, Nebraska

BACON MEAT LOAF WITH OLIVE STUFFING
Number of Servings — 12

1 lb. ground beef
½ lb. ground veal
½ lb. ground pork
2 t. salt
¼ t. pepper
½ lb. sliced bacon

Add salt and pepper to meat and mix well. Place waxed paper on cutting board and press meat into a flat sheet about 8 x 11 inches. Make dressing using:

1½ c. coarse dry bread crumbs
½ t. salt
2 T. butter
1 T. chopped onion
1 egg, slightly beaten
½ c. boiling water
8 stuffed olives

Melt butter and add chopped onion. Cook until onion is clear. Mix with bread crumbs, add salt, sliced olives, and egg. Add boiling water to moisten. Place dressing in center of meat, forming a roll the length of the meat. Roll meat around dressing and pinch edges together. Place meat roll on oiled baking pan with strips of bacon over top. Bake at 325°F. for 1 hour. Garnish with parsley and stuffed olives.

Catherine Dicks, State Supervisor
University Park, New Mexico

MEAT LOAF SURPRISE (Baked)
Number of Servings — 8

1¼ lbs. ground beef
Salt and pepper to taste
1 c. bread crumbs
⅓ c. minced onion
2 T. chopped green pepper
1 T. minced parsley
1 egg, uncooked
4 small eggs, hard cooked
½ c. milk or ½ c. tomato sauce
2 c. whipped potatoes; left-over, plan-over, or
  just whipped

Brown the minced onion in hot fat. Mix well with all the remaining ingredients except the hard cooked eggs. Put half this mixture in a well-greased loaf pan (8¾ x 4¾ x 2½ inch). Down the center place the hard cooked eggs, lengthwise. Pack the remaining meat mixture firmly on top. Bake about an hour in a moderate oven (350°F.). Unmold on a fireproof serving or baking platter or dish. "Frost", like a cake, with the whipped potatoes. Garnish with paprika. Return to oven to brown. If desired, serve with carrots and broccoli or other colorful cooked vegetables arranged around the loaf.

Leora Sayre—Buckskin Valley H. S.
South Salem, Ohio

HAMBURGER RING BARBECUE
Number of Servings — 6-8

2 lbs. hamburger
2½ c. coarsely grated sharp American cheese
1 t. salt
¼ t. pepper
1 t. dry mustard
3 T. chili sauce
1 T. Worcestershire sauce
2 c. corn flakes
1 c. milk
2 eggs

Blend ingredients thoroughly. Press into 9 inch ring mold. Bake in moderate oven at 350°F. for 45 minutes. Unmold on shallow pan; pour Barbecue Sauce over. Place in hot oven (425°F.) 10 minutes to glaze.

Barbecue Sauce: Brown 1 clove garlic in 1 tablespoon salad oil. Add ½ teaspoon salt, ¼ teaspoon pepper, ⅛ teaspoon oregano, ½ cup tomato sauce, and 2 tablespoons honey. Simmer for 30 minutes.

Clara E. Dalton, Piute H. S.
Junction, Utah

MEAT LOAF
Number of Servings — 10

2 c. bread or cracker crumbs
2 T. flour
2½ t. salt
2 T. finely chopped onion
¼ t. mustard
1 hard cooked egg
1 medium sized boiled potato, mashed
½ lb. veal, ground
½ lb. ground beef
½ lb. ground pork
½ c. milk
¾ t. pepper
¼ t. paprika
¼ t. sage
3 T. catsup

Mix and shape in loaf with boiled egg in the center. (When cut the slices of egg will appear). Bake at 350°F.

Bennie Jones, Union Grove H. S.
Gladewater, Texas

QUICKIE HAMBURGER MEAT LOAF
Number of Servings — 4

1 lb. ground beef
1 can tomato soup (condensed)
1½ t. salt
1 t. pepper

Combine the ground beef, salt, and pepper. Form into one large pattie. Place in baking dish and pour undiluted soup over the top. Bake in 350°F. oven for approximately ½ hour or until done.

Carol Vopat, Beverly Rural H. S.
Beverly, Kansas

MEAT LOAF FOR TWO
Number of Servings — 2-4

1½ c. soft bread crumbs
1 egg, slightly beaten
½ c. milk
1 medium onion, peeled
1 lb. ground beef
½ medium green pepper, minced
2 t. salt
Speck pepper
½ t. dried thyme
¾ t. celery salt
1 T. catsup

Combine first 3 ingredients. Cut 2 slices from onion; set aside; mince rest. Add onion, green pepper, and seasoning to crumbs; blend. Add ground beef and shape into oval loaf on shallow pan. Spread with catsup. Insert onion slices on top; brush with salad oil. Bake in moderately hot oven of 400°F. for 45 minutes.

Beatrice Nuppenau, Winnebago H. S.
Winnebago, Illinois

SAVORY MEAT LOAF
Number of Servings — 6-8

1½ lbs. ground beef, chuck
1½ t. salt
Dash pepper
4 slices white bread, cubed
½ c. catsup
1 c. apple sauce
Onion rings for garnish

Place meat in bowl, add salt and pepper and mix well. Add bread cubes, catsup, and apple sauce; mix until well blended. Place meat in greased loaf pan and spread smooth. Bake at 350°F. for 1½ hours. Place platter over loaf pan and turn upside down. Garnish with onion rings.

Elizabeth Miller, Itawamba Jr. College and H. S.
Fulton, Mississippi

SAVORY BEEF LOAF
Number of Servings — 8

2 lbs. ground beef
1 t. salt
¼ t. pepper
4 slices dry bread (broken into small crumbs)
2 T. onion, chopped fine
2 eggs
3-4 slices bacon or salt pork, cut into small strips

Place meat, seasonings, bread crumbs, onion and eggs into a bowl, and blend well, using fork or finger tips. Turn mixture into a loaf pan. Press into the corners and smooth over the top. Decorate the top with an even pattern of strips of bacon or salt pork.

Mrs. Adrianna H. Mills, Johnson H. S.
Johnson, Vermont

MINIATURE MEAT LOAVES
Number of Servings — 6

1½ lb. ground beef
¾ c. quick or old fashioned, uncooked
    Mother's Oats
1½ t. salt
¼ t. pepper
¼ c. chopped onion
1 8-oz. can tomato sauce
1 egg, beaten
1 T. prepared mustard
1 1-lb. 13 oz. can cling peach halves
Currant jelly

Heat oven to moderate (350°F.). Combine all ingredients for meat loaves thoroughly. Shape into 6 individual meat loaves; place in shallow baking pan. Bake in preheated oven (350°F.) 20 minutes. Drain peach halves; fill with jelly and place between meat loaves; bake 15 additional minutes. Makes 6 loaves.

Naomi M. Vaught, Manatee H. S.
Bradenton, Florida

WONDERFUL MEAT LOAF
Number of Servings — 8

2 slices bread
1 c. milk
1½ lbs. ground beef
2 eggs, beaten
¼ c. minced onion
1 t. salt
½ t. sage
⅛ t. pepper
1 small can mushroom sauce

Soak bread in milk; mix to break bread into small particles. Add other ingredients and mix thoroughly. Shape into loaf and spread with mixture of 3 tablespoons brown sugar, ¼ cup catsup, ¼ teaspoon nutmeg, and 1 teaspoon dry mustard. Bake 1 hour at 350°F.

Mrs. Doris E. Jackson, Clay City Com. H. S.
Clay City, Illinois

APRICOT MEAT LOAF
Number of Servings — 8

2 lbs. ground beef
1 c. chopped dried apricots
½ c. dry bread crumbs
2 eggs
2 T. chopped parsley
1½ t. salt
⅛ t. pepper

Combine all ingredients and shape into roll. Place on greased shallow pan. Bake uncovered at 350°F. 1 hour. GLAZE: Mix ½ cup brown sugar with 1 teaspoon water: heat until sugar melts. Spread evenly over hot meat loaf. Continue baking 5 to 10 minutes. Serve hot.

Helen C. Sockman, Mechanicsburg Jr. H. S.
Mechanicsburg, Pennsylvania

PERFECT MEAT LOAF
Number of Servings — 6-8

1½ lbs. ground beef
¾ c. quick-cooking raw oats
2 eggs, beaten slightly
¼ c. chopped onion
2 t. salt
¼ t. pepper
2 8-oz. cans tomato sauce

Combine first 6 ingredients thoroughly with 1 can of tomato sauce. Pack firmly into an 8 x 4 x 3 inch loaf pan. Chill about 1 hour. Unmold into a shallow baking pan. Bake in moderate oven (350°F.) for 1 hour. Pour second can of sauce over loaf. Bake 20 minutes more until loaf is nicely glazed.

Patsy Edmunds, Momence Com. H. S.
Momence, Illinois

MEAT LOAF
Number of Servings — 8-10

2 lbs. ground beef
2 eggs
1 t. salt
Dash pepper
½ c. catsup
*2 T. wheat germ
½ c. catsup

Loosen ground beef. Add eggs, salt and pepper. Stir well. Add ½ cup catsup. Stir well. Add wheat germ. Stir well. Put into casserole. Use last ½ cup catsup to cover meat loaf. Bake at 350°F. for 1 hour, or until done.
*Use 2-4 tablespoons wheat germ for firmer loaf.

Mrs. Vada Nixon, Atkinson County Com. H. S.
Effingham, Kansas

EVERYDAY MEAT LOAF
Number of Servings — 6-8

1½ lbs. ground beef
3 eggs, slightly beaten
¼ c. grated onion
½ c. finely chopped celery
½ c. evaporated milk
½ c. tomato catsup
1 t. salt
⅛ t. pepper
⅔ c. three minute oats

Thoroughly mix all ingredients in a large bowl. Form in individual loaves and place in greased muffin pans. Cover meat loaves with piquant sauce. Bake in moderate oven (350°F.) 45-55 minutes. Or form in two loaves and spread over sauce and bake 1 hour.
Piquant Sauce: Combine 6 tablespoons brown sugar, ¼ cup catsup, ¼ teaspoon nutmeg and 1 teaspoon dry mustard.

Lois Salter, Zwolle H. S.
Zwolle, Louisiana

EVERYDAY MEAT LOAF WITH PIQUANT SAUCE
Number of Servings — 8

⅔ c. dry bread crumbs
1 c. milk
1½ lbs. ground beef
2 eggs, beaten
¼ c. grated onion
1 t. salt
½ t. sage
Dash pepper

Soak bread crumbs in milk; add meat, eggs, onion, and seasoning; mix well. Form in individual loaves; place in greased muffin pans. Cover with Piquant Sauce. Bake in moderate oven (350°F.) 45 minutes. Or form 1 loaf in 8½ x 4½ x 2½ pan. Spread with sauce; bake 1 hour.
Piquant Sauce: Combine 3 tablespoons brown sugar, ¼ cup catsup, ¼ teaspoon nutmeg, and 1 teaspoon dry mustard.

Alice Sue Fairless, Murray College H. S.
Murray, Kentucky

MEAT LOAF PIQUANT
Number of Servings — 8

⅔ c. dry bread crumbs
1 c. milk
1½ lbs. ground beef
2 beaten eggs
¼ c. chopped onion
1 t. salt
½ t. sage
Dash pepper
PIQUANT SAUCE
Combine the following ingredients:
6 T. brown sugar
½ c. catsup
½ t. nutmeg
2 t. dry mustard

Soak bread crumbs in milk, add meat, eggs, onion and seasonings; mix well. Place in two 3x6x2 inch pans and cover with Piquant Sauce. Bake in moderate oven (350°F.) 45 minutes.

Patricia Wells, Clearview Regional H. S.
Mullica Hill, New Jersey

MEAT LOAF
Number of Servings — 6-8

1 lb. ground beef
½ lb. ground pork
½ c. minced onions
1 t. salt
1 c. bread crumbs
1 whole egg
½ can tomato soup (thick)

Blend and place in greased loaf pan. Pour remainder of tomato soup over top and bake in 400°F. oven for 45 minutes.

Lou Hampson, Antlers H. S.
Antlers, Oklahoma

CHEESEBURGER LOAF
Number of Servings — 6

½ c. undiluted evaporated milk
1 egg, beaten
1 c. cracker crumbs
1½ lbs. ground beef
2 T. chopped onion
1½ t. salt
1 t. dry mustard
1 T. catsup
1 c. grated American cheese

Blend all ingredients, except cheese, until thoroughly mixed. Line loaf pan with heavy waxed paper. Place ½ cup cheese in bottom of pan, spread evenly. Cover with ½ meat loaf mixture. Repeat with remaining cheese and meal layers. Bake in moderate oven (350° F.) about 1 hour. Allow loaf to stand about 10 minutes before turning out on platter. Remove paper; slice for serving.

Mrs. Ella Furr Long, Woodville Attendance Center
Woodville, Mississippi

FAVORITE MEAT LOAF
Number of Servings — 6-8

3 slices soft bread
1 c. milk
1 egg
¼ c. minced onion
1¼ t. salt
1 T. Worcestershire sauce
1 lb. ground beef
¼ lb. ground pork
¼ lb. ground veal or
1½ lbs. ground meat loaf mixture
¼ t. each of pepper, mustard, sage,
    celery salt, garlic salt

Heat oven to 350° F. (med.). Tear bread into large mixing bowl; add milk and eggs. Add meat and seasonings; mix thoroughly. Form lightly into loaf and place in shallow baking pan. Bake 1 hour.

Mrs. Lennis Sonne, Wakonda H. S.
Wakonda, South Dakota

FAVORITE MEAT LOAF
Number of Servings — 8-10

2 lbs. ground beef
1 egg
1 can consomme
1 c. Special K
2 T. chopped onion
2 T. chopped parsley
1 t. salt

Combine all ingredients. Mix well. Mound mixture in shallow pan—it will brown on 3 sides. This recipe makes 2 small or 1 large loaf. Bake 1 hour at 375° F.

Laura E. Peterson, Axtell Park Jr. H. S.
Sioux Falls, South Dakota

MUSHROOM MEAT LOAF WITH CREAM SAUCE
Number of Servings — 6

1 can (1¼ c.) condensed cream of mushroom
   soup
2 lbs. ground beef
½ c. fine dry bread crumbs
1 small onion, chopped
2 T. chopped parsley
1 egg, slightly beaten
1 T. Worcestershire sauce
1 t. salt
For sauce:
1 can condensed cream of mushroom soup
⅓ c. drippings
⅓ c. chopped pimento

Preheat oven (350°F.). Combine soup with other
loaf ingredients. Pack lightly into a greased loaf
pan. Bake about 1¼ hours or until cooked
through. Remove loaf from pan. Combine ingredients for sauce. Heat for 2 minutes. Serve hot
sauce with loaf.

Mrs. Ann Hall, Rollingcrest Jr. H. S.
W. Hyattsville, Maryland

MOIST MEAT LOAF
Number of Servings — 6

1 lb. ground beef
2 eggs
1 can Spanish rice
1 t. salt
1 can cream of tomato soup

Mix meat, salt, Spanish rice and eggs thoroughly.
Pour into a loaf pan moistened with Wesson oil.
Bake 40 minutes in a 350°F. oven. Remove from
oven and pour a can of cream of tomato soup on
top. Return to oven and cook 10 or 12 minutes
at 325°F. Serve hot.

Mrs. Aline M. Milholland, Waldron H. S.
Waldron, Arkansas

MOIST MEATLOAF
Number of Servings — 6

1½ lbs. ground beef or hamburger
3 slices soft bread crumbs
1 c. milk
2 eggs
1 medium onion, minced
½ c. celery, chopped
¼ c. chopped green pepper
1 t. poultry seasoning
Salt and pepper to taste
Dash of garlic powder

Mix together with your hands and form into a
loaf. Bake in a 375°F. oven for 45-50 minutes.
If desired, before baking, pour over the top of the
meat loaf 1 small can of tomato sauce.

Roberta Bailey, Tahoma H. S.
Maple Valley, Washington

MEAT LOAF
Number of Servings — 4-6

1½ lb. ground beef
½ t. salt
1 egg
½ onion, finely chopped
1 c. bread crumbs
½ c. tomatoes or juice
3 T. tomato catsup
3 slices bacon

Set oven at 350° F. Mix well: meat, beaten eggs,
salt, bread crumbs, chopped onions, tomatoes, and
catsup. Shape into a loaf, place in pan, and place
the bacon strips on the top. Bake about 1 hour.

Helen Doris Stephens, Rabun Co. H. S.
Clayton, Georgia

JUICY MEAT LOAF
Number of Servings — 6

1 lb. ground beef
1 c. canned tomatoes
1 egg
⅔ c. uncooked oatmeal
1 medium onion, chopped finely
1½ t. salt
½ t. pepper
⅓ c. powdered milk

Combine ingredients. Mix well. Put into slightly
greased baking dish and cook for 45 minutes at
350°F. oven temperature.

Mrs. Mary S. Overman, Harmony H. S.
Harmony, North Carolina

SAVORY BEEF LOAVES
Number of Servings — 12

3 lbs. ground beef
2½ t. salt
1½ c. milk
2 c. soft stale bread crumbs
2 slightly beaten eggs
2 minced small onions
1 t. ground savory
½ t. pepper
½ t. celery salt and a few drops hot-pepper
   sauce

Mix well. Pack about half into a 9x5x3 inch loaf
pan and top with 3 bacon slices. Put remaining
meat mixture into 1 quart ring mold, and bake
in moderate oven (350°F.) for about 1 hour. Each
meat loaf makes 6 servings. Serve loaf hot with
bacon curls, stuffed baked potatoes sprinkled with
cheese, and baked tomatoes filled with peas. Serve
ring cold with center filled with chilled pickled
beets, top with onion rings and surround with
chilled cooked green beans marinated in French
dressing. Garnish with deviled eggs.

Jerry Jane Watts, Cumby H. S.
Cumby, Texas

71

ECONOMICAL MEAT LOAF WITH SAVORY STUFFING

Number of Servings — 12

2 lbs. ground beef
1 c. uncooked oatmeal
1 c. dry milk
1 egg, large
1 t. salt
½ t. pepper
2 t. Bell seasoning
¼ c. finely chopped onion

Combine all ingredients in large bowl. Mix thoroughly. Divide into two equal parts. Place one part in loaf pan. Cover with favorite stuffing (using 2 teaspoons of Bell seasoning for 2 cups of stuffing). Cover stuffing with remainder of hamburg mixture, packing down firmly. Bake one hour at 350° F.

Mrs. Barbara B. Clark, Dover H. S.
Dover, New Hampshire

SAVORY MEAT LOAF

Number of Servings — 4-5

1 lb. ground beef
1 can tomato sauce
1 small onion
¼ lb. ground pork
1½ T. Worcestershire sauce
1 egg

Grate the onion into a bowl and blend with the egg, salt, and pepper. Add the ground meat and mix the ingredients well. Shape into a loaf and place into a skillet or other suitable container. Cover the loaf with the tomato sauce and cook at 350°F. for about 1½ hours.

Mrs. Camille Maier, Flora H. S.
Flora, Mississippi

MINUTE MEAT LOAVES

Number of Servings — 12

½ c. can milk
1½ c. soft bread crumbs
2 lbs. ground beef
1 T. salt
½ c. catsup
½ t. pepper
1 egg
½ c. chopped celery
⅓ c. chopped onions
⅓ c. chopped dill pickles
1 small can tomato sauce

Add milk to bread crumbs. Combine ground beef, salt, pepper, egg, celery, onions, and pickles. Add bread crumbs and milk, catsup and tomato sauce, and mix well. Shape into balls and place meat balls in muffin pan. Bake in moderate oven (375° F.) for 15-20 minutes. Serves 12.

Mrs. Dorothy Jean Gibson, Colmesneil H. S.
Colmesneil, Texas

HAMBURGER LOAF

Number of Servings — 8-10

8 square saltine crackers (crisp)
½ c. milk
1 egg, unbeaten
1½ lbs. hamburger
¼ c. catsup
¾ t. poultry seasoning
1 t. salt
½ t. black pepper (scant)

Break crackers into small pieces and place in mixing bowl. Soften with milk. Add all other ingredients and mix well. Form into a loaf and bake in an ungreased pan for one hour at 325° F. Serve hot or cold sliced.

Dorothy J. Clark, Tawas Area H. S.
Tawas City, Michigan

MEAT LOAF DELUXE

Number of Servings — 6-8

1 lb. ground beef
1 egg
1 t. salt
½ c. bread crumbs
1 can vegetable soup
1 medium sweet pickle
¼ c. diced onion

Combine meat, egg, salt, bread crumbs, undiluted soup, pickle, and onion; mix well. Place in loaf pan and bake 1 hour at 350° F.

Norma Jean Bewley, Edmonson Co. H. S.
Brownsville, Kentucky

MEAT RING

Number of Servings — 8

4 lbs. ground beef or pork
1 c. green pepper and onion, diced
½ c. cracker meal
½ c. tomato juice or milk
3 eggs
Dash of salt and pepper

Combine ingredients and mix well. Pack into tube pan and pour over them ¼ cup water, ½ cup catsup, and ¼ cup brown sugar, thoroughly blended. Bake 1½ hours at 350° F.

Mrs. Howard Jackson, Jr., Fairforest H. S.
Fairforest, South Carolina

HEAVENLY MEAT LOAF

Number of Servings — 6

2 lbs. ground beef (choice round steak)
2 eggs, well beaten
1 t. salt
½ c. catsup
½ diced onion

Mix in order given. Put in a two quart baking dish and bake at 325°F. for 60 minutes.

Emma Jane Welch, Okeene H. S.
Okeene, Oklahoma

SUPREME MEAT LOAF
Number of Servings — 8

1½ lbs. ground beef
¾ c. oatmeal (uncooked)
2 eggs (beaten)
¼ c. onion
2 t. salt
¼ t. pepper
1 can tomato soup
½ c. pickle relish
⅛ lb. cheddar cheese (cut in strips)

Thoroughly combine all ingredients except pickles and cheese. Pack one half of the meat mixture into a one pound loaf pan. Press pickle and cheese down thru the center. Add remainder of meat. Bake one hour (350°F.).

Mrs. Velma Crosby, Carlisle Cons. School
Carlisle, Iowa

BANANA MEAT LOAF
Number of Servings — 5

1 lb. ground beef, round
¾ c. mashed banana (not overly ripe)
1 c. soft bread crumbs
1 T. chopped onion
½ t. dry mustard
¼ t. pepper

Combine meat, crumbs, onion, salt and pepper. Mix together thoroughly and form into a loaf. Place in baking dish with 2 tablespoons of water, or put aluminum foil in dish and omit water. Bake 350°F. for about 1 hour.

Mrs. Nerine Cavins, Ringling H. S.
Ringling, Oklahoma

MEAT LOAF VEGETABLE ROLL
Number of Servings — 6

2 eggs
¾ lbs. ground beef
¾ lbs. ground pork
¼ c. fine bread crumbs
1 t. salt
1 bouillon cube
¼ t. pepper
1 small onion (chopped)
½ c. frozen green beans
⅓ c. water (to be boiled)

Cook 1 egg for 20 minutes in enough water to cover. Set oven at 350°F. Mix raw egg, meat, crumbs and seasonings. On waxed paper, put mixture into rectangular shape ½″ thick. Chop hard cooked egg, onion and pimento; mix with beans and spread over meat. Roll lengthwise and press ends together. Lift into 9x15 inch loaf pan. Boil water, dissolve bouillon cube in it. Pour over loaf. Bake for 1 hour.

Mrs. Betty H. Ballard, Pageland H. S.
Pageland, South Carolina

MEAT AND VEGETABLE LOAF
Number of Servings — 6

1 lb. fresh lean beef
1 T. beef suet
1 medium sized chopped onion
1 c. canned or stewed tomatoes
½ lb. coarse ground string beans
4 stalks coarse ground celery
2 carrots, coarsely grated
2 T. chopped parsley
2 T. butter
2 t. salt
½ t. ground pepper
½ t. dry mustard
¼ t. thyme
2 T. Worcestershire sauce
1 egg
½ c. milk

Combine the meat, vegetables and seasonings, blend thoroughly. Moisten with the egg yolk and milk and fold the stiffly beaten egg white in. Turn into a greased baking dish generously sprinkled with bread crumbs. Cover and set the dish in a pan of hot water. Bake 2 hours, having the oven hot (400° F.) for the remainder of the baking. Unmold, garnish by covering with soft fluffy mashed potatoes and brown slightly.

Mrs. Joyce Real, La Vernia H. S.
La Vernia, Texas

MEAT LOAF DINNER
Number of Servings — 6

2 lbs. ground beef
Salt and pepper
1 c. chopped onion
1 small can evaporated milk
1 egg
4 medium carrots
4 medium potatoes
1 small can tomato sauce

Mix all ingredients with the exception of the carrots and potatoes and shape 3 or 4 small meat loaves. Brown in a small amount of grease in an electric fry pan. Add ½ cup water and the carrots, potatoes and tomato sauce. Cook at medium temperature for 1 hour.

Reva Wilson, Drummond H. S.
Drummond, Montana

BEEF AND POTATO LOAF
Number of Servings — 6

6 c. thinly sliced, peeled potatoes
1½ T. onion
1½ t. salt
¼ t. pepper
⅜ c. chopped onion
1½ t. parsley flakes
1½ lbs. ground beef
1⅛ c. evaporated milk
¾ c. uncooked oatmeal

(Continued on Next Page)

73

⅜ c. catsup
1½ t. salt and ⅛ t. pepper

Arrange potatoes evenly in greased 2 quart baking dish. Sprinkle with 1½ tablespoons onion, 1½ teaspoons salt, ¼ teaspoon pepper, and 1½ teaspoon parsley flake. Mix ground beef, milk, oatmeal, catsup, ⅜ cup onion, 1½ teaspoons salt, and ⅛ teaspoon pepper. Spread evenly over the potatoes. Bake in 350° F. oven 1 hour.

Frances Shipley, Coon Rapids Community H. S.
Coon Rapids, Iowa

BEEF AND POTATO LOAF
Number of Servings — 4

4 c. thinly sliced peeled raw potatoes
1 T. cut-up onion
1 t. salt
⅛ t. pepper
1 t. parsley flakes (can omit)
1 lb. ground lean beef
¾ c. evaporated milk
½ c. soda cracker crumbs
¼ c. catsup or chili sauce
¼ c. cut-up onion
1 t. salt and ⅛ t. pepper

Arrange first five ingredients evenly in greased 2-quart baking dish. Mix balance of ingredients and spread evenly over potatoes. Decorate top with more catsup if desired. Bake in 350°F. oven 1 hour, until potatoes are tender.

Josephine Mei, Turrell H. S.
Turrell, Arkansas

MEAT-POTATO LOAF
Number of Servings — 4

1 lb. ground beef
2 eggs
1 c. cracker crumbs
⅓ c. diced onions
2 t. salt
2 T. milk
2 T. catsup
1½ c. mashed potatoes

Mix the first seven ingredients together. Then roll meat mixture out on wax paper. Place mashed potatoes on meat and fold meat over potatoes. Place roll in a baking dish and garnish with strips of bacon. Bake 45 minutes in 350°F. oven.

Lillian Thompson, Kansas H. S.
Kansas, Oklahoma

HAMBURG-CHEESE LOAF
Number of Servings — 8

1 lb. hamburger
½ lb. (2 c. shredded cheese)
4 eggs beaten
2 T. finely chopped green pepper
¼ c. chopped onion
1 t. salt

Mix all ingredients thoroughly. Pack into a well-greased loaf pan. Bake in a moderate oven (350° F.)—40 minutes.

Ruth Wingo, Kemp H. S.
Kemp, Texas

MEAT AND CHEESE LOAF
Number of Servings — 10

2 lbs. ground beef
1½ c. diced cheese
2 eggs, beaten
1 large onion, chopped
1 large pepper, chopped
2 t. salt
1 t. pepper
1 t. celery salt
½ t. paprika
3 c. milk
1 c. dry bread crumbs

Combine ingredients in order given; mix well. Press into 2 greased loaf pans and bake at 350° F. about 1½ hours.

Ethel Spradling, Bixby H. S.
Bixby, Oklahoma

ROAST BEEF WITH BARBECUE SAUCE
Number of Servings — 6-8

1½ lbs. ground beef
¾ c. uncooked rolled oats
1 c. condensed milk
3 T. cut onion
1½ t. salt
¼ t. pepper

Set oven at 350°F. Rinse mold with cold water. Mix above ingredients thoroughly and pack into mold. Turn into larger greased baking pan. Bake 10 minutes. Pour over the loaf a mixture of 2 tablespoons Worcestershire sauce, 3 tablespoons vinegar, 2 tablespoons sugar, 1 cup catsup, ½ cup water, 6 tablespoons cut onion. Bake until meat is brown (about 1 hour). Baste at 10 minute intervals with sauce in pan.

Mrs. Amy Redfearn, Cheraw H. S.
Cheraw, South Carolina

BARBECUED MEAT LOAF
Number of Servings — 12

2 eggs, beaten
2 lbs. ground beef
2 t. finely chopped onion
2 c. fresh bread crumbs
⅔ c. barbecue sauce
1½ t. salt
Dash of pepper

Combine all ingredients into shallow loaf pan or baking dish. Bake one hour at 350° F. Spread with ⅓ cup barbecue sauce and bake 15 minutes longer.

Nona L. Dutson, Marsh Valley H. S.
Arimo, Idaho

INDIVIDUAL BARBECUED MEAT LOAVES
Number of Servings — 4-6

Meat Loaves
1 lb. ground beef
1 c. rolled bread crumbs
½ c. cream to moisten
¼ c. chopped onion
1 t. salt
¼ t. pepper
Barbecue Sauce
3 T. brown sugar
1 T. vinegar
1 T. Worcestershire sauce
¼ c. chili sauce
¼ c. catsup
½ c. water

Set oven at 375°. Form into loaves and place in casserole. Pour barbecue sauce over loaves, and bake 30 minutes with cover on, then uncover and baste occasionally, for another 30 minutes, or 1 hour altogether.

Jane Baker, Mingo Community H. S.
Mingo, Iowa

HAMBURGER SUPREME
Number of Servings — 4

1 lb. ground beef
Salt and pepper
1 T. Worcestershire sauce
1 can cream of mushroom soup
½ to 1 can whole milk (measure in soup can)
  can be as thick as you like it

Combine meat, salt and pepper to taste and Worcestershire sauce; mix well and form into patties. Fry quickly in a little hot fat until brown on both sides; reduce heat to simmer (pour off extra grease). Mix mushroom soup with milk and pour over patties; continue to simmer until serving time. (Can be kept hot indefinitely). We like it served with rice and a salad.

Mrs. Fred Kruse, Chandlerville H. S.
Chandlerville, Illinois

HAMBURGER DINNER
Number of Servings — 6

¼ c. chopped onion
¼ c. minced green pepper
1½ c. sliced carrots
½ c. sliced celery
½ t. salt
1 lb. hamburger meat
¼ c. of dry bread crumbs
½ c. water
1 c. yellow cream style corn
½ c. of sharp cheddar cheese
1 egg, slightly beaten

Simmer the first 5 ingredients in the water until tender and stir in the can of corn. Add slightly beaten egg, cheese and bread crumbs. Pour into 2-quart baking dish. Make hamburger meat and

a ½ teaspoon salt into meat balls and fry until brown and mix with other foods in the baking dish. Bake at 375° F. for 40 minutes. Serve hot.

Bernice Marshall, Texas Sr. H. S.
Texarkana, Texas

BEEF AND BEAN HASTY
Number of Servings — 4

1 lb. ground meat
1 t. salt
Pepper
Garlic salt (optional)
1 T. Worcestershire sauce
1 can pork and beans
3 T. prepared mustard
¼ c. brown sugar

Combine meat, salts, pepper and Worcestershire sauce and spread evenly in slightly greased pie pan. Combine beans, mustard, and sugar and spread on top of beef mixture. Place in preheated oven at 350°F. for 30 minutes.

Mrs. Artie Norman, Jim Ned H. S.
Tuscola, Texas

CHEESEBURGER LOGS
Number of Servings — 8

1 lb. ground beef
½ c. crisp rice cereal
½ c. dry bread crumbs
¼ c. catsup
½ t. salt
Dash pepper
1 egg
Sharp cheese
8 coney buns

Combine ground beef, cereal, bread crumbs, catsup, salt, pepper, and egg. Mix well. Form into 8 logs to fit buns. Make groove down center of each log. Cut cheese in narrow strips. Press into groove. Broil 3 to 5 inches from heat, 10 to 15 minutes or until done. Serve in coney buns.

Marjorie G. Dye, Homer Com. H. S.
Homer, Michigan

BROILED SALISBURY STEAKS
Number of Servings — 4-6

1 lb. ground beef
½ t. Worcestershire sauce
4 T. barbecue sauce
1 c. corn flakes (crushed)
1 T. Parmesan cheese
Salt and pepper to season

Mix ingredients in ground beef. Pat into cakes and place on broiler pan. Broil 5 minutes on each side. Serve while juicy and hot.

Mrs. Dixie Dunn Ruby,
Charles Town Jr. and Sr. H. S.
Charles Town, West Virginia

HOBO SUPPER

Number of Servings — Number desired

⅓ lb. ground beef (per person), seasoned
   with salt and pepper
Irish potatoes, cut for French fries
Carrots, peeled and split lengthwise
Onions, sliced ¼-in. thick
Celery, cut in 3-in. lengths
Sauce:
½ c. vinegar
½ c. tomato catsup
2 T. Worcestershire sauce
2 T. butter
1 t. prepared mustard
Juice of 1 lemon
Salt and pepper to taste

Take a square of aluminum foil, place in center
a large hamburger of the seasoned ground beef.
On this place a slice of onion, 4-6 strips of potato,
4-6 strips of carrot, and 2 pieces of celery. Pull
the foil up to form a cup and over each pour a
tablespoon of sauce, then twist the foil edges
tighty. Place on a cookie sheet and bake in a
325°F. oven for 45 minutes.

Mrs. Garnet C. Jackson, Indio H. S.
Indio, California

HOBO MEAL

Number of Servings — 3-4

1 lb. ground beef
Seasoned with salt and pepper
Irish potatoes, cut in thin slices
Carrots, peeled and split lengthwise
Onions, sliced ¼ inch thick
Celery, cut in 3-inch lengths
Butter or margarine

On a square of aluminum foil, place in center a
large hamburger of the ground beef. On this
place a slice of onion, 4-6 pieces of potato and
4-6 pieces of carrot, and 2 pieces celery. Dot
vegetables with butter. Season with salt and pepper. Wrap "drug store style." Place on baking
tray and bake in 325° F. oven for 45 minutes.
Loosen foil and brown if desired. May substitute
chicken, pork chop or round steak for ground
meat.

Lillian Sandlin, Pawhuska H. S.
Pawhuska, Oklahoma

BACON AND BEEF ROLL-UPS

Number of Servings — 8-10

8-10 slices bacon
1 egg
1½ lbs. ground beef
¾ t. salt
¾ c. grated cheese
½ t. pepper
3 T. catsup
¼ c. chopped onion
2 T. Worcestershire sauce

Place bacon on board. Combine ground beef and
the other ingredients. Shape into oblong roll and
place on the bacon. Draw bacon strips around the
ground mixture. Fasten with toothpicks. Slice between strips. Broil 5-7 minutes on each side.

Mrs. Delores Ferg, Little Wolf H. S.
Manawa, Wisconsin

GROUND BEEF

Number of Servings — 6

1 medium onion, chopped
1 lb. ground beef
Salt and pepper
1 No. 2 can (2½ c.) or ½ lb. cooked green beans
1 10½ or 11 oz. can condensed tomato soup
5 medium potatoes
½ c. warm milk
1 egg, beaten
Salt and pepper

Cook onion in hot fat till golden; add meat and
seasonings; brown. Add drained beans and soup;
pour into greased 1½ quart casserole. Mash the
potatoes; add the milk, egg, and the seasonings.
Spoon in mounds over meat. Bake in moderate
oven (350°F.) for 30 minutes.

Sharon Daughtry, Williamston H. S.
Williamston, North Carolina

PASTIES

Number of Servings — 8

1 box hot roll mix
1 lb. hamburger
1 medium size head cabbage
½ c. onions, chopped
½ c. vinegar

Shred cabbage fine, stew with chopped onion
and vinegar 'till done. Salt and pepper to taste.
Stew under very low heat. If dry add water to
keep from burning. Then brown hamburger and
more onions—salt and pepper to taste. Put 1½
tablespoons on a 4-in. square dough. Fold over
and put on well-greased sheet or pan—let raise—
about 10 minutes. Bake 'till brown at 375°-400° F.

Mrs. Dorothy Schulz, McIntosh H. S.
McIntosh, South Dakota

DELICIOUS MEAT PATTIES

Number of Servings — 6

1 lb. ground lean beef
1 t. salt
⅛ t. pepper
¼ t. of monosodium glutamate

Blend together, and make into six medium sized
patties. Fry in small amount of hot fat or cook
in a no-stick skillet. Turn once and cook slowly
to desired doneness. NOTE: Excellent for a
low-fat-diet.

Mrs. Mary Kibler, Lynchburg H. S.
Lynchburg, Ohio

PASTIES
Number of Servings — 1

Crust for 1 pasty:
1 c. flour
¼ c. finely chopped suet
¼ c. lard
¼ c. cold water
¼ t. salt
Filling for one pasty:
¼ lb. ground chuck or round
1 chopped onion
1 large potato (cubed)
Carrot (if desired)
Salt and pepper to taste

Crust: Mix flour, salt, suet and lard. Cut in, add cold water gradually and knead vigorously (this crust does not suffer from overkneading). Roll in circle on lightly floured board. Filling: Mix all ingredients. Place on one half the circle. Fold other half over. Seal. Cut slit in top. Bake 1 hour at 450° F. Put 2 teaspoons butter in slit. Return to oven at 350° F. for ½ hour.

Mrs. Grace E. Kukuk, Negaunee, H. S.
Negaunee, Michigan

BEEF PATTIES WITH MUSHROOM SAUCE
Number of Servings — 4

1 lb. ground round steak
½ can beef bouillon
Lawrie's savory salt
Onion salt
2 T. bacon fat
1 can mushroom soup
Salt
Crescent blended seasoning salt
Garlic salt
Dash of "Accent"

Shape patties. Sprinkle with seasoning salts. Brown in bacon fat. Spoon mushroom soup over the patties. Pour ½ can bouillon around the patties. Cover and simmer for about one-half hour. A good meat preparation to hold for an indefinite dinner hour.

Ruth C. Peabody, Sunnyside Jr. H. S.
Sunnyside, Washington

LOW CALORIE CRUNCHY BEEF PATTIES
Number of Servings — 6

2 c. corn flakes
½ c. nonfat dry milk (prepared) or ½ c.
   tomato juice
1 lb. ground lean beef
1 t. salt
⅛ t. pepper

Crush corn flakes slightly. Add remaining ingredients and mix well. Shape into six patties. Arrange on broiler rack. Broil 8 minutes. Turn, broil 5 minutes.

Lorraine Schwer, Sleepy Eye Public H. S.
Sleepy Eye, Minnesota

HAMBURGER STEAK SUPREME A LA RUBINOFF*
Number of Servings — 7-8

Meat Ingredients:
3 lbs. hamburger
1 c. half and half coffee cream
¼ c. cracker crumbs
1 t. salt
½ c. water
Sauce Ingredients:
1 t. BV meat extract
2 4-oz. cans whole mushrooms
1 c. plain consomme
½ doz. green onions, chopped fine
Dash salt
3 t. flour
½ stick oleo
½ c. white sauterne wine

Mix cream, crumbs, and water. Let stand 5 minutes. Add salt and meat and mix thoroughly. Shape in oval forms—½ pound to each serving. Sauce preparation: Melt oleo, saute onions and mushrooms. Add flour, blend, then add consomme. Cook for 2-3 minutes. Then add meat extract. Place hamburger ovals on rack 1-2 inches beneath fire. Broil well done on both sides, turning only once. Serve meat with sauce on top.
Note: This recipe has been passed along by the famous musician—Rubinoff.

Mrs. Ruth Volz, Palatine Twp. H. S.
Palatine, Illinois

HAMBURGERS
Number of Servings — 20

4 lbs. ground meat
4 eggs
1 can tomato soup
½ c. tomato catsup
¼ c. Worcestershire sauce
Salt and pepper to taste

Mix ingredients with meat and make into patties. Place in pan and cook in oven until done; then put under flame until brown.

Sauce:
4 c. chopped onions
2 c. chopped celery
1 large can tomato juice

Cook slowly for about 2 hours; then add ½ cup Worcestershire sauce and ¼ cup mustard and let cook for 15 minutes longer, also add salt and pepper. Using an earthenware crock place alternate layers of hamburgers and sauce until all are used. This can be cooled and placed in the refrigerator and used the next day.

Bert Hearn, Columbia H. S.
Columbia, Louisiana

BEEF AND CHEESE PATTIES
Number of Servings — 4

⅓ lb. ground beef
¼ c. soft bread crumbs
2 T. catsup
1 T. fat
1 t. mustard
¼ t. salt
dash of pepper
1 T. milk
1 T. flour
¼ t. salt
½ c. milk
¼ c. grated cheese

Combine and form into four patties beef, bread crumbs, salt, pepper, catsup and milk. Melt fat in skillet and brown patties in the hot fat. Remove patties and stir into the fat the flour, mustard and salt. Then gradually add milk, stirring constantly until smooth. Then stir in cheese. Pour sauce over patties and bake in slow oven for 20 minutes.

Marion McMurrey, Shepherd H. S.
Shepherd, Texas

CHEESE SURPRISE HAMBURGER PATTIES
Number of Servings — 4

1 lb. ground beef
⅔ c. milk
⅓ c. rolled oats (quick cooking)
2 T. chopped onion
1 t. salt
⅛ t. pepper
4 slices cheese—¼ in. thick and 2 ins. square
4 slices of thin sliced bacon

Combine meat, milk, rolled oats, onion, salt, pepper and mix thoroughly. Form into eight flat patties. Lay cheese squares on top of four patties and place a patty on top of each. Blend edges together and place a strip of bacon around the edge. Fasten bacon ends together with a toothpick. Broil each side of patties for ten minutes about four inches from heat.

Elsie C. Dolin, Newberry H. S.
Newberry, Florida

DELUXE FAVORITE
Number of Servings — 4

1 lb. ground beef
Salt and pepper to taste
1 can condensed onion soup
1 T. flour

Season ground beef and form into four patties. Brown in skillet. Pour can of onion soup over patties, cover and simmer for 10-15 minutes. If desired a gravy may be made from juices remaining with flour.

Mrs. Mary Ellen Hoadley, University H. S.
Laramie, Wyoming

GROUND BEEF PATTIES IN SOUR-CREAM SAUCE
Number of Servings — 4

1 c. sour cream
1 lb. ground beef (or venison)
1 T. Worcestershire sauce
1 t. salt
3 T. milk
1 t. grated onion
2 T. flour
1 can (No. 1) tomatoes
½ c. dry bread crumbs
1 egg
3 T. butter (or margarine)

Mix together ground beef, bread crumbs, milk, egg, Worcestershire sauce, grated onion and salt; shape into 4 patties. Brown well on both sides in butter in skillet; remove from pan. Add flour to butter in pan; blend well; gradually add tomatoes and sour cream. Return meat patties to sauce and simmer about 10 minutes. Serves 4. Cooking time 25 minutes.

Mary Irey, Red Bluff Union H. S.
Red Bluff, California

MEAT PATTIES IN SWEET & SOUR SAUCE
Number of Servings — 4-5

2 c. bread crumbs
¼ c. chopped onion
1 t. salt
⅛ t. thyme
½ c. water
1 lb. ground beef
1 c. sliced onion
⅓ c. brown sugar
1 T. flour
¼ c. vinegar
2 T. water
2 t. prepared mustard

Combine crumbs, chopped onions, seasonings and ½ cup water. Let it stand for five minutes. Mix in meat. Shape into patties; brown in small amount of hot fat. Cover with sliced onion. Combine brown sugar, flour, vinegar, 2 tablespoons water and mustard. Pour over meat. Cover and simmer for 35 minutes.

Mrs. Manuel Cox, Scappoose Union H. S.
Scappoose, Oregon

BAR B-QUE HAMBURGERS
Number of Servings — 6

1 lb. ground beef
¼ c. catsup
1 small onion, diced
1 10½-oz. can chicken gumbo soup
1 t. bar-b-que sauce, if desired

Brown ground beef in a skillet. Add onion, catsup, sauce and soup. Simmer 1 hour. Spoon onto buns and serve.

Jeanette Sanks, Oakfield H. S.
Oakfield, Wisconsin

BARBECUED PATTIES
Number of Servings — 4

½ c. soft bread crumbs
½ lb. ground beef
½ c. catsup
1 T. vinegar
¼ c. milk
2 T. fat
2 T. Worcestershire sauce
1 chopped onion
1 T. sugar
Salt and pepper

Moisten crumbs with milk. Add onion, salt, pepper and meat. Shape into patties and brown in the 2 tablespoons fat. Mix other ingredients together with ½ cup water to form sauce. Pour sauce over patties. Cover and cook slowly 30 minutes on top of stove.

Mrs. Lillian Rhodes, Neshoba County H. S.
Philadelphia, Mississippi

MEAT PUFFS WITH MUSHROOM SAUCE
Number of Servings — 6

1½ lbs. lean beef, ground
1½ medium-sized onions, grated
1½ c. soft bread crumbs
2 eggs, well beaten
½ to ¾ t. salt
½ c. water
¼ t. pepper
Dash of paprika
¼ c. flour
¼ c. fat
1 can condensed mushroom soup

Combine meat, onions, bread crumbs, eggs and seasonings; form lightly into small balls and sprinkle with flour. Brown in fat; add mushroom soup and water, cover and simmer 10 minutes.

Mrs. Gladys H. Frye, Chilhowie H. S.
Chilhowie, Virginia

BROILED BEEF PATTIES IN MUSHROOM SAUCE
Number of Servings — 6

1½ lbs. ground lean beef
½ t. salt
¼ t. pepper
2 T. Worcestershire sauce
1 t. garlic salt
1 can cream of mushroom soup

Combine meat, salt, pepper, and Worcestershire sauce. Mix well and form in patties. Broil three inches from heat five minutes, turn; broil about three minutes or until light brown. Place in saucepan. Add garlic salt and mushroom soup with one-half can of water. Cover patties with the mixture. Allow to simmer on top burner for fifteen minutes. Serve hot.

Lou Penton, Piner Jr. H. S.
Sherman, Texas

MEAT LOAF PATTIES
Number of Servings — 6-8

1½ lbs. ground beef
Salt and pepper
1 egg
¼ c. chopped onion
1 can tomato sauce (small)
¼ cup chopped green pepper
¼ c. chopped celery
1 T. Worcestershire sauce
¾ c. crushed cornflakes
10 slices of bacon

Combine ground beef, cornflakes, egg, onion, green pepper, salt and pepper, Worcestershire sauce, and ½ of the tomato sauce; mix well and form into patties. Wrap each pattie with a slice of bacon and cover with remaining tomato sauce. Bake in a moderate oven of 350° F. for about 40-45 minutes or until done.

Mary Alice Mock, Sloan-Hendrix H. S.
Imboden, Arkansas

MOCK FILLET
Number of Servings — 4-6

2 T. minced onion
1 T. flour
½ c. evaporated milk
Salt and pepper
2 T. of Worcestershire sauce
1 c. soft bread crumbs
⅓ c. tomato puree
1½ lbs. ground meat
½ t. garlic powder
4-6 strips of bacon

Mix dry ingredients (salt, pepper, garlic, flour) and add to milk and puree to make a smooth paste. Add bread crumbs and onion to the meat and thoroughly mix adding the paste. Form into patties approx. 3 inches in diameter and 1 inch thick. Wrap with a bacon strip and sprinkle with Worcestershire Sauce or A-1 Sauce. Bake in a moderately hot oven 350° F. for 40 minutes.

Elaine R. Rotter, Pettus H. S.
Pettus, Texas

PENNYWISE STEAKS
Number of Servings — 6

½ c. fine bread crumbs
¾ c. milk
1½ lbs. hamburger
1½ t. salt
½ t. pepper
1 t. onion juice

Combine crumbs and milk. Combine all other ingredients, add to crumb mixture, blend. Shape meat in form of T-bone steak, sprinkle with Worcestershire sauce and spread with cooking oil. Broil 6-10 minutes. Turn and broil other side.

Mrs. Odelle T. Lakeman, Haleyville H. S.
Haleyville, Alabama

HAMBURGER ROLL-UPS
Number of Servings — 8-10

2 lbs. hamburger
8-10 slices bacon
¼ c. chopped onion
1 egg, beaten
1 c. shredded cheese
3 T. catsup
2 T. Worcestershire sauce
1 t. salt
½ t. pepper

Combine the hamburger, onion, egg, cheese, Worcestershire sauce, salt and pepper, and mix well. Shape into patties (8-10) one inch thick. Place one slice bacon around each pattie securing with toothpick. Broil 5 minutes on each side.

Annie Ruth White, Hamilton H. S.
Hamilton, Mississippi

HAMBURGER FILLETS
Number of Servings — 6

1½ lbs. ground beef
1 t. salt
1 t. onion salt
1 T. Worcestershire sauce
6 slices bacon
3 toothpicks

Place the first four ingredients in a bowl and mix well with a fork. Shape into large patties and wrap each patty with a strip of bacon. Fasten each strip of bacon with ½ of a toothpick. Broil in the oven or over a charcoal fire for about twelve minutes or until done to suit your taste. Makes six large patties.

Mrs. Frances Blount, Northwest Jr. H. S.
R. R. Justin, Texas

DOUBLE HAMBURGERS
Number of Servings — 6

1 lb. hamburger
1 t. salt
1 egg
¼ c. milk
2 T. prepared mustard
6 thin slices onion
2 T. pickle relish or chili sauce

Combine hamburger, salt, egg, and milk. Mix well. Make 12 small flat patties. Spread mustard on 6 patties. Top each with onion slice and a teaspoon of relish. Place remaining patties on top of relish. Press patties together, sealing well around edges. Broil 3 inches from heat ·for 5 minutes on each side—or pan fry in 1 tablespoon fat in a heavy skillet.

Wanda Schaper, Morton H. S.
Kinnear, Wyoming

ECONOMY BURGERS
Number of Servings — 4

1 lb. hamburger meat
1 egg, slightly beaten
1 c. dry bread crumbs
1 t. Worcestershire sauce
1 t. salt
⅛ t. pepper

Beat egg; add Worcestershire sauce, salt, and pepper. Pour over bread crumbs and allow to marinate five minutes. Add to hamburger meat; mix well and shape into patties. Broil 10 minutes on each side or until browned. Serve hot with catsup or mustard.

Mrs. Anne McCord, Kilgore H. S.
Kilgore, Texas

FIESTA HAMBURGERS
Number of Servings — 6-8

1 lb. hamburger
8 slices bacon
1 c. crushed cornflakes
1 c. canned tomatoes
1 egg
1 small onion, minced
1 t. salt
⅛ t. pepper

Combine beef, cornflakes, tomatoes, eggs and seasoning. Shape into patties ¾ to 1 inch thick. Wrap slice of bacon around patty and fasten with tooth pick. Broil 10 to 12 minutes on one side, 8 minutes on other.

Maggie Q. Gardner, Franklin Co. H. S.
Rocky Mount, Virginia

ROYAL HAMBURGERS
Number of Servings — 4-5

1 lb. ground beef
½ c. evaporated milk
2½ T. crushed cereal flakes
1 t. grated onion
⅔ c. crushed cereal flakes
1 t. salt
Dash pepper
4 or 5 slices American cheese
⅓ c. evaporated milk

Combine meat, ½ cup milk, 2½ tablespoons crushed cereal flakes, onion and seasoning. Shape into flat, thin patties. Put two patties together with slice of cheese between. Dip in the ⅓ cup milk and roll in the ⅔ cup crushed cereal flakes. Cook slowly in hot fat for 15 minutes.

Era King, Lamar H. S.
Lamar, Arkansas

HAMBURGER HUMMER (BROILED)
Number of Servings — 2

½ lb. ground beef
2 T. instant non-fat dry milk
3 T. catsup
1 T. mustard
1 T. garlic salt
3 T. chopped sweet pickles

Combine meat, milk, catsup and mustard; mix well and form into two patties. Sprinkle garlic salt. Broil 3 inches from heat 5 minutes, turn and cover top with pickles and cook 5 minutes. Serve hot.

Elwanda Barber, Greenville H. S.
Greenville, Florida

BROILED HAMBURGER ON TOAST
Number of Servings — 10

1 lb. raw hamburger
1 t. salt
10 slices of bread
½ c. of milk
Dash of pepper

Season meat with salt and pepper and add ½ cup milk and mix well. Mixture should be soft enough to spread with a knife. Broil bread on one side. Spread the untoasted side with the meat mixture, covering evenly to the very edge. Dot with butter. Broil for 4-5 minues. Serve hot.

Mrs. Margaret Givens, Page County H. S.
Shenandoah, Virginia

SMOTHERED HAMBURGER STEAKS
Number of Servings — 4

1 lb. ground beef
1 t. salt
¼ t. pepper
¼ c. fine dry bread crumbs
4 medium onions, sliced
10¾-oz. can beef gravy

Mix beef with ½ cup water and remaining ingredients, except onions and gravy. Shape in four large patties about ½ inch thick. Brown on one side; turn; add onion, and brown slightly. Add gravy, cover, and simmer about 35 minutes. Serve with mashed potatoes.

Flora Ward, Newville H. S.
Newville, Alabama

SPECIAL HAMBURGERS
Number of Servings — 4-6

1 lb. ground beef
2 T. finely chopped green pepper
¼ c. chopped onion
1 T. horse-radish
3 T. catsup
1 t. salt
½ t. dry mustard

Combine all ingredients and mix well. Form in patties. Broil, grill, or place in greased shallow baking dish and bake in moderate oven (375° F.) for 30 minutes.

Barbara Neitzel, Trego Community H. S.
WaKeeney, Kansas

TASTY BEEF BURGERS
Number of Servings — 8

1 lb. hamburger
1 t. salt
3 T. catsup
1 t. prepared mustard
1 t. prepared horse-radish
1 t. Worcestershire sauce
1 T. finely chopped onion
½ c. fine bread crumbs
¼ c. milk
1 T. fat

Combine all ingredients except fat. Shape into 8 patties. Pan-fry in fat in heavy skillet, about 4 minutes on each side.

Sharon Fraser, Armada H. S.
Armada, Michigan

TENDER, JUICY HAMBURGER PATTIES
Number of Servings — 4 thick patties

1 lb. ground beef
1 t. salt
¼ t. pepper
2 T. chopped onion
½ c. milk
Flavor extender
Worcestershire sauce
Mustard with horse-radish

Toss together lightly. Divide and form into patties. Handle as little as possible. Arrange thick patties on cold broiler pan. Broil 3 inches from heat, turning once. Broil 8 minutes for rare, 12 for medium, 16 for well done.

Mrs. Laura H. Wilkins, Pickens Co. H. S.
Reform, Alabama

BAR-B-Q-BURGERS
Number of Servings — 8

2 T. fat
1 lb. ground beef
⅔ c. chopped onion
1 T. catsup
½ t. salt and dash pepper
¼ c. water
1 T. mustard
1 can condensed chicken gumbo soup
8 burger buns

Cook meat and onion together in hot fat until lightly browned. Stir frequently with wooden spoon. Add other ingredients. Cover: simmer gently over low heat for 30 minutes. Stir occasionally. Spoon into eight buns.

Carolyn S. Unger, Rowlesburg H. S.
Rowlesburg, West Virginia

BEST BAR-B-Q
Number of Servings — 10-12

1 lb. ground beef
1 large onion, chopped
1 T. flour
1 T. sugar
1 t. salt
¼ t. pepper
1 bottle catsup
1 T. mustard
1 T. Worcestershire sauce

Fry ground beef and chopped onion over moderate heat until done. Mix flour, sugar, salt, pepper and add to beef, stirring well. Add catsup, mustard, Worcestershire sauce to mixture, mixing well. Heat and serve on hamburger buns.

Mrs. Joan M. Hughes, Southern Area Jr. H. S.
Numidia, Pennsylvania

BARBECUE ON BUN (Sloppy Joes)
Number of Servings — 6

1 lb. ground beef
1 can tomato paste
¼ c. catsup
⅓ c. chopped onion
⅓ c. chopped celery
½ c. water
1 T. prepared mustard
½ t. chili powder
½ t. paprika
½ t. garlic salt
Salt and pepper

Brown beef and onions. Simmer celery in water. Combine beef, onions, celery, and remaining ingredients. Simmer. Serve on hamburger buns.

Martha C. Kern, Caro Community H. S.
Caro, Michigan

SLOPPY JOES
Number of Servings — 12-15

2 lbs. hamburger
1 onion, chopped
4 stalks celery (chopped fine)
1 T. mustard
1 T. Worcestershire sauce
1 c. catsup
1 can tomato soup
1 can water
Salt and pepper

Brown hamburger. Mix with browned onion and celery. Add mustard, Worcestershire sauce, catsup, soup and water. Mix well. Add salt and pepper to taste. Simmer one hour. Serve on buttered hamburger buns with celery and carrot sticks.

Jo Ann Kangas, Virginia Jr. H. S.
Virginia, Minnesota

BARBECUED HAMBURGERS (Sloppy Joes)
Number of Servings — 6

1 lb. hamburger
¼ c. chopped onion
2 T. chopped celery
2 T. chopped green pepper
½ bottle catsup
2 T. vinegar
1 T. sugar
1 t. prepared mustard
½ t. chili powder

Brown hamburger, onions, celery and green pepper. Add catsup and seasonings. Simmer. Serve on hamburger buns.

Dorothy Parks, North Huron H. S.
Kinde, Michigan

BARBECUE HAMBURGER
Number of Servings — 12

2 lbs. ground beef
½ c. catsup
1 T. prepared mustard
1 T. chili powder
1 small onion, chopped
Salt

Combine meat, salt, and onion. Brown in skillet. Add catsup, mustard and chili powder. Cook in double boiler 1 hour. Maybe cooked in less time in skillet (25 to 30 minutes). Serve on hot buns.

Pearlie Mae Butler, Middle River Com. H. S.

DEVILED CHEESEBURGERS
Number of Servings — 10-12

1 lb. ground beef
⅔ c. evaporated milk
½ c. finely chopped onion
½ c. finely chopped pepper
1 t. salt
½ t. accent
Dash of pepper
10 to 12 buns (split and toasted)
10 to 12 thin slices of cheese

Mix the ingredients and shape into 10 or 12 thin patties. Place in baking pan and bake at 350° F. for 30 minutes. Place each patty on the bottom half of a toasted bun and top with a cheese slice. Return to the oven until the cheese melts. Top with other half of toasted bun.

Eileen Miller, Deuel Co. H. S.
Chappell, Nebraska

CHEESE AND TOMATO DOUBLE DECKERS
Number of Servings — 4

1 lb. ground chuck
Salt and pepper
4 slices tomato
4 slices onion
4 half slices American cheese
4 T. catsup

(Continued on Next Page)

Combine meat, salt and pepper. Shape into eight large very thin patties. On four patties place one slice each of tomato and onion and one-half slice cheese. Place remaining patties on top and seal edges firmly. Bake on ungreased shallow pan at 450° F. for 10 minutes. Remove from oven; glaze tops with one tablespoon catsup each. Return to oven for 10 more minutes. Serve on toasted buns with dill pickles as a garnish.

Mrs. Donald R. Turley, Penns Manor Joint Jr.-Sr. H. S., Clymer, Pennsylvania

GOLDEN HAMBURGERS
Number of Servings — 5

1 lb. ground beef
1 egg
2 slices fresh bread, crumbed
½ c. milk
¾ t. salt
⅛ t. sage
⅛ t. garlic salt
½ c. chopped onion
5 cubes sharp cheese
1 small can cream of tomato soup

Combine meat, egg, crumbs, milk and seasonings. Form into 5 large patties. Press a cube of cheese into each pattie. Brown in 1 tablespoon fat in hot frying pan. Turn and brown other side. Pour tomato soup over patties, reduce heat to simmer, cover pan and simmer for 15 minutes. Serve as open sandwich on ½ bun.

Mrs. Erma Little, Creswell H. S. Creswell, Oregon

BUSY-DAY BEEFBURGERS
Number of Servings — 6

1 lb. ground beef
1½ c. chopped celery
½ c. extra hot catsup
Dash of pepper
1½ c. chopped onion
1 can condensed tomato soup
1 t. salt
6 hamburger buns

Brown ground beef, add onion and celery. Cook until tender but not brown. Add soup, catsup and seasoning. Simmer uncovered about 20 minutes or until it's the consistency you like. Salt to taste. Spoon between or over toasted bun halves.

Mrs. Faye McNeill, Pearl River Central H. S. McNeill, Mississippi

DAKOTA BURGERS
Number of Servings — 2

½ lb. ground beef
½ t. salt
⅛ t. pepper
1 T. chopped onion
¼ c. milk or water
Worcestershire sauce or mustard to taste

Shape gently into 2 balls and flatten ¾" thick. Brush lightly with salad oil or melted butter. Broil 3" from heat, 4 to 6 minutes on each side. Serve hot on split buns.

Mrs. Beverly Haas, Tappen H. S. Tappen, North Dakota

CREOLE BURGERS
Number of Servings — 8

1 lb. ground beef
½ c. chopped onion
1 can chicken gumbo soup
8 slices cheese
8 hamburger buns
2 T. catsup
2 T. prepared mustard
1 t. salt or to taste
½ t. pepper

Brown ground beef and onion in heavy skillet, stirring to separate pieces. Add 1 can chicken gumbo soup, catsup, mustard, salt and pepper. Simmer 5 minutes or longer. Spoon on 8 split hamburger buns. Top with a slice of cheese and place under the broiler, just until the cheese melts. Serve hot.

. Inez Dykstra, Lovington H. S. Lovington, New Mexico

BROILBURGERS
Number of Servings — 4

4 slices sandwich bread
2 T. margarine
½ t. sage
⅛ t. pepper
¾ lb. of ground beef
2 T. grated onion
¾ t. salt
1 T. Worcestershire sauce
¼ cup tomato sauce

Toast bread on one side, mix margarine and sage, spread on untoasted side. Mix all other ingredients together except the tomato sauce and spread on the untoasted side. Broil 3 inches from your source of heat for 15 minutes. Place a tablespoon of hot tomato sauce on each Broilburger and serve at once.

Nancy W. Sensabaugh, Rockbridge H. S. Fairfield, Virginia

BEEF BUNBURGERS
Number of Servings — 6-8

1½ lbs. ground beef
1 T. fat
½ c. minced onion
⅓ c. chopped green pepper
1 can condensed tomato soup
1 t. salt
1 t. dry mustard
1 t. poultry seasoning

(Continued on Next Page)

½ t. thyme
1½ t. vinegar
6 to 8 hamburger buns

Brown meat in fat. Add onion, green pepper and cook until tender. Add remaining ingredients except buns. Simmer, uncovered, 30 minutes. Serve with dill-pickle slices on toasted buns.

Faye Pearson, Hayneville H. S.
Hayneville, Alabama

TEXAS TAVERN BURGERS
Number of Servings — 10

1 c. chopped onion
3 T. butter
1 can tomato soup
½ c. water
¼ c. vinegar
2 T. prepared mustard
2 T. Lee and Perrin sauce
2 T. brown sugar

Combine and cook onions and butter until clear and tender. Remove from fire and add remaining ingredients. Simmer for 10 minutes. Cook 2 pounds of ground beef and ½ cup onions until brown. Add to mixture. Salt and pepper to season. Spread on toasted buns.

Mrs. Floyd Craig, Divide H. S.
Nolan, Texas

HAMBURGER HACIENDA
Number of Servings — 4-6

¾ c. rice
2 T. oil
1 lb. hamburger
¾ c. chopped onions
1 c. sliced celery
1½ t. salt
¼ t. black pepper
1 No. 2 can tomatoes
2 c. wide noodles
1 c. diced American cheese

Cut olives into small pieces. Heat oil, add meat and cook about 5 minutes, stirring frequently. Stir in onions and celery and cook about 5 minutes longer. Add salt, pepper, tomatoes, olives, uncooked noodles and cheese. Cover tightly and cook until mixture is boiling. Remove cover and stir lightly, but thoroughly. Cover and cook slowly until noodles are cooked.

Mrs. H. L. Mangum, Mize Attendance Center
Mize, Mississippi

SPOONBURGERS
Number of Servings — 6

1 lb. hamburger meat
1 can chicken gumbo soup
½ c. catsup
Garlic, celery, and onion salt to desired taste
Small amount of fat (1 t.)

Brown the meat in the fat after seasoning the meat with the garlic, celery and onion salt. (Do not use table salt). Add the chicken gumbo soup and the catsup and simmer until the mixture is thickened. Take 6 hamburger buns and put a spoonful of the mixture on the bottom and top of the bun. Place a slice on top and put in a slow oven to melt the cheese. (A tablespoon of the grated cheese may be used instead of the sliced cheese). Also cream of chicken soup is used just as well.

Mrs. Myrtle Bailey, Albany H. S.
Albany, Texas

SPOON-BURGERS
Number of Servings — 4-5

1 lb. ground beef
¼ c. chopped peppers
¼ c. chopped onion
1 can tomato paste
1 t. salt
½ t. black pepper
1 T. Worcestershire sauce
1 T. flour

Brown onion and peppers in fat or drippings. Add ground beef, tomato paste, salt, black pepper, Worcestershire sauce and flour. Cook over low heat for 20 minutes.

Mrs. Dean Garland, D.A.R. H. S.
Tamassee, South Carolina

PUMPKIN BERGERS
Special: Circleville Ohio Pumpkin Show
Number of Servings — 6-8 (or 10 small buns)

2 lbs. ground meat (beef)
1 T. fat or Wesson oil
1 medium onion, chopped
¾ c. hot water
1 c. catsup
½ c. tomato juice
¼ t. nutmeg
½ t. cloves
1 t. chili powder
1 t. salt
½ t. black pepper
2 c. canned pumpkin
8 hamburger buns

Brown the ground beef in heavy skillet with the 1 tablespoon fat or oil. Add chopped onion. Continue to cook for five minutes. In a large stew pan cook the following: 1 cup catsup, ½ cup tomato juice, ¼ teaspoon nutmeg, ½ teaspoon cloves, 1 teaspoon chili powder, teaspoon salt and ½ teaspoon black pepper. Boil to rolling boil. Add the meat, onions and the 2 cups of pumpkin. Simmer for 15 minutes. Serve on hamburger buns, garnished with pickle slices.

Katharine Rigby, Triad Schools
Woodstock, Ohio

RANCH BURGERS
Number of Servings — 6

Cook until brown:
½ c. chopped onions
½ c. chopped green pepper
½ c. chopped celery
1 T. fat
Add and cook until meat is done:
1 lb. ground beef
½ t. salt
Stirring all the time.
Add ½ cup catsup
1 t. chili powder
¼ t. garlic salt

Cover and steam 15 minutes. Spoon on heated buns—serve hot with pickles and sliced tomatoes. May also be served with home made buns.

Mrs. Ollie Lee Arter, Kiawa H. S.
Kiawa, Oklahoma

GUMBO BURGERS
Number of Servings — 4-6

1 small onion
2 T. fat
1 lb. ground meat
1 can chicken gumbo soup
½ c. water
Salt, pepper, mustard, catsup, hot sauce,
  Worcestershire sauce, garlic powder to taste

Brown chopped onion in hot fat. Add meat and brown. Add all other ingredients. Mix well. Cover, turn flame low, and simmer for 20 minutes. Serve hot on toasted hamburger buns.

Hilda Whitley, Grand Saline H. S.
Grand Saline, Texas

MUSHROOMBURGERS
Number of Servings — 6-8

1 lb. hamburger
1½ c. chopped onion
1½ c. chopped celery
1 t. salt—pepper to taste
1 can mushroom soup
1 can tomato paste
1 T. Worcestershire sauce
½ t. garlic salt or 1 clove garlic

Brown meat in small amount of hot fat. Add onions and celery; cook 'till tender. Add remaining ingredients. Cover. Simmer 30-45 minutes. Serve on toasted buns. Strips of cheese on top add extra flavor.

Ramona Lawton, Ribault Sr. H. S. No. 96
Jacksonville 8, Florida

BARBECUE
Number of Servings — 6-8

2 lbs. ground beef—salt and pepper and brown.
Combine for sauce:
⅓ c. vinegar

⅓ c. brown sugar
⅔ c. water
1 T. flour
½ c. catsup
2 T. chopped onion
⅔ c. chopped celery
3 T. prepared mustard.

Pour over meat and cook, until celery is cooked.

Ann Held, Horicon H. S.
Horicon, Wisconsin

BAR-B-QUED HAMBURGER
Number of Servings — 6-8

1 lb. ground beef
1 c. chopped onions
½ c. chopped celery
1 finely chopped clove garlic
2 T. brown sugar
1 can tomatoes
½ can tomato paste
4 T. butter
2 T. Worcestershire sauce
1 t. Tobasco sauce
5 T. vinegar
4 T. tomato catsup
1 t. salt
1 t. black pepper

Brown meat in large skillet. Add onions, celery, garlic, and butter. Cook until onion is transparent. Add remaining ingredients and bring to a boil. Reduce heat to simmer and cook 1 hour.

Cleo Codas, Northern H. S.
Durham, North Carolina

BARBECUED HAMBURGER
Number of Servings — 8

2 lbs. hamburger
1 medium onion, diced
½ bottle of catsup
½ c. of water
1½ t. chili powder
1 T. Worcestershire sauce
1 T. prepared mustard
Salt and pepper
Dash of red pepper

Brown hamburger and onion. Add remaining ingredients and simmer slowly for one hour.

Carole Robinson, Pella Community H. S.
Pella, Iowa

BARBECUED BEEF
Number of Servings — 12

1½ lbs. hamburger
½ lb. sausage
1½ c. diced celery
2 c. cracker crumbs
1 c. tomato juice
1 medium onion, minced

(Continued on Next Page)

2 eggs
1½ quart milk (to moisten)

Brown hamburger and sausage, when starts to brown add celery. Saute onions till golden brown. Then mix hamburger mixture, onions, cracker crumbs, tomato juice, eggs and enough milk to moisten together in roaster. Stir occasionally. Bake at 350°F. for one hour.

Janis Main, Utica H. S.
Utica, Ohio

BARBECUED BEEFIES
Number of Servings — 9

1½ lbs. ground beef
½ lb. ground pork
3 slices bread, broken up
1 c. milk
1 egg, beaten
¼ c. minced onion
1¼ t. salt
¼ t. pepper
¼ t. dry mustard
¼ t. sage
¼ t. celery salt
¼ t. garlic salt
1 T. Worcestershire sauce

Combine all ingredients and shape into 9 individual loaves. (1x2x3 inches). Place in shallow greased pan with a thin slice of onion on each. Pour Texas Barbecue Sauce over all and baste often with it during baking. Bake at 350°F. for one hour.

Texas Barbecue Sauce:
2 T. brown sugar
1 T. paprika
1 t. salt
1 t. dry mustard
¼ t. chili powder
⅛ t. cayenne
2 T. Worcestershire sauce
¼ c. vinegar
¾ c. tomato juice
¼ c. catsup
¾ c. water

Combine all ingredients and pour over Barbecued Beefies before baking. Baste often during the baking period.

Judy Kettler, Sabetha H. S.
Sabetha, Kansas

BARBECUED BEEF
Number of Servings — 8

2 lbs. ground beef
1 large onion, chopped
1 c. chopped celery (optional)

1 bottle chili sauce or 2 c. catsup
1 green pepper, chopped
2 T. vinegar
2 T. Worcestershire sauce
5-7 drops Tabasco sauce
2 T. horseradish
2 T. dry mustard
Salt and pepper to taste

Brown meat in fat. Add rest of ingredients. Cook in 250°F. oven for 2 hours. Serve on toasted buns.

Margaret Ledbetter, Black Rock H. S.
Black Rock, Arkansas

BARBECUED HAMBURGER STEAKS
Number of Servings — 6-8

2 large onions, sliced
½ c. catsup
2 c. tomatoes
2 T. sugar
3 T. vinegar
1 T. butter
1½-2 lbs. ground beef
1½ t. salt

Shape meat into patties; brown well in butter; remove to cake pan, or oblong casserole. Place remaining ingredients in frying pan in which meat was browned, simmer 10 minutes. Pour over meat patties. Bake in 325°F. oven 1½ hours. May be served in buns or as a dinner meat, with baked potatoes.

Mrs. Dorothy Soderlund, Milaca H. S.
Milaca, Minnesota

STUFFED HAMBURGERS
Number of Servings — 4

1 lb. ground beef
1 t. salt
¼ t. pepper
¼ c. catsup
¼ c. onion
3 T. chopped green pepper
1 small clove garlic
1 T. margarine
1½ c. dry bread cubes
¼ t. salt
Dash pepper
⅓ c. mayonnaise
3 T. milk

Combine ground beef, salt, pepper and catsup. Form into 4 patties. Shape each patty into a cup by making an indentation in center and pressing firmly around edge. Place in baking pan and sit aside. Saute onion, green pepper and garlic in margarine over low heat until tender. Mix with bread cubes and seasoning. Blend mayonnaise and milk and toss with bread mixture. Fill hamburger cups evenly and press down with bowl of spoon. Bake in very hot oven (450°F.) 20 minutes.

Mrs. Otis Jones, Bude Attendance Center
Bude, Mississippi

BEEFIES
Number of Servings — 8

1 lb. ground beef
1 t. salt
1 t. mustard
1 t. Worcestershire sauce
¼ c. chopped onions
¾ c. fine bread crumbs
1 egg
Fat for frying

Combine all ingredients except ½ cup bread crumbs. Shape into rolls. Roll in bread crumbs. Brown in deep fat. Cover frying pan and cook about 15 minutes.

Foye Davis, Horatio H. S.
Horatio, Arkansas

TALLORINE
Number of Servings — 12

2 lbs. ground beef
2 large onions
2 large bell peppers
2 cloves garlic
Sear above ingredients then add:
1 can tomato soup
1 can whole grain corn
1 can mushroom soup
2 T. Worcestershire sauce

Simmer 30 minutes. Add ½ pound velveta cheese to first mixture. Cook one 10 ounce package egg noodles until tender in salted water. Drain and add to the above mixture. Add a small jar of stuffed olives sliced. Serve with green salad.

Mrs. Carl Taylor, Augusta H. S.
Augusta, Arkansas

MEAL-IN-A-SKILLET
Number of Servings — 4-6

1 lb. ground beef
1 clove garlic, minced
1 c. chopped onion
¼ t. mace
¼ t. allspice
½ t. dry mustard
¼ t. pepper
4 ozs. (1¼ c.) dry spaghetti
1½ t. salt
3 c. tomato juice
Parmesan cheese

Brown beef, garlic, onion well in skillet. Sprinkle on mace, allspice, mustard and pepper. Break spaghetti into 2 to 3 inch lengths; measure. Place in layer over ground beef. Stir salt into tomato juice and. pour over spaghetti; be sure all spaghetti is moistened. Cover closely and cook over high heat until steam escapes. Turn heat low and cook 30 minutes. Turn out onto platter and serve with Parmesan cheese.

Mary Kathryn Lands, Amanda-Clear Creek H. S.
Amanda, Ohio

MEAL-IN-A-SKILLET
Number of Servings — 6-8

1 lb. ground beef
Salt and pepper
1 c. bread crumbs
2 c. whole kernel corn (drained)
2 c. whole tomatoes
1 t. salt
1 c. onion rings

Combine ground beef and bread crumbs; season to taste. Brown in hot fat until well-done. Arrange in bottom of skillet. Place corn over meat. Place tomatoes in corn. Add salt. Arrange onion rings over tomatoes. Cover. Simmer for about 20 minutes or until onions are tender. Serve from skillet —leaving vegetables in layers.

Sarah Kahla, Spring H. S.
Spring, Texas

SIMPLY DELICIOUS SKILLET DINNER
Number of Servings — 4

1 T. fat
½ lb. ground beef
1 medium onion, chopped
1 small clove garlic, minced
2 T. minced parsley
¾ c. tomato paste (6-oz. can)
2¼ c. water
1 t. sugar
1 t. salt
Dash of pepper
4 ozs. noodles
Grated Parmesan cheese

Melt fat in heavy skillet. Add ground beef, onion, garlic and parsley, and brown lightly. Combine tomato paste with water, sugar, salt, and pepper, mixing until smooth. Add to meat mixture, mixing well. Cover, reduce heat and simmer 10 minutes. Add noodles, cover and cook until noodles are tender (about 5 minutes longer), stirring occasionally. Serve with grated cheese.

Mrs. Johnnie Mae Proctor, Dilley H. S.
Dilley, Texas

SKILLET DINNER
Number of Servings — 4

Saute in large skillet 1 tablespoon fat or drippings, ½ pound beef, 1 chopped onion, 1 teaspoon garlic salt, 2 tablespoons minced parsley. Add 1 can tomato paste, 2½ cups water, 1 teaspoon sugar, 1 teaspoon salt, ¼ teaspoon pepper and 4 ounces small egg noodles. Cover and simmer for 15 minutes. Stir frequently. Serve with grated Parmesan cheese and French garlic bread.

Mildred S. Whiteside, Milton Consolidated H. S.
Milton, Delaware

JONNI-MAJARIZY
Number of Servings — 6-8

1 lb. ground beef
1 green pepper
6 small onions
1 can mushroom soup
1 package noodles
1 can tomato soup plus ½ can water
¼ lb. cheese
1 c. bread crumbs

Cook noodles 7 minutes, cut pepper, add to meat and cook well. In another pan cut up onion and fry in butter. Add mixtures together. Mix into meat mixture the mushroom soup, tomato soup, water and noodles. Put into pan, sprinkle with bread crumbs and put cheese on top. Bake 45 minutes at 350°F.

Mrs. Emma Frances McCluskey,
Cotton Center H. S.
Cotton Center, Texas

HAMBURGER CROWN
Number of Servings — 6

2 beaten eggs
1 lb. ground beef
1 c. rolled bread crumbs
1 t. salt
¼ t. pepper
2 T. grated onion
¾ c. milk

Mix ingredients in order given and pack in buttered 8-inch ring mold. Bake 45-60 minutes at 350° F. Turn ring out on platter and fill center with mashed potatoes, buttered peas, or fluffy cooked rice.

Delores Kluckman, DeSmet Public H. S.
DeSmet, South Dakota

SKILLET BEEF AND NOODLES
Number of Servings — 6

2 c. (¼-lb.) wide noodles
3 T. bacon fat
1 c. chopped onions
1 c. chopped celery
1 lb. ground beef
1 c. cooked diced carrots
2¼ c. (#2 can) tomatoes
2 t. salt
½ t. chili powder
¼ t. pepper
½ t. Worcestershire sauce

Scrape, dice, cook carrots till done. Cook noodles according to directions. Drain. Add onions and celery to fat in skillet. Saute about 5 minutes. Add broken-up ground beef. Brown. Add remaining ingredients. Simmer, stirring occasionally, about 5 minutes to blend flavors.

Mrs. Carol Walker, Yuma H. S.
Yuma, Arizona

BEEF, BEAN AND RICE SKILLET MEAL
Number of Servings — 6

4 T. shortening
1 large onion, diced
1 lb. ground beef
2 T. chili powder
2 t. black pepper
1 c. rice (left-over cooked or quick cooking)
1 can red kidney beans (No. 300)
1 can tomatoes (No. 300)
¼ t. garlic salt
2 t. salt

Brown meat and onions in shortening. Add dry seasoning, rice, beans, and tomatoes. Cook on low heat about 30 minutes.

Mrs. Marion Sebastian, Arkadelphia H. S.
Arkadelphia, Arkansas

BEEF GOULOSH
Number of Servings — 6-8

⅓ c. chopped onions
½ c. chopped celery
2 T. fat
1 lb. ground beef
1 8-oz. can of tomato sauce
1 c. water
1 large bay leaf
½ t. salt
1 t. black pepper
1½ T. chili powder
1½ c. uncooked elbow macaroni

Cook onions and celery in hot fat 'till golden. Add meat; brown lightly. Add tomato sauce, water and seasonings. Simmer 30 to 40 minutes. Cook the macaroni in boiling salted water; drain. Add the drained macaroni to the sauce and let simmer 10 minutes. Sprinkle with grated Parmesian cheese, if desired. Makes 6 to 8 servings.

Mrs. Carolene Wood, Perkins H. S.
Perkins, Oklahoma

GOULASH
Number of Servings — 6

1 lb. ground beef
1 T. fat
1 t. salt
¼ t. black pepper
1 7-oz. package macaroni
1 medium onion
1 can tomato sauce
½ lb. cheese, grated
1 t. chili powder

Brown meat in large heavy pan. Add chopped onion and let cook until onion wilts. Cook macaroni according to directions on the package; drain and add to the meat. Add all other ingredients. Cover and cook very slowly until cheese is melted.

Ruth Marshall, Borger Sr. H. S.
Borger, Texas

GOULASH
Number of Servings — 8-10

¼ c. bacon drippings
1 c. chopped onions
1 medium bell pepper, chopped
2 T. chili powder
1 lb. sharp cheese, grated
2 lbs. ground beef
1 t. salt
1 t. garlic salt
1 t. black pepper
1 c. catsup or 1 can tomato soup
1 package Italian spaghetti, cooked

Saute onions, bell pepper, in bacon drippings. Add ground beef and cook until brown. Add seasonings and catsup. Simmer about 10 minutes. Drain and fold in cooked spaghetti, cover with grated cheese. Cover pan and simmer until cheese is melted. Serves 8 to 10.

Mrs. Harold Bartlett, Dubberly H. S.
Dubberly, Louisiana

HAMBURGER GOULASH
Number of Servings — 6

½ c. onions
1 lb. ground beef
1 No. 2 can tomatoes
3 c. macaroni
2 t. salt
¼ t. pepper

Brown onions and hamburger in small amount of fat. Add tomatoes, salt, and pepper and bring to boiling. Add macaroni and cook until soft—about 20 minutes.

Carolyn Smith, Kermit H. S.
Kermit, Texas

RICE-HAMBURGER GOULASH
Number of Servings — 8-10

1 lb. ground beef
1 green pepper
1 large onion
1 c. cooked rice
1 pint tomatoes
1 t. sugar
Salt and pepper to taste

Brown meat in large skillet. Add onion and pepper. Cook one minute. Add rice, tomatoes, salt, pepper, and sugar. Simmer for 2 hours.

Sandra E. Hillman, Rye Cove H. S.
Clinchport, Virginia

BEEF SKILLET DISH
Number of Servings — 6

1 lb. lean ground meat
½ c. chopped onion
½ c. chopped celery
½ c. chopped green pepper

1 t. salt
½ t. freshly ground pepper
2 T. soy sauce
2 T. Louisiana hot sauce
½ t. garlic powder
1 can corn (12-oz. Mexican style niblets)
½ lb. grated cheddar cheese
1 can chow mein noodles

In electric skillet, brown the ground meat, adding small amount of oil, if necessary, add onion and cook until transparent. Lower the temperature and set control at 250°F.; add salt, pepper, soy sauce, garlic powder, hot sauce, celery, and green pepper. Place lid on skillet and close the steam vent. Cook slowly about 7 minutes, stirring occasionally. Add drained Mexican style corn and heat thoroughly. Serve over noodles and top with grated cheese. Serves six generously.

Mrs. Freddie Morrison, Marshall H. S.
Marshall, Texas

SKILLET MEAL
Number of Servings — 8

1 lb. ground beef
1 No. 3 can tomatoes
1 No. 2 can peas, drained (optional)
1 c. ripe olives (optional)
1 T. Worcestershire sauce
1 medium sized onion, minced
¼ c. butter
1 pimento
1½ c. uncooked noodles
½ lb. American cheese
Salt and pepper to taste

Saute onion and meat in butter. Add all of the other ingredients except the cheese. After the mixture steams freely, cook on low heat for 30 minutes. Add grated cheese and cook 5 minutes.

Vara Boyd, Vernon H. S.
Vernon, Texas

HAMBURGER HEAVEN
Number of Servings — 6

1 lb. ground beef
1 c. chopped onions
½ lb. American cheese, sliced
1 c. chopped celery
1 No. 2 can stewing tomatoes
1 small can ripe olives, sliced
2 c. fine dry noodles

Brown meat slightly in a skillet. Stir in onions and season with salt and pepper. Arrange the remaining ingredients in layers (as listed) over the browned beef. Sprinkle salt and pepper over noodles. Rinse out tomato can with about ¼ cup water and pour over noodles. Cover. Bring to boil on high heat, then reduce to simmer and cook for 30 minutes. Occasionally, remove cover and press noodles into the liquid.

Ardis A. Williams, Rio Vista H. S.
Rio Vista, California

HAMBURGER RICE PARMESAN
Number of Servings — 5-6

1 lb. ground beef
1 large can tomato sauce
¼ c. chopped onions
1 can condensed beef bouillon
Salt to taste
1⅓ c. precooked rice
2 T. Parmesan cheese

Brown onions and hamburger in small amount of fat in large skillet. Pour tomato sauce over it and simmer for approximately 1 hour. Meanwhile cook rice as directed on package, using bouillon, plus water to make 1½ cups. Add hamburger and Parmesan cheese to rice, stir together.

June Miller, Glenwood H. S.
Glenwood, Georgia

SKILLETBURGERS
Number of Servings — 6-8

1 lb. ground beef
1 c. chopped onion
¾ c. chopped celery
1 t. salt
Dash of pepper
1 10½ or 11-oz. can condensed tomato soup
2 t. barbecue sauce

Brown meat in a small amount of fat. Add onion and celery; cook until tender, but not brown. Add remaining ingredients. Cover pan and simmer for 30 minutes. Serve on warm or toasted buns.

Barbara H. Thompson, Bovina H. S.
Bovina, Texas

COMPANY BEEF CASSEROLE
Number of Servings — 8-10

1 lb. hamburger
1 T. butter
16 oz. tomato sauce
1 8-oz. package noodles
1 c. cottage cheese
8 ozs. cream cheese
¼ c. thick sour cream
⅓ c. onions, chopped
1 T. green pepper, chopped
2 T. butter, melted

Brown meat in butter. Stir in tomato sauce, remove from heat. Boil noodles, drain. Combine cheese, sour cream, onions, peppers. Butter casserole, put in half the noodles. Cover with cheese mixture. Put in rest of noodles. Pour over the melted butter. Put hamburger sauce over all this. Bake for 20-30 minutes at 350°F.

Nancy Matthews, Coordinator of Special Studies
Home Economics Staff
West Virginia State Dept. of Education

HAMBURG STEW
Number of Servings — 6-8

2 lbs. lean hamburger
1 good sized onion, cut fine
Butter
Salt and pepper
Boiling water
1 bay leaf
¼ t. basil
¼ t. oregano
¼ c. catsup
¼ c. water
⅛ c. flour
6-8 sliced carrots

Break hamburger into small pieces and cut up onion. Put in pan, season with salt and pepper and brown the meat. Add enough boiling water to cover the meat and keep it covered at all times. Add basil, oregano, bay leaf and catsup. Stir, and cook over low heat. If a pressure saucepan is to be used, cook 15-20 minutes at the pressure required for stews, adding sliced carrots before cooking begins. If a saucepan is to be used, cook over low heat approximately 1½ hours, adding the sliced carrots ½ to ¾ hour before completion, and cooking until tender. Before serving remove bay leaf and thicken with flour and water paste, adding slowly and stirring constantly to prevent lumping. The gravy should be relatively thin. Serve over mashed potatoes. Variation: Poach an egg in the heated left-over stew, then serve on toast for breakfast.

Sandra L. Anderson, Groveton H. S.
Groveton, New Hampshire

SIX-LAYER DINNER
Number of Servings — 6-8

2 c. ground beef
2 c. sliced raw potatoes
2 c. chopped celery
½ c. diced onions
2 t. salt
¼ t. pepper
1 c. diced green pepper
2 c. canned tomatoes

Place potatoes in bottom of greased casserole. Add celery, then ground beef, onions and pepper. Sprinkle salt and pepper on each layer. Pour tomatoes over mixture in dish and garnish with green pepper rings. Bake at 350°F. for 2 hours.

Mrs. Jean A. Ross, North Hartford H. S.
Pylesville, Maryland

MUSHROOM HAMBURGER BALLS
Number of Servings — 4-5

1 lb. ground beef
1 egg, beaten
¼ c. onion, minced
1 slice bread
1 t. salt
¼ c. milk
1 can cream of mushroom soup
2 T. flour, blended with ½ c. water

(Continued on Next Page)

Crumble bread and soak in milk. Add egg, salt, onion, and ground beef. Mix well, shape into 20 small balls. Brown. Remove from skillet and add mushroom soup and flour and water mixture to drippings. Stir till smooth. Add meat balls. Serve on hot rice or noodles.

Nancy Wooten, Lakeview H. S.
Rossville, Georgia

OLD-FASHIONED BEEF STEW
Number of Servings — 6

¼ c. flour
2 t. salt
¼ t. pepper
2 lbs. boneless beef, chuck or round, cut into
  1½ inch cubes
3-4 T. fat or oil
3 c. boiling water
1 bay leaf
½ t. marjoram
1 t. Worcestershire sauce
½ c. diced celery
3 medium white potatoes, diced
12 small white onions, peeled
1 c. sliced carrots
1 c. cut green beans

Sift together flour with salt and pepper. Roll meat in flour mixture. Melt fat in Dutch oven, add meat and brown well. Then add water, bay leaf, marjoram and Worcestershire sauce. Cover and simmer for 2 hours. Then add vegetables, and more salt if needed, and simmer 20-30 minutes or until vegetables are tender. If a thicker stew is desired, mix 2 tablespoons flour with ⅓ cup cold water and add slowly to stew. Stir and cook until mixture thickens. Serve in pie wedges.

Mrs. Imelda Watson, Leesville H. S.
Leesville, Louisiana

SPANISH NOODLES
Number of Servings — 6

2 c. noodles, uncooked
¼ c. chopped green pepper
1 lb. ground beef
⅛ t. pepper
1½ t. sugar
3 c. tomatoes
¼ c. chopped onion
1½ t. salt
2 T. fat (bacon drippings)

Mix 1½ teaspoons salt and ⅛ teaspoon pepper with 1 pound ground meat. Melt 2 tablespoons bacon drippings in a heavy skillet, add meat and cook until nicely brown. Add 3 cups tomatoes, ¼ cup green pepper, ¼ cup chopped onions, 1½ teaspoons sugar, 2 cups noodles, and cook over high heat to steaming. Reduce heat to simmer, cover and continue to cook for 45 minutes. Serve in platter with garnish.

Virginia Dale Rawls, Pearl River Jr. H. S.
Pearl River, Louisiana

SPANISH RICE
Number of Servings — 6

1 lb. ground meat
¼ c. chopped onion
¼ c. chopped celery
¼ c. chopped green pepper
1 c. rice
1 can tomato paste
2 c. water
2 t. salt
Pepper to taste

Brown meat, onion, celery and green pepper in skillet. Add rice, tomato paste, water and seasonings. Cover and simmer 30-40 minutes, or until rice is well done.

Mrs. Rita S. Walters, Forest K. White Jr. H. S.
Lake Charles, Louisiana

HAMBURGER PIE
Number of Servings — 4-6

1 medium sized onion, chopped
1 lb. ground beef
½ t. salt
⅛ t. pepper
½ can vegetable soup
½ can tomato soup
1-5 medium sized potatoes, mashed
½ c. warm milk
1 beaten egg

Brown onion in hot fat and add meat and seasonings. Brown. Add soups, pour into greased casserole. Mash potatoes, add milk, egg and seasonings. Spoon potatoes over meat. Bake in 350°F. oven for 30 minutes. Longer baking will make the dish more flavorful.

Dixie Lee Golden, Hobson H. S.
Hobson, Montana

HAMBURGER UPSIDE DOWN BAKE
Number of Servings — 4

1 lb. hamburger meat
¼ c. chopped onion
1 t. salt
½ t. chili powder
¼ c. catsup
1-12-oz. can golden whole corn
Corn bread batter or 8-oz. package corn muffin
  mix.

Combine first 5 ingredients in 10″ skillet. Break meat apart and fry until brown. Push meat evenly around edge of skillet, forming ring. Spread undrained corn in center. Mix corn bread batter and pour evenly over meat and corn. Bake in hot oven (425° F.) 20-25 minutes or 'till corn bread is done and brown. Remove from oven and let stand 5 minutes, turn upside down on hot serving plate.

Mary Emma Bristow, Yale H. S.
Yale, Oklahoma

HAMBURGER PIE
Number of Servings — 6

1 small onion
1 lb. ground beef
½ t. salt
¼ t. pepper
½ t. Accent
1 No. 2 can green beans
1 (10½-oz.) can tomato soup
2 c. mashed potatoes

Heat oven to 350°F. Cook onion in hot fat until yellow; add meat and cook until brown. Add seasonings, drained beans, and soup; pour into 1½ quart baking dish. Spoon mashed potatoes over mixture. Bake 30 minutes.

Ruth Elizabeth Cook, University H. S.
Morgantown, West Virginia

HAMBURGER PIE
Number of Servings — 6

1 medium onion, chopped
1 lb. ground beef
Salt and pepper
1 No. 2 can (2½ c.) or ½ lb. cooked green beans
1 10½- or 11-oz. can condensed tomato soup
5 medium potatoes, cooked
½ c. warm milk
1 beaten egg
Salt and pepper

Cook onion in hot fat till golden; add meat and seasonings; brown. Add drained beans and soup; pour into greased 1½-quart casserole. Mash the potatoes; add the milk, egg, and the seasonings. Spoon in mounds over meat. Bake in moderate oven (350°F.) 30 minutes.

Bonnie Sprayberry, Ocean Springs H. S.
Ocean Springs, Mississippi

PIEBURGER
Number of Servings — 6

¼ c. shortening
1 lb. ground hamburger
1½ c. chopped onions
1½ c. chopped celery
½ c. chopped green pepper
1 can condensed tomato soup
¼ c. catsup
1½ t. salt
½ c. grated cheese
1 package pastry mix (2 crust)

Melt shortening. Cook hamburger, onion, celery, green pepper until onion and celery are soft. Pour off excess grease. Add soup, catsup, salt. Mix cheese with pastry. Fit pastry into 9 inch pie plate. Pour hamburger mixture into pastry. Top with remaining pastry. Bake 350°F. for 45-60 minutes.

Mrs. Linda Barnes, Warren Central H. S.
Indianapolis, Indiana

HAMBURGER PIE
Number of Servings — 6

1 medium onion, chopped
1 lb. ground beef
Salt and pepper
1 No. 2 can (2½ c.) or ½ lb. cooked green beans
1 10½- or 11-oz. can condensed tomato soup
5 medium potatoes, cooked
½ c. warm milk
1 beaten egg
Salt and pepper

Cook onion in hot fat till golden; add meat and seasonings; brown. Add drained beans and soup; pour into greased 1½-quart casserole. Mash the potatoes; add the milk, egg, and the seasonings. Spoon in mounds over meat. Bake in moderate oven (350°F.) 30 minutes.

Ellen B. Robinson, Deshler H. S.
Tuscumbia, Alabama

HAMBURGER UPSIDE DOWN
Number of Servings — 6-8

1 lb. ground beef
2 T. fat
1 c. cut-up celery
¼ c. minced onion
¼ c. cut-up green pepper
Salt and pepper
¼ t. chili powder
1 can tomato soup
Biscuit dough

Brown—ground beef in fat in a 10″ skillet. Add—remaining ingredients. Simmer—10 minutes. Drop—Biscuit topping over hot mixture in skillet. Bake—375°F. oven for 20 minutes. Turn—out onto large platter. Serve—immediately. Cut into wedge-shaped pieces.

Delores Vondrak, Elk Point H. S.
Elk Point, South Dakota

MEAT-ZA PIE
Number of Servings — 4-5

1 lb. ground beef
⅔ c. evaporated milk
½ c. fine dry bread crumbs
1 t. garlic salt
⅓ c. tomato paste or catsup
1 2-oz. can sliced mushrooms
1 c. shredded sharp cheddar cheese
¼ t. oregano, crumbled finely
2 T. grated Parmesan cheese

Place meat, milk, bread crumbs, garlic salt in a pie plate. Mix thoroughly. Pat this mixture evenly on the bottom and sides of pie plate. Pull up over rim and press firmly into place. Spread tomato paste over meat. Sprinkle mushrooms over. Top with cheese and sprinkle with oregano. Bake at 375°F. for 25 minutes.

Mary F. Ragsdale, Dumas Sr. H. S.
Dumas, Texas

HAMBURGER UPSIDE DOWN PIE
Number of Servings — 6-8

2 T. salad oil
1 medium sized onion, cut fine
½ c. chopped green pepper
1 lb. ground chuck or hamburger
1 8-oz. can tomato sauce
1 t. salt
¼ t. pepper
2 T. catsup

Pour oil in skillet, saute onion, green pepper and meat until brown. Add the tomato sauce, salt, pepper and catsup. Turn into 2-quart round casserole. Cover with topping.

Topping:
½ c. all-purpose flour, sifted
2 t. baking powder
1 t. salt
1 T. sugar
¾ c. yellow cornmeal
1 egg
½ c. milk
2 T. salad oil

Sift together all-purpose flour, baking powder, salt and sugar into a mixing bowl. Add the cornmeal. Combine the egg, milk and salad oil. Add to the dry ingredients and stir to moisten. Spread on meat in casserole. Bake at 425°F. in a hot oven, for approximately 25 minutes or until done. Turn upside down on a serving plate and cut in wedges. Makes about six or eight servings.

SUGGESTIONS: If desired, you may use an 8 ounce package of muffin mix. Follow directions on package and use for the topping. Or, use ½ recipe for biscuits. Roll and fit casserole.

Grace M. Benjamin, East H. S.
Bremerton, Washington

UPSIDE-DOWN HAMBURGER PIE
Number of Servings — 6

½ lb. hamburger
1 T. fat
¾ c. chopped onion
¼ c. chopped green pepper
1 can cream of tomato soup
1 t. barbecue sauce
½ t. salt
2 c. biscuit mix
⅔ c. milk
1 T. chopped parsley
½ t. celery seed

Brown meat in hot fat. Add onion, celery, and green pepper; cook until onion is golden. Stir in soup and barbecue sauce, salt and pepper. Turn mixture into a baking dish. Make biscuit dough of other ingredients. Roll to fit pan. Bake in 450°F. oven for 20-30 minutes. (Canned biscuits may be used instead of biscuit dough).

Mrs. Ialeen S. Mode, Franklinton H. S.
Franklinton, North Carolina

MEAT-ZA PIE
Number of Servings — 4

1 lb. ground beef
½ to 1 t. garlic salt
½ c. fine dry bread crumbs
⅔ c. evaporated milk
1 can (2-oz.) sliced mushrooms, drained
2 or 3 slices processed American cheese, cut
   in strips
¼ t. oregano, crumbled finely
2 T. grated Parmesan cheese

Place beef, garlic salt and bread crumbs in a 9 inch pie pan. Add evaporated milk, and mix together with a fork. With the fork, spread mixture evenly over bottom of pan, raising a rim about a half inch high around edge. Spread catsup or tomato paste over meat to the rim. Arrange drained sliced mushrooms on tomato paste. Place cheese strips casually in criss-cross pattern over top. Sprinkle with oregano (or poultry seasoning). Sprinkle generously with grated Parmesan cheese. Bake in preheated hot oven (400°F.) 20 minutes, or until cheese is melted and lightly browned. Cut in wedges and serve. NOTE: ¼ cup finely chopped green pepper may be used in place of mushrooms. 1 cup soft bread crumbs or ½ cup fine cracker crumbs may be used in place of the ½ cup fine dry bread crumbs.

MENU
Meat-za Pie
Buttered Green Beans
Hot Buttered Crusty Bread
Tray of Relishes (Carrots, Celery, Radishes,
Green Pepper Rings, Tomato Wedges)
or Tossed Salad
Chocolate Mint Pudding   Cookies
Beverage

Mrs. Mary Sue E. Spencer, Princess Anne H. S.
Lynnhaven, Virginia

HAMBURGER PIE
Number of Servings — 6

1 medium onion, chopped
1 lb. ground beef
1 No. 2 can or 2½ c. cooked green beans
1 10½ or 11-oz. can condensed tomato soup
3 T. Worcestershire sauce
5 medium potatoes, cooked
½ c. warm milk
1 egg, beaten
Salt and pepper

Cook onion in hot fat until golden. Add meat and seasonings; brown. Add Worcestershire sauce. Add drained beans and soup; pour into greased 1½ quart casserole. Mash the potatoes, add the milk, egg and seasoning. Spoon in mounds over meat. Bake in moderate oven (350°F.) 30 minutes.

Mrs. Joan Brittingham, Union H. S.
Leslie, Georgia

COUNTRY PIE-BEEF MAKES CRUST
Number of Servings — 5-6

Crust:

½ 8-oz. can tomato sauce
½ c. bread crumbs
¼ c. chopped onion
⅛ t. pepper
1 lb. ground beef
¼ c. chopped green pepper
1½ t. salt
⅛ t. oregano

Combine, mix well, pat mixture into bottom and sides of 9 inch greased pie plate. Set aside.

Filling:

1⅓ c. minute rice
1 c. water
1½ 8-oz. can tomato paste
1 c. grated cheese
½ t. salt

Combine rice, tomato sauce, salt, water and ¼ cup cheese. Spoon rice mixture into meat shell. Cover with aluminum foil. Bake in 350°F. oven 25 minutes. Uncover and sprinkle top with remaining cheese. Return to oven and bake uncovered 10-15 minutes longer. Cut into pie shaped pieces. Makes 5-6 servings.

Delaine Blankenship, Elk Garden H. S.
Elk Garden, West Virginia

MEATZZIA
Number of Servings — 4-6

1 lb. ground beef
½ t. garlic salt
½ c. dry bread crumbs
⅔ c. evaporated milk
⅓ c. catsup
1 can mushrooms, drained
4 slices of processed cheese
¼ t. oregano
2 T. grated cheese

Mix the first four ingredients together, then arrange in an 8 inch pie pan. Spread the catsup over the mixture, dot with mushrooms. Arrange the cheese slices on top and sprinkle with oregano and grated cheese. Bake at 400°F. for 20 minutes.

Patricia Moore, Ionia H. S.
Ionia, Michigan

BEEF PIE
Number of Servings — 4-5

1 lb. ground beef
2 T. bacon fat
1 c. tomatoes
1 small onion, chopped fine
2 c. lima beans, (canned) drained
Salt and pepper to taste
Biscuit dough, using 1 c. flour
¼ c. catsup

Sear ground beef in bacon fat until red color disappears. Add tomatoes, lima beans, onions, and seasonings. Pour into casserole. Roll biscuit dough thin; spread with catsup and roll dough jelly roll fashion. Cut dough in ¾ inch slices and lay on top of casserole. Bake at 425°F. until brown.

Mrs. Margery W. Fitzsimmons, Butler H. S.
Butler, Georgia

OLIVE BURGER PIE
Number of Servings — 6

1½ c. ripe olives
1 large onion
1 lb. ground beef
2 T. drippings
1 8-oz. can tomato sauce
¼ c. water
1 t. salt
1 t. mustard
2 t. chili powder
4-5 slices American cheese
Pastry for 2 crust pie

Cut olives into large pieces. Chop onion and cook with beef until lightly browned. Blend in tomato sauce, water, salt, mustard, and chili powder. Simmer 15 minutes. Pat into pastry lined pie tin, with meat layer and a layer of olives. Top with cheese slices. Put top crust on. Bake in hot oven (400°F.) for 25-30 minutes.

Florence Marzoff, Hortonville Union H. S.
Hortonville, Wisconsin

HAMBURGER RICE PIE
Number of Servings — 6-8

1 lb. ground beef
½ c. fine bread crumbs
¼ c. chopped onion
¼ c. chopped green pepper
1½ t. salt
¼ t. pepper
½ c. canned tomato sauce

Combine meat, crumbs, vegetables, seasonings, and tomato sauce. Spread evenly on sides and bottom of greased, deep 10-inch pie pan: 3 cups cooked white rice, ½ cup grated processed American cheese, 1½ cups canned tomato sauce. Mix lightly. Pile into meat shell. Bake at 350°F. for 30 minutes. Serve in wedges while hot.

Mrs. Ava Bush, Latexo Independent H. S.
Latexo, Texas

HAMBURGER-ONION PIE
Number of Servings — 6

1 c. Bisquick
⅓ c. light cream
1 lb. ground beef
2 medium onions, sliced
1 t. salt
¼ t. pepper

(Continued on Next Page)

½ t. flavor extender
2 T. Bisquick
2 eggs
1 c. small curd cottage cheese

Mix Bisquick and cream well. Knead gently 10 times on floured board. Roll dough into circle to fit 9 inch pie pan. Saute beef and onions until brown. Add seasoning and Bisquick. Spread in dough lined pan. Beat eggs slightly and blend with cottage cheese. Pour over meat. Sprinkle with paprika. Bake 30 minutes at 375°F.

Barbara Owens, Casey H. S.
Casey, Illinois

HAMBURGER CORN-PONE PIE
Number of Servings — 4

1 lb. ground beef
⅓ c. chopped onion
1 T. shortening
2 t. chili powder
1 t. Worcestershire sauce
1 c. canned tomatoes
1 c. drained canned kidney beans
1 c. cornbread batter (½ package corn muffin
   mix or ½ standard cornbread recipe)

Brown meat and chopped onion in melted shortening. Add seasonings and tomatoes. Cover and simmer over heat for 15 minutes, then add kidney beans. Pour meat mixture into a greased 1 or 1½-quart casserole (or other baking dish of same capacity). Top with cornbread by spreading carefully with knife. Bake at 450°F. for 20 minutes.

Mrs. Ray L. Evers, McGregor H. S.
McGregor, Texas

CORN PONE PIE

1 lb. ground beef
Salt and pepper
1 medium onion
2 t. chili powder
1 t. Worcestershire sauce
¼ c. catsup
1 can tomatoes
1 can kidney beans (drained)
1 can whole kernel corn (drained)
Cornbread batter (about ½ recipe)

Brown meat and onion in skillet, add salt and pepper, chili powder, Worcestershire sauce and catsup, then tomatoes, corn and beans. Cook all together about 5 minutes. Pour in large baking dish and top with cornbread batter. Bake at 400°F. until cornbread is done.

Velma Grizzle, Tipton H. S.
Tipton, Oklahoma

CORN PONE PIE
Number of Servings — 4-5

1 lb. ground beef
⅓ c. chopped onion
1 T. shortening
2 c. tomato juice

1 t. Worcestershire sauce
1 No. 303 can undrained kidney beans
Cornbread batter

Brown meat and onions in fat. Add seasonings and tomato juice. Cover and simmer for fifteen minutes. Add beans. Pour into greased casserole. Top with cornbread batter, using 1 cup meal and no flour. Bake at 425°F. about 20 minutes or until bread is brown.

Mrs. Mary Jane Kiker, Allison H. S.
Allison, Texas

BURGERPIZZA
Number of Servings — 8

1 c. packaged biscuit mix or ½ recipe biscuits
Pure vegetable oil
½ lb. ground chuck
Salt, pepper, garlic salt
¼ t. oregano or basil
1 8-oz. can tomato sauce
1 T. chopped parsley
¼ lb. Swiss cheese, cut triangle shape slices

Prepare dough according to package directions. Divide dough in half. Roll each piece to fit bottom and sides of 8-inch pie pan. Brush with oil. Put half of the remaining ingredients on each pie in the following order: crumble beef evenly over the dough, sprinkle with salt, pepper, garlic salt and crumbled oregano or basil. Cover with tomato sauce and parsley. Arrange cheese triangle on top. Bake in hot oven (400°F.) about 20 minutes, or until brown and cheese has melted. Cut into wedges, and serve it right away!

Mrs. Lloyd Smittle, Laneburg H. S.
Laneburg, Arkansas

GROUND BEEF STEW
Number of Servings — 6

1 lb. ground beef
1 large onion, chopped
6 carrots, sliced
6 potatoes, cubed
1 c. canned tomatoes
1 t. salt

Saute beef and onions in dry skillet. Add carrots, potatoes, tomatoes and salt. Cover and cook slowly until vegetables are done.

Mrs. Laurena Ward, Ashford H. S.
Ashford, Alabama

TEXAS HASH
Number of Servings — 6

2 large onions, sliced
2 green peppers, sliced
3 T. shortening
1 lb. hamburger
2 c. canned tomatoes
1 c. cooked rice
1 t. chili powder

(Continued on Next Page)

1 t. salt
Dash of pepper

Melt fat in skillet, saute the sliced green peppers and onions until tender. Add hamburger meat and brown, stirring with a fork. Add tomatoes, rice and seasoning, put into greased baking dish, top with bread crumbs. Brown slowly in 350°F. oven.

Mrs. May Calicutt, Luling H. S.
Luling, Texas

BEEF AND BEAN BARBECUE
Number of Servings — 6-8

1 lb. ground beef
¼ c. diced green pepper
½ c. minced onion
½ c. diced celery
1 8-oz. can tomato sauce
1 clove garlic, minced
2 T. wine vinegar
1 t. dry mustard
½ t. thyme
1 T. brown sugar, salt and pepper
2 T. Worcestershire sauce
1 No. 2 can pork and beans

Cook ground beef and vegetables in hot fat until vegetables are soft. Add tomato sauce, water, garlic, vinegar, mustard, thyme, brown sugar, and seasonings. Blend well and simmer 5 minutes. Pour beans into 1½ quart casserole. Pour meat mixture over them. Bake at 375°F. for 45 minutes.

Mrs. Marian S. Hanchett, White Pine Co. H. S.
Ely, Nevada

BARBECUED BEANS
Number of Servings — 10-15

2 c. dried red beans
⅓ c. salad oil
2 or 3 garlic cloves, minced
1 large onion, chopped
Dash of cayenne
1 6-oz. can tomato paste
2 to 4 t. chili powder
1 T. catsup
1 t. salt
1 lb. hamburger

Cook beans until almost done. Brown onion and garlic in salad oil, add meat and brown. Add to beans. Add remaining ingredients. Simmer until beans are done, about 15 minutes.

Lucille King, Nazareth H. S.
Nazareth, Texas

BAKED BEANS WITH HAMBURGER
Number of Servings — 6

1 lb. hamburger meat
½ c. minced onion
1 t. vinegar
1 t. Worcestershire sauce
½ c. catsup

¼ c. green pepper
1 No. 300 can pork and beans

Turn heat low and cook onions. Increase heat and add hamburger meat to onions. Add vinegar and Worcestershire sauce to catsup. After hamburger is brown, add catsup mixture to meat. Let this come to a boil and then add beans and peppers. Cook until it boils. Put in casserole dish and bake for 20 minutes at 300°F.

Mrs. Emma Ruth Everett, Decatur H. S.
Decatur, Mississippi

BAKED BEANS WITH MEAT
Number of Servings — 20

1 lb. hamburger meat
½ stick oleo
2 onions
2 cans pork and beans
3 cans ranch style beans
¼ c. prepared mustard
1 c. brown sugar
¼ c. maple syrup
1 c. catsup

Brown meat and chopped onion in oleo. Mix all together and bake in slow oven at 300°F. for 2 hours or simmer slowly on top of stove until bubbly.

Nellie S. Moore, Perrin H. S.
Perrin, Texas

HAMBURGER PINWHEELS
Number of Servings — 6

½ c. minced onion
2 T. fat
¾ lbs. ground beef
1 t. salt
½ t. pepper
½ c. fine soft bread crumbs
⅓ c. milk
1 recipe biscuit dough

Saute onions in fat in covered saucepan 5 minutes; measure 2 tablespoons and add to meat with salt, pepper, bread crumbs, and milk; mix thoroughly. (Ground lamb may be used or ham, tuna, or left over meat). Mix biscuit dough, adding remaining onions to flour with shortening. Roll dough into 12x9 inch rectangle. Spread with hamburger mixture and roll lengthwise as for jelly roll, wetting edge to seal. Cut 12 slices; place cut side up, on greased baking sheet. Bake in hot oven (450°F.) 20 minutes or until done. Serve hot with green pea sauce. Make 2 cups white sauce, browning butter and adding 2 bouillon cubes. Add ¾ cup drained cooked peas.

Mrs. Peggy M. Ivey, Monahans H. S.
Monahans, Texas

GROUND MEAT PINWHEELS
Number of Servings — 12

⅓ c. chopped onion
3 T. Snowdrift
¼ c. chopped green pepper
¼ c. chopped celery
1 lb. ground beef (ground once)
1 t. salt
Dash pepper
2 T. flour
2 beef bouillon cubes
1 c. hot water
1 recipe biscuits

In skillet, saute onion in shortening 5 minutes. Add next 5 ingredients; cook over medium heat until meat is cooked, but not dry. Blend in flour. Dissolve bouillon cubes in hot water, add gradually. Cook until mixture is thickened, stirring constantly. Cool. Spread filling on rectangle of biscuit dough, roll up, cut crosswise in 1 inch slices, place one inch apart on greased cookie sheet and bake 18 minutes at 425°F. Serve with mushroom or tomato sauce.

Mrs. Trudy Fulmer, Springfield H. S.
Springfield, South Carolina

SOUTHERN BEEF ROLL
Number of Servings — 6

Pastry:
2 c. flour
1 c. shortening
1 t. salt
1 egg
Cold water

Sift and measure flour—sift again together with other dry ingredients. Cut fat into dry ingredients until like coarse meal. Break egg into measuring cup, beat slightly; fill cup to ½ full with water, mix well. Place on ighty floured board. Knead, roll to ⅓ inch thickness into rectangular sheet. Spread with beef mixture (dipping beef out of sauce). Roll as a jelly roll. Bake in hot oven (400°F.) for 30 minutes, remove from oven. Add sauce left from beef mixture, return to oven for 10 minutes.

Filling:
2 c. ground beef
¼ c. catsup
1 can tomato sauce
2 T. minced onion
2 T. chopped pepper
1 T. Worcestershire sauce

Saute onions and pepper in 2 tablespoons melted oleo. Add ground beef. Cook over low heat until light in color. Add: tomato sauce, catsup, Worcestershire sauce, salt, also garlic salt if desired. Simmer for 10 minutes.

Marjorie L. Tinsley, Macon County H. S.
Notasulga, Alabama

BEEF PINWHEELS
Number of Servings — 6

1 lb. hamburger
1½ t. salt
⅛ t. pepper
1 egg
2 T. melted fat
6 T. bread crumbs
2 T. milk
1½ c. mashed potatoes, seasoned
½ c. condensed green pea soup

Mix together all ingredients except the potatoes and pea soup. Pat on waxed paper to form rectangular sheet ½ inch thick. Spread potatoes on half the meat, pea soup on the other half. Roll meat jelly roll style, starting with the end covered with pea soup. Wrap and chill several hours. When ready to cook, cut into six 1-inch slices and broil 3 to 4 inches below heat for about 5 minutes. Turn and broil other side.

Mrs. Richard D. Hempel, Lennox H. S.
Lennox, South Dakota

BEEF BISCUIT ROLL
Number of Servings — 5-6

1 lb. ground beef
½ c. chopped onion
½ c. chopped green pepper
½ t. salt
⅛ t. pepper
Butter or bacon fat

Brown onion, green pepper and beef in fat in a frying pan. Add seasonings. Make a regular biscuit dough and spread dough with meat mixture and roll like jelly roll. Chill, then cut in 1½ inch slices. Place in greased pan, cut side up, brush tops with melted butter. Bake 20-25 minutes at 450°F. Serve with brown gravy, cheese sauce, creamed or buttered peas or celery.

Mrs. Mary Witt, Johnson County H. S.
Buffalo, Wyoming

GROUND BEEF STROGANOFF
Number of Servings — 4

1 lb. ground beef
Salt and pepper
Wide noodles, rice or potatoes
1 can mushroom soup
½ pt. sour cream

Brown ground beef in small amount of shortening in heavy frying pan. Add seasonings, mushroom soup and sour cream. Simmer a few minutes and serve over hot cooked noodles, rice or mashed potatoes. Simple to make for a working or busy housewife.

Mrs. Dolores Vernon, Clare H. S.
Clare, Michigan

GROUND BEEF STROGANOFF
Number of Servings — 4-6

1 c. sour cream
1 lb. ground beef (lean)
2 T. flour
1¼ t. salt
¼ t. pepper
¼ t. paprika
1 can condensed cream of chicken soup
1 small can chopped mushrooms
1 can water packed chestnuts (sliced)
½ c. chopped onion
½ stick butter or oleomargarine

Cook onion in butter until golden, not brown. Add meat mixed with flour, salt, pepper and paprika and brown while stirring. Add the soup, mushrooms, and chestnuts and cook for 5 minutes. Add sour cream and heat thoroughly. Serve on Chinese noodles, rice, or waffles.

Mrs. Suanne Black, Sidney Lanier H. S.
Montgomery, Alabama

EASY BEEF STROGANOFF
Number of Servings — 6

1 lb. round steak, cut in ¾ inch cubes
¼ c. flour
½ t. salt
⅛ t. pepper
2 T. shortening
½ c. onion
½ c. diced green pepper
1 can (6-oz.) sliced mushrooms
1 clove garlic, minced
1 c. thick sour cream
1 can (10½-oz.) cream of tomato soup
1 T. Worcestershire sauce
¼ t. Tabasco sauce

Dredge meat cubes with flour seasoned with salt and pepper. Brown in hot fat on medium heat. Add remaining ingredients and stir until all ingredients are well blended. Cover skillet and cook on medium high heat until steaming, then reduce to low heat and cook 30-40 minutes. Serve with hot fluffy rice or buttered egg noodles.

Mrs. Helen Gardner, South Marshall H. S.
Benton, Kentucky

BEEF STROGANOFF
Number of Servings — 6-8

1 lb. hamburger
1 small onion
1 10½-oz. can cream of mushroom soup
1 c. commercial sour cream

Brown hamburger and diced onion, add cream of mushroom soup and simmer, salt and pepper to taste. Just before serving add sour cream. Serve over mashed potatoes, rice, or biscuits.

Mary Lou Larson, Montezuma Com. H. S.
Montezuma, Iowa

HAMBURGER STROGANOFF
Number of Servings — 6

¼ c. butter or margarine
1 onion, chopped
1 clove garlic, finely chopped
1 lb. ground beef
½ t. pepper
1 t. salt
1 8-oz. can of mushrooms
2 T. flour
1 10-oz. can mushroom soup
1 c. cultured sour cream
¼ c. minced parsley

Melt butter in an electric fry pan at 325°F. Add onion and garlic and cook until lightly browned. Add beef, cook only until redness disappears. Add salt and pepper, mushrooms, flour and soup. Stir thoroughly and cook slowly 20 minutes. Add sour cream, top with parsley, before serving. Serve over cooked noodles.

Edith Bacon, Johnson H. S.
St. Paul, Minnesota

BEEF STROGANOFF
Number of Servings — 4-6

2 lbs. tenderloin tips
3 T. butter
½ lb. mushrooms
1 medium sized onion, chopped
½ clove garlic
1 c. sour cream
1 c. consomme
Salt and pepper

Preheat electric skillet to 350°F. Melt butter in skillet; add onion and saute until yellow. Add beef, turning to brown on all sides. Push to one side of skillet and saute sliced mushrooms. Season with salt, pepper, and garlic. Combine with beef; add cream, consomme, and simmer about 5 minutes and serve.

Mary A. Gallagher, Plainwell H. S.
Plainwell, Michigan

AMERICAN STROGANOFF
Number of Servings — 6

½ c. finely minced onion
1 minced clove garlic
1 lb. ground beef
2 T. flour
1 T. paprika
¼ t. pepper
1 8-oz. can mushroom pieces
1 can cream of chicken soup, undiluted

Combine the above in skillet and cook 5 minutes on controlled gas burner at 300°F. Then add the mushroom pieces and the cream of chicken soup. Cover, reduce dial setting to 200°F. and continue cooking 10 minutes. Just before serving stir in 1 cup commercial sour cream.

Floy Jones, Taylor H. S.
Taylor, Texas

HAMBURGER STRAGONOFF
Number of Servings — 4-6

¼ c. butter or margarine
½ c. minced onions
1 lb. chuck, ground
1 minced clove garlic
2 T. flour
2 t. salt
¼ t. monosodium glutamate
¼ t. pepper
¼ t. paprika
1 lb. sliced mushrooms
1 can undiluted condensed cream of chicken
  soup
1 c. commercial sour cream
Snipped parsley, chives, or fresh dill
Note: May omit mushrooms and use mushroom
soup instead of chicken soup

In hot butter in skillet, saute onions till golden.
Stir in meat, garlic, flour, salt, monosodium glutamate, pepper, paprika, mushrooms; saute 5 minutes. Add soup; simmer, uncovered, 10 minutes.
Stir in sour cream; sprinkle with parsley. Serve on
hot mashed potatoes, fluffy rice, buttered noodles,
or toast. Makes 4-6 servings.

Betty J. Wade, McMinnville Sr. H. S.
McMinnville, Oregon

BEEF STROGANOFF USING HAMBURGER
Number of Servings — 5-6

½ c. minced onion
¼ c. butter or margarine
1 lb. lean ground beef
1 clove garlic, minced
2 T. garlic, minced
2 T. flour
1 t. salt
¼ t. pepper
¼ t. paprika
1 can button mushrooms
1 c. sour cream
1 can cream of chicken soup

Saute onion in butter, add beef and next mix ingredients. Saute 5 minutes, add soup and simmer
10 minutes more. Just before serving add sour
cream. Serve on French fried Chinese noodles.

Mrs. Edith Wilson, Helena Sr. H. S.
Helena, Montana

HAMBURGER STROGANOFF
Number of Servings — 4-6

½ c. minced onion
1 clove garlic, minced
¼ c. butter
1 lb. ground beef
10½ oz. can cream of chicken soup, undiluted
1 c. sour cream
2 T. flour
2 t. salt
¼ t. pepper

1 lb. fresh mushrooms, or 8-oz. can mushrooms,
  sliced
2 T. minced parsley

Saute onion and garlic in butter over medium
heat. Add meat and brown. Add flour, salt, pepper
and mushrooms. Cook 5 minutes. Add soup, simmer uncovered 10 minutes. Stir in sour cream.
Heat through. Sprinkle with parsley. Serve with
noodles.

Sharon Strange, Springville H. S.
Springville, Alabama

HAMBURGER STRAGONOFF
Number of Servings — 6

½ c. minced onion
2 T. hydrogenated fat
1 lb. ground chuck meat
1 cut, peeled clove garlic
1 t. salt
¼ t. pepper
1 8-oz. can mushrooms, drained
2 T. flour
1 10-oz. can cream of mushroom soup,
  undiluted
½ c. sour cream
¼ c. grated American cheese
Minced parsley
¼ c. chopped pimento

Melt shortening in electric fry pan at 340°F.
Brown onion and meat. Add all ingredients except
sour cream and parsley. Cover, reduce heat to
200°F. and cook 10 minutes. Stir in sour cream;
sprinkle with parsley and cheese.

Mrs. Betty Tipton, Everman H. S.
Everman, Texas

HAMBURGER STRAGONOFF
Number of Servings — 6

1 lb. ground chuck beef
½ c. quick-cooking rolled oats
1 t. salt
¼ t. pepper
¼ c. butter or margarine
½ c. chopped onions
2 T. flour
1 chicken bouillon cube
1 c. condensed cream of celery soup
½ lb. sliced mushrooms
1 T. chopped parsley
¾ c. commercial sour cream

Combine beef, rolled oats, salt, pepper, and milk.
Shape into twelve balls. Melt butter in a frying
pan and brown meat balls over a low heat. Remove from the frying pan. Saute onions until soft,
not brown. Add flour, bouillon cube, soup, and
mushrooms. Stir until well blended. Add the meat
balls. Cover and cook over a low heat for 15 minutes. Add sour cream and mix gently. Heat thoroughly. Sprinkle with parsley, and serve at once.

Jane Otwell, Oconee County H. S.
Watkinsville, Georgia

GROUND BEEF STRAGONOFF
Number of Servings — 6-8

1 lb. ground beef
2 T. flour
1 t. salt
¼ t. black pepper
¼ t. paprika
1 can condensed cream of chicken soup
1 can sliced mushrooms
1 can chestnuts, water packed
¼ c. chopped onion
½ stick butter or oleo
1 c. sour cream

Cook onions and flour in butter until golden brown. Add meat mixed with salt, pepper and paprika. Brown well. Add mushrooms, chestnuts and soup. Cook five minutes. Add sour cream and heat until all of the mixture is hot. Serve on toast, Chinese noodles or rice.

Leacy Newell, Wilcox County H. S.
Camden, Alabama

STUFFED GREEN PEPPERS
Number of Servings — 6

6 large green peppers (stems and seeds
    removed)
½ lb. ground beef
1 c. coarse dry bread crumbs
1 t. salt
¼ t. pepper
1 T. chopped onion
2 eggs

Cook peppers in boiling water 5 minutes. Drain. Mix the other six ingredients and stuff peppers with the mixture. Stand upright in small baking dish. Pour a small amount of catsup over top of each pepper. Bake 45 minutes covered, 15 uncovered at 350°F.

Theresa A. Zettel, Reedsville H. S.
Reedsville, Wisconsin

STUFFED BELL PEPPERS
Number of Servings — 4

1 lb. ground round steak
½ c. minced onion
¼ c. minced bell pepper
1 T. butter
1 t. hot sauce (Tabasco)
1 T. Worcestershire sauce
4 large bell peppers
¼ t. pepper
1 t. salt

Saute bell pepper and onion in butter. Add ground beef and other ingredients. Simmer for 30 minutes. Core peppers, boil until tender. Stuff with meat mixture. Top with grated cheese if desired. Bake in 300°F. oven for 30 minutes.

Minnie Van Williams, Livingston H. S.
Livingston, Alabama

STUFFED GREEN PEPPERS
Number of Servings — 4

¼ c. finely chopped onions
2 T. butter
1 c. 1 inch bread cubes
1 lb. ground beef
1 c. drained canned tomatoes
¼ t. chili powder
½ t. salt
⅛ t. pepper
⅛ t. garlic powder

Brown onions in one half of butter. Add bread cubes and brown. Remove onions and bread cubes. Brown hamburger in rest of butter. Combine onions, bread cubes, hamburger, tomatoes, and seasonings. Spoon mixture into green peppers which have been parboiled five minutes. Bake in 350°F. oven for 20 minutes.

Mrs. Myrtle Weed, Wilson Jr. H. S.
Bozeman, Montana

STUFFED BELL PEPPERS
Number of Servings — 6

6 (average size) bell (green) peppers
1 pound ground beef
3 T. oleomargarine or bacon grease
1 medium onion, chopped fine
2 cups tomatoes (one No. 2½ can)
1 t. celery salt
1 c. bread crumbs
1 T. parsley, chopped fine
Salt and pepper to taste

Cut tops off pepper about ¾ inch down. Remove all seeds. Parboil about 5 to 8 minutes. Brown meat in fat; add onion and brown slightly. Add all the other ingredients and bring to a simmer. Mixture should be stiff enough to hold shape of a spoon. Stuff peppers. Place tops on and place in a baking dish. Add approximately ½ cup water. Bake at 350°F. for 45 minutes to one hour.

Mrs. Melba M. Sanders, Pike County H. S.
Brundidge, Alabama

STUFFED PEPPERS
Number of Servings — 6

6 green peppers (seeded)
2 lbs. ground beef
2 T. salt
½ c. bread crumbs
1 egg beaten
½ c. catsup
½ c. tomato juice
1 small onion

Boil peppers until tender. Mix other ingredients and stuff. Bake at 350°F. about 1 hour.

Maria Adams, Spring Garden H. S.
Chatham, Virginia

PIZZA
Number of Servings — 6

1 lb. ground meat (beef)
1 medium onion, minced
½ to 1 t. salt, to taste
¼ t. pepper
¼ t. garlic salt, if desired
1 t. basil
1 t. oregano
1 8-oz. can tomato sauce
1 c. grated cheese (cheddar or mozzarella)

Brown meat in large frying pan. Add onion and cook on medium heat until onion is transparent. Add seasonings, salt and pepper. Use ½ of dough from recipe of yeast bread (use rest for rolls). Roll dough to fit 12 inch round pan (or can use cookie sheet and make it rectangular pizza). Dough should be thin. Oil pan, place dough on pan, make a good high ridge at the edge. Place meat mixture on dough. Add tomato sauce. Sprinkle grated cheese on top. Bake 20-25 minutes at 375°F. Crust should be a golden brown.

YEAST BREAD—FOR PIZZA

1 cake or package yeast
¼ c. warm water
1 c. milk
1½ T. shortening
1 T. sugar
1 t. salt
3 c. sifted flour
Extra shortening and flour

Soften the yeast in the warm water. Scald milk, add shortening, salt and sugar. Cool to lukewarm. Combine yeast with milk, in a large bowl. Add enough flour to make a stiff dough, mix thoroughly, and turn out on a floured board. Knead 5-10 minutes—keep dough soft. Place the dough in a greased bowl, brush the top with shortening, cover with wax paper and towel. Allow to rise in a warm place to double in size. Punch down with fist. Fold over so smooth side is on top, cover and let rise again. Turn out on board. Divide in half, cover with bowl and allow to rest 10 minutes. Roll out ½ for pizza, ½ for rolls. Shape rolls, place in greased pan and let rise. Bake at 400°F. Follow pizza recipe for finishing pizza.

Mrs. Ruth M. Wachtler, Chowchilla Union H. S.
Chowchilla, California

INDIVIDUAL PIZZA PIES
Number of Servings — 10

1 can tomato paste
½ t. salt
½ t. Worcestershire sauce
½ t. garlic salt
2 or 3 drops tabasco
¼ t. thyme
1 can biscuits
½ lb. ground beef
¾-1 c. grated cheese
Oregano

Combine first six ingredients. Mix well. On floured board, roll each biscuit to a thin circle 4 inches across. Cover with thin layer of uncooked ground beef. Spread with tomato paste mixture and sprinkle with sharp cheese and oregano. Place on ungreased cookie sheet and bake in 425°F. oven for 10 minutes.

Mrs. R. J. Traynor, Boise City H. S.
Boise City, Oklahoma

TINY PIZZAS
Number of Servings — 5

1 can tomato paste
½ t. salt
1½ t. Worcestershire sauce
½ t. garlic salt
¼ t. tabasco sauce
¾ lbs. ground beef
¾ c. grated sharp cheese
1 can biscuits
Oregano

Combine the first five ingredients; mix well. Roll or stretch each biscuit to a thin circle about 4 inches in diameter. Cover each thin circle with a layer (about ¼ inch) of uncooked ground beef. Spread with tomato paste mixture, sprinkle with cheese and oregano. Place on an ungreased baking sheet and bake for 10 minutes at 425°F. Serve hot.

Mrs. Ina Mae Perry, Lexington H. S.
Lexington, Texas

JUMBO PIZZA LOAF
Number of Servings — 8 good sized servings

1 loaf French bread about 18x4
¾ lbs. ground beef
⅓ c. grated chopped onion
¼ c. finely chopped onion
¼ c. finely chopped ripe olives
1 t. salt
½ t. oregano
Dash of pepper
1 6-oz. can tomato paste (⅔ c.)
3 tomatoes, thinly sliced
5 slices sharp process cheese, halved

Cut loaf in half lengthwise. Combine meat, Parmesan cheese, onion, olives, seasonings and tomato paste; spread evenly on each half loaf. Broil about five inches from heat 12 minutes, or until meat is

(Continued on Next Page)

done. Top with tomato and cheese slices; broil 1 to 2 minutes, just till cheese begins to melt.

Margaret Ann Brown, Peabody H. S.
Peabody, Kansas

TEXAS STYLE PIZZA
Number of Servings — 8

1 loaf French bread (18"x4")
¾ lb. ground beef
⅓ c. grated Parmesan cheese
¼ c. finely chopped onion
¼ c. chopped ripe olives
1 t. salt
½ t. oregano
Dash of pepper
1 6-oz. can tomato paste
3 thinly sliced tomatoes
3 slices sharp process cheese, halved

Cut loaf in half lengthwise. Combine the meat, Parmesan cheese, onion, olives, seasoning and tomato paste; spread evenly on both halves of the loaf. Broil about 5 inches from flame for 12 minutes or until meat is done. Top with tomato and cheese slice. Broil 1 to 2 minutes, just until cheese begins to melt. Makes 8 servings. (Can leave off tomatoes and place cheese slices like lacing on football).

Jan Harris, Calallen H. S.
Calallen, Texas

PIZZA BURGERS
Number of Servings — 8

1 6-oz. can tomato paste
¼ t. catsup
1½ t. oregano
¾ t. garlic salt
2 T. flour
½ c. instant milk (in dry form)
¾ c. water
1 c. grated process American cheese
1 lb. ground lean beef
1 T. shortening
8 sandwich buns
½ c. grated Parmesan cheese

Mix tomato paste, catsup, oregano and garlic salt in small bowl. Mix in saucepan flour and instant milk, add water gradually until smooth. Cook and stir over medium heat, but do not boil. Add grated cheese and stir until melted. Brown ground beef in the shortening. Arrange on cookie sheet, cut sides up—8 round buns—split and toasted. Spread tomato mixture over each, top with cheese sauce. Cover cheese sauce with equal parts of cooked meat, sprinkle Parmesan cheese over top. Bake near center of oven 12 to 15 minutes, or until bubbly hot.

Mrs. Mary Jane Shipway, Allegany H. S.
Cumberland, Maryland

PIZZA-BURGERS
Number of Servings — 8

4 hamburger buns
¾ c. chili sauce
1 lb. ground beef
1 T. minced onion (optional)
1 t. salt
½ t. oregano
¼ t. red pepper
1 T. chopped parsley
4 slices Provolone (or American cheese)

Split buns and spread with chili sauce, using about ½ cup. Mix beef with remaining chili sauce, onion, parsley, salt, oregano, and pepper. Divide into 8 patties. Broil 3 minutes on each side, 3 inches from broiler unit. Place patties on bun halves, top each with 2 strips of cheese, criss-crossed. Return to broiler for 2 or 3 minutes or until cheese has melted.

Mrs. Betty Dean Suber, Whitmire H. S.
Whitmire, South Carolina

HOMEMADE CHILI
(in 30 minutes)
Number of Servings — 6-8

1 lb. ground beef
2 (8-oz.) cans tomato paste
1 (1-lb.) can kidney beans
½ c. finely cut onion
1 heavy pinch garlic powder
½ c. finely cut green pepper
1 t. salt
Black pepper to taste
2 T. bacon drippings
1 t. chili powder

Using a large skillet or Dutch oven, start browning meat with garlic powder in the bacon drippings. When the meat begins to turn color, add the onions so that they will be limp and translucent about the time the meat is browned. Add green pepper and tomato sauce and cook the mixture for about 10 minutes, stirring occasionally. Add beans, juice and all salt and pepper. Cook 15 minutes. Add chili powder just before removing from heat.

Mrs. Christine Dale, Toccopola H. S.
University, Mississippi

CHILI CON CARNE
Number of Servings — 4

1 large onion, chopped
1 lb. ground beef
½ lb. bulk pork sausage
No. 2 can tomatoes
No. 2 can kidney beans
1-2 T. chili powder
½-1 t. salt

Brown meat in large kettle; crumble with fork. Add rest of ingredients. Simmer 1 hour.

Eleanor Weatherhead, Northridge H. S.
Dayton, Ohio

CHILI CON CARNE
Number of Servings — 4-6

2 T. bacon fat
¾ c. chopped onion
1 clove garlic
1 lb. ground beef
1 T. flour
½ t. salt
⅛ t. pepper
2 or 3 T. chili powder
1 No. 2 can kidney beans
1 No. 2½ can tomatoes
1 6½-oz. can tomato puree

Heat bacon fat in a large deep skillet. Chop onions and garlic very fine. Cook this mixture in fat until it turns slightly yellow. Add meat, sprinkle with flour, salt, pepper and chili powder. Cook over medium heat, until meat is browned. Add tomatoes, tomato puree and drained beans. Cover and simmer for one hour.

This makes a fine meal for 4 to 6 persons on cold winter nights. Try it with a tossed salad and your favorite dressing. Crackers or crusty bread and lime sherbert for dessert.

Madeline Cleere, Lawrence County H. S.
Moulton, Alabama

CHILI
Number of Servings — 3-4

2 lbs. hamburger meat
1½ t. salt
1½ t. black pepper
1½-3 t. chili powder
1 clove garlic or ¼ t. garlic powder
1 medium onion (approx. 2″ in diameter)
2 cans tomato sauce

Combine all ingredients except tomato sauce in heavy skillet. Cook until meat loses its pink color and onion becomes transparent. Add tomato sauce and simmer 30 minutes to an hour. This is especially good served with rice and a green salad for a quick and easy meal.

Mrs. Elizabeth Cleveland, Nederland H. S.
Nederland, Texas

QUICK CHILI SOUP
Number of Servings — 4-6

1 lb. hamburger
1 small onion, chopped
1 No. 2 can red kidney beans
1 can tomato soup
1 t. chili powder
1 t. salt
½ t. pepper

Crumble hamburger. Brown hamburger and chopped onion in a heavy skillet. Add beans, tomato soup, and seasonings. Simmer 15-20 minutes.

Melba Baldwin, Litchfield H. S.
Litchfield, Nebraska

CHILI CON CARNE PIE
Number of Servings — 4

½ c. flour
2 T. melted shortening
½ c. cornmeal
2 t. baking powder
1 egg
½ c. milk
¼ t. salt
1 lb. hamburger
1 t. chili powder
1 16-oz. can tomatoes
1 16-oz. can chili beans
1 small can tomato sauce
1 small onion
2 T. shortening

Mix cornmeal, flour, baking powder, and salt. Add egg and milk and beat thoroughly. Then add shortening and stir until completely mixed. Grease bottom of 8 x 8 inch baking dish and pour ¾ of above mixture in dish. Scramble hamburger in 2 tablespoons shortening with onions added. When done add tomatoes, tomato sauce and chili beans with additional chili powder. Simmer for 20 minutes. Pour in baking dish and top with remaining cornbread mixture. Bake in preheated (375°F.) oven for 25 to 30 minutes.

Glenyce Nell Chinn, Ranum H. S.
Westminster, Colorado

BROWN'S SPECIAL CHILI
Number of Servings — 6

1 lb. ground beef
1 can whole tomatoes
1 6-oz. can tomato paste
1 4-oz. can mushrooms (button)
1 medium onion, chopped
1 medium green pepper, chopped
1 can kidney beans
Salt and pepper to taste

Combine all ingredients in large saucepan or kettle. Simmer until vegetables are cooked through and beef is brown. Serve over fluffy white rice.

Charlotte Batalden, Madison Public Schools
Madison, Minnesota

"SUMMER CHILI" ONE DISH MEAL
Number of Servings — 6-8

1½ lbs. ground beef
1 chopped onion

Brown together for five minutes. Run one number two can tomatoes through colander. Add to meat and onions, with one number two can red beans. Add chili powder to suit taste. Let simmer until thick, about twenty minutes. Place Fritoes over the dinner plate. Add chopped lettuce, then sliced tomatoes over Fritoes, and pour chili over the lettuce, tomatoes and Fritoes and serve.

Mrs. Zelma Gum Goben, Antelope Valley H. S.
Lancaster, California

CHILI MOI
Number of Servings — 6-8

2 T. fat
1 onion
1 lb. ground beef
1 c. catsup
1 green pepper
1 c. spaghetti (cooked)
2 T. chili powder
2 T. sugar
Salt, paprika

Chop onion. Brown onion in hot fat. Add remaining ingredients, cook slowly 30-40 minutes. Serve hot.

Mrs. B. M. Davenport, Boyd H. S.
Frederick, Oklahoma

CHILI
Number of Servings — 4

2 lbs. ground beef (or chuck)
1 T. fat
¼ c. minced onion
1 t. powdered garlic
2 T. chili powder
½ t. red pepper
1 t. salt
1 can condensed tomato soup
½ c. tomato puree
1 c. water

Brown onion in hot fat; add ground meat. Stir until beef is broken into small bits and semi-browned. Add garlic, chili powder, salt and red pepper. Cook until beef is well browned. Remove excess fat from skillet, preferably before adding spices. Add remaining ingredients. Cook or simmer 30 minutes to 1 hour.

Carolyn Smith, Van Buren H. S.
Van Buren, Arkansas

MEXICAN CASSEROLE
Number of Servings — 8

1 lb. ground beef
1 large onion
¼ t. salt
1 can chili (1 lb.)
1 can (10-oz.) tomato soup
1 medium size package Fritos
1 c. grated cheese
Dash of catsup

Put ground beef in skillet and brown. Then let simmer until done. Add chopped onion and salt. Add chili to tomato soup. Let simmer while stirring. Mixture should be consistency of gravy. If dry, add small amount of water. Line large casserole with ½ of Fritos. Pour in the meat mixture, then rest of Fritos on top. Sprinkle cheese and catsup on top. Bake in 400°F. oven until cheese is melted. Serve hot.

Pauline K. Brown, Lone Wolf H. S.
Lone Wolf, Oklahoma

BEANS — ARIZONA STYLE
Plenty of meat, and plenty hot
Number of Servings — 8-10

2 c. brown beans
4 c. water (more if needed)
2 t. table salt
1 t. garlic salt
2 t. chili powder
1½ lbs. ground beef
¼ c. chopped onion
2 T. chopped fresh hot pepper
2 bouillon cubes
1 6-oz. can tomato sauce

Soak beans and cook at low temperature until tender (3-4 hours). Add salt, garlic salt, chili powder, ground beef, chopped onions and pepper. Continue to cook for 20 to 30 minutes. Add tomato sauce and bouillon cubes. Keep hot until time to serve. Can be stored and reheated.

Serve large portions. Hard rolls; a relish of carrot and celery sticks, pickles, and olives; and a simple fruit dessert completes a meal. Ideal for pot luck or picnics.

Ellen S. Massey, Advisor Shoshone FHA
Shoshone, Idaho

TAMALE PIE
Number of Servings — 6-8

1 lb. ground meat
1 large onion, minced
1 clove garlic, minced
1 or more T. chili powder
1 t. oregano
1 t. marjoram
2 c. water
1 can Contidena tomato paste

Brown onion, garlic, and meat. Add other seasoning, water and paste. Simmer 10 minutes. Pour into pyrex dish, top with cornmeal mush, and cook in moderate oven 30 minutes.
Mush—½ cup cornmeal stirred gradually into 2 cups boiling salted water (stirring constantly). If mush becomes lumpy, beat until smooth with rotary beater.

Mrs. Ruby Walker, Kate Griffin Jr. H. S.
Meridian, Mississippi

OKLAHOMA TAMALE PIE
Number of Servings — 8

2 c. hominy grits
6 c. salted water
½ c. chopped green pepper
3 T. cooking fat
1 c. sliced onion
1 minced clove garlic
1 lb. hamburger
½ lb. lean pork
2 c. condensed beef bouillon
2 T. chili powder
Sliced olives
Grated cheddar cheese

(Continued on Next Page)

Boil hominy grits in salted water for 30 minutes. In the meantime saute chopped green peppers, cooking fat, sliced onion, and garlic. Cook until tender, then add hamburger and pork. Stir and cook until red color disappears, then add bouillon and chili powder. Simmer for 45 minutes. On the bottom of a shallow baking dish spread a ½ inch layer of grits, 1 inch layer of meat mixture, layer of sliced ripe olives, and layer of grated cheddar cheese. Repeat the layers and top with remaining grits. Cover and bake at 325°F. for 1 hour.

Ola Maye Veley, Waynoka H. S.
Waynoka, Oklahoma

HOT TAMALE PIE
Number of Servings — 8

2 c. cornmeal
6 c. boiling water
2 T. fat
2 lbs. hamburger meat
1 clove garlic
1 large onion, chopped
1 green pepper, chopped
1 No. 2 can tomatoes
3 t. salt
2 T. chili powder

Sift cornmeal into rapidly boiling water, stirring constantly. Cook until thick and salt to taste. Line bottom and sides of large (11 x 7 x 2 inch) baking dish with the mush, reserving some for the top. Brown the hamburger, garlic, onion and green pepper in the melted fat; add tomatoes, seasonings and enough water to simmer 10 minutes. Turn into mush lined pan and dot with remaining mush. Bake in a 350°F. oven for 30 minutes.

Mrs. Maurine Taylor, East Mountain H. S.
Gilmer, Texas

GOLUBTZI (CABBAGE BUNDLES)
Number of Servings — 6

1 large head cabbage
1 lb. hamburger
1 c. rice, cooked
1 onion, minced
2 T. fat
1 t. salt
¼ t. pepper
2 8-oz. cans tomato sauce
½ c. sour cream

Remove outer leaves from cabbage head, and cook in salt water about 5 minutes. Drain and cool. Slightly brown onion in fat. Add meat, cooked or minute rice, and seasoning. Drop a tablespoon of mixture on the stem end of each cabbage leaf, roll and fasten with toothpicks. Place in baking dish and pour tomato sauce over the bundles. Bake at 350°F. for 1 hour. Add sour cream 5 minutes before serving.

Mrs. Laura Martens, Shafter H. S.
Shafter, California

CORN BREAD TAMALE PIE
Number of Servings — 6

1 lb. ground beef
1 large onion, chopped
1 can tomato soup
2 c. water
1 t. salt
¼ t. pepper
1 T. chili powder
1 cup whole kernel corn (drained)
½ c. chopped green pepper
¾ c. cornmeal
1 T. flour
1 T. sugar
½ t. salt
1 beaten egg
⅓ c. milk
1 T. Mazola
1½ t. baking powder

Brown ground beef and onion in skillet; add tomato soup, water, seasonings, corn and green pepper; simmer for 15 minutes. For topping, sift together dry ingredients. Add beaten egg and milk stirring lightly until combined. Fold in melted fat. Place meat mixture in greased baking dish, cover with cornbread topping. The topping will disappear but will rise during baking and form a good layer of cornbread. Bake in hot oven (425°F.) 20 to 25 minutes until cornbread is brown.

Mrs. Marion Montgomery, McKinney H. S.
McKinney, Kentucky

STUFFED CABBAGE ROLLS
Number of Servings — 4

1 head cabbage (2 lbs.)
1 lb. ground beef
1 T. pre-cooked rice
2 T. chopped onion
1 t. salt
¼ t. pepper
¼ t. paprika
2 T. bacon drippings
1 large onion, minced
¼ t. paprika
½ t. salt
Dash pepper
½ c. hot water
2 8-oz. cans tomato sauce

Wash, core, and cook whole cabbage in boiling water until barely tender. Separate about 8 large leaves from cabbage. Combine beef, rice, onion, salt, pepper, and paprika; place one spoonful of meat mixture on each cabbage leaf; roll up, tucking in ends to make neat compact bundles. In hot fat in Dutch oven saute minced onion, salt, pepper, and paprika about 10 minutes. Add hot water; place cabbage rolls on top of onion. Top with tomato sauce. Cook over low heat about 2 hours.

Mrs. Pat Thompson, Central H. S.
Delhi, Louisiana

CALIFORNIA TAMALE PIE
Number of Servings — 8-10

1 onion, chopped
1 green pepper, chopped
1 clove garlic, minced
3 T. salad oil
1 lb. ground beef
2 cans (8-oz. each) tomato sauce
1 can (12-oz.) whole kernel corn
1 can pitted ripe olives
2 c. milk
1 c. cornmeal
1 t. salt
1 t. Spanish seasoning powder

Saute onion, green pepper, and garlic in oil until limp. Add ground beef; stirring, cook until meat is brown and crumbly. Pour in tomato sauce, corn, olives, and milk. Heat, then gradually stir in cornmeal. Season with salt, Spanish seasoning. Turn into a greased 3-quart casserole. Cover and bake in a moderately slow oven (325°F.) for 1 hour; uncover, and continue baking for 30 minutes.

Mrs. Carole Bajala, South H. S.
Bakersfield, California

CHILI PORCUPINE BALLS
Number of Servings — 4

1 lb. ground beef
1 lb. ground lean pork
1 beaten egg
½ c. milk
2 T. chopped onion
1 t. chili powder
⅔ c. rice
1 t. chili powder
2 t. salt
1 No. 2 can (2½ c.) tomatoes
1 t. salt
2½ c. water

Mix meat; add egg, milk, rice, 1 teaspoon chili powder, and 2 teaspoons salt. Form in 1½-inch balls; brown in fat. Combine tomatoes, water, onion, remaining seasonings; bring to a boil; drop meat balls in. Cover; cook slowly 1½ hours. Chili powder may be omitted.

Mrs. Jessie Sue Smith, West Point H. S.
Cullman, Alabama

HAMBURGER CHOW MEIN
Number of Servings — 4

1 lb. ground beef
2 c. chopped celery

1 c. chopped onion
1 c. raw rice
⅓ c. soy sauce
½ t. salt
½ t. pepper
2 c. boiling water
1 can cream of mushroom soup

Brown meat. Add rest of ingredients and bake about one hour in 350° oven. Stir several times during baking.

Mrs. John Trierweiler, Balaton H. S.
Balaton, Minn.

CHOP SUEY
Number of Servings — 6-8

1½ lbs. hamburger (browned)
1 c. celery (chopped)
1 c. onions (chopped)
½ c. raw rice (not minute)
1 can cream of mushroom soup
1 can chicken soup
3 c. water
2 T. soy sauce

Brown hamburger, then add celery, onions, rice, soup, water and soy sauce. Bake at 350° for ½ hour. Remove from oven, add 1 can chow mein noodles and continue baking for 1 hour.

Doris Balbach, Warren Community H. S.
Warren, Illinois

BEEF SWIRLS
Number of Servings — 4

1 lb. ground beef
1 c. fine fresh bread crumbs
¾ c. grated cheddar cheese
¼ c. chopped green pepper
¼ c. grated onion
1 t. Worcestershire sauce
1 t. salt
⅛ t. pepper
1 egg, well beaten
1 can condensed tomato soup

Combine bread crumbs, cheese, green pepper, onion, Worcestershire sauce, salt, pepper, egg, and half of tomato soup. Gently press beef into triangle on waxed paper. Spread with bread crumbs mixture; roll as for jelly roll. Cut into 4 slices. Place in shallow pan. Add remaining soup. Bake at 350°F. 35 minutes.

Mrs. Glen Byars, Fairfield H. S.
Fairfield, Illinois

FOR ADDITIONAL GROUND BEEF RECIPES SEE CASSEROLES, FOREIGN DISHES AND SANDWICH SECTIONS

Veal

VEAL CHART
Veal Cuts and How to Cook Them

Retail Cuts   Wholesale Cuts   Retail Cuts

Standing Rump Roast   **Rolled Rump Roast**

— Roast or Braise —

Loin Chop   1 **Sirloin Steak**   3 **Kidney Chop**

— Braise or Panfry —

Crown Roast   **Rib Chop** (Frenched)   **Rib Roast**

— Roast — ● — Braise or Panfry — ● — Roast —

Blade Roast   **Arm Roast**

— Roast or Braise —

1 **Blade Steak**   2 **Arm Steak**

— Braise or Panfry —

Rolled Shoulder Roast   **City Chicken**

— Roast or Braise — ● — Braise, Panfry —

LEG (Round)

LOIN

RIB   BREAST

SHOULDER

SHANK

Heel of Round   **Hind Shank**

— Braise or Cook in Liquid —

Round Steak (Cutlet)   **Leg (Round) Center-Cut Roast**

— Braise or Panfry — ● — Roast or Braise —

Scallops   **Rosettes**

— Braise or Panfry —

Breast

— Roast, Braise, Cook in Liquid —

Mock Chicken Legs   **Loaf**

— Braise or Panfry — ● — Roast (Bake) —

Riblets   **Stew Meat**

— Braise or Cook in Liquid —

Fore Shank   **Patties**

— Braise, Cook in Liquid — ● — Braise or Panfry —

NATIONAL LIVE STOCK AND MEAT BOARD

407 South Dearborn Street, Chicago 5, Illinois

Selection of VEAL Cuts

WHOLESALE CUTS	RETAIL CUTS	CHARACTERISTICS	COOKING METHODS
Leg (Round)	Shank Half of Leg	Lower half of leg. Hock and part of shank bone usually removed.	Roast; braise
	Rump Half of Leg	Upper half of leg, including the rump.	Roast; braise
	Center Cut of Leg (Round)	Leg with rump and shank off.	Roast; braise
	Round Steak (Cutlet)	Same muscle and bone structure as beef round steaks.	Braise; panfry
	Standing Rump Roast	Contains aitch or rump bone, tail bone, and usually a part of leg bone.	Roast; braise
	Rolled Rump Roast	Boneless roll.	Roast; braise
	Heel of Round	Wedge-shaped boneless piece—same as in beef.	Braise; cook in liquid
	Hind Shank	Shank bone surrounded by varying amounts of shank meat.	Cook in liquid; braise
	Scallops	Thin boneless slices from any part of carcass.	Braise; panfry
	Rosettes	Solid boneless pieces or slices wrapped with bacon.	Braise; panfry
Loin	Sirloin Roast	Corresponds to sirloin of beef. Contains hip and back bones.	Roast; braise
	Sirloin Steak	Same as above except cut into steaks.	Braise; panfry
	Loin Roast	Corresponds to beef short loin. Contains back bone and three separate muscles—loin eye, tenderloin and flank.	Roast; braise
	Loin Chop	Same as above except cut into chops. Corresponds to porterhouse, T-bone, and club beef steaks.	Braise; panfry
	Kidney Chop	Cut to contain cross section of kidney. Made from rib end of loin.	Braise; panfry
Rib	Rib Roast	Similar to standing beef rib roast.	Roast
	Crown Roast	Rib sections "frenched" and formed into shape of crown.	Roast
	Rib Chop	Contains rib bone and rib eye, except chops cut between ribs have no rib bone.	Braise; panfry
Shouder	Blade Roast	Includes that section of the shoulder which contains the blade bone.	Roast; braise
	Blade Steak (Chop)	Contains blade bone and rib bone except chops cut between ribs have no rib bone.	Braise; panfry
	Arm Roast	Includes arm section of shoulder. Contains arm bone and cross sections of 3 to 5 ribs.	Roast; braise
	Arm Steak (Chop)	Same as above except cut into slices.	Braise; panfry
	Rolled Shoulder Roast	Boneless roll.	Roast; braise
	City Chicken	Boneless cubes of veal fastened together on a wooden or metal skewer.	Braise
Breast	Breast	Corresponds to short plate and brisket of beef. Thin, flat cut containing rib ends and breast bone.	Braise; cook in liquid
	Breast with pocket	Same as above with pocket cut between ribs and lean.	Roast; braise
	Rolled Breast	Boned and rolled breast.	Roast; braise
	Riblets	Breast bone is removed (usually). Breast is separated into riblets by cutting between ribs.	Braise; cook in liquid
	Stew Meat	Small bone-in or boneless pieces of meat. Also made from the shoulder, shank and leg.	Braise; cook in liquid
Fore Shank	Fore Shank	Contains considerable bone and connective tissue. Varying amounts of lean. Rich in gelatin-forming substance.	Braise; cook in liquid
Ground Veal	Loaf and Patties	Usually made from flank, breast, shank and neck.	Roast; braise; panfry
	Mock Chicken Legs	Ground veal molded into shape of chicken legs with wooden skewer to represent leg bone.	Braise; panfry

Arm Roast (Shoulder)

Roast, Braise

Blade Roast (Shoulder)

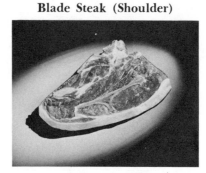

Roast, Braise

Rib Roast

Roast

Arm Steak (Shoulder)

Braise, Panfry

Blade Steak (Shoulder)

Braise, Panfry

Rib Chop

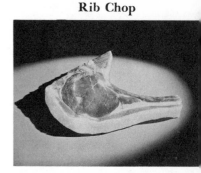

Braise, Panfry

Rolled Shoulder

Roast, Braise

Breast

Roast, Braise, Cook in Liquid

Riblets (Breast)

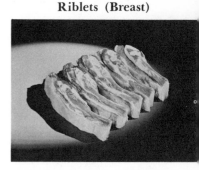

Braise, Cook in Liquid

Fore Shank

Braise, Cook in Liquid

City Chicken

Braise, Panfry

Mock Chicken Legs

Braise, Panfry

the Best Methods for Cooking Them

Standing Rump

Roast, Braise

Center Cut of Leg

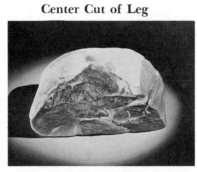

Roast, Braise

Shank Half of Leg

Roast, Braise

Boneless Rump

Roast, Braise

Round Steak (Cutlet)

Braise, Panfry

Heel of Round

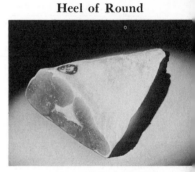

Braise, Cook in Liquid

Sirloin Roast

Roast, Braise

Sirloin Steak

Braise, Panfry

Boneless Stew

Braise, Cook in Liquid

Loin Roast

Roast, Braise

Loin Chop

Braise, Panfry

Kidney Chop

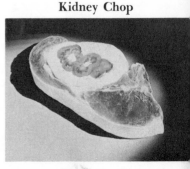

Braise, Panfry

VEAL—Methods of Cooking

VEAL HAS VERY LITTLE FAT. In high quality veal, the fat is clear, firm and white. The lean is light pink with no marbling. The texture of the lean is very fine, fairly firm—though not so firm as beef— and velvety in appearance. Since veal is the young of beef, the bones are porous and soft, with a reddish tinge; the ends of some of them are still in the cartilage stage.

Most wholesale veal cuts are very much like those of beef, except they are considerably smaller, consequently the retail cuts made from them are smaller. In general, veal cuts are from one-third to one-half the size of comparable cuts of beef. The cuts from the loin of veal are called loin chops instead of steaks, as they are in beef. The loin of veal is also sold as a roast. The chops from the rib section are known as rib chops.

Veal has certain characteristics which make its cooking somewhat different from that of the other meats. It lacks fat and, while it is tender, it has considerable connective tissue which means that it requires long, slow cooking. Veal is delicate in color, becoming lighter when cooked. It also has a fine delicate flavor. Cooking methods which intensify color and make the flavor more pronounced should be used. The best methods of cooking veal are roasting, frying and braising. Veal is also cooked in liquid for stews. Veal chops, steaks and cutlets are best if fried or braised. Rich, colorful sauces and gravies are delicious with veal. For broiling or panbroiling, only loin and rib chops from high quality heavy veal should be used; and a lower cooking temperature than that for beef and lamb is advisable. Always cook veal to the well-done stage.

TIME-TABLE FOR COOKING VEAL[1]

CUT	ROASTED AT 300° F. OVEN TEMPERATURE		BROILED		BRAISED	COOKED IN LIQUID
	Meat Thermometer Reading	Time	Meat Thermometer Reading	Total Time	Total Time	Total Time
Leg	Degrees F. 170	Minutes per lb. 25	Degrees F.	Minutes	Hours	Hours
Loin	170	30 to 35	Veal is seldom broiled			
Rack	170	30 to 35				
Shoulder Whole	170	25				
Rolled	170	40 to 45				
Cushion	170	30 to 35				
Breast Stuffed	170	40 to 45			1½ to 2	
Rolled	170	40 to 45			1½ to 2	
Loaf	170	25 to 30				
Birds					¾ to 1	
Chops					¾ to 1	
Steaks					¾ to 1	
Stew						2 to 2½

[1]*For frying see discussion page 6.*

VEAL BIRDS
Number of Servings — 8

2 slices veal steak, from round, cut very thin
Salt and pepper to season
For breading the birds:
1 egg
2 T. milk
Flour
Fine bread crumbs

Cut veal into four-inch squares. Season with salt and pepper. Place a spoonful of your favorite dressing in center and roll meat around it. Fasten with skewers. Roll in flour, dip in egg and milk and then roll in crumbs. Brown in skillet, place in a casserole with 1 cup liquid (water, milk or cream). Bake covered at 325° F. for 1½ hours. Uncover last ½ hour.

BASIC DRESSING

3 c. dry bread cubes—slightly moistened
    with milk
1 small onion, minced and browned in butter
2 t. lemon juice
⅓ c. melted butter
½ t. sage
Salt and pepper to taste

Toss all ingredients together lightly in a bowl. Use as is or with variations.

Mrs. Marie Strand, Stillwater Jr. H. S.
Stillwater, Minnesota

VEAL BIRDS
Number of Servings — 5

1 lb. veal cutlets, sliced very thin
1 egg
1 t. salt
½ t. celery salt
3 dashes pepper
⅓ c. flour
¾ c. boiling water
⅛ t. thyme
2 ozs. salt pork
½ onion
1 T. lemon juice
¾ c. soft bread crumbs
2 T. butter
¾ c. milk

Cut veal into 5 pieces. Beat egg slightly. Add dry seasoning materials. Put salt pork and onion through a meat chopper. Add to egg mixture. Add lemon juice and bread crumbs. Place a portion on each piece of veal. Fasten together with toothpicks. Sprinkle with flour. Melt butter. Brown veal birds. Add remaining flour to hot fat. Stir. Add boiling water and milk. Cover and cook in moderate oven 275° F. for 1½ hours or until tender.

Mrs. Vivian Harwood, Harbor Beach Com. H. S.
Harbor Beach, Michigan

VEAL BIRDS
Number of Servings — 4

1 lb. veal steak
1 c. bread crumbs
1 T. minced onion
½ t. sage
⅔ t. salt
¼ t. pepper
3 T. fat
1 c. evaporated milk
½ c. water

Cut meat into portions for serving; pound to spread. Combine crumbs, onion, salt and seasonings, add enough moisture so that it will stick together. (I like to use melted butter or margarine.) Put a little on each slice of meat. Roll up, fasten with toothpicks or tie. Brown in heated fat. Add liquids. Cover and bake at 350° F. one hour.

Joan M. Kleinert, White Bear Lake Sr. H. S.
White Bear Lake, Minnesota

STUFFED VEAL BIRDS
Number of Servings — 6

1½ lbs. veal steak cut into six oblong pieces
4 c. dry cubes of bread
¼ c. chopped celery
¼ c. chopped onion
1½ t. salt
¼ t. pepper
¼ t. poultry seasoning
½ c. melted butter or shortening

Moisten with liquid. Combine all ingredients and divide on six oblongs of meat. Roll and fasten with toothpicks. Brown in hot shortening. Add ½ cup hot water. Cover with lid and simmer for 1½ hours.

Margaret S. Yoder, Upper Perkiomen H. S.
East Greenville, Pennsylvania

VEAL BIRDS
Number of Servings — 6

2 lbs. veal cutlets, sliced thin
2 c. bread crumbs, stale
½ t. sage
1 T. parsley, minced
¼ t. salt
⅛ t. pepper
4 T. fat, melted
2 T. onion, chopped

Combine bread crumbs with seasonings. Blend with melted fat. Add stock or milk to hold. Add one beaten egg. Cut veal in 3-inch squares. Place stuffing on each, roll, tie with string or fasten with toothpicks. Brown in hot fat. Place in casserole, cover with 1 cup hot water. Cook in slow oven 1½ to 2 hours.

Lola T. St. Romain, Bunkie H. S.
Bunkie, Louisiana

VEAL BIRDS
Number of Servings — 6

2 lbs. veal steaks, ½ inch thick
2 c. soft bread crumbs
2 T. salt pork ground
½ t. salt
2 T. water
¼ t. paprika
1 T. grated onion
¼ t. celery salt
2 T. melted butter
4 T. fat, for browning
1 egg

Mix all the ingredients for the dressing well, and form into small balls. Cut the thin veal steak into squares and place a ball of dressing in the center of each. Wrap meat around it and fasten with string or toothpick. Brown in the fat and place birds in casserole. Bake at medium heat for an hour covered part of the time.

Mrs. Nora Estrem, Battle Lake H. S.
Battle Lake, Minnesota

VEAL BIRDS
Number of Servings — 5

2 lbs. veal shoulder steak cut about ⅜ in. thick
2 c. coarse fresh bread crumbs
1 T. chopped onion
1 egg, beaten
½ t. poultry seasoning
2 t. salt
Dash black pepper
½ c. meat stock (or 1 bouillon cube in
    ½ c. hot water

Wipe steak with damp cloth and cut into serving-size portions. Combine remaining ingredients thoroughly. Pile a portion of the dressing in center of each piece of veal, roll up, and tie securely with fine twine. Thicken liquid with flour mixed to a smooth paste with cold water, using 2 tablespoons flour to each cup of liquid and stirring until it boils.

Jeanne Geers, Leroy Community H. S.
Leroy, Michigan

SCALLOPED VEAL
Number of Servings — 8

1 lb. veal
1 medium onion
3 eggs
1 c. bread crumbs
1 c. broth
1 c. milk
¾ t. salt

Cook cut up veal with minced onion until tender. Broth should yield 1 cupful. Combine all ingredients. Pour into buttered custard cups. Set in pan of water to bake. Bake at 350°F. for 30 minutes. Serve with mushroom sauce.

Mrs. Merle Twesme, Arcadia H. S.
Arcadia, Wisconsin

VEAL PARMESAN
Number of Servings — 4

¼ c. enriched flour
½ t. garlic salt
1 t. salt
½ t. paprika
Dash pepper
4 veal loin chops, ¾ inch thick
½ c. fine dry bread crumbs
¼ c. grated Parmesan cheese
1 egg, beaten
2 T. olive or salad oil
4 thin slices Mozzarella cheese
1 lb. tiny new potatoes, scraped
1 8-oz. can seasoned tomato sauce
1½ T. crushed oregano

Combine flour and seasonings; coat chops. Mix crumbs and Parmesan cheese. Dip chops in egg, then in crumb mixture. Brown slowly in hot oil. Place a slice of Mozzarella cheese atop each chop; arrange potatoes around meat. Pour tomato sauce over; sprinkle with oregano. Cover; simmer 50 minutes or till meat and potatoes are done.

Mrs. Mary Kay S. Bisignani
Hempfield Area Sr. H. S.
Greensburg, Pennsylvania

BREADED VEAL CUTLETS
Number of Servings — 6

2 veal round steaks
3 T. sweet milk
1 egg
15 soda crackers
Few grains salt and pepper

Cut veal in serving size pieces. Beat milk into whole egg. Roll crackers to fine crumb stage. Dip veal in egg mixture, then in crumbs, and brown on both sides in hot fat in heavy skillet. Salt and pepper to taste. Remove browned veal to casserole. When all of meat is browned, add ¼ cup water to hot fat drippings, and pour over meat. Cover casserole and bake 1 hour at 325°F. Remove cover the last 5 minutes. Veal chops may be prepared by same method. Veal prepared in this way is especially good for buffet luncheons or dinners because it is so tender that no knife is needed.

Mrs. Frances S. McDonough, Morrison H. S.
Morrison, Tennessee

VEAL CUTLETS POJARSKI
Number of Servings — 5

1 lb. ground lean veal
½ t. salt
½ c. thick cream

Form into cutlets; dip into flour; fry until brown on both sides; garnish with a little parsley.

Dorothy T. Waugh

VEAL CUTLETS
Number of Servings — 6

2 lbs. veal steak (cubed by butcher)
1 egg
1 T. milk
¾ c. cracker crumbs
1 t. salt
⅛ t. pepper
2 T. butter

Break egg into flat dish and beat. Add salt, pepper and milk. Beat again. Pour cracker crumbs into another flat dish. Melt butter into skillet (use medium heat to fry with butter). Dip meat (one at a time) into egg, then into cracker crumbs, cover well. Fry in skillet until brown on each side. Cover and steam 20 minutes (low heat).

Laurel R. Brice, Blanchard Public School
Blanchard, Michigan

VEAL BAKED IN MILK
Number of Servings — 5

2 lbs. veal steak or cutlets
2 t. salt
1 egg, beaten
Flour for dipping
¼ c. butter
2 c. milk or 1 c. milk and 1 c. cream

Cut meat into serving-size pieces. Sprinkle with the salt; dip in beaten egg, and then in flour. Heat fat in a heavy skillet and brown meat slowly on both sides. Transfer meat and fat to a glass baking casserole. Add milk. Cover, and bake in a slow oven (300° to 325° F.) for 2 hours or until tender. Note: ½ pounds fresh or canned mushrooms can be added to top of meat in casserole cover and bake.

Jimmie Hankins, Lexington H. S.
Lexington, Alabama

VEAL LOAF
Number of Servings — 8

2 lbs. boneless veal
Small bag of noodles
½ green pepper
3 t. of pimento
3 eggs
2 c. of milk
2 t. of salt
3 t. of parsley
¼ lb. mild cheese
1 small onion
½ c. dry bread crumbs
¼ lb. of butter
¼ t. of pepper

Cook veal until tender. May use left over veal from a roast if you prefer. Cook noodles and drain. Send the following items through a food grinder: veal, noodles, green pepper, pimento, parsley, cheese, and onion. Heat milk and butter and add to the ground mixture. Add dry bread crumbs, eggs, salt and pepper. Mix. Place this mixture in a 13 x 9 inch oblong pan and bake about one hour at 350° F. This loaf may be made the night before and stored in the refrigerator. While baking, heat one can of cream of mushroom soup diluted with ¼ can of milk. Use as a topping or gravy for the loaf.

Joyce Niedenthal, Parkway Jr. H. S.
Fort Lauderdale, Florida

VEAL LOAF
Number of Servings — 10-12

3 lbs. ground veal
½ lb. ground pork
3 eggs, beaten
½ c. soda cracker crumbs
Juice of 1 lemon
⅔ c. of catsup
1 t. salt
¼ t. pepper

Mix all ingredients, well. Mold in baking pan and cover top and sides with additional crumbs. Add one cup warm water. Bake at 350° F. for one and one-half hours.

Mrs. Beth W. Wiley, Weiser H. S.
Weiser, Idaho

VEAL FRICASSEE
Number of Servings — 6

2 lbs. veal, ½ to ¾ inch thick
1 T. flour
1 c. sour cream
Salt and pepper to taste
⅛ t. paprika
½ c. meat stock or water

Cut veal in serving pieces, season; dip in flour and brown in hot fat. Combine 1 tablespoon flour, paprika, sour cream, and stock or water; pour over meat. Cover and cook slowly 1 hour.

Anna L. Tellor, Cahokia H. S.
Cahokia, Illinois

CORDON BLEU
Number of Servings — 2

1 slice veal cutlet or round steak
½ slice cooked ham
Sliced Velvetta cheese

Place cooked ham on one half of veal slice. Place Velvetta cheese on other half of veal. Brush around edges of veal with egg white; fold over and press edges together. Dredge meat with egg yolk and flour. Deep fry in oil (375°F.) until veal is brown and done.

Mrs. Ann B. Redic, Dalton H. S.
Dalton, Georgia

VEAL AND MUSHROOMS
Number of Servings — 8-10

2 cans (4½-oz.) mushroom caps
½ c. cooking oil
3 lbs. veal, cut in 1 inch cubes
2 cans cream of mushroom soup
1 c. chicken bouillon (or 1 c. white wine)
½ c. chopped onion
1 t. oregano
1 c. sour cream
5⅓ c. fluffy rice

Drain mushrooms, measure liquid, and add enough to make 1 cup. Heat oil in saucepan. Add veal and saute until browned. Then stir in mushroom liquid, soup, ½ cup bouillon, the onions and oregano. Bring to a boil, cover and reduce heat. Simmer about 1¼ hours, stirring the mixture occasionally. Just before serving add remaining bouillon, mushrooms and sour cream. Serve over hot rice.

Terri Reasor, Milton Jr. H. S.
Milton, West Virginia

VEAL STROGANOFF
Number of Servings — 4-6

1 lb. veal, thinly sliced
¼ c. flour
1 t. salt
¼ t. pepper
¼ c. shortening or salad oil
1 medium onion
½ lb. mushrooms or 6-oz. can
½ c. water
1 chicken bouillon cube
1 t. paprika
1 c. sour cream

Combine flour, salt and pepper; dip meat into it to coat lightly. Heat shortening in large skillet or frypan; quickly brown meat. Add onion and mushooms. Cook 5 minutes. Add water, bouillon and paprika; bring to boil. Reduce heat; blend in sour cream. Cover and simmer gently 15 minutes. Serve with noodles.

Mrs. Margaret K. Shollenberger, Rice Ave.
Union H. S., Girard, Pennsylvania

CRISSCROSS VEAL ROAST
Number of Servings — 6-8

3-4 lbs. boned veal shoulder
½ t. salt
½ t. basil
1 medium-size onion, sliced and rings separated
6 slices bacon

Rub meat well with mixture of salt, basil and pepper. Place on rack in small roaster. Lay onion rings over meat. Crisscross bacon slices on top. Roast in slow oven (325° F.) allowing 40 minutes per pound, or about 2 hours for a 3-pound cut) or 180°F. on meat thermometer).

Grace G. Mount, Beauregard H. S.
Opelika, Alabama

VEAL DINNER
Number of Servings — 4

2 center cuts of veal
6 onions, chopped
1 pt. sour cream
Salt and pepper to taste
Accent to taste
Milk, about 3 cups
Then prepare your dinner accompaniments.
8 carrots
4 potatoes

This is an old home recipe that we have enjoyed. First brown your veal. Then take out your meat and put on a side plate. Put your chopped onions into your skillet and brown. Put meat back into your skillet (be sure to put meat juice, that might be on your plate back into your skillet) and place onions on top. Take a spoon and spread your sour cream over this, then add your milk (water can be used if desired). Now you are ready to put in your carrots and potatoes. Garnish with paprika for looks. Cook until potatoes and carrots are done (about 1 hour to 1½ hour). Cover skillet and let the steam do the work! Cook on medium or low speed on top of your range.

Laura E. Godin, Lakeview H. S.
Lakeview, Michigan

INDIVIDUAL VEAL FILLET ROLLS
Number of Servings — 4

2 lbs. boned veal steak, 1 inch thick
¾ lb. sausage meat
Favorite seasonings
2 c. chicken bouillon

Pound steak to flatten to ½" to ¾" thickness. Cut into four serving pieces. Spread each piece with sausage meat, roll, and fasten securely with a skewer or string. Season. Brown in hot fat. Place rolls in baking dish and pour over them the bouillon. Cover and simmer gently in 325° F. oven 1½ hours or until done. Place rolls on hot serving dish and serve with hot gravy made from stock.

Virginia C. Hoar, Kearney Jr. H. S.
Adams City, Colorado

MINIATURE MEAT BALLS
Number of Servings — 8

Meatballs:

2 T. salad oil
1½ lbs. veal, ground
1 large onion, chopped
½ t. garlic salt
2 T. grated parmesan cheese
1 c. bread crumbs
2 eggs
Salt and pepper

Sauce:

2 T. salad oil
2 medium-sized sliced onions
1 No. 2½ can tomatoes
1 6-oz. can tomato paste
2 6-oz. cans water
1 T. chopped parsley
½ t. garlic salt
1 t. oregano
¼ t. powdered cloves
4 whole bay leaves

Make sauce by browning onions in oil. Add remaining ingredients and simmer for one and one-half hours. Allow sauce to cook for about one-half hour before adding meatballs. To make the meatballs: brown onions in oil. Mix remaining ingredients in large bowl and add browned onions. Form into one-inch balls and brown in fat in skillet, add to sauce and let simmer for about an hour. Meatballs may be removed from sauce and served with cocktail picks, or the meatballs and sauce may be poured over cooked spaghetti or noodles.

Leoda Mestrovic, Wellsburg H. S.
Wellsburg, West Virginia

CHOP SUEY
Number of Servings — 6

1¼ lbs. veal steak
3 c. diced celery
2 c. diced onions
1½ c. LaChoy sprouts
1 c. water from sprouts
2 T. LaChoy soy sauce
4 T. vegetable shortening
1 t. salt
2 T. flour
2 T. water

Cut veal in small pieces, roll in flour. Add shortening to frying pan and brown the veal. Add celery, onions and one cup of water from sprouts. Cook until veal and vegetables are tender. Add sprouts, salt, and make a thickening, using the two tablespoons of flour, two tablespoons of water and two tablespoons of LaChoy sauce. Add the thickening to the Chop Suey mixture, cook two minutes. Serve with rice or canned soy noodles.

Grace L. Engelbrecht, Frederick H. S.
Frederick, Maryland

CHOP SUEY
Number of Servings — 4

2 T. butter or frying oil
Soy sauce to suit taste
¼ t. salt
½ lb. lean pork
¾ lbs. veal, cut into small cubes
2 c. chopped celery
1 c. chopped onion
¾ c. chopped green pepper
½ sweet red pepper (for color)
1 can bean sprouts
1 can chow mein noodles
1 can water chestnuts, sliced
1 small can mushrooms

Place a large frying pan over moderate heat, into which place the butter or oil and 2 or 3 tablespoons of soy sauce. Fry meat in this until nearly done, then remove and keep warm, ready to add later. Into the meat stock put the celery and onions, adding more butter if necessary, and cook, stirring all the time until the vegetables are cooked thru. Add the meat, turn flame a little lower and let simmer for 5 to 10 minutes. (If the water chestnuts are used they may be added with the meat to the vegetables). The green peppers are now added. Add mushrooms if desired. Pour the liquid from the bean sprouts and let drain for a short time. Also pour off the stock from the meat and vegetables, letting them cool while adding the sprouts to the frying pan. Add the meat, celery and peppers to the sprouts. Let all simmer and in another pan make a thick gravy from the stock, using more soy sauce if desired. The chop suey is now ready to serve, but be sure you have let the sprouts heat thru. Place on a platter and pour the gravy over the top or serve the gravy separately. Garnish with fried egg yolks shredded or any bits of green pepper or chopped parsley.

Mrs. Gladys Collier, Muskegon Sr. H. S.
Muskegon, Michigan

VEAL-CHEESE ROLL-UPS
Number of Servings — 4

1 lb. cubed veal cutlets
½ c. cracker crumbs
1 c. shredded Mozenella cheese
1 T. minced onion
1 t. basil leaves
Salt and pepper to taste
1½ c. tomato sauce
½ c. mushrooms, sauteed
2 slices bacon

Roll the first five ingredients in the veal (as for a jelly roll) and fasten with toothpicks. Place roll-ups in a baking dish and cover with tomato sauce, bacon strip and mushrooms. Add ½ cup cheese during last 15 minutes of cooking time. Bake at 350° F. 1 hour and 15 minutes.

Phyllis Richards, Bald Eagle Nittany H. S.
Mill Hall, Pennsylvania

AMERICAN CHOP SUEY
Number of Servings — 4

3 T. table fat
½ lb. veal, cut in ½ inch cubes
¼ c. coarsely cut onion
¾ c. hot water
½ t. salt
⅛ t. freshly ground peppercorns
¾ c. coarsely chopped celery
2 T. chopped green pepper
1½ T. cornstarch
1½ t. molasses
1 T. water
1 package (5-oz.) quick-cooking rice

Heat fat in large skillet. Add veal and onions; cook until onion is golden, stirring 2 or 3 times. Add water, seasonings, and vegetables to veal mixture. Cook covered for 25 minutes or until veal is tender. Mix molasses, cornstarch and water; add to veal mixture, stirring. Cook for 5 more minutes. Cook rice, following directions on package. Serve veal mixture over rice.

Mrs. Carroll K. Busselen, Highland H. S.
North Highlands, California

ITALIAN MEAT LOAF
Number of Servings — 8-10

1 lb. veal, ground
½ lb. cured ham, ground
1 c. bread crumbs
3 eggs, slightly beaten
½ c. cooked spaghetti
½ c. grated cheese
1 small onion, finely chopped
1 garlic bud, chopped
½ pimento, chopped
1 t. salt
1 t. pepper

Mix in order given. Moisten as you like with milk. Place in a greased ring mold and bake at 375°F. for 45 minutes. Serve on a large round platter, pile center with fresh garden peas, surround loaf with various fruits such as sliced pineapple, peach halves, whole canned plums. This is also delicious to serve as a cold platter.

Mrs. Anna Grace Hodges, Berkeley Springs H. S.
Berkeley Springs, West Virginia

CARNE ALLA FORNO
Number of Servings — 6

2 lbs. veal steak
2 c. bread crumbs
½ c. Parmesan cheese, grated
¾ t. oregano
1 t. basil
2 large onions, sliced
¼ c. olive oil
1 c. peeled tomatoes
Tomato paste to moisten

Mix bread crumbs, cheese, basil, oregano and seasonings. Place layer of veal steaks (cut into serving pieces) in casserole. Sprinkle generously with bread crumb mixture, then onions. Dot with tomatoes; repeat until all is used. Pour olive oil over top and bake in moderate oven (350°F.) about 1 hour.

M. Malinda McClure, Erie Com. H. S.
Erie, Illinois

RIC A TONI
Number of Servings — 12

Sauce:

1 square butter
1 large onion, chopped
1 garlic bud, chopped
2 c. tomato juice
1 c. tomato paste
1 c. tomato sauce
½ t. thyme
½ t. marjoram
½ t. rosemary
4 bay leaves
¼ t. cayenne pepper (or less)
1 c. mushrooms
3 shakes tabasco sauce
2 t. vinegar
1 T. Worcestershire sauce
2 T. sugar
1 t. salt.

Add 4 cups water and simmer 5 hours. Cook package of Ricatoni in boiling salt water until tender. Be careful not to over cook. Cool and stuff with meat mixture.

Meat Mixture:

1 lb. ground veal
½ lb. ground pork
1 egg
1 large onion, chopped
1 t. sage
¼ t. salt
Dash pepper
¼ c. canned milk to hold together

Combine above ingredients. Bake 1½ hours at 350°F. Bake in baking dish. One layer of stuffed ricatoni and then of sauce. Pour rest of sauce over top.

MaRee Nelson, Jordan H. S.
Sandy, Utah

Pork

PORK CHART
Pork Cuts and How to Cook Them

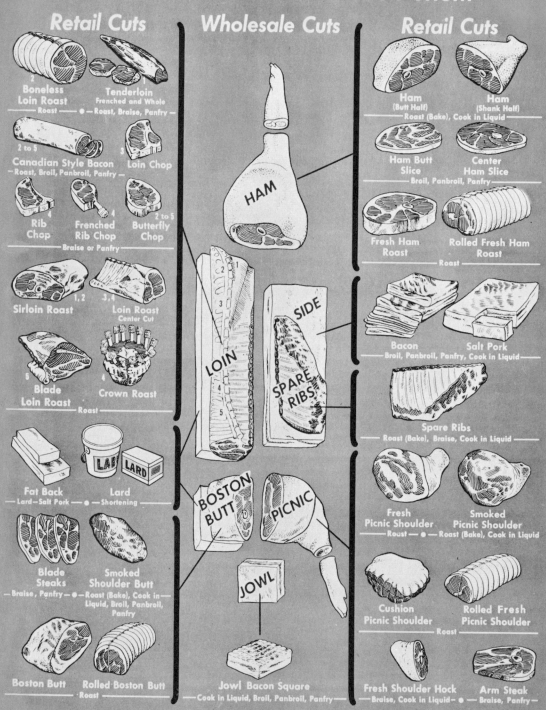

Retail Cuts | Wholesale Cuts | Retail Cuts

Boneless Loin Roast
— Roast —

Tenderloin
Frenched and Whole
— Roast, Braise, Panfry —

Canadian Style Bacon
— Roast, Broil, Panbroil, Panfry —

Loin Chop

Rib Chop

Frenched Rib Chop

Butterfly Chop
— Braise or Panfry —

Sirloin Roast

Loin Roast
Center Cut

Blade Loin Roast

Crown Roast
— Roast —

Fat Back
— Lard—Salt Pork —

Lard
— Shortening —

Blade Steaks
— Braise, Panfry —

Smoked Shoulder Butt
— Roast (Bake), Cook in Liquid, Broil, Panbroil, Panfry —

Boston Butt

Rolled Boston Butt
— Roast —

HAM

LOIN

SIDE

SPARE RIBS

BOSTON BUTT

PICNIC

JOWL

Jowl Bacon Square
— Cook in Liquid, Broil, Panbroil, Panfry —

Ham (Butt Half)

Ham (Shank Half)
— Roast (Bake), Cook in Liquid —

Ham Butt Slice

Center Ham Slice
— Broil, Panbroil, Panfry —

Fresh Ham Roast

Rolled Fresh Ham Roast
— Roast —

Bacon

Salt Pork
— Broil, Panbroil, Panfry, Cook in Liquid —

Spare Ribs
— Roast (Bake), Braise, Cook in Liquid —

Fresh Picnic Shoulder

Smoked Picnic Shoulder
— Roast — • — Roast (Bake), Cook in Liquid —

Cushion Picnic Shoulder

Rolled Fresh Picnic Shoulder
— Roast —

Fresh Shoulder Hock
— Braise, Cook in Liquid — •

Arm Steak
— Braise, Panfry —

NATIONAL LIVE STOCK AND MEAT BOARD

Selection of PORK Cuts

WHOLESALE CUTS	RETAIL CUTS	CHARACTERISTICS	COOKING METHODS
Ham Fresh Pickled, or Smoked	Ham, Whole	Corresponds to beef round with tail bone and portion of backbone removed. Outer skin or rind is left on the regular ham but it is removed, with excess fat, from the skinned ham.	Roast (bake); cook in liquid
	Ham, Shank Half	Lower half of ham. Includes shank and ½ of center section.	Roast (bake); cook in liquid
	Ham Shank	Cone-shaped, rind-covered piece containing shank bones.	Cook in liquid
	Ham, Butt Half	Upper half of ham. Includes butt and ½ of center section.	Roast (bake); cook in liquid
	Ham Butt	Same as above minus most of center section.	Roast (bake); cook in liquid
	Ham, Center Baking Piece	Center section of ham. Both cut surfaces look like center slices.	Roast (bake); cook in liquid
	Ham, Center Slice	Oval shape, small round bone, four separate muscles.	Broil, panbroil, panfry
	Ham, Boneless	Boneless roll. Fresh, pickled, or smoked.	Roast (bake); cook in liquid
Loin Also Tenderloin, Boneless Back Strip and Canadian Style Bacon	Tenderloin	Long tapering round muscle. Weighs ½ to 1 pound.	Roast; braise
	Frenched Tenderloin	Piece cut from tenderloin and flattened.	Braise; panfry
	Boneless Loin Roast	Boneless back strip. Two pieces sometimes tied together.	Roast
	Canadian Style Bacon	Boneless back strip, cured and smoked.	Roast; broil; panbroil; panfry
	Butterfly Chop	Double chop, hinged together, cut from boneless loin strip.	Braise; panfry
	Sirloin Roast	Ham end of loin containing hip bone.	Roast
	Blade Loin Roast	Shoulder end of loin containing rib bones and blade bone.	Roast
	Loin Chop	T-shaped bone and two muscles (back strip and tenderloin).	Braise; panfry
	Rib Chop	Alternate chops have rib bone. May be "frenched".	Braise; panfry
	Crown Roast	Rib sections "frenched" and formed in shape of crown.	Roast
Picnic Shoulder Fresh, Pickled, or Smoked	Picnic Shoulder	Includes arm and shank sections of the shoulder.	Roast (bake); cook in liquid
	Rolled Picnic Shoulder	Boneless roll. Fresh, pickled or smoked.	Roast (bake); cook in liquid
	Cushion Picnic Shoulder	Arm section of fresh picnic with pocket for stuffing.	Roast
	Arm Steak	Oval at one end, squared off at other. Small round bone.	Braise; panfry
	Pork Hock	Round, tapering, skin-covered piece containing shank bones.	Braise; cook in liquid
Boston Butt Also Smoked Shoulder Butt	Boston Butt	Upper half of shoulder. Contains part of blade bone.	Roast
	Blade Steak	Cut from Boston butt. Most steaks have section of blade bone.	Braise; panfry
	Smoked Shoulder Butt	Eye of Boston butt. Cured and smoked boneless roll.	Roast (bake); cook in liquid
	Sm. Sh. Butt Slices	Round boneless slices. Lean and fat intermixed.	Broil; panbroil; panfry
Side (Belly) Fresh, Salt, Pickled, or Smoked	Fresh Side Pork	Usually sliced. Alternating layers of lean and fat.	Braise; panfry
	Pickled Side Pork	Same as above but cured in a sweet pickle solution.	Braise; panfry
	Salt Side Pork	Same as above but cured with dry salt.	Panfry; cook in liquid
	Sliced Bacon	Same as above but cured, dry or in pickle, then smoked.	Broil; panbroil; panfry
Spareribs	Spareribs	Ribs and breastbone which have been removed from the bacon strip.	Roast ; braise; cook in liquid
Jowl	Jowl Bacon Square	Jowl, trimmed square, then cured and smoked. High percentage of fat. May be sliced.	Cook in liquid; broil; panbroil; panfry
Feet	Pig's Feet, Fresh	Contains bones and tendons of foot and ankle. Little lean meat.	Cook in liquid
	Pig's Feet, Pickled	Pickled, cooked and ready to eat.	No cooking necessary

Boston Butt (Shoulder)

Roast

Blade Loin Roast

Roast

Loin Roast (Center Cut)

Roast

Blade Steak (Shoulder)

Braise, Panfry

Fresh Picnic Shoulder

Roast

Loin Chops

Braise, Panfry

Arm Roast (Shoulder)

Roast

Smoked Picnic Shoulder

Roast (Bake), Cook in Liquid

Rib Chops

Braise, Panfry

Arm Steak (Shoulder)

Braise, Panfry

Hocks

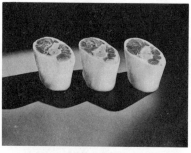

Braise, Cook in Liquid

Crown Roast

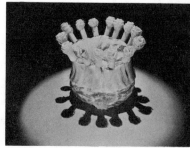

Roast

the Best Methods for Cooking Them

Sirloin Roast

Roast

Half Ham (Shank End)

Roast (Bake), Cook in Liquid

Half Ham (Butt End)

Roast (Bake), Cook in Liquid

Tenderloin

Roast, Braise, Panfry

Center Slice Ham

Broil, Panbroil, Panfry

Sliced Bacon

Broil, Panbroil, Panfry

Boneless Sirloin Roast

Roast

Jowl Bacon Square

Cook in Liquid, Broil, Panbroil, Panfry

Salt Pork (Side)

Cook in Liquid, Panbroil, Panfry

Canadian Style Bacon

Roast, Broil, Panbroil, Panfry

Smoked Shoulder Butt

*Roast, Cook in Liquid, Broil,
Panbroil, Panfry*

Spareribs

*Roast (Bake), Braise,
Cook in Liquid*

PORK–Methods of Cooking

THE FAT OF PORK indicates quality and is largely responsible for the desirable flavor of this meat. In high quality pork, the exterior is well covered with a layer of fairly firm white fat. The color of the lean of young pork is grayish pink, turning to a delicate rose color in older animals. The lean is well marbled with fat. The texture of the lean is firm and fine grained. The bones are porous and pinkish in color, since pork is usually young.

Some cuts are in demand as fresh pork, while others are in greatest demand as cured pork. Many pork cuts are sold both fresh and cured.

All cuts of pork are tender, therefore all large or chunky cuts, both fresh and cured, may be cooked by roasting. Fresh pork is usually roasted at 350° F., and cured pork at 300° F.

Pork chops, cutlets, sliced fresh ham or shoulder, and sliced pork liver are best if cooked by braising, rather than by broiling, panbroiling or griddle-broiling. Braising cooks them well done without drying them out. They may also be cooked by frying. Sliced cured ham and bacon may be broiled, panbroiled or griddle-broiled. Ham also may be panfried, and bacon may be panfried, deep-fat fried or oven-cooked (on a rack in an open roasting pan, at 325° F.). Pork should always be cooked well done. The cooked lean of fresh pork should be grayish white without even a tinge of pink.

TIME-TABLE FOR COOKING PORK [1]

CUT	ROASTED AT 300°-350° F. OVEN TEMPERATURE [2]		BROILED		BRAISED	COOKED IN LIQUID
	Meat Thermometer Reading	Time	Meat Thermometer Reading	Total Time	Total Time	Time
	Degrees F.	Minutes per lb.	Degrees F.	Minutes	Hours	Minutes per lb.
FRESH Loin Center	185	35 to 40	Fresh pork is never broiled			
Whole	185	15 to 20				
Ends	185	45 to 50				
Shoulder Rolled	185	40 to 45				
Cushion	185	35 to 40				
Boston Butt	185	45 to 50				
Leg or Ham	185	30 to 35				
Chops					¾ to 1	
Steaks					¾ to 1	
Spareribs		30 to 35			1½	30
Pork and Ham Loaf		30 to 35				
SMOKED Ham Large	160	15 to 18				
Medium	160	18 to 22				18 to 20
Small	160	22 to 25				
Half	160	25 to 30				25
Ham Loaf	160	30 to 35				
Ham Slice (½ inch)			160 to 170	10 to 12		
(1 inch)			160 to 170	16 to 20		
Picnic	170	35				35 to 45
Shoulder Butt	170	35				
Bacon				4 to 5		

[1] *For frying see discussion page 6.*

[2] *350°F. oven temperature is recommended for fresh pork and 300°F. oven temperature for smoked pork.*

Pork

PORK CHOPS
Number of Servings — 1

1 pork chop
2 T. fat
1¼ in. slice of onion
1¼ in- ring of bell pepper
1 T. uncooked rice
1 small can English peas
1 c. tomatoes

Brown pork chop in fat. Place in a greased baking dish. Place the onion, bell pepper and rice on top of the pork chop. Add tomatoes and English peas around the chop. Cover and cook slowly at 325° F. for 1 hour. (This recipe may be varied to suit the individual taste by addition of different vegetables.)

Inez Galloway, Columbia H. S.
Lake City, Florida

PORK CHOPS
Number of Servings — 5

5 thick pork chops
5 T. rice
5 ½-in. large slices Bermuda onions
5 ½-in. slices green pepper
1 No. 2 can tomatoes
¼ c. chopped celery

Steam rice in small amount of water for 5 minutes. Season chops to taste. Brown in Dutch oven over moderately high heat. Top each browned chop with an onion slice and green pepper ring. Put rice inside ring. Add tomatoes and celery over all. Cover and simmer over low heat 1 hour or until chops are tender.

Mrs. Burchie Johnston, John A. Wilkinson H. S.
Belhaven, North Carolina

PORK CHOP-APPLE KRAUT DINNER
Number of Servings — 4

4 pork chops or shoulder steaks
Salt
Pepper
1 t. caraway seed
⅓ c. brown sugar
1 No. 2 can sauerkraut (2½ c.)
3 T. chopped onion
2 apples

Brown pork chops in a little fat in dutch oven or electric skillet, season with salt and pepper. Remove chops from pan and pour off fat. Add sauerkraut, caraway seed, brown sugar, onions and sliced apples mixed thoroughly. Top with pork chops. Cover and let cook at low heat one hour or until meat is tender, basting chops with juices in pan.

Mrs. Sara L. Stump, New Paris H. S.
New Paris, Indiana

PORK CHOPS A LA PINEAPPLE
Number of Servings — 6

6 pork chops
¾ c. mushrooms
1 c. pineapple juice
1 T. fat
6 slices pineapple
½ c. mushroom liquid
Salt to taste

Brown pork chops in fat. Remove from pan. Brown pineapple quickly and remove from pan. Brown mushrooms and remove from pan. Place pork chops in pan, put a slice of pineapple on each chop. Cover with mushrooms and juices. Cover pan and cook on low heat 1 hour. Serve hot.

Helen Sergent, Gate City, H. S.
Gate City, Virginia

PORK CHOP SKILLET
Number of Servings — 4

4 pork chops, 1½ inch thick
Salt and pepper
4 rounded T. rice, uncooked
1 No. 2 can tomatoes
2 small onions, halved
2 whole cloves
Bay leaf
Few grains thyme

Salt and pepper chops and brown on both sides in fat (grease skillet with fat on chop). Arrange chops in fry pan or skillet. Place rounded tablespoon uncooked rice on each. Place solid parts of tomatoes on rice and pour liquid around chops. Add onions, cloves, bay leaf and thyme. Cover. Simmer 1½ hours. Add tomato juice if necessary; do not let it get dry. Serve with green salad.

Brooks Rector, Richmond-Burton Com. H. S.
Richmond, Illinois

PORK CHOP SKILLET MEAL
Number of Servings — 4

4 T. fat
4 pork chops (1 inch thick)
4 slices Bermuda onion
4 rings green pepper
4 T. uncooked rice
3 c. stewed tomatoes
1 c. diced celery

Heat fat in skillet on high. Turn to medium low and brown chops until well browned on both sides, approximately 15 minutes. Place a slice of onion and one green pepper ring on each pork chop. Place 1 tablespoon rice in each ring. Pour tomatoes around the meat; add celery. Place cover on skillet and when steam appears, switch to simmer and allow to cook for 1 hour.

Lucy H. Kittrell, Sunbury H. S.
Sunbury, North Carolina

STUFFED PORK CHOPS (SKILLET)
Number of Servings — 6

1 large onion, chopped
½ c. chopped celery
1 clove garlic, minced
2 T. cooking oil
1 c. meat or chicken stock or 1 c. water and
    bouillon cube
3 c. bread cubes
¼ c. minced parsley
6 double pork chops, split
2 T. cooking oil or shortening
1 can tomato sauce
½ c. water

Cook onion, celery and garlic in oil slowly about
5 minutes—this softens them and develops the
good taste of each. Add stock and simmer about
10 minutes. Toss in the bread cubes and parsley.
Stuff pork chops, fasten edges with picks and
lacing with string. In a large skillet, brown the
chops in oil or shortening. Add tomato sauce
and water; cover and simmer about 1 hour until
pork is tender.

Mrs. Don Sport, Dozier H. S.
Dozier, Alabama

PORK CHOP SKILLET MEAL
Number of Servings — 6

6 pork chops
½ c. rice
1 green pepper
6 onions
6 tomatoes or 1 can tomatoes
3 potatoes
1-2 c. water
Salt and pepper

Brown pork chops in skillet. Remove. Prepare
vegetables. Wash rice and brown in pork drippings. Slice pepper rings, potatoes. Remove rice
from skillet. Place pork chops in bottom. Place
pepper, onion, tomatoes, potatoes, and rice over
them. Season. Add 1-2 cups of water. Cover. Simmer 45 minutes to 1 hour.

Alice R. McCreary, Monroe Co. H. S.
Monroeville, Alabama

CRANBERRY PORK CHOPS
Number of Servings — 4

4 pork chops
1 c. canned jellied cranberry sauce
1 t. grated orange rind
½ c. crushed pineapple (optional)
¼ c. water

Flour chops and brown in a small amount of hot
fat in a skillet. Mix rest of ingredients and pour
over chops. Cover and simmer for 1 hour or until
fork tender.

Pollyanna Rogers, Howe H. S.
Howe, Oklahoma

SKILLET PORK CHOP SUPPER

5 pork chops (¾″ thick)
1 large can tomatoes
1 large onion
2½ c. rice (partially cooked)

In skillet brown pork chops on both sides. Drain
off surplus grease. On the top of each chop, place
½ cup cooked rice, ¼ cup canned tomatoes and
1 thick slice of onion. Place remainder of canned
tomatoes around the chops. Salt and pepper generously. Cook slowly for 1½ hours.

Mrs. Florence B. Fisackerly, Inverness H. S.
Inverness, Mississippi

BAKED PORK CHOPS
Number of Servings — 6

6 to 8 loin pork chops, ¾ inch thick
6-8 T. brown sugar
1 t. dry mustard
Salt to taste
Pepper to taste
Dash of Accent on each chop

Combine brown sugar and dry mustard. Set aside.
Bake pork chops on broil pan for ½ hour at
400°F. Turn, spoon on top of chops the brown
sugar, mustard and other ingredients. Bake for
approximately ½ hour.

Margaret G. Wilson, Waynesboro Area H. S.
Waynesboro, Pennsylvania

BAKED PORK CHOPS
Number of Servings — 6

6 large loin pork chops
1 egg
1 c. crumbs (crushed Post Toasties)
1 t. salt
⅛ t. pepper
3 T. melted fat, salad oil or bacon drippings

Beat egg, combine with milk and mix. Dip each
chop first in egg, then in crumbs. Brown in hot
fat, season with salt and pepper. After browning,
place chops in well greased casserole, add a little
water. Cover and bake in a moderate oven until
tender, about 1 hour. Garnish with parsley.

May Lohmann, Miami H. S.
Miami, Oklahoma

PORK CHOP BAKE
Number of Servings — 4

4 pork chops, medium thick
Salt and pepper to taste
1 can cream of mushroom soup

Brown chops on both sides. Season. Place browned
chops in a casserole. Pour cream of mushroom
soup over chops. Cover. Bake 40 minutes at 350°F.

Florence Hannewald, Benzonia H. S.
Benzonia, Michigan

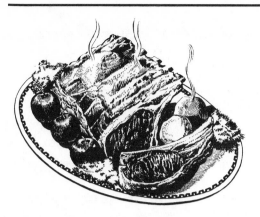

BAKED PORK CHOPS SUPREME
Number of Servings — 6

½ c. chopped celery
2 T. minced onions
1 c. catsup
½ c. water
2 T. prepared mustard
¼ t. salt
⅛ t. pepper
½ t. sage
1 T. fat
6 pork chops (loin chops)

Measure and mix all ingredients except fat and pork chops in medium size bowl and set aside. Heat fat in a large heavy skillet over medium heat. Salt and pepper pork chops on both sides and brown lightly in fat. Place chops in a large shallow baking dish. Cover with catsup mixture, spooning generously over each chop. Cover dish with aluminum foil and bake at 350 ° F. for 30 minutes. Serve from baking dish. Serves six.

Betty T. Doyle, Sunnyside-McKenney H. S.
McKenney, Virginia

GRAVY-BAKED PORK CHOPS
Number of Servings — 6

6 lean pork chops (½-in. thick)
½ t. salt
¼ t. pepper (about)
1 T. shortening
⅔ c. evaporated milk
⅓ c. water
1 can mushroom soup

Sprinkle pork chops with salt and pepper. In 10-inch skillet heat the fat. Brown the pork chops on both sides. Pour off drippings. Pour around the chops a mixture of cream of mushroom soup, ⅔ cup evaporated milk (1 small can) and ⅓ cup water. Bake in 350° F. oven 45 minutes, until chops are tender. Stir gravy well. Makes 6 servings. Tip: Instead of baking, you can cover and cook chops and gravy about 45 minutes over low heat.

Mrs. Sara H. Barlow, Whitesburg H. S.
Whitesburg, Tennessee

GRAVY-BAKED PORK CHOPS
Number of Servings — 4

4 lean pork chops
Salt
Pepper
1 can condensed cream of mushroom soup
⅔ c. evaporated milk
⅓ c. water

Sprinkle 4 lean pork chops, ½ to ¾ inch thick, with salt and pepper. Brown in skillet in 1 tablespoon hot shortening. Pour off drippings. Pour around the chops a mixture of 1 can condensed cream of mushroom soup, ⅔ cup evaporated milk, and ⅓ cup water. Bake in 350° F. oven for 45 minutes, or until chops are tender. Stir gravy well. Makes 4 servings.

Wanda M. Stacke, Abbotsford H. S.
Abbotsford, Wisconsin

BAKED PORK CHOPS
Number of Servings — 6

6 pork chops (¾-in. thick)
1 t. salt
2 c. boiling water
2 T. A.1. sauce
2 T. flour
½ c. rolled bread crumbs

Brown chops on both sides in hot frying pan. Remove to buttered baking dish. Add salt, water and A.1. sauce to pan and heat. Thicken with 2 tablespoons flour, mixed with ¼ cup cold water. Stir until smooth. Pour over chops, top with bread crumbs and bake 45 minutes at 350° F.

Mrs. Louise McKamey, Belfast H. S.
Hillsboro, Ohio

PORK CHOPS WITH PRUNES
Number of Servings — 6

¼ c. catsup
2 T. lemon juice, fresh or frozen
½ t. dry mustard
½ lb. prunes
1 t. Worcestershire sauce
6 thick pork chops
1 small onion, sliced
¼ c. hot water

Combine catsup, lemon juice, mustard and Worcestershire sauce; rub into both sides of chops. Brown into hot fat. Top with onion and add water. Cover and bake in moderate oven (350°F.) 1 hour. Serve with spiced prunes. Cook ½ pound prunes in 1½ cups hot water until tender, about 30 minutes. Add 2 tablespoons vinegar, ½ teaspoon cinnamon, 3 whole cloves, and 2 tablespoons brown sugar; cook slowly 10 minutes. Do not pit prunes.

WadeDelle Squires, Bamberg H. S.
Bamberg, South Carolina

BAKED PORK CHOPS WITH CORN
Number of Servings — 4

1 can condensed cream of chicken
   or cream of mushroom soup
2 c. whole kernel corn
4 pork chops
Salt and pepper to taste
2 bay leaves

Combine soup and drained corn in a shallow casserole dish. Season pork chops with salt and pepper. Arrange the pork chops on top of the soup-corn mixture, placing a half bay leaf under each chop. Bake covered in a slow oven (325° F.) about 45 minutes. Uncover and continue to bake about 15 minutes until chops are brown.

Mrs. Carol Horne, Lorena H. S.
Lorena, Texas

BAKED PORK CHOPS WITH TOMATO SOUP
Number of Servings — 6

6 center cut pork chops
2 T. fat
Salt and pepper
1 can tomato soup
1 can water

Trim excess fat from pork chops. Brown quickly in frying pan, using fat. Salt and pepper chops and place in baking dish. Pour tomato soup, mixed with water, over chops. Cover dish. Bake at 375° F. for one hour.

Mrs. Dorothy M. Jenkins, Springfield Local H. S.
Petersburg, Ohio

PORK CHOPS AND DRESSING
Number of Servings — 6

6 pork chops
6 c. dry bread crumbs
2 (10½ oz.) can cream of chicken soup

Brown pork chops in fat on top unit. Place in baking dish. Mix bread crumbs with undiluted cream of chicken soup. Spread over top of pork chops. Bake at 325° F. for approximately 30 minutes.

Elizabeth Kessinger, Sherrard H. S.
Sherrard, West Virginia

PORK CHOPS AND MUSHROOM GRAVY
Number of Servings — 4-5

Salt and pepper fine lean and tender pork chops. Roll in flour and brown in hot fat. Mix 1 can mushroom (soup or sauce) with ½ cup milk and pour over chops. Turn heat to simmer and cook in tightly covered skillet for approximately 25-30 minutes. Place chops on platter and pour gravy over. Sprinkle lightly with paprika. This meat dish is tasty enough for a king.

Mrs. Ethel A. Nale, Indianola H. S.
Indianola, Oklahoma

PORK CHOPS IN MUSHROOM SAUCE
Number of Servings — 8

8 lean pork chops
½ stick butter or margarine
1 can cream of mushroom soup
1 cup water

Melt butter in skillet, brown pork chops. Return chops to skillet, add soup and water. Bake at 350° F. for 1 hour.

Lucy Dennison, Caneyville H. S.
Caneyville, Kentucky

PORK CHOPS WITH MUSHROOM SAUCE
Number of Servings — 6

1½ lbs. lean pork chops (approx. 6)
2 T. cooking oil or fat
½ c. flour
¼ t. pepper
1 t. salt
1 can mushroom soup
1 can milk (water may be substituted)

Dredge chops with flour, salt and pepper. Brown quickly in hot skillet with cooking oil or fat. Pour mushroom soup and milk over chops—cover; reduce heat and cook slowly for 45 minutes, or until very tender.

Louise N. Penington, Louisa County H. S.
Mineral, Virginia

SMOTHERED PORK CHOPS
Number of Servings — 4

4 pork chops
8 T. minute rice
4 green pepper rings
4 T. chopped onion
1 No. 303 can stewed tomatoes
Salt and pepper
1 c. water

Brown pork chops on both sides. Salt and pepper to taste. Place pepper ring on each pork chop, fill with 2 tablespoons minute rice. Top with 1 tablespoon chopped onion. Add stewed tomatoes and water. Simmer for 30 minutes. Serves 4.

Pat Hurst, Western Heights H. S.
Oklahoma City, Oklahoma

SMOTHERED PORK CHOPS
Number of Servings — 6

6 pork chops
Prepared mustard
Seasoned flour
2 T. fat
1 can chicken and rice soup

Spread chops with prepared mustard, then dip into seasoned flour. Brown in fat. Place in casserole. Pour soup over chops. Bake covered at 350°F. for 1 hour.

Eleanor J. Lewis, Union Point H. S.
Union Point, Georgia

BAKED STUFFED PORK CHOPS
Number of Servings — 6

6 double-thick pork chops
¼ c. butter
1 T. chopped onion
3 c. soft bread cubes
½ c. chopped celery
2 t. chopped parsley
¼ t. salt
⅛ t. pepper

Melt butter in saucepan. Add onion and saute until lightly browned. Add remaining ingredients and mix well. Slit double-thick pork chops from outer edge to bone to make a pocket. Sprinkle chops with salt and pepper inside and out. Stuff loosely with dressing mixture. Brown in fat in skillet on both sides—15 to 20 minutes. Bake covered in greased baking dish in moderate oven (350° F.) for 45 minutes. Then uncover and bake 15 minutes longer, or until chops are tender.

Jane Johnson, Princeton H. S.
Princeton, Indiana

STUFFED PORK CHOPS
Number of Servings — 6

¼ c. catsup
2 T. lemon juice
1 t. Worcestershire sauce
1 small onion
¼ c. hot water
2 T. lemon juice

Have 6 pork chops cut 1 to 1½ inches thick with pockets cut next to bone. Fill pockets with ½ recipe of bread stuffing combining ½ cup chopped apples. Season chops with salt and pepper. Coat with flour. Dip in (2) beaten eggs, then in bread crumbs, brown in fat on both sides (with medium heat). Top chops with onion. Combine other ingredients and pour over chops.

Mrs. Helen Larabee, Central H. S.
Elizabeth City, North Carolina

STUFFED PORK CHOPS
Number of Servings — 6

6 double pork chops
2 c. bread crumbs
¾ t. salt
¼ t. pepper
1½ T. minced parsley
1 t. sage
1 T. grated onion
3 T. milk
Fat

Cut a pocket on the bone side of each chop. Combine next 7 ingredients and mix well. Stuff each chop with mixture. Brown chops in fat, season, add a little water and bake in moderate oven (350°F.) about 1 hour or until tender.

Mrs. Willa Dine Powell, Hatfield H. S.
Hatfield, Arkansas

STUFFED PORK CHOPS
Number of Servings — 6

6 loin pork chops, 1½″ thick
Apple-raising dressing
½ t. salt
⅛ t. pepper
2 c. chicken broth (canned or use bouillon cubes)
4 T. flour
1 c. water

Cut a slit or pocket next to the bone on inside of chop or through center of outer or fat edge. Fill pocket with spoonful of dressing (bake rest of dressing in separate pan). Secure with skewer or toothpick. Season chops. Place in baking pan, add one cup broth; cover and bake (350°F.) in moderate oven for one hour. Uncover and continue baking 30 minutes to brown. Remove chops to hot platter while making gravy. Pour off excess fat. Add flour to residue in bottom of pan. Add remaining chicken broth and about one cup water to mixture; cook 5 minutes. Season if needed.

APPLE-RAISIN DRESSING

3 c. finely diced tart apples, unpeeled
¾ c. diced celery
2 T. sugar
⅓ c. butter
⅓ c. water
6 c. cubed raisin bread
1½ t. salt
1 t. poultry seasoning
¼ t. marjoram
½ c. chicken broth
1 egg, beaten

Combine apples, celery, sugar, butter and water in sauce pan. Bring to boil. Cover and cook 5 minutes. Combine bread and seasonings. (Rubbed sage may be used). Combine chicken broth and egg; add to bread. Add hot apple mixture; toss with fork to mix. Turn into buttered 1½ quart loaf pan or casserole. Bake uncovered in moderate oven (350°F.) 35 minutes (10-15 minutes longer gives a crisper top). Serves 6.

Blanche Maxwell, Spring Valley P. S.
Spring Valley, Wisconsin

SMOTHERED PORK CHOPS
Number of Servings — 6

6 center-cut 1″ pork chops
Milk to cover
1 t. salt
Pepper to taste

Brown pork chops in small amount of fat. Place in casserole and cover with sweet milk. Add salt and pepper. Cover and bake at 350°F. 2 hours or until tender.

Leuty Quaid, Wynnewood Jr. H. S.

STUFFED PORK CHOPS
Number of Servings — 6

6 rib chops, 1½" thick
Celery stuffing
Flour
3 tart red apples
Salt and pepper

Wipe chops, cut halfway through lean to bone. Sprinkle with salt and pepper and rub lightly with flour. Sear both sides quickly in hot, heavy frying pan. Stuff, fasten with small wooden skewer (toothpicks). Lay flat on rack in baking dish. Place half a cored apple on each, cut side down. Cover closely, bake in moderate oven (350°F.) until meat is tender (about 45 minutes). Remove skewers.

CELERY STUFFING

4 c. bread crumbs or half cracker crumbs
½ c. melted butter or savory fat such as bacon, sausage or chicken
1 t. salt
Seasoning
1 c. finely cut celery

Mix ingredients lightly with fork. Season to taste. If a compact stuffing is desired, moisten with hot water or scalded milk.

Josephine L. Grissette, Robert E. Lee H. S.
Montgomery, Alabama

STUFFED PORK CHOPS
Number of Servings — 6

6 pork chops, center-cut or rib-cut about 1¼ inches thick
2 c. soft bread crumbs
¼ c. melted butter or margarine
¼ t. poultry seasoning
2 T. minced onion
Salt and pepper
½ c. water

Have meat man cut pockets in the chops or, with a sharp knife, cut a slit from the fat side to the bone. Combine bread crumbs and next 3 ingredients in a bowl; season to taste with salt and pepper. Fill the meat pockets with stuffing mixture. (Not too full because stuffing will expand). Fasten with wooden picks. Heat a skillet over low heat. Place chops in the skillet and fry until brown, about 10 to 12 minutes, turn once. Dip out excess fat in the skillet. Season with additional salt and pepper. Add water. Cover; simmer 1 hour or until chops are fully cooked and tender. Remove wooden picks. Arrange on a heated platter with sauteed bananas and garnish with parsley, *if desired.* Make gravy, *if desired,* by mixing 1 tablespoon flour with pan drippings in skillet, mix in a little water or milk. Return to heat; bring to boiling, stirring constanly, and cook abou 3 minutes. Pour over chops or serve in a gravy boat.

Sharon Kinsey, Hot Springs County H. S.
Thermopolis, Wyoming

PORK CHOPS WITH CURRY STUFFING
Number of Servings — 4

4 1-in. thick pork chops
1 T. fat
¾ c. diced apple
2 T. onion
¼ c. chopped celery
1½ c. bread crumbs
¼ c. milk
1 t. curry powder
3 T. flour
½ t. salt

Have pockets cut into chops. Melt fat and add onion, apple and celery. Cook over low heat. Fold in rest of mixture and stuff chops. Arrange in casserole, cover and bake in 350°F. oven for one hour. Remove cover last 15 minutes.

Mrs. Ramona Warwick, Castlewood H. S.
Castlewood, South Dakota

STUFFED PORK CHOPS
Number of Servings — 6

2 c. dry bread cubes
1½ T. chopped onion
½ t. salt
⅛ t. pepper
¼ t. sage
3 T. melted butter
½ c. chopped apples
Hot water to moisten

Have pocket cut in 6 double pork chops. Fill chops with bread stuffing and bake uncovered in moderate (350°F.) oven for 1 hour.

Mrs. Arlene Dettmeier, Big Rapids H. S.
Big Rapids, Michigan

STUFFED PORK CHOPS
Number of Servings — 8

8 double pork chops
4 cups bread crumbs
1½ t. salt
½ t. pepper
3 T. minced parsley
2 t. sage
2 t. grated onion
6 t. milk
1 egg, beaten
3 T. celery

Cut a pocket on the bone side of each chop. Mix salt and pepper and use one-half to salt each chop. Combine all other ingredients and mix well. Stuff each chop with the mixture and hold together with tooth picks. Brown each chop in hot fat. Place chops in baking dish with a rack. Add 1 cup water and bake in a 350°F. oven for 1 hour or until tender.

Reba Rowan, Claxton H. S.
Claxton, Georgia

CORN-STUFFED PORK CHOPS

Slowly brown six ¾ inch pork chops in 4 table-spoons shortening. When pork chops are brown spread lightly with prepared mustard. Combine one 1-pound can cream-style corn, one 12 ounce can whole kernel corn, drained, 1 beaten egg, 1 cup soft bread crumbs, ¼ cup each, chopped onion and green pepper, 2 tablespoons chopped pimento, 1 teaspoon salt, dash pepper. Arrange chops in baking dish, fatty side standing up; spoon stuffing between and around chops. Bake at 350°F. for 1 hour.

Mrs. Mary Frances Sibley, Holly Bluff H. S.
Holly Bluff, Mississippi

STUFFED BAKED PORK CHOPS
Number of Servings — 6

6 double pork chops
2 c. bread crumbs
4 T. butter
1 small onion, minced
½ t. Worcestershire sauce
¼ t. salt
Dash of pepper
1½ c. water
3 T. Heinz Tomato Ketchup

Cut pocket in each chop. Make a dressing of bread crumbs and seasonings. Place dressing in the pocket of the chops. Brown. Place in roasting pan, cover with sauce made of water and ketchup. Bake in hot oven (400°F.) about 45 minutes, basting frequently.

Mrs. Catherine R. Mordan, Millville Joint H. S.
Millville, Pennsylvania

STUFFED PORK CHOPS
Number of Servings — 4

4 rib pork chops, 1½″ thick cut through the
  lean part to make a pocket
2 c. soft bread crumbs
1½ t. poultry seasoning
¼ t. celery salt
¼ t. onion salt
2 T. melted butter
¼ c. water or stock
2 T. sauted onion
⅛ t. table salt

Combine the bread crumbs, poultry seasoning, celery salt, onion salt, salt, sauted onion, butter and stock, and lightly mix. Stuff the pork chops with dressing. Secure opening in pork chops with toothpicks. Brown chops in 2 tablespoons hot fat in a heavy skillet. Add ½ cup hot water and cover. Place in moderate oven 350°F.) and bake for one hour.

Mrs. Carrie Tobler, Preston Sr. H. S.
Preston, Idaho

PORK CHOPS A LA STUFFING
Number of Servings — 6

6 pork chops
Bread crumbs (8 sticks bread)
¼ c. butter
3 T. chopped onion
3 T. chopped celery
Sprinkle of Tabasco, salt and pepper
2 eggs

Brown and then simmer chops for 20 minutes. Melt butter in saucepan and add onion, celery and desired seasonings. Cook until tender. Add butter mixture to bread crumbs. Blend in well, 2 eggs. Place chops in baking dish and with an ice cream scoop, scoop on balls of stuffing on each chop. Bake in 350°F. oven 15 to 20 minutes. Serve immediately.

Mrs. Adalu English, Danville H. S.
Danville, Pennsylvania

STUFFED BAKED PORK CHOPS
Number of Servings — 6

6 pork chops, cut 1 in. thick (slit to bone
  forming a pocket)
1 c. bread crumbs
2 T. melted butter
½ t. sage
¼ t. thyme
1 t. salt
⅛ t. pepper
3 T. water or stock

Fill pocket with bread dressing to which ½ cup chopped apples have been added. Brown chops on both sides in hot skillet. Sprinkle with salt and pepper to taste. Add water to cover bottom of pan. Cover closely and simmer over very low heat or bake in 325°F. oven for 45 minutes. Move chops occasionally, add a little water if needed.

Ruby Akers, McDowell H. S.
McDowell, Kentucky

STUFFED PORK CHOPS
Number of Servings — 6

6 rib pork chops (¾ to 1 inch thick)
1 c. bread crumbs
¼ c. chopped celery
¼ t. salt
¼ c. chopped onions
2 T. chopped parsley
⅛ t. paprika
Milk to moisten dressing

Wipe meat with damp cloth and trim. Cut large gash into side of each chop. Prepare dressing with above ingredients. Fill the pockets of chops with dressing. Fasten edges with picks and lace with string. Brown chops slightly in small amount of fat. Then place chops in ¼ inch of milk in a baking pan and cover. Bake at 350°F. until done (¾ to 1 hour). Make gravy with drippings.

Vivian M. Chaffin, Central H. S.
Florence, Alabama

FAVORITE PORK CHOPS
Number of Servings — 4-6

4-6 lean pork chops
4-6 heaping T. long grain rice
1 can condensed cream of mushroom soup
1 can water

Brown chops (in lightly oiled skillet) on both sides. Place in covered baking dish. Wash rice and pile heaping tablespoon on each chop. Cover with soup; add water; place cover on dish and bake 1 hour at 350°F. Note: For added flavor, place water in skillet chops were browned in—then pour over other ingredients

Mrs. Wanda Reeves, Sanger H. S.
Sanger, Texas

FESTIVE PORK CHOPS
Number of Servings — 4

8 medium pork chops
Curry powder
Salt
8 pineapple slices
4 spiced red crabapples
Parsley

Sprinkle pork chops generously on both sides with curry powder. Place in electric fry pan. Cook on 340°F. until brown on both sides. Salt to taste. Arrange on platter with pineapple slices, apples and parsley. (Do not add cooking oil to pan. Do not roll in flour).

Mrs. Loetta Thomason, James F. Byrnes H. S.
Duncan, South Carolina

GLAZED PORK CHOPS
Number of Servings — 6

Use a large, shallow baking dish and aluminum foil to cover. Wipe with a damp cloth 6 pork chops, cut about 1 inch thick. Coat chops evenly with a mixture of ¼ cup flour, 2 teaspoons salt, ½ teaspoon Accent and ¼ teaspoon pepper. Heat 1 teaspoon fat in a large heavy skillet over medium heat. Place chops in skillet and brown lightly on both sides over medium heat. Remove to baking dish. Add ⅔ cup hot water, 3 tablespoons minced onion and 2 tablespoons minced parsley. Cover and bake at 350°F. about 45 minutes. While chops bake, mix together ½ cup apple jelly, broken in pieces with a fork, ¼ cup hot water, ¼ teaspoon cinnamon and ¼ teaspoon cloves. Heat over simmering water, stirring occasionally, until jelly is melted. Uncover baking dish and spread jelly glaze over the chops. Bake uncovered 20 minutes longer, or until chops are tender and thoroughly cooked. (To test for doneness, cut a slit near the bone; no pink color should be visible).

Mrs. Judy Mirka, West Jefferson H. S.
West Jefferson, Ohio

GLAZED PORK CHOPS
Number of Servings — 4

4 pork chops
1 orange
1 apple
1 can of beef broth
1 T. of brown sugar
1 T. of cornstarch

In skillet, brown 4 pork chops on both sides; pour off drippings. Top each with slice of apple and orange, sprinkle with ground cinnamon and cloves. Add 1 can of beef broth, 1 tablespoon of brown sugar. Cover; cook over low heat for 35 minutes. Stir 1 tablespoon cornstarch into 2 tablespoons orange juice 'till smooth; gradually blend into beef broth. Cook; stir constantly 'till slightly thickened; simmer a few minutes. 4 delicious servings.

Mrs. Glenda Wiggins, Greenville H. S.
Greenville, Alabama

BRAISED PORK CHOPS
Number of Servings —

6 pork chops
Salt and pepper to season
½ to ⅔ c. catsup
2 T. vinegar

Brown pork chops in small amount of fat. Drain; season with salt and pepper. Blend catsup and vinegar together. Place pork chops in casserole; pour catsup and vinegar over them being sure to cover each chop. Cover and bake in oven at 325° F. for 1 hour.

Frances Rudd, State Dept. of Education
Little Rock, Arkansas

PORK 'N' CORN ROASTS
Number of Servings — 4-6

4-6 ½-inch pork chops
1 T. prepared mustard
1 No. 303 can (2 c.) golden cream style corn
⅔ c. soft bread crumbs
2 T. finely chopped onion
1 T. finely chopped green pepper
1 t. salt
Dash pepper
1 c. water

Spread pork chops lightly with mustard. Brown well. Combine corn, bread crumbs, onion, green pepper, salt, and pepper. Arrange chops in one layer in baking dish. Drain fat from skillet—do not add to chops. Add water to skillet; heat to a boil. Pour around chops. Top with corn mixture. Cover and bake 15 minutes. Uncover and bake 45 minutes.

Mrs. Lila Gerber, Litchfield H. S.
Litchfield, Michigan

PACKAGE DINNER (OVEN)

½ c. cooked rice
1 browned pork chop
½ c. drained English peas or string beans
½ c. of mushroom soup
Salt and pepper

Cook rice. Brown pork chop on both sides in skillet. Place cooked rice in the center of a square of foil; place browned pork chop on top of rice, then add drained vegetables (English peas or string beans). Next, add mushroom soup. Season to taste. Close the foil, making a tight package. Bake on a cookie sheet in pre-heated oven at 350°F. for about 1 hour. Serve in package.

Nancy Capell, Lowndes County H. S.
Ft. Deposit, Alabama

SWEET AND PUNGENT PORK CHOPS
Number of Servings — 6

6 loin pork chops, 1" thick
½ t. salt
3 large tart apples
5 T. flour
3 T. molasses
2 c. hot water
1 c. cider vinegar
⅓ c. golden seedless raisins
12 maraschino cherries

Score fat edges of chops; brown fat edges in frying pan, then brown chops on both sides. Arrange in shallow baking dish. Sprinkle with salt. Core apples; do not peel; cut into thick rings. Place on chops. Add flour to fat in frying pan; stir until browned. Combine molasses and water; add; stir over low heat until mixture thickens. Add vinegar and raisins; pour over chops and apples. Cover; bake in moderate oven, (350°F.) 1 hour. Add maraschino cherries.

Mrs. Norine Bydalek, Franklin H. S.
Franklin, Nebraska

PORK CHOP DELIGHT
Number of Servings — 4

4 center cut pork chops
2 beef cubes
2 tomatoes (fresh)
1 large onion
1 c. uncooked rice
3 c. water
Pepper and salt to taste

Brown pork chops on both sides in a large, heavy skillet. Add sliced tomatoes and onion, placing one piece on each pork chop. Add the uncooked rice, beef cubes, pepper, salt and 3 cups of water to the pork chops. Cook over medium heat 1 hour.

Mrs. Don Schierholt, Ludington H. S.
Ludington, Michigan

BREADED PORK CHOPS
Number of Servings — 6

6 pork chops (¾-to 1-in. thick)
2 egg yolks
4 T. cold water
2 t. salt
1½ c. cracker crumbs
4 T. fat
6 slices onion
½ c. hot water

Thoroughly beat egg yolks, salt and cold water. Heat fat in frying pan. Wipe chops with damp cloth, dip into egg mixture and then into cracker crumbs. Place in hot fat and brown well on both sides. Lay onion slices on top of chops and add hot water. Cover and oven bake 45 minutes at 350° F.

Effie Lois Greene, Tishomingo H. S.
Paden, Mississippi

PARTY PORK CHOPS
Number of Servings — 6

6 center loin pork chops
1 green pepper
1 Spanish onion
1 can condensed mushroom soup
1 c. milk
Salt and pepper

Fry pork chops until brown. Place in a large flat pan such as a broiler pan. Season with salt and pepper. Slice green pepper and onion in ¼" slices. Place slice of onion on pork chop. Place green pepper ring on onion slice. Mix soup with one cup of milk. Pour mixture over chops and bake at 350°F. for one hour.

Barbara Snyder, Selinsgrove Area Jr. H. S.
Selinsgrove, Pennsylvania

SWEET AND SOUR PORK CHOPS
Number of Servings — 6

1 t. ginger
1 t. salt
½ t. pepper
1 t. paprika
¼ c. flour
1 T. fat
1 c. pineapple juice
2 T. vinegar
3 T. brown sugar
6 pork chops, loin or shoulder

Mix ginger, salt, pepper, paprika, flour together. Coat both sides of the chops in this dry mixture. Brown chops in melted fat. Then pour in pineapple juice and vinegar. Sprinkle with sugar. Cook over a low heat for 40 minutes or until chops are tender.

Marie Gantzert, Thornridge H. S.
Dolton, Illinois

PORK CHOP, SWEET POTATO AND PINEAPPLE DINNER
Number of Servings — 6

6 pork chops
3 large sweet potatoes
6 slices pineapple
12 large prunes
½ c. pineapple juice
12 whole cloves

Brown seasoned pork chops in small amount of fat in skillet. Peel sweet potatoes, cut in half and rub with lemon juice. Place on meat! add pineapple slices. Wash and remove pits from prunes and insert cloves. Add prunes and pineapple juice. Cover, turn heat high until steaming. Turn down low. Cook 45 minutes. Serve hot.

Mrs. Nina Parker, Bear Grass H. S.
Williamston, North Carolina

WILD RICE AND PORK CHOPS
Number of Servings — 6

1 c. wild rice
8 slices bacon
1 medium-sized onion
1 t. salt
¼ t. pepper
½ t. crushed oregano
6 pork chops, cut 1½ inch thick

Wash the wild rice well. Cover generously with hot water and allow to boil about 5 minutes. Drain and rinse with hot water. Cover again with hot water. Add salt. Bring to a boil and cook about 20 minutes or until the rice is tender. Stir gently with a fork a few times during the cooking process. Drain well. Dice the bacon and saute with the minced onion until the bacon is crisp and the onion tender. Add the rice and seasonings and toss to blend well. Place the mixture in a large covered baking dish. Brown the chops well on both sides, sprinkle with salt, pepper, and a little poultry seasoning if desired. Place over the rice. Cover and set the casserole in a pan of hot water. Bake at 325°F. about 1½ hours or until the chops are tender. *Gravy:* Make the gravy in the pan in which the chops were browned. Add 1 (4-oz.) can of mushroom slices, with the liquid.

Darlene Letnes, Nogales H. S.
Nogales, Arizona

PORK CHOPS AND RICE
Number of Servings — 6

6 pork chops
1 small package minute rice
2 cans cream of chicken soup
1½ c. cooked celery

Brown pork chops, season to taste. Cook rice and celery separate, then put rice and celery and soup over chops and simmer 15 minutes.

Donna Mae Hurst, Box Elder H. S.
Brigham City, Utah

PORK CHOPS ON RICE
Number of Servings — 6

6 medium pork chops
½ c. uncooked rice
3 ripe tomatoes or a No. 303 can stewing
    tomatoes
1 medium onion

Brown and season pork chops. Put the *uncooked* rice in a baking dish and lay the pork chops on top. Place a slice of tomato or a spoonful of stewed tomatoes and a slice of onion on each chop. Pour over this a can of consomme soup. Bake in a covered dish 45 minutes at 300°F. *Uncover* and bake 15 minutes longer. Be sure to have baking dish large enough to take care of the rice as it cooks.

Diana Herman, Bowman Public H. S.
Bowman, North Dakota

PORK CHOPS AND RICE
Number of Servings — 4

4 pork chops (1½" thick)
3 c. tomato juice
1 onion, sliced
4 T. chopped celery
4 T. chopped green pepper
¼ t. salt
½ c. cooked rice

Brown pork chops on medium heat (use deep well cooker or sauce pan). Add tomato juice, chopped pepper, salt, and rice. Celery may be omitted. Cook on high heat until steaming; turn to low heat or simmer and cook for 1½ hours.

Mary W. Hull, Pickens H. S.
Pickens, South Carolina

CREOLE PORK CHOPS
Number of Servings — 6

6 pork chops
½ c. flour
4 T. fat
Salt and pepper
2 c. cooked rice
6 green pepper rings
1 c. water
1 No. 2 can tomatoes

Dredge pork chops with flour and brown in hot fat. Season with salt and pepper. Put browned chops into a greased baking dish. Put a pepper ring on top of each chop. Fill pepper ring with cooked rice and top with tomato. Sprinkle with salt and pepper. Pour remaining tomatoes and juice and water around the chops. Bake in moderate oven (350° F.) about 30 minutes.

Mrs. Mary Eula Cowles, Newkirk H. S.
Newkirk, Oklahoma

PORK 'N RICE
Number of Servings — 4

4 lean pork chops
1 T. butter or margarine
¾ t. salt
6 T. uncooked rice
1 16-oz. can tomato juice
¼ t. pepper

Set oven for 300°F. Use heavy skillet. Brown chops rapidly in butter. Sprinkle uncooked rice over browned chops. Pour tomato juice over chops and rice until well covered. Sprinkle salt and pepper over all. Bake from 1 to 1½ hours, or until rice is tender. Add more tomato juice or water from time to time if product becomes dry.

Fern A. Vincent, Henderson Jr. H. S.
Henderson, Nevada

LOUISIANA PORK CHOP CREOLE
Number of Servings — 6

6 pork chops
1 onion, chopped
4 T. fat
1 green pepper, chopped
1 can tomatoes
1 small can tomato sauce
½ c. water

Brown pork chops; remove from pan and saute onion and green pepper in fat. Place pork chops in pan over onions and peppers, add tomatoes, tomato sauce and water. Simmer slowly over low heat for 50 minutes. Serve chops and gravy over rice.

Sue Farmer, Haughton H. S.
Haughton, Louisiana

SURPRISE CHOPS AND BEANS
Number of Servings — 4

2 cans (1-lb. each) pork and beans
4 pork chops (½" thick)
¼ t. caraway seeds
¼ c. apple jelly

Pour pork and beans into a greased 1½-quart baking dish. Brown chops and place on top of beans. Stir caraway seeds into jelly and spread on top of chops. Cover and bake at 350°F. for 35 minutes. Uncover and bake 10 to 15 minutes longer, or until chops are done.

Mrs. Catherine R. Trotter, Independence H. S.
Independence, Louisiana

FARMER'S PORK CHOPS
Number of Servings — 4

4 pork chops
1 clove garlic, chopped
Salt and pepper
4 potatoes, sliced
2 onions, sliced

1½ c. sour cream
1½ t. salt
½ t. dry mustard

Heat oven to 350° F. Trim excess fat from chops and roll in flour. Brown chops and garlic in hot fat. Season. Place potatoes in baking pan; top with browned chops. Onions over chops. Blend sour cream, salt, mustard; pour over potatoes, chops and onions. Bake 1½ hours.

Mrs. O. K. Vorthmann, Sumner Community H. S.
Sumner, Iowa

PORK CHOPS IN SAUCE
Number of Servings — 6

6 medium pork chops
6 green pepper slices
6 onion slices
1 can tomato soup
Salt and pepper
Small amount fat

Brown seasoned chops in very small amount of fat. Pour off fat; cover each chop with a green pepper and onion slice and 2 to 3 tablespoons tomato soup. Cover and cook at a low temperature from 45 minutes to 1 hour.

Mrs. Sue Riddle, Wakita H. S.
Wakita, Oklahoma

PORK CHOPS SUPREME
Number of Servings — 4

4 thick pork chops (seasoned and browned)
4 thin onion slices
4 thin lemon slices
4 T. brown sugar
4 T. catsup
¼ c. water

Top each seasoned and browned pork chop with 1 slice onion, 1 slice lemon, 1 tablespoon brown sugar, and 1 tablespoon catsup. Add water, cover, and bake 1½ hours at 350°F.

Mrs. Anne Marie Farning, Plainview H. S.
Plainview, Minnesota

DIXIE PORK CHOPS
Number of Servings — 7

7 pork chops
2 cans tomato sauce
4 cans water (measure in sauce can)
7 slices green pepper
7 slices onion
1 c. uncooked rice
Salt to taste
Pepper to taste

Brown pork chops in skillet and then add rice. Place slices of green pepper and onion over chops. Pour tomato sauce and water into skillet. Add salt and pepper. Cover and cook on top of stove over very low heat for one hour.

Jo Ann Joffrion, Linwood Jr. H. S.
Shreveport, Louisiana

DIXIE PORK CHOPS
Number of Servings — 8

8 pork chops
½ t. salt
4 tart apples, cored and cut in rings
¼ cup brown sugar
2 T. enriched flour
1 c. hot water
1 T. vinegar
½ c. seedless raisins

Brown chops in hot fat; sprinkle with salt. Place in baking dish; top with apple rings; sprinkle with sugar. Add flour to fat in skillet; blend. Add water, vinegar; cook 'till thick. Add raisins; pour over chops. Bake uncovered in moderate oven (350° F.) 1 hour.

Mrs. Nancy King, Hallsville H. S.
Hallsville, Texas

PORK CHOPS EN CASSEROLE
Number of Servings — 6

6 pork chops (⅝ inch thick)
½ c. partially cooked rice
2 green peppers
1 large onion
1½ c. water
1 small can tomato paste
1 can tomato puree
Salt, pepper and garlic powder to taste

Brown meat in frying pan. Place chops in casserole, topping each with a ring of pepper, which has been filled with rice; top with slice of onion. Mix paste and puree along with water and spices. Bake at 350°F. for 1 hour.

Veronica Iva Peters, Eatonville H. S.
Eatonville, Washington

PORK CHOP CASSEROLE
Number of Servings — 6

6 pork chops
2 medium onions, cut in rings
1 large bell pepper, cut in rings
⅔ c. uncooked rice
1 pt. tomatoes
1 fresh tomato (optional)

Brown pork chops in small amount of fat. Make a thin flour gravy. Arrange the ingredients in alternate layers, saving some pepper and tomatoes for top layer. Pour gravy over all and cook in a covered dish in oven until done. It will be done when the rice is done. Remove lid and continue cooking at 400°F. for approximately 1 hour or until brown.

Mrs. Ferrel C. Lovett, Screven County H. S.
Sylvania, Georgia

PORK CHOPS PIQUANT

Dip each pork chop in a mixture of slightly beaten egg and water (use 3 tablespoons to each egg), then in fine dry bread crumbs. Brown chops lightly in small amount of fat in a large frying pan. Top each chop with 1 tablespoon condensed mushroom soup to which ½ teaspoon Worcestershire sauce has been added and sprinkle with salt and pepper. Top each chop with a slice of Bermuda onion. Cover and simmer slowly, about 45 minutes or until chops are tender.

Mrs. Miriam B. Templeton, Hickory Tavern H. S.
Gray Court, South Carolina

BAR-BE QUE PORK CHOPS
Number of Servings — 3

6 pork chops
1 can condensed chicken soup
1 medium onion slice
3 T. catsup
2 t. Worcestershire sauce

Fry pork chops in fat. Combine in separate bowl; soups, onion, catsup, and Worcestershire sauce and blend well. Place mixture between and on top of drained pork chops in greased casserole dish (uncovered) and bake one hour at 350° F.

Jane Roberts, Quincy Comm. H. S.
Quincy, Michigan

BARBECUED PORK CHOPS
Number of Servings — 4

4 1-in. lean pork chops
¼ c. catsup
½ t. salt
½ t. celery seed
¼ t. nutmeg
¼ c. vinegar
½ c. water
1 bay leaf

Brown chops in hot fat. Combine remaining ingredients; pour over chops. Bake in slow oven (325° F.) for 1½ hours. Turn chops once during baking.

Mrs. Laura Johnson Little, Bessemer H. S.
Greensboro, North Carolina

BARBECUED PORK CHOPS
Number of Servings — 6

6 ¾-in. pork chops
Salt and pepper
1 8-oz. can seasoned tomato sauce
½ c. catsup
1 t. Worcestershire sauce
1 t. liquid smoke or 1 T. commercial
barbeque sauce
½ t. onion salt

Brown pork chops in heavy skillet. Season with salt and pepper. Combine remaining ingredients and pour over chops. Simmer 'till tender, about 1 hour, turning occasionally. Makes 6 servings.

Mrs. Ann Irvine, Milford H. S.
Milford, Nebraska

BARBECUED PORK CHOPS
Number of Servings — 8

8 lean pork chops
½ c. catsup
1 t. salt
1 t. celery seed
½ t. nutmeg
⅓ c. vinegar
1 c. water
1 bay leaf

Brown chops in hot fat. Pour over combined remaining ingredients. Cover and bake in moderate oven (325°F.) 1½ hours. Turn chops once half way through cooking period. Cover may be removed the last half of the cooking period if desired.

Pat Ireland, Oakwood Township H. S.
Fithian, Illinois

BARBECUED PORK CHOPS
Number of Servings — 8

8 lean pork chops
½ c. catsup
1 t. salt
1 t. celery seed
½ t. nutmeg
⅓ c. vinegar
1 c. water
1 bay leaf (optional)

Brown the chops in hot fat. Combine the remaining ingredients in order and pour over the chops which have been placed in a baking dish. Cover and bake in moderate oven (325° F.) for 1½ hours. Note: For a browner surface, remove cover during last 20 minutes.

Frances L. Lynch, Buckhannon-Upshur Sr. H. S.
Buckhannon, West Virginia

BARBECUED PORK CHOPS
Number of Servings — 6-8

8 pork chops, ¾-in. thick
½ c. minced onion
¼ c. salad oil
1½ c. chili sauce
⅓ c. bottled meat sauce
1 t. dry mustard
3 dashes Tabasco
1 T. Worcestershire sauce
1 t. salt

Brown pork chops on both sides in fat trimmed from chops. Cook onions in salad oil until tender. Add remaining ingredients to cooked onions and mix well. Pour barbecue sauce over pork chops. Cover. Simmer 1 hour or until tender. Remove cover and cool.

Mrs. Helen C. Borders, Belwood H. S.
Lawndale, North Carolina

BARBECUED PORK CHOPS
Number of Servings — 6

6 or 8 pork chops
½ c. vinegar
½ c. catsup
1 t. salt
⅛ t. cinnamon
1 t. sugar
1 t. celery salt
½ t. nutmeg
¾ c. water
1 bay leaf

Brown pork chops. Mix ingredients and bring to a boil. Pour sauce over pork chops. Cover. Bake at 350° F. for 1 hour or until done.

Emma Jo Roberts, Winterboro H. S.
Alpine, Alabama

PORK CUTLETS CREOLE
Number of Servings — 6

1 lb. pork cutlets
½ c. thinly sliced onions
1½ T. fat
½ c. chopped celery
2½ c. cooked tomatoes (No. 2 can)
1 t. celery salt
½ t. chili powder
½ c. flour

Dip cutlets in salt, pepper and flour mixture. Brown onions in fat. Add meat and brown thoroughly. Remove excess fat. Add celery, tomatoes, celery salt and chili powder. Cover tightly and simmer over low heat or bake in moderate oven (350°F.) until tender, about 1½ hours.

Geraldine B. Wise, Buckeye H. S.
Buckeye, Louisiana

BRAISED PORK STEAK
Number of Servings — 4

3 T. catsup
2 T. lemon juice
½ t. mustard (paste)
1 t. Worcestershire sauce
4 pork steaks
1 small onion
¼ c. water

Combine catsup, lemon juice, mustard, and Worcestershire sauce; rub into both sides of steak. Brown in hot fat. Top with onion slices, add water. Cover and bake in moderate oven (325-350°F.) for one hour. Serve with spiced prunes!

Patricia Tigert, Armour H. S.
Armour, South Dakota

PORK WITH PINEAPPLE TIDBITS
Number of Servings — 4

1 lb. pork, sliced thin
1 c. flour
1 t. salt

(Continued on Next Page)

1 t. pepper
Corn oil for frying
2 small cans pineapple cubes
1 green pepper
2 T. chopped onion
1½ c. canned chicken soup
2 T. catsup
3 T. sugar
1 t. salt
2 T. vinegar
2 T. flour

Dip the pork in the flour mixture and fry in hot corn oil until lightly brown, and place on serving dish. Cut the green pepper and onion in small pieces. Mix the chicken soup, flour and seasonings together and bring to a boil. Add the pineapple, green pepper and onion and cook until of sauce texture (thin). Pour the mixture over the fried pork and serve.

Mrs. Euzelia M. Vollbracht,
Burns at Fallston H. S.
Fallston, North Carolina

HAWAIIAN BAKED PORK
Number of Servings — 4

2 c. crushed pineapple
3 medium sweet potatoes
2 T. brown sugar
4 pork steaks
4 strips bacon
Salt and pepper

Place pineapple in large baking dish. Place slices of sweet potato over pineapple. Sprinkle brown sugar over this. Season pork steak with salt and pepper and place these over sweet potatoes. On top arrange bacon strips. Cover and bake about 1 hour at 350°F.

Linda Oldenburg, Osseo H. S.
Osseo, Wisconsin

ORANGE-GLAZED PORK ROAST
Number of Servings — 8-10

1 5-lb. pork loin roast
Salt and pepper to taste
6 orange slices
12 whole cloves
1 c. orange juice
½ c. honey
2 sticks cinnamon
1 t. grated orange peel

Trim excess fat from roast and score. Sprinkle with salt and pepper. Attach orange slices to roast with cloves. Place on rack, fat side up, in roasting pan. Bake in slow oven (325° F.) 3 to 3½ hours, or until internal temperature reaches 185° F. Combine orange juice, honey, and cinnamon; bring to a boil and simmer uncovered 15 minutes. Add orange peel. Baste roast with orange juice mixture every 20 minutes during last hour of roasting.

Mrs. Jo Ann Albright, Lytton Community H. S.
Lytton, Iowa

ROAST LOIN OF PORK WITH ORANGE SAUCE
Number of Servings — 5-6

4 or 5 lb. loin of pork
Salt
Pepper
1 small onion, sliced
½ an orange, peeled and divided into segments
¼ c. chopped celery
A little oregano
1 c. orange juice
2 T. wine vinegar

Sprinkle a loin of pork with salt and freshly ground black pepper and put in a roasting pan, fat side up. Add onion, orange segments, chopped celery, oregano, orange juice, and wine vinegar. Roast in a moderate oven (350° F.) for 25 to 30 minutes per pound, basting frequently with the pan juices. When the roast is done, put it on a heated serving platter. Remove the excess fat from the pan and strain the pan juices into a sauce boat. If desired, the sauce may be thickened with a little cornstarch or arrowroot mixed with cold water.

Ellen T. Rakestraw, Deshler Local H. S.
Deshler, Ohio

ROAST WITH TOMATO SAUCE

Marinating sauce for roast:
1 head of garlic, mashed
1 T. of oregano
2-3 T. olive oil
Juice of two lemons
1 T. salt
1 t. pepper
Mix and spread over roast and let stand over night.

Sauce for roast:
1 large can tomatoes, mashed
½ c. chopped celery
1 can water
1 large onion, finely minced
3 or 4 garlic pods, finely minced
1 bell papper, cut in small bits
1 large bay leaf
Salt and pepper according to taste
Juice of one lemon
1 t. oregano
4 T. olive oil

Pound flour on roast and brown in olive oil. Heat oil and saute onions, garlic, celery and bell pepper until soft. Add tomatoes and water and mix well. Add remaining ingredients and mix well. Place roast in a large roast pan and pour sauce over roast; then cover. Cook on top of stove or in oven. About 45 minutes before roast is done vegetables may be added, such as potatoes, carrots, bell peppers and whole onions.

Josephine P. Clark, West H. S.
Fairview, Tennessee

SOUTHERN STUFFED PORK ROLL
Number of Servings — 8

1 smoked boneless butt of pork
2 medium-size sweet potatoes
½ c. chopped celery
1 c. bread crumbs
1 t. salt
1 can (1 lb.) apricot halves

Brown meat slowly in its own fat in heavy kettle or Dutch oven; remove from kettle; cool. Mix sweet potatoes, celery, bread crumbs and salt in medium size bowl. Make slashes about 2 inches deep and 2 inches apart in top of meat to form pockets for stuffing; fill with potato mixture. Hold roll in shape by inserting metal skewer at each end. Drain syrup from apricots; pour over meat; cover. Bake in slow oven (325° F.) 2 hours or until meat is tender. Uncover; baste meat with pan juices; place apricot halves around meat. Bake for 30 minutes longer, or until top is glazed. Slice meat through stuffing; arrange with apricot halves on heated platter; serve with pan juices to spoon over. Wrap and chill any remaining meat to make over for another meal.

Norma Hillberry, Basin H. S.
Basin, Wyoming

PORK 'N APPLE PIE
Number of Servings — 6

3 cups pork cubes (leftover)
2 tart apples, pared and sliced
4 T. brown sugar
½ t. cinnamon

Arrange in layers in 8 inch square pan. Sprinkle layers with sugar and cinnamon mixture. Pour 1 cup pork gravy over all. Top with mashed potatoes. Bake at 350°F. about 45 minutes.

Mrs. Mary K. Adams, Galien Twp. H. S.
Galien, Michigan

CUSHION STYLE PORK SHOULDER WITH APPLE AND PRUNE STUFFING
Number of Servings — 8

Pork shoulder (picnic)
8 to 10 prunes
3 tart apples
2 T. butter
1 c. bread crumbs
½ lemon rind, grated
½ t. brown sugar
¼ t. cinnamon
Salt and pepper

Bone picnic shoulder. Sew three sides. Cook prunes 'till tender, pit and cut in halves. Pare apples. Cut into wedges ¾ inch thick. Melt butter, add bread crumbs, prunes and apples. Sprinkle with lemon rind, brown sugar and cinnamon. Season shoulder with salt and pepper and fill opening with prune and apple stuffing. Place on rack in open roaster. Cook at 350°F., 35 to 45 minutes per pound.

Mrs. Esther M. Hight, Weare H. S.
Weare, New Hampshire

BARBECUED SPARERIBS
Number of Servings — 6

1 t. salt
½ t. dry mustard
1 T. paprika
¼ t. chili powder
¼ t. cayenne and red pepper
¼ c. vinegar
¼ c. tomato catsup
1 c. tomato sauce
2 c. water
2 T. Worcestershire sauce

Combine the above ingredients and pour over spareribs that have been seasoned, rolled in flour and browned in hot fat. Bake at 300°F. for 1½ hours or until ribs are tender and sauce is thick.

Ruth Conn, Cave-in-Rock H. S.
Cave-in-Rock, Illinois

BARBECUED SPARERIBS
Number of Servings — 4-5

3-4 lbs. ribs, cut in pieces
2 lemons, thinly sliced
1 medium sized onion, thinly sliced
2 c. tomato sauce
¼ c. Worcestershire sauce
2 t. chili powder
2 t. salt
4 dashes Tabasco sauce
2 c. water

Place ribs, meaty side up in shallow pan with onion and lemon slices on each piece. Roast 30 minutes in 450°F. oven. Combine remaining ingredients, pour over ribs and bake in 350°F. oven about 45 minutes to 1 hour, until tender, basting every 15 minutes.

Coral Albiani, Zion Benton Twp. H. S.
Zion, Illinois

BARBECUED SPARERIBS
Number of Servings — 6

4 lbs. lean, meaty spareribs cut into serving
  pieces
1½ t. salt
¼ t. pepper
1 t. chili powder
1 t. celery seed
1 t. salt
2 T. brown sugar
¼ c. vinegar
Few drops Tabasco sauce
¼ c. Worcestershire sauce

(Continued on Next Page)

1 c. catsup
1 c. water

Brown ribs on both sides in a skillet. Season with the 1½ teaspoons salt and pepper. Remove from skillet and place in 4-quart roasting pan. Combine remaining ingredients and boil 2 to 3 minutes. Pour over browned ribs. Cover. Bake in slow oven (325°F.) for 2 to 2½ hours or until tender. Baste frequently. Remove cover and increase heat to 350° during last half-hour to brown ribs. Remove to warm platter.

Mrs. Mary Carroll, Greenville Jr. H. S.
Greenville, Texas

OVEN BARBECUED SPARERIBS
Number of Servings — 8

7 lbs. spareribs
1 lb. brown sugar
4 T. liquid smoke
1 medium size can pineapple juice
Juice of 3 oranges
Salt and pepper
1 bottle barbecue sauce

Combine all the ingredients. Place the ribs in a large roaster. Cover with the sauce and marinate over night. Cook for two hours at 350°F. After the first hour, drain off the excess grease, turn the ribs and continue baking.

Gail Navens, Grandville H. S.
Grandville, Michigan

TEXAS BARBECUED SPARERIBS
Number of Servings — 6

3 lbs. spare or loin ribs
½ c. chopped onion
2 lemons

On each piece of rib, place one lemon slice. Sprinkle ½ cup of chopped onion over this. Bake in hot oven (450°F.) about 30 minutes. Pour over ribs Texas Barbecue Sauce. Continue baking in moderate oven (350°F.) 1½ to 2 hours. Baste with sauce every 15 minutes. If sauce thickens, add a little hot water. To prevent ribs from browning too much, cover last 30 minutes of baking.

TEXAS BARBECUE SAUCE

2 T. brown sugar
¼ t. chili powder
1 t. salt
2 T. Worcestershire sauce
1 c. tomato juice
½ c. water
1 T. paprika
1 t. dry mustard
⅛ t. cayenne pepper
¼ c. vinegar
¼ c. catsup

Mix these ingredients in saucepan and simmer 15 minutes or until slightly thickened.

Mary Ann C. Brock, Moore Academy
Pine Apple, Alabama

BARBECUED SPARERIBS
Number of Servings — 3

1 T. chili powder
1 T. salt
1 T. celery seed
¼ c. brown sugar (firmly packed)
1 t. paprika
2 lbs. spareribs
½ c. vinegar
1 1-lb. can cream of tomato soup

Mix together first five ingredients, and rub over spareribs. Broil on each side 8 minutes, with top of meat about 3 inches from heat. Place in roasting pan in such a position that the bones hold the meat up from the bottom of the pan. Mix vinegar and tomato soup, and pour over spareribs. Bake in moderate oven (350°F.) for 1½ hours, basting every 30 minutes.

Mrs. Marjorie West, Northeast Voc. H. S.
Lauderdale, Mississippi

BARBECUED SPARERIBS
Number of Servings — 4-5

3 to 4 lbs. ribs, cut in pieces
1 lemon
1 large onion
1 c. catsup
⅓ c. Worcestershire sauce
1 t. chili powder
1 t. salt
2 dashes Tabasco sauce
2 c. water

Place ribs in shallow roasting pan, meaty side up. On each piece place a slice of unpeeled lemon, a thin slice of onion. Roast in hot oven (450°F.) 30 minutes. Combine remaining ingredients; bring to boiling and pour over ribs. Continue baking in moderate oven (350°F.) until tender, about 1½ hours. Baste ribs with the sauce every 15 minutes. If sauce gets too thick, add more water. If you wish to avoid so much basting, cover the ribs for the last part of cooking time.

Mrs. Mary Elizabeth Jackson, Bad Axe H. S.
Bad Axe, Michigan

BARBECUED SPARERIBS
Number of Servings — 4

3-4 pounds spareribs
2 chopped onions
2 T. vinegar
2 T. Worcestershire sauce
1 T. salt
¾ c. catsup
1 t. paprika
½ t. black pepper
1 t. chili powder
¾ c. water

Place spareribs in pan for roasting. Combine all of the other ingredients and pour over spareribs. Bake at 350°F. for one hour.

Polly C. Hinckley, Lyman Memorial Jr.-Sr. H. S.
Lebanon, Connecticut

BARBECUED SPARERIBS
Number of Servings — 7-8

3 lbs. spareribs
1 T. salt
1 t. red pepper
1 t. black pepper
¾ c. catsup
2 T. Worcestershire sauce
2 small onions
2 T. vinegar
1 t. paprika
1 t. chili powder
¾ c. water

Have spareribs cut in serving pieces. Season with salt and pepper. Place in baking dish and brown in oven at 450°F. Cover with sliced onions. Combine remaining ingredients and pour over meat. Cover tightly and bake in oven at 350°F. for 1½ hours.

Mrs. Edythe Darden, Boone Trail H. S.
Mamers, North Carolina

BARBECUED SPARERIBS
Number of Servings — 6

2 lbs. spareribs
2 T. flour
1½ t. dry mustard
½ c. chopped onion
½ t. ground cloves
¼ c. vinegar
1 c. catsup
2 t. salt
1 t. pepper
3 T. Worcestershire sauce
5 drops Tabasco sauce
¾ c. orange juice

Place spareribs in bottom of baking dish. Mix all ingredients together in mixing bowl and pour over spareribs. Bake at 350°F. for one hour. Pork chops or chicken may be substituted for spareribs.

Patricia Y. Crook, East Coweta H. S.
Senoia, Georgia

SPARERIBS WITH SOY SAUCE
Number of Servings — 6

2 lbs. spareribs
2 T. flour
2 T. brown sugar
½ c. soy sauce
1¼ c. water
Medium sized onion, sliced thin

Combine flour and sugar and mix well. Add the soy sauce and water and mix. Place the onion slices over the spareribs in a baking dish and pour sauce over the spareribs. Bake at 350°F. for 1 hour covered and 1 hour uncovered. (Note: Do not add any salt). Serve with steamed rice.

Marilyn Gies, Eastmont Sr. H. S.
East Wenatchee, Washington

BARBECUED SPARERIBS
Number of Servings — 4

¼ c. chopped onions
1 T. drippings or other fat
½ c. water
2 T. vinegar
1 T. Worcestershire sauce
3 lbs. spareribs
¼ c. lemon juice
2 T. brown sugar
1 c. chili sauce
½ t. salt
¼ t. paprika

Saute onions until brown in drippings or fat. Add and simmer for 20 minutes water, vinegar, Worcestershire sauce, lemon juice, brown sugar, chili sauce, salt and paprika. Cut spareribs into pieces for serving and place them in a pan. Cover them with waxed paper. Bake the ribs in a very hot oven (500°F.) for 15 minutes. Reduce the heat to 350°F. Remove the paper and pour the barbecue sauce over the meat. Bake the spareribs for 1 hour longer. Baste them frequently with the pan liquor.

Mrs. Bette Deane Nelson, Saltsburg Joint H. S.
Saltsburg, Pennsylvania

BARBECUED SPARERIBS (BAKED)
Number of Servings — 4-5

4 lbs. spareribs
1 medium size onion, cut fine
2 T. butter
2 T. vinegar
⅛ t. cayenne pepper
¼ c. lemon juice
2 T. brown sugar
1 c. catsup
3 T. Worcestershire sauce
½ T. ground mustard
1 c. water
½ c. celery, chopped fine
2 T. Mazola

Brown the ribs in a large skillet using the Mazola. When brown on both sides, transfer to baking pan. Melt butter in small saucepan, add onions and brown them. Add the remainder of the ingredients. When very hot, pour over the ribs. Bake in preheated oven at 350°F. for 2 hours.

Mrs. F. E. Dey, Litchfield Sr. H. S.
Litchfield, Illinois

OVEN-BARBECUED SPARERIBS
Number of Servings — 4

2 lbs. meaty spareribs
½ c. chopped onion
1 T. hot fat
2 T. brown sugar
4 T. lemon juice
1 c. tomato catsup
1 c. toamto juice
2 T. Worcestershire sauce
2 T. vinegar
1 T. prepared mustard

(Continued on Next Page)

1 t. salt
Dash of pepper
⅛ t. chili powder

Brown onion in hot fat. Add remaining ingredients and simmer 15 minutes. Place spareribs in casserole, pour sauce over and cover. Bake two hours at 350°F. or until tender. Baste ribs with sauce occasionally.

Annette Fisher, Foulkton H. S.
Foulkton, South Dakota

LANAI SPARERIBS
Number of Servings — 4

1 side (2 to 3 lbs.) spareribs
Salt and pepper
¼ c. chopped onion
¼ c. chopped celery
¼ c. chopped green pepper
2 T. butter or margarine
1 T. cornstarch
1 can (20½-oz.) crushed pineapple
¼ c. vinegar
1 T. soy sauce

Season spareribs on both sides. Place ribs, cut side down, on rack in roasting pan. Roast in a moderate oven (350°F.) for 1 hour. Cook onion, celery, and green pepper in butter or margarine, about 5 minutes. Stir in cornstarch and add pineapple. Cook until thickened, stirring constantly. Add vinegar and soy sauce. Turn ribs and spread pineapple mixture over ribs and continue cooking for 45 minutes or until meat is tender.

Patricia Anderle, Lemont Twp. H. S.
Lemont, Illinois

SPARE RIBS ALOHA
Number of Servings — 8

3 lbs. pork ribs, cut in 2-in. pieces
2 t. salt
1 t. pepper
1 bouillon cube
¼ c. boiling water
2 T. brown sugar
2 T. cornstarch
½ t. salt
½ t. monosodium glutamate
¼ c. cold water
1 c. orange juice
1 T. soy sauce
½ c. diced onion
1 c. pressed kumquats

Season spareribs with salt and pepper. Broil 10 minutes on each side. Place in flat casserole. Make sauce: Dissolve bouillon cube in hot water. Combine with remaining ingredients except kumquats. Cook 5 minutes. Add kumquats. Cover ribs. Bake for 1 hour at 350°F., or until tender. Toasted almonds may be sprinkled over top. Serve over rice.

Mrs. Joan Baber, Union H. S.
College Corner, Ohio

SWEET-SOUR SPARERIBS
Number of Servings — 6

½ t. powdered ginger
1 t. salt
½ c. sugar
½ c. vinegar
½ c. water
1 T. soy sauce
2 lbs. pork spareribs, cut in 2 inch pieces
2 T. cornstarch

Combine salt, ginger, sugar, vinegar, water and soy sauce; pour over spareribs, in shallow dish or bowl. Marinate overnight (or at least 4 hours). Drain off marinade and bake spareribs on a rack in uncovered baking pan in moderate oven (350°F.) 1 hour. Dissolve cornstarch in small amount of water; add to marinade in saucepan. Bring to a boil, stirring occasionally, and boil about 5 minutes, or until smooth and thickened. Pour over spareribs in serving dish. Serve with turnip sticks.

Turnip Sticks: Combine 2 cups thinly sliced white turnips and 1 tablespoon salt in a bowl. Let stand 15 minutes, drain off liquid. Add ¼ cup water and 2 tablespoons vinegar and let stand about 1 hour. Drain and press out any excess liquid. Serve with Sweet-Sour Spareribs.

Christine Boneta, Brookwood H. S.
Brookwood, Alabama

SWEET AND SOUR SPARERIBS
Number of Servings — 4

2 slices bacon, chopped
2 lbs. spareribs, cut in 2-in. pieces
1 large onion, sliced
1 No. 211 can pineapple tidbits
2 medium green peppers, chopped
2 T. cornstarch
½ c. brown sugar
¼ c. vinegar
2 t. soy sauce
2 T. water

Fry bacon in electric frypan, remove bacon. Save. Brown spareribs and onion in bacon drippings, then pour off fat. Add pineapple juice. Cover. Simmer 40 minutes. Add pepper, pineapple, bacon, brown sugar, and soy sauce. Then add cornstarch mixed with water. Simmer 20 minutes and until sauce is thick. Serve immediately with Chinese noodles.

Mrs. Loraine Top, Nooksack Valley H. S.
Nooksack, Washington

SWEET AND SOUR SPARERIBS
Number of Servings — 4

1½ lbs. ribs (2″ length)
1½ T. brown sugar
1 green pepper or pimento
1½ T. cornstarch
3 slices pineapple

(Continued on Next Page)

3 T. vinegar
3/16 pepper
3/16 c. cold water
1½ t. salt
¾ c. pineapple juice
¾ large onion, chopped
¾ t. soy sauce

Mix sugar, cornstarch and salt in skillet. Stir in vinegar, cold water, juice and soy sauce. Cook slowly, stirring until juice becomes transparent. Add pepper, cut in bits and cook 3 minutes. Add remaining ingredients and heat through. Cook ribs in oven 1½ hours at 350°F. Serve in large dish with sauce poured over.

Peggy Rogers, Inman Rural H. S.
Inman, Kansas

SPARERIBS IN SWEET-SOUP CHERRY SAUCE
Number of Servings — 4-6

2 pieces loin ribs
1 T. fat
1 No. 2 can sour cherries
¼ t. ground cloves
1 clove garlic, crushed
¼ c. brown sugar
¼ t. dry mustard
½ t. salt
2 T. flour
3 T. vinegar
1 c. water

Cut spareribs into 3-rib portions. Brown in hot fat. Remove and keep hot. Drain cherries, pouring juice into skillet. Add cloves, garlic, brown sugar, mustard, salt, flour, vinegar, and water. Stir and cook until sauce is thick and smooth. Return ribs to skillet, add cherries. Cover and cook slowly on surface or in 350°F. oven 1½ hours. Dip sauce over ribs 2 or 3 times while cooking.

Ruth E. Briggs, Clinton Com. H. S.
Clinton, Illinois

STUFFED SAUSAGE ROLL
Number of Servings — 6

2 lbs. bulk sausage meat
2 c. diced raw apples
2 c. bread crumbs
2 small onions, chopped

On waxed paper, pat sausage into a flat rectangular shape, ½ inch thick. Mix apples, bread crumbs, and onion together, and spread over meat. Roll like a jelly roll; tuck in edges to keep filling in. Place in a shallow pan or baking dish and bake in a preheated oven at 350° F. for 45 minutes. Cut in 1 inch slices and serve.

Eleanor L. Sturman, Blue Ridge Joint School
New Milford, R. D., Pennsylvania

STUFFED SAUSAGE ROLL
Number of Servings — 8

2 c. finely chopped raw apples
⅓ c. chopped onions
⅓ c. chopped celery
1 c. bread crumbs
1 c. All Bran
2 lbs. bulk pork sausage

Combine apples, onions, celery, bread crumbs, All Bran for stuffing. Pat sausage into rectangle of tin foil about 12″x10″. Spread stuffing over meat. Roll up and bring foil together at top and seal. Seal ends. Lay in shallow pan and bake in moderate oven (350°F.) 1 hour. When sausage is done, cut in slices and serve.

Donna Kay Peak, Geneva Public H. S.
Geneva, Nebraska

SAUSAGE CORN SURPRISE
Number of Servings — 6

1 lb. sausage links
3 T. sausage fat
1 can whole cranberry sauce
1 orange, sliced
1 package corn muffin mix
1 egg
⅔ c. milk

Brown sausage and pour off fat. Use the sausage fat to grease pan. Place cooked sausage in flat pan and put the cranberry sauce and sliced orange on top. Blend the muffin mix, egg, and milk and pour over sausage. (Be sure to get to edge). Bake at 375°F. for 20 or more minutes. Cool 5 minutes and turn out on platter.

Mrs. Helen R. Bigger
Newton-Ransom Jr.-Sr. H. S.
Clarks Summit, Pennsylvania

SWEET-SOUR SAUSAGE BRACKETTES
Number of Servings — 5

1 package (½-lb.) Brown 'N Serve Sausage
    Links
1 lb. can pineapple chunks
½ c. pineapple juice
1 T. cornstarch
¼ c. vinegar
½ c. water
½ c. brown sugar
½ t. dry mustard

Cut sausages in half crosswise. Thread pieces of sausage on metal skewers alternately with pineapple chunks. Place in a shallow baking dish. Combine remaining ingredients in a sauce pan. Stir and cook over low heat until thick. Pour over meat and pineapple skewers. Bake in a moderate oven (350°F.) for 20 minutes.

Mrs. Ruth Horner, Georgetown H. S.
Georgetown, Indiana

SAUSAGE PINWHEELS
Number of Servings — 12

Cornmeal Biscuits:

1½ c. Quaker Enriched Cornmeal
2½ c. sifted enriched flour
6 t. baking powder
2 t. salt
½ c. shortening
1⅓ c. milk

Filling:

2 lbs. bulk pork sausage, cooked
2 c. grated sharp cheese (about ¼ lb.)
Tomato Sauce:
2 6-oz. cans tomato paste
2 c. water
½ t. oregano
1 t. salt
¼ t. pepper
½ c. sliced pimento olives

For biscuits, sift together dry ingredients into bowl. Cut in shortening until mixture resembles coarse crumbs. Add milk; stir lightly until mixture is just dampened. Divide dough into two parts. Knead one part gently a few seconds on lightly floured board. Roll to form rectangle 10 x 16 inches. Spread half the cooked sausage meat and half the grated cheese over dough. Roll lengthwise as for jelly roll. Cut into 12 slices each about 1⅜ inches wide. Repeat with second half of dough. Place in greased large muffin cups. Bake in hot oven (400°F.) 15 to 18 minutes. (Or place in greased 8-inch square pan. Bake 20 to 25 minutes). Serve immediately with hot tomato sauce (made by combining all ingredients and heating thoroughly).

Sula Mae Majure, Tchula H. S.
Tchula, Mississippi

SURPRISE STICKS
Number of Servings — 16

1¼ lbs. link pork sausage (16)
½ c. milk
¼ c. shortening
3 T. sugar
¼ c. cold water
1 package dry granular yeast
¼ c. warm water
About 2¾ c. sifted self-rising flour
½ lb. sharp Cheddar cheese cut into 32 strips
   of about 3½ x ¼ inches
1 T. melted butter

Cook sausages thoroughly, and until lightly browned all over; set aside. Scald milk; add shortening, sugar and cold water; mix well; cool to lukewarm. Dissolve yeast in warm water; add to lukewarm milk mixture; mix well. Add flour gradually, about ½ cupful at one time; mix well to form roll dough. Turn out onto lightly floured board. Knead about 3 minutes, until quite smooth. Place in greased bowl; cover with towel; let rise in warm place about 30 minutes, or until doubled

in bulk. Punch dough down, turn out on lightly floured board; knead 3 minutes. Roll dough into a 16-inch square. With a sharp knife cut into 16 4-inch squares. Place a cooked sausage in the center of each square. Add two strips of cheese, one on each side of the sausage. Fold dough over sausage and cheese; press edges together. Place, seam side down, 1 inch apart on greased baking sheet. Cover lightly and let rise for 20 minutes. Bake in a 425°F. (hot) oven 10-12 minutes. Brush with melted butter and serve hot.

Mrs. Ruth M. Smith, D. W. Daniel H. S.
Central, South Carolina

SAUSAGE BALLS
Number of Servings — 8

1 lb. pork sausage
1 lb. fresh ground pork
½ c. uncooked rice
1 t. cinnamon
2 c. milk
1 c. boiling water
½ t. salt
3 T. flour
⅛ t. ground cloves

Combine salt, pork, sausage and rice. Shape into balls about 1 inch in diameter. Brown slowly 10-12 minutes. Add water and simmer about 1 hour, until water is gone. Remove balls, blend flour into fat, add milk, spices and cook until thickened.

June Houchins, Tuslaw H. S.
Massillon, Ohio

HOMEWOOD BAKED STUFFED HAM
Number of Servings — 20

14 lb. ham
Remove the bone. Take about ½ pound of meat from the cavity and grind it. Add it to the following stuffing:
1½ lbs. shelled and ground pecans
1 onion, chopped fine
1 can truffle paste
2 bay leaves
2 sprigs thyme
2 t. sage
1 t. powdered cloves
½ coffee spoon cayenne
(1 glass wine, optional)

Mix well and stuff firmly into cavity of ham and sew in tightly. Place the following seasoning in large cloth: 1 onion, chopped; 2 bay leaves; 1 tablespoon sage; 1 teaspoon powdered cloves. Sew the cloth firmly around the ham. Put the ham in roaster in water and wine. Put all the same seasoning in water that you put inside cloth. Add, also, 1 apple, 1 cup cane syrup. Bake 3 hours for a pre-cooked ham. Cool in water. Remove the skin and dress with sugar and bread crumbs. Heat until sugar melts. May be served hot or cold.

Mrs. Dixie Giannini, Caldwell County H. S.
Princeton, Kentucky

BAKED HAM

10 or 12 pound ham. Plunge into kettle of boiling water, the ham must be completely covered. Then add following:

1 T. whole cloves
1 stick cinnamon
3 cloves garlic or 1 button
1 c. vinegar
1 c. white sugar

Let remain in kettle over very slow heat for 3¼ hours. *Do not* let the liquid boil, but you can see the little bubbles underneath in the liquid. Turn heat off but let ham stand in the liquid and seasonings for at least four hours or over night. Take ham from the liquid, remove skin and surplus fat and pat into ham the following:

1 c. brown sugar
1 T. dry mustard
Blend together

Put ham in baking pan and add ¼ cup vinegar and ¾ cup water. Bake at 350°F. for 1 hour, basting frequently.

Roma Jean Brown, Meridian H. S.
Meridian, Idaho

BAKED HAM
Number of Servings — 10-12

6-8 lb. whole boneless, semi-boneless or
   butt end of ham
2 c. flour
¼ c. brown sugar
1 t. ground cloves
1 t. cinnamon
½ t. dry mustard

Combine above ingredients adding enough water to make a dough. Place the ham in an open roasting pan with fat side up (trim fat if there is too much) and cover with the dough which has been rolled into a sheet large enough to cover the ham on the top, ends and sides. Put no water in the pan. Place in a *cold* oven. Bake at 350°F. for 20 minutes per pound plus 30 minutes for the cold oven. When baked, the crust will be hard. Crack it off and discard.

Carolyn Rose, Bradford H. S.
Bradford, Ohio

BAKED HAM
Number of Servings — 5

5 T. granulated sugar
1¼ t. dry mustard
1 center slice of ham (1½" thick)
1½ c. standard milk (do not use homogenized)

Mix sugar and mustard together until thoroughly mixed. In a skillet, rub ham slice with one-half of the sugar-mustard mixture, turn ham to other side and use remaining amount of mixture. Pour milk around ham. Cover, bake at 325°F. for 45 minutes. Remove cover, baste with liquid in skillet. Continue to bake until tender and golden brown, basting occasionally.

Mrs. Evelyn E. McConnell, West Shore Jr. H.S.
Lemoyne, Pennsylvania

FESTIVE BAKED HAM
Number of Servings — 4

1 can (3-4½ lb.) ham
½ c. brown sugar, firmly packed
½ c. honey
Cherry sauce
1½ T. cornstarch
¼ c. sugar
¼ t. allspice
¼ t. ground cloves
1 can red sour pitted cherries

Remove ham from can; place ham, fat side up, on shallow pan. Combine brown sugar and honey; spoon over ham. Bake in slow oven (325°F.) 1¼ to 2 hours. Baste occasionally with drippings. Cherry Sauce: Combine dry ingredients, slowly add juice from cherries. Cook until thick and clear. Add cherries and red food coloring. Serve hot, spooned over baked ham.

Mrs. Maggie Beth Watts, Era H. S.
Era, Texas

BAKED HAM IN A "BLANKET"
Number of Servings — 20-25

1 whole ham (12-14 lbs.)
2 c. flour
1 c. brown sugar
1 t. dry mustard
¼ t. cloves
1 c. pineapple juice (or enough to make a soft
   dough)

Wash the ham well, trim off rind and part of fat; place the whole ham in a shallow roasting pan. Make a soft dough and spread over to cover the ham, leaving it on through the entire cooking period. Bake until ham is tender, at 300°F., approximately 25 minutes per pound, or until the interior temperature is 170°F. If quick cured, 15 minutes per pound, or until interior temperature is 150° to 160°F. Remove and discard "blanket." If desired, the ham may be returned to the oven for about ½ hour to brown.

Mrs. Bess Snyder Mohl, Petersburg H. S.
Petersburg, West Virginia

HAM IN THE BLANKET
Number of Servings — 8

4 c. flour
1 c. brown sugar
2 T. cloves
2 T. cinnamon
2 T. mustard
1 t. black pepper
Small ham

Cut off small end of ham and trim off greater part of fat. Mix ingredients above with pineapple juice to make a dough. Cover ham with this and bake 18 minutes per pound.

Mrs. Lillian Wise, Rabun Gap School
Rabun Gap, Georgia

WHOLE OR ONE-HALF HAM — BAKED

1 c. concentrated orange juice
1 c. pineapple juice (unsweetened)
½ c. brown sugar
1 t. dry mustard
1 T. Worcestershire sauce

Mix ingredients together and rub on ham. Bake at 400°F.—14 to 18 minutes per pound.

Nan Lindsey, Wade Hampton H. S.
Greenville, South Carolina

CRANBERRY GLAZED HAM

½ ham, shank end (about 5 lbs.)
1 can (1 lb.) whole cranberry sauce
½ c. brown sugar, firmly packed

Place ham, fat side up, in uncovered baking pan. Bake in slow oven (325°F.) 2½ hours, or until meat thermometer registers 170°F. Combine cranberry sauce and brown sugar; spoon over ham. Return to oven and bake 20 to 30 minutes longer, spooning glaze over top once more.

Mrs. June Potter, Tomah H. S.
Tomah, Wisconsin

BAKED HAM SLICE MAPLE AND PINEAPPLE
Number of Servings — 4

2 T. dry mustard
1 slice uncooked ham, 2" thick
Whole cloves
Maple syrup
½ c. pineapple juice
4 slices pineapple

Rub ham slice with dry mustard. Place in shallow baking dish. Stick whole cloves into the fat of the ham. Pour into the pan enough maple syrup to nearly cover the slice, add the pineapple juice. Bake at 350°F. for 2 hours. After the first hour, turn ham slice over. Place slices of pineapple on ham and bake the last half hour.

Dorothy B. Joslyn, Peoples Academy
Morrisville, Vermont

BAKED HAM SPECIAL
Number of Servings — 6

1 large slice of ham, cut ½ inch thick
6 slices of pineapple
3 c. mashed sweet potatoes
⅓ c. brown sugar
1 T. flour
3 T. butter
½ c. pineapple juice
Wheaties

Cut ham into 6 servings the size of the pineapple slices. Place in a flat baking pan with a slice of pineapple on top of each ham slice. Make 6 sweet potato cakes and put one on top of each of the above. This may be topped with a marshmallow, if desired. Mix the sugar, flour, butter, and pineapple juice together and pour over each serving. Sprinkle each with crushed Wheaties. Bake 1 hour at 325°F.

Kathy Stauffacher, Boscobel H. S.
Boscobel, Wisconsin

BROILED HAM — PEACH HALVES
Number of Servings — 4-6

1 1-inch slice ham, center cut
¼ c. orange juice
1 can peach halves
¼ c. brown sugar
1 T. dry mustard
Brown sugar

Place ham on broiler pan, brush with brown sugar, orange juice, and dry mustard mixture. Place top of ham 4-5 inches from broiler, broil 10 minutes, turn and brush second side with sugar mixture. Place ½ teaspoon brown sugar in center of each peach halve. Arrange around ham. Broil eight minutes.

Sue Wilkins, Delhi H. S.
Delhi, Louisiana

JELLY GLAZED HAM SLICE
Number of Servings — 4

1 ½" slice ready-to-eat ham
Whole cloves
½ c. currant or apple jelly
1 T. vinegar
½ t. dry mustard
¼ t. cinnamon
⅛ t. ground cloves

Slash fat edge of ham at 2 inch intervals. Insert whole cloves in fat. Place slice in shallow baking dish and bake in slow oven (325°F.) 30 minutes. Make jelly glaze, heat jelly over low heat, stirring till smooth. Add remaining ingredients. Remove ham from oven. Spoon half the glaze over ham and return to oven; bake 10 minutes. Spoon on remaining glaze, bake 10 minutes longer or till well glazed.

Eulyn Dynes, Phillips H. S.
Phillips, Texas

BAKED HAM WITH GINGERSNAP SAUCE
Number of Servings — 8

8 slices baked ham
8 gingersnaps
½ c. vinegar
Juice of 2 lemons
1 c. brown sugar
2 c. water
½ c. seedless raisins

Crush the gingersnaps. Add remaining ingredients. Cook mixture until smooth and transparent. Serve on the slices of baked ham.

Mrs. Lettie M. Davis, South Harriman H. S.
Harriman, Tennessee

BAKED HAM SLICE
Number of Servings — 2-4

1 1-inch thick center cut slice of cured ham
1 t. dry mustard
¼ c. brown sugar
Milk enough to barely cover

Cut slashes in edge of ham slice. Sprinkle with dry mustard and brown sugar. Place in heavy skillet or baking pan. Pour on milk at side of ham slice until it barely reaches top of ham. Bake uncovered in moderate oven (350°F.) 1¼ hours.

Elaine Joyce Zuehlke, Sandwich Com. H. S.
Sandwich, Illinois

PINEAPPLE GLAZED HAM
For Your Electric Skillet
Number of Servings — 5-6

Slice of ham (cut from center) ½" thick
¾ c. orange juice
¼ c. brown sugar
6 slices pineapple

Preheat skillet to 350°F. Place ham slice in skillet and cook for about 10 minutes on each side. Remove from skillet and keep hot. Pour orange juice into skillet and add the brown sugar. Bring to a boil. Add 6 pineapple slices and glaze the fruit. Arrange fruit on top of ham and pour orange mixture over ham and serve at once.

Manona Brewer, Orestimba Union H. S.
Newman, California

BROILED HAM

1 slice ham (½" thick and a center cut)
¼ c. prepared mustard
⅓ c. brown sugar

Prepare broiler pan. In bottom pan add 2 cups of water. Place rack over the water and put the ham on the rack. Broil for 15 minutes. Turn the ham over, spread the ham slice with mustard then sprinkle the brown sugar over the mustard. Broil for 12 minutes and brown slightly. (The water helps keep the broiler cleaner).

Mrs. Audra Rasco, Monahans Sr. H. S.
Monahans, Texas

HAM DINNER
Number of Servings — 6

1 thick ham slice (2½ lbs.)
6 sweet potatoes, peeled
1 c. brown sugar
8 slices pineapple

Grease Dutch oven with a bit of fat cut from ham. Brown ham on one side; turn. Reduce heat to very low. Put potatoes around meat and sprinkle with sugar. After cooking 1 hour, turn, and arrange pineapple slices over ham, and pour juice over all. Turn potatoes in liquor and cook 30 minutes more.

Oleta Hayden, Milford H. S.
Milford, Texas

HAM
Number of Servings — 8

8 average slices of baked ham
1 small can chunk pineapple
16 large marshmallows

Put ham slices in baking dish, pour chunks of pineapple and juice over ham. Cook 10 minutes and put marshmallows over top, put back into oven until marshmallows melt and begin to brown.

Mrs. Jennie Johnson, Colera H. S.
Colera, Alabama

HAWAIIAN HAM
Number of Servings — 6

Ham, one inch thick center slice
1 t. prepared mustard
1 can pineapple (large size)
6 cloves

Spread mustard over the ham and place in a baking dish. Pour pineapple syrup (¾ to 1 cup) over ham and stick with the cloves. Bake until tender (about one hour). Arrange pineapple rings on ham. Continue cooking until pineapple is brown, basting frequently with juices from around ham.

Mrs. Rhoda Aday, Midlothian H. S.
Midlothian, Texas

SOUTHERN FRIED HAM
WITH RED-EYE GRAVY
Number of Servings — 4

1 lb. country cured ham, sliced med. thick
2 T. shortening (lard preferred)
½ c. cold water

Place shortening and ham in cold skillet. Cook slowly on medium heat with lid on skillet 25 minutes; turning frequently. Remove lid and cook 5 minutes. Remove ham. Drain. Add ½ cup cold water to drippings in skillet. Let come to boil. Serve immediately with ham and hot biscuits.

Hilda Harman, Smithville H. S.
Smithville, Mississippi

STUFFED HAM STEAK
Number of Servings — 6

2 c. soft bread crumbs
½ c. raisins
½ c. peanuts, chopped
2 T. dark corn syrup
½ t. dry mustard
¼ c. butter
2 slices ham, ½ inch thick

Combine all ingredients except ham. Place one slice of ham in shallow baking pan, spread stuffing over and top with second slice of ham. Stick whole cloves in fat. Bake in slow oven 300° F. 1 hour. Garnish with orange slices and parsley.

Luella V. Henderson, Madison Consolidated H. S.
Lore City, Ohio

HAM ROLLS
Number of Servings — 4

8 slices boiled ham (⅛" thick)
8 slices lean bacon
8 thin slices pimento cheese
Catsup
Prepared mustard

On each slice of ham place a slice of cheese, ½ teaspoon catsup, and ½ teaspoon prepared mustard. Roll and wrap with bacon strips. Fasten bacon end with toothpick. Bake in 350°F. oven for 20-25 minutes. Serves 4. A nice main dish for a luncheon.

Mrs. Pauline Miller, Elk City Sr. H. S.
Elk City, Oklahoma

HARVEST HAM SLICE
Number of Servings — 4-6

Smoked ham slice, cut 1" thick
⅔ c. apple butter
1 T. grated orange rind

Combine apple butter and grated orange rind. Place ham slice on rack in roasting pan. Spread apple butter mixture on top surface of ham slice. Bake in a moderate oven (300°F.) for 1 hour.

Janette Swanson, Ainsworth Public Schools
Ainsworth, Nebraska

CURRIED HAM ROLLS
Number of Servings — 4

2 c. cooked rice
1 medium onion, minced
¼ c. parsley, chopped fine
1 T. melted butter or margarine
½ t. salt
½ t. curry powder
8 slices boiled ham (not too thin)
4 hard-cooked eggs

Mix cooked rice, onion, parsley, melted butter or margarine, salt, and curry powder together. Place about ⅓ cup (#16 dipper) of the cooked rice mixture on each slice of ham. Roll up and place, seam side down, in baking dish. You may cut hard-cooked eggs in half lengthwise and place ½ egg, cut side down, on ham roll. Pour curry sauce over rolls. Bake at 375°F. for 30 to 35 minutes. May be served on thin wedges of toast, if desired.

CURRY SAUCE

¼ c. butter or margarine or butter-margarine mixture
½ t. curry powder
½ t. monosodium glutamate
2 T. cornstarch
½ t. salt
2 c. milk

Melt butter or margarine in sauce pan. Add curry powder, monosodium glutamate, cornstarch, and salt. Blend well. Add milk. Cook over medium heat until thick.

Mrs. Maxine Miller, University H. S.
Iowa City, Iowa

GRILLED HAM SLICES
Number of Servings — 6

1 c. water
1 c. brown sugar
3 T. catsup
1 T. soy sauce
1 t. dry mustard
1 c. crushed pineapple
2 T. bell pepper flakes
1½ T. cornstarch
¼ c. cold water
1 inch thick ham slice (ready to eat)

Mix together one cup water and brown sugar. Add catsup, soy sauce, mustard, pineapple and pepper flakes. Bring to boil; simmer 10 minutes. Dissolve cornstarch in ¼ cup cold water; add to sauce and cook, stirring, until sauce clears and thickens. Makes about 3 cups. Score edges of ham about ¼ inch deep. Cook on grill over hot coals about 8 minutes. Baste frequently with the tropical sauce.

Mrs. Marie W. Davis, John Rundle H. S.
Grenada, Mississippi

HAM WITH BARBECUE SAUCE

2 lb. slice of smoked ham
¼ c. chopped onion
½ clove garlic, chopped
¼ c. tomato catsup
2 T. Worcestershire sauce
¼ c. cider vinegar
1 (10½-oz.) can tomato soup
2 t. butter
1 t. brown sugar
⅛ t. pepper

Combine all listed ingredients and pour over ham. Cover and bake in a moderate oven (350°F.) 1 hour (or until tender). A Dutch oven may be used to cook this on top of stove. An electric skillet is also suitable.

Anne Stevens Glynn, Frankfort H. S.
Frankfort, Kansas

STUFFED HAM STEAK
Number of Servings — 6

2 c. soft bread crumbs
½ c. raisins
½ c. black walnuts
2 T. dark corn syrup
½ t. dry mustard
¼ c. butter or margarine
2 slices ham, ½ inch thick

Combine all ingredients except ham. Place one slice of ham in shallow baking pan; spread stuffing over ham and top with second slice of ham. Stick whole cloves in fat. Bake in slow oven (300° F.) 1 hour. Garnish with parsley and orange slices.

Elaine Holbert, Corydon H. S.
Corydon, Iowa

HAM, DRIED APPLES AND DUMPLINGS

2 c. dried apples
1½ lb. ham, cured or 2½ lbs. ham hock
2 T. brown sugar

Cover dried apples with water and soak over night. In morning cover ham with cold water and cook slowly for 3 hours. Add the soaked apples and brown sugar. Cook this for 1 hour more.

Now for the Knepp:
2 c. flour
3½ t. baking powder
½ t. salt
1 egg, beaten
2 T. melted butter
⅓ to ½ c. milk

Mix together the dry ingredients. Add egg and butter. Add milk until batter is stiff enough to drop from a spoon. Drop batter by spoonfuls into boiling ham and apples. Cover pan tightly and cook 10 to 12 minutes. Do not lift cover until ready to serve.

Laura J. Willcox, Oscar F. Smith H. S.
South Norfolk, Virginia

SWEET AND PUNGENT HAM STEAK
Number of Servings — 4

1 1½-lb. ham steak, 1 inch thick
1 t. kitchen bouquet
1 T. fat
1 c. well-seasoned chicken bouillon
2 T. cornstarch
¼ c. vinegar
2 T. brown sugar
½ t. dry mustard
½ t. powdered ginger
4 slices canned pineapple
1 large green pepper

Brush ham on both sides with kitchen bouquet. Melt fat in 9 inch frying pan. Add ham and brown over moderate heat on both sides about 5 minutes. Remove to warm place. Add chicken bouillon to frying pan and heat. Blend together cornstarch and vinegar and add gradually, stirring constantly until sauce thickens. Add brown sugar and seasonings. Cut each pineapple slice into 6 pieces and add. Return ham to frying pan and cook over moderate heat for 20 minutes. Dice and add green pepper. Cook covered for an additional 10 minutes. Serve immediately.

Mrs. Aliese Paschall, Sullivan H. S.
Sullivan, Illinois

EULALIA'S STUFFED PEPPERS
Number of Servings — 6

4 green peppers
1½ lbs. ham, diced
2 c. day-old biscuits or bread, broken in pieces
1 c. day-old cornbread, broken in pieces
2 T. sugar
2 c. tomatoes (fresh or canned)
2 c. whole kernel corn
Salt to taste

Cut three of the peppers in half, remove seeds, set aside. Dice remaining pepper, combine with ham, breads, tomatoes, corn, sugar and salt. Mix well and stuff pepper halves with the mixture. Place any remaining stuffing in a greased baking pan. Place peppers on top. Bake at 350°F. 45 to 60 minutes, or until peppers are tender.

Frances Moore, Riverton H. S.
Riverton, Illinois

BAKED CANADIAN BACON
Number of Servings — 8

½ c. brown sugar
½ t. dry mustard
½ c. unsweetened pineapple juice
2 lbs. Canadian bacon, in one piece

Combine sugar, mustard, and pineapple juice; spread over bacon and bake uncovered at 325°F. 1 hour. Baste every 15 minutes. When sliced in 1-inch slices, may be served with broiled pineapple slices on top of each slice of meat.

Mrs. Doris G. Kruger, Peotone H. S.
Peotone, Illinois

SPICED HAM SLICES
Number of Servings — 8

8 slices tenderized picnic ham
   (Have butcher slice ½ in. thick)
1 No. 2½ can whole spiced peaches.

Arrange ham slices on broiler pan. Drain spiced peaches. Pour juice over ham slices and bake for 1 hour at 350° F. Baste occasionally. Serve garnished with whole spiced peaches.

Mrs. Annie Glenn Templeton, Boonshill H. S.
Petersburg, Tenn.

HAM MUSTARDINE
Number of Servings — 6

1 2-lb. slice ham (center cut)
Prepared mustard
1 pint milk

Trim and score ham. Spread both sides of ham liberally with mustard. Place in heavy frying pan, add milk, cover tightly, and simmer for 1½ to 2 hours.

Margaret Matthews, A. L. Miller Jr. H. S.
Macon, Georgia

HAM AND LIMA BEANS
Number of Servings — 6

¾ inch slice of center ham
¼ lb. grated cheese
1 No. 2 can lima beans

Cut gashes into outer edge of ham to prevent curling. Broil ham 5 inches from heat for 6 minutes while heating lima beans. Turn ham over and broil 6 minutes. Cover ham with heated lima beans and grated cheese. Return to broiler and cook until cheese is melted and slightly browned.

Fay R. Lewis, Malakoff H. S.
Malakoff, Texas

HAM MARINADE
Number of Servings — 6

⅓ c. water
⅓ c. wine vinegar
1½ T. dry mustard
2 T. brown sugar
2 T. melted butter
1 t. paprika
½ t. ground cloves
Dash garlic powder
2 ready-to-eat ham slices, cut ¾ inch thick

Combine all ingredients except ham in a plastic sack and mix well. Add ham slices and let stand in refrigerator over night. Slash edges of ham to prevent curling. Broil ham slices 3 to 4 inches from heat for about 10 minutes on each side. Baste often with remaining marinade.

Mrs. Iva Stringer, J. Z George H. S.
North Carrollton, Mississippi

STUFFED HAM STEAK
Number of Servings — 6

2 c. soft bread crumbs
½ c. peanuts, chopped
½ t. dry mustard
2 slices ham, ½ inch thick
½ c. raisins
2 T. dark corn syrup
¼ c. butter or margarine

Combine all ingredients except ham. Place one slice of ham in shallow baking pan; spread stuffing over ham and top with second slice of ham. Stick whole cloves in fat. Bake in slow oven (300°F.) 1 hour.

Nadine Calvin, Ravenna H. S.
Ravenna, Nebraska

HAM BALLS WITH SOUR CREAM GRAVY
Number of Servings — 6

2 c. ground ham
½ t. dry mustard
¾ c. dry bread crumbs, fine
⅔ cup milk
1 egg
2 T. butter
1 T. shortening
¼ c. water

Blend ham, mustard, crumbs, milk and egg and form into balls 1½ inch in diameter. Brown balls in butter and shortening, add water, cover and cook over low heat for 15 minutes if ham is precooked, and for 25 minutes if ham is uncooked. Serve with "Sour Cream Gravy".

SOUR CREAM GRAVY
2 T. flour
2 T. ham drippings
1 c. cultured sour cream
1 T. sugar
¼ t. marjoram
1 t. dill seed
½ t. salt

Blend flour into ham drippings, then add sour cream and sugar. Cook and stir until sauce is thoroughly heated and is slightly thickened. Add seasonings and serve over ham balls.

Mrs. Clarice Hubbard, Mitchell Jr. H. S.
Mitchell, S. D.

GLAZED HAM BALLS
Number of Servings — 6-8

1½ lbs. ground fresh pork
1 lb. ground ham
1 egg
1 c. milk
1 c. cracker crumbs
SYRUP:
1½ c. brown sugar
½ c. vinegar

(Continued on Next Page)

½ c. water
1 t. mustard

Shape into meat balls. Pour syrup over meat balls. Bake uncovered for 1½ hours at 350°F.

Mrs. Helen Campbell, Clark H. S.
Clark, South Dakota

HAM LOAF
Number of Servings — 12

2 lbs. ground ham
1 lb. ground lean pork
2 eggs (beaten)
1 c. cracker crumbs
1 c. can tomato soup
1 c. milk
1 T. sugar
1 t. paprika
1 t. salt

Combine all ingredients and mix well. Put into loaf pan and bake at 350° F. for 1 hour 15 minutes. May be served hot or cold with or without mustard sauce.

Mustard Sauce
¼ T. dry mustard
1 c. brown sugar
1 c. vinegar
1 c. water
2 T. flour
3 eggs (beaten)

Combine dry ingredients, add eggs, vinegar, and water. Mix and cook slowly, stirring constantly until it thickens.

Thelma Abbey, Wink H. S.
Wink, Texas

HAM LOAF
Number of Servings — 10

1 lb. ground cooked ham
1 lb. ground fresh pork
2 eggs, slightly beaten
1 c. cracker crumbs
1 c. milk
¼ t. salt
⅛ t. pepper
1 c. pineapple chunks
5 maraschino cherries
¾ c. brown sugar
2 t. dry mustard
¼ c. vinegar

Combine ham, pork, eggs, crackers, milk, salt and pepper. Mix thoroughly. Arrange pineapple and cherries in bottom of 10x5x3″ loaf pan. Combine sugar, mustard and vinegar. Spread half over fruit in bottom of pan. Top with meat mixture. Add remaining sugar mixture over top. Bake 1½ hours in 375° F. oven.

Mrs. Christine Preston, Bokoshe H. S.
Bokoshe, Okla.

HAM LOAF

2 lbs. ground ham
2 lbs. ground pork
2 c. milk
2 eggs
3 c. cracker crumbs
1 t. salt

Mix ingredients in the order that they are listed. When they are well blended shape into a loaf. Bake at 350°F. for 50 minutes.

Leona Bates, Lakewood (Woodland) H. S.
Woodland, Michigan

HAM LOAF
Number of Servings — 8

2 lbs. fresh ground ham
1 lb. ground beef
1 c. dry bread crumbs
1 t. salt
¼ t. pepper
1 egg, beaten
1 T. chopped onion
¼ c. chopped celery
¼ c. chopped green pepper

Combine above ingredients. Place in shallow pan, place strips of bacon on top. Pour over sauce made from ¼ cup water, ¼ cup vinegar, ⅓ cup brown sugar and 1 teaspoon dried mustard. Bake at 350°F. for 45 minutes.

Mrs. Louise Burleson, Swansboro H. S.
Swansboro, North Carolina

HAM LOAF
Number of Servings — 6

1 lb. ham, smoked and lean
½ lb. pork
½ lb. ground beef
2 c. cracker crumbs
2 eggs
¼ t. salt
2 c. milk

Mix well and shape into a loaf. Pour water around the loaf. Bake in moderate oven (350°F.) for 2 to 2½ hours.

Mrs. Jean Curtis, St. Louis H. S.
St. Louis, Michigan

HAM LOAF
Number of Servings — 6-8

⅔ lb. ground ham
1⅓ lbs. ground pork
1 c. dry bread crumbs
¼ t. pepper
2 eggs, beaten
1 c. milk

Combine meats, crumbs, pepper, eggs, and milk. Mix thoroughly; form in loaf in 4½ x 8½ inch loaf pan. Bake in moderate oven (350°F.) 1 hour. Serve.

Addie Jo Curry, La Poyner H. S.
La Rue, Texas

HAM LOAF
Number of Servings — 10

Loaf:

1 lb. ham (cured ham-end cuts)
1½ lbs. pork
1 c. soft bread crumbs
1 c. sweet milk
2 eggs, beaten

Glaze:

½ c. brown sugar
½ t. dry mustard
¼ c. vinegar

Grind together ham and pork. Add bread crumbs, sweet milk and eggs to ham mixture. Pack in baking dish and bake for 1 hour at 350°F. Combine ingredients for glaze and add to ham loaf 30 minutes before it is done.

Mrs. Gail Coppenger, Godley H. S.
Godley, Texas

HAM LOAF
Number of Servings — 8

1 lb. ham
½ lb. pork
½ lb. veal
½ t. salt
Pepper to taste
2 T. green pepper or onion
2 eggs
1 c. milk
2 c. corn flakes

Grind the ham, pork and veal together and mix all the ingredients in with the ground meat and pack in a small sack. Sew sack together at the top. Cover with water and let simmer for 1½ hours. Remove sack from water and let cool with meat in sack. When ready to use peel sack back and slice as needed.

Mrs. Edna Crow, Hollis H. S.
Hollis, Oklahoma

HAM LOAF
Number of Servings — 10

1 lb. smoked ham and
1½ lbs. lean pork (ground together)
1 c. bread crumbs
1 c. milk
2 eggs
Dash pepper

Mix all together and shape into loaf. Bake at 300° F. for 2 hours. After first hour, pour off excess fat drippings and pour the following sauce over loaf and continue baking, basting often.
Sauce: 1½ cups brown sugar; 1 teaspoon dry mustard; ½ cup water and ⅓ cup vinegar. Bring to boil before pouring over ham. May be garnished with pineapple slices.

Mrs. Marguerite McGinness, Danbury H. S.
Danbury, Texas

HAM LOAF
Number of Servings — 6

½ lb. ground lean pork
½ lb. ground beef
½ lb. ground smoked ham
1 egg, beaten
1 c. bread crumbs
½ t. salt
½ t. black pepper
½ t. marjorum
¼ c. milk

Combine all ingredients in order given and mix thoroughly. Put into a greased meatloaf pan and bake for 1 hr. at 325° F.

Mrs. Alza Dunn, Addison H. S.
Addison, Michigan

HAM LOAF
Number of Servings — 6-8

1 lb. smoked ham
1 lb. fresh ham
1 c. cracker or bread crumbs
2 eggs
1 T. dry mustard
½ c. + 2 T. milk
¼ c. chili sauce
1 c. brown sugar
⅔ c. vinegar
⅔ c. water

Mix meats which have been ground together. Add crumbs, milk, chili sauce. Mold into a loaf and place in pan. Add brown sugar, mustard, vinegar and water and bring to a boil in a separate pan. Pour this syrup over the loaf and bake 1 hour at 325°F. Baste often.

Mrs. June C. McIsaac, Hampton Twp. H. S.
Allison Park, Pennsylvania

BAKED HAM LOAF
Number of Servings — 8 large

2 lbs. cured ham
2 lbs. fresh pork
2 c. graham crackers (crumbed)
3 eggs
1 c. milk

Have cured ham and fresh pork ground together twice. Mix graham cracker crumbs, eggs and milk with meat. Mold in loaf, bake 2 hours 250-300° F.

Serve with following sauce.

1 can tomato soup
½ c. water
½ c. vinegar
2 t. powdered mustard
1½ c. brown sugar

Mix ingredients all together, bring to boil, boil for a few minutes. Serve.

Mrs. Maxine M. Miller, Fairview H. S.
Fairview, West Virginia

HAM LOAF
Number of Servings — 6

1 lb. cured ham
½ lb. fresh pork
2 c. rice flakes
1 t. Worcestershire sauce
1 egg
¾ c. milk

Grind ham and pork together twice. Mix all ingredients thoroughly. Put into loaf. Place in greased roaster. Bake uncovered at 375° for one hour.

Mrs. Pauline McKinley, West Lafayette H. S.
West Lafayette, Ohio

HAM LOAF
Number of Servings — 15

2 lbs. smoked ham, ground
1½ lbs. pork, ground
3 c. corn flakes
3 eggs
1 c. milk
¼ t. nutmeg
Pepper to taste

Mix meats and corn flakes. Beat eggs and add milk. Add seasonings. Shape meat mixture into loaf or loaves and bake at 350°F. for about 1 hour.

Mary E. Myers, Barry Com. Unit H. S.
Barry, Illinois

HAM LOAF
Number of Servings — 10-12

1 lb. fresh pork
2 lbs. cured ham
2 eggs
¾ c. bread crumbs
¼ c. chopped onion

Combine meat, slightly beaten eggs, bread crumbs, onion and milk; mix well and make into a loaf. Bake slowly for one hour covered. Spread with the following sauce. ½ cup brown sugar, 2 teaspoons dry mustard and vinegar enough to moisten and bake uncovered one-half hour longer. Serves 10-12.

Jeanne C. Jackson, Lehi H. S.
Lehi, Utah

QUICKY HAM LOAF
Number of Servings — 8-10

1 lb. ham and 1 lb. pork, ground together
2 eggs
1¼ c. milk

Mix the ingredients together in a mixing bowl. Shape in loaf pan 5 x 10 inches and bake in a slow oven (325°F.) for 1¼ hours. Garnish with parsley for serving, if desired.

Wilma Keeler, Cadillac Sr. H. S.
Cadillac, Michigan

HAM LOAF
Number of Servings — 8-10

1½ c. ground fresh pork
1 lb. ground smoked ham
2 eggs
1 c. bread crumbs
1 c. milk
½ t. salt
½ t. pepper

Combine all ingredients and mix well. Form into a large loaf or 2 small loaves.

Sauce
½ c. brown sugar
¼ c. vinegar
½ c. water
1 t. prepared mustard

Combine all ingredients. Boil together 5 minutes. Pour over loaf. Bake at 350° F. for 45 minutes.

Laura Belle Holmes, Perry Joint Jr.-Sr. H. S.
New Bloomfield, Pennsylvania

UPSIDE HAM LOAF
Number of Servings — 6-8

⅔ lb. ground pork
⅔ lb. ground smoked ham
⅔ lb. ground beef
2 c. soft bread crumbs
1 egg, well beaten
¾ c. milk
1 t. salt
¼ t. pepper

Blend the ground meats, add bread crumbs and remaining ingredients. Put 3 tablespoons melted butter in bottom of 4 x 7 or 8 x 3 inch pan, 3 slices canned pineapple, one maraschino cherry in center of each ring. Sprinkle ½ cup light brown sugar over pineapple. Spread meat over this and bake for 1 hour at 375°F.

Mrs. Kathryn Leischner, DeLand-Weldon H. S.
DeLand, Illinois

HAM LOAF
Number of Servings — 16

2 lbs. cured ham, ground
1 lb. fresh ham, ground
1½ c. cracker crumbs
1 No. 1 flat can crushed pineapple
3 eggs, well beaten
1 No. 2 can apricot halves, drained
½ c. water
¼ c. brown sugar

Combine ham, cracker crumbs and pineapple. Add beaten eggs. Shape into large loaf or individual loaves. Dot with whole cloves and apricot halves. Mix together water, brown sugar and apricot juice. Pour around ham. Bake 1½ hours at 325°F.

Jeanette Phillips, Bridgeport H. S.
Bridgeport, Texas

HAM LOAF
Number of Servings — 8

½ c. brown sugar
1 t. whole cloves
1 lb. smoked ham, ground
1 lb. lean pork, ground
½ t. salt
⅛ t. pepper
3 T. chopped green pepper
2 eggs, beaten well
1 c. milk
4 c. corn flakes

Lightly grease loaf pan 9½x5½x2¾ inches and pat sugar evenly over bottom. Arrange cloves over the sugar. Combine meats, add seasonings and chopped pepper and mix thoroughly. Beat eggs, add milk and add to meat mixture with the corn flakes. Mix until thoroughly blended and mixture firm. Pack carefully over sugar mixture. Press down evenly and smooth top with spatula. Bake 1 to 1¼ hours in a moderate oven 375° F. until nicely browned. To serve, invert on a hot platter and discard cloves.

Mrs. Ruth E. Johnson, Syracuse H. S.
Syracuse, Kansas

HAM LOAF
Number of Servings — 10

1 lb. ground ham
1½ lbs. fresh pork, ground
1 c. dry bread crumbs
2 eggs, beaten
1 c. milk
1 T. dry mustard
½ c. brown sugar
½ c. vinegar
½ c. water

Combine meat, bread crumbs, eggs and milk—pack in loaf pan. Combine brown sugar, dry mustard, vinegar and water. (Let sugar dissolve.) Pour over meat. Baste occasionally. Bake 1¼ hours at 350° F.

Mrs. Ruth Reich, Meyersdale Jt. H. S.
Meyersdale, Pennsylvania

HAM LOAF
Number of Servings — 6

1½ lbs. lean smoked ham, ground
¾ lb. lean fresh pork, ground
1½ c. soft bread crumbs
1 slightly beaten egg
½ c. milk
2 T. finely chopped parsley
⅛ t. pepper
¼ t. poultry seasoning

Mix together meats, crumbs, parsley, seasonings, egg, and milk. Pack ingredients into an oiled loaf pan. Bake in moderately hot oven (350° F.) for about one hour. Turn out on warm platter and garnish with parsley.

Mrs. Marshall Reynolds, Baxter Springs H. S.
Baxter Springs, Kansas

HAM LOAF
Number of Servings — 8

1 lb. ground smoked ham
½ lb. ground lean pork
3 c. moderately dry bread crumbs
2 eggs, beaten
1 t. salt
⅛ t. pepper

Mix thoroughly. Shape into a rounded mold in a lightly greased roasting pan which accommodates the meat mixture without crowding. Bake in 350° F. oven 1½ hours. Serve hot . . . or serve cold.

Accompaniment: 1 cup whipped cream into which 2 tablespoons horse-radish has been folded.

Dorothy C. Smith, Stratton H. S.
Stratton, Colorado

HAM LOAF
Number of Servings — 6-8

1 lb. pork, ground
1 lb. ham, ground
1 c. dry bread crumbs
1 c. tomato juice
2 eggs, beaten
1 T. finely chopped onions
⅓ c. brown sugar
½ c. crushed pineapple
¼ c. maraschino cherries, chopped

Combine pork, ham, bread crumbs, tomato juice, eggs and onions. In the bottom of a greased loaf pan, 8x4x3, place in layers in this order; brown sugar, crushed pineapple and maraschino cherries. Place meat loaf mixture on top and bake at 350° F. about one hour.

Virginia B. Smith, Bradford Academy
Bradford, Vermont

HAM LOAF

1½ lbs. cured ham, ground
¾ lb. fresh lean pork, ground
¾ lb. lean beef, ground
1 c. fine cracker crumbs
1 medium onion
2 eggs, well beaten
1 can tomato soup (10½-oz.)
1 c. milk
½ t. mustard
1 t. granulated sugar

Scald milk, let cool. Roll cracker crumbs, place in mixing bowl. Pour milk over crumbs, let stand. Beat eggs ,add to crumb mixture. Chop onion very fine, add to above. Add also soup, sugar, mustard and meat. Mix the ingredients and shape into individual loaves or one large loaf. Place in baking pan. Pour water around loaves until it is ½ inch deep. Bake at 325° F. 2 hours or until done. This recipe has been used for F.H.A. banquets, etc., and is always enjoyed and eaten. 30 pounds of the above mix makes 117 individual loaves.

Mrs. Elizabeth G. Volsud, Franklin Com. H. S.
Franklin, Indiana

HAM LOAF
Number of Servings — 6-8

1 lb. ground ham
¾ lb. ground fresh pork
1 c. soft bread crumbs
⅓ c. chopped onion
1 beaten egg
½ c. milk

Thoroughly combine meats, crumbs, onion, egg, and milk. Shape in loaf in shallow baking dish. Bake at 350°F. 1¼ hours or 'till done. Serve with horse-radish sauce.

Freda C. Rickey, Marshall Co. H. S.
Guntersville, Alabama

HAM LOAF
Number of Servings — 6-8

½ lb. cured ham
1 lb. lean fresh pork
1 beaten egg
½ c. sweet milk
¾ c. cracker crumbs
1 can tomato soup
¾ t. paprika
1 t. salt

Grind meat and mix all ingredients together except ¼ cup crumbs and the soup. Place loaf in roaster. Sprinkle with the ¼ cup crumbs. Pour the soup over it. Cook in slow oven (325° F.) for 2 hours.

Mona Thomas, Prentice H. S.
Prentice, Wisconsin

HAM LOAF WITH HOT MUSTARD SAUCE
Number of Servings — 8

2 lbs. finely ground ham (no fat)
1 lb. fresh ground pork
2 c. bread crumbs
¾ c. milk
2 eggs
¾ t. salt (add to tomatoes only)
1½ t. sugar (add to tomatoes only)
1 c. canned tomatoes

Mix ham, pork, bread crumbs, eggs and milk. Mold in loaf form, place in baking dish. Add salt and sugar to tomatoes and cook 10 minutes. Pour ½ of tomato mixture over loaf. Save rest for basting during baking. Bake uncovered at 350°F. for 30 minutes. Cover and bake 1 hour longer or more. Serve with Hot Mustard Sauce.

HOT MUSTARD SAUCE

2 eggs
2 T. flour
1 T. dry mustard
1 c. brown sugar
1 c. vinegar
1 c. consomme (clear beef broth)

Combine ingredients. Cook in double boiler until thick. Serves 8.

Mrs. Rachel H. Bissitt, Upland H. S.
Upland, California

HAM LOAF
Number of Servings — 12

2 lbs. ground smoked ham
2 lbs. lean ground fresh pork
2 c. finely rolled cracker crumbs
4 whole eggs
2 c. milk
1 T. prepared mustard

Combine all ingredients. Mix well and shape into two loaves. Place in roasting pan and bake at 350°F. 2 hours until golden brown. If desired, baste the loaves during baking with the following sauce: 1½ cups brown sugar, ½ cup water, ½ cup vinegar and 1 teaspoon dry mustard. Combine in small saucepan and bring to boiling.

Mrs. Adelaide Wolf, Harbor Creek H. S.
Harbor Creek, Pennsylvania

HAM LOAF
Number of Servings — 12-16

2 lbs. ground pork
1½ lbs. cured ham
3 eggs beaten
1 c cracker crumbs
1½ c. milk
Basting Sauce (mix together)
1 c. brown sugar
½ c. vinegar
½ c. water
2 T. prepared mustard

Mix first five ingredients together and shape into loaf. Place in open roast pan and pour basting sauce over it. Cook in moderately hot oven about two hours. Baste several times during cooking.

Mrs. Mayme Veach, Holdenville H. S.
Holdenville, Oklahoma

HAM LOAF SUPREME
Number of Servings — 8

1½ lbs. ground ham
¾ lb. ground fresh pork
¾ lb. ground veal
2 eggs, well beaten
1 c. bread crumbs
½ t. pepper
Salt lightly
1 c. pineapple juice
1½ t. dry mustard
2 T. brown sugar
3 rings pineapple
3 maraschino cherries

Mix together meats, eggs, crumbs, pepper and salt. Form into loaf. Combine sugar, mustard and juice. Baste loaf with about ¼ of this mixture. Baste again about every 20 minutes during baking. Garnish top with pineapple rings and cherries 15 minutes before serving. Bake 2 hours at 350° F.

Mrs. Marjorie F. Rendulic, Edgewater H. S.
Orlando, Florida

DELICIOUS HAM LOAF
Number of Servings — 6

¾ lb. ground ham
¼ lb. ground pork
1 c. bread crumbs
2 eggs, beaten
1 t. celery seed
1 c. milk
⅓ c. chopped green pepper
Salt and pepper

Mix above ingredients and make into loaf. Place in bottom of pan pineapple slices, 3 tablespoons butter, ½ cup brown sugar. Place ham loaf on top. Bake at 350° F. for 30-40 minutes.

Mrs. Edward A. Whitescarver, Flemington H. S.
Flemington, West Virginia

PORK LOAF
Number of Servings — 12

1 lb. ground pork
1 lb. ground cured ham
2 slightly beaten eggs
1 c. cracker crumbs
1 c. milk
Pinch of salt

Mix pork, ham, crumbs, salt, milk, and eggs together well and form into a loaf. Over the loaf pour the following glaze and baste occasionally during baking.

1½ c. brown sugar
½ c. vinegar
½ c. water

Mix together.

Mrs Rama G. Steen, Caldwell H. S.
Caldwell, Ohio

HAM AND PORK LOAF
Number of Servings — 6

1 lb. ground ham
1 lb. ground pork
1 egg
1 c. milk
1 c. dried bread crumbs
Salt and pepper
¾ t. dry mustard
6 T. vinegar
6 T. water
1 c. brown sugar

Add egg, milk and crumbs to meat with seasonings to taste. Form a loaf and place in a greased pan. Place in moderate oven. When beginning to brown baste with sugar, mustard, vinegar and water which have been brought to a boil. Continue to baste from time to time during the baking allowing about an hour and a half for the baking. Temperature 350°F.

Mrs. Myrtle Hawk, Lincoln Sr. H. S.
Warren, Michigan

HAM LOAF IN MOLD
Number of Servings — 6

1 lb. ground lean pork
1 lb. ground cured ham
1 egg beaten
½ c. milk
1½ c. Wheaties

Combine all ingredients and mix well. Press into favorite mold. Combine ¼ cup brown sugar, 1 teaspoon prepared mustard, ¼ teaspoon cloves. Mix well and put on top of ham loaf. Bake at 350°F. for 1 to 1½ hours.

Mrs. Marguerite Craig, Fulton Local H. S.
Swanton, Ohio

GLAZED HAM LOAF
Number of Servings — 12

2 c. ground smoked ham
3 c. ground fresh pork
1 c. soft bread crumbs
1 c. milk
2 eggs, slightly beaten
1 c. brown sugar
½ t. dry mustard
½ c. diluted vinegar

Grind ham and fresh pork together and combine with bread crumbs. Add milk and eggs. Shape into a loaf and place in shallow pan. Bake in moderate oven (350°F.) about 1½ hours. Baste with vinegar mixture. *Note:* 1 cup crushed pineapple may be substituted for the vinegar.

Audrey Gerbyshak, Crivitz H. S.
Crivitz, Wisconsin

GLAZED HAM LOAF
Number of Servings — 8

½ c. brown sugar
2 T. pineapple syrup
1 No. 1 can sliced pineapple
1½ lb. ground uncooked ham
1 lb. ground pork
¾ c. crushed crackers
1 t. dry mustard
1 c. milk

Mix brown sugar and syrup in 10x5x3 inch loaf pan. Cut pineapple slices into wedges and arrange in loaf pan. Beat eggs (in bowl), add remaining ingredients, and mix well. Pack ham mixture into loaf pan. Bake in 350° F. oven for 1½ hours. Serve with horse-radish sauce.

Horse-radish Sauce

⅓ c. heavy cream, whipped
⅓ c. cooked salad dressing
1 T. horse-radish

Fold together above ingredients.

Mary A. Hugus, Fairless Sr. H. S.
Navarre, Ohio

GLAZED HAM LOAF
Number of Servings — 10

1 lb. ground smoked ham, raw
½ lb. ground pork shoulder
2 eggs, beaten
¾ c. milk
¼ c. pineapple juice
1 t. dry mustard
2 T. vinegar
1 c. bread crumbs
½ t. salt
⅛ t. pepper
1 T. dry mustard
3 slices pineapple or ¾ c. chunks
¼ c. brown sugar

Combine ham, pork, eggs, milk, juice, crumbs, salt, pepper and mix thoroughly. Place in greased 9x5x3 inch loaf pan. Arrange pineapple slices or chunks on top. Mix brown sugar, mustard and vinegar together, pour over pineapple. Bake in a 350° oven for 1 hour.

Betty Joyce Hardman, Valley Head H. S.
Valley Head, Alabama

GLAZED HAM LOAF
Number of Servings — 10

1 lb. cured ham
1½ lbs. pork steak
2 eggs
1 c. milk
1 c. cracker crumbs
Salt and pepper to taste
Mix and make into loaf and bake a few minutes at 350° F. Then add following sauce.
1½ c. brown sugar
1 T. prepared mustard
½ c. vinegar and ½ c. water

After cooking 5 minutes, bake loaf about 2 hours, at 300° F., basting with this mixture.

Pearl E. Reuter, Fayetteville H. S.
Bedford, Indiana

INDIVIDUAL HAM LOAVES IN APRICOT SAUCE
Number of Servings — 8

1 lb. ground ham
1 lb. ground pork
1 c. graham cracker crumbs
2 eggs
½ c. apricot nectar
¼ c. catsup
¼ c. drained, crushed pineapple
1 t. lemon juice

Combine meat, beaten eggs and crumbs; mix well and form into eight individual loaves. Combine remaining ingredients and pour over loaves in a baking dish. Bake at 350° F. for 1 hour.

Gladys C. Clemens, Connellsville Joint Sr. H. S.
Connellsville, Pennsylvania

GLAZED HAM LOAF
Number of Servings — 8

2 lbs. cured ham (ground)
2 lbs. fresh pork (ground)
3 eggs
1½ c. cracker crumbs
½ t. pepper
½ c. milk

Mix all ingredients together and mold into loaf. Cover with glaze and bake at 350° F. for 1 hour or until glaze thickens. **Glaze**—Mix together 1 cup brown sugar, 1 teaspoon dry mustard, ½ cup vinegar, and ½ cup water. Stir until dissolved and pour over loaf.

Beverly Raven, Woodlin H. S.
Woodrow, Colorado

PINEAPPLE UPSIDE-DOWN HAM LOAF
Number of Servings — 6-8

2 c. ground cooked ham
1½ c. ground pork shoulder
2 eggs
1 c. milk
1 c. finely crushed cracker crumbs
½ t. salt
⅛ t. pepper
¼ c. brown sugar, packed
1 t. dry mustard
3 T. vinegar
3 slices canned pineapple

Combine first 7 ingredients. Combine sugar, mustard and vinegar. Pour into loaf pan 10 x 5 x 3 inches. Arrange pineapple on top of sugar mixture in a design. Pack meat on top. Bake at 375° F. for 1½ hours. Unmold.

Mrs. Laverne Littrel, Wapello Com. Schools
Wapello, Iowa

PINEAPPLE HAM LOAF
Number of Servings — 6-8

2 c. ground ham
1½ c. ground pork shoulder
2 eggs
1 c. milk
1 c. crushed crackers
½ t. salt
⅛ t. pepper
¼ c. brown sugar
1 t. dry mustard
2 T. vinegar
3 slices canned pineapple

Combine first 7 ingredients. Combine last four ingredients, pour into 10x5x3 inch loaf pan. Arrange pineapple in any design. Pack meat on top of pineapple. Bake at 375° F. for 1½ hours. Invert on platter. (1 can pork and ham loaf, ground, may be substituted for the 2 cups ground ham).

Ellen McCallum, Wauneta H. S.
Wauneta, Nebraska

PARTY PINEAPPLE HAM LOAF
Number of Servings — 8

1 lb. ground smoked ham
1 lb. ground lean fresh pork
2 eggs
¾ c. bread crumbs
¾ c. milk
8 T. catsup
8 slices pineapple, drained

Mix all ingredients except pineapple. Divide into 9 patties. In a shallow baking dish, form a long roll, alternating a patty and pineapple slice, starting and ending with meat. Bake 30 minutes in slow oven (325°F.) Baste with Spicy Glaze and bake 1 more hour. *Spicy Glaze:* 1 cup light brown sugar, ¼ cup pineapple juice, 2 tablespoons vinegar and 1 teaspoon prepared mustard.

Grace E. Randell, Van Buren Com. H. S.
Keosauqua, Iowa

HAM LUNCHEON PIE
Number of Servings — 6

1 stack pack crushed crackers
⅓ c. margarine
1 lb. ground ham
1 medium chopped onion
1 c. cooked rice
1 c. milk
3 eggs, beaten
2 T. chopped green pepper
½ lb. cheese, grated

Blend cracker crumbs and softened margarine. Reserve ⅔ cup crumb mixture for topping. Firmly press remainder against bottom of baking dish. Combine ham, onion, and rice in baking dish. Add milk to eggs. Stir in green pepper and cheese. Pour over mixture and sprinkle with remaining crumbs. Bake at 350°F. for 45 minutes.

Nancy Simonton, Wade Hampton H. S.
Greenville, South Carolina

SAILBOAT BUNS
Number of Servings — 6-8

2 c. chopped ham
¼ c. mayonnaise
2 T. minced onion
2 T. chopped pickle
4 slices American cheese
3 or 4 oval buns

Combine the ham, mayonnaise, onion and pickle. Split the oval buns, butter and spread with ham mixture. Cut cheese slices diagonally. Mount on toothpick to represent the sail of the boat. Delightful for a children's party at the lake.

Mrs. Thelma Hause, Charlestown H. S.
Charlestown, New Hampshire

HEALTH HAM LOAF
Number of Servings — 6-8

2 lbs. cured ham, ground
1 lb. ground fresh pork
2 eggs, well beaten
1 c. bread crumbs
¾ c. sweet milk
½ t. dry mustard

Mix the above ingredients together well. Stuff into a small cloth sack and boil two hours in water to which ½ cup vinegar has been added. Serve with a horse-radish sauce.

Mrs. Eunice Cole Salomonson, Berthoud H. S.
Berthoud, Colorado

CANDIED HAM LOAF
Number of Servings — 8

¾ lb. ground ham
¾ lb. ground pork
¾ lb. ground beef
¼ can tomato soup
½ c. milk
1 c. cracker crumbs
1½ t. Worcestershire sauce
¼ c. catsup
1½ t. prepared mustard

Mix and mold into loaf day before serving. Bake 2 hours at 300° F., basting with ¾ cup brown sugar, ¼ cup vinegar, ¼ cup water, ⅛ teaspoon dry mustard, heated to boiling.

Zoe Dunn, Holton H. S.
Holton, Kansas

FOR ADDITIONAL PORK RECIPES SEE CASSEROLES, SANDWICHES, SALADS AND FOREIGN DISHES SECTIONS

Lamb

LAMB CHART
Lamb Cuts and How to Cook Them

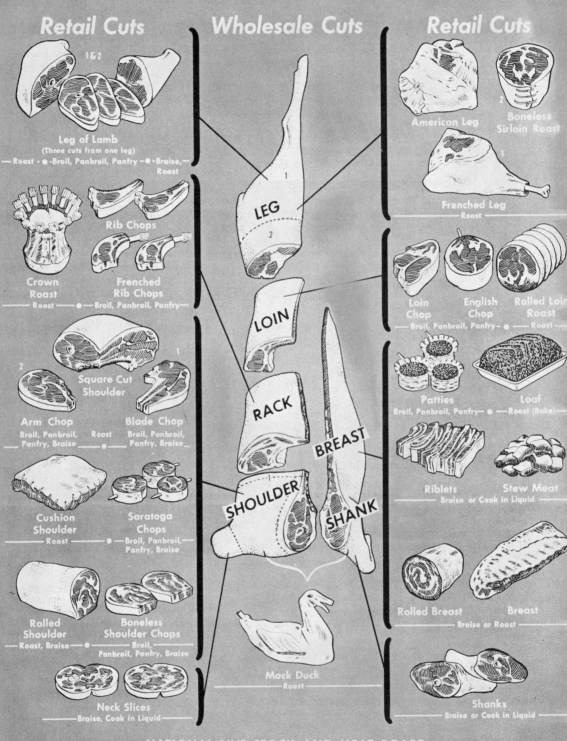

Retail Cuts — **Wholesale Cuts** — **Retail Cuts**

Leg of Lamb
(Three cuts from one leg)
—Roast - ●-Broil, Panbroil, Panfry -●-Braise,—
Roast

Rib Chops

Crown Roast

Frenched Rib Chops
— Roast —●— Broil, Panbroil, Panfry—

Square Cut Shoulder

Arm Chop
Broil, Panbroil, Panfry, Braise

Roast

Blade Chop
Broil, Panbroil, Panfry, Braise

Cushion Shoulder
— Roast —

Saratoga Chops
● — Broil, Panbroil, Panfry, Braise

Rolled Shoulder
—Roast, Braise—●—

Boneless Shoulder Chops
Broil, Panbroil, Panfry, Braise

Neck Slices
—Braise, Cook in Liquid—

LEG

LOIN

RACK

BREAST

SHOULDER

SHANK

Mock Duck
—Roast—

American Leg

Boneless Sirloin Roast

Frenched Leg
— Roast —

Loin Chop   **English Chop**   **Rolled Loin Roast**
— Broil, Panbroil, Panfry – ● — Roast —

Patties   **Loaf**
Broil, Panbroil, Panfry— ● —Roast (Bake)—

Riblets   **Stew Meat**
— Braise or Cook in Liquid —

Rolled Breast   **Breast**
— Braise or Roast —

Shanks
— Braise or Cook in Liquid —

NATIONAL LIVE STOCK AND MEAT BOARD

Selection of LAMB Cuts

WHOLESALE CUTS	RETAIL CUTS	CHARACTERISTICS	COOKING METHODS
Leg	Frenched Leg	Shank bone is "frenched", that is, meat is removed to expose one inch or more of lower end of shank bone.	Roast
	American Leg	Shank meat is removed at stifle joint. Shank meat is tucked into pocket under fell and pinned into place.	Roast
	Half of Leg	Either the shank or the loin half.	Roast
	Leg Chops (Steaks)	May contain cross section of back bone and aitch bone. Center cut steaks look like miniature beef round steaks.	Broil; panbroil; panfry
	Sirloin Chops	Corresponds to beef sirloin steaks. Pinbone chops have considerable bone.	Broil; panbroil; panfry
	Boneless Sirloin Roast	Small boneless roll weighing from 2 to 3½ pounds.	Roast
Loin	Loin Roast	Corresponds to beef short loin. It can be the unsplit loin but is usually one side of the split loin.	Roast
	Rolled Loin Roast	Boned and rolled loin.	Roast
	Loin Chops	Contain T-shaped bones; correspond to porterhouse, T-Bone, and club beef steaks.	Broil; panbroil; panfry
	English Chops	Cut across the unsplit loin. Back bone removed and boneless chop skewered into shape.	Broil; panbroil; panfry
Rack	Rib (Rack) Roast	Contains rib bones and rib eye muscle.	Roast
	Crown Roast	Ribs are "frenched", that is, meat is removed from rib ends, then two or more rib sections are shaped and tied into a "crown".	Roast
	Rib Chops	Contain rib bone and rib eye muscle.	Broil; panbroil; panfry
	Frenched Chops	Same as rib chops except meat is removed from ends of ribs.	Broil; panbroil; panfry
Shoulder	Square Cut Shoulder	Thickest part of forequarter, with shank, breast, rib (rack), and neck removed.	Roast
	Cushion Shoulder	Boned and left flat. Sewed on two sides. One side may be left open for stuffing, then skewered or sewed.	Roast
	Rolled Shoulder	Boneless roll made from square cut shoulder.	Roast
	Boneless Shoulder Chops	Cut from boneless rolled shoulder.	Broil; panbroil; panfry; braise
	Mock Duck	Made from outside of shoulder. Shaped like a duck.	Roast
	Arm Chops	Contain small round bone and usually the cross sections of 4 or 5 rib bones.	Broil; panbroil; panfry; braise
	Blade Chops	Contain portions of rib, back and blade bones.	Broil; panbroil; panfry; braise
	Saratoga Chops	Boneless chops made from the inside shoulder muscle.	Broil; panbroil; panfry; braise
	Neck Slices	Round slice with neck vertebrae in center.	Braise; cook in liquid
Breast	Breast	Corresponds to veal breast and to short plate and brisket of beef. Narrow strip of meat containing breast bone and ends of 12 ribs.	Roast; braise; cook in liquid
	Breast with Pocket	Same as above but with pocket between ribs and lean.	Roast; braise
	Rolled Breast	Small boneless roll. Alternating layers of lean and fat.	Roast; braise
	Riblets	Breast bone removed and breast cut between ribs. Each small piece contains part of a rib bone.	Braise; cook in liquid
Shank	Shank	Contains shank and elbow bones.	Braise; cook in liquid
Ground Lamb	Loaf	Usually made from flank, breast, shank, and neck. May be straight ground lamb or combined with varying amounts of beef, pork or veal.	Roast (bake)
	Patties	Ground lamb formed into patties. May be encircled with sliced bacon.	Broil; panbroil; panfry

Square Cut Shoulder

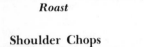

Roast

Cushion Shoulder

Roast

Breast

Braise, Roast

Shoulder Chops

Broil, Panbroil, Panfry, Braise

Rolled Shoulder

Roast, Braise

Riblets (Breast)

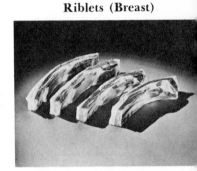

Braise, Cook in Liquid

Saratoga Chops (Shoulder)

Broil, Panbroil, Panfry, Braise

Ground Lamb

Roast (Bake)

Rolled Breast

Braise, Roast

Neck Slices

Braise, Cook in Liquid

Patties

Broil, Panbroil, Panfry

Shanks

Braise, Cook in Liquid

the Best Methods for Cooking Them

Rib Roast (Rack)

Roast

Loin Roast

Roast

Frenched Leg

Roast

Rib Chops

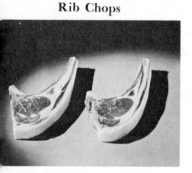

Broil, Panbroil, Panfry

Loin Chops

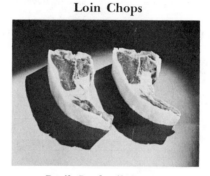

Broil, Panbroil, Panfry

American Leg

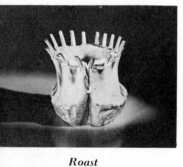

Roast

Crown Roast

Roast

Rolled Loin

Roast

Boneless Sirloin Roast

Roast

Frenched Chops (Rib)

Broil, Panbroil, Panfry

English Chops

Broil, Panbroil, Panfry

Sirloin Chops

Broil, Panbroil, Panfry

LAMB–Methods of Cooking

HIGH QUALITY lamb has a smooth covering of clear, white, brittle fat over most of the exterior. The lean is pinkish red in color; in yearling lamb and mutton it is a deeper red. The texture of the lean is fine grained and velvety in appearance.

The bones are porous and reddish in color. In older lamb and mutton they become hard and white. In young lamb, the fore feet when broken off expose eight well-defined ridges, known as the *break joint*. In yearlings, the break joint is hard and white instead of porous, moist and reddish. This joint cannot be broken by the time the mutton stage is reached. The break joint is a sure and simple way, therefore, of identifying lamb; however, about 90 per cent of the sheep in this country are marketed as lambs.

The thin, paper-like covering over the outside of the lamb carcass is known as the *fell*. It does not affect the flavor unless the lamb has been aged for some time. Under normal conditions, the fell should not be removed from the leg, since this cut keeps it shape better, cooks in less time and is juicier when the fell is left on. Chops, however, will be more desirable if the fell is removed before cooking.

Most cuts of high quality lamb are tender, therefore roasting, broiling and panbroiling or griddle-broiling are the cooking methods most used.

The neck, shanks and breasts may be prepared for braising or cut into small pieces for stew, which is cooked in liquid. The meat from these cuts also may be ground for patties or loaf, then cooked by dry heat. Most cuts of Utility lamb are best if cooked by moist heat. Lamb is cooked medium or well done. If cooked so that it is still slightly pink on the inside, there will be less shrinkage and the meat will be very juicy and delicious.

Lamb should be served very hot or cold, but it should never be served lukewarm.

TIME-TABLE FOR COOKING LAMB [1]

CUT	ROASTED AT 300° F. OVEN TEMPERATURE		BROILED [2]		BRAISED	COOKED IN LIQUID
	Meat Thermometer Reading	Time	Meat Thermometer Reading	Time	Total Time	Time
Leg	Degrees F. 175 to 180	Minutes per lb. 30 to 35	Degrees F.	Minutes	Hours	Hours
Shoulder Whole	175 to 180	30 to 35				
Rolled	175 to 180	40 to 45				
Cushion	175 to 180	30 to 35				
Breast Stuffed					1½ to 2	
Rolled	175 to 180	30 to 35			1½ to 2	
Lamb Loaf	175 to 180	30 to 35				
Chops (1 inch)	175 to 180	30 to 35	170	12		
Chops (1½ inch)			170	18		
Chops (2 inch)			170	22		
Lamb Patties (1 inch)				15 to 18		
Neck Slices					1	
Shanks					1½	
Stew						1½ to 2

[1] *For frying see discussion page 6.*

[2] *Panbroiling or griddle-broiling requires approximately one-half the time of broiling.*

Lamb

ROAST LEG OF LAMB
Number of Servings — 8

Use heavy roaster for top of range roasting. Have butcher cut off bone at first joint. Do not remove fell; rub with garlic. Heat roaster over high heat until hot. Reduce heat to medium; add meat; brown on all sides. Reduce heat to low; cover; cook 35 minutes per pound. Season with salt, pepper near end of cooking. Serve with mint jelly.

Lorna Carswell, Lone Rock H. S.
Lone Rock, Wisconsin

LEG OF LAMB — SOUTH OF THE BORDER
Number of Servings — 12

8 lb. leg of lamb
1 clove garlic
½ t. marjoram
½ t. salt
2 T. lemon juice
¼ t. tabasco
2 strips bacon
1 bottle small stuffed green olives

Mash and mix garlic, marjoram, and salt together. Add lemon juice and tabasco. Cut bacon into ½ inch pieces. Cut excess fat off lamb and wipe with clean damp cloth. Make 10 holes with handle of a wooden spoon about 1½ inches deep. Push small olive in hole, then piece of bacon, ½ teaspoon of garlic mixture, then another stuffed olive until all holes are filled. Roast in moderate oven 325° F., allowing 30 to 35 minutes per pound or use meat thermometer and roast until temperature is 175°.

Mrs. Martha Foster, Marshall H. S.
Marshall, Michigan

BARBECUED LEG OF LAMB
Number of Servings — 12

4 or 5 lb. leg of lamb
2 chopped onions
¼ c. vinegar
½ t. dry mustard
4 T. catsup
2 T. sugar
2 T. Worcestershire sauce
4 c. water

Salt and pepper leg of lamb, roll in flour. Put in roaster with ingredients listed above. Put lid on roaster and bake in a moderate oven (350°F.) for 3 or 4 hours or until meat is tender. Meat should be turned and basted with sauce every half hour. Remove lid from roaster half hour before meat is ready, to permit browning. Serve with the sauce.

Mrs. Patricia Nixon, St. Louis H. S.
St. Louis, Oklahoma

BARBECUED LAMB
Number of Servings — Depends on size of roast

Rub a leg of lamb with 2 teaspoons salt and dredge well with flour. Brown quickly in a hot oven (450°F.). Make sauce with the drippings in the pan by pouring over the lamb 1 cup water, ½ cup tomato catsup, 2 tablespoons pepper sauce, 2 teaspoons Worcestershire sauce and ¼ teaspoon cayenne, mixed together. Add 1 onion, sliced, to the sauce in the bottom of the pan. Roast until tender, basting every 20 minutes with the sauce. Frequent basting is necessary so that the meat may absorb the flavor of the sauce. The time of roasting depends on the size of the roast. (For a small roast, the amount of sauce may be reduced but be sure that there is enough to baste often).

Eleanor L. Miller, Wahama H. S.
Mason, West Virginia

ROAST LAMB SHOULDER
Number of Servings — 8-10

½ t. salt
¼ t. pepper
1 T. dry mustard
3 T. flour
½ c. cold water
4-5 lb. lamb shoulder, boned and rolled
1 c. currant jelly

Mix seasonings and flour; add water and blend. Spread over lamb shoulder. Roast uncovered in slow oven (300°F.) 30-35 minutes per pound, or 3½ hours. Spread with currant jelly the last hour. Baste every 15 minutes.

Mrs. Mary G. Meyer, Griggsville H. S.
Griggsville, Illinois

BREAST OF LAMB WITH APRICOT STUFFING
Number of Servings — 8

1 breast of lamb with pocket (about 2 lbs.)
Salt and pepper
Lemon juice or garlic

APRICOT STUFFING

¾ t. salt
¼ t. pepper
¼ t. thyme or poultry seasoning
1⅓ c. dried apricots (cut in small pieces)
½ c. minced onion
1 c. chopped celery
⅓ c. melted butter
6 c. soft bread cubes

Have your dealer remove the fell and crack the bones of the breast, so it can easily be carved between the ribs when served. Have a pocket made in the breast by cutting through the flesh, close to the ribs. Rub the inside of pocket and outside with salt and pepper; use a little lemon or garlic if you wish additional seasonings. Place apricots in a saucepan and cover with a little water. Cover the pan; when water is boiling remove from heat and let stand about a minute or until apricots are slightly tender. Drain off liquid. Cook onions and celery in the melted butter over

(Continued on Next Page)

low heat until tender but not browned. Add to bread mixture along with the apricots. Fill lamb pocket with apricot stuffing and fasten opening with skewers and string as you would poultry. Place breast ribs down in a shallow baking dish. Cook in 325°F. oven about 1¾ hours. Serve piping hot.

Mrs. Dorothy Tyler, Dalton H. S.
Dalton, Nebraska

FRICASSED LAMB JARDINIERE
Number of Servings — 6

3 lb. shoulder of lamb
1 sliced onion (½ c.)
½ c. sliced carrots
½ c. celery sliced
⅛ c. diced red sweet pepper
1 clove garlic, sliced very fine
1 bay leaf
½ t. Rosemary leaves
¼ c. dry sherry wine

Cut and braise lamb. Add onion, carrots, celery, pepper, garlic, bay leaf, and Rosemary leaves. Simmer until meat is done, about 1 hour. Add sherry wine.

Jo Anne Kralich, Fort Benton H. S.
Fort Benton, Montana

LAMB POT ROAST
Number of Servings — 6-8

5 lbs. lamb roast
2 large onions
3 large potatoes or 6 very small
2 to 3 cups water
1 large can tomato sauce or 2 small
Salt and pepper to taste

Cook roast until almost done—about 1½ hours. Add onions, cut in quarters; potatoes, cut in quarters or if they are small, add whole. Cook until potatoes are done. Add tomato sauce and simmer for 30 minutes.

Mrs. Mary Lee Haby, La Pryor H. S.
La Pryor, Texas

LAMB CHOPS
Number of Servings — 6

6 thick lamb shoulder chops
Salt and pepper
1 green pepper (cut in rings)
1 large onion (sliced)
1 lemon (sliced)
2 c. tomato juice

Brown chops in hot fat; season. Place in baking pan; top each with green-pepper ring, onion ring, lemon slice. Pour tomato juice over chops. Cover; bake in slow oven (325° F.) 1½ hours.

Pruda Caudill Prather, Carter H. S.
Carter City, Kentucky

CHOPS IN PACKAGE
Number of Servings — 1

1 or 2 lamb, veal or pork chops
1 white potato
1 small onion
Package frozen green peas
Can condensed cream of celery soup
Salt and pepper
1 T. meat sauce

For each person cut two 18 inch lengths of heavy duty aluminum foil. Cross them and turn up the edges. Place raw sliced potatoes in the center of each. Salt and pepper the chops and rub with favorite meat sauce. Place on potatoes and top with celery soup. Arrange onion slices on top. Bring slightly thawed green peas around the sides, sprinkle with salt and pepper. Bring aluminum foil together and close snugly. Bake at 325°F. for 1½ hours.

Mrs. Ivy West Cross, Patrick Henry H. S.
Ashland, Virginia

SWEET 'N SOUR LAMB CHOPS
Number of Servings — 4

4 shoulder lamb chops about 1-inch thick
¼ c. vinegar
¼ c. brown sugar, firmly packed
1 medium lemon
1 t. salt
⅛ t. pepper
¼ t. ginger
1 medium orange

Cook chops over low heat until browned on both sides, best broiled. Test for doneness. While meat is cooking, peel and slice orange and cut lemon in narrow wedges. Combine vinegar, sugar, salt, pepper and ginger. Mix well, pour sugar mixture over chops after they are done. Add orange slices and lemon wedges and cook over low heat about 30 minutes or until chops are tender. This is delicious with pork chops and ham.

Mrs. T. R. Sparkman, Crystal River H. S.
Crystal River, Florida

DINNER CHOPS
Number of Servings — 6

6 thick lamb shoulder chops
Salt and pepper
1 green pepper, cut in rings
1 large sliced onion
1 lemon, sliced
2 c. tomato juice

Brown chops in hot fat; season. Place in baking pan; top each with green pepper ring, onion slice, lemon slice. Pour tomato juice over chops. Cover; bake in slow oven (325°F.) for 1½ hours.

Marialice Tatom, East Dougherty Jr. H. S.
Albany, Georgia

ORANGE GLAZED LAMB CHOPS
Number of Servings — 4

4 double lamb chops, rib or loin
4 T. frozen concentrated orange juice

Brown lamb chops quickly in skillet. Remove to baking dish and pour drippings and concentrated orange juice over the top. Bake uncovered in moderate oven (350°F.) until done, basting frequently with pan drippings. Cook 30 to 45 minutes for desired degree of doneness.

Grace F. Harrison,
Connecticut State Dept. of Education
Hartford, Connecticut

LAMB CHOP GRILL
Number of Servings — 6

6 lamb chops, 1 inch thick
6 link sausages
3 medium sized tomatoes
2 T. dry bread crumbs
2 T. grated American cheese
1 t. grated onion
6 slices bacon
6 pineapple spears

Broil chops and sausages on one side 8 minutes. Halve unpeeled tomatoes; sprinkle cut side with mixture of crumbs, cheese, and onion. Wrap bacon slices around pineapple spears. Season chops; turn meats; arrange tomatoes and pineapple on broiler rack; continue broiling 6 minutes. Turn pineapple once.

Mrs. Mary G. Meyer, Griggsville H. S.
Griggsville, Illinois

LAMB OR BEEF STEW
Number of Servings — 6

"Be an artist of the range and bring happiness into your home."
1½ lbs. meat
¾ c. flour
1 T. salt
¼ t. pepper
3 T. bacon drippings
1 t. Worcestershire Sauce
8 small onions
1 bunch carrots
6 or 8 medium potatoes
1 can tomato sauce
1 turnip (if desired)

Cut meat into pieces 2 inches square. Put meat into flour, press flour into meat. Brown meat in the hot drippings. Add 3 onions, cut fine, cover with water. Cook 1 hour. Other onions are left whole. Dice other vegetables and add to the stew. Add remaining ingredients and cook slowly for 1 hour.

Betty Kandt, Herington H. S.
Herington, Kansas

LAMB
Number of Servings — 10

4 c. soft bread crumbs
½ c. water
2 lbs. lamb ground, uncooked
1 T. salt
¼ t. pepper
2 eggs
1 clove garlic, minced
½ c. chopped onion
¼ c. chopped parsley
½ c. grated carrots (fine)

Combine bread crumbs and water; add remaining ingredients and mix well. Form into patties. Melt 2 tablespoons bacon fat or shortening in a frying pan, add meat patties, brown on side (six minutes) then turn and brown other side (six minutes). Serve with catsup or chili sauce.

Naomi K. Ingwalson, Chinook H. S.
Chinook, Montana

BARBECUED GRILLED LAMBURGERS
Number of Servings — 8

2 lbs. ground lamb
2 T. salt
1 t. pepper
Dash of curry powder
Dash of thyme
½ c. sweet pickle relish

Mix dry ingredients with ground lamb. Shape patties lightly. For extra juicy burgers, cook in foil pockets sealed to hold in juices—a favorite barbecue sauce may be spooned into the pocket just before sealing; if desired—these burgers will be moist. For crusty burgers, cook on open grill top. In grilling, cooking should start with a fire at greatest distance from food so as fire cools, food can be adjusted closer for more heat.

Sue S. Lacklear, Fairgrove H. S.
Fairmont, North Carolina

LAMBURGERS
Number of Servings — 8

2 lbs. of ground lamb
1 c. bread crumbs
½ c. tomato sauce
1 T. vinegar
1 T. sugar
1 T. garlic salt
1 t. dry mustard
1 t. lemon juice

Work seasonings into ground lamb, shape burgers lightly, handle ground lamb as little as possible to obtain the best product. Panfry or grill. Sprinkle with red pepper.

Sue S. Lacklear, Fairgrove H. S.
Fairmont, North Carolina

BROILED LAMB & BACON PATTIES
Number of Servings — 6

½ lb. lean bacon
1 lb. lamb (ground)
½ t. salt

Lay bacon out slightly overlapping it; spread with seasoned ground lamb and roll up jelly roll form; chill; cut in 1½ inch slices; broil 5 inches from heat 6 to 8 minutes per side.

Dorothy K. Heidlebaugh, Mendon Union H. S.
Mendon, Ohio

LAMB CURRY
Number of Servings — 6

3 large apples, pared, cored and sliced
1 onion, sliced
1 clove garlic
2 to 3 T. flour
1 T. curry powder
1 T. lemon juice
2 c. meat stock or bouillion
1 t. gravy flavoring
Grated rind of ½ lemon
½ c. raisins
3 whole cloves
2 c. cubed leftover cooked lamb

Saute in butter the apples, onion and garlic until golden brown—then remove garlic. Blend well and add flour and curry powder to apple mixture. Combine lemon juice, meat stock and gravy flavoring and stir in gradually to mixture. Then add lemon rind, raisins and cloves. Cover and simmer 30 minutes. Add lamb, heat thoroughly and serve with rice on hot platter.

Mrs. Dortha Cooper, Van Buren H. S.
Spencer, Tennessee

LAMB LIVER BAKED IN SOUR CREAM
(original)

Number of Servings — 2-4

Note: In many parts of the United States (N.J. and N.Y. specifically) it is necessary to buy a lamb haslet to get the liver. This includes liver, heart and lungs. The heart may be par boiled, stuffed with sage dressing and baked at the same time.
1 lamb liver (whole)
1 small carton commercial sour cream
1 medium sized onion
Flour, salt, pepper, bacon drippings

Method: Buy one or more lamb livers. Rinse and wipe whole liver. Roll in flour, to which salt and pepper has been added. Sear in hot bacon fat and place in a shallow table serving dish. Spread generously with commercial sour cream. Arrange slices of raw onion over top and bake about an hour at 325°F. or until done. The size of the liver determines the baking time. There will be sour cream gravy to serve with each serving of meat.

Linda Paulson, St. John's H. S.
John's Island, South Carolina

LAMB KABOBS
Number of Servings — 6

2 green peppers
1 large onion
2 firm tomatoes

Have 1½ pounds lamb shoulder cut into 1 inch cubes. Marinate in French dressing (with garlic) 1 hour or over night. Alternate meat cubes, pieces of pepper, onion, and tomato on metal skewers. Roll in salad oil. Broil 3 inches from heat, allowing 30 minutes. Turn as meat and vegetables brown.

Kathryn Williams, Ruidoso H. S.
Ruidoso, New Mexico

LAMB SHISH-KABOB
Number of Servings — 8

2 lbs. boned leg of lamb
1 T. lemon juice
1 T. vegetable oil
1 round sliced medium onion
⅛ t. pepper
3 whole tomatoes
3 round sliced green peppers
3 round sliced egg plant
3 bay leaves
Dash salt

Cut meat in 1-inch cubes. Mix oil, lemon juice, salt, and pepper, and rub on meat thoroughly. Cover with sliced onion, pepper, and bay leaves and refrigerate for 4-5 hours in covered bowl or overnight. Arrange meat on skewers alternately with vegetables dipped in the seasoning. Broil over charcoal or woodfire or in range broiler turning as needed. Serve hot as part of a balanced meal.

Bertha K. Benthien, Clermont Northeastern H. S.
Owensville, Ohio

SHEPHERD'S PIE
Number of Servings — 6-8

1½ lbs. lean raw lamb
Salt
Pepper
Flour
Fat
1 onion, sliced
3 c. diced turnips
1 green pepper, chopped
Mashed potatoes

Cut meat into inch cubes; sprinkle with salt, pepper, and flour; and brown in 2 to 3 tablespoons fat. Add onion and water. Cover and simmer for 1½ hours until meat is tender. Add turnips and green peppers and cook until tender. If stew is not thick enough, thicken by adding a flour paste to the stew. When stew is done put into a large baking dish and cover with seasoned mashed potatoes and bake until the pie is hot throughout and browned on top.

Rosie Laughlin, Olathe H.S.
Olathe, Colorado

Poultry

Poultry

CHICKEN AND DRESSING
Number of Servings — 6
1 4-lb. dressed hen
Water to cover
1½ T. salt

Boil hen until almost tender. Remove from broth and bake 40 minutes at 400°F. until well-browned and tender.

SOUTHERN DRESSING
4 c. cornbread crumbs
3 c. hot chicken broth
1 c. finely chopped celery
2 chopped boiled eggs
1 t. sage
5 biscuits (crumbled)
3 T. minced onion
½ t. black pepper
2 raw eggs
3 c. hot chicken broth

Crumble bread into mixing bowl. Add boiling broth. Cover and let set 5 minutes. Add other ingredients in order given. Pour into greased baking dish and bake 1 hour at 400°F. Serve with chicken, and giblet gravy.

GIBLET GRAVY
Melt ¼ cup butter. Add ¼ cup flour and ½ teaspoon salt. Blend well. Add 2 cups chicken broth and finely chopped gizzard and liver. Add 1 chopped hard boiled egg. Cook until thick, stirring constantly.

Hilda Harman, Smithville H. S.
Smithville, Mississippi

STUFFED CHICKEN BREASTS
Number of Servings — 4
4 c. herb stuffing
4 chicken breasts
¼ c. flour
1 t. salt
½ t. paprika
⅛ t. pepper
6 T. melted butter
1 can mushroom soup
1 c. commercial sour cream
2 t. parsley flakes

Make herb stuffing (recipe below). Shake chicken in paper bag with flour, salt, paprika and pepper. Cut breasts from neck and toward lower tip to make a pocket. Fill with stuffing; skewer with picks; dip in melted butter; place in baking dish. Bake in slow oven (325°F.) 1½ hours, or until tender. It will not need turning. Serve with mushroom sauce.

HERB STUFFING—Combine 4 cups dry bread cubes, 2 tablespoons chopped onion, ½ teaspoon salt, ½ teaspoon poultry seasoning, ¼ teaspoon pepper, 4 tablespoons melted butter, ½ cup hot water in small bowl; toss lightly.

MUSHROOM SAUCE—Heat 1 can cream of mushroom soup. Stir in 1 cup sour cream and parsley flakes. Do not boil. Serve with chicken. Chicken quarters may be prepared as above, except not stuffed.

Faye Sadler, Perryville H. S.
Perryville, Arkansas

CHICKEN DRESSING
Number of Servings — 8
4 c. left over biscuit and loaf bread
4 c. egg cornbread (use several eggs to make)
½ c. finely chopped onion
1 c. chopped celery
⅓ c. butter or oleo
1 c. milk
3 c. chicken broth (about)
Salt
Pepper

Crumble the bread in large bowl. Add onion, celery, and seasonings. Add enough hot chicken broth to make a soft mixture. Mix well. Add butter and milk. Mixture should be very soft to allow for loss of moisture during baking. Add more broth if necessary. Pour in greased pan and bake in moderate oven (350°F.) for about an hour. Stir occasionally. Serve with giblet gravy.

Sue Batchelor, Palmetto H. S.
Reform, Alabama

ROASTED CHICKEN BREAST
Place chicken breast in a shallow baking dish, skin side up. Sprinkle with salt, pepper and ½ teaspoon thyme per chicken. Brush with melted butter. Roast 1 hour at 350°F.

Carolyn Ellington, Glynn Academy
Brunswick, Georgia

CHICKEN BREASTS BAKED IN CREAM OF MUSHROOM SOUP
Number of Servings — 6-8
3 T. hot fat
3 lbs. chicken breasts
1 can cream of mushroom soup
½ can of canned milk
2 t. salt
⅛ t. pepper

Brown chicken breasts in hot fat and add cream of mushroom soup, canned milk and salt. Blend soup and canned milk well. Pour over chicken. Cover tightly. Bake until tender. Just before serving, remove chicken and keep warm while making gravy. Temperature 300°F. Bake about 2 hours. For the gravy, blend mixture of 2 tablespoons flour and ½ cup water into drippings in baking pan. Cook 2 to 3 minutes. If too thick, thin with milk.

Janet Walp, Mifflinville Jr. H. S.
Mifflinville, Pennsylvania

CHICKEN WITH ORANGE-RICE
Number of Servings — 4-5

4 chicken breasts, split in half or one 2½-lb.
  chicken, cut into pieces
Flour
Salt
Pepper
Paprika
2 10½-oz. cans cream of chicken soup
1 4-oz. can mushrooms

Dredge chicken in seasoned flour and brown in
shortening. Pour chicken soup diluted with milk
over the chicken and let simmer until chicken is
tender. This may be cooked in electric skillet,
covered; top of stove, or in the oven. A heavy,
covered pan or casserole may be used in a 300°F.
oven for about an hour. Add mushrooms to gravy
to be served with rice. Gravy may need to be
thinned or thickened depending on method used.

RICE

2 T. margarine or shortening
½ c. chopped onion
1 c. chopped celery
1 c. regular rice
Grated rind of 1 orange
Juice of 2 oranges, or 1 c. diluted frozen orange
  juice
Water enough to make 2½ c. liquid with juice
½ t. salt
⅛ t. thyme, if desired

Melt shortening in heavy pan. Saute onion and
celery until clear and golden, but not brown. Add
rice, grated rind, salt, thyme, orange juice and
water. Cook over low heat for 25 minutes or more.
Rice may be cooked by baking in a casserole in
the oven at the same time as chicken, if using
oven for chicken.

Princess Egbert, Grants Pass Sr. H. S.
Grants Pass, Oregon

BAKED CHICKEN BREAST
Number of Servings — 6

6 chicken breasts (skinned)
2 t. salt
½ t. pepper
¾ t. thyme
¾ t. marjoram
1 t. paprika
6 T. salad oil
1½ c. non-fat milk solids
2½ c. cornflakes (crushed)

Sprinkle chicken with salt, pepper, paprika,
thyme, and marjoram. Dip each piece in oil and
then in corn flakes to coat both sides. Set chicken
breasts on a rack in a shallow baking dish. Fill
dish with water to a depth of ¼ inch. Bake
chicken for 35 minutes in an oven of 375 degrees.
Do not turn.

Mrs. Vergie E. Stephens, Castle H. S.
Newburgh, Indiana

CHICKEN SUPREME
Number of Servings — 6-8

6-8 chicken breasts or 1 whole chicken
1½ sticks butter or oleo
½ c. flour
1 t. salt
¼ t. pepper
1 t. paprika
½ c. cooking sherry

Preheat oven to 400°F. Flour chicken breasts.
Melt the butter in a large baking dish. Lay the
chicken skin side down in the dish of melted
butter. Bake 30 minutes or until brown. Turn
chicken pieces and add 2 cans cream of chicken
soup, (a little water to rinse can) to which the
cooking sherry has been added. (Mushroom soup
may be used if desired). Bake until bubbly. Reduce oven heat to 350°F. Cover dish with foil.
Bake 1 hour. Can be prepared in advance and
reheated.

Maralee Garland and Clarice Snider,
Union County H. S.
Erwin, Tennessee

BAKED CHICKEN BREASTS WITH ALMOND SAUCE
Number of Servings — 6-8

4 whole chicken breasts
Garlic salt to taste
¼ cup melted butter
1 T. paprika
1 T. lemon juice
⅓ oz. can mushrooms, stems and pieces
½ t. Worcestershire sauce
¼ c. sherry wine
¼ c. slivered almonds

Split chicken breasts in half and salt both sides
with garlic salts. Dip in melted butter to which
paprika and lemon juice has been added. Place
in shallow baking dish with skin side up. Bake
for 30 min. at 350°. Mix remaining ingredients
listed and spoon over chicken breasts. Sprinkle
with slivered almonds and continue baking for
30 additional minutes. Remove chicken; thicken
sauce with 2 tablespoons flour and stir in ¼ cup
sour cream. Serve over chicken breasts and rice.

Mary Free, Assistant Supervisor
Carrollton, Georgia

BAKED CHICKEN BREASTS
Number of Servings — 6

6 chicken breasts
1 stick margarine
Ritz crackers (crumbed)

Melt margarine. Dip chicken breasts in margarine
and roll in Ritz cracker crumbs. Bake in 350°F.
oven until tender (about 1 hour). (I usually bake
mine in an iron skillet).

Mrs. Mary J. Higgins, Marietta H. S.
Marietta, Georgia

GOURMET CHICKEN
210 calories each serving
Number of Servings — 6

3 whole chicken breasts, split
3 drumsticks
3 thighs
1 can (1-lb.) diet-pack whole purple plums
Juice of 1 lemon
1 medium onion (chopped)
¼ c. chili sauce
¼ c. soy sauce
1 T. Worcestershire sauce
1 t. ginger
2 t. prepared mustard
2 drops tobasco

Arrange chicken in a single layer 9 x 13 x 2 inch baking pan. Seed and puree plums and add to remaining ingredients to make a sauce, and pour over chicken. Cook 350° for 1¼ hours.

Lucille B. McGehee, Southwest DeKalb H. S.
South Decatur, Georgia

BAKED CHICKEN WITH SAUCE
Number of Servings — 4

2 lbs. chicken breasts
2 cans cream of chicken soup
½ c. milk
¼ c. green peppers, chopped
¼ c. chopped celery
1 small onion, chopped
Salt and pepper
2 T. lemon juice
2 T. Worcestershire sauce
Butter slices

Combine all ingredients, pour over chicken breasts in casserole dish. Bake at 325°F. until tender (approximately 1 hour). Place butter slices on top of dish when nearly done. Sauce is good served over rice.

Mrs. Evelyn R. Sheets, Yatesville H. S.
Yatesville, Georgia

PECAN STUFFED CHICKEN BREASTS
Number of Servings — 4

4 small chicken breasts
Lemon juice
¾ stick butter, melted
3 c. crumpled toasted bread
¼ t. Accent
⅓ c. chopped onion
½ c. chopped celery
2 t. parsley flakes (or fresh)
¾ c. chopped pecans
Salt and pepper

Mix toast crumbs, half the butter, onion, celery, parsley, pecans and Accent with enough water to moisten. Make four mounds of stuffing and arrange minutes more at 400°F. until brown.

Mrs. T. Juett, Mississinawa Valley H. S.
Union City (Ohio), Indiana

BAKED CHICKEN BREASTS
Number of Servings — 4-6

4 breasts split in halves
2 T. melted butter
1 t. salt
½ t. pepper
4 T. lemon juice
1 t. paprika

Preheat oven to 350°F. Remove skins from fresh or thawed frozen breasts, wash and pat dry. Place flesh side up in greased baking pan. Pour over melted butter and lemon juice. Add salt, pepper and paprika. Cover and bake 30 minutes. Uncover and bake until delicately brown and tender, depending on thickness of breast meat.

Dorothy E. Brevoort, State Dept. of Education
Trenton, New Jersey

CHICKEN BREAST WITH MUSHROOMS
Number of Servings — 8-10

8 or 10 frozen or fresh breast
2 sticks of margarine
2 cans mushroom soup
2 or 3 cans of mushrooms
Paprika
Parmesan cheese

Brown breast of chicken in skillet with 2 sticks of margarine. Place in flat baking dish. Pour 2 cans of mushroom soup over chicken breast. Put in 2 or 3 cans of mushrooms also. Sprinkle paprika and Parmesan cheese liberally over all. Bake 2 hours at 325° or 350°. Serve with wild rice.

Nelle B. Underwood, Flomaton H. S.
Flomaton, Alabama

BAKED CHICKEN BREASTS
Number of Servings — as many as needed

One chicken breast per person
Be sure meat is clean and dry. Roll the meat in seasoned flour and brown it lightly in fat in a frying pan. Put the breasts in a casserole; add a bit of sweet basil or rosemary (or paprika) and enough water to provide steam. Cover and bake in a moderately slow oven (325°F.) for 45 to 60 minutes, depending upon the tenderness of the meat.

Mrs. Louise Forsythe, Butler Co. H. S.
Morgantown, Kentucky

CHICKEN BREASTS — BAKED
Number of Servings — 4

1 box frozen chicken breasts (4)
¼ lb. butter
1½ c. crushed potato chips

Thaw chicken and dip each piece in melted butter, then roll in potato chip crumbs. Place in pan to bake, not touching each other. Bake about 1 hour at 325°F. Baste with extra butter if needed.

Mrs. Audrey Bailey, Northfield Jr.-Sr. H. S.
Northfield, Minnesota

OVEN BAKED CHICKEN BREASTS
Number of Servings — 8

2 c. crushed potato chips
½ c. margarine
8 chicken breasts
1 t. salt

Crush potato chips and melt margarine. Add salt to melted margarine and stir. Dip breast first into melted margarine, then into potato chip crumbs. Place in large pan, skin side up, in oven and bake uncovered for 1 to 1¼ hours at 350°F.

Mrs. Elwanda M. Brewer, East Tallahatchie H. S.
Charleston, Mississippi

CHICKEN BREAST

4 large whole breast of chicken
1 can mushroom soup
⅔ c. mushrooms
1 c. dairy sour cream
½ c. cooking sherry wine

Salt, pepper and flour chicken. Brown and place in baking dish. Combine soup, mushrooms, cream and sherry, pour over chicken. Bake one hour in 350°F. oven, uncovered. Serve with rice.

Mrs. Ruth T. Hanegan, Hope H. S.
Hope, Arkansas

CHICKEN ENTREE
Number of Servings — 4-6

4-6 halves of chicken breasts
1 t. curry powder
1 can chicken soup 10½-oz.)
½ c. commercial cream (sour)
Flour and fat and seasonings

Dip chicken breasts in seasoned flour and brown in fat slightly. Arrange in baking pan. Stir curry powder into cream of chicken soup and pour over chicken. Cover and bake in moderate oven about 40 minutes until tender. Stir in cream and serve with cooked rice or on toast.

Myrtis L. McAlhany, St. George H. S.
St. George, South Carolina

BROILED CHICKEN
Number of Servings — 3

6 medium pieces of chicken
3 T. Worcestershire sauce
2 T. butter
Juice of 1 lemon

Salt and pepper chicken, then place in broiler pan. Put lemon juice, Worcestershire sauce and butter on chicken and broil for 30 minutes or until chicken is brown.

Janette Yates, Baldwin County H. S.
Bay Minette, Alabama

MARVELOUS BROILED CHICKEN

1 broiler (1½ to 2½ lbs.)
1 t. salt
1 t. sugar
¼ t. paprika
¼ t. pepper
Juice of 1 lemon
Butter or margarine

Have chicken split in half lengthwise. Break drumstick, hip and wing joints. Rub the entire surface of the chicken with lemon juice. Sprinkle with a mixture of the salt, sugar, paprika and pepper. Coat with melted butter or margarine. Place in the bottom of the broiling pan (no rack) skin side down. Place broiler pan 5 to 7 inches from the heat. Regulate the heat so that chicken just begins to brown in 10 minutes. Turn and brush with fat about every 15 minutes. Total cooking time varies from 35 to 50 minutes. Drumstick and wing joints will yield easily to fork pressure when done. Serve on a warm platter, skin side up. Pour drippings over chicken.

Ruth Wiman, Roscoe H. S.
Roscoe, Texas

OVEN BROILED CHICKEN
Number of Servings — 2-4

1 frying size chicken
1 package chicken livers
1 can small potatoes
Juice of 1 lemon
6 to 8 T. Worcestershire sauce
8 T. oleomargarine
Garlic, salt, pepper to taste
½ c. dry sherry

Split chicken in half, sprinkle with garlic salt, salt and pepper. Place in deep pan, with livers, pour over juice of 1 lemon, and Worcestershire sauce. Place in 500°F. oven for ½ hour (uncovered). Turn, dot with oleomargarine, add potatoes, drained, and sprinkled with paprika, salt and pepper. Cover with foil and continue cooking for ½ hour or until chicken is tender. Add sherry to gravy. Heat and pour over chicken.

Mrs. Dorothy M. King, Palestine H. S.
Palestine, Texas

BROILED CHICKEN WITH WINE SAUCE
Number of Servings — 4

1 fryer
Salt
⅔ c. honey
⅓ c. Madeira wine

Mix wine and honey. Cut fryer in serving pieces. Place on broiler. Brown and cook until tender (20 minutes). Salt. Paint each piece with honey mixture. Allow honey to brown into chicken. Turn. Paint each side at least twice.

Betty Otteson, Pearl City Unit No. 200
Pearl City, Illinois

OVEN BROILED CHICKEN
Number of Servings — 4

1 frying-size chicken
¼ c. cooking oil or
¼ cup melted butter
Salt and pepper

Cut chicken into quarters, brush with ¼ cup oil or melted butter and sprinkle with salt and pepper. Place chicken pieces in a 2-inch heavy iron skillet or similar utensil. Cover tightly with aluminum foil. Cook at 475°F. for 40 minutes. Remove foil and continue baking for approximately 15 minutes or until golden brown. Turn pieces only once during the browning period.

Mrs. Jerry M. Cook, Live Oak H. S.
Watson, Louisiana

GINGER-BROILED CHICKEN
Number of Servings — 2

2½ lb. chicken, split for broiling
1 t. onion salt
¼ c. melted butter
¾ c. apple juice
1 t. cinnamon
Ground ginger

Season chicken with onion salt. Place on oven-broiler pan cut side up, or on outdoor grill cut side down. Brush with part of melted butter. Place 6 to 7 inches from heat source. Combine apple juice and cinnamon with remaining butter. During cooking time, turn chicken and baste with sauce every 10 minutes. After 20 minutes sprinkle chicken very lightly with ginger. Broil 40 minutes or until tender.

Harriet J. Harless, Logan Sr. H. S.
Logan, West Virginia

BARBECUED CHICKEN
Number of Servings — 4-6

1½ c. tomato juice
1 t. pepper
2½ t. salt
1 t. powdered mustard
1 T. sugar
¾ c. vinegar
4½ T. Worcestershire sauce
4 T. salad oil
1 bay leaf
1 small onion, chopped fine
Dash of garlic salt
¼ c. catsup, if desired
1 fryer, or equivalent in select pieces

Combine ingredients and heat for 10 minutes. While sauce is heating prepare fryer as though frying (salt, dredge and brown in small amount of fat). Pour sauce over chicken. Cover and cook on top of range or uncovered in oven at 300°F. for 1½ hours. Turn chicken several times during cooking.

Mary Jim Combs, Carrollton H. S.
Carrollton, Georgia

BARBECUED CHICKEN
Number of Servings — 4

1 frying chicken
½ c. flour
2 t. salt
¼ t. pepper
1 medium onion, chopped
2 T. vegetable fat
2 T. vinegar
¼ c. lemon juice
1 c. catsup
3 T. Worcestershire sauce
1½ t. prepared mustard
1 c. water
¼ c. chopped celery
⅛ t. red pepper
Salt to taste

Cut chicken in serving pieces. Flour by shaking several pieces at a time in a paper bag containing flour, salt and pepper. Preheat ¼ inch vegetable fat in skillet and brown chicken. Brown onion in vegetable fat. Add remaining ingredients of barbecue sauce and simmer for 30 minutes. Place browned chicken in a deep baking dish. Pour hot sauce over the chicken. Bake uncovered in a slow oven (325°F.) for one hour.

Mrs. Jean Borden, Marysville Jr. H. S.
Marysville, Ohio

BARBECUED CHICKEN
Number of Servings — 8

4 breasts
4 legs
Salt
Pepper
Vinegar
Butter

Place chicken in oblong pyrex dish and fill dish ⅔ full of vinegar (undiluted). Sprinkle with salt and pepper. Dart with butter. Cook uncovered for 1 hour at 325°F.

Mary R. Copley, Bluestone H. S.
Skipwirth, Virginia

BARBECUED CHICKEN
Number of Servings — 6

3½ to 4 lb. fryer
Cut in halves, quarters, or pieces. Wash, dry well, and flour pieces by shaking several at a time in a paper bag containing:
1 c. flour
2 t. salt
1 t. paprika
¼ t. pepper
½ t celery salt

After browning, pour Texas Barbecue Sauce over the chicken and cook over low heat on top of stove, or bake in a preheated oven (325°F.) until tender (45-60 minutes).

TEXAS BARBECUE SAUCE

Mix together and simmer 15 minutes
½ c. finely chopped onion (1 medium sized)
2 T. brown sugar
1 T. paprika
1 t. salt
1 t. dry mustard
¼ t. chili powder
⅛ t. cayenne pepper
2 T. Worcestershire sauce
¼ c. vinegar
1 c. tomato juice
¼ c. catsup
½ c. water

Mrs. Charlotte Brainerd,
Fennimore Community Schools Jt#1
Fennimore, Wisconsin

BARBECUED CHICKEN
Number of Servings — 4

1 2½-3 lb. fryer
1 medium onion, chopped fine
2 T. fat
2 T. vinegar
2 T. brown sugar
¼ c. lemon juice
1 c. catsup
3 T. Worcestershire sauce
½ T. prepared mustard
1 c. water
⅛ t. garlic salt
⅛ t. celery seed
⅛ t. chili powder
⅛ t. paprika
⅛ t. dry mustard
⅛ t. Tabasco sauce
Several drops Hot Pete

Brown chicken in fat (do not flour). To make sauce—cook onions in fat until tender and slightly brown. Combine all other ingredients, pour into onions and simmer for 30 minutes. Pour sauce over browned chicken and cook in oven at 300°F. 1 hour, or until tender. Sauce delicious for barbecuing on grill and also suitable for other meats.

Mrs Joan M. Miller, Jefferson H. S.
Jefferson, South Carolina

BARBECUED CHICKEN
Number of Servings — 4

3 T. tomato catsup
3 T. brown sugar
Juice of 1 lemon
1 t. paprika
Red pepper as desired
2 T. Worcestershire sauce
4 T. water
1 t. mustard
1 t. chili powder
Little garlic salt

Combine sauce ingredients and simmer until blended. Season chicken with salt and pepper, dip in sauce and place in aluminum foil lined pan. Pour remaining sauce over chicken. Cover over completely with foil. Cook 450°F. for 15 minutes, reduce heat to 350°F. and cook about 1 hour and 15 minutes.

Mildred R. Buck, Linden H. S.
Linden, Alabama

BARBECUED CHICKEN
Number of Servings — 6

1 3-3½ lb. ready to cook frying chicken
1 medium onion
2 T. fat
2 T. vinegar
2 T. brown sugar
¼ c. lemon juice
1 c. catsup
3 T. Worcestershire sauce
½ T. prepared mustard
1 c. water
½ c. chopped celery
Salt and red pepper

Brown chicken in hot fat. Brown onion in 2 tablespoons fat; add remaining ingredients. Simmer 30 minutes. Pour over chicken. Bake uncovered in 325°F. oven 1 hour. Sauce may be used for meats also.

Mary Ann Buresh, Jesup Community School
Jesup, Iowa

OVEN BARBECUED CHICKEN
Number of Servings — 6

1 chicken
2 T. butter
3 T. catsup
3 T. Worcestershire sauce
1 T. lemon juice
½ t. hot sauce
1 t sugar (optional)

Place pieces of chicken in casserole dish. Combine above ingredients, melt and pour over chicken. Cover with aluminum foil. Cook in hot oven (450°F.) for 15 minutes. Then reduce temperature to 250°F. Cook about two hours.

Mrs. Harold H. Jones, Jr., Elbert County H. S.
Elberton, Georgia

BARBECUED CHICKEN
Number of Servings — 6-8

2 broilers
Melted fat
⅓ c. vinegar
2 t. Worcestershire sauce
¼ t. garlic salt
½ t. salt
⅛ t. pepper
Dash paprika
1 T. tomato paste
½ t. onion salt
½ c. melted fat

Split broilers. Brush with fat and place on heated broiler, skin side down. Place rack 5 inches from heat. Cook 15 minutes, turn, brush with fat, cook 15 minutes and turn again, allowing 40-60 minutes for cooking through. Combine sauce and baste, skin side up, until browned good.

Mrs. Dorothy Chapman, Irwin County H. S.
Ocilla, Georgia

BARBECUED CHICKEN
Number of Servings — 6

2 large fryers, 3 or 3½ lbs.
1 medium onion, sliced
½ t. salt
2 c. tomato juice
3 T. margarine
½ t. black pepper
1 clove garlic
1 bay leaf
1 t. dry mustard
1 t. red pepper
1 t. celery seed
3 T. vinegar
½ t. Tabasco sauce
½ t. curry powder

Quarter chicken, turn skin side up in baking dish, dot with margarine and sprinkle with salt. Cut garlic in half and place in baking dish—bake uncovered 30 minutes. Meanwhile make sauce of ingredients remaining. Cook 10-15 minutes. Remove garlic, add sauce and continue cooking 1½ hours, basting every 15 or 20 minutes.

Mrs. Virginia Lee, Technical H. S.
Memphis, Tennessee

CHICKEN BARBECUE
Number of Servings — 6-8

2 fryers
1½ c. barbecue sauce

Have your butcher split each fryer into 4 pieces for baking. Arrange chicken in baking pan or pans, skin side up. Place in 300°F. oven and bake until skin is crisp and meat tender—1 to 1½ hours. Pour over each piece some of barbecue sauce and replace in oven until barbecue sauce bubbles— 15 to 20 minutes.

Margaret Crawford, Silverton P. S.
Silverton, Colorado

BARBECUED CHICKEN
Number of Servings — 6

3 T. brown sugar
6 T. lemon juice
1 T. Worcestershire sauce
1 c. chili sauce
Few grains pepper
3 T. chopped onion
3 T. vinegar
3 T. water
1½ t. salt
1 medium green pepper, chopped

Prepare chicken as for frying. Brown in hot fat if desired. Place in baking dish. Combine all ingredients and add to the chicken. Bake 1 hour at 350 degrees.

Nancy Matthews, State Dept. of Education
West Virginia

BARBECUED CHICKEN
Number of Servings — 2-3

1 fryer (cut up)
2 t. catsup
2 t. vinegar
2 t. butter
2 t. Worcestershire sauce
4 t. water
2 t. prepared mustard
1 t. paprika
1 t. chili powder
½ t. red pepper
A well-greased paper bag

In a bowl large enough to dip the chicken, mix thoroughly catsup, vinegar, melted butter, Worcestershire sauce, water, lemon juice, mustard, paprika, chili powder, red pepper, salt and pepper. Dip in sauce. Place in well greased paper bag and tie lightly with string. Place in baking pan and cook in a 375°F. oven for 1 hour.

Nita Whitfield, Clinton H. S.
Clinton, Tennessee

BARBECUED CHICKEN
Number of Servings — 6

1 chicken, cut up (skinned if desired)
1 c. water
¼ c. vinegar
1 onion, sliced
1 stick margarine
¼ t. red pepper
½ lemon

Put water, vinegar, margarine, onion, red pepper and lemon juice in pan. Flour and salt chicken. Put chicken in pan. Bake at 425°F. for 20 minutes and then cut heat down to 300°F. for 45 more minutes. If you want dry crisp chicken, put chicken on rack above sauce and baste every 10 minutes instead of putting chicken directly in sauce.

Alta Ann Morrison, Tuscaloosa County H. S.
Northport, Alabama

BARBECUED CHICKEN (in a paper bag)
Number of Servings — 6

3 T. tomato catsup
2 T. vinegar
2 T. lemon juice
2 T. Worcestershire sauce
4 T. water
2 T. butter
3 T. brown sugar
1 t. salt
1 t. mustard (dry or prepared)
1 t. chili powder
1 t. paprika
½ t. cayenne pepper
1 t. sodium glutamate

Mix all of these ingredients together and heat to blend. Cut up a 3 pound chicken or use 3 pounds of pieces. Grease the inside of a medium-size heavy-paper sack and place in a roaster or Dutch oven. Set oven at 500°F. Salt and pepper the chicken, dip in hot sauce and place in the bag. Pour the remaining sauce over the chicken in the bag. Carefully fold sack opening in a double fold and secure with paper clips so that sauce will not leak out. (Place sack in roaster with seam up to prevent sack from coming apart). Cover roaster, cook 15 minutes at 500°F. Lower heat to 350°F. and cook for 1 hour and 15 minutes. Do not open bag until cooking time is over. You may cook chicken, cool and freeze after wrapping in Reynolds Wrap. To serve, place in oven directly from freezer in 350°F. oven for additional 1 hour.

Mrs. Pauline G. Adkins, Sandy Hook H. S.
Sandy Hook, Kentucky

BARBECUED CHICKEN WITH KENTUCKY SAUCE
Number of Servings — 10

2½ c. water
1 T. sugar
2½ t. black pepper
2 T. butter
1 t. mustard
1 bud garlic
½ t. red pepper
¼ c. vinegar
2½ t. salt
2 T. Worcestershire sauce
¼ onion
2 t. chili powder
½ t. Tabasco sauce

After the fire has burned down to a bed of coals, put the ten halves of chicken on the grill, skin side up. This seals the cut side so the natural juices will not run out. Baste repeatedly during the entire barbecuing period, particularly during the last 30 minutes. Turn every 5-10 minutes, basting each time turned. Broil from 1¼ to 2 hours.

Mary Denton Pierce, Clinton County H. S.

TEXAS BARBECUED CHICKEN
Number of Servings — 5-6

2 large or 3 small cut up fryers
1 t. salt
⅛ t. pepper
½ c. butter
¼ c. granulated sugar
2 T. flour
½ t. salt
½ to 1 T. chili powder
¼ t. dry mustard
¼ t. pepper
⅓ c. vinegar
1 T. Worcestershire sauce
3 T. hot water

About 3 hours before serving start heating oven to 300°. Place chicken in casserole or roasting pan; sprinkle with 1 teaspoon salt and ⅛ teaspoon pepper .Cover (if roaster has no cover use foil). Bake 2 hours. Meanwhile, in double boiler, melt butter, stir in sugar with flour, salt, chili powder, dry mustard and pepper; then vinegar, Worcestershire sauce and hot water. Cook, stirring till thickened. Keep hot. About 15 minutes before serving brush with generous amount of sauce and turn oven to 350°. When serving, pass extra sauce.

Kathleen Story, Harvard H. S.
Harvard, Illinois

BARBECUED CHICKEN
Number of Servings — 4-6

2 T. brown sugar
1 T. paprika
1 t. salt
1 t. dry mustard
¼ c. catsup
½ c. water
¼ t. chili powder
⅛ t. cayenne pepper
2 T. Worcestershire sauce
¼ c. vinegar
1 c. tomato juice
½ c. chopped onions

Mix above ingredients in saucepan; simmer 15 minutes, or until slightly thickened. Meanwhile, brown chicken in 2 tablespoons fat. Pour ½ sauce over chicken and cover. Cook over medium low heat. Baste wit hsauce every 10 minutes until chicken is tender.

Mrs. Jean Crane, Burnsville H. S.
Burnsville, Mississippi

BARBECUED CHICKEN
Number of Servings — 4-6

2 or 2½ lb. frying chicken
2 T. catsup
2 T. vinegar
1 T. lemon juice
2 T. Worcestershire sauce
4 T. water

(Continued on Next Page)

2 T. butter
1 t. mustard
2 T. brown sugar
1 t. salt
1 t. chili powder
1 t. paprika
½ t. red pepper

Set chicken aside. Mix all ingredients together and heat till butter melts. Place a large piece of aluminum foil on a baking pan. Dip each piece of chicken in sauce and place on pan in foil. Pour remaining sauce over chicken. Fold edges of foil to seal airtight. Place in oven at 500°F. for 15 minutes. Reduce heat to 350°F. and bake for 1 hour. Open foil and serve chicken hot.

Mrs. Edward Felknor, White Pine H. S.
White Pine, Tennessee

CHICKEN A LA BARBECUE SAUCE
Number of Servings — 16

4 2-2½ lb. fryers quartered
1 bottle catsup
½ bottle Worcestershire sauce
1 c. tomato sauce
Salt and pepper, as desired
Juice of 2 lemons
1 c. Wesson oil
1 c. vinegar

Quarter fryers. Salt and pepper as desired. Mix catsup, Worcestershire sauce, tomato sauce, lemon juice, Wesson oil, and vinegar together. Dip seasoned chicken into sauce, and put in roaster or baking dish. Bake covered in a 350°F. oven for 2 hours. Turn chicken and baste with sauce occasionally. May be uncovered for last 20 minutes for browning, if desired.

Nellie Merrill, St. David H. S.
St. David, Arizona

BARBECUED CHICKEN
Number of Servings — 4

3 T. catsup
1 T. lemon juice
3 T. vinegar
3 T. brown sugar
2 T. Worcestershire sauce
4 T. water
2 T. butter
1 t. salt
1 t. mustard
1 t. paprika
1 t. chili powder
½ t. red pepper

Mix all ingredients; heat until dissolved. Cut chicken into serving pieces. Dip each piece into sauce. Line pan with foil and grease, leaving foil so it will cover chicken. Place in foil and pour remaining sauce over it. Seal in foil and place in 500°F. oven. Cook 15 minutes and reduce heat to 350°F. Cook 1 hour and 15 minutes longer.

Martha Sue Stout, Joshua H. S.
Joshua, Texas

WAISTLINE BARBECUED CHICKEN
Number of Servings — 8

One serving original, 571 calories—streamlined 415 calories
2 T. salad oil
2 3-lb. ready-to-cook fryers
The Sauce:
3 c. tomato juice
½ c. vinegar
1 T. sugar
4 medium onions, sliced
3 T. Worcestershire sauce
½ c. catsup
4 t. prepared mustard
1 t. pepper
2 t. salt

Start heating oven to 350°F. In hot salad oil in skillet, brown chicken well on all sides. Remove to shallow baking pan. In saucepan, combine tomato juice, vinegar, sugar, onions, Worcestershire sauce, catsup, mustard, pepper, salt; heat. Pour over chicken. Bake chicken, uncovered, 1 hour, or until tender, basting every 10 minutes with sauce.

Mrs. Elsie Kitchens, Grady H. S.
Grady, New Mexico

BARBECUED CHICKEN
Number of Servings — 8

2 T. salad oil
2 3-lb. ready to cook broiler fryers, quartered
3 c. tomato juice
½ c. vinegar
4 medium onions, sliced
1 T. sugar
3 T. Worcestershire sauce
½ c. catsup
4 t. prepared mustard
1 t. salt
1 t. pepper

Start heating oven to 350°F. In saucepan, combine tomato juice, vinegar, sugar, onions, catsup, Worcestershire sauce, mustard, salt and pepper. Heat and pour over chicken. Bake chicken, uncovered, 1 hour or until tender, basting every 10 minutes with sauce. A little water may be added to sauce if too thick. Suggestion: Serve sauce over rice.

Lois Ousley, Hartsville Jr. H. S.
Hartsville, South Carolina

BARBECUED CHICKEN
Number of Servings — 6-8

1 3-3½ lb. frying chicken
1 medium onion
3 T. fat
2 T. vinegar
3 T. brown sugar
1 c. chopped celery
¼ c. lemon juice, fresh or canned
1 c. tomato catsup
3 T. Worcestershire sauce

(Continued on Next Page)

½ T. prepared mustard
1 c. water
1 T. green pepper, chopped

Sprinkle brown sugar in bottom of pan, place chicken (fat side up) in the pan. Brown onion in fat; add remaining ingredients. Simmer 30 minutes. Sprinkle salt over chicken. pour mixture over chicken. Cover with aluminum foil, bake 350°F. slow oven for 1 hour, or until tender. Extra sauce may be put in container and frozen to be used at a later date with chicken or other meats.

Mrs. Sallie P. Satterly, F.H.A. Adviser H. S.
Hitchins, Kentucky

BAR-B-Q CHICKEN
Number of Servings — 4

1 frying size chicken
Flour
Salt
1 medium onion
2 T. fat
2 T. vinegar
2 T. brown sugar
1 c. tomato catsup
3 T. cream mustard
1 c. water
½ c. chopped celery
½ t. red pepper

Salt cut up chicken to taste. Roll in flour to coat and brown in 2 tablespoons fat. When golden brown, remove chicken and add remaining ingrediens to the fat left in skillet. Simmer 30 minutes. Pour over browned chicken and bake uncovered in low oven (325°F.) for one hour. Excellent dish to prepare ahead of time and bake at meal time.

Mrs. Mildred Tate, Henderson City H. S.
Henderson, Kentucky

BARBECUED CHICKEN
Number of Servings — 6

1 3-3½ lb. ready-to-cook frying chicken
1 medium onion
2 T. fat
1 c. catsup
3 T. Worcestershire sauce
½ T. prepared mustard
1 c. water
½ c. chopped celery
2 T. vinegar
2 T. brown sugar
¼ c. lemon juice, fresh, frozen or canned
Salt
Red pepper

Brown chicken in hot fat. Brown onion in 2 tablespoons fat; add remaining ingredients. Simmer 30 minutes. Pour over chicken. Bake uncovered in slow oven (325°) 1 hour. Sauce may be used for meats also.

Virginia E. Hart, Whitestown H. S.
Whitestown, Indiana

SPECIAL BARBECUED CHICKEN
Number of Servings — 6

½ c. butter or margarine, melted
1½ t. salt
1 large clove garlic, minced
2 T. lemon juice
½ c. catsup
⅓ c. diced onion
1 T. Worcestershire sauce
4 drops Tabacco
Quick-frozen split broilers or cut-up fryers

Prepare barbecue sauce by melting butter or margarine and mixing with other ingredients. Store covered in refrigerator. Thaw chicken according to package directions. Place chicken on grill and set grill no higher than 2 to 3 inches above bed of glowing coals. Brush chicken with barbecue sauce. Turn chicken every 5 minutes with long-handled fork or tongs (avoid piercing meat) and brush with barbecue sauce. Watch closely. Reserve some of sauce for sprinkling over chicken before serving. Grill chicken 45 minutes to 1 hour, or until knife cuts easily into thickest part of drumstick and no pink color shows at bone.

Ruth E. Boyett, Gordo H. S.
Gordo, Alabama

OVEN BARBECUED CHICKEN
Number of Servings — 5

Barbecue Sauce:
Cook until soft 1 c. chopped onions
Add
1 c. chopped onions
½ c. oil
¾ c. tomato catsup
¾ c. water
⅓ c. lemon juice
¼ c. Worcestershire sauce
3 T. sugar
1 T. dry mustard
2 T. salt
½ t. pepper

Simmer all of above ingredients over low heat for 15 minutes. Disjoint frying chicken and place in a flat baking dish without stacking the pieces. Spread about ¾ cup of the barbecue sauce over the chicken and bake in oven set at 375°F. for 1 hour. Turn the chicken and spread another ¾ cup of sauce over the chicken. Cook another hour.

Mrs. Blanche Hitson, Lordsburg H. S.
Lordsburg, New Mexico

OVEN BARBECUED CHICKEN
Number of Servings — 6-8

2 2-lb. broiler chickens, cut in fourths
½ c. Mazola oil
2 T. vinegar
1 can tomato sauce
½ t. Tabasco sauce
3 T. sugar
1 t. salt
Black pepper to taste

(Continued on Next Page)

1 T. Worcestershire sauce
½ T. soy sauce

Brush chicken with Mazola oil and vinegar. Arrange skin side up in shallow pan. Cook at 325°F. for 25 minutes. Turn, brush again and cook for 20 minutes. Mix together over low heat tomato sauce, Tabasco sauce, sugar, salt, pepper, Worcestershire sauce and soy sauce. Add oil and vinegar left in pan. Mix well and dip chickens in sauce. Serve warm. (Cover with foil if meal is delayed).

Mrs. Joyce Nance, Nixon H. S.
Nixon, Texas

LEMON BARBECUED CHICKEN
Number of Servings — 6

¼ c. fat (half butter)
2½ lb. frying chicken, cut in pieces
1 small clove garlic
¼ c. salad oil
½ t. salt
½ c. lemon juice
2 T. finely chopped onion
1 t. black pepper
½ t. thyme

Melt fat in shallow baking pan in 400°F. oven. Dip chicken pieces in seasoned flour. Place in baking pan in single layer, skin side down. Bake 30 minutes. Turn skin side up and pour over Lemon Barbecue Sauce made as follows: Mash garlic with salt. Add and mix well salad oil, lemon juice, pepper, onion, and thyme. Continue baking until tender, about 30 minutes.

Helen E. Snyder, Hughesville H. S.
Hughesville, Pennsylvania

OVEN BARBECUED CHICKEN
Number of Servings — 8

6 lbs. frying chicken parts
⅔ c. lemon juice
½ c. soy sauce
2 T. chopped parsley
1½ c. salad oil
8 drops Tabasco sauce
⅛ t. salt
¼ t. pepper
1 T. garlic salt
1 c. (about) bread crumbs or flour

Place chicken parts in a shallow pan. Combine lemon juice, soy sauce, parsley, salad oil, Tabasco sauce, salt, pepper, and garlic salt. Mix well. Pour over chicken and let stand 4 hours. Turn pieces occasionally. Then drain chicken and roll lightly in bread crumbs or flour. Shake off excess. Arrange chicken in a shallow pan and bake in a moderate oven (350°F.) for bout 1 hour, or until tender. Makes 8 servings.

Mrs. Marilyn M. Cannon, Berry H. S.
Berry, Alabama

ROTISSERIE OF CHICKEN WITH BARBECUE SAUCE
Number of Servings — 8

1 T. shortening
¼ c. finely chopped onion
1 c. red catsup
½ c. water
2 T. brown sugar
½ t. salt
⅛ t. black pepper
2 T. white vinegar
2 T. Worcestershire sauce
½ t. prepared mustard
¼ c. lemon juice
½ c. finely chopped celery

Heat fat in frying pan. Add onion and cook until golden brown, stirring 3 or 4 times. Mix catsup, water, seasonings and celery, then add onion. Cover pan and simmer this mixture for 15 or 20 minutes, stirring 3 or 4 times. Makes 2¼ cups. Select a 2½-pound chicken, clean, rub with butter and sprinkle with salt. Place on spit of rotisserie and tie firmly. Start rotisserie and cook for 1 hour (longer if needed to make tender). Baste every 15 minutes with melted butter. Serve with sauce.

Mrs. Claude Elliott, Minonk Dana Rutland H. S.
Minonk, Illinois

BARBECUED CHICKEN
Number of Servings — 6

1 3 to 3½ lb. ready-to-cook frying chicken
1 medium onion
2 T. fat
2 T. vinegar
2 T. brown sugar
Red pepper
¼ c. lemon juice, fresh, frozen, or canned
1 c. catsup
3 T. Worcestershire sauce
½ T. prepared mustard
1 c. water
Salt

Brown chicken in hot fat. Brown onion in 2 tablespoons fat; add remaining ingredients. Simmer 30 minutes. Pour over chicken. Bake uncovered in slow oven (325°F.) 1 hour. Sauce may be used for meats also.

Betty Jean Wade, Unadilla H. S.
Unadilla, Georgia

OVEN BARBECUED CHICKEN
Number of Servings — 6-8

1 fryer, cut in servings
Favorite barebecue sauce

Roll chicken pieces in barbecue sauce until well coated; place in casserole (do not stack). Cover and bake at 325°F. about 1¼ hours.

Mrs. E. T. Parker, La Vega H. S.
Bellmead Branch; Waco, Texas

OVEN BARBECUED CHICKEN
Number of Servings — 6

3 T. catsup
2 T. Worcestershire sauce
3 T. brown sugar
4 T. water
Juice one lemon
1 t. mustard
1 t. paprika
1 t. chili powder
Dash of red pepper and garlic salt
1 fryer cut up

Combine sauce ingredients and simmer till blended. Season chicken with salt and pepper. Dip in sauce and place in aluminum foil-lined pan. Pour remaining sauce over chicken and cover completely with foil. Bake at 450°F. for 15 minutes and cook one hour and 15 minutes.

Mrs. Flora R. Nowell, Cottonwood H. S.
Cottonwood, Alabama

OVEN BARBECUED CHICKEN
Number of Servings — 8

2 frying-size chickens
½ c. cooking oil
¾ c. chopped onion
¾ c. catsup
¾ c. water
⅓ c. lemon juice
3 T. sugar
3 T. Worcestershire sauce
2 t. salt
½ t. pepper

Place cut up chicken in aluminum foil 9 x 13 pan in oven set at 400°. Bake about one hour—or until tender. Cook onion till soft in hot cooking oil; add remaining ingredients; simmer 15 minutes. When chicken is tender, cover with sauce and bake—without foil over chicken, about 15 minutes.

Mrs. Peggy Green, Zion-Benton Twp. H. S.
Zion, Illinois

BARBECUED CHICKEN
Number of Servings — 8

1 c. cooking oil
¾ c. chopped onion
¾ c. catsup
¾ c. water
⅓ c. lemon juice
3 T. brown sugar
3 T. Worcestershire sauce
2 T. prepared mustard
2 t. salt
½ t. pepper

Cut up two fryers. Combine all ingredients above. Marinate chicken in sauce (above) overnight. Cook chicken and sauce in slow oven (300°F.) 3 hours or until brownness desired.

Wanda Frix, Mojave H. S.
Mojave, California

HERB-GARDEN FRIED CHICKEN
Number of Servings — 4

1 3-lb. frying chicken, cut
½ c. buttermilk
1 c. flour
1½ t. salt
⅛ t. pepper
½ t. paprika
½ t. powdered thyme
½ t. powdered marjoram

Dip prepared pieces of chicken in buttermilk; drain. Combine flour and remaining ingredients in paper bag. Place one piece of chicken at a time in bag and shake to coat evenly with flour. Fry chicken in fat preheated to 375°F. until golden brown on both sides, about 10 to 12 minutes.

Mary Lou Miller, Grantsburg H. S.
Grantsburg, Wisconsin

SESAME FRIED CHICKEN
Number of Servings — 4

1 chicken (cut up for frying)
1 egg, beaten
½ c. milk
1 c. flour
1 t. baking powder
2 t. paprika
2 t. salt
¼ t. pepper
¼ c. chopped nuts
2 T. sesame seeds
½ c. butter

Dip chicken pieces into egg and milk mixture, then into mixture of flour, baking powder, salt, paprika, pepper, nuts, and sesame seeds. Melt butter in a shallow pan (400°F.) and bake in oven until tender and golden brown. About 1½ to 2 hours.

Mrs. Roselynn A. Cobb, Mosinee H. S.
Mosinee, Wisconsin

SOUTHERN FRIED CHICKEN
Number of Servings — 4-5

1 fryer (about 1½ lbs.)
1 egg, beaten
½ c. evaporated milk
1 c. flour
Salt
Pepper

Disjoint fryer. Season with salt and pepper. Dip pieces in milk. Coat with flour. Dip into egg and coat again with flour. Lower into deep fat heated to 350°F. The temperature will drop to about 300°F. Cook at this temperature (300°F.) until brown and tender, about 20 minutes. Drain on absorbent paper. If unsure of doneness for larger pieces, place drained meat in a shallow pan and cook in slow oven (325°F.) about 20 minutes.

Mrs. Jane S. Funderburk, Seminary H. S.
Seminary, Mississippi

BATTER FRIED CHICKEN
Number of Servings — 4-5

1 fryer
1 egg
2 T. milk
½ c. flour
Salt
Shortening

Beat the egg until frothy, then stir in milk. Salt pieces of chicken, dip into batter, then flour. Fry in a deep heavy skillet or electric fryer. Have fat deep enough to cover the chicken, and heat to 365°F. Remove from fat when golden brown, and drain on absorbent paper.

Mildred N. Mallette, Greenville H. S.
Greenville, Alabama

SPICY FRIED CHICKEN

1 3-lb. chicken
Flour
Paprika
Salt and pepper
2 eggs
1½ c. buttermilk
2 T. water

Cut up chicken and salt. Put into the flour, paprika (quite a bit so it can be seen). Batter—2 eggs, 1½ cups buttermilk and 2 tablespoons water. Flour each piece of chicken and dip in batter. Flour again. Have skillet well filled with margarine and Crisco. Pieces should not touch. Turn once when golden brown. Drain.

Marilyn Ziegler, University H. S.
Bloomington, Indiana

TENDER GOLDEN FRIED CHICKEN
Number of Servings — 6

1 medium size fryer
2 c. flour
Salt
Fat

Cut chicken into pieces. Add salt to chicken. Place flour into paper bag. Drop chicken into bag and shake until all pieces are covered with flour. Place chicken into skillet containing 1 inch hot fat. Cover skillet. Turn heat to low and cook until brown. Turn and cook second side until brown. Drain, and serve.

Linda P. Davis, McAdory H. S.
McCalla, Alabama

DEEP FAT FRIED CHICKEN
Number of Servings — 4

1 frying chicken (2½- 3-lb. chicken)

Salt individual pieces to taste, shake in flour in paper bag. Fry in popcorn oil. Fry approximately 8 to 10 minutes at 350°F.

Mrs. Jane Mosbacher, Dupo H. S.
Dupo, Illinois

DELMARVA FRIED CHICKEN
Number of Servings — 5

2½ lbs. frying chicken
½ c. flour
1 t. salt
¼ t. pepper
⅛ t. paprika
1 c. shortening

Melt ½ inch shortening in heavy frying pan. Combine flour, salt, pepper and paprika in a paper bag. Cover pieces with flour mixture by shaking chicken in bag. Brown slowly on both sides. Total cooking time about ½ hour.

Jean Brittingham, John M. Clayton H. S.
Dagsboro-Frankford, Delaware

STEWED FRIED CHICKEN
Number of Servings — 4

1 chicken

Cut chicken into fourths. Roll chicken in flour. Dip chicken in egg and milk batter. Roll the dipped chicken in flour. Fry until golden brown. Place golden brown chicken into casserole dish. Place casserole dish into a 250° oven for 1 hour. Batter for chicken: 1 egg to 2 cups of milk; the milk may be powdered.

Mrs. B. D. Funderburk, West Lamar H. S.
Petty, Texas

CRISPY CHICKEN
Number of Servings — 4-6

3 lb. fryer
3-4 c. crisp cereal
⅔ c. margarine
1 t. salt
½ t. pepper

Dip pieces of chicken in melted margarine, coating each piece well; roll in crushed cereal patting the cereal into an even coating. Line cookie sheet with foil and arrange chicken pieces one layer deep. Bake in moderate oven (350°F.) for 1 hour, or until very tender and golden brown.

Joan Johnson, Gallup H. S.
Gallup, New Mexico

OVEN FRIED CHICKEN
Number of Servings — 4

1½ t. salt
1 t. paprika
1 t. dry mustard
½ c. melted butter
1 2½- 3-lb. ready-to-cook fryer cut up

Combine seasonings and melted butter. Rub chicken pieces in butter mixture. Place in 1½ x 7⅜ x 1½-in. baking dish. Bake uncovered at 450°F. for 50 to 60 minutes, or until tender. Turn once during baking period.

Mrs. Ruth Gamble, Northern Potter Joint H. S.
Ulysses, Pennsylvania

OVEN FRIED "BUTTER CRISP" CHICKEN
Number of Servings — 6-8

1 2- to 3-lb. ready-to-cook frying chicken
1 c. flour
1 t. salt
½ t. pepper
2 t. paprika
½ c. butter
¼ c. shortening

Melt butter and shortening in shallow baking pan. Pre-heat oven at 350° F. Put flour, salt, pepper and paprika in a paper bag. Shake 3 or 4 pieces of chicken in the bag to coat thoroughly. Place pieces—one layer deep—skin side up—in pan. Brush with butter and put in oven. Bake 50-55 minutes. Brush with butter at intervals. The last 10 minutes cover and reduce oven to 300° F. (Oven browned potatoes are delicious with this chicken.)

Mrs. Doris Swinehart, Muscoda H. S.
Muscoda, Wisconsin

OVEN FRIED HERB CHICKEN
Number of Servings — 4

1 2½- to 3-lb. ready-to-cook broiler or fryer
½ envelope garlic-salad dressing mix
2 T. flour
¼ t. salt
¼ c. soft butter or margarine
1 T. lemon juice

Dry chicken with paper towels. Combine salad dressing mix with flour, salt. Blend in butter and then lemon juice. Spread mixture evenly over top of chicken. Place pieces skin side up, not touching, on jelly roll pan or cookie sheet. (Bake in 350°F. oven 1¼ hours or until tender).

Jane Cole, Geneva H. S.
Geneva, Illinois

OVEN-FRIED CHICKEN
Number of Servings — 4

1 3 lb. frying chicken (cut)
¼ c. shortening
1½ c. flour
1 T. salt
1 t. paprika
1 t. celery seed
½ t. pepper
½ t. garlic salt
1 egg
1⅓ c. milk

Preheat oven to 375°F. Place a sheet of aluminum foil on a cookie sheet with sides. Place shortening on cookie sheet and place in oven. Mix dry ingredients together in paper sack. Beat egg and milk together. Dip chicken pieces in egg mixture and then shake in flour mixture. Place on cookie sheet, skin side down. Bake for 45 minutes, turning once.

Mrs. Barbara Bringhurst, Stayton Union H. S.
Stayton, Oregon

FRYER
Number of Servings — 8

1 fryer
Salt and pepper
1 stick margarine
Juice of 1 lemon
3 T. flour
1 c. milk

Cut chicken as for frying; salt and pepper to taste. Arrange pieces of chicken in heavy baking dish and sprinkle juice of lemon over it. Cut the margarine in slices and put over chicken. Put top on baking dish and put in 350°F. preheated oven. Bake 40 minutes and turn pieces of chicken over. Bake 20 minutes and then add mixture of flour and milk. Bake 25 minutes and serve immediately.

Mrs. Rachel Nicholson, Union H. S.
Union, Mississippi

CRUSTY CHIP FRIED CHICKEN
Number of Servings — 4

1 4-oz. package of potato chips (2 cups crushed)
¼ t. garlic salt
Dash of pepper
1 2½- to 3-lb. ready-to-cook frying chicken, disjointed
½ cup melted butter or margarine (1 stick equal ½ c.)

Combine crushed chips, garlic salt and pepper. Dip chicken in melted butter; roll in the chip mixture. Place the pieces skin side up, so they do not touch in a greased shallow pan, which may be lined with foil. Bake in moderate oven at 375°F. 1 hour, or until tender (do not turn). Meat should shrink a little from the bone ends. When you cut thickest part to bone, no pink should show. Makes four or more servings.

Mrs. Norma Piboin, Madisonville H. S.
Madisonville, Texas

CHICKEN IN THE OVEN
Number of Servings — 8

2 chickens (large fryers)
½ c. margarine (melted)
2 c. dry bread crumbs
¾ c. Parmesan cheese
¼ c. parsley
1 clove garlic or garlic salt
2 t. salt
Pepper

Combine bread crumbs, cheese, parsley, garlic, salt and pepper; mix well. Cut large fryers in serving sized pieces. Dip pieces into margarine, then into crumb mixture. Place in a long flat, uncovered baking pan or broiler pan. If any is left over the crumb mixture is good on top of chicken. Bake one hour at 350°F.

Esther Magill, Kimball H. S.
Kimball, South Dakota

FRYER
Number of Servings — 4-5

1 tender frying chicken
1 stick margarine or butter
Salt to taste
2½ c. cracker crumbs or crushed corn flakes

Cut chicken in serving pieces. Roll each piece in melted butter or margarine, then in cracker crumbs or corn flakes. Bake on an uncovered broiler pan, leaving space between each piece. Bake uncovered for 1 hour at 325°F. until brown and tender. Makes 4 or 5 servings. (If you use salty crackers, use less salt).

Mrs. Margaret Kemp, Mountain View H. S.
Mountain View, Arkansas

CORN FLAKE CHICKEN
Number of Servings — 4

1 2 or 2½-lb. chicken
2 c. crushed corn flakes
Juice of 1 lemon
¾ c. Wesson oil
2 T. salt
1 t. pepper
2 T. Wesson oil

Cut chicken into serving pieces. Salt and pepper. Add lemon juice to Wesson oil, roll in crushed corn flakes. Place in casserole. Add 2 tablespoons Wesson oil over chicken. Bake in 500°F. oven 20 minutes. Turn oven to 300°F. and bake 30 minutes longer. For variety dip chicken in Pet milk instead of oil.

Marjorie Ellzey, Bunker Hill H. S.
Columbia, Mississippi

OVEN-FRIED CHICKEN PARMESAN
Number of Servings — 4

1 c. crushed packaged herb stuffing
⅔ c. grated Parmesan cheese
¼ c. chopped parsley
1 clove garlic, minced
1 2½-3 lb. frying chicken, cut up
½ c. butter or margarine, melted

Combine stuffing crumbs, cheese, parsley, and garlic. Dip chicken in melted butter and roll in crumb mixture. Place pieces skin side up so they don't touch in a shallow pan. Sprinkle with remaining butter and crumb mixture. Bake at 375°F. for 45 minutes or until tender. Turning is unnecessary.

Carolyn Baldwin, Pontiac Central H. S.
Pontiac, Michigan

OVEN-FRIED CHICKEN
Number of Servings — 6

1 frying chicken, 2½ lbs. (cut up)
¼ c. margarine
1 c. flour
1 t. salt
¼ t. pepper

Melt margarine in shallow baking pan in moderate oven (400°F.). Combine flour, salt and pepper in paper sack. Add chicken pieces and shake to cover. Place chicken in baking pan in single layer, skin side down. Bake 30 minutes. Turn skin side up. Continue baking until tender, about 30 minutes. Remove chicken from pan. Make milk gravy in same pan.

Leva A. Brown, Tecumseh H. S.
Tecumseh, Michigan

OVEN-FRIED CHICKEN
Number of Servings — 4

2½ lb. fryer
Flour
Salt
Paprika
Cooking oil

Allow ¼ chicken for each serving. Have 2½ pound fryer quartered. Wash and dry with a soft towel. Dip into sifted flour seasoned with salt, pepper and a generous amount of paprika. Dip into cooking oil and back into flour mixture. Place in a pan which has been greased with oil. Place bony side down. Place in 325°F. oven for one hour. Do not turn chicken while cooking. Remove from pan and make gravy.

Mrs. Howard Yarbrough, Cherokee H. S.
Canton, Georgia

OVEN-FRIED CHICKEN
Number of Servings — 8

2 frying chickens, cut up
1 t. salt
½ t. pepper
½ c. butter or margarine
2 c. dry cereal

Dry chicken thoroughly. Add salt and pepper to butter or margarine (melted). Crush dry cereal on waxed paper. Dip chicken in seasoned butter and then roll in cereal. Place chicken separately on foil-lined flat pan. Cook in moderate oven (350°F.) for 1 hour.

Mrs. Kay Thompson, Ladoga H. S.
Ladoga, Indiana

OVEN-FRIED CHICKEN
Number of Servings — 6

½ c. flour
½ t. salt
3-3½ lb. chicken, cut in pieces
½ c. melted shortening

Sift flour and salt together. Roll pieces in flour mixture. Place in shallow baking dish. Pour shortening over pieces. Bake at 350°F. for 60 minutes, covered tightly, turning three or four times. Remove cover last 20 minutes.

Mrs. Ben Elkin, Beulaville H. S.
Beulaville, North Carolina

OVEN-FRIED CHICKEN
Number of Servings — 4-8

2 broilers 1½ lbs. or less (halves or quarters)
1 c. flour
1 t. salt
½ t. pepper
2 t. paprika
1 t. dry mustard
½ c. butter or oleo

Combine dry ingredients in a paper bag; shake each piece of chicken in it. Place on broiling pan, bony sides up. Brush with melted butter. Place broiler in pre-heated oven 325°F. Turn in half an hour and baste as necessary. Bake 1½ hours. Make gravy with some of remaining dry ingredients.

Mrs. Eunice C. Peters, Hopewell Memorial H. S.
Aliquippa, Pennsylvania

OVEN-FRIED CHICKEN
Number of Servings — 6

1 c. flour
¼ t. pepper
¼ lb. butter
2 t. salt
2 t. paprika
6 servings of chicken

Mix flour, salt, pepper and paprika in a paper sack and shake three or four pieces of chicken in a sack at a time to coat them thoroughly. Then melt butter in a shallow baking pan in a moderately hot oven, about 400°F. When butter is melted remove pan from oven, and place the chicken, skin side down, in a single layer. Bake in that same moderately hot oven for a ½ hour; turn the chicken. Bake another 30 minutes or until tender. If you can't serve at once, then reduce the oven heat and brush the chicken with more melted butter. This will also give a nice gold crust to the chicken.

Nancy Davis, Mechanicsburg H. S.
Mechanicsburg, Ohio

OVEN-FRIED CHICKEN
Number of Servings — 6

1 (2½ or 3 lb.) fryer cut southern style
1 c. crushed corn flakes
1½ t. salt
¼ t. pepper
¼ c. butter or margarine

Coat chicken with seasoned corn flakes. Melt fat in 9 x 12 x 2 inch pan. Arrange chicken in single layer on melted fat with skin side down. Cover or wrap with heavy aluminum foil. Bake (400°F.) for 30 minutes in preheated oven. Turn chicken; bake 30 minutes longer or until golden brown and tender.

Georgia Matthews, Oliver Springs H. S.
Oliver Springs, Tennessee

OVEN-FRIED CHICKEN
Number of Servings — 6

1 2½ lb. fryer
1 large package potato chips
1 clove garlic
¼ lb. butter or margarine

Cut chicken as desired. Soften butter. Crush garlic in butter. Roll chicken in butter and garlic, then in crushed potato chips. Place on flat pan. Bake in oven for 45 minutes at 350°F.

Mrs. Dorsey Long, Laverne H. S.
Laverne, Oklahoma

OVEN-FRIED CHICKEN
Number of Servings — 4-6

½ c. fine dry bread crumbs
2 t. salt
1 t. paprika
¼ t. pepper
1 broiler-fryer chicken (cut in pieces)

Combine bread crumbs, salt, paprika and pepper. Brush each piece of chicken with corn oil, then roll in bread crumb mixture. Place chicken pieces, skin side up, in shallow baking pan. Bake in 425°F. (hot) oven 35 to 45 minutes, or until chicken is tender.

Nancy Kimball, University H. S.
Tallahassee, Florida

OVEN-FRIED CHICKEN
Number of Servings — 4

1 (3 to 4 lb.) chicken, cut in serving pieces
1 c. biscuit mix
2 t. salt
1 t. paprika
1 t. oregano
¼ c. butter

Dip chicken in mix, seasoned with salt, paprika and oregano. Put butter in shallow pan. Add chicken pieces. Bake 1½ to 2 hours in 350°F. oven. Baste frequently.

Helen McSparrin, Quakertown Sr. H. S.
Quakertown, Pennsylvania

OVEN-FRIED CHICKEN
Number of Servings — 4

2 frying chickens
⅛ lb. butter
2 T. Crisco
Salt and pepper

Have chicken quartered. Clean and pat dry. Melt shortening in a pan and dip each piece into fat. Lay chicken on a shallow pan, skin side down. Place in pre-heated oven 450°F. 15 minutes. Season and turn chicken, also season skin side, lower temperature to 350°F. Bake 1 hour or until tender.

Sylvia Stephenson, Lomira Community School
Lomira, Wisconsin

OVEN-FRIED CHICKEN
Number of Servings — 6-8

1 fryer size chicken
Salt and pepper to taste
¾ c. evaporated milk, full strength
1 medium sized bag potato chips, crushed

Cut up chicken in pieces. Season to taste with salt and pepper. Dip each piece in the evaporated milk and roll in crushed potato chips. Place chicken in greased oblong Pyrex baking dish and cook in medium oven (350°F.) for 45 minutes. For variety, substitute ½ cup melted butter or shortening for milk.

Nancy J. Ross, Del Rio H. S.
Del Rio, Texas

CORN-CRISPED CHICKEN
Number of Servings — 4-5

1 broiler-fryer chicken, cut in serving pieces
1 t. Ac'cent
1 t. salt
4 c. corn flakes
1 t. pepper
Heavy duty aluminum foil

Crush corn flakes into fine crumbs if using flake form. Add salt, pepper and Ac'cent to corn flake crumbs. Dip chicken pieces into undiluted evaporated milk, then roll in seasoned corn flake crumbs. Place chicken pieces, skin side up in an aluminum lined shallow pan, do not crowd. Bake at 350°F. for about an hour or until tender. Cover lightly with foil if a less crisp crust is desired; no need for turning pieces. No shortening needed.

Mrs. Albert T. Butler, Eau Gallie Jr. H. S.
Eau Gallie, Florida

OVEN-FRIED CHICKEN, DRESSING
Number of Servings — 6

1 4 lb. ready-to-cook chicken
6 c. dry bread cubes
1 t. salt
Dash pepper
1¼ t. sage
2 T. chopped onion
½ c. melted butter or margarine
1 10½ or 11 oz. can condensed cream of
   chicken soup

Dip chicken into flour seasoned with salt and pepper; brown in hot fat. Combine bread cubes, salt, pepper, sage, onion, and butter, using ½ cup soup. Arrange chicken in Dutch oven. Pile dressing in center. Make gravy of pan drippings, using 2 tablespoons flour and enough water with remaining soup to make 2 cups; pour over chicken. Cover closely; bake in moderate oven (350°F.) 1 hour.

Sadie G. McIlwain, Fairview H. S.
Cullman, Alabama

OVEN-FRIED CHICKEN, DRESSING
Number of Servings — 6

1 4 lb. chicken
6 c. dry bread crumbs
1 t. salt
Dash pepper
1¼ t. sage
2 T. chopped onion
½ c. melted butter
1 can cream of chicken soup

Dip chicken in seasoned flour and salt. Brown in hot fat. Combine bread cubes, salt, pepper, sage, onion, butter, ½ cup soup. Arrange chicken in Dutch oven. Pile dressing in center. Make a gravy of pan drippings, 2 tablespoons flour, soup, and 1½ cups water. Pour over chicken. Cover. Bake at 350°F. for one hour.

Ramona Reisch, Middlebury Union H. S.
Middlebury, Vermont

OVEN-FRIED CHICKEN
Number of Servings — 4-5

1 3 lb. fryer, cut up
¼ lb. (½ c.) butter or margarine, melted
1 c. cereal or cracker crumbs
½ t. salt
Dash of pepper

Dip pieces of chicken in melted fat, then in seasoned crumbs. Place in foil-lined shallow baking dish, without crowding. Bake 1 hour at 325°F. (An excellent dish to place in automatic oven, to cook while you're at church! And the dish is so easy to clean!)

Joyce P. Davis, Henderson County H. S.
Henderson, Kentucky

BAKED CHICKEN
Number of Servings — 4

1 fryer, cut up
½ c. flour
½ t. salt
¼ t. paprika
½ lb. butter (could use less)*
1 medium onion, sliced
1 4 oz. can mushrooms, drained
1 c. sour cream
Black pepper

Coat pieces of chicken in mixture of flour, salt, and paprika; brown pieces in butter in heavy skillet. Remove to casserole. Lightly brown onion and mushrooms; place over chicken. Sprinkle with black pepper. Place, uncovered, in 350°F. oven for 20 minutes. Reduce heat to 325°F.; add sour cream. Cover and bake for an hour, or until tender. The sauce makes a good gravy. (If commercially soured cream is used, dilute with some coffee cream.)
*A more economical cooking fat could be used.

Mrs. Barbara Rippe, Valley City Central H. S.
Valley City, North Dakota

CHICKEN COUNTRY CAPTAIN
Number of Servings — 6

6 chicken breasts
⅓ c. flour
½ t. salt
Dash pepper
½ c. shortening
1 c. chopped onions
1 c. chopped green pepper
1½ t. garlic salt
½ t. thyme
2 t. curry powder
1 t. chopped parsley
4 c. tomatoes
½ c. almonds
¼ c. currants (optional)

Remove skin from chicken. Roll in seasoned flour. Brown in hot fat, and remove. Add onions and green pepper to fat and cook until tender. Add salt, pepper, curry, thyme, garlic salt, parsley and tomatoes, mix thoroughly and replace chicken in vegetable mixture. Add water if liquid does not cover chicken. Cover, reduce heat and cook 45 minutes. Serve chicken in rice ring, add currants to sauce and pour over rice. Sprinkle shredded almonds on top.

Sue Boyet, North Caddo H. S.
Vivian, Louisiana

CRUNCHY BAKED CHICKEN
Number of Servings — 4-6

1 frying chicken
½ c. melted butter or margarine
1½ c. crushed corn flakes
1 package dry onion soup

Roll each piece of chicken in the melted butter, then in corn flakes. Place in greased baking pan. Dribble any remaining butter over chicken and sprinkle with onion soup. Bake at 325°F. for 1½ hours.

Billie Jane Blankinship, Kofa H. S.
Yuma, Arizona

BAKED CHICKEN
Number of Servings — 6-7

2½ lb. fryer (breasts best)
½ c. flour
1 t. salt
⅛ t. pepper
Paprika (optional)
½ c. butter
¼ c. French dressing

Put flour, salt and pepper in plastic bag and shake well. Then add the pieces of chicken. Put in a dripper. Place a chunk of butter on top of each piece of chicken. Then pour the dressing on top of each piece of chicken. Cook in 350°F. oven uncovered for 1 hour.

Emogene Graff, Enterprise H. S.
Enterprise, Utah

GOLDEN CHICKEN
Number of Servings — 6

3 whole chicken breasts
3 chicken thighs
2 T. lemon juice
1 t. soy sauce
3 chicken drumsticks
1 can (about 1 lb.) diet-packed cling peach
  halves

Arrange chicken in single layer in shallow baking dish 12x8x2 inches. Drain peach syrup into a cup. Add lemon juice and soy sauce, brush half over chicken. Bake in hot oven (400°F.), brushing every 15 minutes with remaining peach syrup and pan juices, 1 hour, or until chicken browns and is tender. Place peach halves around chicken; brush with pan juices; bake five minutes longer to heat peaches.

Joann Parks, Hopewell-London H. S.
Bascom, Ohio

CHICKEN BREASTS SUPREME
Number of Servings — 4-6

4-6 chicken breasts
2 T. butter
2 T. minced onion
½ c. chicken broth (canned)
½ c. sherry
¼ c. slivered almonds
2 T. toasted slivered almonds
1 small can mushrooms

Brown chicken breasts in melted butter. Add onions and saute. Add liquids, mushrooms, and ¼ cup almonds, and cook 40 minutes. Thicken gravy with cornstarch. Serve chicken and thickened gravy on a bed of rice, topped with toasted almonds.

Mrs. Jane Morris, Hardin-Jefferson H. S.
Sour Lake, Texas

CHICKEN IMPERIAL
Number of Servings — 5

5 chicken legs and thighs
⅓ c. butter or margarine
2 c. dry bread or cracker crumbs
2 t. salt
½ t. pepper
1½ t. oregano
⅓ c. grated Parmesan cheese

Melt butter in 13x9 inch baking pan. Combine crumbs, salt, pepper, oregano, and grated cheese. Dip chicken legs in butter and then dip into crumb mixture. Place legs in baking pan, skin side up. Legs should not be crowded in pan. Pour any remaining butter over chicken. Sprinkle with Parmesan cheese. Bake in moderate oven, 350°F., for 1½ hours.

Kathleen M. Foltz, Shippensburg Sr. H. S.
Shippensburg, Pennsylvania

CHICKEN IMPERIAL
Number of Servings — 4-6

2-3 lbs. chicken, cut up
½ c. melted butter
½ t. salt
⅛ t. pepper
¼ t. oregano
2 c. ground bread crumbs
⅓ c. Parmesan cheese

Dip chicken in melted butter. Roll chicken in mixture of remaining ingredients. Place on baking sheet. Bake at 350°F. for 1½ hours, or until tender.

Ruth C. Gordon, South Western H. S.
Hanover, Pennsylvania

EASY CHICKEN
Number of Servings — 8

2 chickens (fryers) quartered
3 T. heavy cream
2 t. salt
¼ t. ground pepper

Wash chicken and dry thoroughly. Place in one layer in a roasting pan after salting each piece on both sides. Have skin side up. Some overlapping of pieces is permissible. Place in pre-heated oven (350°F.) uncovered. Baste every half hour with pan drippings. Sprinkle with pepper ½ hour before serving. Bake 1½ hours or until chicken is rich brown and very tender.

Merle M. Shurpit, Westfield H. S.
Westfield, Wisconsin

CHICKEN IN ONION SOUP
Number of Servings — 6

Boil 3 cups of water with ½ stick butter. Remove from heat and add 1 package of Onion Soup. Cover, let stand for 15 minutes. 1 large fryer (3 to 3½ pounds) cut in serving pieces. Wash and flour by shaking several pieces at a time in a paper bag containing 1 cup flour, 1 teaspoon salt, ¼ teaspoon pepper, and 1 teaspoon paprika. Place chicken in single layer in 13 x 9 inch oblong pan. Pour soup mixture over chicken. Bake in moderate oven (350°F.) until tender (45 to 60 minutes).

Mrs. Agnes Beers, Henry County H. S.
McDonough, Georgia

CHICKEN SIMPLICITY
Number of Servings — 4-6

In bottom of fry pan or baking pan: Sprinkle ½ package of dry onion soup mix. Over this sprinkle 1 cup uncooked brown (or white) rice. Place cut up pieces of one uncooked chicken over rice (do not salt or pepper). Dilute 1 can of cream of chicken soup, or cream of mushroom soup and pour over the chicken. Cover. Bake at 300-325°F. for about 1 hour and 15 minutes, or until done.

Lucile Forrester, Kelso H. S.
Kelso, Washington

CHICKEN 'N GOLDEN SAUCE
Number of Servings — 6

1 2½ lb. chicken or 6 chicken breasts
⅓ c. flour
½ t. paprika
Dash of black pepper
¼ c. melted butter or margarine
1 10½ oz. can condensed cream of chicken soup
1 T. minced parsley

Place chicken, flour, paprika and pepper in brown paper bag and shake to coat chicken with flour mixture. Arrange chicken in a single layer (skin side down) in a buttered shallow baking dish (12x7½x2) inches. Dribble melted butter over chicken. Bake in a moderate oven (375°F.) for 20 minutes. Turn chicken and bake 20 minutes longer. Stir cream of chicken soup; pour over chicken; sprinkle parsley on top. Bake an additional 20 minutes.

Nancye H. Shannon, Greenbrier H. S.
Greenbrier, Tennessee

BUTTER-BAKED CHICKEN AND GRAVY
Number of Servings — 6

1 cut up frying chicken
½ c. evaporated milk
1 c. flour
1½ t. salt
⅛ t. pepper
¼ c. butter or margarine
1 can cream of chicken soup
¾ c. milk
¼ c. water

Dip chicken pieces in canned milk—then roll in mixture of flour, salt, and pepper. Melt margarine in baking dish. Put floured chicken pieces in pan, skin side down and bake uncovered in hot oven (400 to 425°F.) for 30 minutes. Turn chicken over and pour around chicken mixture of soup, milk and water. Bake 30 minutes longer or until tender.

Claudia Marotz, Douglas County H. S.
Gardnerville, Nevada

CHICKEN DELIGHT
Number of Servings — 8

1 fryer, cut in serving pieces
1 stick margarine
2 cans cream of mushroom soup
1 c. water
Salt
Pepper

Heat oven to 350°F. Season chicken pieces with salt and pepper. Melt margarine in baking pan large enough so chicken can be placed in only one layer. Place chicken in pan and cover with aluminum foil. Bake 20 minutes, remove from oven, turn chicken. Recover and bake 20 minutes longer. Remove foil. Spoon on soup that has been thinned with water. Bake uncovered 20 minutes. Serve hot.

Mrs. Mildred Klawinsky, New Caney H. S.
New Caney, Texas

BAKED CHICKEN CAMILLE
Number of Servings — 6

2 packages (1 lb. each) quick frozen chicken
   drumsticks or thighs
½ c. flour
2 t. salt
¼ t. pepper
3 T. butter or other fat
1 can condensed cream of mushroom soup
⅔ c. water

Thaw chicken until pieces can be separated. Mix flour, salt and pepper. Roll chicken in seasoned flour. Saute in hot fat in skillet, turning to brown. Remove chicken to 2 quart baking dish. Combine soup and water with drippings in skillet, blending well. Pour over chicken. Cover and bake in moderate oven (350°F.) for 45 minutes. Then uncover and bake until tender—15 to 30 minutes.

Mrs. Elizabeth T. Hammond
Northwest Area H. S.
Shickshinny, Pennsylvania

BAKED SESAME CHICKEN
Number of Servings — 5-6

1 3 lb. fryer, cut up
1 egg, slightly beaten
½ c. evaporated milk
½ c. flour
¼ t. baking powder
1 t. salt
4 t. paprika
¼ t. pepper
3 t. sesame seeds
¼ c. ground nuts (optional)
½ c. butter

Combine egg and milk. Mix dry ingredients. Dip chicken in egg mixture, then in dry mixture to coat. Melt butter in shallow pan in 400°F. oven. Place chicken, skin side down, in single layer in pan. Bake uncovered 25 minutes. Turn and bake 25-35 minutes more until tender. Baste if kept longer. (Use a 9x13 baking pan).

Mrs. Verna Zeeb, Tripp H. S.
Tripp, South Dakota

"TANGY" CHICKEN

Temperature 350°F.
Cooking time—about 1 hr.
1 2 lb. chicken (cut)
¼ c. butter or margarine
¼ c. vinegar
¼ c. lemon juice
¼ t. garlic salt
¼ t. thyme
¼ t. pepper

Melt butter. Add other ingredients. Pour over chicken and bake uncovered for about 1 hour, or until chicken is a golden brown. Baste often while chicken is cooking.

Charlotte Burns, Spalding Jr. H. S.
Griffin, Georgia

SESAME SEED CHICKEN
Number of Servings — 6

1 2½ lb. chicken cut up for frying
1 c. flour
1 t. baking powder
2 t. salt
2 t. paprika
2 T. sesame seed
¼ t. pepper
¼ c. nuts, chopped or ground
½ c. butter
1 egg, beaten
½ c. milk

Sift flour, baking powder, paprika, salt and pepper together. Add nuts and sesame seed. Mix egg and milk together. Dip chicken into egg and milk mixture, then in mixture of dry ingredients. Melt butter in shallow pan. Place chicken in melted fat. Turn each piece to coat with butter. Bake skin side down in a single layer 20 minutes. Turn and bake 30 minutes more. Bake in a 400°F. oven.

E. L. Huston, Greenwood Jr. H. S.
Greenwood, Mississippi

OVEN-CHICKEN
Number of Servings — 6

1 large chicken
1 can mushroom soup
½ c. milk or 1 can evaporated
Salt
Pepper
Paprika

Cut chicken into serving pieces. Salt and pepper to taste. Place in 1 layer on a shallow pan. Cover with the mixed soup and milk. Sprinkle generously with paprika. Bake at 300°F. for 2 hours (time depends on size of chicken).

Mrs. Arline C. Miles, Watertown H. S.
Watertown, South Dakota

CHICKEN DINNER (SPECIAL)

For each package use:
1 fryer, halved
1 slice onion
1 slice tomato
2 slices potato
3 strips carrots
2 pieces celery

Place halved fryer in the center of a square of foil. Add a slice of onion on top, then add potato slices. Next add tomatoes and place carrot strips and celery to sides. Season to taste, top with butter if desired and close the foil, making a tight package. Bake on a cookie sheet in preheated oven at 350°F. for 1 hour and 30 minutes. Serve in package to retain vegetable-chicken juices as a natural gravy.

Mrs. Donald Webb, Gaylesville H. S.
Gaylesville, Alabama

OVEN BAKED CHICKEN AND BISCUITS
Number of Servings — 4

Heat oven to 425°
Mix in a paper bag:
1 c. plain flour
2 t. salt
¼ t. pepper

Place ½ cup shortening (half butter) in 13x9 inch oblong pan and set in oven to melt. Shake 3 or 4 pieces of chicken at a time in bag to coat thoroughly. Place chicken, skin side down, in single layer in hot shortening. Bake 45 minutes; then turn. Meanwhile, make dough for biscuits. Drain No. 2½ can of peach halves. Push chicken to one end of pan; place biscuits in single layer on the other end. Place peach halves on top of chicken. Bake another 15 minutes, or until biscuits are brown.

Mrs. Maurice E. Eskridge, Tryon H. S.
Bessemer City, North Carolina

DELICIOUS OVEN-COOKED CHICKEN
Number of Servings — 4

1 large frying chicken
Salt and pepper
⅛ c. soy sauce
¼ c. Worcestershire sauce
½ stick margarine or butter

Cut chicken into frying-size pieces. Salt and pepper to taste. Brush with mixture of soy sauce and Worcestershire sauce. Place chicken in baking pan. Dot with butter. Bake at 350°F. for 1 hour. Turn chicken once or twice and baste with remaining sauce. Delicious!

Jean Russell Yarborough, Mooreville H. S.
Mooreville, Mississippi

OVEN EASY GARLIC CHICKEN
Number of Servings — 4

1 chicken or legs and breasts
Garlic salt
¼ c. flour
½ t. paprika
Salt and pepper
1 c. chicken bouillon or broth

Rinse chicken in cold water and dry. Sprinkle garlic salt over each piece. Put chicken into a paper bag along with the flour mixture. In a shallow baking pan, place ½ cup chicken broth. Place chicken, skin side down in the broth. Bake in a 400°F. oven for 30 minutes. Turn chicken. Add remaining chicken broth. Bake another 30 minutes. After chicken is done, pan may be placed on top of the range and gravy can be made by adding milk or water. Chicken broth can be made by cooking the neck, heart, and gizzard in two cups water with celery leaves, one small bay leaf and salt. Cook until tender.

Darlene M. Johnson, Elmore H. S.
Elmore, Minnesota

GOLDEN CHICKEN SURPRISE
Number of Servings — 4

1 broiler-fryer (3 lbs.) cut in pieces
½ c. butter
1 clove garlic
½ t. salt
⅛ t. pepper
¼ t. poultry seasoning
1 c. finely crushed potato chips
1 c. finely crushed corn flakes

Remove skin from chicken pieces, wash and dry well. Melt butter, add all seasonings. Mix potato chips and corn flakes in pie plate. Dip chicken in fat, then in chips. Arrange in baking pan. Remove clove garlic from fat, pour over chicken. Bake at 350°F. for 1 hour.

Lee Ann Lilly, Ford City H. S.
Ford City, Pennsylvania

OVEN BAKED FRYER
Number of Servings — 4

4 halves of fryer
4 T. melted butter
2 T. lemon juice
1 T. salt
2 T. paprika

Combine melted butter, lemon juice, and salt. Rub fryer halves with combined mixture. Place on heavy duty aluminum foil. Sprinkle paprika over the chicken. Wrap and seal as for freezing. Place in 400°F. oven for 50 minutes. This is delicious if prepared ahead of time and left in the oven. Heat in the aluminum foil before serving or remove foil if a crusty finish is desired.

Mrs. Roy Cousins, Hogansville H. S.
Hogansville, Georgia

BAKED SOUTHERN CHICKEN

1 med. fryer (salted)
1 c. butter
2 c. ground cracker crumbs

Dip chicken in melted butter, roll in crumbs. Bake in heavy skillet in 350°F. oven until tender.

Mrs. Belva M. Woodard, Sharpsburg H. S.
Sharpsburg, Kentucky

CHICKEN
Number of Servings — 2-4

1 medium size broiler
Salt or poultry seasoning
Pepper if desired
¼ c. water or vegetable broth

Split chicken lengthwise. Rub with seasonings. Place cut side down in a baking dish. Cover, aluminum foil will do. Add liquid. Bake 1½ hours at 300°F. or until meat is very tender. Remove cover last 30 minutes to let chicken brown.

Mrs. Gladyce Davis, Poteau H. S.
Poteau, Oklahoma

LEMON BAKED CHICKEN
Number of Servings — 6

1 broiler-fryer chicken (cut in serving pieces)
1 T. flour
1 t. Ac'cent
½ t. salt
⅛ t. pepper
½ t. paprika
1 T. margarine
3 T. lemon juice

Place chicken in shallow baking dish. Combine flour and seasoning, salt, pepper and paprika; sprinkle over chicken pieces. Dot with butter. Bake uncovered in a moderate oven (375°F.) 30 minutes. Sprinkle with lemon juice, bake 20 minutes longer. Serve with heated spiced peaches. Yield 6 servings, 200 calories per serving.

Mrs. Mary R. Cole, North Marshall H. S.
Calvert City, Kentucky

LEMON-KIST CHICKEN
Number of Servings — 4-6

1 cut-up fryer
1 egg
⅓ c. milk
2 c. yellow cornmeal
¼ lb. butter
3 T. lemon juice
2 small onions

Dip chicken pieces into beaten egg and milk mixture. Coat with cornmeal. Pour melted butter and lemon juice together over chicken laid in a loaf pan. Place sliced onion rings over chicken. Season as desired. Bake for 1 hour at 350°F. without turning.

Lois Jacobson, Badger H. S.
Lake Geneva, Wisconsin

CHICKEN AND DUMPLINGS
Number of Servings — 4

2½ lb. fryer, cut up
1 medium onion, grated
1 bay leaf, crumbled
1 whole clove
5 peppercorns, cracked
1½ t. salt
1 stalk celery, cut up
1 c. self-rising flour, sifted
2 T. shortening
⅓ c. milk

Put chicken in heavy pot with next five ingredients and water to cover. Simmer until almost tender (about ¾ hour). Add celery and cook 15 minutes. Remove chicken and keep warm. Add milk to broth to make 4 cups. For dumplings, cut shortening into flour, stir in milk, drop dough by spoonsful into simmering broth. Cover and cook gently for 15 minutes. Arrange chicken on large platter with dumplings around it. Pour gravy over all. Sprinkle with parsley.

Ida Cecil, Griffin H. S.
Griffin, Georgia

CHICKEN AND DUMPLINGS
Number of Servings — 6-8

3 lb. chicken
Salt and pepper
1 bay leaf
1 small carrot
1 stalk celery
DUMPLINGS
1 c. flour
½ t. salt
½ t. baking powder
⅛ t. baking soda
¼ c. buttermilk
2 T. fat

Cook cut up chicken pieces and seasonings together until chicken is tender, usually 45 minutes. Remove chicken and seasonings from liquid. Sift flour and dry ingredients together. Cut shortening into flour mixture. Add egg beaten and buttermilk to flour mixture. Additional flour is used for kneading dough; knead thoroughly. Roll to a thin dough on a bread board or pastry cloth. Use plenty of flour on board as dough is kneaded or rolled. Let stand 2 to 3 hours. When ready to cook, heat broth to boiling temperature. Cut dough into strips approximately 1 inch in width and 3 to 4 inches in length. Add strip to gently boiling chicken liquid. Keep adding until all dough is added. From time to time, during adding of dumplings, push dumplings down in liquid. Cover vessel. Boil gently for 20 minutes. Add ¼ cup sweet milk. If liquid is not as thick as desired, add flour stirred into milk that is added. Chicken can be kept warm in the oven (low temperature). Seconds may be served for later meals. Add cut up chicken to dumplings for variety.

Alma Keys, Director Home Economics Education
Little Rock, Arkansas

CHICKEN WITH DUMPLINGS
Number of Servings — 6

1 (4 to 5 lb.) chicken

Cook chicken in boiling salted water until tender, or pressure cook. Season with desired seasoning, celery, or marjoram. Add ¾ teaspoons of monosodium glutamate. Strip meat from the bones, leave in large pieces.

Dumplings
¾ c. sifted flour
2½ t. baking powder
½ t. salt
1 egg
⅓ c. milk

Sift the flour, baking powder, and salt together. Beat the egg until very foamy, add the milk, and mix quickly with dry ingredients, stirring just enough to mix. Drop by small spoonfuls into thickened broth, cover tightly, steam without lifting the lid for 15 minutes.

Marie Green, Newton H. S.
Newton, Illinois

CHICKEN WITH DUMPLINGS

1 stewing chicken cut in pieces and stewed
3 to 4 c. broth
Salt and pepper
3 to 6 T. flour
6 T. fat

Remove chicken from broth. Skim fat from broth. Blend fat and flour. Stir in several spoonfuls of broth. Pour mixture into broth, stirring constantly. Cook this gravy until it is slightly thickened. Season to taste.

Dumplings:
¾ c. sifted flour
2½ t. baking powder
½ t. salt
1 egg
⅓ c. milk

Sift flour, baking powder and salt together. Beat eggs, add milk, and mix with the dry ingredients. Drop, by small spoonfuls, on boiling chicken gravy. Cover tightly and cook 15 minutes. The cover must not be removed while the dumplings are cooking. If steam escapes they will not be light.

Mrs. Nell Inez Lawless, Pearl H. S.
Jackson 8, Mississippi

CHICKEN AND DUMPLINGS
Number of Servings — 6-8

4 to 6 lb. chicken, cut up
2 t. salt
1 small onion
2-3 ribs celery, cut up
1 carrot, sliced
2-3 whole cloves
1 bay leaf
1 sprig parsley, cut up
2 c. water

Put everything in pressure pan. Exhaust air. Cook 30 minutes at 10 lbs. pressure. Let pressure down rapidly. Mix your favorite dumplings. Drop on chicken. Cook uncovered 5 minutes. Put on lid and cook 5 to 10 minutes more.

Mrs. Forrest A Stewart,
Sandoval Com. Unit H. S.
Sandoval, Illinois

CHICKEN AND DUMPLINGS

Boil 1 chicken until tender (hen preferred). Season with salt and pepper. *Dumplings:* 1 cup of broth; 1 egg, whipped together until foamy. Add flour until stiff as for biscuits. Roll very thin. Cut into small pieces and drop into rest of broth. Be sure broth is boiling rapidly, when all dumplings have been added, lower flame. Simmer for 45 minutes. Add 1 cup of milk the last 5 minutes. Season to taste. (Be sure to keep enough liquid—add hot water if more is needed).

Ola Mae Hawkins, Santa Fe H. S.
Alta Loma, Texas

CHICKEN AND DUMPLINGS
Number of Servings — 8

4 lbs. chicken
2 c. sifted flour
4 t. baking powder
3 c. water
3 t. salt
½ t. salt
1 c. milk

Prepare chicken for cooking, cutting in serving portions. Cook until tender with salt and water. The exact time will depend upon the age and weight of the fowl. Remove chicken. Bake batter for dumplings by teaspoonfuls and cook 10 minutes. Thicken broth and serve.

Ruby Jo Chancey, Hale County H. S.
Moundville, Alabama

COUNTRY STYLE "SLICKER" DUMPLINGS WITH CHICKEN
Number of Servings — 6-8

Chicken:
1 stewing hen
1 T. salt
½ t. black pepper
2 qts. water

Dumplings:
3 c. all-purpose flour
1½ t. baking powder
1 T. salt
1 beaten egg
Broth to make a stiff dough

Stew chicken until tender in 1 quart of water. Cool and remove from bones. Cut chicken into desired-size pieces. Add 1 quart water, salt and pepper to broth and heat to simmering. Mix dry ingredients. Mix egg with 1 cup broth and add. Use as much broth as needed for dough. Knead on a floured board. Roll very thin. Cut into 1-inch squares. Cook 20 minutes in boiling broth. Add chicken, heat again and serve.

Kathryn Davis, Community H. S.
Pinckneyville, Illinois

CHICKEN SPAGHETTI

1 hen
1 box spaghetti
1 t. chili powder
1 onion, chopped
2 garlic buttons
1 small can mushrooms
1 pt. can tomatoes

Cook hen till tender and cut fine. Cook spaghetti in broth. (Save some for later use). Salt to taste. Add chili powder. Cook tomatoes, onions and garlic till tender enough to sieve. Pour this over spaghetti. Add chicken and mushrooms that have been sauted in butter. Cook slowly for 1 hour.

Mrs. Buddy Fallin, Stamps H. S.
Stamps, Arkansas

CHICKEN AND SPAGHETTI
Number of Servings — 24

1 4 lb. hen
1 onion
1 c. celery
1 bell pepper
1 8 oz. package spaghetti
1 can pimento
1 lb. cheese
1 can mushrooms

Cook hen, chop meat. Simmer onion, pepper, and celery in broth. Cook spaghetti. Chop pimento, grate cheese and mushrooms. Mix all ingredients together. Put in greased baking dish and top with grated cheese. Bake before serving.

Mrs. Mona Faye Fordham, Sikes H. S.
Sikes, Louisiana

CHICKEN SPAGHETTI
Number of Servings — 10-12

1 hen, stewed
1 onion
1 button garlic
1 c. celery, diced
1 No. 2 can tomatoes
1 can tomato paste
1 can mushrooms
2 c. chicken stock (may absorb a little more)
1 box Italian spaghetti
1 No. 2 can peas or box frozen peas
½ lb. cheese, grated over top

Saute onion, garlic, and celery in butter or chicken broth. Add tomatoes and tomato paste and simmer for 30 minutes. Add chicken, mushrooms, stock, cooked spaghetti, and cook together for 30 minutes, or until well heated. Add peas just before serving time. Grate the cheese over the top. Serves 10-12 generously.

Mrs. Ann Hoit, Ousley Jr. H. S.
Arlington, Texas

CHICKEN SPAGHETTI
Number of Servings — 8

3 large onions, sliced
3 T. shortening
1 c. celery, diced
2 No. 2 cans tomatoes
1 c. mushrooms
2 T. chili powder
1 green pepper, chopped
3 lb. chicken, boiled and chopped
2 9 oz. boxes spaghetti
6 qts. water (boiling)

Saute onions to a rich brown in shortening; add celery, green pepper and chicken. Mix well, add tomatoes, mushrooms, and chili powder. Season with salt and pepper. Cook 45 minutes. Add some chicken stock if it becomes dry. Cook spaghetti 9 minutes, add to chicken mixture and mix well. Serve with grated cheese.

Mrs. Yvonne McCoy, Pewitt H. S.
Naples, Texas

CHICKEN AND SPAGHETTI
Number of Servings — 10

1 3-4 lb. hen, stewed
1 box spaghetti
1 can cream of mushroom soup
1 can cream of chicken soup
1 can pimientos, chopped
½ c. green olives, chopped
½ c. celery, chopped
1 green pepper, chopped
1 medium onion, chopped

Cook spaghetti in chicken broth, leaving it somewhat soupy. Lightly brown celery, pepper, and onion in 2 tablespoons bacon fat. Remove chicken from bone and combine with all other ingredients. Place in baking dish, top with grated American cheese, and bake 20 minutes at 350°F.

Betty Addison, Lipan H. S.
Lipan, Texas

CHICKEN SPAGHETTI
Number of Servings — 8-10

1 baking hen
2 boxes long spaghetti
2 large onions, chopped
2 No. 303 cans tomatoes
½ lb. oleo (may want to omit if hen is fat)
1 clove garlic
1 lb. American cheese, grated
Hot pepper or sauce, if desired

Cook hen, save broth, cut meat from chicken bones. Cook onions in melted oleo, simmer, add garlic, tomatoes and seasonings. Cook slowly 45 minutes to 2 hours. Cook spaghetti in chicken broth, do not drain. Combine spaghetti, chicken and sauce. Add grated cheese and mix well, serve hot.

Jo Ann Seymour, Roosevelt H. S.
Roosevelt, Oklahoma

CHICKEN AND SPAGHETTI
Number of Servings — 10

1 chicken, stewed and cut into small cubes
1 T. butter
2 buttons garlic, chopped
1 c. minced onion
1 T. green peppers, chopped
2 small cans tomato paste
1 t. chili powder
1 can mushroom soup
1 package spaghetti,

Saute in heavy skillet, butter, garlic, onion, peppers and add tomato paste, chili powder, mushroom soup and simmer well. Add the spaghetti cooked in chicken broth and simmer until flavors are blended.

Mrs. Laura E. Sumner, Cobre H. S.
Bayard, New Mexico

SPAGHETTI CHICKEN

Number of Servings — 8

1 hen, boned
1 box spaghetti, cooked
1 onion
1 No. 2 can tomatoes, drained
Salt and pepper to taste
1 can mushrooms
½ c. ripe olives
1 T. Worcestershire sauce
½ c. grated cheese

Saute onion and mushrooms in butter, add tomatoes and seasoning to 1 pint chicken broth. Add 2 tablespoons flour and simmer 15 minutes. Add chicken, spaghetti, olives, etc. Sprinkle top with cheese. Bake 275°F. for 1 hour.

Mrs. Betty Hall, Fort Cobb H. S.
Fort Cobb, Oklahoma

CHICKEN SPAGHETTI

Number of Servings — 8

1 medium cooked chicken (boned and cubed)
¾ c. chopped onion
½ c. chopped green pepper and celery
2 T. butter or oil
1 can tomatoes
1 can pimiento
1 c. velveta cheese
Broth of chicken
1 t. salt and pepper
1 box long spaghetti

Cook spaghetti in chicken broth until tender. Do not drain. While spaghetti is cooking saute onion, green pepper, and celery in heavy skillet with butter. Add tomatoes, chicken, pimientos, and seasoning to skillet. Combine all ingredients in with spaghetti and mix well. Put in casserole dish and bake in 350° F. oven until cheese melts. Serve hot.

Ruth Dietz, Hamlin Jr. H. S.
Corpus Christi, Texas

CHICKEN SAUCE FOR SPAGHETTI

Number of Servings — 6-8

6 T. flour
2 T. butter
½ c. green pepper
¾ c. shallots
1 c. tomato sauce
1 4-oz. can sliced mushrooms
1½ T. Worcestershire sauce
Salt and pepper to taste
½ c. water
1½ c. chicken broth
2 c. boned cooked chicken

Brown flour in dry skillet. Saute green pepper and shallots in butter. Add browned flour, tomato sauce, mushrooms, seasonings, and liquids and simmer for 10 minutes. Before serving, combine with boned chicken and pour over cooked spaghetti. Top with Parmesan cheese if desired.

Mrs. Doris B. Lutz, Westdale Jr. H. S.
Baton Rouge, Louisiana

CHICKEN AND SPAGHETTI

Number of Servings — 10-12

1 large hen (3 lbs.) or 2 fat frying chickens
   stewed in enough water to make about 2
   qts. stock
1 c. chopped celery
1 green pepper, chopped
3 buttons garlic (left whole)
1 c. chicken fat
1 c. flour
2 qts. stock
1 can condensed tomato soup
1 can condensed cream of mushroom soup
½ lb. thin spaghetti
½ lb. grated cheese

Cook celery, pepper and garlic in chicken fat until tender. Remove garlic. Stir the flour into fat mixture until well blended. Gradually add stock and cook until thickened. Add undiluted tomato and mushroom soups. Last, add the chicken cut into small pieces. Cook the spaghetti according to directions on package, drain well, and add to chicken mixture. Place in greased casserole, sprinkle with the grated cheese and place in 350°F. oven until the cheese melts. Ripe olives can be added if desired.

Mrs. Marian L. Carpenter, Farmersville H. S.
Farmersville, Texas

"MAC'S CHICKEN SPECIAL"

Number of Servings — 6-8

1 5 lb. stewing chicken
2 lbs. spaghetti (any style)
2 T. butter
1 clove garlic, chopped
1 large onion, chopped
1 No. 2½ can tomatoes
1 t. comina seed
3 T. Worcestershire sauce
Salt to taste
Black pepper, if desired

Cook chicken till tender, cut in bite size pieces. Cook spaghetti in chicken broth. Brown chopped onions and garlic in butter. Add remaining ingredients, tomatoes, salt, spices and chicken. Combine with spaghetti. Simmer 1½ hours on low temperature surface unit or in covered baking dish in oven at 300°F. for 1 hour or more. Garnish with pimentos and parsley.

Ninta A. McAninch, Raton Sr. H. S.
Raton, New Mexico

CHICKEN AND SPAGHETTI

Number of Servings — 10-12

1 large fat hen
3 medium-size packages of vermicelli
2 large onions or 4 buttons of garlic
1 medium-size can pimiento
1 large green pepper
1 4-oz. can sliced mushrooms
2 c. grated cheese
2 c. chopped celery

(Continued on Next Page)

Boil hen until tender, remove from broth, take from bones and chop. Cook the vermicelli, chopped onion or garlic in the broth, when tender add the chopped chicken and all other ingredients except the cheese. Stir to mix well, this should be a fairly dry mixture, in other words, judge the amount of broth to use. In case the hen did not have sufficient fat some butter should be added. Serve hot with the grated cheese sprinkled over the top.

Mrs. H. M. Thomas, Breckinridge Sr. H. S.
Breckinridge, Texas

CHICKEN SPAGHETTI
Number of Servings — 12

1 large chicken (5 to 7 lbs.)
2 large cans tomatoes
2 small cans tomato paste
1½ c. chopped onions
1 small garlic
1 small bottle stuffed olives
1 large bell pepper
1 lb. spaghetti
1 lemon
3 pieces celery
1 c. chicken fat (about)
2 cans mushroom soup
Salt and pepper to taste

Cook chicken until tender. Remove from bone. Cook spaghetti in salted water until tender, drain well. Cook onions and garlic in fat. Add bell pepper and celery, cook until tender. Add tomatoes, paste, lemon juice and grated rind, 1 cup chicken fat and finally chicken. Simmer for about 10 minutes. Add spaghetti, cream of mushroom soup and finally chopped olives. Simmer until ready to serve. (If more liquid is needed, use broth from chicken or tomato juice). More garlic salt may be added. Sprinkle with cheese when ready to serve.

Mrs. Carolyn C. Burton, Doyline, H. S.
Doyline, Louisiana

CHICKEN SPAGHETTI
Number of Servings — 10-12

1 hen or 2 broilers (hen has more flavor)
2 T. fat
1 onion, diced
1 green pepper, diced
1 limb celery, diced
1 T. flour
1 can tomato sauce
1 can tomato paste
1 can mushrooms and juice (cut or whole)
2 t. salt
Black pepper
2 c. water
1 lb. spaghetti
2 c. grated cheese

Cut chicken into pieces as for frying. Brown in fat in Dutch oven, steam cooker, or large skillet. Re-

move chicken. To fat in cooker, add onion, green pepper, celery, and flour. Cook till golden brown. Add tomato sauce, paste, mushrooms, salt, black pepper and water. When mixture comes to boil, add chicken pieces, and cook slowly until meat almost falls from bones. Add more water if necessary during cooking. Arrange cooked spaghetti on dish, sprinkle generously with cheese, add sauce; place serving piece of chicken on top.

Mrs. Mary R. Abney, Bay Springs H. S.
Bay Springs, Mississippi

CHICKEN SPAGHETTI
Number of Servings — 10-12

1 stewing chicken
1 c. celery, chopped
1 green pepper, chopped
1 can pimentos
1 can sliced mushrooms
1 clove garlic, grated
1½ c. yellow cheese, grated
2 packages spaghetti
Salt and pepper to taste

Stew chicken until tender in plenty of water so there will be 3 quarts of broth left. Cut chicken in small chunks. If broth is too fat, remove part of grease. Cook spaghetti in remaining broth with the garlic. About 10 minutes before the spaghetti is done, add celery, green pepper and pimentos. Remove from fire and combine with chicken. The mixture should be very juicy. Immediately before serving, add the mushrooms and cheese and heat thoroughly in a covered pan in the oven—350°F.

Vera Periman, Snyder H. S.
Snyder, Texas

CHICKEN SPAGHETTI
Number of Servings — 20-25

1 hen, boiled and boned
1½ to 2 boxes spaghetti
1 clove garlic
2 large onions
4 branches celery
1 large can pimentos
1 large green pepper
1 can tomato soup
1 can tomatoes
1 can mushroom soup
1 qt. milk
1 lb. pasteurized cheese

Boil spaghetti in the broth from the hen. Chop and saute in butter: the onions, garlic, celery and green pepper. Combine in large roaster, the chopped hen, drained spaghetti, sauted vegetables, chopped pimentos, canned soups, tomatoes and milk. Season to taste. Put grated cheese on top. Bake 1 hour in 325°F. oven for 1 hour.

Lois Page, McLean H. S.
McLean, Texas

CHICKEN AND SPAGHETTI
Number of Servings — 20

1 large hen
1 bunch celery, chopped
2 bell peppers, chopped
2 medium onions, chopped
1 large can ripe olives, chopped
1 4-oz. can mushrooms, chopped
1 4-oz. can pimentos, chopped
3 cloves garlic, chopped
2 bay leaves
1 can tomato paste
2 packages spaghetti, cooked

Boil chicken until tender; cool, and cut into bite size chunks. Saute celery, pepper, onions. Add olives, mushrooms, pimento, garlic, tomato paste, chicken, and enough chicken broth to make a watery sauce. Salt and pepper to taste. Simmer for 1 hour. Add spaghetti to sauce; add more broth if needed. Serve with grated cheese if desired.

Mrs. Carla Sue Park, Dayton H. S.
Dayton, Texas

CHICKEN — SOUTHERN SPECIAL
Number of Servings — 10

Corn Bread Ring

2 c. cornmeal plus 2 T. flour
3 t. baking powder
1 t. salt
½ t. soda
1 t. thyme
2 T. finely chopped parsley
2 eggs, slightly beaten
1 c. buttermilk

Sift dry ingredients together. Beat eggs slightly and add milk. Add dry ingredients and parsley. Bake in 400°F. oven for 30 minutes or until brown in a ring mold.

Creamed Chicken

1 c. milk and 1 c. broth
4 T. flour
4 T. chicken fat
¼ cup chopped pimento
2 c. chopped chicken
½ t. salt

Make a white sauce of fat, flour and liquids. Fold in chicken and pimento. Add salt. Serve cornbread ring with creamed chicken poured over the top.

Mrs. Eileen Wilson, Poolville H. S.
Poolville, Texas

SAVORY CHICKEN
Number of Servings — 2-3

1 package (1-lb. size) frozen chicken breasts, thighs, drumsticks, or wings, or use one fresh chicken
1 egg

1 t. salt
1 t. prepared mustard
Dash black pepper
⅔ c. fine dry bread crumbs
¼ c. butter or margarine
1½ c. V-8 juice (12-oz. can)

Thaw chicken as directed on package. Beat together egg, salt, mustard, pepper. Dip chicken in egg mixture; roll in bread crumbs. Brown chicken in butter in skillet. Add V-8 juice; cover and cook over low heat about 45 minutes or until chicken is tender. Stir occasionally.

Shirley Dockery, J. D. Leftwich H. S.
Magazine, Arkansas

DEVILED CHICKEN
Number of Servings — 4-6

1 broiling or frying chicken
Salt and pepper
½ c. melted fat
2 T. flour
1 c. soup stock
1½ t. dry mustard
2 T. tomato catsup
⅛ t. paprika

Cut chicken into serving pieces. Season with salt and pepper. Brown in fat. Remove from pan. Stir flour into fat. Add soup stock. Cook until mixture thickens. Add next four ingredients. Place chicken in sauce. Cover pan and simmer 1 hour.

Helen Hoermann, Jamestown Sr. H. S.
Jamestown, North Dakota

CHICKEN IN WINE SAUCE
Number of Servings — 6-8

1 chicken (2 to 3 lb. fryer)
2 cans onion soup
1 c. white port wine
1 large can tomato juice
1 large can mushrooms (diced)

After chicken is cleaned, cut into fourths. Salt and pepper parts slightly. Fry in deep fat until golden brown. Pour off excess fat. Combine other ingredients; pour over chicken and simmer slowly until chicken is well done (about 2½ hrs.).

Mrs. Aline Burruss, Bogalusa Jr. H. S.
Bogalusa, Louisiana

CHICKEN-FRYER
Number of Servings — 4

1 fryer, cut up
1 onion, diced
1 can consomme soup
1 c. rice

Roll chicken in mixture of flour, salt and pepper, then brown in hot fat. Meanwhile saute onions in small amount of fat, then add rice and consomme and then put browned chicken on top of mixture. Cover and cook in 350°F. oven for 1 hour.

Donna Jo Beard, Cameron H. S.
Cameron, Oklahoma

CHICKEN BREASTS IN WHITE WINE SAUCE
Number of Servings — 8

8 frozen or fresh chicken breasts
3 c. rich white sauce (medium thick)
1 c. button mushrooms
½ c. slivered toasted almonds
Seasoning to taste
½ c. white wine

Saute chicken breasts in butter to a light brown. Arrange in glass heatproof baking dish or casserole. Add wine and seasoning to white sauce. Add mushrooms and pour over the chicken. If desired, two cans of cream of mushroom soup may be used in place of white sauce and mushrooms. Bake one hour at 350° F. Sprinkle with toasted almonds 10 minutes before removing from oven.

Evelyn Cotney, Home Economics Education
Montevallo, Alabama

BISCUIT TOPPED CHICKEN PIE
Number of Servings — 6

3 T. butter
3 T. flour
1 t. salt
½ t. pepper
2 T. diced onion
2 c. diced cooked chicken
1 c. mixed vegetables (drained)
3 c. chicken broth

Melt butter. Add flour and salt. Add chicken broth slowly and bring to boil. In a 2-quart casserole dish place chicken, vegetables, onion and pepper. Pour hot broth mixture over chicken and vegetables. Top with biscuits: 3 tablespoons melted lard, ½ cup buttermilk, (about) 1 cup self-rising flour. Mix above ingredients quickly. Roll ⅜ inch thick. Cut biscuits and place on hot broth mixture. Bake in hot oven (425°F). about 30 minutes. Serve hot.

Hilda Harman, Smithville H. S.
Smithville, Mississippi

CHICKEN PIE
Number of Servings — 6-10

Cook full grown hen, covered with water, until
   tender
4 hard cooked eggs—sliced
3 c. of chopped chicken
1 can cream of mushroom soup
2 cans of rich chicken broth
   (measure with mushroom can)
¼ t. of black pepper
Salt as needed
Pastry—use mix or your favorite recipe
2 T. of butter

Place chicken over bottom of baking dish; cover with sliced eggs; sprinkle with pepper and salt. Mix broth and soup; pour over chicken and eggs. Cover with pastry; dot with butter. Bake in 400 degree oven until brown; serve hot.

Mrs. Eunice Broussard, Monterey H. S.
Monterey, Louisiana

CHEESY-CHICKEN PIE
Number of Servings — 6-8

Chicken Filling:
3 T. shortening
3 T. flour
¼ t. salt
¼ t. pepper
1 c. milk
1 5-oz. jar pimento cheese
½ c. chopped celery
½ c. drained cooked peas
Pie Crust:
½ c. corn meal
1½ c. sifted flour
1 t. salt
½ c. shortening
4 T. water

Bone well cooked chicken, or use boneless canned chicken, drained. For filling, melt shortening; blend in flour, salt and pepper. Add milk all at once; stir constantly. Cook over low heat until thickened. Remove from heat; beat in cheese until mixture is smooth. Stir in celery, peas and chicken. Heat oven to hot (400°F.). For pie crust, sift together cornmeal, flour and salt into bowl. Cut in shortening until mixture resembles coarse crumbs. Add water, a tablespoon at a time, mix until a ball can be formed. Use more water if necessary. Form into a ball, let stand 5 minutes. Divide dough in half. Roll one half on lightly floured board or canvas until it is 1½ inches larger than inverted pie plate. Fit pastry loosely into 9 inch pie plate trim. Fill with chicken filling. Roll other half of dough 1½ inches larger than pie plate. Cut slits to allow steam to escape. Adjust cover over filling; trim ½ inch beyond rim. Fold top crust under bottom crust. Flute to seal. Bake in preheated oven (400°F). 40 minutes or until evenly browned. Cool 10 minutes.

Tamzon Petter Jr. H. S.
Hot Springs, South Dakota

CHICKEN PIE
Number of Servings — 6

2 T. poultry fat
1 c. diced celery
¼ c. chopped green pepper
½ c. chopped onion
2 c. chopped cooked chicken
4 T. flour
2 c. stock
1 c. milk
Salt to taste

Slowly brown onion, pepper, and celery in fat, stirring constantly. Make thin white sauce with flour, stock, and milk. Add above mixture and chopped chicken. Heat thoroughly. Pour into shallow baking dish. Cover with rich thin biscuits. Bake at 450°F. for about 45 minutes.

Augusta Richardson, Caddo H. S.
Caddo, Oklahoma

CHICKEN PIE
Number of Servings — 6

1 4 lb. fowl
1 sliced carrot
1 stalk celery
1 sprig parsley
1 sliced onion
1 t. salt
⅛ t. pepper
Plain pie paste
4 T. flour
½ lb. sliced sauteed mushrooms

Dress fowl and wipe with cold, damp cloth. Put in saucepan and cover with water. Add carrot, celery, parsley and onion. Bring to boiling point. Reduce heat, cover, and let simmer until fowl is tender. Season with salt and pepper when half done. Remove fowl from pan. Remove skin and bones, keeping meat in large pieces. Line sides of baking dish with plain pie paste. Put in chicken. Reduce chicken stock to three cups by boiling. Skim off fat and strain. Mix flour to a smooth paste in cold water. Add to stock. Bring stock to boiling point, stirring constantly. Add stock and mushrooms to chicken. Cover with pie paste. Bake at 450° F. for 15 minutes or until well browned.

Bettye T. Brumley, Weston H. S.
Jonesboro, Louisiana

CHICKEN TAMALE PIE
Number of Servings — 6

2 small roasting chickens, disjointed
4 large ripe tomatoes, peeled
1 lime or ½ orange, juiced
1 sweet red pepper, minced
1 T. chili powder
Butter or oil
Clove of garlic, minced
2 onions, sliced thin
1 green pepper, minced
1 T. parsley, minced
Salt and pepper
1 c. corn pulp

Fry chickens in butter or oil with garlic, until tender. Bone and dice chicken meat, place in a stew pan with tomatoes, onions, lime or orange juice, minced peppers, parsley and chili powder. Add salt and pepper to taste and simmer gently until vegetables are tender. Add the corn pulp. Continue cooking over a low flame, stirring occasionally, until consistency is good. Make paste crust by mixing 1 cup of cornmeal, 2 large eggs, well beaten, with salt and pepper to taste. Roll out crust and line casserole dish. Pour in meat mixture, set the casserole in a pan of hot water, and bake until nicely browned at 425°F.

Esther Darst Minton, Peoria H. S.
Peoria, Arizona

CREAMED BAKED CHICKEN
Number of Servings — 12

1 large hen
1 T. salt
1 lb. soda crackers
12 hard boiled eggs
1 pt. milk
½ t. pepper
½ c. flour
1 c. butter

Cover whole chicken with water, add salt and boil until tender. Cool chicken quickly and remove from bones. Stack chicken in three piles—large pieces, small pieces, and skin and giblets. Grind skin and giblets. Line a large, flat oiled baking dish (10x14 inches) with cracker crumbs. Place 12 large pieces of chicken in rows. Fill in around chicken with small pieces and ground skin and giblets. Cover with a layer of egg slices. Add thickened gravy. Salt and pepper to taste. Cover with ½ pound cracker crumbs. Dot with butter. Bake 45 minutes in 350°F. oven. Cut in squares and remove with spatula. Note: This can be prepared days ahead and frozen, then baked.

Cathilene Gleason,
Angola, Indiana

CREAMED CHICKEN WITH MUSHROOMS

1 medium sized hen
1 small white onion
2 stalks of celery
Salt to taste

Use heavy pot and cook fowl half covered with water to which has been added a small onion and two stalks of celery, salt to taste. Add water as chicken cooks. Cool and remove meat from bones. Cut into small pieces about 1 by 2 inches.

1 can mushrooms (4 oz. or more)
  (save water for sauce)
Saute mushrooms in butter
4 T. poultry fat
5 T. flour
2 egg yolks, well beaten
1 c. chicken broth (fat removed)
  and water from mushrooms
½ t. salt
2 t. Worcestershire sauce
½ t. paprika
¼ t. curry powder
½ c. sherry
1 can cream of mushroom or celery soup
  (do not dilute)

Make white sauce of the poultry fat, flour, egg, chicken broth, and water from mushrooms. Add salt, Worcestershire sauce, paprika, and curry powder and cook until mixture thickens. Add mushroom soup and sherry. Add chicken and reheat. Let mixture stand several hours before serving so that flavors are absorbed in the meat; reheat, and serve in timbles or on rice cooked dry.

Mrs. Marvolin Stephens, Thompson H. S.
Siluria, Alabama

CREAMED CHICKEN
Number of Servings — 8

2 T. butter or oleo
½ c. broth
2 c. diced chicken
Dash red pepper
1 T. flour, rounded
1½ c. cream of mushroom soup
2 hard boiled eggs, diced
Salt to taste

Melt butter in a heavy skillet. Add flour and stir until creamy, but not browned. Add broth to make thick sauce. Add mushroom soup and blend thoroughly. Add salt and pepper, then chicken and eggs and heat through. Serve in timbale cases.
TIMBALE CASES
Separate 2 eggs. Beat the yolks until lemon colored. Add 1 cup of water, 1 tablespoon of Wesson oil and 1½ cups flour. Beat until smooth and fold in beaten egg whites. Pour the batter in a small deep mixing bowl. Heat timbale iron in Wesson oil that has temperature of 365°F., drain iron, wipe off excess fat and dip in batter, being careful to have batter adhere only to the outside of the iron. Fry in hot fat until medium brown. Remove from iron and place on absorbent paper. Makes 18 cases.

Mrs. B. A. Woods, Kirbyville H. S.
Kirbyville, Texas

CREAMED CHICKEN
Number of Servings — 8

1 c. chopped celery
4 T. butter
½ c. flour
3 c. chicken broth
½ c. milk
3 c. diced cooked chicken
Salt

Cook celery in the butter for a few minutes. Stir in flour and blend thoroughly. Then stir in broth and milk and cook until smooth and thick. Season to taste with salt. Add chicken. Heat mixture thoroughly and serve hot in a rice or noodle ring, in patty shells, on waffles, on crisp toast, or in toasted bread baskets.

Berenice S. Phillips, Winfield H. S.
Winfield, Alabama

CHICKEN A LA KING
Number of Servings — 6

1 T. butter or margarine
½ c. sliced mushrooms
¼ c. green pepper, chopped
3 T. flour
3 T. butter or margarine
1½ c. milk
1 egg yolk, slightly beaten
1 t. salt
¼ c. cream
2 T. pimento, chopped

1½ c. cooked, diced chicken

Melt butter in a 2-quart saucepan. Add mushrooms and green pepper, cook until mushrooms are browned. Remove mushrooms and pepper from the saucepan. Add butter to saucepan and melt. Add flour, salt and pepper and blend well. Add milk and stir constantly until mixture thickens. Cook 5 minutes. Add mushrooms, green pepper, cream pimento and chicken to white sauce; heat thoroughly. Add egg yolk gradually, stirring constantly for 1 minute.

Julia Cox, Wynn H. S.
Habersham, Tennessee

CHICKEN A LA KING
Number of Servings — 4

⅓ c. butter or margarine
2 T. minced onion
¼ c. finely chopped celery
⅓ c. flour
2 c. chicken broth
1 c. milk
1 t. salt
½ t. pepper
1 t. paprika
1 4-oz. can pimentos, diced
1 hard-cooked egg, chopped
1 c. diced, cooked chicken
4 toast cups
Toasted bread crumbs

In heavy skillet lightly brown onion and celery in butter. Add flour; mix till smooth; then add chicken broth, milk, salt, pepper, and paprika. Cook slowly, stirring constantly, till slightly thickened. Add pimento, egg, and chicken. Simmer till all ingredients are heated through and mixture is thick. Pour into toast cups, sprinkle top with bread crumbs, and serve immediately.

Mrs. Betty Thompson, Star H. S.
Star, Texas

CHICKEN A LA KING
Number of Servings — 6

2 c. diced chicken
5 T. salad or chicken fat
3 T. pimento, chopped
6 T. green pepper, chopped
½ t. salt
1 c. cream
2 T. flour
2 egg yolks
1 c. cream of mushroom soup

Cook green peppers 6 minutes in oil or fat. Add chicken, pimento and salt. Prepare white sauce with flour, 1 tablespoon fat and cream. When sauce is thick add beaten egg yolks and soup to chicken mixture and heat thoroughly. Serve on toast or patty shells. Add paprika for more color if desired.

Mrs. Verna F. Carruth, Improve H. S.
Columbia, Mississippi

CHICKEN A LA KING
Number of Servings — 6

1 c. sliced mushrooms
¼ c. green pepper, chopped
¼ c. butter or margarine
3 T. enriched flour
2 c. milk
Salt and pepper
1 beaten egg yolk
2½ c. diced, cooked chicken
2 T. finely cut pimento

Lightly brown mushrooms, green pepper in butter; add flour; blend; add milk, seasonings; cook until thick, stirring constantly. Stir some of hot mixture into egg yolk; add to remaining hot mixture. Cook a minute or two, stirring constantly. Add chicken and pimento. Serve on biscuits, hot buttered toast, or in Swedish timbales.

Joyce Mauldin Redstone, Weir H. S.
Weir, Mississippi

CHICKEN A LA KING
Number of Servings — 10

2 c. cooked chicken
1 T. green pepper, chopped
1 pimento
2 c. chicken stock
1 t. salt
1 c. mushrooms (No. 1 can)
2 egg yolks
¼ c. butter or chicken fat
1 c. cream

Remove the meat from the bones, cut in pieces. Add mushrooms, browned in 2 tablespoons butter. Make a sauce of butter, cream, stock, and combine with chicken, minced pepper and pimento. Season well and just before heating, add beaten egg yolks. Serve in timbale cases or pastry shells.

Alice J. Gardner, Parowan H. S.
Parowan, Utah

ESCALLOPED CHICKEN
Number of Servings — 16

1 large boiled chicken, boned and ½ broth
1 loaf bread
6 eggs
2 c. diced celery
1 c. mushrooms, cut up
2 T. minced onions
1 c. raw rice, cooked
1 t. pepper
2 t. salt
½ c. butter, melted

Mix all ingredients except chicken with ½ broth. Put ¾ in roaster. Cover with chicken. Add rest of dressing. To rest of broth add 1 or 2 cans of cream of mushroom soup. Pour part over dressing. Bake at 350°F. 1 to 1½ hours.

Mrs. Mary Belle Meredith, Onsted Com. H. S.
Onsted, Michigan

ESCALLOPED CHICKEN
Number of Servings — 12-15

6 c. cooked chicken, diced
6 c. cooked rice or noodles
4 c. chicken broth
3 c. milk
6 T. butter
¾ c. flour
1 c. blanched almonds
1 sm. can pimento, cut fine
2 small cans mushrooms, drained
Salt and pepper to taste

Into a large casserole, put a layer of rice (or noodles); then a layer of chicken, and cover with gravy made from the broth, milk, butter and flour. Dot with pimento, almonds, and mushrooms. Repeat with a second layer of each and sprinkle with buttered bread crumbs and paprika. Bake in a moderate oven for 45 minutes.

Clotile Pease, Kasson-Mantorville H. S.
Kasson, Minnesota

SCALLOPED CHICKEN
Number of Servings — 12

1 qt. coarsely cut chicken
Make gravy of: 1 qt. broth, free from fat, 4 T. fat, and 4 T. flour. Salt to taste.
1½ qts. bread cut into ½-in. cubes
¾ c. chicken fat or butter
Saute the above slightly in skillet.
Mix with a fork lightly, 1 t. sage, and ¾ t. salt
If desired add 2 T. minced onions, chives or parsley
¼ c. cream or stock

Arrange chicken in a 9 x 13 inch greased pan. Cover with ¾ of the gravy. Arrange dressing over the top and add the remaining gravy. Bake 25 to 35 minutes at 350°F. Cut in squares, garnish with parsley spring, celery leaf or green and red pepper strips. (If chicken does not have enough flavor, add a can or two of cream of chicken soup.

Mrs. Corinne Brown, Story City Com. H. S.
Story City, Iowa

SCALLOPED CHICKEN
Number of Servings — 12

1 hen, 5 lbs.
1 carrot
1 onion
4 t. salt
⅓ c. pimento
2 stalks celery
⅛ t. white pepper
1 c. milk
¾ c. sifted flour
1 c. chicken fat
4 eggs

Cook carrot, sliced onion, 2 teaspoons salt and hen in 2 quarts boiling water until meat leaves the bones. Cool in own liquid. Pull meat from bones. Put skins through meat chopper. Cut up 2

(Continued on Next Page)

stalks celery and cook in broth. Skim fat off top of chicken broth and heat 1 cup in heavy saucepan. Heat 4 cups chicken, celery, broth and 1 cup milk together. Stir 1 cup sifted flour into melted fat until smooth. Add broth mixture gradually, stirring constantly. Add 2 teaspoons salt and 1/3 cup pimento. Cook until thickened. Beat 4 eggs slightly and add sauce gradually to the eggs. Cook over low heat 3 or 4 minutes. Add the ground chicken skin and chicken. Serve over rice or toast squares. Good in casseroles.

Mrs. Mae Plummer, Woodrow Wilson Jr. H. S.
Danville, Virginia

SCALLOPED CHICKEN SUPREME
Number of Servings — 10

6 c. cooked chicken
4 c. chicken broth
6 c. cooked rice (3½ c. uncooked rice)
3 c. milk
4 T. butter
¾ c. flour
1 T. salt
⅛ t. pepper
1 c. blanched almonds
1 small can pimento
2 cans mushrooms (buttered bread crumbs and paprika)

Cut chicken into 1 inch pieces and measure. Pour 1 cup chicken broth over cooked rice. Make white sauce (or use mushroom soup). Slice almonds, cut pimento fine. Slice mushrooms and brown in butter. Butter casserole. Cover bottom with rice. Place layer of chicken over rice and gravy. Dot with almonds, pimento and mushrooms. Repeat. Sprinkle with buttered crumbs. Bake 45 minutes in a 350°F. oven.

Mrs. Erline Ryan, Hampshire H. S.
Hampshire, Illinois

SCALLOPED CHICKEN SUPREME
Number of Servings — 8

3 c. cooked cut-up chicken
1 c. chicken stock
2 c. boiled rice (⅔ c. uncooked)
3 c. chicken gravy seasoned with celery salt or poultry seasoning
½ c. slivered almonds
2 T. chopped pimento
1 c. sauteed sliced mushrooms
½ c. buttered bread crumbs

Pour chicken stock over rice. Place in alternate layers in greased 11 x 7 inch oblong baking dish: rice, chicken, and gravy. Sprinkle over each layer some of the almonds, pimento and mushrooms. Top with buttered bread crumbs. Bake in moderate oven (350°F.) 45 minutes. This is an excellent recipe to serve guests because it can be prepared hours ahead of time and popped in the oven just before serving.

Mrs. Carolyn Sage, Woodlan H. S.
Woodburn, Indiana

SCALLOPED CHICKEN
Number of Servings — 12-16

5 c. cooked chopped chicken (4 to 5 lb. ready to cook stewing chicken)
1 stick (½ c.) butter or margarine
¾ c. chopped onion
½ c. flour
2 t. salt
1 qt. milk
4 oz. jar (⅓ c.) chopped pimento
2 cans (1 lb. each) peas, drained
3 oz. can sliced mushrooms, drained
2 cans (5 ozs. each) chow mein noodles

Melt butter in a large skillet. Cook onion in melted butter until tender. Blend in flour and salt. Gradually add milk. Cook, stirring constantly, until sauce is smooth and thickened. Add all the remaining ingredients except chow mein noodles. Pour mixture into a 3 quart shallow casserole or baking pan. Bake in moderate oven (350°F.) for 30 minutes. Serve hot over chow mein noodles.

Violet Shaffner, Marshall H. S.
Marshall, Illinois

SCALLOPED CHICKEN
Number of Servings — 12

1 4-lb. hen, boiled till meat can be separated
1 qt. chicken stock
1 lb. loaf white bread
4 eggs
1 can condensed mushroom soup
Salt and pepper to taste
½ c. chopped onion
½ c. chopped celery
1 t. dried parsley flakes
3 T. chicken fat

Separate chicken meat in large pieces. Save skin—put thru food grinder with onion and celery. Crumble outside brown crust of bread fine. Mix with fat for topping. Cut inside white crumbs of bread into ½ inch cubes. Heat stock, soup, ground skin, onions and celery. Add eggs and cook until thickened. Alternate layers of soft crumbs, chicken and sauce. Top with brown crumbs in casserole. Brown 30 minutes in a 350°F. oven.

Mrs. Helen P. Sims, Spearsville H. S.
Spearsville, Louisiana

ESCALLOPED CHICKEN
Number of Servings — 8

4 c. coarsely cubed stewed chicken

Gravy:
1 qt. broth
4 T. flour
4 T. chicken fat or butter
Dressing:
1½ qts. bread (rather stale), cut in ½ inch squares
¾ c. butter, melted
1¼ t. powdered sage

(Continued on Next Page)

¼ c. cream
¾ t. salt
2 T. finely chopped onion

Put layer of chicken in the 13 x 9 x 2 inch pan. Cover with the dressing. Pour gravy over the top of the dressing. Bake in 425°F. oven until dressing is slightly brown, about 35 minutes. Cut into squares and serve.

Mrs. Nancy Davis, Auburn H. S.
Auburn, Nebraska

CHICKEN SURPRISE
Number of Servings — 20

1 fat hen
2 c. uncooked rice
2 cans mushroom soup
1 T. chopped parsley
1 T. minced onion
Salt
Pepper
2 c. rolled dried bread crumbs

Cover hen with salted water and stew until tender. Let it cool in the broth. Skim off fat and reserve. Remove chicken from bones and cut in small pieces. Wash rice and cook in chicken broth, boiling rapidly for 20 minutes. Add mushroom soup, onion, salt and pepper. Combine with chicken and pour into greased baking dish. Heat a few tablespoons of skimmed fat in a skillet and saute bread crumbs in it. Do not neglect or overlook this point. Mix thoroughly and spread over chicken-rice mixture. Bake in moderate oven 1½ to 2 hours. Cook in a flat pan and serve in squares. Baking temperature 325° to 350°.

Joan Haines, Cle Elnm H. S.
Cle Elum, Washington

CHICKEN LOAF WITH MUSHROOM SAUCE

1-4 lbs. chicken
2 c. fresh bread crumbs
1 c. cooked rice
1½ t. salt
⅛ c. chopped pimentos
3 c. liquid (milk, chicken broth or half and half)
4 eggs, well beaten

Boil chicken until meat leaves bone. Cut up in small pieces like you make chicken salad. Mix all together. Add eggs last. Bake in well greased and floured pan, 8 x 12 x 2 inches, 1 hour at 350°F. Cut in squares and serve with mushroom sauce.

Mushroom Sauce:

¼ c. butter or margarine
¼ c. flour
1 pt. chicken broth
¼ c. cream
¼ lb. mushrooms or ½ lb. can mushrooms or 1 can mushroom soup
⅛ t. paprika
½ t. chopped parsley
⅛ t. lemon juice
Salt to taste

Melt butter in saucepan, add flour, mix smoothly. Add chicken broth, mushrooms or mushroom soup. Cook and stir constantly until thick like gravy. Add cream, paprika, parsley, lemon juice, and salt. Let stand in hot water until ready to serve on chicken loaf. Cut chicken livers and gizzards up in mushroom sauce.

Mrs. Georgie H. Putney, Cumberland H. S.
Cumberland, Virginia

CHICKEN LOAF
Number of Servings — 8

4 lb. chicken (shredded)
2 c. soft bread crumbs
1 c. cooked rice
1 t. salt
½ t. paprika
¼ c. chopped pimento
4 well beaten eggs
¼ c. chicken fat
3 c. chicken broth and milk (half and half)

Combine and bake 1 hour in very slow oven. Serve with Mushroom Sauce.

Mushroom Sauce:

¼ c. butter
½ lb. mushrooms
¼ c. flour
2 c. chicken stock
2 egg yolks, beaten
¼ c. cream
¼ t. salt
⅛ t. paprika
1 T. chopped parsley
1 T. lemon juice

Cook mushrooms in butter but do not brown. Make a sauce by adding flour and chicken stock. Add egg yolks and cook until thickened. Add remaining ingredients and mushrooms and serve.

Helen M. Brauns, Batavia H. S.
Batavia, Illinois

CHICKEN LOAF—CASSEROLE STYLE

1 4-lb. stewing chicken, cut up
1½ c. cooked rice
2 c. fresh bread crumbs
1 t. salt
¼ t. pepper
¼ c. chopped pimento
3 c. chicken broth
4 eggs, beaten
¼ c. non-fat dry powdered milk

Simmer chicken till tender; cool quickly; refrigerate unboned chicken and broth. About 2 hours before serving, cook rice as package directs. Start heating oven at 325°F. Remove skin from chicken. Grind and dice chicken meat coarsely. Combine skin and meat with rice and next 7 ingredients. Pour into well-greased 3 quart casserole. Bake 1½ to 1¾ hours.

Margaret N. Phillips, Carthage Com. H. S.
Carthage, Illinois

CHICKEN LOAF — MUSHROOM SAUCE
Number of Servings — 8

4 c. cooked chicken, chopped
1½ c. cooked rice
2 c. fresh bread crumbs
1½ t. salt
2 T. chopped pimento
3 c. chicken broth

Mix the above well with hands. Add 4 well beaten eggs and mix well. Put into well greased loaf pans and cook 1 hour at 225°F. Serves 8.

Nita P. Lowery, South Mountain H. S.
Phoenix, Arizona

CHICKEN LOAF
Number of Servings — 8

1 T. butter
1 4-oz. can sliced mushrooms
1½ c. soft bread crumbs
1 c. milk
1 c. chicken broth, well seasoned
2 eggs
½ t. salt
¼ t. pepper
¼ c. pimento, finely cut
3 c. small pieces of cooked chicken

Saute drained mushrooms in butter until only lightly brown. Combine in loaf if desired, or use in sauce. Beat eggs. Combine with all other ingredients. Pour into greased 9 x 5 x 3 inch loaf pan. Set pan in water 1 inch deep. Bake at 350°F. (moderate oven) for 55 to 60 minutes. Turn out on platter. Serve sliced with mushroom sauce, if desired. *Mushroom Sauce:* Use drained liquid from mushrooms. Measure and finish filling with canned milk, to make 1 cup. Add 1 tablespoon flour to sauted mushrooms and stir well. Cook 2 minutes. Add ¼ teaspoon salt to liquid and boil 2 minutes. Serve on meat loaf.

Madge H. Tuckett, American Fork H. S.
American Fork, Utah

CHICKEN LOAF
Number of Servings — 6

2 c. soft bread crumbs
2 beaten egg yolks
1 c. thin cream
1½ c. minced chicken
1½ c. cooked peas
1 T. minced onion
¼ t. sage
Salt and pepper to taste
3 beaten egg whites

Mix in order given, adding beaten egg whites last. Pour into greased loaf pan. Bake in slow oven (325°F.) 1½ hours. Serve with sauce made of chicken broth to which a little cream has been added.

Mrs. Betty Kirschten, Rosebud H. S.
Rosebud, Montana

CHICKEN LOAF
Number of Servings — 12

3 lb. hen—cook separate dark meat from white
Grind meat
8 hard-cooked eggs—put through food chopper
½ pkg. gelatine with ½ c. cold water
Add 1½ c. chicken stock
Divide stock—gelatine mix into 3 parts
Add 1 part to egg and 1 part to each lb. of chicken

Season according to taste with salt, white pepper, celery salt. Press the dark layer in bottom of pyrex loaf pan. Then place layer of eggs. Last layer is white meat. Chill in refrigerator. Slice, serve as a salad or cold plate.

Ruth Owen, Bonham Jr. H. S.
Odessa, Texas

CHICKEN LOAF
Number of Servings — 8

3 c. stewed chicken
1 c. soft bread crumbs
2 T. chopped green pepper
2 T. chopped pimentos
1 T. chopped parsley
2 T. melted butter
½ t. salt
¼ t. paprika
4 beaten eggs
⅔ c. milk or broth

Mix together and press in greased loaf pan. Bake for 35 minutes in 325°F. oven. Let stand for 5 minutes before unmolding.

Mrs. Joalice Poehler, Reagan County H. S.
Big Lake, Texas

CHICKEN LOAF
Number of Servings — 12

1 fryer, 2 to 3 lbs.
1 c. bread crumbs
½ c. uncooked rice
1 pimento, chopped
1 c. liquid (broth or milk)
3 eggs, well-beaten
¾ t. salt

Cook rice in chicken broth. Cut up chicken, after cooking. Add all ingredients and mix well. Bake in pyrex or shallow pan until brown and firm. When done, cut in blocks. Pour over blocks a sauce made of white sauce and mushroom soup.

Kay Rodgers, Rutledge H. S.
Rutledge, Tennessee

CHICKEN LOAF
Number of Servings — 6

1 pt. sweet milk
1½ c. crumbs
1 T. butter
2 eggs, well beaten
Salt, pepper and onion

(Continued on Next Page)

1 chicken (meat ground)

Place milk on stove; when it bubbles stir in crumbs. Let stand a few minutes then remove from heat and add butter, eggs, salt, pepper, onions, and meat. Form in loaf. Place in a greased pan and cover with crumbs. Let set at least 2 hours, then bake in 350°F. oven until brown.

Katherine Stackpole, Guthie H. S.
Guthrie, Kentucky

CHICKEN LOAF OR RING
Number of Servings — 6

1 c. soft bread crumbs
2 c. milk
2 eggs, slightly beaten, or 3 egg yolks
½ t. salt
¼ t. paprika
1 t. Worcestershire sauce
3 c. cooked chicken, diced
½ c. celery, chopped
1 green pepper, chopped
Juice of ½ lemon

Mix ingredients well. Pack into buttered 1½ quart mold. Set in pan of hot water. Bake at 325°F. about 40 minutes. Let stand 10 minutes before unmolding. Serves 6 or more.

Mrs. Charlene Strickland, Madison County H. S.
Danielsville, Georgia

PRESSED CHICKEN
Number of Servings — 6

1 chicken
1 package unflavored gelatin

Cook chicken in water until tender, dissolve unflavored gelatin in ½ cup cold water. Add boiling broth, approximately 2 cups. Bone chicken and grind through coarse food chopper. Add broth and gelatin to chicken. Flavor to taste with dash of celery salt and pepper. Place mixture in bread pan and chill until firm. Slice and serve. Excellent for school lunches.

Martha L. Finkbeiner, Middleville H. S.
Middleville, Michigan

PRESSED CHICKEN
Number of Servings — 30

2 cooked hens, ground in food chopper
1 bottle dressing
½ c. vinegar
1 bunch celery, diced
Juice of 1 lemon

Season to taste with sat, pepper, Worcestershire sauce, and add a dash of tabasco sauce. Cook chicken broth down to 4 cups. Dissolve 1 envelope of plain gelatin in broth and allow to cool. Add to meat mixture. When congealed, slice and serve on lettuce and top with mayonnaise.

Mrs. Prince A. Hodgson, Elbert County H. S.
Elberton, Georgia

PRESSED CHICKEN

1 hen, cooked and ground
½ c. crushed crackers
1 small onion, minced
5 hard boiled eggs
Salt and pepper to taste
2 T. butter
1 T. sugar
1 t. dry mustard
½ c. vinegar
1½ c. chicken stock

Separate hard boiled eggs and mash whites with a fork. Add to chicken, cracker and onion mixture. Mash yolks with salt, pepper, butter, sugar, mustard and vinegar. Add this to meat mixture. Mix in about 1½ cups chicken stock to the above until it will mold. Chill overnight. Cut in squares and serve on lettuce.

Rose Chandler, Calhoun City H. S.
Calhoun City, Mississippi

PRESSED CHICKEN
Number of Servings — 16

1 hen (cooked and cut fine)
1 c. mayonnaise
1 can pimento (cut)
2 c. celery (cut fine)
6 hard boiled eggs (sliced)
2 T. pickle relish
2 envelopes gelatin
1 c. chicken stock

Dissolve gelatin in 1 cup cold water, add hot chicken stock. Salt ingredients to taste and mix thoroughly, adding mayonnaise last. Press in shallow pan and place in refrigerator overnight. Cut in squares, and serve on lettuce. Top with mayonnaise and olive.

Ethel F. Johnson, New Brockton H. S.
New Brockton, Alabama

PRESSED CHICKEN
Number of Servings — 10-12

1 3½ to 4 lb. ready-to-cook chicken
Hot water
1½ t. salt
Pepper

Cut chicken in serving pieces; cover with hot water; cook until tender. Remove the chicken from the broth and cool until the chicken can be removed from the bones; dice. Add the salt and pepper to taste, and approximately ¾ to 1 cup of the broth. Reheat the mixture, stirring just to mix thoroughly. Pour mixture into a bowl and place weight on chicken. Chill overnight. Unmold and slice for serving.

Lila F. Book, Custer H. S.
Custer, Oklahoma

CHICKEN ALMOND SKILLET
Number of Servings — 6

2 c. diced cooked chicken
2 T. butter
¾ c. celery, cut in 1 inch pieces
¼ c. sliced onions
½ c. canned mushrooms
1 T. cornstarch
3 T. soy sauce
1 c. canned clear chicken consomme
1 c. toasted almonds
Cooked rice

Melt butter in a skillet. Add celery and onion. Stir and cook 2 minutes. Add chicken and mushrooms. Heat 8 minutes. Combine cornstarch, soy sauce and consomme. Stir slowly into chicken mixture. Stir and cook slowly 5 minutes. Stir in almonds. Serve hot on fluffy rice.

Mrs. Thelma B. Lee, Seneca H. S.
Seneca, South Carolina

CASHEW CHICKEN
Number of Servings — 6

2 T. margarine
1 medium onion, sliced
1 medium green pepper, sliced
1¼ c. chicken broth
3 c. sliced celery
1 T. Soy sauce
2 c. cut-up chicken, cooked (fryer or hen may be used)
1 3-oz. can mushrooms, drained (save liquid)
2 T. cornstarch
3 T. mushroom liquid
½ c. broken cashew nuts (or more)

Saute onion and green pepper in hot margarine until tender. Add chicken broth, celery, Soy sauce. Simmer, covered, 10 minutes. Stir in chicken, mushrooms. Mix cornstarch with mushroom liquid, stir into chicken mixture, and bring to a boil. Add cashew nuts just before serving. Serve on cooked rice. (Cook 1 cup raw rice as cashew chicken is being prepared).

Mrs. Annie Lillian Brewton, Escambia H. S.
Pensacola, Florida

CHICKEN FRICASSE
Number of Servings — 5

1 large chicken
3 T. shortening
1 medium onion
1 can cream of mushroom soup
1 can water
2 T. cooking sherry

Cut up chicken; salt, pepper, flour. Brown chicken on all sides. Drain off fat. Add onions, soup, water, and sherry. Reduce heat and cook for 1½ hours at low temperature. The sauce formed may be served over rice.

Dorothy Minton, Littlefield H. S.
Littlefield, Texas

CHICKEN COUNTRY CAPTAIN
Number of Servings — 6-8

1 4-lb. hen or ready cut pieces
Flour, salt, pepper
2 finely chopped medium onions
2 finely chopped green peppers
1 clove garlic, cut fine
1 t. salt
1 t. sugar
2 t. curry powder
2 No. 2 cans tomatoes
1 t. finely cut parsley
½ t. thyme
½ lb. chopped roasted almonds
3 T. currants or white raisins
2 c. cooked rice

Roll chicken in mixture of flour, salt, and pepper. Place in frying pan enough shortening to make ½ inch deep. Fry chicken until golden brown. Remove from pan. Into drippings place onion, green pepper, and garlic. Cook about 5 minutes very slowly, stirring constantly. Add salt, curry powder, tomatoes, sugar, chopped parsley, and thyme. Place chicken in roaster or Dutch oven and pour mixture over. Add hot water, if needed, to cover chicken. Cover tightly and place in moderate oven. Cook about 45 minutes until chicken is tender. Place rice on large platter. Sprinkle with currants and chopped almonds. Arrange chicken around edge of platter. Place sauce in separate bowl. Pour over rice when serving each individual.

Inez Wallace, Home Economics Education
Atlanta, Georgia

COUNTRY CAPTAIN
Number of Servings — 6-8

2½ or 3 lb. chicken, disjointed
1 T. butter
1 medium white, onion, sliced thin
1 large bell pepper
1 or 2 beans garlic
2 cans tomatoes
1 t. salt
½ t. white pepper
1 t. curry powder
1 t. chopped parsley
1 t. powdered thyme
2 t. fat, in which chicken was cooked
¼ lb. almonds, blanched and browned
2 T. dried currants

Season the chicken, dredge with flour, fry in frying pan. Brown onion, pepper and garlic in 1 tablespoon butter. Add tomatoes and cook 10 minutes longer. Season with salt, pepper, curry, parsley, and thyme. Cook 5 minutes longer. Place chicken in covered dish. Pour the sauce over and add 2 tablespoons fat in which the chicken was cooked. When ready to serve, mix with ¼ pound almonds, blanched and browned, and 2 tablespoons currants. Serve with dry rice.

Claudia Whitmire, Carolina H. S.
Greenville, South Carolina

CHICKEN COUNTRY CAPTAIN
Number of Servings — 8

1 3½ lb. chicken
2 No. 2 cans tomatoes
½ c. diced celery
½ c. chopped onion
1 small clove garlic
½ t. white pepper
1 t. curry powder
½ t. thyme
1 t. salt
¼ lb. almonds, roasted
3 T. raisins or currants

Disjoint chicken as for frying. Brown in small amount of fat. Remove chicken. Brown very lightly onions, celery and garlic. Season with salt, pepper, curry powder and tomatoes. Add thyme. Combine with chicken and cook slowly in covered roaster for 1 hour. Serve over steamed rice. Sprinkle with currants or raisins. Garnish with almonds and parsley. A dish which is popular in the south, originating in Columbus, Ga.

Mrs. Kathryn Lumpkin, Randolph County H. S.
Wedowee, Alabama

CHICKEN COUNTRY CAPTAIN
Number of Servings — 6

2 c. canned tomatoes
1 c. chopped onion
1 c. chopped bell pepper
1 c. currants
1 t. salt
½ t. thyme

One chicken cut into pieces, covered with flour as for frying. Brown pieces in skillet with small amount of fat. Place pieces in an oven dish with a cover. Pour over chicken the mixture above. Cover and cook in 350°F. oven for 1 hour or until tender. Serve on brown or wild rice.

Jean Trull, Cedartown H. S.
Cedartown, Georgia

DEVILED CHICKEN

1 cut-up broiling or frying chicken
Salt and pepper
½ c. fat, melted
2 T. flour
1 c. hot water or soup stock
1½ t. dry mustard
2 t. Worcestershire sauce
2 t. tomato catsup
Paprika, as desired

Season cut-up chicken with salt and pepper and brown in melted fat; remove from pan. Stir flour into fat; add hot water or soup. Cook until mixture thickens, stirring constantly. Blend together the next 4 ingredients and add to cooked sauce. Place chicken in sauce, cover pan and simmer until chicken is tender, about 1 hour. Allow ¾ pound chicken per serving.

Mrs. Margaret C. Hoffman, Victory Joint H. S.
Harrisville, Pennsylvania

CHICKEN A LA PILAF
Number of Servings — 6-8

2-2½-lb. broiler-fryer, cut up
¼ c. butter
1 clove garlic, chopped fine
½ c. onion, chopped fine
¼ c. parsley, chopped fine
¼ c. celery leaves, chopped fine
2 t. dried basil leaves
2 t. salt
¼ t. pepper
1 c. Fisher's Ala, uncooked

Wash chicken parts; dry. Using a Dutch oven, melt the butter, add chicken and brown well. Remove chicken — set aside. Add onion, parsley, celery leaves, and garlic. Saute until tender. Add basil, salt, pepper, and 3 cups water. Mix well. Turn heat low, place chicken in liquid mixture. Simmer covered 55 to 60 minutes until chicken is tender. Remove chicken from skillet, place in foil covered pan to keep warm. Stir Ala into liquid mixture. (Add chicken bouillon and hot water to make 2 cups if liquid has cooked down below that amount). Simmer covered for 15 to 20 minutes. Stir occasionally. The Ala should be tender and all liquid absorbed. Serve chicken on platter, with the Ala around the edges. Garnish with fresh parsley.

Beulah V. Swanson, Raft River H. S.
Malta, Idaho

CHICKEN CURRY
Number of Servings — 8

1 stewing chicken (4 to 5 lbs.), cut up
1 qt. water
1 large onion, sliced
1 bay leaf
4 whole cloves
3 peppercorns
2 t. salt
1 clove garlic, mashed
½ c. finely chopped onion
½ c. finely chopped celery
2 T. butter
2 T. flour
1 t. curry powder
1 t. ginger
1 t. salt
1 t. grated lemon rind
1 T. lemon juice
1 tomato, peeled and chopped

Place chicken, water, onion, bay leaf, peppercorns, and salt in deep pan and simmer covered 3 to 4 hours. Cool. Cut chicken in small pieces. Strain broth; reserve. Cook garlic, onion and celery in butter until soft. Stir in flour, curry, ginger, 1 teaspoon salt, pepper and 2 cups broth. Cook, stirring constantly, until thickened. Reduce heat, cook 10 minutes. Add lemon rind, juice, tomato, chicken and heat thoroughly. Serve over rice or spaghetti.

Mrs. Jo Marler, Forest H. S.
Forest, Mississippi

CHICKEN CURRY
Number of Servings — 8

½ large white onion
¼ c. butter
½ c. chicken fat
1 c. flour
1 can condensed milk
1 qt. chicken broth
12 sliced green olives
2 small cans mushrooms
2 t. curry powder
⅛ t. pepper
Salt to taste
Boned chicken
½ c. sherry (optional)

Stew 1 whole stewing chicken, 1 stock celery, 1 onion, 1 carrot and 2 teaspoons salt until tender. Drain off broth and let set. Cool and remove chicken from bones. Brown onion in butter and chicken fat. Add flour, condensed milk and chicken broth and stir until thick. Add olives, mushrooms, curry powder, pepper, salt, boned chicken and sherry to sauce. Serve over steamed rice or in patty shell.

Mrs. Luola Walch, Coeurd'Alene Jr. H. S.
Coeurd'Alene, Idaho

BEAN POT CHICKEN
Number of Servings — 4

4 chicken legs and thighs
2 whole chicken breasts
2 T. minced onion
¾ stick butter or margarine
Juice ½ lemon
½ can mushroom soup

Place chicken, onion and butter in bean pot. Cover. Bake 3 to 4 hours at low heat in oven or in electric bean pot. Strain liquid and combine with mushroom soup. Pour over chicken. Heat in pot and serve.

Grace F. Harrison,
Connecticut State Dept. of Education
Hartford, Connecticut

CHICKEN DELIGHT
Number of Servings — 24

2 16-oz. packages noodles
2 small cans mushrooms
2 lb. can of asparagus
1 5-lb. chicken cooked and cut in small pieces
2 green peppers cut fine
2 c. grated cheese
1 t. salt
¼ t. pepper
2 c. medium white sauce

Boil noodles for 3 minutes in 4 cups of water. Let stand 5 minutes. Mix all ingredients except enough cheese to sprinkle over top. Pour into casserole and bake 30 to 40 minutes.

Ann Dean Carr, Caverna H. S.
Cave City, Kentucky

CURRIED CHICKEN
Number of Servings — 8

½ c. slivered or chopped blanched almonds
½ c. butter
1⅓ c. chopped onions
1 c. diced green pepper
1 c. flour
6 c. chicken broth
1 t. salt
2 T. curry powder
4 c. diced cooked chicken
Almond-Currant Rice*

Saute almonds in butter until golden brown. Remove almonds and set aside. (Almonds are used later in rice mixture). Add onions and green pepper to remaining butter in skillet; saute until tender. Stir in flour. Gradually blend in the chicken broth, salt, and curry powder. Cook until sauce is thickened, stirring occasionally. Then, add chicken. Continue to cook until thoroughly heated. Serve over Almond-Currant Rice.

Almond-Currant Rice: Stir 2⅔ cups packaged pre-cooked rice, 1 teaspoon salt, 6 tablespoons currants, and 2 tablespoons butter into 2⅔ cups boiling water in saucepan. Cover, remove from heat, and let stand 5 minutes. Stir in sauteed almonds with a fork.

Mrs. Beverly J. Huth, Lakewood H. S.
Hebron, Ohio

PARMESAN CHICKEN
Number of Servings — 4-5

1 chicken, cut
1 c. bread crumbs or corn flake crumbs
½ c. parmesan cheese
Sprinkle very generously with garlic salt
Pepper

Mix well. Brush each piece with melted butter. Roll in bread crumb mixture. Place in heavy skillet. Bake at 300° F. until nicely browned. Cover and continue baking until done. (Approximately 2-3 hrs.).

Lois Erickson, Cambridge H. S.
Cambridge, Minnesota

CHICKEN BROCCOLI CASSEROLE
Number of Servings — 6

2 pkgs. frozen broccoli cooked according to directions
Meat from 1 chicken (stewed or baked)
2 T. butter
2 c. thin white sauce
1 c. grated cheese

Prepare broccoli as directed. Into a greased casserole dish, place one layer of cooked broccoli, one layer of boneless chicken, cover with white sauce which has had the grated cheese melted into it. Place under broiler until warm and serve.

Mrs. Arlee Rylander Barton, Burnet H .S.
Burnet, Texas

CHICKEN TETRAZZINI
Number of Servings — 8

2 slices bacon, finely cut
⅓ c. minced onion
½ c. minced green pepper
2 c. shredded American cheese
¼ c. cut-up pimento
¼ c. toasted shaved almonds
1¾ c. cooked peas
2 c. cut-up cooked chicken

Cook bacon until brown and crisp. Add onion and pepper and brown lightly in bacon fat. Add cheese, pimento, almonds, peas and chicken. Heat using chicken broth to moisten. Serve hot over boiled rice or macaroni. Garnish with tomato slices, parsley or ripe olives.

Mrs. Ralph Ayers, Hale Center H. S.
Hale Center, Texas

CHICKEN TETRAZZINI
Number of Servings — 10-12

1 hen
1 c. chicken stock
1 can mushroom soup
2 c. grated cheese, sharp
2 heaping t. flour
1 t. powdered mustard
2 t. Worcestershire sauce

Prepare hen as for salad, except cut in larger pieces; salt to taste, add stock and heat. Add soup, stirring all the time. Fold in grated cheese, then thicken with flour, mustard; add Worcestershire sauce—add more sauce and mustard if taste demands. The mixture should be creamy thick. Serve on nest of cooked, well drained spaghetti, or rice.

Mrs. Katherine M. Simons, Cross H. S.
Cross, South Carolina

CHICKEN TETRAZZINI
Number of Servings — 8-10

3 T. butter
2 T. flour
2 c. chicken broth
⅓ c. minced onion (browned in butter)
½ c. minced green pepper (browned with onions)
2 c. grated American cheese (½-lb.)
¼ c. toasted shaved almonds
¼ c. cut-up pimento
1¾ c. cooked green peas
3 c. cut-up cooked chicken

Make a sauce of the butter, flour and chicken broth. Add to the sauce the browned onions and pepper. Then add the remaining ingredients. Mix lightly with hot drained boiled macaroni (1 cup uncooked). Heat using chicken stock to moisten, generally it is needed. If one wishes, one may add 1 cup sauteed mushrooms to macaroni before adding remainder of mixture. Serve hot.

Mrs. Janice Watson, Florence H. S.
Florence, Mississippi

CHICKEN TETRAZZINI
Number of Servings — 8

5 T. maragarine
2 c. chicken or turkey broth
1 c. light cream
⅓ c. flour
½ c. sliced mushrooms
1 6-oz. box cooked spaghetti
2 c. chopped turkey or chicken
Parmesan cheese
½ t. salt
⅛ t. pepper

Melt margarine, add flour, salt, pepper and blend well. Add turkey or chicken broth and cook over medium heat, stirring constantly, until thick. Add cream. Divide sauce in half, to one half add mushrooms and spaghetti, to second part add turkey or chicken. Place alternate layers in a greased casserole. Top with Parmesan cheese. Bake at 350°F. for 30 minutes.

Mrs. Frances Hicks, Utopia H. S.
Utopia, Texas

PAPRIKA CHICKEN
Number of Servings — 6

1 young chicken, cut as for frying
1 T. chopped onion
4 thin slices lemon
Salt
2 t. Worcestershire sauce
1 T. paprika
1 c. cream

Sprinkle chicken with small quantity of flour and sear in hot butter. Add onion, Worcestershire sauce, salt, paprika, lemon and small quantity of hot water. Put cover on and allow to steam until chicken is done. Just before serving add one cup of cream and heat, but do not boil. Cubed Irish potatoes added to this gravy are delicious.

Marion A. Cloud, Cuthbert H. S.
Cuthbert, Georgia

CHICKEN PAPRIKA
Number of Servings — 6

3 broilers
3 T. chopped onions
4 T. butter
1½ t. paprika
2 T. lemon juice
2 T. flour
1½ c. sour cream
1 t. salt
½ t. pepper

Saute onions in butter until lightly browned. Cut chicken in halves and brown lightly; add paprika and lemon juice. Cover and cook over low heat until tender. Remove chicken and keep hot. Add flour, salt and pepper. Blend in sour cream, stirring constantly until smooth and thick. Pour sauce over chicken and serve hot.

Mrs. Mary Light, King H. S.
Kingsville, Texas

PAPRIKA ROLLS
Number of Servings — 12

1 lb. each chicken breasts and thighs
2 t. salt
1 t. pepper
1 T. paprika
2 T. flour
12 thin slices bacon (warmed)
¼ c. water
1 clove garlic
¼ t. Accent

Remove skin and bones and spread chicken meat on cutting board. Sprinkle with Accent, then with salt, pepper, paprika and flour which have been mixed together in a bowl. Make 12 rolls of the meat, wrapping a bacon slice around each on the bias from end to end. Lay close together in a skillet that has been rubbed with a cut clove of garlic (discard garlic). Cook uncovered on medium heat until bacon browns. Turn once. Pour off any excess fat; add water, cover and cook on low heat until tender; about 30 minutes.

Christine Stage, New Lexington H. S.
New Lexington, Ohio

CHICKEN MARENGO
Number of Servings — 5-6

2 to 3 lbs. chicken parts
⅓ c. flour
1 t. salt
¼ t. pepper
¼ c. olive oil
1 clove garlic, crushed
3 T. onion, chopped
4 tomatoes, quartered
1 c. white wine
1 herb bouquet: 3-4 sprigs parsley, 1 sprig thyme, 1 bay leaf, wrapped in cheesecloth
2 T. butter
1 c. (4 oz.) mushrooms, sliced
½ c. olives, sliced
½ c. cold consomme
2 T. flour

Rinse chicken and pat dry with absorbent paper. Coat chicken evenly in a bag with a mixture of flour, salt, and pepper. Brown chicken in a heavy skillet in the olive oil which has been heated. Add the garlic, onion, tomatoes, white wine, and herb bouquet. Cover and simmer over a low heat for about ½ hour or until thickest pieces of chicken are tender. Saute in a small skillet; the mushrooms in the butter. Add to the chicken with sliced olives. Place consomme in a screw-top jar and sprinkle flour on top. Cover and shake well. Remove chicken and herb bouquet from the skillet. Gradually add consomme-flour liquid to mixture in skillet, stirring constantly. Boil 3 to 5 minutes or until thickened. Return chicken to sauce, cover and simmer 10 minutes. Arrange chicken on a hot platter. Cover with the sauce.

Shirley M. Griffiths, Wilson Boro Area Joint H. S.
Easton, Pennsylvania

CHICKEN SUPREME
Number of Servings — 6

2 T. butter
1 clove garlic, crushed
½ small green pepper, chopped
¼ pimento, chopped
1 t. Worcestershire sauce
1 t. salt
½ t. paprika
½ t. pepper
1 can cream of chicken soup
1½ c. cooked chicken, chopped
1¾ c. chicken broth
1¾ c. pre-cooked or minute rice

Melt butter at 300°F. in the controlled skillet. Add pepper and garlic, cook until pepper is softened. Add rest of ingredients, combine well, and bring to boil. Cover, switch to 200°F. for about 10 minutes. Garnish with green pepper rings.

Kay S. Frantz, Biglerville H. S.
Biglerville, Pennsylvania

CHICKEN WIGGLE
Number of Servings — 15

1 fat hen
1 can English peas
2 cans mushrooms
1 large can pimento
2 large onions
2 large green peppers
Salt and pepper
Worcestershire sauce to taste
Hot Luzanne sauce to taste
2 to 3 packages egg noodles

Cook hen, cool, and chop meat. Add to chicken broth, peas, mushrooms, pimento, onions, and pepper. Cook until tender. Add chopped meat, salt, pepper, Worcestershire and Luzanne sauces. Add egg noodles and simmer for 1 hour.

Pat Helms, Barbour County H. S.
Clio, Alabama

CHICKEN OR PHEASANT
Number of Servings — 5

1 pkg. dried onion soup
1 c. rice
1 chicken
1 can cream of chicken soup
1 can of milk (rinse soup can)
1 can onion rings

Grease 2 quart casserole. Sprinkle onion soup over bottom of casserole. Spread rice over this. Brown meat and put over rice. Dilute can of soup and pour over top. Bake, covered, for 1 hour, 15 minutes at 350°F. Uncover and add onion rings. Cook 15 minutes longer. Wild rice can be used with this also.

Rose Schottenbauer, Hopkins H. S.
Hopkins, Minnesota

QUICK CHICKEN STROGANOFF
Number of Servings — 4-6

1 2½-3 lb. broiler, cut up
2 T. butter or margarine
1 clove garlic, minced
¼ c. minced onion
1 t. salt
⅛ t. pepper
1 8-oz. can tomato sauce
1 c. commercial sour cream
1 4-oz. can whole mushrooms
1 8-oz. package noodles

In a large skillet, brown chicken lightly in butter; push to one side. Add garlic and onion and cook until lightly browned and tender. Sprinkle with salt and pepper. Put tomato sauce in a bowl. Add sour cream gradually, stirring to combine. Pour over chicken. Simmer, covered, about 30 minutes or until fork tender, turning and basting once or twice. Garnish with whole drained, canned mushrooms. Serve with hot boiled rice or noodles.

Rosemary Anderson, Spring Branch H. S.
Houston, Texas

YELLOW RICE AND CHICKEN
Number of Servings — 8

1 fryer
2 button garlic
1 onion
1 bay leaf
Pinch of saffron
2 c. rice
4 oz. lard or ½ pt. of olive oil
1 2-oz. can Petit Pois (small size)
2 pimentos
1 green pepper
2 T. salt
6 oz. tomatoes
1½ quarts of water

Cut chicken in quarters and fry with onions and garlic; when done, add tomatoes and water. Boil for five minutes. Add bay leaf, salt, rice, saffron and green peppers. Stir thoroughly and place in moderately heated oven for 20 minutes. Garnish with Petit Pois and pimientos. Serves 8.

Jessie L. Fielding, Plant City Sr. H. S.
Plant City, Florida

CHICKEN AND RICE
Number of Servings — 6-8

2 c. chicken cut in bite size pieces
Chicken broth
1 c. uncooked rice
½ t. chili powder
¼ c. chopped green pepper
¼ c. chopped onion
1 garlic button or ¼ t. garlic powder
½ small can mushrooms
1 c. tomatoes
Grated cheese

Cook rice in chicken broth. Salt to taste. Add chili powder. Cook tomatoes, onion, pepper and garlic until tender enough to sieve. Pour over rice. Add chicken and the mushrooms that have been browned in butter. Cook slowly about 1 hour. Before serving top with grated cheese and allow to melt. May substitute ½ can (303) stewed tomatoes for onions, tomatoes, and pepper.

Mrs. Lloyd Smittle, Willisville H. S.
Willisville, Arkansas

CHICKEN AU McGILL
Number of Servings — 6-8

2 large broilers
4 large red onions, sliced
4 large red peppers, sliced
2 carrots, sliced
1 t. curry
1 large bud garlic, minced
1 t. pepper
1 t. salt
1 can consomme
1 c. sherry wine

Sautee slowly the pieces of chicken until tender. Remove from skillet and then saute onions, peppers, and carrots until golden brown. Return chicken to skillet and add curry, garlic, pepper and salt. Add consomme and simmer for about an hour. Thirty minutes before taking up the dish, add sherry. This dish is served with rice and green salad.

Mrs. Robert Williams, Graceville H. S.
Graceville, Florida

TROPICAL CHICKEN
Number of Servings — 6

1 3-lb. ready-to-cook chicken, cut up
½ c. all-purpose flour
½ t. salt
1 large can peaches
Drained parsley
1 t. dried basil
12 small potatoes
¼ t. pepper
½ t. paprika
½ c. shortening
1 c. orange juice
2 T. brown sugar
2 T. vinegar
1 t. ground nutmeg

About 45 minutes before serving: Lightly coat chicken with combined flour, 1 teaspoon salt, pepper and paprika. In hot shortening in chicken fryer or large skillet, saute chicken until golden on all sides. Sprinkle with 1 teaspoon salt. Combine orange juice, brown sugar, vinegar, nutmeg and basil; pour over chicken. Place well-scrubbed new potatoes between and around chicken pieces. Cook, covered, over medium heat, 25 minutes, or until chicken and potatoes are tender. Then add peaches; heat, covered, 5 minutes. Serve at once, garnished with parsley.

Mrs. Lille McNatt, D. W. Daniel H. S.
Central, South Carolina

CHICKEN SANTE FE
Number of Servings — 8

⅛ c. salad oil
1 small chicken, cut-up
1 onion
1 c. water
2½ t. salt
½ t. pepper
¼ t. dried whole leaf sage
4 ozs. macaroni
1 lb. kidney beans
1 6-oz. can whole kernel corn
2 cans blue lake beans
1 8-oz. can tomatoes
2 dashes tabasco

In hot salad oil in Dutch oven brown chicken well. Add sliced onions and saute. Then add water, salt, pepper and sage. Cook covered about 2 hours, or until chicken is tender. Meanwhile cook and drain macaroni. When chicken is tender, add kidney beans, corn, beans, tomatoes, macaroni, then tabasco—heat. Serve in rimmed soup plates.

Mary C. Shaw, Kress H. S.
Kress, Texas

SAVORY CHICKEN
Number of Servings — 4

1 3-lb. chicken
¼ c. fat
1 T. chopped onion
1 chopped carrot
1 slice turnip
¼ c. flour
1 c. boiling water
1½ c. strained tomatoes
Salt, pepper and paprika
Salt pork fat
1 c. button mushrooms
2 T. chopped olives

Saute chopped onions, carrots, and turnip in melted fat to make a savory sauce. Add flour gradually, boiling water and strained cooked tomatoes. Season with salt, pepper and paprika. Cut up chicken, dredge in flour and saute in salt pork fat. Remove to a saucepan, cover with savory sauce and cook until tender. When done, add mushrooms, and chopped olives. Arrange the chicken on a platter; cover with savory sauce and garnish with hot spiced fruit and stuffed olives.

Videllia M. O'Neal, Goodridge H. S.
Goodridge, Minnesota

PINEAPPLE CHICKEN
Number of Servings — 4

2 T. oil
1½ c. boned raw chicken
1 large green pepper, cut in 1-in. pieces
½ c. mushrooms, sliced
1 c. celery, sliced ¼-in. thick
1 t. sugar
½ t. monosodium glutamate

1½ c. hot chicken broth or stock
2 T. soy sauce
1⅓ c. drained pineapple chunks
¼ c. syrup, drained from pineapple

Pre-heat oil in pan. Saute chicken over moderately high heat about 5 minutes till tender, but not brown. Saute next 3 ingredients with chicken, stirring till hot (about 1 minute). Add remaining ingredients, cover and bring to boil quickly. Simmer, covered 5 minutes. Thicken sauce with cornstarch mixed with cold water (about 2 tablespoons each), stirring constantly. Serve immediately with hot rice. Makes 4 servings.

Mattie Mary Green
McLain, Mississippi

CHICKEN AND SCAMPI
Number of Servings — 6

1 3½-4 lb. chicken, cut up
1 T. salt
½ t. pepper
¼ c. butter or margarine
3 small onions, finely chopped
1 clove garlic, minced
3 T. snipped parsley
½ c. port wine
1 8-oz. can tomato sauce
1 t. dried basil
1 lb. cooked shrimp
Little snipped parsley

Rub chicken with salt and pepper. Saute in hot butter until golden brown. Add onions, garlic, snipped parsley, wine, tomato sauce, and basil. Simmer, covered, about 30 minutes or until tender. Add shrimp and cook, uncovered, 3-4 minutes. Pile chicken in serving dish. Top with shrimp and sauce. Sprinkle with remaining parsley.

Mrs. Ann C. Cartzendafner, Bel Air H. S.
Bel Air, Maryland

SAUCE PE QUA
Number of Servings — 6

1 fryer (cut up)
½ c. cooking oil
½ lb. smoked sausage, cut in small pieces
1 large chopped onion
Clove garlic
2 T. flour
½ c. chopped celery
½ chopped green pepper
1 T. prepared mustard
1 can tomato paste
6 or more cans water
Salt and pepper to taste

Brown chicken in cooking oil. Take out and add chopped onion, garlic, celery, and pepper. Fry until slightly brown, then add flour, mustard, tomato paste, water, the chicken and sausage. Season. Let simmer about 1 hour. Serve on rice.

Mrs. C. P. Hooper, Elizabeth H. S.
Elizabeth, Louisiana

211

CHICKEN NEWBURG
Number of Servings — 8, 1-cup servings

6 T. butter
1 medium onion, chopped
½ c. (4-oz. can) sliced mushrooms, drained
3 T. flour
3 c. light cream
1 8-oz. package process cheese
    shredded
4 c. diced chicken or turkey, cooked
¼ c. sherry (optional)

Melt butter in large skillet or blazer pan of chafing dish over low flame. Add onions and mushrooms; saute until onions are tender. Blend in flour. Add light cream and cheese. Cook over low heat or place blazer pan over hot water. Cook, stirring constantly until cheese is melted and mixture thickens slightly. Add chicken or turkey and sherry. Cover and cook until chicken or turkey is thoroughly heated, about 10 minutes. Serve over toasted frozen waffles.

Martha Ann Andrews, Atwater H. S.
Thomaston, Georgia

CHICKEN COMO
Number of Servings — 6

2-3½ lb. cut-up chicken
1 t. salt
⅛ t. pepper
1 t. monosodium glutamate
½ c. flour
¼ c. salad oil
¼ c. chopped onion
1 green pepper, chopped
1 clove garlic, minced
2 c. canned tomatoes
½ t. sugar
1 T. vinegar
1 c. mushrooms

Dip chicken into mixture of salt, pepper, monosodium glutamate and flour. Heat oil in a skillet and brown chicken. Add onions, peppers, garlic, tomatoes, vinegar and sugar. Cover and simmer gently 1 hour. Add mushrooms, simmer 10 minutes longer.

Mrs. Patricia Hartenstein
Florence Township Memorial H. S.
Florence, New Jersey

CHICKEN BURGERS
Number of Servings — 4

2 cans (No. ½ flat) boned chicken
¼ c. chopped parsley
Seasoning to taste
1 can (No. 303) cranberry jelly
2 t. lemon juice

Shred chicken, combine with lemon juice, chopped parsley and seasoning. Shape as for thick hamburger patties. Cut cranberry jelly into 1 inch rings (thick), place burgers on cranberry rings and place under broiler. Brown lightly and serve.

Sue Ann West, Nicholas County H. S.
Carlisle, Kentucky

SMOTHERED CHICKEN

5 lb. fowl
5 small peeled onions
½ c. butter (1 stick)
1 c. sour cream
Salt and pepper to taste
Bean Pot (improves flavor)

Cut fowl in serving pieces, leave breast whole. Place with onion and butter in pot or casserole and cover. Bake in 300°F. oven or in electric bean pot, 3 to 4 hours, or until tender. Add cream and seasoning; heat to serving temperature and serve.

Grace F. Harrison
Connecticut State Dept. of Education
Hartford, Connecticut

CHICKEN SQUARES WITH MUSHROOM SAUCE
(a luncheon delicacy)
Number of Servings — 6-9

3 c. diced cooked chicken or turkey
1 c. cooked rice
2 c. soft bread crumbs
⅓ c. diced celery
¼ c. chopped pimento
4 beaten eggs
2 t. salt
¼ t. poultry seasoning
2 c. chicken broth

Combine chicken, rice, bread crumbs, celery, and pimento. To the beaten eggs, add salt, poultry seasoning, and broth (or use 2 chicken-bouillon cubes dissolved in 2 cups hot water, then cooled); mix thoroughly. Stir into chicken mixture. Bake in greased 9 x 9 x 2 inch baking dish in moderate oven (350°F.) 55 minutes. Cut in squares and serve with Mushroom Sauce. *Mushroom Sauce:* Add ⅓ cup milk to 1 can condensed mushroom soup; heat thoroughly.

Mrs. Ina P. Vance, Jefferson-Morgan Jr.-Sr. H. S.
Jefferson, Pennsylvania

FOWL BALLS
Number of Servings — 6

1 breast of chicken (large)
½ t. salt
1 egg, beaten
¼ c. cracker crumbs (powdered)
1½ c. light cream

Bone and grind the raw fowl meat seven times. Mix ingredients well, make balls by using a teaspoon, cook in concentrated chicken broth for 15 minutes. If used for main dish, serve them with chicken gravy. As appetizers: Roll in grated Parmesan cheese. Pierce with a long handled fork or wooden stick and hold over a flame until cheese is melted. Serve hot.

Hannah Hoff Brown
Supervisor, Home and Family Life Education
Texas Education Agency
Waco, Texas

CHICKEN RICE RING
Number of Servings — 8

Chicken Mixture:

2 c. cooked chicken, cut in pieces
2 eggs, hard cooked and sliced (additional eggs
   may be used for garnish)
4 T. flour
4 T. butter or margarine
2 c. chicken broth
2 small onions, sliced
2 small carrots, sliced
¼ bay leaf
8 peppercorns
2 sprigs parsley
½ c. heavy cream

Combine flour and butter or margarine in top of double boiler. Simmer chicken broth with carrots, onion, bay leaf, peppercorns and parsley, for 10 minutes. Strain and add broth to flour-butter mixture, stirring constantly. Continue cooking until thickened. Stir in heavy cream and cook 5 minutes. Add chicken and sliced eggs and heat thoroughly.

Rice Ring:

½ c. grated cheese
2 c. uncooked rice
4 c. cold water
2 t. salt
Butter or margarine

Cook rice by 14 minute fluff method. When done, stir in grated cheese and pack into greased 8 or 8½ inch ring mold. Bring rice well up to brim of the mold or the ring will break when it is turned out. Put mold into pan of hot water, cover with foil or waxed paper and let stand until serving time. Loosen ring around edges with knife and unmold on hot platter by turning platter over mold and inverting both quickly. Fill center of rice ring with chicken mixture. Garnish with sliced eggs, parsley, and pimentos. Serves 8.

Mrs. Mildred Spanihel
Louise Independent School Dist.
Louise, Texas

SAN MATEO CHICKEN
Number of Servings — 6

1 4-5 pound chicken
1 c. melted margarine
2 c. of bread or cracker crumbs
Savory salt

Cut up chicken into individual frying pieces. Dry pieces thoroughly. Dip pieces of chicken in melted margarine, then roll skin side in crushed crumbs. Place with skin side up in large baking dish (13 x 9 x 3"). Season each piece with savory salt. Cover pan tightly with aluminum foil and bake in 325° oven for two hours. If you wish crust to be crisp—remove foil last 10 minutes of baking time.

Dorothy G. Scothorn, Windom H. S.
Windom, Minnesota

PAN CHICKEN
Number of Servings — 10-12

1 4-lb. chicken
1 c. celery
¼ lb. crackers
2 c. chicken broth
4 egg yolks
¼ t. Tabasco sauce
4 egg whites
Salt and pepper to taste

Cook hen until tender and remove from bone; dice as for salad. Add chopped celery and rolled crackers to chicken. Mix well. Add chicken broth and well beaten egg yolks and Tabasco sauce to chicken mixture. Fold in beaten egg whites. Place in 12 x 8 inch pan. Bake 350°F. for 30 minutes. Cut in squares to serve.

Emma Lou Garst, Natural Bridge H. S.
Natural Bridge Station, Virginia

CHICKEN SQUARES WITH MUSHROOM SAUCE
Number of Servings — 6

3 c. diced chicken
1 c. cooked rice
2 c. soft bread crumbs
⅓ c. diced celery
¼ c. chopped pimento
4 eggs, beaten
2 t. salt
¼ t. poultry seasoning
2 c. chicken broth

Combine first five ingredients. Beat together the last four ingredients and add to first mixture. Pour into 8 inch square pan and bake at 350°F. 1 hour. Top with mushroom sauce. *Mushroom Sauce:* 1 can cream of mushroom soup, ⅔ can milk and 1 (3 oz.) can drained mushrooms. Heat.

Mrs. Adele Logue, Northern Bedford Co. H. S.
Hopewell, Pennsylvania

CHICKEN 'N RICE BAKE
Number of Servings — 6

1 chicken (cut for frying)
1 stick margarine
1 medium onion (chopped)
1 medium bell pepper (green, chopped)
1 c. long grain rice
1½ c. water
½ t. salt
4 chicken bouillon cubes

Salt and pepper chicken. Brown in margarine. Saute onion and pepper in margarine after removing chicken. Crush cubes with fork. Add to onion and pepper. Stir in rice. Add ½ teaspoon salt and 1½ cups water. Place in baking pan. Lay brown chicken on top of rice. Cover with foil. Bake 1½ hours at 250°F.

Mrs. Mary S. Hatcher, Brooks County H. S.
Quitman, Georgia

CHICKEN FRICASSEE
Number of Servings — 6-8

1 ready-to-cook stewing chicken (about 3½ lbs.), cut up (giblets and neck optional)
3 c. water
2 t. salt
1 medium onion
3 peppercorns
Tip of bay leaf
3 c. broth (chicken)
5 T. chicken fat
5 T. flour
1 c. milk
Salt
Pepper
Baking powder biscuits using 2 c. flour or biscuit mix

Place chicken, giblets, and neck, if used, water, 2 teaspoons salt, onion, peppercorns, and bay leaf in kettle. Simmer covered about 3 hours or until thick pieces are fork-tender. Remove chicken from broth. Strain broth. Skim fat from surface of broth and set aside. Measure broth and if necessary, add enough water to make 3 cups liquid. Bring liquid to simmering. Blend 5 tablespoons of the chicken fat, flour, and milk until free of lumps. Pour slowly, stirring constantly, into the simmering liquid. Cook until uniformly thickened, stirring constantly. Cover and simmer about 5 minutes or until flour is thoroughly cooked. Meanwhile, if giblets and neck were cooked with chicken, remove meat from neck and slice giblets. Place chicken, neck and giblet meat in gravy. Heat thoroughly. Season to taste. Serve chicken and gravy with hot baking powder biscuits.

Judith Bosworth, Whitingham H. S.
Whitingham, Vermont

CHICKEN SQUARES
Number of Servings — 6

3 c. cooked chicken, cut into bite sizes
1 c. cooked rice
1½ T. pimento, chopped
1 t. salt
1 T. butter or melted margarine
1½ T. chopped parsley
⅛ t. black pepper
3 eggs, slightly beaten
1 c. Rice Krispies
1½ c. seasoned chicken stock

Combine chicken, rice, parsley and pimento. Stir in salt, pepper, and slightly beaten eggs. Heat chicken stock and add to chicken mixture, stirring constantly. Pour into greased baking dish or pan 8 x 8 inches; mixture should be about 2 inches deep. Mix melted butter and Rice Krispies together and sprinkle over top of dish. Set in pan of hot water and bake at 350°F. for 50 minutes or until set. Cut in squares and serve hot or cold.

Jewell W. Hunter, Hawkins H. S.
Hawkins, Texas

CHICKEN FRICASSEE AND SPAGHETTI
Served with Creole Sauce
Number of Servings — 6

1 large fryer, cut up
5 oz. vermicelli spaghetti
Creole Sauce ingredients:
4 T. shortening
½ c. minced onion
½ c. minced green pepper
½ c. minced parsley
2 6-oz. cans tomato paste
2 t. salt
4 t. vinegar
½ t. Worcestershire sauce
¼ t. oregano

Dip pieces of chicken in flour. Brown quickly in small amount of fat. Finish cooking in pressure cooker. Make creole sauce by frying for 5 minutes in the 4 tablespoons shortening, the minced onion, green pepper and parsley. Stir in the tomato paste, salt, vinegar, Worcestershire sauce and oregano. Simmer 10 minutes. Boil the spaghetti and drain. Serve chicken pieces over the spaghetti with the creole sauce on top.

Mrs. Mildred Beck, Fairhope Sr. H. S.
Fairhope, Alabama

SESAME CHICKEN
Number of Servings 4 or 5 lbs. Chicken

1 egg, beaten
½ c. milk
1 c. flour
1 t. baking powder
2 t. salt
2 t. paprika
¼ t. pepper
⅓ c. ground almonds
3 T. sesame seed
¼ lb. butter, melted

Mix egg and milk. Combine next seven ingredients. Dip cup-up frying-size chicken in egg and milk mixture. Roll in dry ingredients. Place on greased baking sheet. Pour the melted butter over chicken. Bake 1½ hours at 350°.

Patricia Copeland, Saranac H. S.
Saranac, Michigan

CHICKEN IN MUSHROOM-ALMOND SAUCE
Number of Servings — 6

1 chicken (cut up)
1 can cream of mushroom soup
½ c. toasted slivered almonds

Arrange pieces of chicken in large frying pan, meat side up. Salt lightly. Bake in oven at 350°F. for 40 minutes. Mix cream of mushroom soup (undiluted) and slivered almonds. Pour mixture over chicken in pan and return to oven for 20 minutes. (Suggestion: May add small can of diced or whole mushrooms).

Anida Miller, Morris Com. H. S.
Morris, Illinois

CHICKEN DELICIOUS
Number of Servings — 15

Cook 1 chicken (4 or 5 pounds) until tender. Bone and cut into small pieces. There should be about 6 cups of broth when finished cooking. *Dressing:* Use about 7 cups of whole wheat crumbs. Season with butter, pepper and salt. Cook 1 cup of diced celery in a little of the broth for about 10 minutes. Make a dressing of the crumbs, half of the broth, 2 slightly beaten eggs and the celery. *Custard:* Cook 3 cups of broth with 4 tablespoons of flour until thick. Take off fire, beat into mixture 3 eggs. Return to heat and cook till thick. Season with salt and pepper. Allow to cool completely. Put a layer of dressing in pan or casserole. Add a layer of chicken then a layer of custard. Top with more crumbs. This can be prepared a day in advance and refrigerated. Bake 30 minutes before serving. Serves approximately 15. (Crumbs from biscuits, cornbread, or light bread may be used in place of whole wheat crumbs. Sage and onion to taste may be added).

Mrs. Jean White, Bristow H. S.
Bristow, Oklahoma

CHICKEN BALLS
Number of Servings — 5

2 T. butter
3 T. flour
1 c. milk or chicken broth
2 c. cooked chicken, chopped
3 lbs. fat for frying
1 T. parsley, chopped
Salt and pepper to taste
1 egg, beaten
8 slices day old bread

Melt butter; add flour, stir well. Slowly add milk or broth and cook until thickened. Cool and add chopped chicken and seasonings. Chill 3 hours, then shape into 5 balls. Roll in egg, then in bread. To prepare bread, remove crusts, cut bread in 1/4 inch cubes. Chill 3 hours. Fry in hot fat (375°F.). Drain on absorbent paper. Serve hot with mushroom sauce. These freeze wonderfully well. Remove 1 hour before frying.

Lythene W. Lambert
Cherokee County Rural H. S
Columbus, Kansas

JUG CHICKEN

Prepare chicken as you would for frying. Weigh chicken and add 1 teaspoon salt for each pound of meat. Sprinkle lightly with pepper. Place in covered casserole dish that can be used inside oven. Bake for 30 minutes at 350 degrees, then reduce oven temperature to 250 degrees and continue cooking for 1 hour.

Elizabeth Miller, Itawamba Junior Col. and H. S.
Fulton, Mississippi

CHICKEN CROQUETTES
Number of Servings — 12

3 T. butter
1/3 c. flour
1 c. chicken stock
2 1/4 t. salt
1 1/4 t. pepper
2 c. finely diced (or ground) chicken or turkey
1 t. chopped parsley
2 eggs
2 T. milk
2 T. lemon juice (optional)

Mix butter in saucepan over low heat. Stir in flour. Add stock slowly. Add salt and pepper. Cook over low heat (stir) until thick and creamy. Add the chicken and parsley; blend. Remove from heat. Beat one of the eggs. Add to chicken mixture. Cook 1 minute longer. Cool. Shape into croquettes. Combine remaining egg with milk. Roll croquettes in this—then crumbs. Deep fry, 375°F. approximately 2 minutes on each side. Can use leftover ham or turkey to make these, too.

Eleanor Jones Shields, Bloomfield H. S.
Bloomfield, Kentucky

CHICKEN WITH RICE (in foil)
Number of Servings — 4

4 large pieces chicken
4 onion slices
8 T. minute rice
1 can cream of mushroom soup
1/3 c. sweet milk
4 12-in. square pieces aluminum foil

Place one chicken piece on each piece of foil. One slice of onion on each chicken piece. Top onion slice with two tablespoons rice. Dilute can of mushroom soup with milk and spoon 4 tablespoons of mixture over rice. Wrap with a freezer fold. Place on cookie sheet and bake for 1 1/2 to 2 hours at 250°-275°F.

Barbara D. Stralee, Chelsea H. S.
Chelsea, Michigan

CHICKEN LIVER BALLS
Number of Servings — 10

1/4 c. finely chopped onions
2 T. fat
1/2 lb. chicken liver
2 hard cooked eggs

Saute onions until softened (but not brown) in the fat. Drain and reserve onions. Saute the chicken livers in the fat until well done or use livers cooked in chicken broth. Chop livers fine and add the chopped hard cooked eggs. Mix with onions. Season with salt and pepper. Moisten with the fat or chicken broth. Shape into 1 inch balls. Garnish with sprigs of parsley.

Barbara Wallace, Union H. S.
Union, West Virginia

CHICKEN GIZZARDS—ITALIAN STYLE
Number of Servings — 4

1 lb. fresh chicken gizzards
2 T. vegetable oil
1 large onion, finely chopped
2 t. oregano
1 t. ground sage
¼ t. cinnamon
1 clove garlic, finely minced
¼ c. tomato paste
½ t. pepper (black)
1 t. salt

Saute onion in vegetable oil. Add chicken gizzards to browned onions and let simmer for 10 minutes. Add garlic, oregano, cinnamon, sage, salt and pepper, then add enough water to cover gizzards. Cover and let simmer for 1 hour and 15 minutes. Add tomato paste and simmer for an additional 45 minutes. May serve over dumplings or alone.

Dorothy Fochesato, Powers Spalding H. S.
Powers Spalding, Michigan

CAPON EUGENE
Number of Servings — 4

4 capons
4 slices ham
Mushrooms
Seasonings to taste
1 c. cream
3 oz. sherry
Butter to saute in

In melted butter saute capon face (cone) down over low heat. Turn and repeat, about 10 minutes. Remove. Saute mushrooms and ham. Remove. Pour in wine, simmer to reduce to gravy, 5 minutes. Add cream reduce, 5 minutes. Serve capon, cover with sauce, mushrooms and ham.

Florence Tooke, Reed-Custer Twp. H. S.
Braidwood, Illinois

CHICKEN OR TURKEY DRESSING

4 c. packed bread crumbs (biscuit)
1 c. cornbread crumbs
2 eggs
1 c. chopped celery
¼ c. chopped onion
2 T. sugar
1 t. salt
¼ t. pepper
3-4 T. chicken or turkey fat
1-2 c. milk—or enough to mix well

Combine all ingredients. Keep mixture thick enough to retain shape when spooned onto a well-greased baking sheet. Bake in 400°F. oven for 15 to 20 minutes. Serve hot with giblet gravy.

Mrs. Frances J. Benson, North Edgecombe H. S.
Tarboro, North Carolina

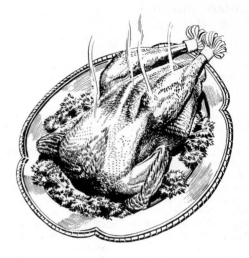

TANGY ROAST TURKEY WITH FRUIT DRESSING
Number of Servings — 10-12

FOWL:

8 to 10 lb. hen turkey
1 medium full ripe grapefruit
1 2 buttons garlic
Salt (to rub turkey)
Melted butter (for greasing turkey)

STUFFING:

4 c. toasted bread cubes
2 c. diced celery
3 T. grated grapefruit peel
½ c. crushed pineapple
½ c. seedless raisins
¼ c. chopped nut meats
⅓ c. melted butter (may be omitted)
Hot water or broth to moisten
1 t. salt

Toss ingredients for stuffing together lightly and set aside. Have bird thoroughly clean and dry. Rub entire bird inside and out with garlic and then salt. Loosely fill bird with stuffing, shaking to fill but do not pack. Tie and fold neck opening, tuck wings, close cavity and tie legs. Grease bird thoroughly and place breast down on a V-rack. Cover with foil. Roast slowly at 325° for about 3½ hours. Turn bird breast-side UP and squeeze ½ of fresh grapefruit over entire bird. Leave uncovered and continue roasting 15 or 20 minutes longer. Squeeze other half of grapefruit over bird and turn up heat to 375° to finish roasting and browning. After squeezing last half of grapefruit over bird, cut the tie that holds the legs together to allow this portion of the bird to completely cook. Finished bird should have a golden brown skin that is crisp and faintly glazed as a result of the grapefruit and butter. Use pan drippings and any remaining grapefruit juice to make gravy.

Barbara A. Jones, Coal City H. S.
Coal City, Illinois

BUTTER BAKED TURKEY AND DRESSING

Stuffing:

3 large loaves of 4 day old bread
½ c. minced onion
½ c. melted butter
1½ c. melted butter
¼ t. pepper
1 t. salt
1½ t. poultry seasoning

Remove crusts from bread and dice to ½ inch in size and toast. Cook minced onion in the ½ cup melted butter until the onion is soft and yellow. Then add the 1½ cups melted butter to the bread along with the cooked onion. Then add the seasonings and toss together. Place the stuffing in a well cleaned, 24 pound bird, and lace. Pat soft butter all over the turkey, with extra amounts on drumsticks, breast, and wings. Place turkey in a shallow roasting pan, breast up; cover with cheese cloth which has been dipped in melted butter. Place in a 300°F. oven. Every 30 minutes brush melted butter onto the cheese cloth. Bake for about 8 to 10 hours. Bird is done when drumstick moves easily up and down, or the meat on the thick part of the leg feels soft when pressed with protected fingers.

Mrs. Mary Louise Sawyer, Smyer H. S.
Smyer, Texas

SOUTHERN TURKEY DRESSING

Number of Servings — 20-25

1 turkey (baked)
12 slices two-day old bread
1 pan cornbread
1 can mushroom soup
3 c. chopped celery
3 c. chopped (white) onion
½ t. sage
Salt and pepper
2 c. liquid from baked turkey
1 doz. eggs
1 c. milk
Salt and pepper

Toast bread lightly. Add baked cornbread (2 cups meal), celery and onions cooked together in one cup turkey fat or butter (¼ pound) until transparent. Cook covered. It takes usually 20 to 30 minutes. Break toasted bread into very small pieces. Mix thoroughly with cornbread. Stir into mixture sage, salt and pepper. Add cooked celery and onions, mushroom soup and liquid from baked turkey. Add giblets. Mix this thoroughly. Add hard cooked eggs cut into small pieces; tossed gently with mixture. When making gravy, add sweet milk and liquid from turkey with several spoonfuls of dressing. Bake the dressing until thoroughly heated. It usually takes 30 minutes at 350°F. The turkey dressing is good for extra meals with left-over turkey.

Alma Keys, Director Home Economics Education
Little Rock, Arkansas

BREAD STUFFING (Turkey)

2 or 3 T. melted fat
1 T. chopped onion
1 c. dry bread crumbs (preferably toasted bread)
1 t. salt
¼ t. pepper
1-2 T. milk or stock
½ t. sage
½ t. chopped celery
½ t. parsley

Melt the fat in the frying pan; add the onion, and saute until tender. Add the bread crumbs and seasonings and mix well. Then add the milk or stock. This makes a loose, light stuffing much preferred by many to the soft moist or compact type.

Uva Seeley, Moore H. S.
Moore, Montana

CHESTNUT DRESSING

For 12 to 16 pound turkey

1½-2 lbs. chestnuts
1 c. butter or margarine
1¾ c. onions
2½ qts. bread crumbs
1 T. salt
½ T. black pepper
2 T. poultry seasoning

Boil chestnuts 20 minutes. Shell and skin them. Chop chestnuts finely. Cook onions in butter, then add other ingredients. Add chestnuts last. Stuff turkey before baking.

Mrs. Mary Davis Faison, Weldon H. S.
Weldon, North Carolina

TURKEY OR CHICKEN CROQUETTES

Number of Servings — 6-8

½ c. milk
½ c. stock
5 T. flour
3 T. fat
½ t. salt
1 or 2 c. finely chopped chicken
1 c. dry bread crumbs
1 egg, slightly beaten
⅛ t. pepper
½ t. parsley

Make very thick sauce of milk, flour, fat, salt, pepper and stock. Fold in chicken and parsley flakes. Cool. Put crumbs in shallow bowl; beat eggs in shallow bowl. Divide cooled mixture into 6 or 8 parts. Shape each into a ball or cylinder. Coat with egg, then with crumbs. Fry in deep, hot fat.

Mrs. Lillian Pursley, Rush Springs H. S.
Rush Springs, Oklahoma

CURRIED TURKEY, SWEET 'N SOUR
Number of Servings — 6

6 scallions, leaving 3 inches of green tops on, chopped
1 clove garlic, minced
½ c. chicken bouillon
1 10-oz. can condensed cream of mushroom soup, undiluted
1 1½-oz. can condensed cream of chicken soup, undiluted
1 to 2 T. curry powder
½ t. ground ginger
⅛ t. monosodium glutamate
⅛ t. black pepper
2 c. leftover or canned turkey or chicken
¼ c. slivered almonds
¼ c. seedless raisins
1 c. pineapple chunks, drained

Place scallions, garlic, and chicken bouillon in electric saucepan. Cover with vent closed. Set temperature control at 200° F. and cook five minutes. Combine all ingredients from mushroom soup thru black pepper in the saucepan and stir until blended. Add remaining ingredients and blend. Cover with vent closed and cook 20 minutes. Serve on chow mein noodles.

Lois Finerty, Chaffey H. S.
Ontario, California

TURKEY ROLLS
Number of Servings — 6-8

2 T. butter or margarine
2 T. flour
1 c. hot milk or chicken broth
2 egg yolks
2 c. diced cooked turkey
1 T. minced parsley
1 T. minced or grated onion
½ t. salt and pepper
Pastry

Melt butter or margarine, add flour, and then add liquid. Cook until thick, and then blend with egg yolks. Add this to turkey with seasonings. Cook over hot water for 10 minutes. Remove from heat and cool, then place in 5 inch pastry squares. Seal squares and bake at 350°F. for 45 minutes. Serve with mushroom sauce. Yield: 6 to 8 servings.

Martha Tate, Stigler H. S.
Stigler, Oklahoma

CREAMED TURKEY
Number of Servings — 6

Melt ¼ cup margarine in saucepan. Blend in ¼ cup flour. Stir in 2 cups milk gradually. Cook, stirring constantly until thick. Add ½ teaspoon salt, dash pepper, ¼ cup pimento (chopped), ¼ cup green peppers (chopped), 1 teaspoon Worcestershire sauce, 2 cups diced turkey, 1 can mushroom soup and 1 tablespoon grated onion. Heat thoroughly. Serve on crisp toast.

Mrs. Sue Jones, Marriott H. S.
St. Stephens Church, Virginia

CALIFORNIA TURKEY SALAD
Number of Servings — 6

2 c. turkey, diced
1 c. celery, cubed
1 c. seedless white grapes (sliced)
1 head lettuce
½ c. mayonnaise
½ t. Accent
1 t. salt or substitute
½ c. toasted almonds

Dice turkey into large cubes, add celery and sliced grapes. Mix in mayonnaise and seasonings. Sprinkle with toasted almonds. Serve on shredded lettuce.

Margaret C. Welks, Highland H. S.
Highland, California

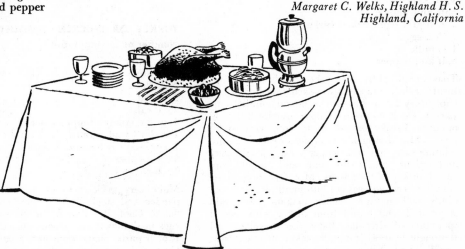

FOR ADDITIONAL POULTRY RECIPES SEE CASSEROLES
SALADS, SANDWICHES AND FOREIGN DISH SECTIONS

Seafoods

Seafoods

BAKED FISH

Any whole fish or fillets suitable for baking
Celery leaves or garden lettuce
Parsley
Lemon juice from half a lemon
⅓ c. butter
Salt and pepper to taste
Seasoning salt

Make a bed of parsley, celery leaves (or garden lettuce) and thinly sliced onion on a double sheet of aluminum foil paper. Place fish for baking on the sheet, sprinkle fish with salt, freshly ground pepper, seasoning salt and lemon juice. Dot with butter. Cover with parsley, celery leaves and sliced onions and fold the foil closed with a "drugstore fold." Bake 30 minutes in oven or over a charcoal fire. Can also be cooked in a campfire.

Beverly Anderson, Rolla H. S.
Rolla, North Dakota

BAKED FISH

Number of Servings — 6

1 c. bread crumbs
1 t. chopped parsley
1 T. chopped pickle
1 t. chopped onion
(Also pimento or salad olives may be added)
1 T. lemon juice
¼ t. salt
⅛ t. pepper
¼ c. melted butter

Mix ingredients. If crumbs seem too dry add hot water or increase butter. Clean and prepare fish for stuffing. Stuff. Sew up. Rub thoroughly with salt and pepper on both sides. Cut gashes in sides about 2 inches apart and fill with thin slices of bacon or salt pork. Lay slices of salt pork on back and head. Put in pan on top of folds of paper toweling or folded cloth. Dredge with flour. Bake 14 minutes to each pound. Baste frequently.

Katherine Schilling, Letcher H. S.
Letcher, South Dakota

BAKED FISH

Number of Servings — 6-8

3 to 5 lb. fish
2 t. salt
1 t. pepper
8 slices salt pork
1 large onion
1 No. 2 can tomatoes
1 No. 2 can water

Dress fish whole. Rub outside and inside with salt and pepper. Place in baking pan. Lay strips of salt pork and slices of onion around and on top of fish. Pour tomatoes and water over fish. Bake covered for one hour at 375°.

Mrs. Bonnie B. Wren, Nicholls H. S.
Nicholls, Georgia

BAKED FISH FILLETS

Number of Servings — 4

1 lb. fish fillets, fresh or frozen
½ can mushroom or cream of tomato soup
¼ c. milk
¼ t. pepper
¼ t. salt
¼ t. onion salt
Extra black pepper
1 T. dried parsley flakes
2 T. butter or margarine

Cut fish into five to six serving pieces. If frozen, let thaw one hour. Arrange in baking dish. Combine soup, milk, salt, pepper and onion salt. Pour mixture around fish. Sprinkle with extra black pepper and parsley flakes. Dot with butter. Bake in moderate oven, 350 degrees, about 20 to 25 minutes, or until fish is fork tender. Serves three to four.

Mrs. Marguerite S. Darnall,
Mt. Empire Unified Jr.-Sr. H. S.
Campo, California

FILLET OF SOLE IN SHERRY WINE

Number of Servings — 4

4 fillet of sole
12 shrimp or prawns cooked and chopped
4 green onions chopped
2 T. butter
2 T. flour
⅓ c. sherry wine

Stuff fillet of sole with chopped shrimp and onions. Make sauce of butter, flour and sherry wine. Pour over top of fillets arranged side by side in greased 8-inch baking dish with cover. Bake at 350°F. 45 minutes. Note: Variety of herbs for fish may be added for additional flavor such as tarragon, oregano, etc.

Mrs. Robert A. Still, Olympia H. S.
Olympia, Washington

BAKED ROCK

Number of Servings — 4

1½ lbs. rock fish
2 c. water
2 strips bacon
1 t. salt
Dash celery salt
3 small potatoes
1 small onion
¼ t. pepper

Place fish, water, salt, pepper, celery salt in a large heavy pan. Slice onion and potatoes and put in water. Cover and bake in a slow oven (300°F.) for 1 hour.

Phyllis Rae Horner, Severna Park H. S.
Severna Park, Maryland

BAKED STUFFED FISH
Number of Servings — 6-8

1 2½-3 lb. red snapper
¼ c. oleo
2 slices bacon
Salt to season
Stuffing:
2 c. cornbread crumbs
2 slices white bread, crumbled
1 whole egg
1 t. salt
1 onion, chopped
½ t. poultry seasoning
Enough hot water to moisten

Have butcher split fish down one side of backbone. Rub cavity with salt. Combine all ingredients for stuffing. Add hot water until it will hold together. Put stuffing inside cavity of fish. Fasten with toothpicks. Pour melted butter or oleo across top of fish. Place bacon on top. Bake at 325°F. for 30 minutes per pound of fish. Serve with tartar sauce.

Ruth D. Jordan, Benjamin Russell H. S.
Alexander City, Alabama

FISHERMAN'S LUCK

½ c. chopped green pepper
½ c. chopped onion
2 T. butter or margarine
1¾ lbs. 1 inch thick frozen halibut
½ c. catsup
½ t. garlic salt
2 small bay leaves

For each person, place one serving halibut in aluminum foil. Sprinkle with salt and pepper. Make sauce by mixing first six ingredients together and simmer 10 to 15 minutes. Pour ¼ of sauce over each serving of fish. Fold over foil so that it is sealed. Cook over glowing coals, or place in shallow pan and bake in extremely hot oven (500°F.) 15 to 20 minutes, or until well done.

Mrs. Marjorie Browning, Pensacola H. S.
Pensacola, Florida

QUICK BAKED FISH

2 large fillets or steaks
1 t. salt
¼ c. milk
1 c. finely crushed corn flakes
2 T. butter, melted
Paprika
Milk

Soak fish in milk for several hours. Pre-heat oven to 500°F. Dip fish in salted milk, then corn flakes. Place on greased baking sheet. Drizzle tops with melted butter. Add dash of paprika. Bake 10 to 15 minutes in 500-550°F. oven, or until fish flakes.

Patricia Meyer, Finley P. S.
Finley, North Dakota

BAKED RED SNAPPER
Number of Servinas — 8

Sauce:
½ c. mayonnaise
½ c. Thousand Island dressing
1 small onion, chopped
3 T. Worcestershire sauce
3 T. lemon juice
3 T. butter, melted

Dressing: about 6 slices bread toasted and soften with milk or water

1 egg, beaten
1 medium onion, grated
½ c. whole kernel corn
¼ c. grated cheese (optional)
1 small tomato, cut up (cubed), or canned tomatoes

Stuff 8 fish, pour sauce over it and bake about 50 minutes at 350°F.

Gayle Scott, Alton H. S.
Alton, Texas

BAKED HADDOCKS
Number of Servings — 4-6

2 lbs. haddock fillet
1 can frozen shrimp soup
½ c. milk
2 T. flour
4 T. butter or margarine
1 t. salt
¼ t. pepper
⅓ to ½ c. soft bread or cracker crumbs

Dust bottom of glass baking dish with flour. Sprinkle with crumbs (use ½). Place fish in serving pieces on crumbs (skin removed). Sprinkle with salt and pepper. Cover with remaining crumbs. Dot each piece of fish with small pieces of butter. Spoon frozen cream shrimp soup over each piece of fish. Rinse can out with milk and pour over all. Bake in 350° oven about one hour or until golden brown. One small can of drained shrimp may be added if desired.

Susan B. Randlett, Molly Stark Jr. H. S.
Bennington, Vermont

BARTER FRIED FISH
Number of Servings — Optional

1 egg
1¼ c. evaporated milk
1 c. flour
2 t. baking powder
¼ t. salt
¼ c. cornmeal

Cut boneless fish in serving pieces, salt and dip in batter made of above ingredients. Fry in deep fat (375°F.) for 5 minutes, or until brown.

Mrs. Shirley Hueftle, Owyhee H. S.
Owyhee, Nevada

FISH — FRIED FLORIDA STYLE

2 small fish
Flour, if desired
½ c. cornmeal
½ t. salt
Dash pepper
Fat (½ to 1 inch)

Clean fish. Scale or remove fins, skin, head and tail. Fillet the fish. (Remove meat from bone). Sift cornmeal with salt and pepper. (If you wish to include flour, do so at this point). Coat each fillet with cornmeal mixture. (The fish should be moist enough for the meal to cling to it. Do not let any excess water from fish or hands drop into hot grease for it will cause the grease to "pop" and "splatter"). The fish is already tender so you need only fry it until the color of the meat is whitish and the color of the coating is golden. Drain on absorbent paper (paper towels). Serve on warmed plates (hold under hot water to heat; dry quickly; serve immediately). Garnish with parsley, lemon wedge or pimento strip.

HUSH PUPPIES

½ c. flour
½ c. cornmeal (white)
1 t. salt
Dash of pepper
1 small onion, chopped
½ c. white corn, drained
1 egg
1 t. baking powder

Sift flour, meal, salt, pepper and baking powder together. Add onion and corn. Combine all ingredients with egg. (If liquid is needed, use juice from corn or milk). Fry in deep fat in which fish has been fried. Serve with seafood.

Mrs. Marolyn K. Whitehead
Miami, Florida

BROOK OR BROWN TROUT

Number of Servings — 4

4 9 inch trout
½ c. flour
1 t. salt
¼ t. pepper
1 T. dried basil leaves or ¾ t. powdered basil
Unsalted butter, oleo, or hydrogenated cooking
    fat

Clean trout, leaving the heads attached. Be sure to remove the black line along the spine. Dry inside and out with a paper towel. Place salt, pepper, and basil in a mortar and grind with a pestle. Mix seasoning with flour on a wax paper. Dredge each fish in the flour mixture, being sure to get the flour mixture inside the fish where seasoning is needed. Place enough fat in the frying pan to make fat ¼ inch deep when melted. Melt fat until it moves in the pan. Add fish to hot fat. Fry over medium heat. Turn when one side is nicely browned (about 5 to 8 minutes). Brown second side. Turn once more to crisp. Fish is done when

meat at the back bone is dry. Serve while hot. If a large quantity of fish must be prepared, the fish can be removed from the pan after the second side is browned and returned to the pan for the crisping just before serving. This recipe makes stocked fish, pond fish, or hatchery raised fish tasty.

Ora Goodrich, Coudersport Area Schools
Coudersport, Pennsylvania

BROILED FROZEN FISH FILLET (Haddock, etc.)

Number of Servings — 4

1 package frozen fish
4 T. Worcestershire sauce
Salt to taste
6 T. butter or margarine
1 lemon
4 T. chili sauce (optional)

Slice frozen fish in half lengthwise. Place on griddle or skillet. Dot with 3 tablespoons of butter. Sprinkle 2 tablespoons Worcestershire sauce and juice of half a lemon. Salt. If desired, sprinkle with 2 tablespoons of chili sauce. Broil about 3 inches below flame for 8 to 10 minutes (until slightly browned). Turn fish and treat second side same as first. Broil 6 to 8 minutes longer. Basting once or twice will prevent undue dryness.

Mrs. Jack Searcy, Lewisville H. S.
Lewisville, Arkansas

CAT FISH STEW

Number of Servings — 4-6

2-3 lb. catfish (fresh dressed)
2 slices bacon (fat back)
1 c. corn
1 c. tomato juice
½ medium onion, chopped

Cover catfish with water, add bacon and cook until done. Remove fish from liquid. Cool. To the liquid add corn, tomato juice and onion. Remove bone from fish. Add flaked fish to liquids. Cook until thick, stirring constantly on low heat. Season to taste.

Mrs. Rodney A. Russell, Johndela Howe H. S.
McCormick, South Carolina

DEVILED CLAMS
Number of Servings — 4-6

2 c. clams
½ c. clam liquor
2 T. minced onion
2 T. minced green pepper and celery leaves
¼ c. chopped celery
4 T. butter or butter substitute
⅛ t. pepper
½ t. prepared mustard
¾ c. cracker crumbs or fine bread crumbs

Chop clams fine and simmer in their own liquor 5 minutes. Cook chopped seasonings, onions, green pepper, celery leaves and celery in melted fat until tender. Mix with remaining ingredients. Combine with clams and mix well. Fill greased scallop shells or custard cups. Bake in moderate (350°F.) oven 20 minutes.

Ruth Adams, Claymont H. S.
Claymont, Delaware

NEW ENGLAND CLAM CHOWDER
Number of Servings — 6

7½ oz. can minced clams or 1 pt. clams, cooked
   and minced
¼ c. chopped bacon or salt pork
¼ c. chopped onion
1 c. liquid drained from clams or liquid and
   water to make 1 cup
1 c. diced potatoes
½ t. salt
Dash pepper
2 c. milk
1 T. chopped parsley

Drain clams and save liquid. Fry bacon or salt pork until lightly browned. Add onion and cook until tender and transparent. Add liquid, potatoes, and seasoning. Cook, covered, over medium heat for 15 minutes or until potatoes are tender. Add milk and clams. Heat, but do not boil. Serve piping hot, sprinkled with parsley.

Mrs. Sarah Plumb, Middlesex H. S.
Middlesex, New Jersey

BARBECUED CLAMS
Number of Servings — 2-4

3 doz. small to medium clams
⅓ c. catsup
¼ lb. very sharp cheese
4 strips lean bacon

Open raw clams. Loosen all parts of clam from shell and keep on half shell. Place in baking pan that has 1½ to 2 inch sides. Pace about ¼ teaspoon catsup on each clam. Next put ½ inch slice cheese and top with ½ inch slice of bacon. Broil until bacon is crisp, about 5 minutes. Serve with crackers and a salad, or may be used as an entree.

Ellen Morgan Schenck, Wilson H. S.
West Lawn, Pennsylvania

IMPERIAL DEVILED CRAB
Number of Servings — 6

1 lb. can crab meat
2 T. green pepper, chopped
2 hard cooked eggs, chopped
¼ c. soft bread crumbs
¼ c. mayonnaise
¼ t. celery seed
¼ c. milk
¼ t. red pepper
1 egg, beaten
¼ t. salt
Juice of ½ lemon
1 t. Worcestershire sauce

Mix all ingredients together. Spread in individual crab "shells" on 9 x 9 inch pan or casserole that has been greased. Spread with dry bread crumbs and pour ¼ cup melted butter over all. Bake at 350°F. for 30 minutes for individuals, 35 to 40 minutes for casserole.

Mrs. Mary G. Moser
Mechanicsburg Area Sr. H. S.
Mechanicsburg, Pennsylvania

MARYLAND CRAB CAKES
Number of Servings — 4-5

1 lb. crab meat
3 slices bread
3 T. mayonnaise
1 t. mustard
1 t. vinegar
1 t. salt
⅛ t. red pepper
1 egg, beaten

Pick over crab meat to remove bits of shells. Break the bread into small pieces. Combine all of the ingredients and mix gently in order not to break up the crab meat. Shape into 6 crab cakes. Brown in butter, using a heavy skillet.

Mary S. Briscoe, Calvert County Jr.-Sr. H. S.
Prince Frederick, Maryland

CRAB COMBO
Number of Servings — 3-4

1 onion, chopped
⅛ t. leaf thyme
2 T. butter
1 can cream of vegetable soup
½ c. milk
½ c. water
½ c. cooked crab meat
¾ c. chopped cooked broccoli

Saute onion and thyme in butter on medium heat until tender. Blend in soup, milk, and water. Add flaked crab and broccoli. Heat on lowest heat (200°F.) until thoroughly warm. Garnish with lemon.

Mrs. Katherine B. Winfree
Port Neches-Jones H. S.
Port Neches, Texas

DEVILED CRABS

1 can Japanese crab meat
2 hard-cooked eggs
2 eggs
3 T. melted butter
¼ c. boiling water
¼ t. salt
⅛ t. prepared mustard
2 T. vinegar
Cayenne pepper to taste

Drain crab meat, remove bones and paper. Hard-cook 2 eggs, chop whites, mash yolks with melted butter, add slightly beaten egg yolks, boiling water, salt, mustard, vinegar, and cayenne. Add crab meat and chopped egg whites to this mixture. Fold in raw egg whites beaten until almost stiff. Place in greased shells or ramekins, cover with bread crumbs. Bake at 350°F. until firm and crumbs are brown.

Frances Bailey, State Dept. of Education
Little Rock, Arkansas

DEVILED CRAB

Number of Servings — 6

1 15-oz. can crab meat
2 hard cooked egg yolks
2 T. melted butter
3 T. vinegar
¼ t. cayenne pepper
¼ t. mustard
Salt to taste

Drain liquor from crab meat. Make a dressing of balance of ingredients. Then stir in the yolk of a well beaten egg, and the beaten egg white. Add the chopped egg whites and ½ cup boiling water. Mix dressing with crab meat. Fill crab shells lightly and bake to a delicate brown. Baste with melted butter while baking.

Mrs. Ruth A. Jennings, Eufaula H. S.
Eufaula, Alabama

DEVILED CRAB DELIGHT

Number of Servings — Approx. 10

1 lb. crab meat
2 T. Worcestershire sauce
½ c. canned milk
½ large green pepper
Salt and pepper to taste
4 T. bacon drippings
1 raw egg, well beaten
4 hard boiled eggs
½ c. mayonnaise
2 T. India relish

Mix all ingredients together. Put in crab shells. Sprinkle top with crushed corn flakes and dot with oleo. Bake in hot oven until brown.

Mrs. Louise H. Motes, Laurens H. S.
Laurens, South Carolina

DEVILED CRABS

Number of Servings — 4-6

¼ t. dry mustard
Salt and pepper
1 t. Worcestershire sauce
½ c. hot water
½ c. soft bread crumbs
1 T. cream
1 T. butter
1 c. crab meat
Buttered crumbs

Combine first 7 ingredients and simmer 5 minutes. Add crab meat. Fill crab shells and cover with buttered crumbs. Bake at 350°F. until brown.

Mrs. Edward Trice, Southampton H. S.
Courtland, Virginia

DEVILED CRAB

Number of Servings — 4-6

2 c. white sauce, seasoned
½ t. Worcestershire sauce
1 T. chopped capers
1 hard cooked egg, chopped
2 c. crab meat
½ c. grated cheese
Paprika

Mix together first 5 ingredients, fill shells and cover with grated cheese. Sprinkle with paprika and bake 20 minutes at 350°F.

Margaret Lopp, Chandler H. S.
Chandler, Arizona

CRAB CAKES

Number of Servings — 6

1 c. crab meat
1 t. mayonnaise
½ c. flour
½ t. salt
1 egg, beaten
¾ t. baking powder

Mix crab meat with mustard, mayonnaise, and egg. Mix separately flour, baking powder and salt. Combine and form patties or drop by spoonful into hot fat.

Mrs. Ann C. Daniels, Escambia H. S.
Pensacola, Florida

CRAB CAKES

Number of Servings — 6

1 lb. crab meat
2 eggs, beaten
1 small onion, cut fine
2 T. prepared mustard
1 T. mayonnaise
1 T. salt
1 c. mashed potatoes

Blend the ingredients and shape into croquettes. Fry in deep fat.

Mrs. Martha B. Godwin, Windsor H. S.
Windsor, Virginia

CRAB PATTIES
Number of Servings — 6

1 lb. crab meat (on ice) or 2 cans
1 c. bread crumbs
½ t. salt
Dash of red pepper
1 T. butter, melted
½ t. dry mustard
1 t. chopped parsley
1 T. lemon juice
2 hard cooked eggs, chopped
1 beaten egg
1 T. flour

Blend. Add ½ cup milk and cook until thick. Add all of the above ingredients. Mix thoroughly. Make into patties. Roll in crumbs. Fry in deep fat until brown or spoon into a buttered casserole, cover with buttered crumbs. Bake at 375°F. until brown.

Mrs. Harriet Knorr, Beaver Twp. Jr. H. S.
Bloomsburg, Pennsylvania

CRAB MEAT SOUFFLE
Number of Servings — 6

3 T. margarine
¼ c. flour
¼ t. salt
⅛ t. white pepper
1 c. milk
3 egg yolks
1 c. cooked crab meat, flaked
1 t. lemon juice
3 egg whites, beaten

Make a white sauce of the margarine, flour, salt, pepper and milk. Set aside to cool and when cool stir in egg yolks. Mix in the crab meat and lemon juice. Fold in the beaten egg whites. Place in ungreased baking dish and bake at 350°F. for 40 minutes or until a knife comes out clean when thrust into the center.

Esther Stufft, Cut Bank H. S.
Cut Bank, Montana

CRAB AND SHRIMP CASSEROLE
Number of Servings — 6

1 c. crab meat
1 c. cooked shrimp
2 cans mushroom soup
1 c. finely sliced celery
½ c. minced onion
⅓ c. chopped green pepper
1 3-oz. can fried noodles
1 c. slightly crushed potato chips
¼ c. slivered almonds

Combine all ingredients except potato chips and place in a greased casserole. Top with the potato chips and bake 30 minutes at 375°F. Serve bubbling hot.

Mrs. Retha George, Biloxi Sr. H. S.
Biloxi, Mississippi

CRAB CAKES
Number of Servings — 6

1 lb. crab meat
½ c. soft bread crumbs
1 egg, beaten
2 T. mayonnaise
2 T. cream
1 T. parsley, chopped
2 T. butter, melted
1 t. Worcestershire sauce
1 t. prepared mustard
Salt and pepper

Combine ingredients, form into cakes and dip in flour. Pan-fry in hot skillet with fat ⅛ inch deep (part butter gives superb flavor), over medium heat until golden brown. Turn and brown other side.

Geraldine M. Glaser, Wicomico Jr. H. S.
Salisbury, Maryland

SOUTHERN CRAB CAKES
Number of Servings — 4

2 c. cooked crab meat, freed of membrane
1½ t. salt
1 t. dry mustard
2 t. Worcestershire sauce
1 egg yolk
1 T. mayonnaise
2 t. minced parsley
Flour
2 T. milk
1 egg, slightly beaten
Finely sifted bread crumbs
Butter

Mix first seven ingredients together. Press mixture into 8 firm cakes. Chill well. Just before serving, dip cakes in flour, then in egg beaten in milk, then in bread crumbs. Melt small amount of butter in frying pan, saute cakes quickly over high heat until golden brown, turning once. Serve on warm platter.

Barbara J. Keithan, Mifflinburg H. S.
Mifflinburg, Pennsylvania

CRABMEAT PINECROFT
Number of Servings — 4-5

1 lb. crabmeat
Salt and pepper
Juice of ½ lemon
2 stalks finely chopped celery
1 t. mustard (prepared)
Dash of Worcestershire sauce
3 t. green pepper, chopped fine
1 t. onion, chopped fine
3 heaping t. mayonnaise
1 to 2 T. milk or cream
3 T. sauterne
1 egg, beaten slightly

Mix crabmeat, seasoned with salt, pepper, lemon juice, celery, onion and pepper. Add mustard,

(Continued on Next Page)

Worcestershire sauce, sauterne, egg to mayonnaise. Lightly toss crabmeat with mayonnaise mixture. Add milk, if needed. Heap into casserole. Top with crushed crackers—dot with butter. Bake in hot oven until bubbly and nicely browned.

Dorothy A. Foster, Mathews H. S.
Mathews, Virginia

CRAB IMPERIAL
Number of Servings — 4

1 lb. lump crab meat
2 pimentos, sliced
¼ c. butter
¾ c. milk
2 T. flour
½ t. Worcestershire sauce
½ t. salt
Pepper to taste

Place butter in saucepan and melt. Add pimentos and flour. Gradually add milk and stir to a boil. Add seasonings and remove from stove. Place with crab meat and gently fold the cream sauce in. Place in crab shells to a high peak. Put in broiler to brown. Bake in oven for 10 to 20 minutes at 350°F. Remove from oven and place crab shells on serving platter.

Mrs. Esther Wasson, Bredgeton H. S.
Bredgeton, New Jersey

CRAB IMPERIAL
Number of Servings — 4

1 lb. crab meat
¼ onion, chopped
¼ green pepper, chopped
1 c. milk
1 T. cornstarch
⅛ t. salt
⅛ t. pepper

Heat milk in double boiler and add cornstarch, stirring constantly. When slightly thickened add finely chopped onion and green pepper. Pour sauce over crabmeat and stir together. Place in baking shells or casserole. Sprinkle cracker crumbs and dot with butter. Bake 35 minutes at 375°.

Mrs. Lucille Glover, North Dorchester H. S.
Hurlock, Maryland

SOUTH CAROLINA DEVILED CRAB
Number of Servings — 4

2 c. fresh crab meat
1 T. flour
1 t. Worcestershire sauce
2 T. butter
Salt and pepper to taste
½ c. milk
2 t. grated onion
¾ c. bread crumbs (toasted)
1 T. chopped green pepper
1 T. chopped pimento
2 t. lemon juice

1 egg yolk
½ t. prepared mustard

Melt butter; stir flour; add milk and cook until it thickens. Add slightly beaten egg yolk and shredded crab meat. Add seasonings. Cook 3 minutes. Stir in onion and lemon juice; also pimento and green pepper. Fill crab shells with mixture. Sprinkle with bread crumbs. Bake at 400°F. for 10 minutes, or until top is brown.

Mrs. Nancy N. Gaston, Rock Hill H. S.
Rock Hill, South Carolina

CRAB MEAT PIE
Number of Servings — 6

1 pt. crab meat
3 eggs, beaten
½ c. butter
½ t. prepared mustard
½ t. Worcestershire sauce
1 t. salt
½ t. pepper
½ c. buttered crumbs
1 c. evaporated milk
½ c. salad dressing
¼ c. minced green pepper
½ c. minced celery
1 T. chopped onion
Dash hot sauce

Combine all ingredients except crumbs. Turn into a deep buttered dish or casserole. Sprinkle with the crumbs, and bake in moderate oven (350°F.) until browned, about 30 minutes.

Adeline Scarborough, Edmunds H. S.
Sumter, South Carolina

CRAB CURRY
Number of Servings — 6

2 medium onions
3 T. butter
3 T. flour
2 T. melted butter
2 c. milk
1 t. curry powder
1 lb. crab
⅛ t. salt
¼ t. black pepper
Dash cayenne pepper

Saute onions and add crab, salt, black pepper and dash of cayenne.
Cream Sauce: Make cream sauce of butter, flour and milk. Add 1 teaspoon curry powder dissolved in 2 tablespoons of water. Mix crab in cream sauce and permit to thicken over a low heat. Serve over cooked rice.

Ruth I. Lamb, Central Kitsap Jr. H. S.
Silverdale, Washington

CRABMEAT MONZA
Number of Servings — 6

1 lb. mushrooms
2 ozs. butter
Meat of 1 crab
2 shallots or green onions
3 T. flour
1 c. table cream
1 t. Worcestershire sauce
¼ c. sherry wine
Salt and pepper
Grated cheese

Cut mushrooms in quarters and simmer in butter. Add chopped onions, blend in flour and seasonings, and add crab and cream. Stir until smooth, and add sherry and Worcestershire. Fill individual shells, sprinkle with grated cheese and paprika, and bake at 350° oven until browned.

Mrs. Mary Guerrant, Liberty H. S.
Pratt, Kansas

CRABMEAT CASSEROLE
Number of Servings — 6

2 c. cooked rice (1 c. minute rice, 1 c. water, ½
    t. salt. Follow cooking directions on box)
1 c. grated cheese
2 T. chopped onion
3 egg yolks, beaten
1 6½-oz. can flaked crabmeat
¼ c. melted butter or margarine
Salt and pepper to taste
1 c. chopped parsley
3 stiffly beaten egg whites
1 can cream of mushroom soup
½ c. milk

Combine all ingredients except egg whites, soup and milk. Fold in beaten whites. Bake in a greased casserole at 350°F. for 30 minutes. Serve with mushroom soup sauce made by mixing ½ cup milk and 1 can soup, heated together.

Agnes K. Boulger
Bradley-Bourbonnais Com. H. S
Bradley, Illinois

CRAB, MOUNT AIRY
Number of Servings — 6

1 lb. crab meat
1 c. medium white sauce
1 egg
1 slice bread, crumbed
2 T. mayonnaise
1 T. chopped parsley
1 T. grated onion
1 T. lemon juice
2 t. Worcestershire sauce
Few drops Tabasco sauce

Pick crab meat over carefully to remove all pieces of shell. Make one cup of medium white sauce (melt 2 tablespoons butter, add 2 tablespoons flour and let bubble, add 1 cup milk and cook slowly until thick). Add to crab along with the

other ingredients. Fill well-greased baking shells or casserole, top with cornflake crumbs and grated cheese. Bake at 400°F. for 20 to 25 minutes.

Mrs. Margaret Martin, Central H. S.
Painter, Virginia

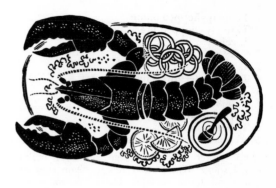

BROILED LOBSTER TAILS
Number of Servings — 4

1 stick butter, melted
2 t. salt
3 t. accent
3 t. garlic salt
3 t. lemon juice

This makes the sauce. Make while lobster tails are boiling. Boil frozen lobster tails in water for 10 minutes. Remove. Take scissors and cut meat loose from shells. Place in pan and baste with above sauce until delicately browned. Have oven 450°.

Mrs. Lettie Stafford Tyner, Covington Co. H. S.
Florala, Alabama

LOBSTER OR SHRIMP BISQUE
Number of Servings — 4-6

2 T. quick cooking Tapioca
1¼ t. salt
⅛ t. pepper
⅛ t. paprika
1 T. minced onion
3 c. milk
1 c. light cream
1 c. (5-6 oz.) lobster or shrimp
    (drained and cut into pieces)
2 T. butter

Combine tapioca, salt, pepper, paprika, onion, milk and cream on top of double boiler. Cook 10-15 minutes over rapidly boiling water, stirring frequently. Add seafood and butter and mix well. Keep over hot water 15-20 minutes to heat thoroughly and blend flavors. Garnish with a thin slice of firm ripe tomato sprinkled with chives or garnish with grated lemon rind.

Edith J. Anderson, Claymont H. S.
Claymon, Delaware

SOUTH AFRICAN DEVILED ROCK LOBSTER
Number of Servings — 6

6 or 7 South African rock lobster tails
¼ lb. butter
6 T. flour
¼ c. cream (half and half)
¾ c. milk
3 T. finely chopped onion
3 T. finely chopped green pepper
2 T. celery
2 t. dry mustard
2 T. catsup
1 T. Worcestershire sauce
1 t. salt
1 t. paprika
1 T. chopped parsley
1 T. lemon juice
½ c. toasted bread crumbs

Drop lobster tails into large kettle of boiling salted water. When water reboils begin counting time; boil for 5 minutes. Drain off water and drench with cold water; cut through undershell with scissors. Remove meat and reserve shells. Flake meat with fork. Melt butter, blend in flour, cream and milk and cook until thickened. Saute onion, pepper and celery in butter. Add this to cream sauce together with mustard, catsup, Worcestershire sauce, salt, paprika and parsley. Add meat. Heat together thoroughly. Fill shells with parsley. Add meat. Heat together thoroughly. Fill shells with mixture, sprinkle tops with bread crumbs. Dot with butter and put under broiler for a few minutes until bread crumbs are a golden brown.

Mrs. Weldon Olson, Cambridge H. S.
Cambridge, Wisconsin

LOBSTER THERMIDOR
Number of Servings — 2

1 2-lb. lobster
4 T. butter
2 T. flour
1 c. cream
Paprika
½ t. salt
½ t. dry mustard
4 T. sherry
1 egg yolk
1 c. fresh mushrooms, quartered
½ c. grated Parmesan cheese

Boil the lobster and split lengthwise. Remove all the meat and cut in 1-inch cubes. Melt 2 tablespoons of the butter in a skillet, add flour, and cook until bubbly, then add cream, salt and mustard; cook until thick; add sherry and egg yolk, stirring thoroughly. Keep warm over hot water. Saute mushrooms in remaining 2 tablespoons of butter and add the lobster meat. Swish around, then add the sherry sauce to it. Sprinkle part of the cheese in the bottom of the lobster shells, add the mixture and sprinkle remaining cheese on top.

Sprinkle with a little paprika and brown in oven at 375° F. You should do these ahead of time and freeze them, then brown when ready to serve.

Mary Ann Worthy, Mexia H. S.
Mexia, Texas

DEVILED LOBSTER
Number of Servings — 6

2 c. diced cooked lobster
1 c. soft bread crumbs
1 hard cooked egg
2 t. lemon juice
1 T. butter
1 T. anchovy paste
1 c. milk
½ t. salt
1 T. flour

Mix lobsters with half the crumbs. Add chopped egg and lemon juice. Melt butter, blend in flour, add milk, and cook until thickened, stirring constantly. Mix well with lobster mixture and fill greased scallop shells. Top with crumbs. Brown in moderate oven (375° F.) about 15 minutes. Crabmeat may be substituted for lobster

Evelyn Hannie, N. P. Moss H. S.
Lafayette, Louisiana

GOLDEN BROILED SALMON STEAKS

Arrange salmon steaks (cut ¾ inch thick) on greased broiler rack. Spread with part of mixture of grated onion, soft butter, lemon juice, salt, and pepper, and a little marjoram. Broil at 375°F. for 10 minutes (2 inches under heat); turn and spread with remaining mixture. Broil until golden brown. Serve hot with parsley.

Hazel B. Pann, Hempfield Sr. H. S.
Landisville, Pennsylvania

SALMON LOAF
Number of Servings — 6-8

1 can salmon
2 eggs, slightly beaten
2 T. chopped onion
2 c. biscuit mix
1½ c. medium white sauce
2 T. lemon juice
1 c. bread crumbs
½ t. salt
10 olives
1 box frozen peas

Put salmon in bowl; remove skin and bones; break into flakes. Add lemon juice, eggs, bread crumbs, onion and salt. Mix thoroughly. Prepare dough from biscuit mix. Roll out to 9 x 12 inches oblong. Press olives into dough, across the 9 inch end. Spread salmon mixture evenly on rest of dough. Roll up like a jelly roll. Bake 50 minutes at 400°F. Serve with peas and white sauce.

Genevieve Williams
Assistant State Supervisor H. E. Education
Bridgeport, West Virginia

SALMON LOAF
Number of Servings — 5-6

1 1-lb. can pink or red salmon
1½ c. bread crumbs
¾ c. chopped celery
2 eggs, beaten
½ c. milk
Fine grain cayenne
½ c. liquid (salmon juice and water)
1 T. lemon juice
½ t. baking powder
1 t. salt

Drain salmon; remove bones and skin, and flake. Grease bread pan. Turn oven to 350°F. Beat 2 eggs; add ½ cup milk and ½ cup liquid. Combine salmon, 1½ cups bread crumbs, 1 tablespoon lemon juice, egg mixture, 1 teaspoon salt, and few grains cayenne. Make into loaf and place in greased pan. Bake in moderate oven (350°F.) for 30 to 40 minutes or until brown and firm. Loosen edges of salmon loaf from pan; invert on warm platter, and garnish with celery tops or parsley. Serve with egg sauce.

Evelyn Wester, Crossville H. S.
Crossville, Alabama

SALMON LOAF

1 lb. can salmon
⅓ c. hot milk
1 c. soft bread crumbs
1 t. minced onion
1 t. lemon juice
½ t. salt (or more)
Dash of cayenne
½ t. nutmeg
1 T. chopped parsley
2 or 3 eggs (separated)

Free salmon from skin and bones; flake; save juice. Combine hot milk and bread crumbs. Add seasonings, salmon juice, and egg yolks. Taste, add more salt if needed. Fold in stiffly beaten egg whites. Pour into greased baking dish. Bake at 350°F. for 45 minutes or until firm in center and delicately browned.

Enid Cobb, Blue Springs H. S.
Blue Springs, Alabama

SALMON LOAF
Number of Servings — 10

1 lb. flaked salmon
1 c. cracker crumbs (18 small)
1 c. sweet cream
3 eggs, well beaten
Salt and pepper to taste

Combine all ingredients; mix only until all cracker crumbs are moistened. Bake in 9 x 5 inch loaf pan for 45 minutes at 350°F.

Grace Abrahamson
Wessington Springs College H. S.
Wessington Springs, South Dakota

CONGEALED SALMON LOAF
Number of Servings — 6

1 envelope gelatin
¼ c. cold water
2 c. pink or red salmon
2 egg yolks
1 t. salt
1 t. prepared mustard
1 t. paprika
1½ T. melted butter
2½ T. lemon juice
¾ c. milk

Mix eggs with salt, mustard, and paprika. Add butter, milk, and lemon juice. Cook slowly until mixture begins to thicken. Remove from heat. Soften gelatin in cold water. Add to hot mixture. Then, add flaked salmon. Turn into mold and chill until firm. Turn onto cold platter and garnish with hard boiled egg slices, lemon wedges, pepper slices or as desired.

Mrs. Mildred Drinkard, Collinsville H. S.
Collinsville, Mississippi

MEAT OR SALMON LOAF

3 c. ground meat or salmon (meat may be cooked or uncooked)
1 or 2 eggs
1 T. chopped parsley
1 slice onion, finely minced
1 c. bread crumbs
1 c. milk
1 t. salt
¼ t. pepper
2 slices bacon, chopped fine, or 2 T. butter

Mix thoroughly; press into a greased bread pan. Bake in moderate oven (350°F.) for 30 to 40 minutes. Serve salmon loaf with 1 cup white sauce No. 2 containing chopped parsley or chopped hard-cooked egg. Serve meat loaf with or without tomato sauce.

Mrs. Margaret T. Rayfield, Weogufka H. S.
Weogufka, Alabama

SALMON CROQUETTES
Number of Servings — 9

1 lb. can pink salmon
1 T. lemon juice
1 egg, beaten
1 c. thick white sauce
1 c. fine bread crumbs

Drain salmon and flake coarsely. Add white sauce and lemon juice and mix thoroughly. Cool and shape into croquettes, roll in beaten egg, then in bread crumbs. Package in moisture-vapor-proof material and freeze. To prepare, take from freezer and let thaw 5 to 10 minutes at room temperature. Cook in deep fat heated to 375°F. until croquettes are golden brown. Serve hot.

Mrs. Joe M. Poston, West Fannin H. S.
Blue Ridge, Georgia

SALMON CROQUETTES

1 can salmon
1 c. white sauce
Black pepper
Salt
1 t. lemon juice
White Sauce:
1 c. milk
4 T. flour
2 T. butter
½ t. salt

Fix white sauce and mix thoroughly with salmon, lemon juice, salt, and pepper. Beat 2 eggs. Roll out cracker crumbs. Roll salmon mixture in cracker crumbs, dip in egg, roll again in cracker crumbs, and fry in deep fat.
White Sauce: Melt butter, add flour, salt and blend well. Warm the milk and stir it into mixture until it is well blended again. Then stir over very low heat for 15 to 20 minutes.

Mary Frances C. Boyd, Stovall H. S.
Stovall, North Carolina

SALMON CROQUETTES

Number of Servings — 7

3 c. salmon
2 c. soft bread crumbs
2 eggs, well beaten
2 T. melted butter
1 T. finely grated onion
1 T. chopped parsley
2 T. baking powder
Salt and pepper to taste

Combine salmon, bread crumbs. Add eggs, seasonings, and butter. Mix thoroughly. Form into small croquettes. Fry in deep fat at 375 to 385°F.

Brenda Swofford, St. Matthews H. S.
St. Matthews, South Carolina

NEW ORLEANS SALMON CHOWDER

Number of Servings — 6

1 lb. can of salmon
1 bouillon cube (or stock)
1 c. boiling water
¾ c. chopped onion
½ c. chopped green pepper
¼ c. melted fat
1 clove garlic
⅓ c. salmon liquid
1 lb. can tomatoes
1 8-oz. can whole kernel corn, or 1 package
    frozen corn
½ t. salt
¼ t. thyme
Dash of black pepper

Drain salmon, preserve liquid. Bread salmon into large pieces. Dissolve bouillon cube in boiling water. Cook onion, green pepper and garlic in butter until tender. Add remaining ingredients and cook for 15 minutes or until vegetables are tender. Serve with warm buttered saltines.

Helen Janis Hale, Somerset H. S.
Somerset, Kentucky

SALMON SOUP

Number of Servings — 6

4 c. milk, scalded
2 c. shredded salmon
Salt and pepper
2 T. butter or butter substitute

Combine salmon, butter or butter substitute, and milk. Season to taste. Heat thoroughly. Stir until well blended. Serve at once.

Elizabeth McClure, Greencastle H. S.
Greencastle, Indiana

SALMON PATTIES

Number of Servings — 6

1 c. or 1 can red salmon
10 soda crackers
2 eggs

Crush crackers with rolling pin. Pour salmon and liquid into bowl. Add 2 eggs and cracker crumbs. Combine and mix well. Make into small patties. Roll in cornmeal. Fry in ¼ inch of hot shortening, but not smoking hot, in a skillet. Turn over when brown. Take up and serve.

Rubena Reeves, Cache H. S.
Cache, Oklahoma

SALMON RECIPE

Number of Servings — 4-6

2 c. flaked salmon
1 T. lemon juice
1 c. medium white sauce
½ c. milk
½ t. salt
1 egg, beaten
½ c. chopped celery
1 c. dry bread crumbs

Add lemon juice to salmon; mix well. Add remaining ingredients and mix. Bake in greased baking dish in moderate oven (350°F.) until brown and set; about 30 minutes.

Mrs. Joe D. Gamble, Ropes H. S.
Ropesville, Texas

SALMON PUFF

Number of Servings — 6

4 eggs, lightly beaten
½ c. milk
1 can cream of mushroom soup
1 can salmon, medium size
2 c. soft bread crumbs
1 T. minced parsley
2 T. butter

Combine eggs, milk and soup. Blend in remaining ingredients and place in buttered casserole. Bake 45 to 50 minutes in a moderately hot oven.

Mildred L. Callahan, Thomas Jefferson H. S.
Miami, Florida

TUNA LOAF WITH TOMATO SAUCE
Number of Servings — 6

Your favorite biscuit recipe
1 6½-, 7-, or 9¼-ounce can tuna, drained and
   flaked
2 boiled eggs, diced
¼ c. chopped green pepper
¼ c. chopped pimiento
½ c. melted butter
¼ c. chopped onion
¼ t. paprika
½ c. grated cheese
Salt and pepper to taste
1 8-oz. can seasoned tomato sauce
1 T. Worcestershire sauce
1 t. lemon juice
1 t. brown sugar

Prepare favorite biscuit recipe and roll into a 12-
inch square, approximately ¼ inch thick. Brush
¼ cup butter on it. Combine tuna, eggs, pepper,
pimiento, onion, cheese, paprika, salt and pepper.
Spread mixture over dough. Carefully roll dough
and place in a 12-inch greased loaf pan. Use
remaining butter to spread over loaf. Bake in a
moderate oven (375°) 30 to 35 minutes, or until
loaf is golden brown and done through and
through. While loaf is baking place tomato sauce,
brown sugar, Worcestershire sauce and lemon
juice in a sauce pan and heat to boiling. Slice loaf
and serve hot with tomato sauce. If preferred,
mushroom or other favorite sauce may be used.

Mrs. Rachel Pearce, Castleberry H. S.
Fort Worth, Texas

TUNA LOAF
Number of Servings — 6

1 large can tuna, flaked
1 can ready-to-serve cream of tomato or
   mushroom soup
2½ c. soft bread crumbs
½ c. milk
¼ c. minced pimiento
3 T. minced parsley
1 t. salt
¼ t. pepper
2 eggs, beaten

Force tuna through food chopper, using small
blade. Combine with soup. Soak crumbs in milk
and add tuna mixture. Pimiento, parsley, seasoning and eggs. Mix thoroughly. Place in greased
loaf pan and bake in moderate oven (350° F.)
30 to 40 minutes.

Judith Carol Hughes, Jefferson Township H. S.
Dayton, Ohio

TUNA LOAF
Number of Servings — 6

2 7-oz. cans tuna fish
2 t. lemon juice
3 slices bread
1 egg

⅛ t. black pepper
¼ c. margarine
½ minced onion
½ c. chopped green pepper
1 tomato, finely chopped
½ t. salt
¼ t. tarragon

Put undrained tuna in a bowl; flake with a fork
and sprinkle with lemon juice. Break bread into
crumbs; add to tuna mixture with egg, and mix
well. Melt butter in a saucepan over low heat;
saute onion, pepper, and tomato until soft and
tender. Add with seasonings to bread and tuna
fish. Blend well. Pack into a greased 9 x 4-inch
loaf pan. Bake in a moderate oven (375°) 40
minutes. Unmold and serve with green peas.

Katherine Harlan, LaGrange Sr. H. S.
Lake Charles, Louisiana

BAKED TUNA RING
Number of Servings — 6

2 7-oz. cans tuna fish, drained and flaked
1 c. oats, uncooked
½ c. cooked peas
2 T. chopped onion
2 T. chopped green pepper
1¼ c. milk
2 T. chopped pimiento
¼ c. slivered almonds
2 t. salt
¼ t. pepper
1 T. Worcestershire sauce
2 eggs, beaten

Heat oven to moderate (350°). Combine all ingredients; place in greased aluminum foil-lined 8-
inch ring mold (5-cup capacity). Bake in pre-
heated oven (350°F.) 50 minutes to 1 hour, or
until set. Invert on platter; fill center with buttered baby lima beans.

Kathleen Burchett, Flatwood H. S.
Jonesville, Virginia

TUNA "N" NOODLES
Number of Servings — 4-6

1 10½- or 11-oz. can condensed mushroom soup
1 c. milk
1 6½- or 7-oz. can tuna, flaked
2 3-oz cans chow mein noodles

Stir milk into soup and heat; add tuna. Pour, piping hot, over crisp noodles. A delicious main dish to make when you get home late for supper.

Mrs. Sarabell S. Dunlap
Northeastern Jr.-Sr. H. S.
Manchester, Pennsylvania

TUNA BALLS (OR CHICKEN)
Number of Servings — 6

2 T. margarine
3 T. flour
1 c. milk
1 can tuna, flaked
1 T. minced parsley
¼ t. salt
Dash of pepper
6 to 8 slices of day-old bread

Melt margarine in saucepan. Add flour and stir until blended. Slowly add milk and stir until very thick. Cool. Add tuna and seasoning and chill 3 or 4 hours. Trim crusts from bread and pull bread apart into small pieces. Dip tuna balls into beaten egg and then roll in bread. Return to refrigerator and let stand for 2 or 3 hours, or make one day and fry the next. Fry in deep fat and serve hot with mushroom sauce. For sauce, add a can of mushrooms to a can of cream of mushroom soup. Heat and pour over tuna balls.

Mrs. Tom Finley, Clayton H. S.
Clayton, Oklahoma

TUNA SOUFFLE
Number of Servings — 4-5

1 T. lemon juice
1 c. flaked tuna
4 T. butter
4 T. flour
½ t. salt
1 c. milk
3 eggs
¼ t. cream of tartar

Sprinkle lemon juice over the tuna. Let mixture set while making white sauce as follows: Melt butter, blend in flour and salt. Remove from heat and stir in milk. Cook over low heat until thick—about 5 minutes. Stir in seafood. Remove from heat and stir in slowly 3 egg yolks, beaten until thick. Beat until frothy 3 egg whites. Add cream of tartar and continue beating until stiff. Fold into seafood. Pour into well greased casserole. Bake in pan of water at 350°F. for 50 minutes. Serve at once.

Marian Wilson, Odessa H. S.
Odessa, Texas

CREAMED TUNA WITH CHEESE ROLLS
Number of Servings — 4

Make 1 cup medium white sauce. Add 1 (7-oz.) can tuna, 1 cup cooked English peas, 2 tablespoons chopped pimiento, ½ teaspoon celery salt. Pour into slightly greased 1-quart casserole. Put into 350 degree oven to heat while preparing rest of ingredients. Mix 1 cup biscuit mix for rolled biscuits (or make 1 cup flour into biscuits) roll into rectangle about ⅜ inch thick. Sprinkle with 1 cup grated cheese and 2 tablespoons chopped, drained pimiento. Roll as jelly roll from wide side. Cut into rolls ¾ inch thick. Place over hot tuna mixture and bake at 350 degrees until biscuits are done. (Note: Cream of mushroom or cream of celery soup with ¼ cup of canned milk added may be substituted for white sauce above.)

Mrs. Francis A Baker, Amarillo H. S.
Amarillo, Texas

TUNA CASHEW CASSEROLE
Number of Servings — 6

1 can chow mein noodles
1 can condensed mushroom soup
½ c. water
1 6-oz. chunk-style tuna (may use chicken)
½ c. broken cashew nuts (salted or unsalted)
1 c. finely diced celery
¼ c. minced onion
Dash of pepper

Reserve ½ cup of noodles. Combine mushroom soup and water, add remaining noodles and rest of ingredients. (If unsalted nuts are used add a little salt). Turn into 1½-quart casserole, sprinkle top with reserved noodles. Bake uncovered in an oven that has been preheated, at 325°, for 25-30 minutes.

Mrs. Irene Robotham, Bellaire Public School
Bellaire, Michigan

TUNA FISH CASSEROLE
Number of Servings — 6

1 can flaked tuna fish
1 can mushroom soup
1 soup can of cold milk
1 (25c) bag potato chips
2 hard cooked sliced eggs
8 stuffed sliced olives (optional)
¼ lb. grated American cheese

Butter the casserole dish lightly. Put a layer of potato chips in the casserole, then the tuna fish, eggs and olives. Alternate all ingredients, then pour soup and milk on the tuna mixture. Cover the top with crushed potato chips and then grated cheese. Bake at 350° F. for thirty minutes covered then remove cover for fifteen minutes and let it brown.

Carolyn Robinson, East Jr. H. S.
Gulfport, Mississippi

TUNA FISH FONDUE
Number of Servings — 5

2 c. toasted bread cubes
1 7-oz. can flaked tuna
¾ c. grated American cheese
3 eggs, beaten
1 c. milk
½ t. chopped onion
¾ t. salt
Dash of paprika

Alternate layers of toasted bread cubes, tuna, and cheese in a greased 1½-quart casserole. Combine eggs, milk, onion, salt and paprika; pour over bread mixture. Bake in 350° F. oven for 45 minutes. Makes 5 servings.

Mrs. Opal Pockrus, Collinsville H. S.
Collinsville, Texas

CURRIED TUNA FISH
Number of Servings — 4

1 onion, sliced
1 6½-oz. can tuna
1 can cream of mushroom soup
1 or 2 t. curry powder
Salt and pepper to taste

Saute sliced onion in melted butter. Add contents of cans of tuna and mushroom soup. Add curry powder, salt and pepper. Heat thoroughly and serve over rice or toast.

Mrs. Elizabeth R. Whisnant, Cool Springs H. S.
Forest City, North Carolina

TUNA PIE
Number of Servings — 4-5

1¼ c. diced potatoes
¼ c. diced celery
1 T. chopped onion
¾ c. frozen or canned peas
1 7-oz. can (1 cup) flaked tuna
¾ t. salt
⅛ t. pepper
1 T. flour

Cook potatoes, celery, and onion in small amount of salt water until tender. Drain. Reserve ½ cup liquor. Combine vegetables and tuna. Pour into greased 1-quart casserole. Add seasonings. Gradually add vegetable liquor to flour; blend. Pour over tuna and vegetables. Arrange Pin-Wheel Cheese Biscuits on top. Bake in hot oven (400°) 20 minutes. Pin-Wheel Cheese Biscuits: Sift 1 cup enriched flour with ¼ teaspoon salt and 2 teaspoons baking powder; cut in 1½ to 2 tablespoons shortening. Add ⅓ cup milk; mix just until flour is moistened. Turn onto lightly floured surface; knead ½ minute. Roll ¼ inch thick. Sprinkle with ¼ cup grated American cheese. Roll as for jelly roll. Cut ½-inch slices.

Margaret Daugherty, Chestnut-Ridge H. S.
Fishertown, Pennsylvania

TUNA FISH PIE WITH CHEESE ROLL CRUST
Number of Servings — 6

½ c. bell pepper, chopped
¼ c. chopped onion
3 T. butter
6 T. flour
3 c. milk
½ t. salt
1 T. lemon juice
1 c. tuna fish, family size

Melt butter, add pepper and onion. Cook until soft. Add flour and stir until well blended. Add salt. Add milk slowly, stirring constantly until thick. Boil 2 minutes. Add remaining ingredients. Pour into baking dish and cover with cheese rolls.

CHEESE ROLLS

1½ c. flour
3 t. baking powder
½ t. salt
Few grains cayenne
3 T. shortening
½ c. milk
¾ c. grated cheese
2 pimientoes, chopped

Make as biscuits. Sprinkle with cheese and pimento. Roll like jelly roll. Slice and place on pie. Cook in 425° oven for 30 minutes.

Nelle H. Woodward, Holt H. S.
Holt, Alabama

TUNA TETRAZZINI
Number of Servings — 5

¼ pkg. (2 oz.) long, thin spaghetti
1 can (6½ oz.) chunk tuna
½ cup undiluted condensed cream of
mushroom soup
¼ c. water
2 T. diced pimento
2 T. chopped green pepper
2 T. chopped onion
Dash of salt
¾ c. grated sharp cheese

Cook and drain spaghetti. Flake tuna with fork. Mix soup with water. Combine all ingredients, except 2 tablespoons of cheese, in a 3-cup casserole. Toss lightly. Sprinkle with cheese. Bake, uncovered, in moderate oven, 350 degrees, 45 minutes.

Mrs. Mary O. Rowe, Gloucester H. S.
Gloucester, Vermont

TUNA TAMALE PIE
Number of Servings — 6

½ c. ripe olives, pitted, whole
⅓ c. chopped onion
2 T. shortening
1 t. garlic salt

(Continued on Next Page)

1 (12 oz.) can whole kernel corn
1 (1 lb.) can tomatoes
1 c. water
¾ c. corn meal
2 cans (7 oz.) tuna fish

Saute onion in shortening until soft. Add garlic salt. Stir in corn, tomatoes, and water. Bring to a boil, lower heat, and simmer 10 minutes. Slowly stir in corn meal and cook, stirring, until mixture is thick. Add olives and tuna. Turn into buttered casserole. Bake at 400 degrees F. for 20 minutes. For variation, turn mixture into a pre-baked pastry shell and bake as above.

Mrs. Kay Oring, Dibble H. S.
Dibble, Oklahoma

TUNA VEGETABLE PIE
Number of Servings — 4

1 9-oz. package pie crust mix
2 10½-oz. cans cream of mushroom soup
1 10-oz. package frozen lima beans or mixed vegetables
1 6½-oz can chunk-style tuna, drained
14 small whole onions, cooked
½ c. milk

Mix the pice crust according to the package directions. Roll out to one-eighth inch thickness on a floured board. Line a shallow eight-inch casserole with pie crust. Mix the remaining ingredients and turn into the lined casserole. Bake in a moderately hot oven (400 degrees) 40 minutes, or until the sauce is bubbly and the crust is browned.

Mrs. Gertrude J. Bennett, Chester H. S.
Chester, Vermont

TUNA ROLL-UPS
Number of Servings — 5-6

2 c. flour
3 t. baking powder
1 t. salt
⅓ c. oil
⅔ c. milk

TUNA FILLING:

1 c. tuna
½ c. minced celery
1 egg, unbeaten

SAUCE:

1 can mushroom soup

Sift flour, baking powder and salt together. Pour liquid over flour mixture all at once. Stir with fork. Form into ball. Knead 10 times. Place between 2 waxed papers. Roll out to 12x12-inch squares. Cut into 9 squares. Spread over each square 2 tablespoons tuna filling. Roll up like jelly roll. Bake 15 minutes. Serve with 1 can mushroom soup thinned with 1 cup milk. Bake on ungreased cookie sheet at 450° F.

Mrs. Lois S. White, Lakeland Joint Schools
Olyphant, Pennsylvania

TUNA STUFFED BAKED POTATO
Number of Servings — about 6

6 medium potatoes
6 T. butter or margarine
Small amount of milk
1 t. salt
⅛ t. pepper
1 can white tuna
1 c. grated American cheese
2 T. onion

Bake potatoes until done at 400° F. (about one hour). Split each potato in half. Remove potato from shell. Add butter, milk and seasonings. Mash until smooth. Add grated onion and tuna. Fill shells again. Sprinkle cheese on top. Return to oven until cheese melts.

Mrs. Martha L. Matthews, Colorado Jr. H. S.
Colorado City, Texas

ROYAL TUNA
Number of Servings — 4

1 c. tuna
1 c. mashed potatoes
2 eggs
salt and pepper

Remove skin and bones from tuna, add eggs and potatoes. Season, mix well. Drop by a tablespoon into hot deep fat. Fry until golden brown. Delicious served with white sauce over it and sliced hard cooked eggs.

Mrs. Bernice W. Moats, Marion Jr. H. S.
Belle Vernon, Pennsylvania

SHRIMP IN BATTER
Number of Servings — 4

1½ c. flour
1 t. baking powder
¼ t. salt
1 egg
1 c. milk
2 lbs. fresh shrimp

Sift together flour, baking powder and salt. Beat egg; add milk. Add to dry ingredients; beat smooth. Dip shrimp singly in batter. Fry in shallow fat or salad oil heated to 375°F. 2 to 3 minutes, or until brown. Drain on absorbent paper. Serve with sauce.

Shrimp Sauce:

1 c. catsup
2 T. lemon juice
½ t. salt
2 T. chili sauce
1 T. Worcestershire sauce
Dash tabasco
2 t. prepared horseradish

Combine catsup, lemon juice, salt, Worcestershire sauce, tabasco, chili sauce, and horseradish; chill.

Elizabeth Stokes, Sulligent H. S.
Sulligent, Alabama

BATTER-FRIED SHRIMP

1½ c. flour
½ c. cornstarch
½ c. white cornmeal
½ t. baking powder
1 t. salt
1 egg, beaten
½ c. whole milk
1½ c. water
2 lbs. raw shrimp

Shell and wash raw shrimp, removing cord. Remove or leave tail as desired. Split down center if you desire a prettier looking shrimp. Mix flour, cornstarch, cornmeal, salt, and baking powder very well. Combine egg, milk, and water and add to flour mixture, mixing quickly and beating with an egg beater until smooth. (If necessary add more water, but I personally prefer a thick batter). Dip shrimp in batter and fry at once in deep hot fat (350°-365°F.) about 2 minutes or until shrimp is pink and coating lightly browned. Don't overload your fryer. The results will be better if you cook fewer shrimp more often for overloading slows the cooking and browning and produces a grease-soaked product. Do not attempt to fry the shrimp too quickly for you do not wish to have a tough product. Keep batter drippings from burning in pan by removing them. This prevents a burned flavor from affecting the delightful flavor of the shrimp. Drain on absorbent paper and serve in warm dish with lemon wedges and tartar sauce.

Mrs. Marolyn K. Whitehead
Miami, Florida

STEWED SHRIMP A LA CREOLE
Number of Servings — 4-6

2 lbs. fresh or frozen shrimp (or 2 cans)
1 large onion, minced
4 T. cooking fat
1 can tomatoes (2 cups)
1½ t. salt
1 t. parsley, finely chopped
1 clove garlic, finely chopped
⅛ t. pepper
Slice lemon
1 t. flour
1 bay leaf
1 sprig thyme
¼ t. celery salt
Dash cayenne

If fresh or frozen shrimp are used, remove shells, wash thoroughly, and drain. Brown onion and flour in hot fat, then shrimp, cooking until pink and slightly brown, stirring constantly. Add tomatoes and remaining ingredients and bring to a boil. Cover. Lower fire and simmer for 20 minutes. Serve with cooked rice.

Lela A. Tomlinson
Director of Home Economics Education
State Department of Education
Baton Rouge, Louisiana

SHRIMP CREOLE
Number of Servings — 6

2 medium onions, sliced
2 celery stalks, diced
1 green pepper, sliced
3 T. bacon drippings
1 T. flour
1 t. salt
1 t. chili powder
2 c. tomatoes
1 c. water
1 T. catsup
1½ c. cooked shrimp

Cook onions, celery, and pepper in hot fat until brown. Stir in flour, salt, chili powder, tomatoes, catsup and water. Cook until slightly thickened, stirring frequently. Add cooked shrimp. Serve over hot rice.

Rebecca Turner, State Dept. of Education
Little Rock, Arkansas

CREOLE SHRIMP GUMBO
Number of Servings — 8

3 T. bacon fat
3 T. flour
1 t. salt
½ t. black pepper
1 T. filet (seasoning)
1 large onion, chopped
2 lbs. shrimp, cleaned
2 qts. water
Cooked rice

Brown the flour in the bacon fat. Brown slowly, stir constantly, brown to a golden brown. Add onion, and stir until onion is brown. Add water. Bring to a boil. Add shrimp and simmer for 30 minutes. Season with salt, pepper, and filet. Serve in bowls with or over rice.

Mrs. Tillie Gandy, Leggett H. S.
Leggett, Texas

SHRIMP CREOLE
Number of Servings — 4-6

¼ c. butter
1 chopped onion
½ c. minced green pepper
1 minced clove garlic
1 t. salt
⅛ t. dried rosemary
⅛ teaspoon paprika
2 c. canned tomatoes
1 lb. cooked, cleaned shrimp
2 to 3 c. hot cooked rice

Melt butter in saucepan. Add onion, green peppers, garlic. Saute 10 minutes, or until tender. Add salt, pepper, rosemary, paprika, tomatoes. Bring to boil; reduce heat and simmer 15 minutes. Add shrimp, heat thoroughly. Serve on hot fluffy rice.

Mrs. Beverly Baker Holcomb, Baker H. S.
Mobile, Alabama

SHRIMP CREOLE
Number of Servings — 6

3-4 lbs. shrimp
5 T. shortening
4 T. flour
1 large onion, chopped
Salt, red and black pepper
¼ c. green pepper, chopped
6 green onions
½ c. celery, chopped
1 small clove garlic, chopped
1 8-oz. can tomato sauce
1 can water
1 T. Worcestershire sauce
1 t. hot sauce

Wash and peel raw shrimp. Remove black vein. Make a roux by heating shortening in a deep skillet. Add flour. Cook on medium heat until dark brown. Stir constantly. Add chopped onions, peppers, celery, garlic. Add tomato sauce and water. Season with salt, pepper and sauces. Let simmer 30 minutes. Bring to boiling point and add shrimp. Cook 20 minutes. Serve over steamed rice.

Mrs. Marlene S. Miller, Fenton H. S.
Fenton, Louisiana

SHRIMP CREOLE
Number of Servings — 4

1 lb. shrimp
2 onions
2 bell peppers
1 pod garlic
4 pieces celery
2 T. cooking fat
1 can tomato sauce
1 t. chili
1 T. La. Red Hot
1 T. Worcestershire sauce
Salt, black and red pepper to taste

Heat fat in large skillet. Add finely chopped onions, bell peppers, celery and garlic. Wilt these ingredients and cook until clear. Add tomato sauce and seasoning. Let simmer for 30 minutes. Add shrimp and cover with tight lid. Cook on low fire about 30-40 minutes or until shrimp is well done. Serve over hot rice.

Mrs. Leavon R. Ladner, Lacassine H. S.
Lacassine, Louisiana

SHRIMP CREOLE
Number of Servings — 6-8

4 T. butter or margarine
1 medium onion, cut fine
1 green pepper, cut fine
4 stalks celery, cut fine
2 T. flour
1 t. salt
⅛ t. pepper
2 small cans tomato sauce
1 T. vinegar
1½ lbs. shrimp, shelled

Peel shell from shrimp. Slit lightly down back, lift out and vein. Wash, sprinkle with salt. Heat fat in broad-bottomed pan. Brown onions, pepper, celery. Blend in flour, salt, pepper. Add tomato sauce and vinegar; cover, simmer 10 minutes. Add shrimp, bring to boil again; cover and simmer 5 minutes. Serve over bed of fluffy rice.

Gayle D. Lee, Forest Hill H. S.
Forest Hill, Louisiana

BOILED SHRIMP
Number of Servings — 8

3 lbs. shrimp
½ c. salt
1 package crab-boil
1 T. black pepper

Enclose crab-boil in some type of loose cloth sack. Add crab-boil, salt, pepper, and shrimp to boiling water. Boil 18 minutes. Let stand in hot water for 15 minutes. Drain and let cool. Serve while still warm or after they have been refrigerated.

Mrs. Dorothy Jean Keller, Cobden Unit H. S.
Cobden, Illinois

BOILED SHRIMP
Number of Servings — 8-10

5 lbs. frozen shrimp (in shell)
½ c. salt
½ sliced lemon
1 small onion, sliced
½ pkg. "Crab-Shrimp boil"

Dip:

1½ c. mayonnaise
(combine with)
1 lb. catsup
1 lb. crackers

Put frozen shrimp in a large pot of boiling water. Add salt, lemon, onion, and "crab shrimp and boil." Cook until tender, about 45 minutes. Serve with dip and crackers.

Christine Moore, Lena H. S.
Lena, Mississippi

SHRIMP ERNIE

1 pt. vegetable oil
1 level t. salt
4 T. catsup
1 t. paprika
1 small pod garlic, chopped fine

Prepare 2 pounds raw jumbo shrimp as for frying (de-vein and remove tails and shells). Marinate 1 or 2 hours in refrigerator in sauce made of above ingredients. Put shrimp on sides in shallow pan; pour over some of the sauce; do not let sauce cover them. Broil under flame until lightly browned on both sides; 3 to 5 minutes on each side at 350°F. or medium flame. Serve on hot plate or frilled toothpicks.

Mrs. J. M. Gay, Baton Rouge Jr. H. S.
Baton Rouge, Louisiana

DE LUXE SHRIMP

8 slices slightly dry bread, trimmed, buttered
   and cubed (5 cups)
2 c. cleaned, cooked, or canned shrimp
⅔ c. (3 ozs.) broiled sliced mushrooms, drained
2 c. milk
3 eggs
½ lb. sharp process cheese, shredded
½ t. salt
½ t. dry mustard
Dash pepper
Dash paprika

Place ½ bread cubes in greased 11 x 7 x 1½ inch baking dish. Add shrimp, mushrooms, and ½ of the cheese. Top with remaining bread and cheese. Beat together eggs and seasonings; add milk and pour over all. Bake at 325°F. for 45 to 50 minutes, or until just set.

Loretta McKnight, Justin F. Kimball H. S.
Dallas, Texas

SHRIMP CHOW MEIN
Number of Servings — 8

2 lbs. raw shrimp
4 T. oil
3 T. soy sauce
2 c. sliced celery
2 c. sliced onions
2 T. Chinese brown sauce
1 medium can water chestnuts cut up
1 can bean sprouts
2 T. corn starch
2 cans fried noodles
Rice

Parboil shrimp 2 minutes in boiling salted water. Drain, clean and cut in pieces. Fry in oil 3 minutes. Add 1 tablespoon soy sauce. Remove from pan. Add to oil remaining in saucepan the onions, celery, soy sauce, liquid from chestnuts and bean sprouts. Moisten corn starch with a little water. Add and stir until slightly thickened. Add shrimp. Serve over rice and sprinkle with fried noodles.

Mrs. George Richardson, Toccoa H. S.
Toccoa, Georgia

THE ROCKY SPREAD SPECIAL
Number of Servings — 4

⅔ c. butter
2 T. Worcestershire sauce
½ t. dry mustard
1 t. paprika
½ c. catsup
¼ c. lemon juice
1 lb. cooked shrimp

Combine first 6 ingredients in mixing bowl. Mix well. Place in a covered skillet and bring to a boil. Add cooked, drained shrimp. Cover with a lid and simmer for 15 minutes.

Mrs. Clara S. Phillips, Moncure H. S.
Moncure, North Carolina

SHRIMP LUNCHEON DISH
Number of Servings — 4

3 T. margarine
1 onion, minced
1 green pepper
1 clove garlic
¼ c. pimento
1 c. rice (3 minute or pre-cooked)
½ c. mushrooms
1½ c. shrimp, diced
1 t. salt
1 bay leaf
2 c. water

Melt butter. Mix all ingredients. Cover. When steaming, turn to low, simmer 30 minutes. Serve with salad.

Mrs. Sue Winston Smith, White Hall H. S.
Pine Bluff, Arkansas

SHRIMP LUNCHEON DISH
Number of Servings — 6

3 T. margarine
1 onion, minced
1 green pepper, minced
1 clove garlic, minced
¼ c. pimento, minced
1 c. rice
½ c. mushrooms
1½ c. shrimp, cleaned
1 t. salt
1 bay leaf
2 c. water

Melt margarine; add onion, green pepper, garlic, pimento, and rice. Add mushrooms and shrimp with the liquids. Add salt, bay leaf, and water. Cover. When steaming, turn to low heat or simmer for 30 minutes.

Joan H. Strople, Escondido H. S.
Escondido, California

SHRIMP REMOULADE

1 c. French dressing
1 c. creole mustard
2 T. paprika
1 t. Worcestershire sauce
1 T. horseradish
Juice of 1 lemon
1 T. grated onion
½ t. celery salt

Clean, boil in seasoned water and peel the required amount of shrimp or use canned ones, if desired. Combine above ingredients in a jar and shake well to blend. Allow them to marinate in this sauce, overnight if need be. This recipe makes quite a bit but it will keep, refrigerated, for weeks.

Mrs. Nina T. Smith, Picayune Mem. H. S.
Picayune, Mississippi

SHRIMP RICE DRESSING
Number of Servings — 10

1½ c. raw rice (cook according to package directions)
2 lbs. shrimp, fresh or canned
1 can whole tomatoes
1 can tomato paste
1 can tomato sauce
Green onion tops, parsley to taste, chopped
1 t. sugar
1 c. chopped onions
1 c. chopped celery
½ c. chopped bell pepper
½ c. cooking oil
Salt, pepper, cayenne

When using fresh shrimp, boil, peel, chop and set aside. Place oil in heavy pot over medium heat. Add onions, celery and bell pepper and cook until onions are wilted. Add tomatoes, tomato paste, and tomato sauce. Season highly with salt, black and red pepper. Add sugar. Cook uncovered about 40 minutes, or until oil separates from tomatoes. Add shrimp and mix well. Cook uncovered another 15 minutes. Add rice, which has been cooked, chopped green onions and parsley. Serve with green combination salad and hot French garlic bread.

JoAnna W. Boyens, Many H. S.
Many, Louisiana

FRIED RICE AND SHRIMP
Number of Servings — 6

3 T. oil
1 t. salt
Dash pepper
2 eggs, beaten
1 lb. raw shrimp, shelled, cleaned and cut in 3 pieces
⅓ c. onion, finely diced
½ c. sliced mushrooms
4 c. cold cooked rice
2 T. soy sauce
½ t. sugar

Place oil, salt, and pepper in a heavy pan. Add eggs and fry until firm. Cut fried egg into small strips. Add shrimp, onions and mushrooms. Cook over moderate heat for 5 minutes, stirring constantly. Add rice, soy sauce and sugar. Cook over moderate heat, stirring constantly until rice is hot.

Mrs. Ruth S. Riale,
Central Columbia County Joint Schools
Bloomsburg, Pennsylvania

HASTY SHRIMP CURRY WITH SAFFRON RICE
Number of Servings — 8

2 T. butter or margarine
2 cans frozen condensed cream of shrimp soup, thawed
2 c. dairy sour cream
4 T. instant minced onion
1 t. curry powder
2 5-oz. cans (2 c.) canned clean shrimp

Place butter and shrimp soup in skillet. Heat at a low temperature and stir until smooth. Stir in sour cream, minced onion, curry powder, and shrimp. Cover and heat, but do not boil. Serve over hot Saffron Rice. Chopped pimento and canned mushrooms add color and texture to the recipe.

SAFFRON RICE

2⅔ c. water
1 t. salt
¼ t. saffron powder (or 15 grains)
2 4⅝-oz. packages or (2⅔ c.) pre-cooked rice

Bring water to boil. Add salt and saffron. Remove utensil from unit and stir rice into water. Let stand 5 minutes. Fluff with fork and serve.

Mrs. Clio S. Reinwald, Dept. of Pub. Instruction
Harrisburg, Pennsylvania

SNACK STYLE SHRIMP
Number of Servings — 8

2½ lbs. shrimp
¼ c. mixed pickling spices
1¼ c. salad oil
2½ t. celery seed
½ c. celery tops
1 pt. sliced onion
¾ c. white vinegar
1½ t. salt
3½ t. salt
7 or 8 bay leaves
2½ T. capers and juice
Dash tabasco sauce

Cover shrimp with boiling water. Add celery tops, pickling spices, and salt. Bring to boil and simmer shrimp 10 to 12 minutes. Drain; cool with cold water. Peel under cold running water. Remove black line. Alternate cleaned shrimp and sliced onions in shallow dish. Add bay leaves. Combine salad oil, vinegar, capers, and juice, celery seed, salt, and tabasco sauce. Mix well; pour over shrimp and onions. Cover and store in refrigerator at least 24 hours for best flavor.

Ms. Variel Garner, Moody H S.
Moody, Texas

SHRIMP CARROT RING
Number of Servings — 6

2 c. diced cooked carrots
½ t. minced onion
1 t. salt
⅛ t. pepper
3 eggs, well beaten
1 c. milk
1 lb. boiled shrimp

Combine ingredients. Pour into a buttered ring mold and bake in a moderate oven (350°F.) 40 minutes. Unmold and fill with seasoned boiled shrimp.

Phyllis A. Hill, Roosevelt Jr. H. S.
Great Bend, Kansas

SURPRISE
Number of Servings — 3-4

2 T. butter
1 medium onion, finely diced
1 can shrimp
1 c. boiled rice
1 c. cream
½ c. catsup
Buttered toast

Melt butter, add onion; cook until soft, but not browned. Add the rice and the shrimp. Mix well. Then add the cream, mixing again. Add catsup. Serve hot on the toast slices. Chopped green pepper may be added. Variation: Use crab meat in place of shrimp.

Fern Soderholm, Willmar Jr. H. S.
Willmar, Minnesota

HOLIDAY SHRIMP
Number of Servings — 12

3 T. butter
1 c. uncooked long-grain rice
1 small garlic, sliced
½ c. minced onion
1 small green pepper
1 t. salt
1 can beef bouillon
½ t. tabasco
3 small cans Pacific tiny shrimp
1 package frozen prawns
1 4-oz. pimento strips (optional)
Pepper to taste

Heat butter, add rice and cook, stirring constantly until rice is golden brown. Add garlic and onion, cook 2 minutes. Add chopped green pepper, salt and pepper. Measure bouillon and add water to make 2 cups. Add this liquid to rice mixture. Simmer until rice is done. Add frozen cooked peas, then shrimp and cook 5 more minutes. Serve hot.

Mrs. Elizabeth Beach, Evergreen H. S.
Vancouver, Washington

SHRIMP LOUISIANA
Number of Servings — 8

1 c. coarsely chopped onions
½ c. butter
2⅔ c. packaged pre-cooked rice
2 to 3 t. salt
4 7-oz. cans shrimp or cook and clean about 2 lbs. raw shrimp
½ c. green pepper strips (about ½-in. long)
3 c. water
4 T. finely chopped parsley

Brown onions in butter in saucepan. Add the rice, salt, and green pepper. Saute 3 minutes, or until lightly browned, stirring constantly. Add shrimp and water; mix lightly with a fork. Cover and simmer 5 minutes. Add parsley. Serve with Worcestershire sauce, if desired.

Margaret E. White, Morrice Area H. S.
Morrice, Michigan

MOLDED SHRIMP IMPERIAL
Number of Servings — 8

1 can tomato soup
1 envelope plain gelatin
2 T. milk
1 package cream cheese
2½ c. cooked shrimp
½ c. chopped celery
½ c. mayonnaise
¼ t. red pepper
¼ c. grated onion
¼ c. sliced stuffed olives
½ t. salt
¼ t. Worcestershire sauce

Dissolve gelatin in ¼ cup cold water. Heat soup and stir in gelatin. Cream cheese with a little milk and stir in soup mixture. Cool and stir in other ingredients. Put into large mold or individual molds and chill until firm.

Mrs. Sara M. Gantt, Wagener H. S.
Wagener, South Carolina

SHRIMP SEA ISLAND
Number of Servings — 12

5 lbs. shrimp, cooked
10 mild, white onions, sliced in thin rings

Into deep, flat pan place a layer of shrimp, then a layer of onion slices, alternating until ingredients are consumed.

Dressing:

1 pt. olive oil or salad oil
¾ pt. good cider vinegar
1 large bottle capers, including juice
Salt, sugar, tabasco and Worcestershire sauce to taste

Mix ingredients thoroughly and pour over shrimp and onions. Cover and place in refrigerator at least 12 hours before serving. To serve, lift out of dressing. Place on large platter and decorate with crisp lettuce leaves or parsley.

Mrs. Sylvia O. Kinder, Briarcliff H. S.
Atlanta, Georgia

MANDARIN SHRIMP
Number of Servings — 4

4 T. cooking oil
1 clove garlic, crushed
½ t. ginger
Salt and pepper
2 lbs. green shrimp (or 2 cans)
¾ c. water
¾ c. catsup
1 T. (heaping) cornstarch
1½ c. rice

Crush clove of garlic in oil and cook gently for 3 to 4 minutes. Remove garlic, add other seasonings and blend. Add shelled, cleaned shrimp to the oil and cook, stirring gently, for 3 minutes. Then add water; cover tightly and cook for 5 min-

(Continued on Next Page)

utes. Add catsup and cook 5 minutes uncovered. (Water and catsup may be added together if canned shrimp are used). Make a paste of the cornstarch and a little water to thicken the juices. Serve over hot rice at once.

Mary P. Sprague, Parksley H. S.
Parksley, Virginia

PAELLA
Number of Servings — 6

½ c. onion, chopped
½ to 1 clove garlic
2 tomatoes
1 to 2 green peppers, chopped
1 package frozen peas
1 package frozen green beans
1 small can pimento
6 pieces chicken, previously broiled
12 large shrimp, previously boiled
1 to 2 c. chopped, cooked picnic ham
1½ c. rice
Olive oil
⅓ package saffron

Use a large cast iron skillet or large electric skillet. Cover the bottom of the skillet with about ⅛ of an inch of olive oil. Add garlic, onions and green pepper, cooking until tender. Add tomatoes, peas and beans allowing a minute between each addition, stirring constantly. Next add to the mixture gradually chicken, ham and shrimp. Then add rice and let cook 5 minutes, before adding 2½ cups of water for every cup of rice. As you add the water turn up heat and let it boil for 5 or 10 minutes. Turn down heat and cook slowly for 30 minutes. Ten minutes before serving add saffron and salt to taste, slice pimentos and decorate Paella. The quantities in this dish can be adjusted to serve a number of people.

Mrs. Helen Borton Parker,
Downington Joint Sr. H. S.
Downington, Pennsylvania

SHRIMP AU GRATIN
Number of Servings — 6

¾ lb. cooked shrimp
3 T. chopped onion
3 T. butter
¼ c. flour
1 c. grated cheese
½ t. salt
¼ t. dry mustard
Dash pepper
1½ c. milk
¼ c. dry bread crumbs

Cut large shrimp in half. Cook onion in butter until tender. Blend in flour and seasoning. Add milk gradually and cook until thick, stirring constantly. Add ¾ cup cheese and heat until melted. Stir in shrimp and pour into individual casseroles. Mix crumbs with butter and remaining cheese. Add to top and bake at 400°F. for 10 minutes.

Kathleen Garrett, Albertville H. S.
Albertville, Alabama

SHRIMP ETOUFFEE
Number of Servings — 6

3 lbs. fresh shrimp
1 c. chopped onion
½ c. chopped celery
¼ t. tomato paste
½ c. margarine
¼ t. cornstarch
½ c. cold water
2 t. salt
¼ t. black pepper
¼ t. red pepper

Shell shrimp and season generously with salt, black and red peppers. Set aside. Melt margarine and add onions, celery and tomato paste. Cook slowly in uncovered heavy pot until onions are wilted. Dissolve cornstarch in water and add to mixture. Add seasoned shrimp and cook over medium heat about 20 minutes. Serve over hot steamed rice.

Mrs. Evelyn B. Fontenot, Church Point H. S.
Church Point, Louisiana

SHRIMP SALAD
Number of Servings — 6-10

5 lbs. shrimp, fresh or frozen
1 doz. eggs, boiled and diced
1 stalk celery, cut in bite size
1 pt. mayonnaise
⅛ lb. blue cheese
¼ lb. butter, melted
1 medium onion, grated
1 head lettuce
1 box crackers

Boil shrimp with favorite seasonings just until it floats. Dress shrimp. Cut in bite size pieces. Season to taste. Add butter. Cut eggs and celery in bite size pieces. Season. Mix gently shrimp, eggs and celery. Add desired amount of mayonnaise to which blue cheese and grated onion have been added. Serve on lettuce in salad plates or in salad bowl. Serve with crackers or your favorite salad accompaniment. (If desired grated cucumbers may be added).

Mrs. Mollie Venn Steger, Montgomery H. S.
Montgomery, Texas

SALASA PICQUANTE
Number of Servings — 8-10

2 lbs. shrimp
1 medium onion
2 garlic buttons
2 celery blades
½ bell pepper
1 can tomato sauce
3 T. shortening
2 T. flour
1 T. salt
¼ t. black pepper
3 c. water
1 small cola

(Continued on Next Page)

1 bottle hot catsup

Chop onions, garlic, celery, and bell pepper. Melt shortening, add flour, stir until light brown. Add chopped onions, garlic, celery, and bell pepper. Stir well. Add tomato sauce, hot catsup and water. Pepper and salt, then add shrimp. Cook 1 hour, turn off heat and add cola.

Mrs. Dorothy Sue T. Hill, Oberlin H. S.
Oberlin, Louisiana

OYSTERS BIENVILLE
Number of Servings — 2

1 doz. oysters on the half shell
1 T. butter
1 bunch shallots, chopped
1 T. flour
½ c. chicken broth
½ c. shrimp, minced
⅓ c. mushrooms, minced
1 egg yolk
⅓ glass white wine
Ice cream salt
Bread crumbs
Grated cheese
Paprika
Preheat oven to 350°F.

Place ice cream salt in pie plate, layer cake pan, or other shallow pan. Place oysters on half shell on salt. Bake until partially done; about 6 to 8 minutes. Meanwhile, prepare sauce by frying shallots in butter until brown. Stir in flour and heat until brown. Add chicken broth, shrimp, and mushrooms. Beat egg yolk with wine and add to sauce, slowly, beating vigorously as you add. Season to taste with salt, pepper, and tabasco, if desired. Simmer for 10 to 15 minutes, stirring constantly. Pour sauce over each oyster; cover with a mixture of bread crumbs, paprika, and grated cheese. Place in oven to brown; about 12 minutes.

Virginia L. Langston, Area Supvr. of Home
Economics, State Dept. of Education
Baton Rouge, Louisiana

DEVILED OYSTERS
Number of Servings — 8

1 pt. oysters
¼ lb. butter or oleo
1 small diced onion
½ c. chopped celery
1 c. cracker crumbs
1 beaten egg
Juice of ½ lemon
Salt and cayenne pepper to taste

Heat oysters until they curl, then chop. Cook celery and onion in melted butter until tender and combine with chopped oysters, cracker crumbs, beaten egg, and seasoning. Put in individual ramekins or casserole. Cover with buttered crumbs and bake until brown.

Ruth Huey, Director Home and Family Life,
State Board of Education
Austin, Texas

BAKED OYSTERS
Number of Servings — 2

½ pt. oysters
Slightly beaten egg
Saltine cracker crumbs
Cracker crumbs
Milk

Drain oysters and save oyster liquior. Dip each oyster in beaten egg and roll in cracker crumbs. Place in layers in baking dish. Pour oyster liquior and milk over oysters about half way. Dot with butter. Bake at 375°F. for about 50 minutes.

Mrs. Margaret Cepelka, Clarke County H. S.
Berryville, Virginia

FRIED OYSTERS

1 pt. oysters
2 eggs, well beaten
1 c. fine cracker crumbs (make by rolling crackers)

Drain oysters on paper towel or cloth. Roll oysters in cracker crumbs, dip into egg and again in cracker crumbs. Place in wire basket and fry in deep hot fat until golden brown and crisp. (Do not overcook).

Mrs. Augusta Peacock, Cleveland H. S.
Merigold, Mississippi

SCALLOPED OYSTERS
Number of Servings — 6

1 pt. oysters
½ c. melted butter
2 c. dry bread crumbs
1 t. salt
¼ t. black pepper
⅓ c. oyster liquor or milk

Mix the crumbs with the salt, pepper and butter; spread ⅓ of them on the bottom of a buttered baking dish; put in ½ of the drained and rinsed oysters, another layer of crumbs and the rest of the oysters; sprinkle crumbs over the top, pour over these the liquid. Bake about 20 minutes in a hot oven (425°F.)

Beulah W. Dowell, Cuba H. S.
Mayfield, Kentucky

SCALLOPED OYSTERS
Number of Servings — 6

1 pt. fresh oysters
¾ c. dry bread crumbs
¾ c. unsalted cracker crumbs
Dash pepper
½ c. butter or margarine, melted
¼ t. Worcestershire sauce
1 c. milk

Drain oysters. Combine crumbs, pepper, and butter. Sprinkle ⅓ of the buttered, seasoned crumbs in a well greased, round baking dish, 8 x 2 inches. Cover with a layer of oysters. Repeat layers. Add

(Continued on Next Page)

Worcestershire sauce to milk; pour over oysters. Sprinkle remaining crumbs over the top. Bake in a hot oven, 400°F. for 20 to 25 minutes, or until brown.

Grace Lunsford, Foley H. S.
Foley, Oklahoma

SCALLOPED OYSTERS
Number of Servings — 4

¾ c. dry bread crumbs
¾ c. cracker crumbs
1 pt. oysters, including liquor
Salt and pepper to taste
2 T. milk
2 T. oil

Oil a shallow baking dish. Mix together the crumbs. Put ½ of this mixture in bottom of dish, cover with a layer of oysters, and repeat once. Season with salt and pepper, pour over it the oyster liquor, the 2 tablespoons milk, and finally 2 tablespoons oil. Bake in 450°F. oven for 30 minutes.

Mrs. Anita H. Reece, Boonville H. S.
Boonville, North Carolina

OYSTER STEW
Number of Servings — 6

1 pt. oysters
4 T. butter
1 qt. milk
1½ t. salt
⅛ t. pepper
Paprika

Melt butter, add drained oysters and cook 3 minutes or until edges curl. Add milk, salt, and pepper and bring almost to boiling point. Serve at once and garnish with paprika.

Mrs. Nina Parker, Bear Grass H. S.
Williamston, North Carolina

OYSTER STEW (WITH MEAT)
Number of Servings — 6

1 qt. oysters
¼ lb. salt pork

Dice salt pork into ⅛ inch cubes and fry. Heat oysters slowly in their own liquor and add the meat and drippings and cook until the oysters are plump and their edges are curled. Add salt and pepper to taste. Serve at once in deep dishes.

Alice I. Jett, Northumberland H. S.
Reedville, Virginia

OYSTER STEW
Number of Servings — 4

1 pt. oysters
1 stick margarine
1 qt. milk
10-12 salted crackers (crushed fine)
½ t. salt
½ t. celery salt

Cook oysters in margarine over low heat until edges of oysters curl. Add salt, celery salt and milk. Heat until milk is hot but does not boil. Add crushed crackers and stir. Serve while hot.

Nell Beasley, Blount Jr. H. S.
Pensacola, Florida

BARBECUED FISH
Number of Servings — 6

1 3-lb. white fish or trout
2 T. chopped onion
1 T. fat
¾ c. tomato catsup
2 T. brown sugar
2 T. cider vinegar
¼ c. lemon juice
2 T. red hot sauce
3 T. Worcestershire sauce
½ t. salt
½ t. pepper

Place fish in greased shallow baking pan. Brown onion lightly in fat; add remaining ingredients and simmer 5 minutes. Pour over fish and bake in hot oven (425°F.) for 30 minutes or until fish is tender. Serve on warm platter. Garnish with parsley and lemon slices.

Mrs. Thelma L. Fowler, South Side School
Counce, Tennessee

SEA-FOOD NEWBURGH

6 shallots, finely minced
1 glassfull sherry wine
Salt and pepper to taste
1 pt. milk
4 oz. butter
1 dash paprika
2 T. flour
1 lb. assorted sea food (crab flakes, lobster, shrimp, and scallops); any kind of fish (white variety only)

Braise shallots in butter; add cooked sea food, paprika and seasoning. Add sherry wine, cover and cook 2 to 3 minutes over low fire, being careful not to burn. Make a sauce by blending flour and butter thoroughly. Add hot milk or if you prefer richer sauce, make with half cream and half milk. Cover and cook 15 minutes. Add sea food to sauce and serve hot.

Mary Joe Whitefield, Lebanon H. S.
Lebanon, Tennessee

COURT BOUILLON (For Poaching Fish) with PIQUANT FISH SAUCE

Number of Servings — 4 halibut steaks or a larger piece of salmon

Piquant Fish Sauce

4 T. tarragon vinegar
1 clove garlic
2 leaves celery
1 bay leaf
1 slice onion
2 T. flour
2 T. butter or margarine
2 eggs, beaten
1 T. butter or margarine
½ t. salt
⅛ t. pepper

Combine first five ingredients. Cook until reduced to about 2 tablespoons; strain. Blend together 2 tablespoons flour and 2 tablespoons butter or margarine. Add gradually 1 cup boiling water. Cook over low heat or in top of double boiler until thick. Add 2 eggs, 1 tablespoon butter or margarine, ½ teaspoon salt and ⅛ teaspoon pepper. Add vinegar mixture. Reheat and serve piping hot over fish.

Court Bouillon

2 qts. water
2 T. salt
½ c. vinegar
1 T. black peppercorns
3 bay leaves
6 cloves
2 sliced carrots
2 sliced onions
4 stalks celery, sliced
2 sprigs parsley

Make enough to cover fish. One quart water will do for 4 halibut steaks. A larger piece of salmon takes 2 quarts. Combine in skillet or kettle the above ingredients. Poach fish in Court Bouillon until just tender. Serve with Piquant Fish Sauce.

Mrs. Barbara S. Peter, Winamac H. S.
Winamac, Indiana

SOLE MARGUERY

Number of Servings — 8

12 strips of sole
½ c. fresh or canned small shrimp
2 eggs
1 can mushroom soup
1 pt. half and half milk
3 drops tabasco

Place sole in butter flat (Pyrex) baking dish. Mix egg, soup, milk, and tabasco together. Pour mixture over sole. Scatter shrimps over sole and mixture. Bake in 450°F. oven for 30 minutes.

Laura Belle Carmany, Carmel H. S.
Carmel, California

FILLET OF FLOUNDER WITH MUSHROOMS (Filetti di Pesce Passara ai Funghi)

Number of Servings — 4-6

4 T. butter
½ lb. sliced mushrooms (canned or fresh)
1 c. milk
2 lbs. fillet of flounder (fresh or frozen)
Salt and pepper to taste
1 T. flour
2 T. grated Parmesan cheese (optional)
½ c. heavy cream
½ lb. white seedless grapes

Saute mushrooms in 3 tablespoons butter for 3-4 minutes, stirring occasionally. Season to taste. Poach fillets in milk, by pouring milk in large skillet; when boiling add fish, salt and pepper to taste, and simmer 5-10 minutes, depending on thickness of fillets. Remove fish. Cream butter and flour and stir into the milk left in skillet. Add cheese and cream and continue stirring until it becomes as thick as medium white sauce. Arrange fish in buttered baking dish in layers with grapes and mushrooms, cover with sauce and bake at 400°F. for 10-12 minutes.

Mrs. Kenneth B. Britt, Tom Bean H. S.
Tom Bean, Texas

SEA-FOOD SAUCE — CRAB AND SHRIMP

Number of Servings — 3

1½ c. medium white sauce
¾ c. grated cheddar or processed cheese
2 hard cooked eggs, sliced
¾ c. green pepper and onion, chopped (boil in small amount of water till soft)
4 t. dry mustard
1 can crab meat
½ t. English mustard
½ lb. shrimp (boiled and deveined)
Cayenne to taste
Garlic salt
2 T. butter
1 T. Parmesan or Romano cheese, grated

Add all ingredients in above order to white sauce. Sprinkle with grated Parmesan cheese. Bake at 350°F. or heat on low flame 15 minutes. This recipe will serve 3 generously. It is easy to double or triple. A heavy cook pot and low heat is the secret to fit preparation.

Lula Lee Smith, Gueydan H. S.
Gueydan, Louisiana

MEAT OR FISH CROQUETTES

Number of Servings — 8

1 c. thick white sauce
1 t. minced onion
1 t. minced parsley
2 c. chopped or coarsely ground cooked meat (roast beef, pork, veal, lamb, chicken or fish)

(Continued on Next Page)

Mix above ingredients together and spread out in a pan; chill thoroughly. Then shape into pyramids or cylinders, and roll them in fine, dry bread crumbs. Let dry 2 to 3 hours. Then dip croquettes in a mixture of 1 egg, slightly beaten, and 2 tablespoons water. Again roll in fine, dry bread crumbs. Dry for about ½ hour. Fry in deep, hot fat (400°F.) until delicately browned (1½ to 2 minutes). Drain on absorbent paper in a warm place. Keep hot in oven until time to serve. Serve hot with any desired hot sauce, such as mushroom, tomato, or mustard.

Mrs. Ina Norris, Albin Consolidated School
Albin, Wyoming

SEA-FOOD CHOWDER
Number of Servings — 4

¼ c. finely cut bacon or salt pork
¼ c. finely cut onion
2 cans (7-oz. each) clams, lobster, or other sea food
2 c. cooked diced potatoes
2 c. milk
1 t. salt
⅛ t. pepper

Cook bacon in large frying pan for 1 to 2 minutes; add onion and cook until golden, stirring 2 or 3 times. Drain sea food in sieve; save the liquid. Add sea food liquid and potatoes to bacon mixture; cook covered until potatoes are thoroughly heated. Mince sea food with a knife and add with milk and seasonings to bacon mixture. Heat slowly to serving temperature.

Mrs. Buena B. Hedden, Hayesville H. S.
Hayesville, North Carolina

SEAFOOD GUMBO
Number of Servings — 8

6 T. bacon drippings
6 T. flour
3 onions, minced
3 cloves garlic, minced
3 t. salt
2 T. tomato paste
6 c. water
1 pt. oysters
1 lb. shrimp
1 can dark crab meat
Pepper
2 t. file (optional)

Make dark roux of bacon drippings and flour, stirring constantly. Wilt onions and garlic in roux,

slowly stir in water, salt and pepper, tomato paste. Add shrimp and cook 30 minutes (simmer); add oysters and crab meat, simmer 5 minutes more. Add file after gumbo is removed from heat. Serve on mounds of hot rice. Garnish with finely minced green onion.

Nell Wall Papizan, Central H. S.

DANISH FISH PUDDING
Number of Servings — 12-15

1½ lbs. fish pulp
4 egg yolks
1 thick slice bread, remove crust
1½ c. milk
¼ lb. butter
3 t. salt
½ t. pepper
1 t. nutmeg
4 egg whites

Use any fish with few bones. Scrape into pulp. Add to pulp, one at a time, eggs. Stir in well. Soak bread in milk and add to mixture. Next add butter, salt, pepper, and nutmeg. Stir well. Fold in egg whites. Pour into a 2 quart mold that has been greased and crumbed and boil 3 hours. Serve with drawn butter, lime juice, and parsley, or with a thick white sauce which has had mushrooms added.

Mrs. Jane W. Duff, Rolesville H. S.
Rolesville, North Carolina

SEA-FOOD CASSEROLE
Number of Servings — 6

1 stick (¼ lb.) oleo
1 onion, chopped
2 c. chopped onion
½ c. flour
2 cans chicken broth
1 pt. sweet milk
1 small can mushrooms
1 can lobster
1 can crab meat
1 lb. raw shrimp
Grated cheese

Melt oleo; add flour to make a smooth paste. Add milk and broth, then all other ingredients. Cook over medium heat, stirring constantly. When it begins to thicken, place in baking dish. Top with cheese and bake 45 minutes in 300°F. oven.

Mrs. Rush Valentine, Starkville H. S.
Starkville, Mississippi

FOR ADDITIONAL SEAFOOD RECIPES SEE CASSEROLES
SALADS, SANDWICHES AND FOREIGN DISH SECTIONS

Wild Game

Wild Game

ROAST COON (DELICIOUS!)

Take one coon, dressed, and skinned the day before, and chilled overnight in the meat compartment of the refrigerator. (The chilling is most important, as the fat has to be removed, and this is possible only when it is very cold). Remove the fat completely. Parboil by simmering gently for 15 minutes or so in water to cover, to which has been added 1 teaspoon soda. Pour away this cooking water. Have ready your favorite stuffing, such as for turkey and skewers or large needle and twine with which to sew up the coon. Stuff the cavity and close well. Place on roasting pan, or roast in tightly sealed aluminum foil as for roast turkey. The time depends upon the size of the animal, 325°F. for open roast, and 450°F. for foil roast. Steam cooking may also be used with a few minutes in the oven at the last for browning. Care must be taken not to let the meat dry out, however.

Mrs. Dorothy F. Bent, Whitcomb H. S.
Bethel, Vermont

SAUTEED DOVES, CARMEL

Number of Servings — 4

6 doves
½ c. butter
2 small onions, minced
2 cloves garlic, minced
½ bay leaf
1 t. peppercorns
1 c. white wine
1 c. water
2 c. heavy cream
½ t. salt
⅛ t. pepper
1 t. chives

Cook butter with onions, garlic, bay leaf and peppercorns 8 minutes, stirring constantly. Saute doves in mixture until well browned. Add wine and water and simmer 30 minutes. Remove doves, strain sauce into casserole and add cream slowly. Add remaining seasonings and dove, cover and heat to boiling point. Serve immediately.

Carolyn Wilson, Abilene H. S.
Abilene, Texas

DOVE IN BLANKET

2 dove breasts for each person. Rub breast with salt and pepper. Wrap with a strip of bacon. Fold each wrapped dove breast in aluminum foil. Place in baking dish. Cook 2 hours in 300° F. oven. Serve hot with steamed wild rice, generously buttered. Garnish with parsley and pickled crab-apples.

Mildred Sanders Williamson, Five Points H. S.
Five Points, Alabama

BROILED DOVE BREASTS

Number of Servings — 4

12-15 doves, depending on size
12-15 bacon strips
Butter

Place cleaned doves, breast side up on broiling pan or in pyrex bowl. Slice breast meat parallel with breast bone once on each side. Insert a slice of butter into each slit; salt and pepper; and use garlic salt, if desired. Wrap each bird with slice of bacon. Broil about 5 inches below heat until done—approximately 20 minutes. You may leave bacon on bird or unwrap it. Bacon and butter help dove meat have a juicier texture and covers up wild taste. Gravy may be made with drippings.

Mrs. Dorothy Pogue, Pawnee H. S.
Pawnee, Texas

ROAST DUCK AND CUMIN RICE

Number of Servings — 6

⅓ c. chopped onion
¼ c. diced green pepper
2 T. bacon drippings
1 c. uncooked rice
2 10½-oz. cans consomme
1 T. Worcestershire
¾ t. salt
¾ t. cumin seed

Rice—In a 3-quart container, on medium heat, saute onions, pepper and rice in bacon drippings until golden brown. Add consomme, Worcestershire, salt and cumin seed. Cover with tight lid, bring to a boil. When steam escapes, turn burner low and cook for 20 minutes.
Duck—Soak ducks in salted water ½ hour. Dry and rub with salt and black pepper. Stuff with onions, carrots, apples and celery. Cook in 400° F. oven.

Nanci Carolyn White, Lepanto H. S.
Lepanto, Arkansas

POTATO DRESSING FOR DUCK

Number of Servings — 6-8

½ c. butter
1 finely chopped onion
2 c. white potatoes, mashed
1½ c. stale bread crumbs
2 t. salt
½ t. black pepper
2 eggs

Combine mashed potatoes, bread crumbs, seasonings and well beaten eggs. Mix thoroughly and fill duck. (Will stuff 2 ducklings or 1 large duck).

Mrs. Mary Elizabeth Watkins, Lily H. S.
Lily, Kentucky

FRIED WILD DUCK
Number of Servings — 6-8

2 or 3 ducks
2 T. cooking oil
½ c. celery (chopped)
½ c. bell pepper (chopped)
1 c. onion
3 cloves garlic

Clean duck well and dry; chop celery, Bell pepper, onion and garlic. Mix well. Make 2 incisions in each side of ducks breast. Bathe ducks inside and out with Louisiana hot sauce. Stuff mixture in incisions and leave in refrigerator overnight. Heat oil in heavy skillet. Put ducks in and cover. Cook at low temperature until they quit steaming (about 30 minutes). Add 2 cups hot water and cook about 2 hours. Thicken gravy. (The ducks are not pepper hot.)

Mrs. Frances Morton, Tallulah H. S.
Tallulah, Louisiana

STEAK 'N GRAVY (ELK)
Number of Servings — 6

1 2½- to 3-lb. elk round steak
1 medium onion
1 bell pepper
1 c. flour
2 t. salt
1 t. pepper
½ c. cooking oil
1 can cream of mushroom soup

Slice onion and bell pepper in rings. Brown lightly in oil. Remove from heat and drain. Mix flour, salt and pepper. Pound into well-trimmed (all fat and connective tissue removed) round steak. Brown on both sides in oil used for pepper and onions. Pour off oil. Place onion and pepper rings on top of steak and spread soup on top of all pieces. Add water to almost cover meat. Simmer for 2 hours adding water as needed to keep meat nearly submerged.

Mrs. Lillian Gibson, Pagosa Springs H. S.
Pagosa Springs, Colorado

WILD GOOSE

1 wild goose
4 slices bacon
2 apples
1 onion
2 celery stalks
Bacon drippings
Salt
Pepper

Rub inside of bird with salt and pepper. Stuff loosely with sliced onions, apples, and celery. Truss bird if large. Brush bacon drippings lightly over entire body. Sprinkle pepper generously over breast and body. Place 3 or 4 bacon strips over the breast. Cover exposed part of bird with aluminum foil. Pour 2 cups of water in roaster. Roast at 300 to 325°F. for 15 minutes per pound until

tender. Baste frequently. Remove foil when ready to brown. Remove stuffing and serve. Allow 1 to 1½ pounds per person.

Mrs. Bill Patrick, Monticello H. S.
Monticello, Kentucky

SAVORY APPLE STUFFING
Number of Servings — Enough for 10-lb. Goose

½ c. salt pork, diced
1 c. celery leaves and stalks, chopped
1 c. onion, chopped
¼ c. parsley, finely chopped
2 qts. tart apples, diced
½ c. brown sugar
1½ t. salt
¼ t. pepper
¼ t. thyme
1¼ t. marjoram
¼ t. sage
1 qt. stale bread crumbs

Fry salt pork in a large heavy skillet until almost crisp; remove from pan. To the pork fat add celery, onion and parsley. Cook over low heat until soft but not browned. Add diced apples, brown sugar and seasonings. Cook over low heat, stirring constantly, about 3 minutes. Add bread crumbs and the fried pork. Stir lightly over low heat about 2 minutes. Makes enough for a 10 pound goose.

Linda Powell, West Fannin H. S.
Blue Ridge, Georgia

LARDED GROUSE

Wash and clean the birds, and if the skin is tough remove it. Since grouse are a dry meat, it is well to lard them before roasting. Cover the entire bird with thin slices of bacon, tying them with a crossing of string if necessary. Place the grouse in a roasting pan in a 350°F. oven for one hour, basting about every ten minutes. Take from the oven, remove the bacon strips and string. Dust with flour, season with salt and pepper, return to the roasting pan and place in a 450°F. oven to brown. Make a gravy, using the liquid in the roaster. Add dry red wine in the proportion of ¼ cup per bird. Cook down, serve as a sauce.

Mrs. Charlie Dalton Bain, Petersburg H. S.
Petersburg, Alaska

GROUSE OR PARTRIDGE
Number of Servings — 4

4 wild grouse or partridge
2 c. sour cream
½ c. flour
Salt and pepper to season
A pinch of marjoram for each bird adds to the
 flavor
4 T. salad oil

Dredge fowl which has been washed and dried with a towel in the ½ cup flour. Brown in salad

(Continued on Next Page)

oil to the desired browness. Season with salt, pepper, and marjoram if desired. Place in a covered baking dish. Add sour cream and bake at 325°F. for one-half hour. Remove cover, bake until tender. Pheasant may be prepared in the same way. Pheasant should be cut in serving size pieces before browning.

Marybelle R. Hickner, Marshall P. S.
Marshall, Minnesota

BAKED PHEASANT WITH BROWN RICE STUFFING
Number of Servings — 4-6

1 lb. brown rice (cook this first, cool slightly,
    drain excess water)
½ c. diced celery
1 medium onion, diced
1 egg, slightly beaten
1 bouillon cube (beef preferably) in ½ c. water
Slivered pheasant giblets (raw)
1 t. sage
2 T. parsley, chopped (fresh preferably)
1 t. salt
Pepper

(Pheasant should have unbroken skin if possible). Cook rice, cool slightly, add rest of stuffing ingredients. Fill body and craw cavities. Pack some in over breast if possible. Excess may be baked alone or packed over body of bird, and bird wrapped in foil to bake. Game tends to be dry and this is always a moist tasty dressing.

Mrs. Dalton Bednarik, Morris H. S.
Morris, Illinois

BARBECUED PHEASANT
Number of Servings — 6-8

2 pheasants (preferably older birds)
Salt and pepper
Flour for coating pheasant
1 medium sized onion, diced
1 T. fat, melted
1 T. brown sugar
1 T. cornstarch
¼ c. tomato catsup
2 T. vinegar
2 T. Worcestershire sauce
½ t. salt
¼ t. pepper
2 c. cooked tomatoes

Cut up birds, coat with seasoned flour, and brown in hot fat. Meanwhile, saute finely chopped onion in the hot fat in a saucepan until limp but not brown. Combine and blend in sugar and cornstarch. Add remaining ingredients gradually, stirring constantly. Cook slowly until sligthy thickened (about 20 minutes), stirring frequently. Pour sauce over browned pheasant; cover and cook in 300°F. oven about 1 hour.

Mrs. Harold Garnick, Ord Public Schools
Ord, Nebraska

SOUTH DAKOTA PHEASANT STEAKETTES
Number of Servings — 4-6

4 pheasants
3 eggs
1 c. flour
Salt and pepper

Clean pheasants and use breasts and thighs. Cut meat of pheasant from bones and chop into steakettes. Roll pheasant steakettes in flour, seasoned with salt and pepper. Dip into egg mixture. Brown on all sides in hot fat for about 30 minutes.

Imogene Van Overschelde
State Supervisor, Homemaking Education
Department of Public Instruction
Pierre, South Dakota

WESTERN PHEASANT CURRY
Number of Servings — 4-6

1 pheasant
½ c. flour
3 T. butter
2 medium-sized onions, chopped
1½ T. curry powder
2 T. flour
3 c. beef broth or bouillon
1 tart apple
2 t. salt

Cut pheasant for frying, roll in flour and brown in hot fat in iron skillet. Take out each piece as it browns, and when all are done, cook onions in same fat. Add curry powder and flour, then the broth and stir until it boils. Put back the pheasant pieces, add the quartered apple and salt. Cover and cook about 1½ hours or till tender.

Mrs. Beverly Witt, Williston Jr. H. S.
Williston, North Dakota

BRAISED PHEASANT WITH MUSHROOMS

1 pheasant, cut in pieces
¼ c. pancake mix
¼ c. butter
1 c. mushrooms
3 T. chopped onion
½ c. stock (may use 1 chicken bouillon cube
    dissolved in ½ c. hot water)
1 T. lemon juice
½ t. salt
½ t. pepper

Dredge cut up pieces of pheasant in pancake mix. Brown pieces in butter until golden brown (approximately 10 minutes). Remove pheasant pieces. In the butter remaining in skillet, saute mushrooms and chopped onion until golden brown. Return meat to skillet, add stock, lemon juice and seasonings. Cover and simmer 1 hour or until tender. Remove cover last 10 to 15 minutes of cooking time to recrisp meat.

Ferne Creamer Floyd, Elkton H. S.
Elkton, South Dakota

BAKED PHEASANT DELUXE
Number of Servings — 6-8

2 pheasants, cut in serving pieces
½ c. flour
1 t. salt
¼ t. pepper
½ c. butter
2 T. onion juice
¼ c. chopped parsley
2 c. thick sour cream

Dredge each piece of pheasant thoroughly in mixture of flour, salt and pepper. Heat butter in a heavy skillet and brown pheasant slowly over medium heat for about 15 minutes. Remove to baking dish. Add onion juice and chopped parsley to sour cream and pour over pheasant. Cover and bake at 325°F. for 1½ hours.

Mrs. D. L. Conner, Hooks H. S.
Hooks, Texas

SOUTH DAKOTA PHEASANT
Number of Servings — 4

1 pheasant cut in desired pieces
Flour
Lawry's seasoned salt
Lawry's seasoned pepper
1 c. sour cream

Roll cut pheasant in flour, seasoned with Lawry's seasoned salt and Lawry's seasoned pepper. Brown in hot fat—butter preferred. Remove to roasting pan—add pan fat. Bake in 250°F. oven about 1 hour. Add 1 cup sour cream and continue baking 1 to 1½ hours in 250°F. oven.

Mrs. Vera Troyer, Bennett County H. S.
Martin, South Dakota

SMOTHERED PHEASANT
Number of Servings — 3-4

½ c. fat
½ c. flour
Salt and pepper
1 c. sliced onion (or 1 medium onion)
1 c. water (milk or light cream can be
   substituted)

Clean bird, cut up, and roll in seasoned flour. Brown pieces slowly in hot fat in electric skillet, turning once. Cover with onion and liquid. Cover tightly and cook at 300°F. until tender (30 minutes to 1 hour depending on age of bird). Make gravy from drippings.

Veleta Vander Zanden, Hillsboro Union H. S.
Hillsboro, Oregon

COUNTRY-STYLE QUAIL

4 to 6 quail
Enough flour to coat
3 T. flour
½ t. salt
Shortening
1 t. salt
½ t. black pepper

Take whole quail, cut down backbone so it will lay flat in skillet. Season with salt and pepper and coat with flour. Put these in skillet of hot fat, enough to cover bottom of skillet good. Brown quail, turning once, then add flour and ½ teaspoon salt. Add water enough to make gravy to half cover birds. Cook until tender to fork prick. Serve hot.

Mrs. Nancy Paul, Aurora H. S.
Aurora, North Carolina

GRILLED QUAIL OR CAILLES GRILLEES BOURGEOISE
Number of Servings — 12

Generous pinch allspice
4 T. minced onion
4 bay leaves
8 peppercorns
1 c. dry white cooking wine
4 T. lemon juice

Clean, open from back, place on wooden board, flatten with broad side of meat cleaver. Salt, pepper to taste. Marinate in marinade prepared from above ingredients, for 2-3 hours. About 20 minutes before serving, roll quail in fine bread crumbs. Broil under flame 20 minutes, place on buttered toast. Serve hot with melted butter, bread sauce, red or white currant jelly.

Mrs. Marguerite Buckley, Lee Jr. H. S.
Roanoke, Virginia

HOT QUAIL PIE
Number of Servings — 4

3 medium size quail, dressed
Salt and pepper
1 small can green peas
1 cup cooked, diced carrots
Small recipe of buttermilk biscuit
3 T. flour
1 small onion
2 T. butter or oleo
Few drops tabasco sauce
1 t. Kitchen Bouquet

Cook quail in about 4 cups water with salt and pepper to taste. Save liquid. Pick all meat from bones and drop in liquid, set aside. Saute onions in oleo until tender, add flour and stir well. To this add the quail pieces and liquid, tabasco sauce and Kitchen Bouquet. Cook over low heat until thick. Add carrots and peas and pour into deep baking dish. Place freshly made biscuit on top and place in oven (375°F.) and bake 20 to 30 minutes. Serve hot.

Genevieve M. Rice, Aransas County H. S.
Rockport, Texas

BRAISED DOMESTIC RABBIT
Number of Servings — 4-6

1 dressed domestic rabbit weighing 2 to 2½ lbs.

Roll moist pieces of rabbit in flour seasoned with

(Continued on Next Page)

salt and pepper. Fry in butter until brown on both sides. Add a little water. Cover and bake in a moderate oven (350°F.) until tender. (Or cook on top of stove in Dutch oven or covered heavy skillet). Will cook in about 1½ to 1¾ hours.

Mrs. Fleta Bruce, Hamburg H. S.
Hamburg, Iowa

RABBIT IN WINE

Cut one rabbit into serving pieces. Brown on all sides in hot oil. Salt and pepper. Add 1 cup red wine, 1 clove garlic, 1 teaspoon chopped parsley and ½ teaspoon rosemary. Cover and simmer until meat is tender, from 45 to 60 minutes.

Mrs. Mildred Christopheno, Baugo Imp. School
Elkhart, Indiana

DOMESTIC RABBIT SALAD
Number of Servings — 4-6

2½ c. diced cooked rabbit
1 c. diced celery
⅓ c. diced sweet pickle
Few grains pepper
2 diced hard cooked eggs
½ c. mayonnaise
2 T. lemon juice
½ t. salt

Rabbit meat may be left over from a previous meal or boil rabbit meat until tender (about 1¼ hours) in water to which ½ teaspoon of salt has been added. (May boil with 2 whole peppers and a bay leaf). Cool meat, then dice. Mix with other ingredients, chill and serve on lettuce or use as a spread for sandwiches.

Mrs. Fleta Bruce, Hamburg H. S.
Hamburg, Iowa

SQUIRREL CHOWDER
Number of Servings — According to the appetites of your guests

2 squirrels
Chicken pieces
1 lb. cubed beef
1 c. celery pieces
1 can corn
2 medium onions
1 can tomato juice
1 can green beans
4 potatoes, cubed
3 carrots, sliced
1 can peas
Seasoning as desired

Combine meats, celery, corn, onions, salt and pepper. Cover with water. Cook until almost tender. Add tomatoes, green beans, potatoes, carrots and peas. Cook until tender. Remove bones and serve to hungry hunters or their appreciate families.

Glenadine Weaver, Robinson H. S.
Robinson, Illinois

SQUABS IN RED WINE
Number of Servings — 2

4 slices bacon
2 squabs (1 lb. or over)
3 T. flour
1 t. salt
¼ t. pepper
1 c. red wine (Burgundy, Claret, but not Port)
½ c. chicken stock
8 small white onions
2 carrots, sliced
2 T. chopped parsley
½ bay leaf
2 squab livers, chopped
¼ lb. mushrooms, sliced

In a skillet, fry bacon till brown and remove and cut into squares, leaving the fat in the skillet. Put bacon squares into a casserole or Pyrex roaster with a top. Sprinkle squabs well with seasoned flour and brown them all over in the bacon fat. Add and blend in any of the flour not used on the squabs. Put squabs in casserole. Add ½ to ¾ of the wine and all the stock to the fat in the skillet in which the squabs have been browned. Bring to a boil, and lower heat to simmering. Stir, being sure to scrape all the drippings from the bottom and sides into the sauce. Cook 5 minutes, stirring constantly, and pour over squabs in the casserole. Add the onions, etc., the remaining wine, and cover. Place in a 325°F. oven. After 30 minutes, add mushrooms, cover and cook another 40 to 45 minutes. Time 2¼ to 2½ hours.

Bernice Q. Campen, Emerson H. S.
Union City, New Jersey

PAN BROILED VENISON
Plain or with PARSLEY BUTTER
Number of Servings — 3-4

1 lb. venison steak
⅛ lb. butter
Salt and pepper

Heat the frying pan, melt the butter, add venison steaks. Broil on one side until nicely browned (approximately 5 minutes). Turn, and brown on the other side for similar time. Venison should be cooked rare, but well browned on surface. Transfer to warm plates or platter and serve *at once*, seasoned with salt and pepper or parsley butter.

PARSLEY BUTTER FOR VENISON STEAKS

½ c. butter
½ t. salt
Dash pepper
½ t. parsley, chopped
1 T. lemon juice

Work butter until creamy, add seasonings and parsley and very slowly work in the lemon juice. Serve over hot venison steaks.

Margaret Thornton, Center Point H. S.
Center Point, Texas

VENISON

4 lbs. venison shoulder
½ c. tomato juice
½ c. red wine
2 T. horseradish
Salt and pepper
Flour and shortening
8 small whole onions
6 medium sliced carrots
6 stalks celery
2 small turnips (halved)
8 peeled potatoes

Roll the shoulder in seasoned flour (salt and pepper to taste) and place it in a hot kettle, browning it on all sides in hot shortening. Add horseradish, tomato juice, and red wine. Cover and cook slowly for 3 hours, adding water to prevent burning. About 45 minutes before end of cooking time, add onions, celery, carrots, potatoes, turnips and salt. Thicken the juice with flour for good gravy.

Kathryn Shea, Superior H. S.
Superior, Wyoming

VENISON ROAST

Number of Servings — 10-12

4 to 5 lb. venison roast
2 lemons
6 slices salt pork, ¼ inch thick
Salt to taste
Black pepper to taste
2 T. Worcestershire sauce
Medium size onion

Remove all fat from venison roast. Season with salt and pepper. Line a roast pan with salt pork that has had excess salt washed off. Place roast in pan. Add the juice of 1 lemon, Worcestershire sauce, chopped onion, and slices of other lemon. Cover and cook slowly until done. Add a small amount of hot water if needed.

Lillian Y. Wynn, Sicily Island H. S.
Sicily Island, Louisiana

ROAST LOIN OF VENISON

Number of Servings — 8

4 lb. loin of venison
1 t. monosodium glutamate or accent
1 t. salt
½ t. pepper
2 T. instant minced onion
4 slices bacon
½ c. beef bouillon
Favorite vegetable salad dressing

If desired, marinate meat over night in salad dressing. Rub in salt, pepper and accent. Sprinkle onion on top of roast. Cover top of roast with bacon slices. Place meat on rack in pan with tight lid. Add bouillon. Cover and roast in 300°F oven for 4 hours, or until tender.

Barbara B. Wise, Converse County H. S.
Douglas, Wyoming

PAN-FRIED VENISON STEAKS

Number of Servings — 4

1 lb. "ham" steaks, ½ inch thick
¼ c. thick cream or evaporated milk
¼ c. flour
3 T. butter or margarine
Salt and pepper to taste

Pound steaks thoroughly with sharp-edged meat pounder. Cut into serving pieces. Dip steaks into cream, dredge in flour. Brown one side in hot butter. Turn. Salt and pepper to taste. Continue browning until second side is well browned. Serve hot.

Mrs. Marjorie Steagall, Scio H. S.
Scio, Oregon

VENISON CHILI

Number of Servings — 8

½ c. beef suet
2 lbs. ground venison
2 cloves garlic, minced
1 t. paprika
2 T. chili powder
1 T. salt
1 T. white pepper
2 T. diced chili pods
1 qt. water

Fry suet in heavy kettle. Add meat and brown. Add seasonings. Add enough water to cover meat. Cook slowly 4 to 5 hours, stirring occasionally. Add remaining water as needed. Serve with pinto beans. Freezes especially well.

Mrs. Fern S. Zimmerman, Clayton H. S.
Cayton, New Mexico

RULLEPOLSE (MEAT ROLL)

Meat (mutton, venison or veal)
2 t. salt
¼ t. (scant) pepper
¼ t. ginger
½ t. thyme
½ t. allspice
Pinch of saltpetre

Remove any bone from meat. Trim meat off the skin. Cut the skin into rectangular shape about 7" x 12". Sew smaller pieces together to form this shape. Cut the meat into strips and lay lengthwise on the skins. Season with the above spices and also use the above amounts for each "Rul" made. Fold over so the edges meet and sew up ends and sides. Wind tightly with strong cord. Place in salt brine until ready for use. Soak out before boiling. Place in boiling water. Pierce meat often with fork the first 15 minutes, so the "Rul" does not burst. Continue boiling slowly until tender. Deer meat takes about 2 hours. After removing from the kettle, cool under heavy weight. Serve thinly sliced for sandwiches or hors d'oeuvres.

Mrs. Charlie Dalton Bain, Petersburg H. S.
Petersburg, Alaska

VENISON POT PIE
Number of Servings — 6

1½ lbs. venison, round or chuck cut in 1 inch
    cubes
2 T. vegetable shortening
2 T. butter
½ c. flour
1 t. salt
Dash of pepper
1 recipe baking powder biscuits
½ c. chopped onion
½ c. diced celery
1 c. diced or sliced carrots

Add salt and pepper to flour and toss meat cubes
in it. Brown in very hot fat. Add ½ cup water and
simmer while preparing biscuits and vegetables.
Make biscuits next and allow to raise on cookie
sheet. Mix vegetables with meat and place in a
large casserole. Add water to pan in which meat
was cooked to loosen brown on pan and make a
gravy.

Olive C. Lambert, Northern Potter Joint H. S.
Ulysses, Pennsylvania

VENISON CUTLETS
Number of Servings — ½ to ¾ lb. per person

Use tender cuts from loin, about ½ to ¾ inch
thick; marinate in oil and grape juice for 1 hour.
Drain, sprinkle with salt and pepper, roll in flour,
dip in slightly beaten egg and roll in dry bread
crumbs. Saute in butter 10 to 12 minutes, turning
frequently. Place meat on hot platter; add ¼ cup
currant jelly to drippings, stir, bring to a boil
and pour over steak.

Mrs. Mary L. Whitt, King William H. S.
King William, Virginia

SWISS VENISON
Number of Servings — 4

4 venison chops or 2 venison rounds
Salt and pepper
Flour
4 T. cooking oil
1 large Bermuda onion
1 can tomatoes
1 can water

Salt, pepper and flour the meat. Brown sides in
cooking oil. Add onion slices, tomatoes and water.
Simmer about 45 minutes. Serve with rice.

Bess Halliday, Galena Park Jr. H. S.
Galena Park, Texas

YUM YUM WILD TURKEY
Number of Servings — 7

1 15-lb. wild turkey
Salt and pepper
1 c. chopped onion
2 c. chopped celery
Bacon fat
1½ c. white wine
1 muslin cloth (about 16" square)

Clean and draw wild turkey. Singe. Wash in warm
water. Dry on outside. Brush with bacon fat. Salt
and pepper. Stuff with onion, celery, and 1 cup
white wine. Truss. Place turkey in shallow pan.
Dip cloth in bacon fat and cover turkey with it.
Roast in slow oven (300°F.) for 3 hours. Baste
several times with drippings in pan and remaining
wine. If turkey varies in size from recipe allow 20
minutes per pound roasting time. Before serving
discard onion and celery stuffing

Mrs. Eileen Blake, T. Jefferson H. S.
El Paso, Texas

FOR ADDITIONAL WILD GAME RECIPES SEE CASSEROLES
SALADS, SANDWICHES AND FOREIGN DISH SECTIONS

Casseroles and Combination Dishes

Beef Casseroles

QUICK SPAGHETTI AND MEAT SAUCE
Number of Servings — 3-4

1 lb. ground beef
½ t. salt
⅛ t. pepper
3 T. shortening
½ c. chopped onion
1 c. chopped celery
½ c. chopped green pepper
4 ozs. fine spaghetti
3 c. canned tomatoes
2 T. Worcestershire sauce
2 t. salt

Mix the ½ teaspoon salt and the pepper with meat. Brown meat in hot fat in a large skillet. Add onion, celery and green pepper. Break uncooked spaghetti into 3 inch pieces and scatter over top of meat and vegetable mixture. Add Worcestershire sauce and the 2 teaspoons salt to the tomatoes and pour over spaghetti. Press spaghetti under liquid. Cover skillet and bring to a boil. Then, turn heat to low to keep mixture simmering. Cook slowly 30 minutes without removing cover.

Mrs. Nolan Crawford, Seven Mile H. S.
Seven Mile, Ohio

BEEF-NOODLE CASSEROLE
Number of Servings — 6

1 lb. ground beef
½ c. chopped onion
2 T. fat
1 can tomato soup
1½ c. water
1 5-oz. package noodles
½ pt. sour cream

Saute ground beef and onions in fat, using a large skillet, until beef is brown. Add soup, water, and noodles. Simmer until noodles are tender (about 30 minutes). Add sour cream and mix well. Garnish with green vegetables and parsley.

Mrs. Pat Baker, Royse City H. S.
Royse City, Texas

SEVEN LAYER CASSEROLE
Number of Servings — 8

One cup uncooked rice, washed and drained; 1 cup whole kernel corn, drained. Sprinkle with salt and pepper. Pour over 1 can tomato sauce and ½ can water; ¼ cup each finely chopped onion and green pepper; ¾ pound uncooked ground beef; sprinkle with salt and pepper. Pour over second can tomato sauce and ¼ can water. Cover meat with 4 strips bacon, cut in half. Set oven at 350°F. Place these ingredients in layers in a 2 quart baking dish with a tight-fitting lid. Bake for 1 hour. Uncover and bake about 30 minutes longer, until bacon is crisped.

Mrs. Gladys McDaniel, Broaddus H. S.
Broaddus, Texas

WEST TEXAS SPAGHETTI
Number of Servings — 4-6

¾ lb. ground beef
1 medium onion, chopped
1 medium green pepper, chopped
2 T. fat
½ lb. spaghetti, cooked
1 small can whole kernel corn
1 can tomato soup
1 small bottle chopped stuffed olives
¼ lb. grated cheese

Brown beef, onion and pepper in fat; mix cooked spaghetti, meat mixture, corn, soup, olives and cheese, reserving a little of the olives and cheese for the top. Pour into baking dish and bake 25 minutes at 350°F. Sprinkle with cheese and olives and serve with a tossed green salad.

Martha J. Moody, Axtell H. S.
Axtell, Texas

MEAT CASSEROLE AND CHOW MEIN NOODLES
Number of Servings — 6

1 lb. ground beef
1 T. margarine
1 t. margarine
3 pieces celery, chopped
1 green pepper, chopped
1 large onion, chopped
1 can cream mushroom soup
½ c. water
1 t. salt
1 can chow mein noodles

Saute ground beef in 1 tablespoon margarine until brown, using medium heat. Remove meat—add 1 teaspoon margarine to fat in skillet; add and cook until light brown celery, green pepper, and onion. Stir in 1 can of mushroom soup, water, salt and meat. Pour into casserole and bake 30 minutes at 325°F. Sprinkle with chow mein noodles and bake 10 minutes longer.

Mrs. J. C. Embry, Forestburg H. S.
Saint Jo, Texas

RICE CASSEROLE
Number of Servings — 6

1 lb. ground beef
Salt and pepper
1 c. diced celery
1 c. diced onion
1 chopped green pepper
1 can mushroom soup
1 can chicken rice soup
½ c. un-cooked rice

Cook beef, salt, pepper, celery, onion and green pepper until brown. Combine remaining ingredients and simmer 15 minutes. Bake in greased baking dish in moderate (350°F.) oven for 20 minutes.

Mrs. Elizabeth Richard, Sunfield H. S.
Sunfield, Michigan

BEEF-NOODLE CASSEROLE
Number of Servings — 6-8

2 No. 303 cans tomatoes
8 ozs. broad noodles
1 lb. ground beef
2 T. salad oil
½ t. garlic salt
½ lb. American cheese, sliced
3 T. flour
¼ c. minced onion
1½ t. salt
¼ t. pepper
1½ t. oregano

Cook and drain the noodles. Brown the ground beef in the salad oil and add garlic salt. Mix ¼ cup tomato liquid with the flour and add it to the ground beef. Add the remaining tomatoes, onion, salt, pepper and oregano. Simmer until slightly thickened (10 to 15 minutes). In a greased 3-quart casserole place alternate layers of noodles and the tomato-beef mixture. Top with a layer of the cheese slices. Sprinkle with Parmesan cheese and bake at 375°F. for 20 to 25 minutes.

Rose Shular, Ottawa H. S.
Ottawa, Kansas

MEAT CASSEROLE
Number of Servings — 10

1½ lbs. ground beef
4 stalks celery
1 large onion
½ lb. mushrooms
½ lb. noodles
2 T. soy sauce
1 c. tomato soup
1 c. vegetable soup

Brown beef in butter; then brown celery chopped fine with onion. Add mushrooms, chopped, but not fine. Add remaining ingredients and place in casserole with cornflakes on top and dot with butter. Bake ½ hour in moderate oven.

Fern Todd, Bloomington H. S.
Bloomington, Wisconsin

BEEF-RICE CASSEROLE
Number of Servings — 6

1 lb. ground beef
1 T. fat
½ c. uncooked rice
1 10½ or 11 oz. can condensed chicken soup
1¼ c. water
1 t. salt
½ c. chopped celery
¼ c. chopped green pepper

Brown beef in hot fat. Add rice, soup, water, salt, celery and green peppers. Mix thoroughly. Place in greased 2 quart casserole. Cover and bake 1 hour and 15 minutes in 350°F. oven. Cool thoroughly. A topping of corn flakes may be added during the last 30 minutes of cooking.

Mrs. J. E. Robertson, Friendship H. S.
Friendship, Tennessee

COMPANY CASSEROLE
Number of Servings — 8-10

1 lb. ground beef
1 onion, minced
1 c. carrots
1 c. peas
1 green pepper, chopped
1 small can mushrooms
2 c. fine noodles, cooked
3 c. tomatoes
2 T. Worcestershire sauce
2 T. shortening
¼ t. pepper
¼ t. celery salt
Buttered bread crumbs

Cook noodles until tender. Saute ground beef and onion. Combine noodles, meat mixture, vegetables, and seasonings in a casserole dish. Top with buttered crumbs. Bake at 350°F. until brown on top.

Mrs. Elaine L. Smith, Union City-Wayne H. S.
Union City, Indiana

SAVORY TEXAS CASSEROLE
Number of Servings — 4

¼ large onion, diced
½ medium green pepper
2 t. chili powder
2 cans tomato sauce (8 oz.) and 2 cans water
4 ozs. macaroni
½ lb. ground beef
1 t. hot pepper sauce
Salt and pepper to taste
1 T. bacon drippings

Fry onion, green pepper, and ground beef in bacon drippings until beef is browned. Add the macaroni and let simmer while adding chili powder, hot sauce, pepper, and salt. Then add the 2 cans of tomato sauce, and the 2 cans of water. Let simmer about 30 minutes or until mixture is very thick. Can be topped with ¼ pound of longhorn cheese.

Mrs. Billy C. Vinson, Dumas Jr. H. S.
Dumas, Texas

MACARONI AND BEEF CASSEROLE
Number of Servings — 6-8

2 T. fat
1 medium onion, chopped
1 lb. ground beef
¼ lb. cubed cheese
1 can tomato soup
1 c. elbow macaroni
1 can mushrooms and juice
1 t. salt

Cook macaroni and drain. Brown beef and onions in fat. Add all other ingredients. Add macaroni and cheese last. Bake about 30 minutes at 400°F.

Inez P. Curvin, Benjamin Russell H. S.
Alexander City, Alabama

SEVEN LAYER CASSEROLE
Number of Servings — 4

1 c. rice, uncooked
1 c. corn
1 chopped onion
1 chopped bell pepper
Salt and pepper
1 can tomato sauce
½ can water
¾ lb. hamburger
1 can tomato sauce
3 strips bacon

Arrange the ingredients in layers in order given; lay bacon strips on top. Cover and bake at 350°F. for 1 hour; then uncover and continue baking 30 minutes.

Mrs. Nancy York, St. Andrew's H. S.
Charleston, South Carolina

SPAGHETTI CASSEROLE
Number of Servings — 6

1 lb. ground beef
1 t. salt
1 T. vegetable oil
1 c. tomato catsup
1 c. tomato puree
½ c. water
1 c. uncooked elbow spaghetti
1 medium onion, chopped fine

Combine beef, salt, onion and salad oil. At high heat cook until the beef has lost its red color. Immediately pour over it the tomato catsup, tomato puree, water and spaghetti. Mix well, turn heat to simmer, cover and cook 35 minutes. Ready to serve.

Clara Davis Ferguson, Spurgeon H. S.
Spurgeon, Indiana

BEEF CASSEROLE
Number of Servings — 6

2 c. left over pot roast or 1 lb. ground beef
1 large onion
3 stalks celery
1 green pepper
2 T. butter
1 can (10½ oz.) mushroom soup
½ c. water
½ t. salt
Dark pepper
1 can (3 oz.) chow mein noodles

Start oven at 325°F. Cut onion, celery and pepper coarsely. Chop leftover beef in small cubes. Cook beef in 1 tablespoon fat (butter) for several minutes (if ground beef, cook until brown) and transfer to medium size casserole. Put remaining butter or margarine in pan, toss in chopped vegetables and cook until limp. Stir in mushroom soup, water, salt, pepper and pour over beef. Mix well. Cover and bake 30 minutes. Remove cover and sprinkle with chow mein noodles and bake 10 minutes.

Mrs. Lucille Jordan, Cary Sr. H. S.
Cary, North Carolina

CHEROKEE CASSEROLE
Number of Servings — 4-6

1 lb. ground beef
1 T. cooking oil
¾ c. finely chopped onion
1½ t. salt
Dash pepper
⅛ t. oregano
⅛ t. garlic
1 can (1 lb.) tomatoes
1 can cream of mushroom soup
1 c. minute rice
6 stuffed olives, sliced
2-3 slices cheese, cut in ½ inch slices

Brown meat in oil; add onion, cook until tender. Stir in all ingredients except cheese and olives. Bring to a boil, reduce heat and simmer for 5 minutes. Stir occasionally. Spoon into baking dish, make lattice top with cheese. Broil till cheese melts. Garnish with olive slices.

Mrs. Sondra Allen, Beckville H. S.
Beckville, Texas

THREE-IN-ONE CASSEROLE
Number of Servings — 6

1 lb. ground beef
1 green pepper, chopped
2 onions, cut fine
1 large can cream style corn
4 sliced tomatoes
Butter
Crumbs
Salt and pepper

Saute pepper and onions in butter until light brown. Add meat and cook until seared. Place alternate layers of meat mixture and corn in buttered baking dish, seasoning with salt and pepper. Cover with buttered crumbs. Bake in moderate oven (350°F.) until crumbs are brown.

Betty Canada, Munford H. S.
Munford, Alabama

GROUND BEEF CASSEROLE
Number of Servings — 10-12

1 lb. ground beef
1 lb. sharp cheese
2 cans tomato soup
1 can Mexicana corn
1 package fine noodles
1½ c. catsup
1 large onion

Cut up onion and cook with beef. Cook noodles separately. Mix meat, noodles, corn and soup and ½ cup water. Divide cheese in half. Cut half into cubes; add with catsup and meat mixture. Put into casserole; cover with rest of cheese (grated). Bake 1 hour at 325°F. Makes 2 large casseroles.

Mrs. Gertrude McRae
Rockingham-Wall St. H. S.
Rockingham, North Carolina

BEEF CASSEROLE
Number of Servings — 6

1½ lbs. round steak, cubed
1 medium size onion
1 can mushroom soup or a can of mushrooms
1 can chop suey vegetables
1 can chop suey noodles
1 c. milk
2 T. flour

Brown steak cubes with onion. Add mushrooms and chop suey vegetables. Place meat and vegetables in casserole. Add milk to liquid in pan used to brown meat. Thicken with flour and pour over meat and vegetables. Bake ½ hour at 350°F. Then add noodles and heat.

Mrs. Arvella Curtis, Fulton H. S.
Middleton, Michigan

RICH BROWN STEAK DINNER
Number of Servings — 6-8

2 lbs. round steak, 1 inch thick, cut in servings
2 t. salt
½ t. pepper
Flour
6 medium onions, sliced
¼ c. shortening
3 large potatoes, halved
1 bay leaf
1 can condensed tomato soup
1 package frozen French cut green beans

Season meat with salt and pepper, roll in flour. Cook onions in hot fat, until tender, but not brown; remove onions and brown meat slowly on both sides. Place meat in 3 quart casserole; add onions, potatoes, and bay leaf; pour soup over. Cover. Bake in moderate oven (350°F.) 1 hour and 45 minutes, or until meat is tender. Add beans; cook 10 to 15 minutes longer.

Patricia A. Harrell, Colonial Heights H. S.
Colonial Heights, Virginia

JOHN BEN GETTY
Number of Servings — 8-12

1½ lbs. hamburger meat
2 chopped onions
1 green pepper
8 ozs. cooked noodles
3 pimentos
1 can (1½ c.) peas
1 can mushroom soup
1 can tomato soup
Salt and pepper to taste
½ c. grated cheese

Brown hamburger, onions, and peppers in skillet. Add pimentos, peas, mushroom soup and tomato soup plus seasoning. Alternate this mixture with noodles in placing in casserole (3 quart dish). Sprinkle ½ cup grated cheese over top for last 15 minutes. Bake 350°F. for 1 hour.

Mrs. Eleanor C. Ginder, Manheim Central H. S.
Manheim, Pennsylvania

RICE HAMBURGER CASSEROLE
Number of Servings — 6

1 lb. hamburger
1 large onion
2-3 stalks celery
1 can cream of mushroom soup
2 cans water
3 oz. bottle soy sauce
1 c. pre-cooked rice
Salt and pepper

Brown hamburger, onion, celery, salt and pepper in small amount of fat until done. Add soup and water. Add soy sauce and rice. Bake until rice is tender, about ½ hour. (For extra richness 2 cans of soup can be used).

Mrs. Curt Stillwell, Lyle H. S.
Lyle, Minnesota

HAMBURGER CASSEROLE
Number of Servings — 8-10

1 medium onion, chopped
1 lb. ground beef
1 No. 2 can green beans
1 can (11 oz.) tomato soup
5 medium potatoes, boil until tender
½ c. warm milk
1 beaten egg
1 t. salt
⅛ t. pepper

Cook onion in hot fat till golden brown; add meat and seasonings. Add drained beans and soup, pour into greased 1½ quart casserole. Mash potatoes, add the milk and egg and salt to season. Spoon in mounds over meat. Bake in 350°F. oven 30 minutes.

Mrs. Aleta B. Nelson, Tidehaven H. S.
Blessing, Texas

HAMBURGER POTATO PIE
Number of Servings — 4-6

1 lb. hamburger
1 medium onion
1 c. peas (cooked)
2 c. tomatoes
½ c. catsup
2 T. butter
½ t. salt
⅛ t. pepper
4-6 potatoes, cooked and mashed
1 egg

Brown in 2 tablespoons butter, 1 medium onion chopped fine. Remove onion and brown hamburger with salt and pepper. Place browned onion, hamburger, 1 cup peas, 2 cups tomatoes and ¼ cup catsup in 2 quart casserole and stir to combine. Mash potatoes, beat in 1 egg and spoon potatoes on top of other mixture. Brown in 375°F. oven till peaks are golden.

Mrs. Mary E. Jensen, Tyndall H. S.
Tyndall, South Dakota

BEEF AND BEAN BARBECUE
Number of Servings — 5-6

1 lb. ground round steak
¼ c. diced green peppers
½ c. minced onion
½ c. celery
1 8-oz. can tomato sauce
½ c. water
1 clove garlic, minced
2 T. vinegar
1 T. dry mustard
½ t. thyme
1 T. brown sugar
Salt and pepper to taste
1 No. 2 can (2½ c.) pork and beans

Cook beef and vegetables in hot fat until soft. Add tomato sauce, water, garlic, vinegar, mustard, thyme, brown sugar, and seasonings; blend well and simmer 5 minutes. Pour beans into casserole. Pour meat mixture over beans. Bake at 375°F. for 45 minutes.

Mrs. Yvonne Taylor Jones, Tallassee H. S.
Tallassee, Alabama

CABBAGE SPECIAL
Number of Servings — 6

1 head cabbage
3 potatoes
3 stalks celery
1 small onion
1 carrot
1 lb. seasoned hamburger

Turn stalk end of cabbage down. Slice off upper end for a cover. Scoop out inside of cabbage until shell is ½ inch thick. Make small patties of hamburger and pack closely in bottom of cabbage. Pare, wash and dice potatoes, 3 stalks celery, onion and carrot. Put vegetables together in the cabbage and sprinkle with salt. Dot with butter or margarine. Replace cover. Tie firmly wih string. Cover with water and boil about 1 hour and 15 minutes. Remove strings. Serve with butter.

Anna D. Williams, Evarts H. S.
Evarts, Kentucky

POTLUCK FAVORITE
Number of Servings — 10

2 c. hamburger
2 c. diced celery
2 c. diced onions
1 green pepper, diced
⅔ c. raw rice
1 can mushroom soup
1 can creamed chicken soup
3 cans water
1 t. salt

Brown hamburger, celery, onions and peppers. Add rest of the ingredients and mix. Place in greased casserole. Cover with crumbs. Bake 2 hours at 300°F.

Mrs. Evelyn E. Tompkins, Shelby H. S.
Shelby, Michigan

BEEF 'N BARLEY
Number of Servings — 8-10

¾ c. chopped onion
1 c. pearled barley
1 T. butter
4 c. water
2 lbs. tenderloin steak
⅓ c. fine bread crumbs
1 T. sesame seed
1 t. salt
1 t. paprika
2 T. shortening
1 can cream of mushroom soup
1 can (4 oz.) button mushrooms, undrained
½ t. salt
1 t. Worcestershire sauce
1 can (4 oz.) pimento, chopped

Saute onion and barley in butter in skillet. Add 2 cups of the water. Cover skillet and simmer gently over medium heat for 15 minutes. Cut steak in strips and roll in mixture of crumbs, sesame seed, salt and paprika. Brown in hot shortening. Combine barley with soup, mushrooms, ½ teaspoon salt, Worcestershire sauce, pimento, remaining 2 cups water. Add browned steak strips. Pour into 3 quart casserole. Cover with lid or foil. Bake at 325°F. for 1½ hours. Uncover and bake 30 minutes more. (Add water if needed). Garnish with melba toast slices and parsley.

Mrs. Robert Biehler, Bidwell Jr. H. S.
Chico, California

ALMOND HOT DISH
Number of Servings — 8

8 oz. package wide noodles, cooked
1 lb. hamburger
2 c. diced celery
2 c. diced onions
1 can chicken rice soup
1 can cream of mushroom soup
½ c. almonds (leave skins on)
Salt and pepper

Cook hamburger in 1 tablespoon of butter. Steam rather than brown it. Add onions, celery, cooked noodles, soups and almonds. Heat well and place in casserole. Season to taste. Bake for 1 hour in 350°F. oven.

Mrs. Mary Nestande, Fairfax P. S.
Fairfax, Minnesota

NOODLE HOT DISH CALLED "MORE"
Number of Servings — 20

Cook 2 boxes noodles until tender. Fry 4 pounds hamburger until brown. Put all this, plus 4 cans tomato sauce, 1½ cans corn, 1½ cups chopped green pepper and 2 tablespoons chili powder into a baking dish or buttered pan. Cover with 1 tablespoon grated cheese and bake for 1 hour.

Mrs. Evelyn Johnson, Bottineau H. S.
Bottineau, North Dakota

"MORE"
Number of Servings — 6

No. 1 Mixture:

1 lb. ground meat
2 diced onions
3 garlic cloves
1 diced green pepper
3 T. chili powder

No. 2 Mixture:

1 can tomatoes or tomato soup
1 small can mushrooms
1 box frozen peas
1 can corn
1½ boxes spaghetti, cooked and drained

Cook mixture No. 1 and No. 2 separately and then combine. This may be baked in the oven. May be frozen and held over for larger servings. Cheese may be grated and put on top if desired; if so it should be done after cooked in the oven.

Dana Ray Owens, Eldorado H. S.
Eldorado, Texas

DINNER IN A DISH
Number of Servings — 6

1½ lbs. ground beef
1 small onion, chopped fine
1 c. diced carrots
1 c. canned peas
1 8-oz. package noodles
1 qt. water
1 t. salt
¼ t. pepper
Cracker crumbs

Cook noodles in 2 quarts boiling water until tender (9 minutes). Drain. Brown meat and onions in skillet with small amount of shortening. Add water and carrots and cook until tender. Combine the two mixtures, add peas, salt and pepper; mix well. Place in well-oiled casserole, cover with cracker crumbs and bits of butter. Bake at 350°F. for 30 minutes or until a golden brown.

Mrs. Madge Addington, Altoona Rural H. S.
Altoona, Kansas

SIX-LAYER DINNER
Number of Servings — 6

2 c. sliced raw potato
2 c. chopped celery
1 lb. ground beef
½ c. sliced raw onion
1 c. minced green pepper
2 c. cooked tomatoes
2 t. salt
¼ t. pepper

Place in layers in greased 2 quart casserole. Garnish with green pepper slices. Bake 2 hours at 350°F. (moderate oven).

Nova Mayer, Windber Area H. S.
Windber, Pennsylvania

BEEF AND MUSHROOM CASSEROLE WITH SOUR CREAM

2 lbs. round steak, cut in ½ inch cubes
2 T. fat
1 large onion, chopped
1 clove garlic, chopped
2 T. flour
1 c. sour cream
1 3-oz. can broiled mushrooms
½ c. chopped celery
1 8-oz. can tomato sauce
1 t. salt
1 T. Worcestershire sauce

Brown steak in hot fat. Remove meat, add onion and garlic and cook until onion is golden. Blend in flour, add cream and cook, stirring constantly until thickened. Return meat to pan, add remaining ingredients, mix well. Turn into greased 3 quart casserole. Bake uncovered in moderate oven (350°F.) until meat is tender, about 1½ hours. Serve over steaming noodles or steamed rice, if desired, or just plain.

Mrs. Sarah Perry, F.H.A.
North Webster, Indiana

MARTHA'S COMPANY CASSEROLE
Number of Servings — 8

½ lb. egg noodles
1½ lbs. ground beef
2 8-oz. cans tomato sauce
½ lb. cottage cheese
2 T. chopped green pepper
½ lb. cream cheese
⅓ c. chopped onion
⅓ c. milk

Cook noodles, drain. Stir in 1 can tomato sauce. Set aside. Combine cheese, milk, onion and green pepper. Place half of the noodle mixture in bottom of 2 quart, greased casserole. Add cheese mixture, then remaining noodles. Top with ground beef and tomato sauce. Bake 1 hour at 350°F.

Mrs. Herwood Curtiss, New London Central H. S.
New London, New Hampshire

RICE HAMBURGER
Number of Servings — 6

1 c. rice
¼ t. salt
No. 2 can tomatoes
1 lb. hamburger
1 large onion
1 large green pepper
1 T. cooking oil

Combine rice, salt and tomatoes in casserole. Brown hamburger, onion, and pepper in oil. Add to other ingredients in casserole. Bake in 350°F. oven about 45 minutes with cover.

Ruth H. Hughes, Abbeville H. S.
Abbeville, South Carolina

MEAL-IN-A-DISH
Number of Servings — 6-8

2 T. fat
1 medium onion, chopped
1 bell pepper, chopped
1½ lbs. ground beef
1½ t. salt
2 eggs
2 c. cream style corn
2 medium tomatoes (fresh or canned)

Saute onion and pepper in 2 tablespoons fat until onion becomes transparent. Add the ground beef and salt and cook until the meat separates into small particles. Remove from heat. Stir in 2 eggs. In 2 quart casserole place 1 cup of the corn and over that spread half the meat mixture. Cover with 1 thinly sliced tomato. Repeat with remaining corn, meat and tomato. Top with buttered bread crumbs. Bake in a 350°F. oven 30 minutes.

Mrs. Ann W. Allen, Sand Hill H. S.
Richton, Mississippi

TEXAS HASH
Number of Servings — 6

3 medium onions, chopped
1 large green pepper, minced
1 lb. ground beef
2 c. canned tomatoes
½ c. washed uncooked rice (or 2 c. uncooked noodles)
1 t. chili powder
2 t. salt
⅛ t. pepper

Cook onions and green pepper in 3 tablespoons fat (or butter) until onions are yellow. Add the ground beef and fry until mixture gets crumbly. Stir into mixture the remaining ingredients. Pour into greased 2 quart casserole (8 inch). Cover and bake 1 hour in 350°F. oven. Remove cover the last 15 minutes of baking. Serve hot.

Mrs. Alberta Lanham, Bellevue H. S.
Bellevue, Kentucky

BEEF AND POTATO HOT DISH
Number of Servings — 6

1 lb. ground meat
1 diced onion
2 large potatoes
1 can tomato soup
4 stalks celery
Salt
Pepper

Add salt and pepper to meat and form into balls. Do not work meat much. Line bottom of pan (2 quart casserole) with diced celery. Peel potatoes and cut into 1 inch cubes. Place potatoes, meat balls and diced onion on top of celery. Season to taste and pour soup over top. Cover and bake 2 hours at 350°F.

Diane Barden, Lakeland H. S.
Minocqua, Wisconsin

BEEF AND NOODLE CASSEROLE
Number of Servings — 6

1 lb. hamburger
2 T. finely chopped onion
2 T. fat
1½ t. salt
⅛ t. pepper
8 ozs. wide noodles, cooked
1 can (10½ oz.) condensed cream of tomato soup
½ c. shredded cheese

Pan-fry onion in hot fat in heavy skillet. Add hamburger and brown thoroughly. Combine meat, seasonings, noodles, and soup in a 2 quart casserole. Top with shredded cheese. Bake in a moderate oven (350°F.) for 30 minutes.

Genevieve E. Snyder, Cocalico Union H. S.
Denver, Pennsylvania

BEEF AND MACARONI DINNER
Number of Servings — 5-6

1 lb. ground beef
2 medium onion, chopped
2 T. fat
1 c. chopped green pepper
1 T. garlic salt and chili powder
2 8-oz. cans tomato sauce
1 t. salt
2 c. grated cheese
2 c. cooked macaroni

Cook onion and green pepper in fat. Add meat, garlic salt and chili powder and brown in greased casserole dish. Put a layer of meat mixture, then macaroni, grated cheese and can of tomato sauce. Repeat. Bake in 400°F. oven until cheese melts (15 to 20 minutes).

Mary Ann Norris, Meriwether H. S.
Woodbury, Georgia

QUICK 'N EASY CASSEROLE
Number of Servings — 6-8

1 lb. ground beef
1 medium onion, chopped
½ t. salt
½ t. pepper
1 small can tomato paste
1 c. cold water
¼ c. diced green pepper
1 small can mushrooms
¼ t. garlic salt

Crumble ground beef into frying pan containing 1 tablespoon cooking oil. Add onion, stirring occasionally until beef and onion are brown. Add salt, pepper, tomato paste, water, pepper, mushrooms and garlic salt. Simmer until flavors are well blended. Mix with 4 cups of cooked spaghetti or macaroni and place in casserole. Cover with thin slices Mozzarelli cheese. Bake in 350°F. oven 15 minutes or until brown on top. Serve while hot.

Mrs. Donald W. Emery, Patterson Union H. S.
Patterson, California

CHUCK WAGON CASSEROLE
Number of Servings — 6

3 T. fat
1 c. medium chopped onions
1 can (10 oz.) tomato sauce
Salt and pepper to taste
1 lb. ground beef
1 c. chopped sweet green bell pepper
¾ c. cornmeal
Parmesan cheese

Saute onion and green pepper in fat; add meat, salt and pepper. Braise in skillet until ¾ way done and add 1 can tomato sauce and 1 can water; bring to boil. Add cornmeal and simmer until done. Serve hot, sprinkling with Parmesan cheese just before serving.

Mrs. Grace Ann Nowlin, Dime Box H. S.
Dime Box, Texas

CHEROKEE CASSEROLE
Number of Servings — 4-6

1 lb. ground beef
1 T. olive oil
¾ c. finely chopped onion
1½ t. salt
⅛ t. garlic
⅛ t. thyme
⅛ t. oregano
1 lb. can tomatoes
1 can cream of mushroom soup
1 c. minute rice
6 stuffed olives, sliced
2-3 slices cheese, cut in ½ inch strips

Brown meat in olive oil. Add onions, cook until tender. Stir in ingredients in order given, except 3 of the olives and cheese. Bring to a boil, reduce heat and simmer for 5 minutes, stirring occasionally. Spoon into baking dish and top with cheese. Broil until cheese is melted. Garnish with olives.

Betsy De Lorme, Rudolph H. S.
Rudolph, Wisconsin

CEDRIC CASSEROLE
Number of Servings — 6

1 medium onion
3 T. butter
½ lb. ground beef
¾ t. salt
⅛ t. pepper
6 c. coarsely shredded cabbage
1 can (10½ oz.) condensed tomato soup

Saute chopped onion in the butter. Add the ground beef; do not brown but heat through. Spread 3 cups of shredded cabbage in the bottom of a 2 quart baking dish. Cover with meat mixture, then add last 3 cups of cabbage. Pour over all condensed soup. Bake 1 hour at 350°F.

Polly Powell, Nordhoff H. S.
Ojai, California

BEEF-NOODLE CASSEROLE
Number of Servings — 10

1½ lbs. ground round steak
1 medium onion, chopped
1 bell pepper, chopped
1 can mushroom soup
½ c. milk
5 oz. package noodles
1 can tomato paste
1 c. grated cheese

Cook noodles according to the directions on the package. Saute onion and bell pepper in small amount of fat until tender. Add ground round steak and continue cooking slowly until it loses its pink color. Mix mushroom soup and milk and add to beef mixture. Add drained cooked noodles and tomato paste and mix well. Pour into casserole and sprinkle with grated cheese. Bake at 300°F. for 1 hour.

Mrs. Eleanor Weatherford
Itawamba Agricultural H. S.
Fulton, Mississippi

HAMBURGER-HARVEST CASSEROLE
Number of Servings — 8

1 lb. ground chuck
1 c. minced onion
1 No. 2 can tomatoes
1 T. Worcestershire sauce
1½ c. grated American cheese
2 t. salt
2 c. sliced pared raw potatoes
⅓ c. flour
1 package frozen cut corn
1 package frozen lima beans

Heat oven to 375°F. Combine ground chuck, onion, tomatoes, Worcestershire sauce, salt. Place in 3 quart casserole. On top, place in layers the potatoes, flour, corn and lima beans. Bake covered for 45 minutes. Sprinkle with cheese and bake uncovered for 30 minutes longer.

Mrs. Betty Goodhue Keeney, Gilbert Com. H. S.
Gilbert, Iowa

HAMBURGER CASSEROLE
Number of Servings — 6

2 small onions
¾ lb. hamburger
1 can tomato soup
1½ c. canned corn
Shortening
Mashed potatoes

Slice onions into frying pan and cook slowly in shortening. Saute meat with onions. Arrange meat and corn in casserole in 4 layers. Season with salt and pepper, and cover with tomato soup. Put mashed potatoes on top. Brush top with beaten egg yolk and bake in a 450°F. oven until potatoes brown.

Christine C. Risher, Noxubee County H. S.
Macon, Mississippi

HAMBURGER CASSEROLE
Number of Servings — 8-10

1 lb. hamburger
1 medium sized onion
1 can cream of chicken soup
1 can cream of mushroom soup
1 c. uncooked noodles
½ to ⅔ c. milk

Brown hamburger and onion together in skillet. Mix in all other ingredients except noodles and let simmer for about 5 or 10 minutes. Mix in noodles and pour into a 7 x 12 inch baking pan that has been greased and bake in a moderate oven for bout 1 hour.

Janice Nielson, Hurricane H. S.
Hurricane, Utah

HAMBURGER CASSEROLE
Number of Servings — 6

1 lb. ground hamburger meat
1 c. uncooked macaroni
1 small onion
1 can tomato soup
1 c. grated cheddar cheese

Cook macaroni; salt both macaroni and uncooked meat, pepper to taste. Place a layer of cooked macaroni, meat, cheese until all has been placed in casserole dish. Pour a can of tomato soup and 1 can water, plus chopped onion over meat, macaroni, cheese. Bake at 325°F. until well done.

Jacquelyn Howell, Theodore H. S.
Theodore, Alabama

CHEROKEE CASSEROLE
Number of Servings — 4-6

1 lb. ground beef
1 T. olive oil
¾ c. finely chopped Bermuda onion
1½ t. salt
Dash of pepper
⅛ t. garlic powder
⅛ t. thyme
⅛ t. oregano
½ small bay leaf
1 can (1 lb.) tomatoes
1 can (10½ oz.) condensed cream of mushroom
   soup
1 c. minute rice
6 stuffed olives, sliced
2 or 3 slices American cheese, cut in ½ in. strips

Brown meat in olive oil. Add onions; cook until tender. Stir in ingredients in order given, except 3 of the olives and cheese. Bring to a boil, reduce heat and simmer for 5 minutes, stirring occasionally. Spoon into baking dish and top with cheese. Broil until cheese is melted. Garnish with olives.

Mrs. Alice Kealhofer, Satartia H. S.
Satartia, Mississippi

NEAPOLITAN CASSEROLE
Number of Servings — 8-10

1 lb. ground chuck beef
½ green pepper, chopped
1 onion, chopped
3 T. butter
¼ t. pepper
½ t. salt
⅓ c. broad noodles
½ c. sliced mushrooms
1 c. tomato soup
1 c. water
½ t. paprika
1 t. meat sauce
¼ c. Parmesan cheese

Saute green pepper and onion in butter; add beef and mushrooms, brown. With a spatula, break up beef into small pieces. Cook noodles in 4 cups boiling water with ½ teaspoon salt for 20 minutes. Drain. Combine soup, water, salt, pepper, paprika and meat sauce. Add to meat. Pour half the meat mixture into a 2 quart casserole. Cover with a layer of noodles, then pour the remainder of the meat mixture over the noodles. Sprinkle with cheese. Bake in a pre-heated oven at 375°F. for 30 minutes.

Mrs. Margaret W. Lyles, Cleveland H. S.
Madison, South Carolina

ALL-AMERICAN LASAGNA
Number of Servings — 8

2 T. cooking oil
¾ c. chopped onion
2 cloves garlic
¾ lbs. ground beef
3½ c. tomatos
1 can (6 oz.) tomato paste
2 t. salt
2 t. oregano
¼ t. black pepper
12 ozs. lasagna noodles, or other broad noodles
1 c. small-curd cottage cheese
2 c. coarsely shredded cheddar cheese
¾ c. grated Parmesan cheese

Heat oil in large heavy saucepan. Add onion and garlic and cook until tender. Add ground beef and cook until meat is brown. Mash tomatoes. Add to ground meat mixture. Stir in tomato paste, salt, oregano, and black pepper. Simmer about 2 hours, or until sauce is thick. Cook lasagna noodles in boiling salted water until tender, about 15 minutes. Rinse lasagna with cool water until noodles are cool enough to handle; drain. Lightly grease a 9 x 13 inch pan. Arrange ⅓ of the noodles in pan; cover with ⅓ of the meat sauce, cottage cheese, cheddar cheese, and Parmesan cheese. Repeat layers twice. Bake in moderate oven (340° F.) for 40 minutes. Serve at once. This food freezes well.

Mrs. Ann Hunt, Nampa Sr. H. S.
Nampa, Idaho

AMERICAN LASAGNA
Number of Servings — 6-8

1 T. fat
1 lb. ground beef
2 cloves garlic, chopped
6 oz. can tomato paste
2½ c. canned tomatoes
1 t. salt
½ t. oregano
¾ t. pepper
8 oz. package wide noodles
1½ c. Swiss cheese, cut-up
12 oz. carton cottage cheese

Brown ground beef and chopped garlic in hot fat. Add tomato paste, canned tomatoes, salt, oregano, and pepper and simmer 20 minutes. Cook wide noodles according to directions on package. In an oblong baking dish (7 x 11 inch) alternate layers of the cooked noodles, Swiss cheese, cottage cheese, and the meat sauce (above). Bake in moderate oven (350°F.) for 20 to 30 minutes. Serve with grated Parmesan cheese.

Mrs. Jeane Myers, Western H. S.
Parma, Michigan

HAMBURGER CASSEROLE
Number of Servings — 6

1½ lbs. chuck ground beef
1 medium onion
3 medium potatoes, thinly sliced
1 can mushroom soup
Less than ¼ c. milk
Cracker crumbs
Garlic salt
Seasonings

Grease a 2 quart baking dish and dust with garlic salt. Make a thin layer of thinly sliced potato, a thin layer of onions, another thin layer of potato and then alternate hamburg and potato, ending with hamburg. Season each layer. Pour on mushroom soup. Sprinkle with cracker crumbs. Moisten with a little milk. Bake at 370°-375°F. until potatoes are done.

Beverly L. Seaver, Northfield H. S.
Northfield, Vermont

HAMBURGER CASSEROLE
Number of Servings — 4

1 lb. hamburger
4 large potatoes
4 cooking onions
1 can tomato soup
1½ t. salt
¼ t. pepper

In a greased casserole, slice alternate layers of potatoes and onions, seasoning each layer and ending with onion. Cover with seasoned hamburger. Pour tomato soup over all. Bake at 350°F. for 1½ hours or until tender.

Mrs. Ann Manzer, Mountain View H. S.
Kingsley, Pennsylvania

BAKED BURGERS
Number of Servings — 6

1 lb. ground beef
½ c. finely chopped green pepper
½ c. finely chopped onion
¼ c. finely chopped celery
Salt and pepper
½ c. mayonnaise or salad dressing
1 beaten egg
1 T. water
¾ c. fine bread or cracker crumbs
¼ c. fat
3 slices sharp process cheese, halved
1 can condensed cream of vegetable soup
⅓ c. milk

Mix beef, green pepper, onion, celery, salt, pepper and mayonnaise. Shape in 6 patties. Blend egg and water, dip patties into egg, then crumbs. Brown lightly in hot fat. Arrange patties in baking dish. Place a cheese triangle on each patty. Combine soup and milk, heat, pour around patties. Bake in moderate oven (350°F.) 20 to 25 minutes.

Mrs. D. J. Dear, Stringer H. S.
Bay Springs, Mississippi

MEAL-IN-ONE OR QUICK SUPPER
Number of Servings — 6

1 lb. ground beef
1 small chopped onion
Salt and pepper
3 T. salad oil
1 can tomato soup
1 can cut green beans
2 T. Worcestershire sauce
2 t. mustard (prepared)
3 medium potatoes, cooked and whipped or mashed

Combine meat, onion, salt, pepper and brown in small amount of salad oil. Add tomato soup (undiluted), Worcestershire sauce and mustard, stirring well. Pour in can green beans (not drained). Simmer 15 to 20 minutes. Pour into ungreased casserole dish. Spread or spoon mashed potatoes over top. Bake in 350°F. oven until peaks on mashed potatoes are brown. (Instant mashed potatoes decrease preparation time).

Lynn Lankford, Carrizo Spring H. S.
Carrizo Springs, Texas

BEEF LA CATCHORIA
Number of Servings — 8

On medium high heat melt 3 tablespoons lard, and brown 1 pound hamburger, diced onion and green pepper. Next add 2 teaspoons salt, ¼ teaspoon pepper, 1 can tomato soup, 1 can water and ⅔ cup uncooked rice. Mix all together and turn to low for 25 or 30 minutes. Cover tightly. Stir once or twice.

Mary Simmons Rakes, William Monroe H. S.
Stanardsville, Virginia

HAMBURGER PIE
Number of Servings — 6

1 medium onion, chopped
1 lb. ground beef
Salt and pepper
1 No. 2 can green beans
1 11-oz. can condensed tomato soup
5 medium potatoes, cooked
½ c. warm milk
1 beaten egg
Salt and pepper

Cook onion in hot fat till golden; add meat and seasonings; brown. Add drained beans and soup; pour into greased 1½ quart casserole. Mash the potatoes; add the milk, egg, and the seasonings. Spoon in mounds over meat. Bake in moderate (350°F.) oven 30 minutes.

Janice Hancock, Groton H. S.
Groton, South Dakota

HAMBURGER PIE
Number of Servings — 6

4 medium size potatoes
1 T. fat
2 slices of medium onion
1 lb. hamburger
1 can string beans
1 can tomato soup
Salt and pepper to season

Peel potatoes, wash and boil until soft. Make into mashed potatoes. Place fat in a saucepan (heavy one or fry pan). Slice into fat onions. Fry to golden brown. Add hamburger loose. Fry until done. Cook string beans until done. Combine hamburger, beans and tomato soup. Season to taste. Place in casserole dish. Top with mashed potatoes. Bake at 400°F. until potatoes are tipped with brown.

Florence Shaffer, Berwick Area Sr. H. S.
Berwick, Pennsylvania

HAMBURGER CASSEROLE
Number of Servings — 4

1 lb. ground beef
1 medium onion
½ green pepper
1 T. butter
1 can tomato soup
3 potatoes
1 T. sugar
1 t. salt
1 c. fresh buttered bread crumbs

Saute chopped onion and pepper in butter until golden. Add hamburger and brown. Slice potatoes and add with tomato soup, sugar and salt. Pour into casserole and top with bread crumbs. Bake at 350°F. for 1 hour or until potatoes are cooked through.

Mrs. Charles C. Housenick, Black Creek
Township H. S., Rock Glenn, Pennsylvania

MEAT PIES
Number of Servings — 8

2 T. flour
½ lb. ground beef
2 large onions, chopped
2 T. chopped parsley
1 T. shortening
1½ lbs. pork
6 green onions, chopped

Make a roux of shortening and flour; add other ingredients and salt and pepper to taste. Cook thoroughly and let cool before placing in dough.

Pastry recipe for dough:

4 c. flour
½ c. shortening
2 t. baking powder
2 eggs
Milk

(Use saucer to cut dough. Place filling in it).

Corinne Dowden, Kisatchie H. S.
Kisatchie, Louisiana

HAMBURGER PIE
Number of Servings — 6

1 medium onion, chopped
1 lb. ground beef
Salt and pepper
1 No. 2 can (2½ c.) or ½ lb. cooked green beans
1 10½-11 oz. can condensed tomato soup
5 medium potatoes, cooked
½ c. warm milk
1 beaten egg
Salt and pepper

Cook onion in hot fat till golden; add meat and seasonings; brown. Add drained beans and soup; pour into greased 1½ quart casserole. Mash the potatoes; add milk, egg, and the seasonings. Spoon in mounds over the meat. Bake in moderate oven (350°F.) 30 minutes.

Norma Kay Jenni, Red Lodge H. S.
Red Lodge, Montana

HAMBURGER CASSEROLE
Number of Servings — 6

1 lb. hamburger
2 T. butter
4 medium size potatoes
2 onions
1 t. salt
dash of pepper
1 c. tomato soup

Brown hamburger in skillet with butter. Cut potatoes in half-inch cubes and spread in a baking dish. Cover with half the meat. Add half the soup and a sliced onion. Season with salt and pepper. Repeat, using remaining ingredients. Bake 1½ hours in a moderate oven (350°F.). More soup may be added during baking, if needed.

Willie Ruth Atchley, Lanier H. S.
Maryville, Tennessee

HAMBURGER CASSEROLE
Number of Servings — 6-8

1 lb. ground beef
1 can cream mushroom soup
½ c. raw rice
1 c. chopped onion
½ clove garlic
1 t. salt
1 c. grated cheese
1 can chicken noodle soup
2 T. fat
⅓ c. chopped bell pepper
½ c. celery, chopped
¼ t. red pepper

Fry onion, celery, bell pepper and garlic in 1 tablespoon of fat until wilted. Fry ground meat in 1 tablespoon fat until brown. Blend the two mixtures. Add cheese, cream mushroom soup, chicken noodle soup, raw rice, salt, pepper and mix thoroughly. Pour into greased 1½ quart casserole. Cover with bread crumbs. Bake 1 hour at 325°F.

Hilda Harmon, Crowley H. S.
Crowley, Louisiana

BEEF CASSEROLE
Number of Servings — 4

1 small onion, chopped
½ lb. ground beef
1 can tomato soup
½ c. water
½ c. cut green beans, cooked
1 c. noodles, cooked and drained
½ c. parmesian cheese or other shredded cheese

Saute onion, then brown hamburger in skillet. Add tomato soup, water, green beans and noodles. Pour mixture in 1-quart casserole. Top with cheese. Bake in moderate oven (375°F.) about 25 minutes. Serve with French bread or hot rolls and a salad.

Marlene Rostetter, Lisle Community H. S.
Lisle, Illinois

HAMBURGER PIE
Number of Servings — 6

1 medium onion, chopped
1 lb. ground beef
Salt and pepper
1 No. 2 can (2½ c.) green beans
1 10½-oz. can tomato soup
5 medium potatoes, cooked
½ c. warm milk
1 beaten egg
Salt and pepper

Cook onion in hot fat until golden brown; add meat and seasonings; brown. Add drained beans and soup; pour into greased 1½ quart casserole. Mash potatoes; add milk, egg, and seasonings. Spoon in mounds over meat. Bake in moderate oven (350°F.) 30 minutes.

Mrs. Ruth Morrill, Edison Jr. H. S.
Sioux Falls, South Dakota

7-LAYER CASSEROLE
Number of Servings — 4-6

1 c. uncooked rice
1 c. canned whole kernel corn, drained
salt and pepper
2 cans tomato sauce
½ can water
½ c. finely chopped onion
½ c. finely chopped green pepper
¾ lb. uncooked ground beef

Sprinkle rice and corn with salt and pepper. Pour over one can tomato sauce and ½ can water. Add onion, green pepper and meat; sprinkle with salt and pepper. Pour over second can tomato sauce and ½ can water. Cover meat with 4 strips bacon, cut in half. Start heating oven to moderate, 350°F. Place the above ingredients in layers in a 2-quart baking dish with a tight-fitting lid. Bake for 1 hour. Uncover and bake about 30 minutes longer, until bacon is crisp.

Mrs. L. R. Boyter, St. Bernard H. S.
St. Bernard, Louisiana

SEVEN LAYER BEEF CASSEROLE
Number of Servings — 4-6

1 c. uncooked rice
1 c. drained whole kernel corn
salt and pepper
2 cans tomato sauce
1¼ cans water
½ c. chopped onion
½ c. green pepper
1 lb. uncooked ground beef
strips of bacon

Sprinkle rice and corn with salt and pepper. Pour over 1 can tomato sauce and 1 can water. Add onion, green pepper and meat. Sprinkle with salt and pepper. Pour over other can tomato sauce and ¼ can water. Place strips of bacon on top. Heat oven to 350°F. Grease a 2-qt. covered casserole. Place ingredients in the dish by layers. A layer of canned whole tomatoes, drained, may be placed between the onion and meat. Cover and bake 1 hour. Uncover and bake until bacon is crisped.

L. Adelaide Towne, Goffstown H. S.
Goffstown, New Hampshire

MEAT-NOODLE CASSEROLE
Number of Servings — 6

Cook 3 ounces of noodles in 1 quart of boiling water with ½ teaspoon of salt. Cook ½ pound of ground beef with 1 teaspoon salt in 2 tablespoons fat until browned. Add 1 small minced onion, ½ cup diced celery, 1½ teaspoons Lea and Perrin sauce. Place a layer of noodles and layer of meat mixture in a casserole—repeat layers. Add 1 can of cream of tomato soup. Cover with ¼ cup grated cheese. Bake at 350°F. for 20 minutes.

Mrs. Ramona Montgomery, Edison H. S.
San Antonio, Texas

HAMBURGER NOODLE CASSEROLE
Number of Servings — 6

1 lb. hamburger
2 T. olive oil
1½ c. sliced onions
1 crushed clove of garlic
1 No. 2½ can tomatoes
1 6-oz. can tomato paste
1 6-oz. can water
1 t. Worcestershire sauce
½ t. paprika
1 T. salt
2 bay leaves
½ t. tabasco
⅛ t. thyme
⅛ t. marjoram

Brown hamburger in olive oil until crumbly. Add remaining ingredients. Bring to a boil and remove from heat. Place half the mixture in a 2½-quart casserole. Add 8 ounces uncooked noodles and top with remaining meat mixture. Bake at 375°F. for 45 minutes. Sprinkle with parmesan cheese.

Nancy Long, Allen County H. S.
Scottsville, Kentucky

SKILLET MACARONI AND BEEF
Number of Servings — 6

1½ lbs. ground beef
½ lb. uncooked macaroni
½ c. minced onion
½ c. chopped green pepper
2 8-oz. cans tomato sauce
1 c. water
1 t. salt
¼ t. pepper
1-1½ T. Worcestershire sauce

Cook beef in large skillet till it loses redness. Remove from skillet and cook macaroni, onion, and green pepper in meat fat until macaroni is yellow. Return meat to skillet along with tomato sauce, water, salt, pepper and Worcestershire sauce. Cover and simmer until macaroni is soft (25 minutes). Makes 6 servings .

Mrs. Jane Brockman, Hardin Houston H. S.
Houston, Ohio

DRIED BEEF NOODLE CASSEROLE
Number of Servings — 25

1 qt. thin white sauce
1 lb. American cheese, grated
1 lb. dried beef, shredded
2 10-oz. cans of cream of mushroom soup
½ c. sliced pimentos
1 lb. broad noodles
2 c. buttered bread crumbs

Make white sauce, and add other ingredients. Mix slightly. Place mixture in greased baking dish and sprinkle with bread crumbs. Bake at 350°F. for 35 to 45 minutes.

Mrs. Virgil W. Olson, Clinton H. S.
Clinton, Wisconsin

GROUND BEEF AND NOODLE CASSEROLE
Number of Servings — 8-10

2 T. salad oil
1 lb. ground beef
2 medium onions, chopped
1 medium bell pepper, chopped
1 8-oz. pkg. small noodles
1 12-oz. can whole kernel corn
1 10½-oz. can condensed tomato soup
¼ t. cummin
¼ t. oregano
¼ t. black pepper
1 t. salt
6 slices bacon (optional)
¼ lb. cheddar cheese (optional)

Brown ground beef in oil, add onions and pepper. Cook noodles according to directions on package. Add noodles, corn, tomato soup and seasonings to beef mixture. Simmer on surface unit at medium heat or bake at 350°F. for 30 minutes. Bacon or grated cheese may be put on top if baked.

Mrs. Evelyn Lewis, Antelope H. S.
Wellton, Arizona

GROUND BEEF AND VEGETABLE CASSEROLE
Number of Servings — 5-6

2 lbs. hamburger steak
½ t. sage
2 t. salt
¼ t. pepper
fried onions
4 T. fat
3 T. enriched all-purpose flour
2 c. unstrained tomatoes
buttered crumbs

Into the bottom of a 2-quart casserole arrange balls of hamburger steak, using 2 pounds of hamburger. Season with sage, salt and pepper. Over this, place a generous layer of fried onions. Melt fat, add flour, then mix well. To this, add tomatoes. Cook until thickened. Pour over onions. Cover with buttered crumbs. Bake uncovered at 375°F. for 1½ hours.

Elsie McCracken, Flippin H. S.
Flippin, Arkansas

HAMBURGER AND POTATO CASSEROLE
Number of Servings — 6

3 medium potatoes
1 c. condensed mushroom soup
2 T. fat
2 medium onions
1 lb. ground beef
1 t. salt

Season meat with salt and brown in hot fat. Pare and slice potatoes thinly. Slice onions. Make alternate layers of potatoes, onions, and meat. Pour mushroom soup over top and bake at 350°F. for 45 minutes.

Mary E. Finley, Baker County H. S.
Macclenny, Florida

MEAT AND POTATO CASSEROLE
Number of Servings — 4

Top Layer:
1 lb. ground lean beef
¾ c. evaporated milk
½ c. fine soda cracker crumbs or rolled oats (uncooked)
¼ c. catsup
¼ c. onion, cut-up
1 t. salt
⅛ t. pepper

Bottom Layer:
4 c. thinly sliced raw potatoes
1 T. onion, cut-up
1 t. salt
1 t. parsley flakes
⅛ t. pepper

Mix ground beef, milk, cracker crumbs, catsup, ¼ cup onion, 1 teaspoon salt and ⅛ teaspoon pepper. Arrange evenly in greased 2 quart baking dish potato slices and 1 tablespoon cut-up onion sprinkled with 1 teaspoon salt, ⅛ teaspoon pepper and 1 teaspoon parsley flakes. Spread meat mixture evenly over potatoes. Decorate with more catsup. Bake 350°F. 1 hour or until potatoes are tender.

Mrs. Martha S. O'Neil, Montgomery Area H. S.
Montgomery, Pennsylvania

STUFFED CABBAGE ROLLS
Number of Servings — 6-8

½ lb. ground beef
½ lb. ground pork
1 t. salt
Dash of pepper
¼ t. thyme
1 c. cooked minute rice
2 onions (large), chopped
1 egg, beaten
8-10 large cabbage leaves
1¼ c. tomato juice
1 c. water
3 beef bouillon cubes
1 T. vegetable shortening
2 T. chopped parsley
1½-2 T. flour
8-10 pieces of string (12-14 inches long)

Mix beef and pork; season with ½ teaspoon salt. pepper and thyme. Add rice, onion and egg. Mix well; shape into 8 to 10 small rolls. Parboil cabbage leaves 5 minutes. Place mixture in cabbage leaf; roll, and tie securely with string. Place rolls in skillet in a mixture of tomato juice, water, bouillon cubes, shortening, onion and 1 teaspoon salt. Cover and simmer for 1 hour. Turn occasionally. Reseason to taste. Thicken sauce with flour that has been blended smooth with cold water. Remove strings; serve with gravy over them.

Carol Packer, Spencerville H. S.
Spencerville, Ohio

BEEF EGGPLANT CASSEROLE
Number of Servings — 6

1½ lbs. ground beef
2 medium eggplants
1 medium onion, chopped fine
¼ c. chopped bell pepper
1½ c. cooked rice
½ c. fine bread crumbs
¼ stick butter
¼ c. diced celery
1 clove garlic, chopped

Peel and boil eggplant in salted water until tender. In a skillet with a small amount of shortening, brown ground beef, bell pepper, celery, onion, garlic, salt and pepper to taste. To the skillet mixture add rice and eggplant; mix well. Turn into casserole, cover with bread crumbs and dot with butter. Bake in 350°F. oven until brown.

Printellia T. Hodges, Starks H. S.
Starks, Louisiana

CASSEROLE OF BARBECUED HAMBURGER AND LIMA BEANS
Number of Servings — 6-8

¾ lb. hamburger
3 T. fat
Barbecue Sauce:
1 medium onion, sliced
2 T. sugar
2 T. Worcestershire sauce
½ lb. dried lima beans or 1 can (4 oz.) lima beans
2 t. salt
½ t. chili powder
¾ c. water
¾ c. catsup

Wash beans and cook in boiling, salted water until tender, about 2 hours. Combine barbecue sauce ingredients and simmer 15 minutes. Brown hamburger in the hot fat. Place cooked lima beans, hamburger and sauce in alternate layers in a 2 quart casserole. Bake in a moderate oven (350° F.) 45 minutes.

Sybil Todd, W. W. Lewis Jr. H. S.
Sulphur, Louisiana

TWO WAY CASSEROLE
Number of Servings — 6

1 lb. ground beef
1 medium onion, finely diced
½ cup diced celery
1 can cream of mushroom soup
1 can cream of chicken soup
1 can water
2 T. soya sauce

Cook meat, onion, celery until nearly done. Add mushroom soup, chicken soup, water, and soya sauce. Mix thoroughly. Place in casserole and bake 1½ hours at 350°F. Serve on toast or noodles or rice or chow mein noodles.

Marval Klecker, Viroqua H. S.
Viroqua, Wisconsin

MEAT BALLS AND VEGETABLE CASSEROLE
Number of Servings — 6

½ lb. ground beef
½ lb. ground veal
½ lb. ground fresh pork
1½ t. salt
⅛ t. pepper
½ small onion, minced
½ c. applesauce
½ c. bread crumbs
2 egg yolks
2 c. canned tomatoes
4 medium potatoes, diced
1 small carrot, diced
½ small onion, minced
1 stalk celery, minced
1 green pepper, minced

Mix first 9 ingredients thoroughly and shape into balls. Roll in flour and brown in two tablespoons fat. Place in casserole. To drippings in frying pan add remaining ingredients. Bring to a boil, turn out over meat balls, bake at 350°F. for 45 minutes.

Jane S. Scates, Rogers H. S.
Florence, Alabama

MUSHROOM AND CHEESE CASSEROLE
Number of Servings — 4-6

1 lb. ground beef
¾ c. chopped onion
Dash pepper
1 can (1 lb.) tomatoes
1 c. uncooked minute rice
6 stuffed sliced olives
1 T. shortening
1½ t. salt
⅛ t. garlic powder
⅛ t. oregano
1 can (10½ oz.) condensed cream of mushroom soup
2 or 3 slices American cheese, cut in ½ in. strips

Brown meat in fat, add onions; cook until tender. Stir in ingredients in order given, except 3 of the olives and cheese. Bring to boil, reduce heat and simmer for 5 minutes, stirring occasionally. Spoon into baking dish and top with cheese. Broil until cheese is melted. Garnish with olives.

Ethel M. Buehl, Junior H. S.
Detroit Lakes, Minnesota

CORN BEEF CASSEROLE

1 can corn beef, cubed
¼ lb. cubed cheese
1 can condensed mushroom soup
1-2 small onions
1 c. buttered bread crumbs
1 8-oz. pkg. noodles

Place in layers in casserole dish and dot with butter. Bake in oven at 350°F. for 45 minutes.

Mrs. Evelyn B. Jordan, Wilcox Central H. S.
Rochelle, Georgia

EASY-DOES-IT MEAT LOAF
Number of Servings — 6

1½ lbs. ground round steak
1 can chicken and rice soup
1 package dried onion soup

Combine meat, dried onion soup and undiluted chicken and rice soup. Mix well and form into a meat loaf. Cook 1½ hours in oven set at 350°F. Serve while hot.

Mrs. Rex Todd Withers, Chief
Homemaking and Family Life Education Service
Division of Vocational Education
Michigan Department of Public Instruction
Lansing, Michigan

SPAGHETTI AND MEAT BALLS
Number of Servings — 10

Meat Balls:

¾ lb. lean pork
¼ lb. beef (chuck)
1 medium onion, finely chopped
¼ c. parsley
1 egg, beaten
½ t. salt
½ t. paprika
1 t. oregano
½ c. bread crumbs
3 T. milk

Mix above ingredients and roll into the size of walnuts. Brown in ¼ cup oil. Follow directions on package for cooking spaghetti.

Sauce: Brown in skillet 1 medium onion, finely chopped; ½ button garlic, ground fine and 3 slices bacon. Add 5 (4 ounce) cans tomato paste, 1 teaspoon sugar, 2 tablespoons vinegar, pinch cayenne pepper (optional), ½ teaspoon paprika and 1 No. 2½ can tomatoes or tomato juice. Bring this to a boil. Pour over brown meat balls and drippings which have been previously placed in a roaster. Bake at 250°F. for 3 hours. (Note: The longer it bakes the more flavor you have).

Elaine Carlson, Horton H. S.
Horton, Kansas

AMERICAN SPAGHETTI
Number of Servings — 6

1 lb. ground bacon (may be cut up in small pieces)
2 pkgs. dried beef
1 large can tomatoes, mashed
1 can peas
1 lb. chopped onions
4 green peppers, chopped (optional)
½ lb. butter

Cook meat and onions until nearly done. Add tomatoes, peas, and peppers and simmer for 1 hour. Cook one box of whole spaghetti, add butter, and pour the sauce over spaghetti on individual plates.

Mrs. Carol Zwolanek, Stanley H. S.
Stanley, Wisconsin

SPAGHETTI CASSEROLE
Number of Servings — 4

1 c. spaghetti, broken
8-10 c. water
2 t. salt
½ medium onion, chopped
2 T. fat
¼ lb. ground beef
½ t. salt
½ t. Worcestershire sauce
1 c. canned tomatoes
½ c. grated cheese

Heat water and add 2 teaspoons salt. When boiling, add spaghetti and cook until tender. Drain. While cooking spaghetti, melt fat in frying pan, add onion and meat and cook until meat begins to brown. Add tomatoes and seasonings and simmer about 10 minutes. Add spaghetti to meat mixture and turn into a greased baking dish. Sprinkle a layer of grated cheese on top. Bake at 350°F. bout 20 minutes.

Wilma House, London H. S.
London, Kentucky

SPAGHETTI
Number of Servings — 15

2 lbs. spaghetti
1 lb. ground beef
1 lb. ground pork
5 large onions
4 buds garlic
1 c. cooking oil
5 stalks celery
6 cans tomato paste
1 large can evaporated milk
1 large can mushrooms
1 lb. cheese, grated
1 can chili powder

Boil spaghetti until done. Cook onions, celery and garlic in cooking oil. Add meat and cook, then add mushrooms and tomato paste. Put in baking dish, a layer of spaghetti, sauce and cheese until all has been used, then pour a can of milk over and through. Sprinkle grated cheese over top and bake in 325°F. oven, until well blended.

Mrs. Dalpha Boley, Splendora H. S.
Splendora, Texas

SPAGHETTI WITH MEAT BALLS
Number of Servings — 6

¾ lb. ground beef
¼ lb. ground pork
1 c. fine dry bread crumbs
½ c. grated parmesan cheese
1 T. minced parsley
2 small cloves garlic, cut fine
½ c. milk
2 eggs, beaten
1½ t. salt
⅛ t. pepper
1 c. minced onion

2 T. flour
5 c. cooked tomatoes (2 No. 2 cans)
6 T. minced green pepper
½ t. pepper
2 small bay leaves, crumbled
6 T. minced parsley
2½ t. salt
3 t. sugar
1 t. Worcestershire sauce

Mix first 10 ingredients and form into 1½-inch balls. Panfry until brown with onions in 4 tablespoons fat. Blend in flour. Then add remaining ingredients and simmer about 1 hour. Serve hot over hot drained boiled spaghetti (8 ounces uncooked) on a hot platter. Sprinkle with grated sharp cheese.

Bonnie Wyland, Elgin H. S.
Elgin, Oregon

GROUND MEAT CASSEROLE
(OR SPAGHETTI CASSEROLE)
Number of Servings — 12 or more

1 lb. ground steak
1 box spaghetti
3 onions, cut fine
3 t. chili powder
1 can (large) English peas
salt and pepper to taste
1 button garlic, cut fine (or garlic salt)
4 T. grease
1 can tomato paste
1 can mushrooms (may be omitted)
grated cheese for topping

Brown meat in grease and add onions and garlic. Cook spaghetti in boiling water until tender: about 20 minutes. Drain and add to meat mixture which has had chili powder and paste added. Add peas, mushrooms, salt and pepper to taste and 2 tomato paste cans of water; simmer in casserole in oven for about 30 minutes. Top with grated cheese just few minutes before removing from oven.

Mrs. Evelyn Newsom, Mt. Vernon H. S.
Mt. Vernon, Texas

TEXAS HASH
Number of Servings — 6

3 large onions, sliced
1 large green pepper, minced
1 lb. ground beef
2 c. cooked tomatoes (No. 303 can)
½ c. uncooked rice
1 t. chili powder
2 t. salt
⅛ t. pepper

Saute the onions and green pepper until onions are yellow. Add the ground beef and fry until mixture falls apart. Stir in the tomatoes, rice, chili powder, salt and pepper. Pour into greased 2-quart baking dish. Cover and bake at 350°F. for 1 hour, removing cover last 15 minutes.

Joan Williams, Parkrose H. S.
Portland, Oregon

LOUISIANA JAMBALAYA
Number of Servings — 10

1½ lbs. ground beef
½ lb. ground pork
½ c. salad oil
2 c. chopped onions
1 c. chopped bell pepper
1 c. chopped celery
2 cloves garlic, minced
1 t. tomato paste (optional)
1 c. stock or water
½ c. parsley, minced
½ c. onion tops, chopped
½ t. Kitchen Bouquet
3 c. cooked rice
2 t. salt
½ t. black pepper
¼ t. cayenne (red pepper)

Put salad oil in heavy iron pot. Brown meat. Add onions, pepper, celery, paste and garlic. Cook over low heat until soft, stirring constantly. Add stock to cover. Season (little more than desired after rice is added). Cook uncovered, over medium heat until meat separates; do not allow to get dry. Add more stock or water, if necessary. Cook 45 minutes, stirring often. This makes a thick gravy. Add Kitchen Bouquet to give rich brown color. Add parsley and onion tops. Cook 5 minutes. Add more stock or water to slightly cover meat. Fold in cooked rice and serve.

Variations:

Giblet Jambalaya: Boil giblets and necks in seasoned water until tender. Use stock to cover meat mixture. Grind or chop giblets and meat and add to Louisiana Jambalaya mixture. Fold in rice. Serves 12.

Meat and Lobster Dressing: Add flaked lobster (1 or 2 cans) to meat mixture in Louisiana Jambalaya recipe. Fold in rice. Serves 12.

Meat and Oyster Jambalaya: Use oyster water in meat mixture instead of water. Add 2 dozen or more cleaned, small oysters to meat mixture. Cook 3 to 5 minutes. Fold in rice. Serves 12.

Mrs. Ethel B. Douglas, Kaplan H. S.
Kaplan, Louisiana

NUTRIA CASSEROLED
Number of Servings — 12

10-12 lbs. nutria (meat in pieces)
1 can condensed cream of chicken soup
salt to taste (approximately 2 t.)
pepper to taste

Remove the natural animal fat. Place ½ cup water in the bottom of a large pan. Arrange the nutria pieces in the pan, salting and peppering as you proceed. Spread condensed chicken soup on top of the nutria and cover. Bring to a boil, turn down immediately to simmer. Simmer for 3 to 4 hours. The meat stock makes excellent gravy.

Nancy Ruder, North Adams Public School
North Adams, Michigan

HAMBURGER MOCK CHOW MEIN
Number of Servings — 4-6

1 lb. hamburger
1 small onion, chopped
1 c. chopped celery
2 T. soy sauce
½ c. rice
1 can cream mushroom soup
1 can (soup) water
1 4-oz. can mushrooms

Brown hamburger. Combine all ingredients and mix well. Place in buttered baking dish. Bake one hour at 350°F.

Muriel Olson, Warroad H. S.
Warroad, Minnesota

CHOP SUEY
Number of Servings — 8

1 T. fat
1 lb. round steak, diced
½ lb. lean pork, diced
½ lb. lean veal, diced
salt and pepper
2 large onions, diced
2 T. soy sauce
1 bunch celery, diced
4 T. butter
1 1-lb. can bean sprouts

Heat pan, add fat and brown meat just a little. Season with salt, pepper, onions and soy sauce. Cover and let steam until meat is tender. Simmer celery in butter. Drain liquid from bean sprouts and add with celery to meat. Cover with water and thicken. Serve over chow mein noodles or steamed rice.

Lois H. Leavitt, Union H. S.
Roosevelt, Utah

CORNMEAL DUMPLINGS
Number of Servings — 4-6

1 c. sifted self-rising flour
1 c. self-rising cornmeal
1 t. sugar
¼ c. shortening
1 T. chopped green pepper
1 T. chopped onion
1 T. chopped celery
¾ c. milk
1 egg, beaten
Hot chicken or meat stew with flakes of meat

Combine flour, cornmeal and sugar. Cut in shortening until mixture is fine. Stir in green pepper, onion and celery. Combine milk and egg and add to flour mixture. Stir just until dry ingredients are damp. Mixture will be lumpy. Drop by large tablespoons into simmering meat stew. Cover tightly and cook about 15 minutes without lifting cover. Serve immediately.

This was students winning recipe in the 1960 Victor's Self-Rising Contest.

Mrs. Rodney A. Russell, John de la Howe School,
McCormick, South Carolina

DELICIOUS AMERICAN PIZZA
Number of Servings — 3

2 lbs. ground beef
2 medium onions, chopped
2 6-oz. cans tomato paste
2 t. salt
½ t. red pepper
1 box hot roll mix
½ lb. sharp American cheese, grated
1 8-oz. jar stuffed olives, chopped

Brown meat in skillet. Add onions to meat mixture and let cook till onions are clear. Add tomato paste, salt, and red pepper to meat mixture and cook 10 minutes. Follow the direction on the box for hot rolls. Knead dough, but do not let rise. Divide into 3 equal parts and roll out to 14 inch circles. Place on greased pizza pans or cookie sheets. Sprinkle half of the cheese on the dough. Divide meat mixture into 3 equal parts and spread thinly over dough. Sprinkle with rest of the cheese. Sprinkle chopped olives on top of pizzas. Bake in a 350°F. oven for 35 to 45 minutes. These pizzas may be frozen before baking to be used at some later date.

Mrs. Ann S. Belair, Jennings H. S.
Jennings, Louisiana

GRAND CASSEROLE
Number of Servings — 6

1 lb. ground chuck beef
¼ c. quick oats
¼ c. grated potatoes
¼ c. grated carrots
¼ c. chopped onion
1 egg
1 t. salt
¼ t. pepper
1 T. Worcestershire sauce
2 T. catsup
¼ c. milk
1 can condensed cream of celery soup
2 T. shortening
¾ c. crushed potato chips

Combine all ingredients but the potato chips, soup, and shortening. Shape into 12 balls. Melt shortening in frying pan and brown the balls over low heat. Place browned meat balls in casserole dish, cover with soup and crushed potato chips. Bake in moderate oven (325°F.) 40 minutes.

Betty Capener, Grace H. S.
Grace, Idaho

CASSEROLE DE LUXE
Number of Servings — 10-12

1 c. raw rice
3 c. boiling water
1½ lb. cubed beef
1½ lb. cubed pork
1 c. diced celery
1 chopped onion
½ c. almonds (do not blanch)
4 T. chop suey sauce
1 large can mushrooms

Pour boiling water over rice and let stand while preparing the rest. Brown pork, beef, celery, and onion in small amount of fat. Combine meat mixture with rice mixture. Add almonds, sauce and mushrooms. Mix and bake in moderate oven (350°F.) for 1½ hours.

Dragica Nerbun, Ladysmith H. S.
Ladysmith, Wisconsin

DINNER RING WITH RICE AMANDINE
Number of Servings — 8

½ lb. liver (beef, calves, pork or lamb)
½ lb. well-seasoned pork sausage
2 T. chili sauce
1 T. horseradish
1 T. grated onion
1 egg, beaten
1 c. dry bread crumbs
½ c. water

Cover liver with hot water; cover and simmer 5 minutes. Put through food grinder, using plate, add remaining ingredients. Mix thoroughly, fill with well-oiled 8½ inch ring mold. Bake in moderate oven (350°F.) 1 hour. Serve with chili sauce.

Rice Amandine:
2 c. cooked rice
3 T. melted butter
⅓ t. curry powder
¼ c. slivered toasted almonds

Combine melted butter and curry powder. Pour over well-drained rice. Sprinkle with toasted almonds.

Carrie Williams, Dudley Hughes Voc. School
Macon, Georgia

OVEN ROUND STEAK DINNER
Number of Servings — 6-8

2 lbs. round steak, 1 inch thick, cut in servings
Enriched flour
6 medium onions, sliced
¼ c. fat
3 large potatoes, halved
1 bay leaf
1 can condensed tomato soup
1 1-lb. can (2 c.) French-cut green beans, drained

Season meat with 2 teaspoons salt and dash pepper roll in flour. Cook onions in hot fat until tender but not brown; remove onions and brown meat slowly on both sides. Place meat in 3-quart casserole; add onions, potatoes, and bay leaf. Pour soup over mixture. Cover and bake in moderate oven (350°F.) 1 hour and 45 minutes or until meat is tender. Add beans; cook 10 to 15 minutes more.

Mrs. Madra Fischer, Mendota H. S.
Mendota, Illinois

GOULASH
Number of Servings — 6

1 lb. hamburger
¼ c. chopped onion
2 T. fat
1 c. tomato soup
1½ c. water
4 ozs. packaged noodles
Salt and pepper
1 can creamed corn
¼ c. ripe olives
1 c. grated cheese

Brown hamburger and onion in fat. Add tomato soup and water to the hamburger mixture. Simmer 5 minutes. Add noodles and season with salt and pepper. Simmer 5 minutes. Add corn and olives, mix well. Pour in greased baking dish and sprinkle grated cheese on top. Bake in a moderate oven (325°F.) for 45 minutes.

Mrs. Verda E. McConnell, Adams City Sr. H. S.
Adams City, Colorado

HAMBURGER HEAVEN
Number of Servings — 8

1 lb. ground beef
1 No. 2 can stewed tomatoes
⅓ c. ripe olives, sliced
dash salt, pepper and garlic salt
1 pkg. noodles, cut fine
4 pieces (4 or 5 oz.) sliced American cheese

Cook ground beef until it is gray. Add salt, pepper, and garlic salt. Add noodles and stewed tomatoes. Rinse out the can with ½ cup of water, add to mixture. Sprinkle ripe olives over mixture. Cook at a low boil 15-20 minutes. Stir occasionally. When noodles are done, break cheese slices into fourths and spread over the top. Cook for a few minutes more. Serve hot.

Marguerite Holloway, Petersburg H. S.
Petersburg, Illinois

BEEF AND HAM STEW
Number of Servings — 8

1 lb. stew meat
1 lb. ham cut in small pieces
2 T. shortening
2 t. salt
2 large onions
2 c. carrots
3 c. potatoes
2 c. rutabagas
1 c. celery

Brown stew meat and ham slowly in shortening. Add salt and a quart of water; simmer slowly for about three hours, adding more water if needed. About 45 minutes before serving, add vegetables cut in cubes about an inch square. Serve in soup bowls. This is good served the second day also.

Mrs. Eleanor Howard, Kent-Meridian H. S.
Kent, Washington

SADEY'S SPECIAL
Number of Servings — 12

1½ lbs. ground beef
2 medium onions, chopped
2 c. diced celery
1 c. raw rice
2 cans mushroom soup
2 cans chicken rice soup
2 cans water

Brown meat, onions and celery. Scald rice (may use minute rice and omit scalding) in boiling water for 10 minutes; rinse in cold water. Combine with meat mixture and add soups and water. Mixture will seem watery but thickens as it bakes. Bake 2½ hours at 350°F. This recipe is easy to make in quantity.

Mrs. Marie C. Grieger, Edison Jr. H. S.
Sioux Falls, South Dakota

BEEF CASSEROLE
Number of Servings — 4

1 small onion, chopped
1 T. shortening
½ lb. ground beef
1 c. tomato soup
½ c. water
½ c. cooked green beans
1 c. cooked and drained noodles, macaroni or
   rice
Salt and pepper to taste

Brown onion and ground beef in the shortening. Add the soup, water, green beans and noodles. Pour mixture into a 1 quart casserole. Top with ½ cup shredded cheddar cheese. Bake in moderate oven (375°F.) about 25 minutes.

Marilyn Oelschlager, Herscher H. S.
Herscher, Illinois

LIVER CASSEROLE
Number of Servings — 6

1 lb. liver
2 large potatoes
1 medium size onion
2 c. canned tomatoes
flour
seasoning
bacon grease

Dip liver in flour seasoned with salt and pepper. Brown on both sides in bacon grease—do not overcook. Cut into pieces and put in baking dish in alternate layers with sliced uncooked potatoes. Brown chopped onions in the grease, thicken with small amount of flour; add tomatoes which have been seasoned with salt, pepper and teaspoonful sugar. Pour mixture over liver and potatoes, bake one hour in 350°F. oven.

Elizabeth Davenport, Berea H. S.
Berea, Kentucky

Veal Casseroles

VEAL CASSEROLE
Number of Servings — 6

1 lb. veal steak
5 slices white bread
1 small onion
1 c. frozen peas
Salt and pepper
1 can cream of mushroom soup
½ c. milk
3 T. shortening

Cut veal into cubes and brown in the shortening. Cut bread into cubes and brown also. Place in a greased casserole; add minced onion, salt, pepper, mushroom soup, frozen peas and the milk. Mix well. Bake ½ hour at 375°F.

Pauline Mathews, Richmond Com. H. S.
Richmond, Michigan

VEAL CASSEROLE
Number of Servings — 6-8

1 lb. ground veal (steak or shoulder)
2 T. butter
1 c. water
1 medium onion, diced
1 c. mushrooms
1 package noodles
1 c. sour cream
½ c. buttered bread crumbs

Brown veal in butter, add salt and pepper. Cover with water and simmer until tender. Add diced onion and mushrooms. Simmer 10 minutes. Cook noodles as directed on package. Combine noodles with above ingredients and the sour cream. Put all into a buttered baking dish, cover with buttered crumbs and bake 1 hour at 320°F.

Ruth S. Blomgren, Eastern Jr. H. S.
Silver Spring, Maryland

VEAL CASSEROLE
Number of Servings — 6-8

2 lbs. veal, cut in 1 inch cubes
½ c. butter or oleo
1 can mushroom soup
½ c. milk
1 can pimentos, diced
1 can (8 oz.) mushrooms, broken

Steam veal 20 minutes in butter or oleo. Remove lid and brown. Add mushroom soup, milk, pimentoes and mushrooms. Place in greased casserole. Bake at 350°F. for 45 minutes, covered. Remove casserole cover and top with chow mein noodles or canned onion rings. Continue baking 15 minutes.

Mrs. Ruth McLaughlin, New London Local H. S.
New London, Ohio

CHINESE VEAL CASSEROLE
Number of Servings — 10-12

3 lbs. veal shoulder, cut in 1 inch squares
2 T. shortening
1 c. chopped onion
1 7-oz. can mushrooms
4 c. water
1 can cream of chicken soup
1 can cream of mushroom soup
¼ c. soy sauce
1 t. salt
¼ t. pepper
1 c. uncooked rice
2½ c. coarsely cut celery
1 package frozen peas, thawed
1 c. sliced almonds

Brown veal and onions in shortening; add remaining ingredients, except celery and almonds. Bake in a 4 quart covered casserole 45 minutes, stirring occasionally. Add celery and peas and cook 30 minutes longer. Remove cover, sprinkle almonds on top and bake 15 minutes to brown almonds.

Margaret Taylor, Irving Jr. H. S.
Pocatello, Idaho

VEAL HOT DISH
Number of Servings — 6

1 lb. veal steak
1 medium sized onion
1 c. chopped celery
1 can cream of mushroom soup
1 can chicken and rice soup
2 cans water (use soup can to measure)
½ c. mushroom pieces
½ c. raw washed rice

Cut up and brown the veal steak. Chop up the onion and brown. Add the celery, mushroom soup, chicken rice soup, water, mushroom pieces, and rice. Stir to mix. Pour into 2 quart casserole and bake 2 hours at 325°F.

Mrs. Prudence Sheldon, Airport Com. H. S.
Carleton, Michigan

MUSHROOM MEAT LOAF
Number of Servings — 8

1 lb. veal, ground
1 lb. smoked ham, ground
4 T. tomato catsup
2 T. chopped green pepper
2 eggs, beaten
1 can condensed cream of mushroom soup
1 small onion, finely chopped
1 c. soft bread crumbs
½ t. salt
⅛ t. pepper

Mix all ingredients and pack into loaf pan. Bake at 350°F. for 1 to 1½ hours. Serve hot or cold.

Mrs. Agnes C. Huffman, Ripon Union H. S.
Ripon, California

VEAL AND RICE CASSEROLE
Number of Servings — 8

2 lbs. veal steak or veal knuckle
2 c. celery, chopped
2 c. onion, chopped
1 T. butter or oil
1 c. regular rice
1 can mushroom soup
1 can chicken rice soup
2 c. water
2 t. salt

Soak rice in water to cover for overnight. Saute celery and onion in fat. Brown veal in a small amount of fat and cook until done. Combine all ingredients in an electric skillet and simmer for 1½ hours.

Mrs. Marcia Miller, Petoskey H. S.
Petoskey, Michigan

VEAL WILD RICE DISH
Number of Servings — 8

1½ lbs. veal, cut in cubes
1 onion, chopped
1 can chicken rice soup
1 can cream of mushroom soup
1 soup can water
1 small can mushrooms and juice
½ c. white rice
¼ c. wild rice or 1 can pre-cooked
1 c. finely cut celery
1 T. soy sauce

Saute veal with onion, until onion is golden brown. Combine with remaining ingredients and season with salt and pepper to taste. Place in casserole and bake 1½ hours in 350°F. oven.

Mrs. Marlene Schroeder, Minnesota Lake H. S.
Minnesota Lake, Minnesota

HOLIDAY CASSEROLE
Number of Servings — 6-8

2 lbs. ground veal
1 t. lard
2 c. sliced celery
½ c. finely chopped green pepper
3 T. grated onion
½ c. sliced blanched almonds
1 t. salt
½ t. pepper
3 T. lemon juice
1 c. mayonnaise
¾ c. grated processed cheese
¾ c. crushed potato chips

Brown veal in lard. Pour off drippings. Combine veal, celery, green pepper, onion, almonds, salt, pepper, lemon juice and mayonnaise. Place in greased 2 quart casserole and cover top with grated cheese. Sprinkle potato chips around edge. Bake uncovered in a moderate oven (350°F.) for 40 minutes.

Uvonne Jones Van Hecke, Walnut Grove H. S.
Walnut Grove, Minnesota

CREAM BAKED VEAL
Number of Servings — 6

2 lbs. boneless veal
½ c. butter
2 T. flour
2 c. milk
3 hard-boiled eggs
1 t. salt
Dash of pepper
1 4-oz. can mushrooms
1 No. 2 can chow mein noodles

Cut veal in 1 inch cubes; brown in melted butter. Add flour, stir well. Pour in milk and cook, stirring constantly, until sauce is formed. Put a layer of the meat mixture in a greased 2 quart casserole, cover with the eggs, sliced, and the mushrooms, repeat meat layer. Bake for 45 minutes at 350°F. Put noodles on top and bake 15 minutes longer.

Mrs. Jeanne Bunch, Van Buren H. S.
Van Buren, Ohio

PARTY GOULASH
Number of Servings — 6

½ lb. veal
½ lb. tenderloin
1 t. salt
½ t. paprika
¼ t. pepper
2 T. shortening
2 T. onion flakes
½ c. mushrooms
1 c. tomato sauce
1 c. chopped green pepper
1 c. chopped celery
2 c. carrots, cut into ¼-inch pieces
1 c. sour cream

Cut meat in strips. Mix salt, pepper and paprika and sprinkle on meat. Brown in shortening. Add onion flakes and sliced mushrooms and continue browning. Add tomato sauce and simmer for 1 hour. Add vegetables; simmer for 10 minutes. Just before serving, add sour cream and heat. Serve over noodles and rice.

Katherine Rowland, Central H. S.
Fargo, North Dakota

MOCK CHICKEN DRUMSTICKS
Number of Servings — 6

1 lb. veal steak
1 lb. pork steak
Salt
Pepper
1 egg
Bread crumbs
¼ c. shortening

Cut meat into 1 x 1½ inch pieces. Arrange the veal and pork cubes alternately on 6 skewers. Press the pieces close together into the shape of a drumstick. Dip the sticks into beaten egg, then roll in crumbs. Brown in skillet. Cover the bottom of skillet with water. Cover and put in oven for 1 hour at 325°F.

Mrs. Johnie Adams, Wetumka H. S.
Wetumka, Oklahoma

Pork Casseroles

PORK CHOP CASSEROLE
Number of Servings — 4-6

4 to 6 loin pork chops
Salt and pepper to taste
2 T. vegetable shortening
1 can condensed cream of mushroom soup
½ c. water

Trim excessive fat from pork chops, season with salt and pepper and brown on both sides in a skillet with the 2 tablespoons of fat. Place in baking dish, pour the can of mushroom soup and ½ cup of water over the chops. Bake in pre-heated oven (350°F.) for 45 minutes.

Mary W. Hall, Mabelvale H. S.
Little Rock, Arkansas

PORK CHOP CASSEROLE
Number of Servings — 6

6 pork chops, ½ inch thick
6 Irish potatoes
1½ c. milk
3 T. butter
2 t. salt
½ t. pepper

Arrange sliced potatoes in a greased dish or pan, dot with butter, arrange chops over potatoes; sprinkle salt and pepper, and pour milk over this. Bake at 350°F. for 45 minutes or till golden brown and pork tender.

Mrs. Julia Powers, Gordon Military H. S.
Barnesville, Georgia

BAKED FRUIT PORK CHOPS
Number of Servings — 4

1 lb. prunes
4 lean rib pork chops, 1 inch thick
1 t. cinnamon
¼ t. ground cloves
2 T. fresh frozen, or canned lemon juice
¼ c. brown sugar, packed
2 T. water
1 T. salad oil
1 t. salt
¼ c. hot water

Early in day, soak prunes in hot water, covered for 5 minutes. Meanwhile trim as much fat from chops as possible; then slit each chop from bone side almost to fat, cutting a pocket. Pip prunes; then with scissors, snip prunes; add cinnamon, cloves, lemon juice, brown sugar, and water; cook 2 or 3 minutes; use to stuff chops, saving any leftover prune mixture. In skillet, thoroughly brown pork chops in salad oil; remove to casserole; sprinkle with salt. Add hot water to skillet; stir well to loosen browned bits. Pour over pork chops, then spoon left over prune mixture around chops. Heat oven to 350°F. Bake chops covered 1 hour.

Jo Ann Owens, Cotaco H. S.
Sommerville, Alabama

WILD RICE PORK CHOP CASSEROLE
Number of Servings — 4

4 pork chops, 1½ to 2 inches thick
8 T. wild raw rice
1 green pepper
1 large Bermuda onion
1 fresh ripe tomato
1 can consomme or 1 beef bouillon cube
½ c. white wine
Season as desired

Brown pork chops. Place in casserole. Place one slice of green pepper, tomato, and onion on top of each pork chop. Rinse wild rice in ice water, drain in colander. Pour wild rice in a bowl; pour 1 cup boiling water over rice. Let it stand for 5 to 10 minutes. Remove rice from water and place in casserole. Pour remaining rice water, and consomme into fry pan and bring to a boil. Turn off heat and add wine. Pour into casserole. Cover casserole. Place in 300°F. oven for 1½ to 2 hours. Serve hot.

Bernice Jager, New Prague Public H. S.
New Prague, Minnesota

PORK CHOPS AND POTATOES
Number of Servings — 6

6 pork chops
6 potatoes
1 large onion
1 can cream of mushroom soup
1 c. milk
Salt and pepper

Brown pork chops in skillet and set aside. Slice potatoes and onions and alternate in layers in casserole. Season to taste with salt and pepper. Mix milk and soup and pour ½ of mixture over potatoes and onions. Lay pork chops on top and cover with remainder of soup mixture. Bake at 350°F. for approximately 1 hour.

Mrs. Don Martin, Clay Co. Com. H. S.
Clay Center, Kansas

PORK CHOP AND GREEN TOMATO CASSEROLE
Number of Servings — 6

6 pork chops
Salt
Pepper
3 medium green tomatoes
3 small onions
1 T. curry powder

Salt and pepper all. Brown pork chops and pour off grease. Put in casserole and alternate with a layer of green tomatoes and a layer of onions. Sprinkle with curry powder and bake in moderate oven (350°F.) at least 1 hour.

Mrs. Sue Harrison, Keiser H. S.
Keiser, Arkansas

PORK CHOP CASSEROLE (WITH SWEET POTATOES)
Number of Servings — 6

6 large ½ inch thick slices sweet potato (cooked or uncooked)
6 thin slices unpeeled orange
6 pork chops
1 t. salt
¼ t. pepper
⅓ c. brown sugar

Heat oven to 350°F. (moderate). Place potato slices in greased oblong baking dish; top with orange slices, then pork chops. Season with salt and pepper; sprinkle with brown sugar. Cover and bake 1½ hours, uncovering last half hour.

Mrs. Betty Jo Hill, Gorham Com. H. S.
Gorham, Illinois

PORK CHOPS EN CASSEROLE
Number of Servings — 6

6 pork chops
6 sweet potatoes
Salt and pepper
½ c. brown sugar
1 to 2 c. milk

Place a layer of sweet potatoes, peeled and sliced crosswise, in a greased casserole. Sprinkle with salt and pepper and a little brown sugar; continue layers until casserole is ⅔ full. Heat milk, pour over potatoes to just cover them. Place pork chops on top of potatoes, cover and bake at 350°F. for 1 hour. Remove cover and season with salt and pepper. Continue cooking, uncovered, until chops are tender and nicely browned on top.

Mrs. Josephine Lumpkin, Fairfield Jr. H. S.
Richmond, Virginia

PORK CHOPS EN CASSEROLE
Number of Servings — 6

6 lean pork chops
1 8-oz. can whole kernel corn
1 10-oz. can cream of mushroom soup

Brown pork chops slowly. Season with salt and pepper. Add corn and soup. Bake 1 hour in covered casserole at 350°F.

Mrs. Magdaline Dhuey, Casco H. S.
Casco, Wisconsin

PORK CHOP AND RICE CASSEROLE
Number of Servings — 3-4

1⅓ c. uncooked minute rice
1 can cream of mushroom soup
¾ can water
3-4 pork chops

Combine uncooked rice with cream of mushroom soup. Add ¾ can of water and mix. Put mixture into casserole dish. Brown pork chops on both sides. Put on top of rice mixture. Bake at 350°F. for 1 hour.

Mrs. Diane Ross, Laingsburg H. S.
Laingsburg, Michigan

PORK OR BEEF CABOOSE
Number of Servings — 6

2 or 3 c. left over meat, cut small
1 can condensed vegetable soup
1 T. chopped onion
1 T. chopped celery
1 T. chopped celery leaves
1 T. chopped green pepper
1 tomato, chopped small
Dash oregano
Dash tabasco sauce
Dash pepper
¼ t. salt
1 T. Kitchen Bouquet

Place all ingredients in pot and just cover with water. Bring to a boil over direct heat then lower to simmer for 30 minutes. Serve in toast cups, patties, over waffles, or simply plain. Garnish with fresh parsley.

Sister M. Eleanor, Bishop McDevitt H. S.
Harrisburg, Pennsylvania

SCALLOPED PORK AND RICE
Number of Servings — 8

1 lb. pork, cubed
1 T. shortening
1 onion, diced
1 t. paprika
1 t. salt
1 c. rice
1 small can sauerkraut
½ pt. sour cream

Melt shortening; add diced onion and brown slightly. Add paprika, pork and salt to taste. Cook until meat is done—about 1 hour. Add water to keep meat from burning. Cook rice in boiling salted water. In a casserole arrange a layer of this meat mixture, layer of rice and layer of sauerkraut. Continue this until all ingredients are in casserole. Pour sour cream over all. Bake in 350°F. oven for about an hour, until all is browned. For a richer casserole, another ½ pint sour cream may be used in the layers.

Regina E. Johnson, Memorial Sr. H. S.
Ely, Minnesota

MOCK CHICKEN-NOODLE CASSEROLE
Number of Servings — 4

⅔ lb. pork or veal steak
1 can (11 oz.) chicken soup
1 can (No. 2) whole kernel corn
1 package (6 oz.) noodles
1 T. cooking fat

Cut meat into small pieces and brown in fat. Cook noodles in boiling salted water until done, about 9 minutes. Place meat, corn, and drained noodles in alternate layers in a greased casserole. Pour chicken soup over all and sprinkle with grated cheese. Bake in a 350°F. oven for about 45 minutes or until nicely browned.

Olith Hamilton, W. K. Kellogg H. S.
Nashville, Michigan

MEAT NOODLE CASSEROLE
Number of Servings — 8

1 8-oz. package noodles
1 lb. ground lean pork
2 small onions, chopped
2 c. diced celery
1 small green pepper, chopped
Salt and pepper to taste
1 can condensed tomato soup
1½ t. Worcestershire sauce
½ c. grated American cheese

Cook noodles in boiling, salted water; drain and rinse. Brown meat in small amount of hot fat; add onions, celery, and pepper; cook until tender. Season with salt and pepper. Alternate meat and noodles in greased casserole. Mix tomato soup with Worcestershire sauce. Pour over mixture in casserole. Sprinkle cheese over top of mixture in casserole. Bake in moderate oven (350°F.) for 45 minutes.

Mrs. Jo Frances Weimar, Alto H. S.
Alto, Texas

PORK AND NOODLE CASSEROLE
Number of Servings — 8

2 lbs. cubed pork
1 c. diced celery
1 small onion, diced
1 c. water
1 c. corn
2 t. salt
1 can condensed mushroom soup
1 8-oz. package medium noodles, cooked
1 c. grated cheddar cheese
¼ c. fine bread crumbs
1 T. butter

Cook celery and onion in water until tender (about 8 minutes). Brown pork; add onion, celery and cooking liquid. Cover and cook 20 minutes. Season. Combine with noodles, corn, and soup. Place in 3 quart casserole. Cover with grated cheese. Top with crumbs mixed with melted butter.

Jeanette Pusheck, Denmark H. S.
Denmark, Wisconsin

PORK HOT DISH
Number of Servings — 6

¾ lbs. pork
½ stock celery
1 onion
1 can chicken-rice soup
1 can mushroom soup
½ to ¾ package noodles
1 small package potato chips

Cut meat in cubes and brown in fat. When browned, add celery and onion and cook until tender and well done. Mix with 1 can chicken-rice soup and 1 can mushroom soup and ½ package noodles. Add enough water to soup to make it

nice and juicy. Add salt and pepper. Bake 1½ hours, covered. Last 20 minutes take off cover and put potato chips on top.

Mrs. Linda F. Johnson, Marietta P. S.
Marietta, Minnesota

MOCK CHICKEN CASSEROLE
Number of Servings — 25

3 lbs. crumbled sausage
2 medium onions, chopped
2 c. diced celery
1 large green pepper, diced
10 c. water
2 c. uncooked rice
3 packages chicken noodle soup
1 c. slivered almonds

Fry sausage, onions, celery and green pepper until slightly brown. Add water and uncooked rice; let boil 5 minutes then add chicken noodle soup and almonds. Boil from 5 to 7 minutes. This is an excellent casserole to freeze and have for that unexpected company.

Annie Lewis Varnell, Dora Municipal H. S.
Dora, New Mexico

CITY CHICKEN
Number of Servings — 8

1 lb. cubed beef
1 lb. cubed pork
1 egg, beaten
½ c. flour
Salt and pepper
8 skewers

Place beef and pork alternately on skewers. Roll "drumsticks" in the beaten egg. Place seasonings, flour, and meat in a sack and shake. Brown meat on one side in a small amount of fat. Add 1 cup water or tomato juice and braise on low heat for 1 hour.

Mrs. Caroll Deem, Decker H. S.
Decker, Indiana

CHOP SUEY CASSEROLE
Number of Servings — 10

1 lb. cubed pork steak
1 lb. veal steak
2 c. celery, chopped
½ c. green pepper, chopped
½ c. onions, chopped
1 can mushrooms
3 T. Show-You sauce
1 can chicken rice soup
½ c. raw rice
1 can mushroom soup
2 c. water

Brown meat. Add remaining ingredients, mix, and bake in a casserole for 1½ hours at 350°F.

Irma B. Morley, Allegan H. S.
Allegan, Michigan

AMERICAN CHOP SUEY
Number of Servings — 4

¼ lb. ground pork
¼ lb. ground veal
¼ c. chopped green pepper
1 No. 2½ can tomatoes
¼ c. chopped onion
¼ c. chopped celery
¼ c. rice (uncooked)

Brown meat in skillet in 1 tablespoon fat. Spread evenly over bottom. Sprinkle over meat: pepper, onion and celery which have been mixed together. Add salt and pepper to taste. Pour in tomatoes. Last, sprinkle with rice which has been washed. Cover. Turn to high until steaming then to low for 30 minutes.

Catherine H. Wilder, Contenerea H. S.
Kinston, North Carolina

HAM SURPRISE
Number of Servings — 4-6

2 T. shortening
1 2-oz. can mushrooms
1 chopped onion
½ c. chopped green pepper
2 c. diced ham
1 c. medium cream sauce
1 can whole kernel corn (including liquid)
¼ t. dry mustard

Cook mushrooms, onion, green pepper and ham in shortening until lightly brown. Add cream sauce, corn, and mustard. Can be baked in oven with biscuit baked on top of ham sauce. Serve over biscuit or toast.

Barbara Gaylor, Consultant
Homemaking and Family Life Education Service
Division of Vocational Education
Michigan Department of Public Instruction
Lansing, Michigan

SAVORY HAM-TOMATO CASSEROLE
Number of Servings — 8

1 6-oz. package macaroni
1 No. 2 can tomatoes
1 c. chopped celery
½ c. chopped onions
½ c. chopped green pepper
2½ t. salt
¼ t. pepper
1½ c. chopped, cooked ham
2 T. parsley
1 c. grated American cheese

Cook macaroni according to directions; drain. Cook tomatoes, onions, green pepper, and seasonings together for 30 minutes. Combine all ingredients and ¾ cup cheese. Bake in slow oven (325°F.) for 1 hour. Top with ¼ cup cheese during last 5 minutes.

Bonnie Dickinson, Fort Sumner H. S.
Fort Sumner, New Mexico

FILLED BAKED TOMATOES
Number of Servings — 4

10 large tomatoes
1 T. shortening
¾ c. cooked onion
1 c. cooked ham
1½ t. flour
¾ c. sour cream
2 t. soya sauce
2 t. chives or parsley
1 T. grated cheese
1 T. fine dry bread crumbs

Cut off a thin slice from top of tomatoes. Scoop out pulp. Melt shortening, add onion; saute 5 minutes; chop ham, add and cook until onions are soft. Stir in rice, flour, sour cream, soya sauce, pepper, chives. Season with salt and pepper to taste. Stuff tomatoes with this mixture. Place in buttered baking dish. Sprinkle with cheese and bread crumbs. Bake in moderate oven (375°F.) for 15 to 20 minutes or until golden brown.

Gloria Sawyer, Webb H. S.
Reedsburg, Wisconsin

HAM CASSEROLE
Number of Servings — 6-8

¼ lb. American cheese, diced
1½ c. thin white sauce
2 c. boiled macaroni
1½ c. cooked ham, diced
4 hard cooked eggs, sliced
½ c. bread crumbs, buttered

Add cheese to white sauce and stir until the cheese is melted. Put 1 cup macaroni in bottom of greased casserole, sprinkle with ¾ cup ham, cover with a layer of egg slices and pour ½ of the cheese sauce over the top. Repeat, arranging the remaining ingredients in like layers; cover with buttered crumbs. Bake in a moderate oven (350°F.) about ½ hour or until the crumbs are well browned.

Frances Smith, Rockcreek Center H. S.
Bluffton, Indiana

SMOKED HAM
Number of Servings — 12

1 lb. smoked ham
½ lb. round steak
½ lb. fresh pork
1 c. fresh bread crumbs
1 T. chopped green pepper
2 T. chopped onion
1 t. salt
2 eggs, beaten
1 c. canned tomatoes

Grind the ham, steak and pork together. Mix all ingredients well. Pack into a pyrex loaf baking dish. Bake 3 hours at 325°F. Serve with broiled pineapple slices or a nippy horseradish sauce.

Laura Ryburn, Rantoul Twp. H. S.
Rantoul, Illinois

HAM AND CABBAGE CASSEROLE
Number of Servings — 6

4 c. coarsely shredded cabbage
½ c. water
½ t. salt
¼ c. butter or margarine
¼ c. flour
½ t. salt
⅛ t. pepper
½ t. dry mustard
2 c. milk
1½ c. grated sharp cheese
1½ lbs. cooked ham, cut into 1 inch cubes
½ green pepper, diced
1 c. fresh bread crumbs, buttered

Place cabbage, water and salt in a covered saucepan. Bring to boil, lower heat and cook 3 minutes. Drain. Melt butter, blend in flour, salt, pepper and mustard. Add milk and cook, stirring constantly until thick and smooth. Add cheese and heat until melted. Add cabbage, ham and green pepper. Turn into a casserole and top with bread crumbs. Bake at 350°F. for 20 minutes or until heated through.

Kay Ashdown, Manlius H. S.
Manlius, Illinois

SAUERKRAUT DISH
Number of Servings — 4-5

1 lb. sauerkraut
1 c. water
½ lb. ham, in thin slices (about 1/16 or ⅛ in.)
1½ lbs. potatoes
Milk
Margarine
Nutmeg
Pepper
Bread crumbs

Cook sauerkraut until done. Make mashed potatoes. Roll the sauerkraut in the slices of ham. Put them in a casserole. Put the mashed potatoes on top. Sprinkle bread crumbs over it and some little pieces of margarine. Put the casserole in the middle of the oven. Bake at 350°F. until there is a brown crust.

Gebrouella W. Kroene, Whitehall H. S.
Whitehall, Montana

HAM AND KRAUT ROLLS
Number of Servings — 6

6 slices boiled ham, ⅛ inch thick
1½ c. sauerkraut, drained
¼ lb. grated sharp cheese
¼ t. dry mustard
¼ t. Worcestershire sauce
1 c. seasoned white sauce
¼ c. diced green pepper

Spread each ham slice with ¼ cup sauerkraut and green pepper. Roll each slice up beginning with the narrow end. Arrange in a shallow baking dish. Add cheese, dry mustard, and Worcestershire

sauce to white sauce. Heat slowly, stirring constantly, until cheese is melted. Pour over ham rolls. Bake at 350°F. about 30 minutes.

Mrs. Kathryn Woods, Woodrow Wilson H. S.
Beckley, West Virginia

SAVORY HAM-POTATO BAKE
Number of Servings — 6

2 T. butter
1 medium green pepper, chopped
1 small onion, chopped
3 T. flour
¼ c. crushed corn flakes
½ t. salt
1 c. milk
½ c. grated sharp cheese
2 c. peeled sliced potatoes
2 c. cubed cooked ham
3 slices diced cooked bacon

Cook green pepper, onion in butter until tender. Stir in flour and salt. Add milk and cook until thick, stirring constantly. Add cheese and stir until melted. Layer potatoes, ham, bacon and cheese sauce in 1½-quart casserole. Top with corn flakes. Bake at 350°F. 1 hour or until potatoes are done.

Ruth B. Royer, Warrior Run Area School
Turbotville, Pennsylvania

HAM, MACARONI AND CHEESE FAMILY-STYLE
Number of Servings — 4

½ c. ground or finely chopped cooked ham
¼ c. chopped onion
2 T. butter or margarine
1 can (10½ oz.) condensed cream of mushroom
   soup
½ c. milk
1 c. shredded sharp cheddar cheese
2 c. cooked macaroni
2 T. buttered bread crumbs

In saucepan, lightly brown ham and onion in butter. Stir in soup, milk, and ¾ cup cheese. Heat until cheese melts. Blend sauce with macaroni; pour into a buttered 1½ quart casserole. Sprinkle remaining cheese and crumbs on top. Bake in a moderate oven (350°F.) about 30 minutes, or until nicely browned and bubbling.

Marolyn Westbrook, Lee County H. S.
Leesburg, Georgia

HAM TIMBALE
Number of Servings — 4

2 c. ground cooked ham
1 c. medium white sauce
2 eggs, beaten
¼ t. powdered dry mustard

Mix all ingredients and pour into shallow greased baking dish. Place dish in pan of hot water. Bake at 350°F. (modertae oven) about 50 minutes or until mixture is firm in center. Serve with baked squash, coleslaw and cooked dried fruit.

Mrs. Lela Carlile, Calvin H. S.
Calvin, Oklahoma

THREE-IN-ONE HAM CASSEROLE
Number of Servings — 6-8

1 10-oz. package frozen green beans
1 can (4 oz.) mushrooms
¼ c. butter
¼ c. sifted flour
1 c. thin cream
1 c. milk
1 t. salt
¼ t. pepper
3 c. diced, cooked ham
⅓ c. diced pimento
⅔ c. grated mild cheese

Cook beans until tender in small amount of water. Drain. Lightly brown mushrooms in butter. Reserve several mushrooms for topping. Blend flour into butter and mushrooms. Add cream, milk, and seasonings. Cook until thickened and smooth, stirring constantly. Fold in beans, ham, and pimento. Pour into buttered 2-quart casserole. Top with reserved mushrooms and sprinkle with grated cheese. Bake in moderate oven (350°F.) for 20 minutes or until lightly browned.

Jean Zink, Chrisman H. S.
Chrisman, Illinois

OZARK HAM CASSEROLE
Number of Servings — 4

1 thin center slice smoked ham (¾ lbs.)
2¼ t. flour
1 can condensed cream of mushroom soup, undiluted
1 c. milk
3 c. sliced, pared potatoes
1 c. sliced, scraped carrots
¼ c. minced onion
Salt and pepper

Start heating oven to 375°F. In skillet, brown ham lightly on both sides; remove from skillet and cut into serving-size pieces. Stir flour into fat left in skillet; add soup. Then slowly stir in milk. Heat, stirring, till boiling. In 2 quart casserole, arrange ham, potatoes, carrots, onions until all are used, sprinkling vegetables lightly with salt and pepper. Pour on soup mixture. Bake covered, 1 hour; uncover, bake 15 minutes longer, or until potatoes are fork-tender.

Roxy Ann Pike, Hillcrest Jr. H. S.
Fayetteville, Arkansas

HAM
Number of Servings — 6

1½ c. baked ham, cubed
6 eggs, hard cooked, cubed
1 c. medium white sauce

Cube ham, hard cooked eggs, and mix lightly in casserole. Pour white sauce over ham and egg mixture. Bake in 350°F. oven until brown on top.

Lois B. Jenkins, Franklin Area Joint School
Franklin, Pennsylvania

HAM AND RICE CASSEROLE
Number of Servings — 4

1 c. uncooked rice
2 large slices center cut ham
3 to 4 c. milk

Grease a flat casserole, or a large cast iron skillet. Spread evenly over bottom of casserole the washed uncooked rice. Place slices of ham on top of rice. Add milk; enough to cover ham. Bake in 375°-400°F. oven for 1 hour. Ham will season the rice.

Mary Kathryn Hay, Homer H. S.
Homer, Illinois

HAM AND RICE CASSEROLE
Number of Servings — 10

2 10½-oz. cans cream of celery soup
1 c. light cream
1 c. grated sharp cheddar cheese
½ c. grated Parmesan cheese
1½ T. minced onion
1 T. prepared mustard
⅛ t. pepper
4 c. cooked rice
4 c. cubed cooked ham
1 10-oz. package frozen green peas
1 3½-oz. can French-fried onion rings

In saucepan, combine celery soup and cream. Stir until smooth. Heat over low heat until hot, do not boil. Stir in cheeses. Blend in onion, mustard, pepper. Remove from heat. Combine sauce with rice and cubed ham. In 3 quart casserole, alternate layers of ham and rice mixture with green peas, ending with ham and rice mixture on top. Sprinkle top with French-fried onion rings. Bake, uncovered, at 350°F. for 15 to 20 minutes. If family is small, divide into 2 casseroles and freeze one for a later meal.

Mrs. Martha Jo Bredemyer, Lancaster H. S.
Lancaster, Texas

SAUSAGE-RICE CASSEROLE
Number of Servings — 6-8

1 lb. pork sausage
¾ c. uncooked rice
2 c. canned tomatoes
¾ c. finely chopped onion
1 t. salt
1 t. chili powder
2 c. hot water
½ c. grated sharp cheese

Break sausage into pieces i na cold skillet. Fry slowly for 12 to 15 minutes until evenly browned, pouring off fat as it accumulates. Pour off all but ¼ cup fat. Add rice to fat in skillet. Cook and stir over low heat until rice is lightly browned. Stir in tomatoes, onion, salt, chili powder, hot water, and sausage. Pour into a baking dish and cook, uncovered, at 350°F. for 45 minutes. Sprinkle cheese on top and bake for an additional 10 minutes.

Lynda Hunter Black, Bartow Sr. H. S.
Bartow, Florida

SAUSAGE WITH SWEET POTATO AND APPLE CASSEROLE*

½ lb. sausage
2 medium sized sweet potatoes
3 medium sized apples
½ t. salt
1 T. flour
2 T. sugar
½ c. cold water
1 T. sausage drippings

Cut link sausage into ½ inch pieces. Fry until well done. If bulk sausage is used, shape into small balls before frying or break it up as it cooks. Slice potatoes and apples. Leave peeling on apples for color. Mix salt, flour, and sugar together and blend with cold water. Arrange layers of potatoes, apples, and sausage in a baking dish, pouring flour-sugar mixture over each layer. Top with apples and sausage, and add drippings. Cover and bake in 375°F. oven (moderate) until apples and potatoes are tender, about 45 minutes. To shorten cooking time; precook sweet potatoes with skins on. *Menu Suggestion:* Serve with a crisp green salad. For dessert have a well-chilled creamy rice pudding made with eggs to supplement the protein from the small serving of meat.. If you double the amount of sausage in the main dish you will not need to choose a dessert that supplies additional protein.
*Economy dish.

Mrs. Ann Simon Knutson, South Jr. H. S.
Rapid City, South Dakota

CORN SAUSAGE CASSEROLE

Number of Servings — 6

4 eggs
2½ c. cream style corn (No. 2 can)
1 c. soft bread crumbs
1 lb. sausage meat
1 t. salt
⅛ t. pepper

Mix all ingredients together and pour into a greased round casserole. Spread catsup over the top. Bake in a pan of hot water (1 inch deep) at 350°F. (moderate oven) for 1 hour.

Mrs. John A. Shipe, East Forest Joint H. S.
Marienville, Pennsylvania

BAKED SAUSAGE 'N EGGS

Number of Servings — 8

½ lb. package brown 'N serve sausage patties
2 t. salt
½ t. marjoram
8 eggs
¼ t. pepper
3 T. butter or margarine

Lightly grease the sides of 8 custard cups. Place a sausage patty in the bottom of each cup and break an egg on top of each. Combine salt, pepper, and marjoram. Sprinkle each egg with some of the seasoning. Dot with butter. Bake in a moderate oven (350°F.) for about 20 minutes or until eggs are firm.

Elvira Benne, Columbus Sr. H. S.
Columbus, Nebraska

SAUSAGE CASSEROLE

Number of Servings — 6

1 lb. bulk sausage
½ c. chopped onion
1 c. chopped celery
1 c. brown rice
1 can cream of mushroom soup
1 can water
1 chopped bell pepper
¼ c. grated cheese

In a skillet brown sausage, onion, celery and rice. When the above is golden, add rest of ingredients. Put in casserole. Sprinkle grated cheese on top. Bake at 350°F. for 1 hour, or until rice is tender.

Mrs. Helen Bell, South Jr. H. S.
Grants Pass, Oregon

SAUSAGE BLUE CHEESE CASSEROLE

Number of Servings — 6 generous

1 lb. pork sausage, in balls
2 c. fine noodles
2 T. green pepper
2 T. pimento
1 can chicken soup
½ c. blue cheese
Buttered bread crumbs

Brown sausage balls lightly. Cook noodles in unsalted water and drain. Mix sausage and noodles. Add chopped green pepper and pimento. Place in casserole and add soup in which blue cheese is melted. Cover with buttered bread crumbs and bake at 350°F. for 30 minutes uncovered.

Aldona Klisis, Council H. S.
Council, Idaho

CROQUETTES

Number of Servings — 4-6

1½ c. chopped, cooked eggs or cheese or tuna
    or roast veal or pork
1 c. thick white sauce
2 t. salt
⅛ t. pepper
1 egg
1 T. water

Grind or chop the material and combine with white sauce and seasonings. Allow to cool and stiffen. Shape into balls, cones, or rolls, allowing 1 tablespoon for each croquette. Roll in crumbs, then dip in egg slightly beaten and mixed with cold water. Roll in crumbs again. Fry in deep fat (375°-380°F.) until delicately browned (about 1 minute). Serve hot.

Caroline Brady, Sapulpa Jr. H. S.
Sapulpa, Oklahoma

Poultry Casseroles

HUNTERS HOTDISH
Number of Servings — 6

1 lb. bacon
1 lb. smoked ham
2 cans Italian spaghetti
1 No. 303 can whole kernel corn
1 No. 303 can tomatoes
1 8-oz. can baby lima beans
1 4-oz. can mushrooms

Cut ham and bacon into bite size pieces. Fry until done. Drain liquid from corn, mushrooms, and lima beans. Combine all ingredients in a deep casserole dish. Bake for 3½ hours at 325°F.

Mrs. Delores Dexter, Spearfish H. S.
Spearfish, South Dakota

CHICKEN-HAM SUPREME
Number of Servings — 8

3 whole chicken breasts
8 slices home baked ham
2 packages frozen broccoli
3 T. butter
1½ t. salt
3 T. flour
2 c. milk
½ c. chicken broth
⅔ c. either wine or sharp cheese

Cook chicken in small amount of salted water. Remove skin and bone; use in long, thick pieces. Cook broccoli in salted water and drain. Make white sauce. Add chicken broth and either wine or cheese. Use serving of broccoli. Cover with ham. Place slithers of chicken on top. Cover with sauce. Garnish with browned almonds.

Armitage Coburn, Calhoun H. S.
West Homestead, Pennsylvania

CHICKEN CASSEROLE
Number of Servings — 6-8

2 lbs. chicken breasts
2 c. soft bread crumbs
1 c. grated cheese
¼ c. (½ stick) melted butter
1 10-oz. package frozen mixed vegetables, cooked
Cheese sauce

Simmer chicken in water until tender. Save 1 cup broth. Remove from bone and chop. Mix bread cubes with grated cheese and melted butter for topping. Spoon rest into 2 quart casserole; top with vegetables, chicken and cheese sauce mixed and save bread. Bake in moderate oven (350°F.) for 15 minutes; uncover and bake 10 minutes longer. *Cheese Sauce:* Stir ¼ cup flour, ¾ teaspoon salt and ¼ teaspoon pepper into ¼ cup melted fat in saucepan. Add 1 cup milk and 1 cup saved broth. Cook until thick and add 1½ cups grated cheddar cheese.

Mrs. Louise Simpson, New Site H. S.
Alexander City, Alabama

OLD FASHIONED CHICKEN CASSEROLE
The Hen:

1 hen—cook in enough water so that you have at least 1 quart liquid left when hen is tender. Add 3 or 4 pieces of celery (cut in pieces) to the stock while cooking. Also salt and pepper to taste. When the hen is thoroughly tender, drain off and strain the stock. Remove bones and cut the hen in bite sized pieces.

The Sauce:

Use 1 cup of the fat skimmed off the stock. Add 1 cup flour and mix thoroughly. Heat slowly, adding while heating the remainder of the stock. Cook, stirring constantly until thoroughly thickened. While still hot, put a little of this mixture into 3 or 4 beaten eggs. Gradually add the remaining part to the eggs. Set aside to cool without further cooking. Season with salt and pepper corns (freshly ground).

The Dressing:

Make a good cornbread (see recipe). Crumble ½ of it, crumble ½ loaf of bread into fine pieces, and crumble 6 or 8 crackers. Mix cornbread crumbs, crackers and bread crumbs. Add 1 large onion (chopped), ½ teaspoon sage and 2 or more cupfuls of fresh chopped celery. Add 3 or 4 tablespoons of the sauce (enough to moisten) to the bread crumb mixture.

The Casserole:

Place a 2 inch layer of the dressing in a casserole dish. Over this place a layer of the cooked chicken (about 1 inch). Top this with the sauce spread evenly. Cook for 20 minutes. Serve bubbling hot.

CORNBREAD

1 c. cornmeal (water ground)
4 T. whole wheat flour
1 t. salt
1½ t. baking powder
1 beaten egg
1¼ c. buttermilk
3 T. baking drippings

Mix dry ingredients well, add milk, eggs and fat. Put in hot skillet. Cook 425°F. for 17 minutes. Serve hot.

Mrs. Elsie Evans, Loris H. S.
Loris, South Carolina

CHICKEN SUPREME
Number of Servings — 6

6 chicken thighs
1 can mushroom soup
1 c. bread crumbs
½ c. water

Prepare chicken for frying and brown in deep fat. Place the soup and water in casserole, add the browned chicken, cover with bread crumbs and bake until brown in a moderate oven. Serve hot.

Agnes I. Howell, Andrew Jackson H. S.
Jacksonville, Florida

CHICKEN SUPREME CASSEROLE
Number of Servings — 8-10

1 small box crackers
1 stewing chicken, cooked and boned
1 can mushroom soup
1 can milk (use soup can)

Grease a casserole dish. Place a layer of crushed crackers, then a layer of chicken. Alternate layers. Top with crackers. Pour diluted soup over the crackers and bake for 45 minutes or until bubbly in a moderate oven (350°F.). Salt to taste.

Mrs. Wilma B. Harris, Western H. S.
Russiaville, Indiana

CHICKEN CASSEROLE
Number of Servings — 8

1 cooked chicken, boiled with bones removed
1 c. diced celery
½ lb. mild cream cheese
1 can mushrooms
1 c. cooked shell macaroni
Small bits of pimento
2 c. chicken broth, thickened
1 can mushroom soup

Combine ingredients in casserole dish and bake slowly at 325°F. for 1 hour.

Norma Jeremison, Sundance H. S.
Sundance, Wyoming

CASSEROLE CHICKEN
Number of Servings — 6-8

2 to 2½ lb. chicken (fryer)
1 c. flour, seasoned with salt and pepper
⅓ c. French salad dressing
1 c. hot water
½ c. cooking oil

Prepare chicken as for frying. Coat with flour, seasoned with salt and pepper. Brown quickly in hot oil in skillet. When well brown place chicken, skin side up in casserole. Pour French dressing slowly over each piece of chicken. Add water; cover casserole. Bake in 325°F. oven for 1 hour.

Juanita Patton, Achille P. S.
Achille, Oklahoma

CHICKEN CASSEROLE
Number of Servings — 6-8

3 c. diced chicken
1 can mushroom soup
½ c. chicken broth
¼ c. chopped onion
1 c. diced celery
2 c. chow mein noodles
1 c. broken cashew nuts

Mix together all ingredients except 1 cup of chow mein noodles. Pour mixture into greased casserole. Sprinkle 1 cup chow mein noodles on top. Bake at 350°F. for 30 minutes.

Mary D. Thompson, Owensville H. S.
Owensville, Indiana

CHICKEN CASSEROLE
Number of Servings — 20

3-4 lb. stewing chicken
1½ c. diced celery
1 medium sized onion
1½ c. cubed American cheese
3 eggs, beaten
6 c. broth
½ t. pepper
½ t. salt
1 can mushroom soup
1 can cream of celery soup
4 c. rolled buttered crumbs

Cook chicken, remove meat from the bones and cut into small pieces. Add all other ingredients, except 1 cup buttered crumbs. Mix well. Pour into a large casserole. Cover with remaining crumbs and bake 45 minutes at 350°F.

Mrs. Barbara Deane, Sheridan Com. H. S.
Hoxie, Kansas

CHICKEN CASSEROLE PLUS
Number of Servings — 6

2½ lb. fryer (cut up)
1 t. salt
½ t. black pepper
½ t. celery salt
1 can cream of mushroom soup
Enough flour to dredge chicken
1 can water
1 t. parsley flakes
Few dashes paprika
3 T. corn oil

Combine salts, pepper, parsley flakes and flour; mix well and dredge chicken pieces as for frying. Oil casserole dish well and arrange chicken in dish. Blend soup and water; pour over chicken. Bake covered 45 minutes at 350°F. cook uncovered about 10 minutes. Sprinkle top with paprika. Serve with rice or mashed potatoes.

Mrs. Mary A. Campbell, Fort Necessity H. S.
Fort Necessity, Louisiana

CHICKEN CASSEROLE
Number of Servings — 6

2 c. cooked chicken
2 c. dressing
2 c. gravy
Black pepper
Paprika

Cook chicken, seasoned with salt and pepper, until done; separate from bones. Combine ingredients for your favorite chicken dressing. Make gravy from chicken broth. Combine casserole in deep baking dish beginning with chicken, then dressing, then gravy, chicken, dressing and gravy. Sprinkle with paprika and black pepper. Bake until browned, about 25 minutes in 375°F. oven.

Mrs. Estelle Dobbins, Auburn H. S.
Riner, Virginia

CHICKEN-EGG EN CASSEROLE
Number of Servings — 4

1 young chicken, cut for frying
4 T. butter
1 small onion
1 small carrot
3 hard cooked eggs
2 c. stock or water
1 bay leaf
3 potatoes, thinly sliced
1 small can mushrooms
Salt and pepper
3 T. cooking sherry

Melt butter in frying pan. Add onion and carrot cut in thin slices. Also add pieces of chicken and cook until golden brown, placing them in casserole as they reach this stage. Add potatoes, mushrooms and seasonings. Pour stock over them. Add bay leaf; cover and cook in a slow oven (325°F.) until tender. Add the sherry at last moment before serving. Garnish with egg wedges.

Mrs. B. Fred German, Copper Basin H. S.
Copperhill, Tennessee

CHICKEN CASSEROLE
Number of Servings — 4-5

1 can chow mein noodles
1 c. chicken
1 can cream of chicken soup
1 can cream of mushroom soup
1 can celery soup
½ c. almonds

Grease casserole dish. Cover bottom of dish with ½ of noodles. Add chicken soup, ¼ cup chicken; add mushroom soup, ½ cup chicken; add celery soup and ¼ cup chicken. Sprinkle top with noodles and almonds. Bake at 325°F. for 1½ hours. Cover 1 hour; uncover ½ hour.

Karen Manthei, Springfield H. S.
Springfield, Minnesota

CHICKEN SUPREME
Number of Servings — 4-6

1 3-lb. chicken
1 medium onion
6 medium potatoes
1 10½- or 11-oz. can cream of mushroom soup
Salt and pepper

Cut chicken in serving pieces, salt and pepper to taste. Place in casserole alternately with ½ inch thick slices of potatoes and ¼ inch slices of onion. Pour soup which has been diluted with ⅓ can of water over the chicken and vegetables. Cover casserole. Bake in slow oven (250°F.) about 2 to 2½ hours. For individual serving, place 1 or 2 pieces of chicken, 2 pieces potato and 1 onion slice with 1 heaping tablespoon soup (not thinned) in the center of a sheet of foil large enough to seal and still have air space.

Mrs. Violet C. Moseley, Avon Park H. S.
Avon Park, Florida

CHICKEN CASSEROLE
Number of Servings — 12

4 lbs. stewing chicken
1 6-oz. can mushrooms
1 c. evaporated milk
½ c. butter, oleo or chicken fat
1 12- or 16-oz. package medium sized noodles
½ c. flour
½ T. tumeric
¼ t. oregano
½ c. cheese

Measure liquid from mushrooms. Add enough chicken broth to make 3 cups, and add milk. Melt fat and blend in flour and spices. Add liquid, and cook until thickened. Add ¼ cup of cheese; stir until melted. Spread noodles in greased casserole. Add boned chicken and mushrooms. Pour sauce. Add remaining cheese. Bake at 350°F. for 45 minutes.

Mrs. Marjory Fuller, Seitz Jr. H. S.
Wyandotte, Michigan

CHICKEN CASSEROLE — (Chili)
Number of Servings — 6-8

1 medium sized chicken
1 qt. of broth, drain off fat
½ lb. sharp cheese
1 can (4 ozs.) green chili
1 large onion, diced
1 button garlic, crushed
1 package Fritos (8 oz.)

Cook chicken until done, cool and bone. Simmer onion and garlic in broth until done. Place thin layer of Fritos in the bottom of a 2 quart casserole. Divide remaining ingredients into two parts. For first layer use about ½ chicken, followed by grated cheese, frozen or canned green chili, and Fritos. Continue by second layer as indicated. Top with remaining Fritos. Pour broth over entire mixture, cover and bake 30 minutes at 300°F.

Mrs. Hazel Speake, Washington Jr. H. S.
Albuquerque, New Mexico

CHICKEN
Number of Servings — 8

1 can (5 oz.) boned chicken
1 can cream of chicken soup
1 T. minced onion
½ c. olives
½ t. salt
1 T. lemon juice
½ c. mayonnaise
3 hard cooked eggs, sliced
¾ c. cooked wild rice
1½ c. crushed potato chips

Combine all ingredients and place in casserole. Cover top with additional ½ cup crushed potato chips and bake at 450°F. for 15 minutes.

Mrs. Lucille Clowclis, Gordon H. S.
Decatur, Georgia

CHICKEN CASSEROLE
Number of Servings — 8-10

3 c. cooked, boned chicken
1 can cream of mushroom soup
1 4-oz. can mushrooms
3 T. chopped red sweet peppers
1 pkg. (10-oz.) noodles, cooked
1 pkg. cooked frozen peas
1 T. dried parsley
1 c. crushed potato chips

Combine all the ingredients, except potato chips, in casserole baking dish. Top with crushed potato chips. Bake in 350°F. oven for 35 minutes. Serves 8-10 amply.

Mrs. Joseph Didot, Hartford Center H. S.
Geneva, Indiana

CHICKEN SUPREME
Number of Servings — 6

6 chicken breasts
½ pt. coffee cream
¼ lb. butter
1 t. finely chopped onion
1 t. finely chopped celery
1 t. finely chopped carrot

Place chicken breasts right side up in wide, low baking dish. Pour over coffee cream and melted butter. Sprinkle with the fine chopped vegetables. Bake at 325°F. for 1½ hours. Baste occasionally with the cream-butter mixture to keep chicken moist.

Mary Osborne, Washington H. S.
Massillon, Ohio

CHICKEN CASSEROLE
Number of Servings — 8

¾ lb. processed cheese
8 oz. package macaroni, uncooked
1 small onion, diced
2 cans cream of mushroom soup
2 c. diced chicken
3 hard cooked eggs, diced
1 c. milk

Mix all ingredients together. Refrigerate for 24 hours. Bake in a moderately hot oven (350°F.) for 1 hour or until not soupy.

Avis Jean Johnson, Plymouth H. S.
Plymouth, Illinois

CHICKEN CASSEROLE
Number of Servings — 6

1 frying size chicken
1 can cream of chicken soup
1 onion
Salt
1 c. rice
1 can water
3 T. salad dressing
Pepper

Combine rice, salt and pepper, add to casserole dish. Pour soup over rice, add can of water. Slice onion over rice. Place chicken pieces over rice. Dot salad dressing over chicken pieces and bake 400°F. for 1 hour.

Mrs. Kay Holland, Dexter H. S.
Dexter, Georgia

HERBED CHICKEN CASSEROLE
Number of Servings — 6

2½ to 3 lb. broiler chicken, cut up
6 onion slices, ¼ inch thick
1 can condensed cream of mushroom soup
½ c. ready to cook rice
2 T. chopped parsley
¼ c. chopped celery
1 t. salt
½ c. water

Place pieces of chicken in casserole dish with rice around chicken. Mix remaining ingredients and pour over chicken and rice. Cover and bake in hot oven (450°F.) 40 minutes or till tender.

Ellaine B. Scott, DeKalb H. S.
DeKalb, Mississippi

CHICKEN AND DRESSING CASSEROLE
Number of Servings — 7

Gravy:

1 qt. coarsely cubed stewed chicken
1 qt. chicken broth
4 T. flour
4 T. chicken fat

Dressing:

1½ qt. dry bread cubes
3¼ c. melted butter
1¼ t. powdered sage
1 c. diced celery
1¼ c. cream or broth
¾ t. salt
2 T. chopped onion

Mix dressing lightly with fork. Place dressing, chicken, and gravy in layers in casserole. Bake at 350°F. for 35 minutes until lightly browned.

Karen H. Wahlberg, Madelia H. S.
Madelia, Minnesota

QUICK CHICKEN-NOODLE CASSEROLE
Number of Servings — 6

2 c. noodles
1 10½-oz. can chicken soup
2 5-oz. cans boned chicken
1 t. salt
⅓ c. dry bread crumbs

Cook noodles in boiling, salted water; drain. Butter 2 quart baking dish. Alternate layers of noodles, chicken soup, and boned chicken. Sprinkle with bread crumbs. Bake in moderate oven (350°F.) 30 minutes.

Jane Frudy, Tahleguah Jr. H. S.
Tahleguah, Oklahoma

CHICKEN-ALMOND NOODLES
Number of Servings — 6

2 c. noodles
3 c. chicken
1 can cream of mushroom soup
1 can cream of celery soup
1 small package slivered almonds
¼ c. diced pimento

Cook noodles and drain. Mix undiluted soups, add noodles, chicken, almonds and pimento (if too thick, thin with broth from chicken). Mix and put in baking dish. Cover top with cracker crumbs and grated cheese. Bake at 350°F. until top is brown.

Mrs. Carrie S. Bolton, Pageland H. S.
Pageland, South Carolina

CHICKEN-ALMOND CASSEROLE
Number of Servings — 8

3 c. cooked chicken
½ c. chopped almonds
1 T. minced onion
1½ T. lemon juice
⅛ t. pepper
1 c. mayonnaise
1½ c. grated cheddar cheese
1½ c. crushed potato chips
1½ c. diced celery

Combine chicken, celery, almonds, onion, lemon juice and pepper in mixing bowl. Add mayonnaise and toss. Divide into individual casseroles. Sprinkle top generously with grated cheese and finish with potato chips. Bake in pre-heated oven (375°F.) for 25 minutes. This casserole may be baked in 1 dish also. It can also be frozen successfully.

Mrs. Wilma Adams, Lockney H. S.
Lockney, Texas

CHICKEN ROYAL
Number of Servings — 6

4 c. stale bread cubes
2 c. chopped chicken (an old hen, boiled)
1 sliced hard cooked egg
½ c. raw oysters—if desired, bits of left-over
    cooked ham or bacon
1 T. parsley
1 T. onion
1 T. celery leaves
1 T. pimento
1 T. green pepper

Mix the above with enough hot chicken broth to moisten, but not sloppy. Do not mix till the bread looks stringy or mushy. Season with salt, curry powder, black pepper and paprika. Bake in greased casserole at 400°F. until golden brown and crusty. Serve with creamed peas or hot mushroom soup or good old home made chicken gravy left over from your boiled chicken.

Ruth Hardy, Vernon H. S.
Vernon, Indiana

SCALLOPED CHICKEN CASSEROLE
Number of Servings — 16-20

Broth:
1 5 lb. stewing hen, cut for stewing
2 qts. water
1 onion
2 t. salt
1 carrot
Cook until tender.

Dressing:
1½ loaves of 2 day old bread
½ c. butter
6 sprigs chopped parsley
2 celery stalks and leaves
1 t. salt
1 t. poultry seasoning
6 T. chicken broth
Dash of pepper
Ground cooked giblets

Remove bread crusts, crumble and reserve for top of casserole. Saute celery, onion and parsley in butter 5 minutes. Break bread and add to giblets. Mix with seasonings and sauted ingredients.

Sauce:
1 c. melted chicken fat
1 c. sifted flour
4 c. chicken broth
1 c. milk
2 t. salt
4 eggs, slightly beaten

Heat chicken broth and milk. Do not boil. Make a paste using the flour and melted chicken fat. Stir paste into heated mixture. Heat and stir until thick. Add salt and eggs slowly so as not to cook the eggs before mixture is thoroughly thickened. Grease casserole. Cover bottom with dressing. Add the medium sized pieces of chicken and cover with sauce. Mix crumbled crusts with 4 tablespoons butter and sprinkle on top of casserole. Cook 20 minutes in 375°F. oven.

Myra D. Sorensen, Richfield H. S.
Richfield, Utah

SCALLOPED CHICKEN SUPREME
Number of Servings — 8

1 c. chicken stock
2 c. cooked rice
3 c. cooked cut-up chicken
3 c. cream of celery soup
½ c. toasted slivered almonds
2 T. chopped pimento
1 c. sauteed mushrooms
Buttered crumbs for topping

Pour chicken stock over rice. Place in alternate layers with chicken and soup in buttered oblong 11 x 7 inch baking dish. Sprinkle each layer with almonds, pimento and mushrooms. Top with buttered crumbs. Bake in a moderate oven (350° F.) for 45 minutes.

Marie Shaw Griffin, Thomasville H. S.
Thomasville, Alabama

SCALLOPED CHICKEN
Number of Servings — 20-25

1 5-lb. stewing hen or
  (2 fryers, taking less time to cook)
1 carrot
2 quarts water
1 onion
2 t. salt
1½ loaves bread
1 c. butter
6 sprigs parsley
1 t. sage or poultry seasoning
2 T. chicken broth
1 onion (med.)
2 stalks celery (tops too)
1 t. salt
pepper
1 c. fat, skimmed from broth
1 c. flour
4 c. broth
1 c. milk
2 t. salt
4 eggs

Simmer chicken, 1 carrot, 1 onion, 2 teaspoons salt in 2 quarts water for 2½ hours or until tender. Cool in liquid. Remove meat from bones. Remove crust from bread and crumble for crumbs. Melt butter and add chopped vegetables. Cook for 5 minutes. Mix into bread crumbs and add seasoning, 2 tablespoons broth. Melt fat, blend in flour, add 4 cups broth, milk and salt, cook until thick, add small amount to beaten eggs. Pour into sauce. Heat and stir for 4 minutes. Grease large casserole, put dressing in bottom. Pour ½ sauce over, add cut chicken. Add remaining sauce and cover with crumbs. Bake at 375° for 20 minutes or until brown.

Mrs. Hannah Wells, Dixie H. S.
St. George, Utah

CHICKEN AND RICE
Number of Servings — 8

3-lb. frying chicken, disjointed
½ cube margarine
¾ c. uncooked rice
½ green pepper, chopped
½ t. Worcestershire sauce
½ t. pepper
1 t. salt
4 T. onion, chopped
1 can (3 oz.) sliced mushrooms
1 can (11 oz.) mushroom soup
1 can (11 oz.) celery soup

Brown chicken in margarine. Place in 9 x 14 inch baking dish; add rice, chopped onion and pepper to fat in frying pan. Saute until vegetables are limp. Add drained mushrooms, soup, salt, pepper and Worcestershire sauce; mix well and heat to simmering. Pour mixture over chicken in baking dish. Cover and bake for 1½ hours at 350°F.

Georgia M. Wilson, Prescott H. S.
Prescott, Arizona

CHICKEN AND RICE CASSEROLE

1½ c. uncooked rice
1 can cream of mushroom soup
1 can cream of chicken soup
1 can cream of celery soup
1½ soup cans of water
1 large can mushrooms
½ c. slivered almonds
1 large fryer, cut up
Butter
Salt and pepper

Use large shallow baking dish, well buttered. Cover bottom of dish with rice. This will make a thin layer. Mix the 3 cans of soup with the water and pour over the rice. Dip chicken in melted butter and salt and pepper. Bake at 250°F. for 2½ to 3 hours.

Velma Shaffer, State Dept. of Education
Little Rock, Arkansas

CHICKEN IN RICE
Number of Servings — Any number

pieces of chicken
uncooked rice
milk
salt
pepper
paprika

Select pieces of chicken to please the family. Choose a dutch oven or baking dish in which the chicken may be arranged for baking. Cover bottom of dutch oven or baking dish with uncooked rice. Arrange pieces of chicken on rice. Add milk to cover chicken, salt, pepper and paprika to taste. Bake 1½ to 2 hours in 350°F. oven. Chicken must be tender, rice flaky and milk absorbed. Serve chicken and rice together, garnish with an edging of buttered peas.

Pauline K. Fish, Mt. Lebanon H. S.
Pittsburgh, Pennsylvania

CHICKEN CASSEROLE WITH WILD RICE
Number of Servings — 15

1 5-lb. chicken, cooked
1½ c. wild rice, cooked in stock
1 8-oz. can of mushrooms
1 can pimento
1 c. blanched almonds
Salt and pepper
Make a white sauce from:
1 c. cream
1 c. milk
2 T. fat
4 T. flour

Pheasant is very good instead of chicken. Cut up the cooked chicken. Mix all together and bake for 1 hour, or until heated through.

Bergliot Larson, Cook H. S.
Cook, Minnesota

CHICKEN WITH RICE
Number of Servings — 4

4 medium chicken breasts
1 can cream of mushroom soup
½ can water
1 c. long grain rice
½ envelope dehydrated onion soup

Arrange pieces of chicken in casserole. Add rice, soup and water. Sprinkle dehydrated onion soup over top. No other seasoning is needed. Bake at 350°F. for about 1 hour or until chicken is tender. Check occasionally to see if a little more liquid is needed.

Mrs. Corilda C. Keyser, Eastern Jr. H. S.
Silver Spring, Maryland

BAKED CHICKEN ON RICE
Number of Servings — 4

8 pieces chicken (frying size)
1½ c. uncooked long grain rice (long cooking)
2 cans beef consomme
salt to taste

Measure rice. Pour into baking dish. Place chicken on top of rice. Sprinkle with salt. Pour beef consomme over chicken and rice. Cover. Bake in oven at 350° about 1¼ hours. Serve hot.

Mrs. W. D. Gibbs, La Vega H. S.
Waco, Texas

CHICKEN RICE CASSEROLE
Number of Servings — 4-6

Place 1 cup uncooked rice in a greased casserole. Pour 1 can onion soup over it. Lay 1 quartered chicken over this (do not brown chicken); do not add seasoning. Add 1 can cream of chicken soup or 1 can cream of mushroom or 1 can cream of celery. Then add a small can of evaporated milk. Bake at 350°F. for 1½ to 2 hours. Wild rice could be substituted for white rice.

Dorothea Nevramon, Steele H. S.
Steele, North Dakota

CHICKEN AND RICE CASSEROLE
Number of Servings — 12

1½ c. uncooked rice
1 can cream of celery soup
1 can cream of mushroom soup
1 can cream of chicken soup
1 can mushrooms and juice
½ c. slivered almonds
12 breast's of chicken
1 stick margarine, melted

In a buttered pan place the uncooked rice. Rinse out each soup can with ½ can of water. Mix with soups and pour over rice. Add the mushrooms and juice. Add almonds. Salt and pepper chicken and dip pieces into melted margarine. Place on top of rice mixture. Bake at 250°F. for 3 hours.

Maudalene Patterson, Booneville H. S.
Booneville, Arkansas

CHICKEN AND RICE CASSEROLE
Number of Servings — 6

1-2 lb. chicken, cut in serving pieces
¼ lb. butter or margarine
1 c. long cooking rice
1 can cream of chicken soup
1 can cream of celery soup
Salt and pepper

Place cut chicken on bottom of casserole baking dish. Salt and pepper. Melt butter, add rice, coat rice with butter, add can of celery soup and chicken soup, mix well. Pour over chicken. Cover dish with lid or foil. Bake in 250°F. oven for 2 hours.

Mrs. Audrey R. Colston, Monroney Jr. H. S.
Midwest City, Oklahoma

CHICKEN-RICE CASSEROLE
Number of Servings — 6

1 lb. package of chicken breasts
1 c. rice (uncooked measure)
1 c. sour cream
1 can cream of mushroom soup

Cook chicken breasts in a small amount of water until done. Cook rice according to package directions. Combine chicken, rice, soup, and sour cream. Heat in a 275°F. oven for 30 minutes. Serve in chafing dish. (Cubes of roast instead of the chicken is a good variation).

Mrs. Hazel Jones, Lampasas H. S.
Lampasas, Texas

CHICKEN AND RICE
Number of Servings — 6

3 strips bacon
1 c. raw rice
1 chicken
1 can cream of mushroom soup
2½ cans (soup) milk

Place bacon in bottom of 2½ to 3 quart casserole. Add rice. Place chicken, which has been cut up, salted and seasoned, over rice. Add 1 can cream of mushroom soup, which has been mixed with 2½ cans milk. Cook in 300°F. oven 2 hours.

Mrs. Raymond M. Barton, Sulphur Springs H. S.
Sulphur Springs, Texas

CHICKEN TETRAZZINI
Number of Servings — 8

Cook until brown and crisp, 2 slices bacon, finely cut. Add and brown lightly in bacon fat, ⅓ cup minced onion and ½ cup minced green pepper. Add 2 cups shredded American cheese, ¼ cup cut-up pimento, ¼ cup toasted shaved almonds, 1¾ cups cooked peas and 2 cups cut-up cooked chicken. Mix lightly with hot drained boiled macaroni (8 ounces uncooked). Heat, using chicken broth to moisten. Serve hot on chop plate, garnished with tomato slices, parsley and ripe olives.

Mrs. Verlyne Foster, Rolette H. S.
Rolette, North Dakota

CHICKEN RICE
Number of Servings — 6

1 stick butter
1 large onion, chopped
1 c. uncooked rice
2 c. chicken stock
1 can mushrooms
¼ c. sherry
3 c. cut up chicken
1 c. slivered almonds
Salt and pepper

Steam hen, bone and cut up. Saute onion in butter, add rice and brown. Add other ingredients and pour into buttered casserole. Bake at 325°F. for 1 hour and 20 minutes.

Elizabeth Curry, Marianna H. S.
Marianna, Florida

CHICKEN A LA RICE CASSEROLE
Number of Servings — 4-6

1 chicken 3 to 4 lbs.) cut in pieces
¼ c. butter
¼ c. vegetable shortening
1 pt. coffee cream
1 to 1½ c. rice (pre-cooked type)
Salt and pepper to taste

Melt shortening in casserole or roaster. Flour chicken and place in casserole and brown in oven (30 minutes at 400°F). When brown add rice and cream, salt and pepper and bake covered at 350°F. for 30 minutes.

Mrs. Elaine Petrik, South Winneshiek Com. H .S.
Calmar, Iowa

TIMBALE OF CHICKEN
Number of Servings — 12

1 fowl
1 t. cold water
1 c. rice
2 chopped onions
2 eggs, well beaten
Dressing:
2-3 c. butter or substitute
1 pt. milk
2 T. chopped onions
1 T. flour
2 T. chopped parsley
1 t. curry powder

Boil fowl until tender enough to pick off bones. Boil rice in chicken broth, season with salt, cayenne pepper and chopped onions. Line large shallow pan 1 inch thick with rice. Spread chicken over this, cover with another layer of rice. Prepare dressing. Melt butter, add flour and curry, then milk and other ingredients. Salt to taste. Add 2 eggs, well beaten with 1 teaspoon cold water. Pour over chicken and rice. Bake 20 minutes.

Mrs. Esther Peacock Vogl
Caledonia Community Schools
Caledonia, Michigan

CHICKEN CONTINENTAL
Number of Servings — 8

4 large chicken breasts
½ to ¾ c. water
2 t. salt
2 packages frozen broccoli
1 recipe Hollandaise sauce
Rich cream sauce
¾ c. almonds, slivered
¼ c. butter or margarine
½ c. Parmesan cheese, grated

Steam chicken with 1 teaspoon salt and very little water. When tender remove from liquid, cool and slice. Cook broccoli with 1 teaspoon salt, drain and place in a greased casserole. Top with Hollandaise sauce. Arrange chicken over broccoli, cover with rich cream sauce, sprinkle with almonds which have been browned in butter. Heat in 400°F. oven about 20 minutes. Remove, sprinkle with cheese and broil about 5 minutes.

Hollandaise Sauce:

2 egg yolks
½ c. butter
¼ t. salt
Few grains cayenne
1 T. lemon juice

Place egg yolks with ⅓ of the butter in top of a double boiler. Keep water in bottom hot but not boiling. Stir constantly. When butter melts add another portion and as it melts and mixture thickens add remaining butter. Stir constantly. As soon as mixture thickens, remove from heat and add spices. Should sauce separate, beat in 2 tablespoons boiling water drop by drop. Lemon juice may be increased to 1½ tablespoons. Makes 1 cup.

Rich Cream Sauce:

1½ T. flour
⅓ t. salt
1½ c. rich milk or half-and-half
Follow general directions for making white sauce.

Carolyn Stroup, Childersburg H. S.
Childersburg, Alabama

CHICKEN SMOTHERED IN ONION RINGS
Number of Servings — 4

2 chicken breasts
1 large onion, sliced thin
3 T. butter
1 T. lemon juice
Salt and pepper
1 t. Worcestershire sauce

Start oven at moderate (350°F.). Butter shallow baking dish. Rinse chicken, drain. Place in casserole, cover with onion rings, dot with butter, sprinkle with lemon juice, a little salt and pepper and the Worcestershire sauce. Cover and bake in moderate oven 45 minutes. Uncover dish and bake until tender and done, about 15 minutes longer.

Mrs. Marilynn Trosper, Bryan Station Jr. H. S.
Lexington, Kentucky

PIQUANT CHICKEN CASSEROLE
Number of Servings — 8

2 cans condensed cream of chicken soup
¼ c. finely diced onion
2 t. salt
⅛ t. pepper
1 t. parsley flakes
1 t. celery flakes
¼ t. thyme
2⅔ c. water
2⅔ c. packaged pre-cooked rice
3 c. diced cooked chicken
½ t. paprika

Combine soup, onion, and seasonings in a saucepan, mixing well. Gradually add water, stirring constantly to blend thoroughly. Bring to a boil over medium heat, stirring constantly. Pour half the soup mixture into a 3-quart casserole. Then, making two layers each, add the rice (right from the box) and the chicken. Top with remaining soup mixture. Cover and bake at 375°F. for 15 to 20 minutes. Stir well after 10 minutes and sprinkle with paprika.

Mrs. Bill Pate, Clinton H. S.
Clinton, Arkansas

CHICKEN BROCCOLI CASSEROLE
Number of Servings — 10-12

4 10-oz. boxes frozen broccoli
1 4-lb. hen, stewed
2 cans mushroom soup
1 8-oz. package processed cheese
½ roll garlic cheese
½ c. buttered crumbs
½ c. slivered almonds

Cook broccoli; bone hen; combine mushroom soup and cheeses in double boiler and heat until cheese melts. Into a buttered baking dish place a layer of broccoli, chicken, soup and cheese sauce. Repeat layers and top with crumbs and almonds. Bake at 350°F. for 30 minutes.

Mrs. Nita DeGrand, Thomas J. Rusk Jr. H. S.
Nacogdoches, Texas

CHICKEN BROCCOLI CASSEROLE
Number of Servings — 8

6 chicken breasts
2 packages frozen broccoli
2 cans cream of chicken soup
2 T. cooking sherry (optional)
2 egg yolks
Slivered almonds

Stew chicken in salty water until tender. Cool and remove meat from bones. Cook broccoli according to directions on package. Place broccoli in large utility baking dish. Cover with boned chicken. Combine soup, sherry and egg yolks. Pour over chicken and broccoli. Sprinkle with almonds. Bake at 350°F. for 30 minutes.

Vertrude Jones, Greene County H. S.
Eutaw, Alabama

CHICKEN-BROCCOLI CASSEROLE
Number of Servings — 8

4 chicken breasts (stewed tender)
2 packages broccoli (boiled 5 minutes)
2 cans chicken soup
1 t. curry powder
1 t. lemon juice
1 c. mayonnaise
1 c. bread crumbs

Place layer of chicken in casserole, then layer of chopped broccoli. Combine other ingredients and put over chicken and broccoli. Cover top with bread crumbs or corn flake crumbs. Use a shallow pyrex dish. Bake 30 minutes at 350°F.

Fay Harper, Bell County H. S.
Pineville, Kentucky

CHICKEN AND BROCCOLI CASSEROLE
Number of Servings — 6

1 package frozen broccoli
1 can cream of mushroom soup
2 c. cubed chicken
½ c. grated cheese
2 c. potato chips

Cook broccoli until almost tender. Drain and place in buttered casserole. Cover with cheese. Add the soup and chicken. Cover with slightly crushed potato chips and bake at 350°F. for 30 minutes.

Myrtle Sellie, Ellis Jr. H. S.
Austin, Minnesota

PLANTATION CHICKEN
Number of Servings — 8

1 c. diced celery
1 medium onion (chopped)
2 T. minced green pepper
5 T. butter
6 T. flour
3 c. milk
1 10-oz. can condensed cream of mushroom soup
4 c. diced cooked chicken
2 T. minced canned pimento
salt
1 c. soft bread crumbs
1 c. grated American cheese

Cook the celery in one inch of boiling water until tender. Meanwhile cook the onion and green pepper in the butter in the top of a double boiler over direct heat until soft. Then add the flour and blend. Next add the milk, while stirring; cook over hot water until smooth, then add undiluted mushroom soup, chicken, celery and pimentos. Heat well; then add salt to taste and turn into a greased 2 quart casserole. Top with crumbs mixed with grated cheese and bake in moderately hot oven of 375° for 30 minutes or until golden brown and bubbling hot. May be served in pastry shells (will serve 12).

Mrs. Barbara H. Watts, Chipley H. S.
Chipley, Florida

PLANTATION CHICKEN
Number of Servings — 6 large

1 c. diced celery
1 medium onion, chopped
2 T. green pepper
5 T. butter
6 T. flour
1 can mushroom sauce
2 c. diced cooked ham
2 c. diced cooked chicken
2 T. pimentos
1 c. grated cheese
3 c. milk

Cook celery until tender. Cook onion, green pepper and butter in top of double boiler until soft. Add flour and blend well. Add milk, cook over hot water until smooth and thickened. Then add the mushroom soup, cooked ham, cooked chicken and pimentos. Season to taste. Place in greased casserole. Top with the bread crumbs which have been mixed with cheese. Bake in a 375°F. oven for 30 minutes.

Mrs. Frances Detmer, Weeping Water H. S.
Weeping Water, Nebraska

PLANTATION CHICKEN
Number of Servings — 12

1 large onion, minced
1 c. celery, diced
5 T. butter
6 T. flour
Seasoning to taste
3 c. milk
1 can mushroom soup
4 c. chicken, diced
1 small can pimento
Grated cheese and bread crumbs

Cook onions and celery in butter until soft. Add flour which makes a paste. Add milk, soup, chicken, pimento and seasoning. Place in buttered dish, cover with cheese and crumbs and bake at 350°F. for 30 minutes. This may be prepared the day ahead and baked before serving.

Jo Anne Tuttle, Spencer H. S.
Spencer, Iowa

WORCESTERSHIRE CHICKEN
Number of Servings — 4

1 fryer (cut and salted)
1 stick oleo
1½ c. water
¼ c. Worcestershire sauce
2 t. sherry flavoring

Brown fryer in oleo (cut fryer as desired). Place browned chicken in casserole dish. Pour butter and other ingredients which have been mixed over chicken. Cook covered in oven at 325° for 1¼ hours. Chicken livers are good prepared this same way.

Willie Kathryn Roney, Headland H. S.
Headland, Alabama

CHICKEN AVOCADO CASSEROLE
Number of Servings — 8

2 c. water
1 diced onion
2-3 sprigs celery
2 t. salt
¼ t. pepper
5-6 lb. chicken
2 T. butter or chicken fat
3 T. flour
1 c. stock
1 c. light cream
½ c. sharp cheese, grated
½ t. salt
½ t. hot pepper sauce
1 pinch basil and rosemary
½ lb. sliced mushrooms, sauteed in butter

Into a pressure saucepan place 2 cups water, diced onion, celery, 2 teaspoons salt, and pepper. Cut chicken into frying size pieces and add. Process at 15 pounds pressure for 40 minutes. Pour off broth and chill. Skim off fat. Bone chicken and cut meat into ½ inch cubes. In a saucepan melt 2 tablespoons butter or chicken fat. Blend in 3 tablespoons flour. Stir in 1 cup stock and 1 cup light cream. Cook gently, stirring constantly until thickened. Add cheese, ½ teaspoon salt, hot pepper sauce, basil and rosemary. Into bottom of a casserole place cubed chicken and sliced mushrooms. Sprinkle lightly with salt and pepper. Pour sauce over chicken-mushroom mixture and bake 25 minutes in moderate oven (350°F.). Remove from oven and scatter meat from 2 diced avocadoes over the surface of the casserole. Heat in oven in covered casserole until avocadoes are warmed, about 10 minutes.

Norene Young, Comfort H. S.
Comfort, Texas

TREASURE ISLAND CHICKEN
Number of Servings — 8

5 lb. fowl
1 c. mayonnaise
1 t. salt
⅓ c. butter
2 No. 2 cans green asparagus spears
½ c. flour
1 c. milk
2 c. broth
1 t. lemon juice
½ c. toasted bread crumbs

Cook chicken and bone it. Leave in fairly large pieces. Melt butter, add flour. Combine milk and broth, add gradually to butter and flour mixture. Cook until thick and smooth. Remove from range and beat in mayonnaise and lemon juice. Mix well. Arrange chicken and asparagus in layers. Pour sauce over all and garnish with pimento strips, paprika, and buttered bread crumbs. Place in 375°F. oven for 45 minutes.

Evelyn G. Nicholas, Amherst County H. S.
Amherst, Virginia

CATERER'S BUFFET CHICKEN DISH
Number of Servings — 12

5 lb. stewing hen
1 carrot
2 medium onions
1 loaf 2 day-old bread
½ c. butter
6 sprigs parsley
2 large celery stalks, diced
1 T. poultry seasoning or sage
3 t. salt
Dash pepper
1 c. fat from broth
4 c. and 6 T. chicken broth
1 c. milk
1 c. flour
4 eggs, beaten
1 package frozen peas (optional) or
1 small can pimento (optional)

Simmer hen in 2 quarts water with 1 carrot and 1 onion until done. Cool in liquid, drain and cube. Prepare stuffing by cubing bread. Saute butter in parsley, 1 diced onion, and diced celery. Cook for 5 minutes. Combine with bread crumbs, salt and pepper to taste, poultry seasoning or sage and mix with 6 tablespoons chicken broth. Prepare sauce by skimming 1 cup fat and melting it in pan. Stir in 1 cup flour until smooth. Heat 4 cups broth and 1 cup milk in pan. Add broth mixture and 2 teaspoons salt to fat mixture. Cook and stir until very thick. Add 4 beaten eggs and cook over low heat for 3 minutes more. Combine as follows: Place layer of stuffing in greased 3 quart or two 1½ quart casseroles. Pour ½ of sauce over stuffing. Add layer of chicken, pour on remaining sauce. Top with sauteed crumbs. Bake at 350°F. for 30 minutes. (Peas or pimento may be added to the sauce).

Mrs. Patricia Larson, Milaca H. S.
Milaca, Minnesota

CHICKEN AND SPAGHETTI
Number of Servings — 12

7-8 lbs. stewed chicken, removed from bones
2 large onions
1 cube butter
Several cloves garlic (according to desire)
1 stalk celery
2 small cans tomato paste
2 c. chicken broth
1 can pimentos
1 large can mushrooms
2 c. grated cheese
1 package spaghetti, boiled and drained before adding
Black and red pepper
3 t. salt

Mix all together and put in roaster or large baking dish. Bake 1 hour at 300°F.

Mrs. Edith Donaldson, Gadsden H. S.
Anthony, New Mexico

CHICKEN SPAGHETTI
Number of Servings — 25

2 chickens (10-14 lbs.)
4 large cans tomatoes
4 small cans tomato paste
3 c. chopped onion
1 c. flour
1 c. fat
3 stalks celery
1 can mushrooms
1 small garlic
6 hard-cooked eggs
1 lemon
1 bell pepper
Salt and pepper to taste

Cook onions and garlic in fat until tender. Add flour and mix thoroughly. Add tomatoes and tomato paste. Add chopped celery and bell pepper, and lemon cut in small pieces (use all of lemon). Cook until well-blended. Fry chicken, if young, and add to tomato sauce and cook until chicken comes off bones. Serve with 2 or 3 pounds of spaghetti.

Gussie Mae Beard, Pelican H. S.
Pelican, Louisiana

CHICKEN SPAGHETTI
Number of Servings — 6-8

⅓ c. chicken fat or butter
¼ c. chopped onion
1 clove finely chopped garlic
1 c. sliced mushrooms
¼ c. flour
2 c. chicken stock
2-3 c. diced chicken
1 c. stewed tomatoes
¼ c. grated cheese
8 ozs. boiled spaghetti
½ c. bread crumbs

Heat fat, add onion, garlic and mushrooms; cook until lightly browned. Add flour until blended; slowly add stock and stir over low heat until thick and smooth. Salt and pepper to taste. Add chicken, tomatoes, and cheese. Arrange chicken mixture and spaghetti in layers in a greased casserole. Top with buttered bread crumbs and a dash of paprika. Bake 375°F. for 25 minutes.

Mrs. Grace Yates, Stephen F. Austin Jr. H. S.
Borger, Texas

CHICKEN-MUSHROOM CASSEROLE
Number of Servings — 6-8

2 c. boned chicken
1 package potato chips (medium)
1 can mushroom soup
2 c. medium white sauce
White sauce recipe:
3 T. butter
4 T. flour
1 t. salt
2 c. milk

(Continued on Next Page)

Melt butter, blend in flour and salt, add milk and cook over medium heat until smooth and thickened. Use a flat baking dish (9 x 15 inch), butter it well. Put a layer of boned chicken in dish, cover with white sauce, follow with a layer of potato chips, then one of the soup. Top with white sauce. Sprinkle top with grated cheese. Bake at 350°F. until brown and cheese is melted. About 45 minutes.

Evelyn Wilson, Waurika H. S.
Waurika, Oklahoma

CHICKEN-ALMOND CASSEROLE
Number of Servings — 8

5 lb. stewing chicken, cut up
2 celery stalks
2 carrots, cut up
1 medium onion, sliced
2 t. salt
½ t. pepper
8 c. boiling water
2 c. cooked rice
1 4-oz. can sliced mushrooms
¼ c. chopped pimento
1 c. blanched slivered almonds
4 T. butter or chicken fat
2 T. flour
¼ t. marjoram
¼ t. thyme
½ c. fine bread crumbs

Simmer chicken until tender with vegetables, salt and pepper. Remove chicken from bones in large pieces. Combine rice, chicken, mushrooms, and pimento with ¾ cup almonds. Make sauce with 2 tablespoons butter, flour and 2 cups chicken broth. Add marjoram and thyme, stir into chicken mixture. Put into 11 x 7½ x 1½ inch baking dish. Sprinkle with bread crumbs and remaining almonds. Dot with 2 tablespoons butter. Bake 1 hour at 350°F. Serve with gravy made from remaining broth.

Janet Malone, Callaway Public H. S.
Callaway, Nebraska

CHICKEN ALMOND BAKE
Number of Servings — 6

1 can cream of mushroom soup
1 c. evaporated milk
1 c. cooked chicken
1 c. blanched almonds, sliced
1 c. celery, cut
½ t. onion
¼ t. Worcestershire sauce
1 large can Chinese noodles or 2 small cans

Blend soup and milk. Combine with chicken, celery, almonds, onions, and Worcestershire sauce. Sprinkle half of noodles in bottom of baking dish. Spoon chicken mixture over noodles. Top with remaining noodles. Bake at 350°F. for 30 minutes.

Mrs. Anne Dodenhoff Nelson, J. E. B. Stuart H. S.
Falls Church, Virginia

CHICKEN WITH ALMONDS
Number of Servings — 4

2½ to 3 lb. broiler fryer, cut up
3 T. butter
1 garlic clove, chopped
2 T. onion, chopped
1 T. tomato paste
2 T. flour
1½ c. chicken stock
2 T. shredded almonds
½ t. dry tarragon
2 T. sherry
Salt and pepper to taste
¾ c. sour cream
1 T. grated cheese
1 tomato, skinned (optional)

Brown chicken in the hot butter. Remove chicken. Saute garlic and onion 2 to 3 minutes. Remove from heat. Stir in tomato paste and flour. Then blend in chicken stock and sherry, stirring over low heat until mixture comes to a boil. Add browned chicken, almonds, tarragon, salt and pepper. Cover and cook slowly 45 to 50 minutes. Arrange chicken in a shallow casserole. Stir sour cream into the sauce and pour over the chicken. Sprinkle with cheese. Garnish with the tomato and brown under the broiler.

Phyllis J. Taylor, George Washington H. S.
Alexandria, Virginia

A NEW CASSEROLE
Number of Servings — 8

1 large hen, cooked and boned (large pieces)
1 c. each, onions, bell peppers, celery
6 large green olives, chopped
2 small glasses pimento
1 small can mushrooms

Brown above ingredients in one stick butter. Add ½ cup chicken broth, one can mushroom soup, juice of 3 lemons and ½ pound grated cheese. Simmer 20 minutes and add chicken. Cook two packages of noodles in remaining chicken broth. Drain noodles and add to mixture. Serve in casserole.

Mrs. John Y. Smith, Greenwood H. S.
Greenwood, Mississippi

CLUB CHICKEN
Number of Servings — 8-10

Melt ¼ cup butter or margarine. Blend in ¼ cup flour. Gradually add 1 cup chicken broth, 1 14½ ounce can evaporated milk and ½ cup water. Cook over low heat until thick, stirring constantly. Add 1½ teaspoons salt, 2½ cups diced cooked chicken, 3 cups cooked rice, one 3 ounce can sliced mushrooms, ¼ cup chopped pimento, and ⅓ cup chopped green pepper. Pour into greased 11½ x 7½ x 1½ inch baking dish. Bake at 350°F. about 30 minutes. Sprinkle with toasted almonds.

Joyce M. Wingate, Marshall H. S.
Marshall, Michigan

CHICKEN SURPRISE
Number of Servings — 12

Simmer until tender 1 stewing chicken in salted water with 1 carrot, tops of 5 stalks of celery and 1 bay leaf. Strain stock into a bowl. Remove chicken meat from the bones and cut in bite size pieces. Make a sauce by melting 6 tablespoons of chicken fat; blend in 6 tablespoons flour; stir in 2 cups of stock. Stir constantly while cooking until thickened. Add 1 cup cream or rich milk, 6 ounces mushrooms, one 4 ounce can pimentos and ¼ teaspoon salt. Stir in chicken and 1 cup slivered toasted almonds. In buttered 3 quart casserole place alternate layers of cooked rice (6 cups) and chicken mixture, sprinkle (1 cup buttered soft bread crumbs) buttered crumbs around edges. Bake in 350°F. oven about 1 hour, until sauce bubbles around the edge and crumbs are brown. To toast almonds: Melt 1½ tablespoons of butter in medium sized frying pan, add almonds and toast over low heat till almonds are lightly browned.

Verna Danley, State Supvr. of Home Economics
State Department of Education
Trenton, New Jersey

PARISIAN BAKED CHICKEN
Number of Servings — 6

6 halves of chicken breast
salt and pepper
1 can cream of mushroom soup
½ pt. sour cream
beau monde seasoning
1 small can whole button mushrooms

Remove skin from chicken pieces. Sprinkle each piece with salt and pepper, then place it in a casserole dish. Combine mushroom soup and sour cream. Spread this over the chicken pieces. Spread the whole button mushrooms on top of this. Sprinkle with seasoning. Bake covered in oven at 350° for 30 minutes. Uncover and bake 30 minutes longer.

Virginia S. Sharbutt, Vincent School
Vincent, Alabama

CHICKEN AND CHIPS CASSEROLE
Number of Servings — 4

1 c. condensed cream of chicken soup
1 c. cubed cooked chicken (6 oz. can boned chicken)
½ c. milk
¼ c. crushed potato chips
1 c. potato chips
1 c. cooked green peas, drained (small can)

Preheat oven (375°F.). Empty soup into 1 quart casserole. Add milk and mix thoroughly. Add chicken, 1 cup potato chips, and peas to soup. Stir well. Sprinkle top with ¼ cup crushed potato chips. Bake for 25 minutes.

Mrs. Geneva H. Davis, Rock Ridge H. S.
Wilson, North Carolina

ORIENTAL CHICKEN
Number of Servings — 8

2 disjointed chickens
2 c. unwashed rice
1 orange
1 onion
1 qt. milk
2 t. salt
Rosemary or marjoram or thyme
Frying fat

Flour and saute chickens. Remove from fry pan. Saute in remaining fat 2 cups of unwashed rice. Grind 1 orange and 1 onion. Add to browned rice and pour into a baking pan or glass baking dish. Add 4 cups of milk and 2 teaspoons salt. Arrange chicken on top of rice. Sprinkle generously with rosemary or marjoram or thyme. Cover with foil so that it steams. Bake at 325°F. for 1 hour. Uncover. Let dry a little before serving.

Genevieve P. Pieretti, State Supervisor
Home Economics Education
State Department of Education
Carson City, Nevada

CHICKEN MARGUERY
Number of Servings — 8

8 to 10 pieces of frying chicken browned in 4 T. fat (half vegetable shorten and half butter)
3½ c. water, added to drippings in skillet where chicken was browned
1 No. 1 can condensed celery soup
1 No. 1 can condensed mushroom soup
1 envelope dry onion soup

Place washed rice in a 3 quart casserole. Add water, drippings, celery soup and onion soup and mix thoroughly. Lay pieces of chicken in this mixture. Beat the mushroom soup until smooth and spread over top of the casserole. Bake at 325°F. for 2½ hours. Remove the cover and brown for 15 minutes.

Margery S. Gibeaut, Cowan H. S.
Cowan, Indiana

CHICKEN 'N GARLIC
Number of Servings — 5

1½ sticks margarine
¼ t. garlic
½ c. flour
½ c. cornmeal
Paprika
1 fryer (cut up)
Salt

Melt margarine in casserole dish, sprinkle with garlic salt. Sift flour and cornmeal together. Dredge the salted chicken in the meal mixture and place meaty side down into the margarine. Cover and bake for 20 minutes at 350°F. Turn chicken over and sprinkle with paprika. Bake until done (20 minutes). Serve from casserole dish.

Glenda F. McSwain, Forrest County A. H. S.
Hattiesburg, Mississippi

CHICKEN SUNDAY DINNER
Number of Servings — 6

1 c. uncooked rice
1 fryer, cut-up
Salt and pepper
1 package onion soup mix
1 can cream of mushroom soup

Grease 9 x 9 inch pan or casserole dish. Spread rice evenly over bottom. Add cut up fryer over rice. Season with salt and pepper. Sprinkle onion soup mix over chicken. Top with mushroom soup and 1 soup can milk or water. Bake approximately 2 hours at 325°F.

Mrs. Emely Sundbeck, Manor H. S.
Manor, Texas

TURKEY CHARADE CASSEROLE
Number of Servings — 6

¼ c. butter
2 T. minced onion
¼ c. flour
1 c. chicken or turkey broth or water
1 c. water
2 chicken bouillon cubes
2 eggs, slightly beaten
½ c. mayonnaise
2 c. diced turkey
¼ c. slivered almonds, toasted
2 T. minced pimento
1 can chow mein noodles

Melt butter in saucepan. Add onion; cover and cook over low flame until softened. Blend in flour. Add broth, milk and bouillon cubes. Cook over medium flame, stirring constantly until mixture thickens. Stir some of the sauce into beaten egg; return to saucepan; cook 1 minute. Remove from flame. Fold in remaining ingredients. Turn into a greased 1½ quart casserole. Bake in an oven that has not been preheated at 350°F. for 35 minutes. Do not overcook.

Marjorie Mouser, Grant H. S.
Grant, Michigan

SEAFOOD OR CHICKEN HOT DISH
Number of Servings — 6-8

1 can cream of mushroom soup
1 can cream of chicken soup
1 small can evaporated milk
2 c. Chinese noodles (1 can)
Green pepper and pimento, if desired
1 c. cooked celery
1 c. chicken, tuna, crab, lobster or shrimp
1 small can mushroom buttons
Slivered almonds

Bake in a dish set in a pan of hot water for 1½ hours at 275°F. and ½ hour more at 325°F. (This allows for time for the liquid to evaporate). Garnish with hard-boiled eggs (mashed egg yolks and strips of whites). This needs no sauce.

Geneveve K. Johnston, Advisory Editor
Minneapolis Public Schools

Seafood Casseroles

CRAB CASSEROLE
Number of Servings — 4-6

1 can hominy (No. 2 or 2¼)
½ lb. fresh crab
1 can cream of mushroom soup
¾ c. milk
1 c. grated cheese

Drain hominy; put through food grinder. Mix soup and milk together. Butter a 1½ quart casserole. Put in a layer of hominy, layer of crab, ½ of soup mixture and ½ of the cheese. Repeat. Top with buttered crumbs or crushed cereal. Bake at 350°F. for 45 minutes. YUMMY!

Mrs. Lillian Englmann, Battle Ground Sr. H. S.
Battle Ground, Washington

SEAFOOD FANCY
Number of Servings — 6-8

¾ c. chopped green pepper
¾ c. minced onion
1 c. canned flaked crab meat
1 c. canned or cooked shrimp
½ t. salt
Dash of pepper
1 t. Worcestershire sauce
1 c. mayonnaise
1 c. soft bread crumbs
2 T. melted butter

Combine vegetables, crab meat, shrimp, salt, pepper, Worcestershire sauce and mayonnaise. Put mixture in greased 1 quart casserole or 8 individual dishes. Toss bread crumbs in butter; sprinkle over top. Bake in moderate oven (350°F.) for 30 minutes or till hot and crumbs are golden brown.

Clara Deiter, Dodge City Jr. H. S.
Dodge City, Kansas

SHRIMP AND CRAB CASSEROLE
Number of Servings — 4

1 lb. shrimp
1 pt. crab meat
½ c. catsup
½ green pepper
½ onion
2 T. Worcestershire sauce
1 t. tabasco
¾ c. cracker crumbs

Boil shrimp, peel. Combine crab meat, catsup, Worcestershire sauce, tabasco and cracker crumbs in medium size bowl. Add finely diced onion and green pepper. Place shrimp in casserole dish. Cover with crab mixture. Bake at 350°F. for 30 minutes.

Paula E. Reeves, Myers Jr. H. S.
Savannah, Georgia

BAKED CRAB MEAT AND SHRIMP CASSEROLE
Number of Servings — 8

1 c. crab meat
1½ c. shrimp (cleaned)
1 medium green pepper
1 medium onion, chopped
1 c. finely diced celery
½ t. salt
1 t. Worcestershire sauce
¾ c. mayonnaise
1 c. buttered crumbs
Dash pepper

Combine all ingredients, except crumbs; place in buttered casserole. Sprinkle with buttered crumbs and bake in 350°F. oven for 30 minutes.

Louise Crosby Roebuck, Semmes H. S.
Semmes, Alabama

GOLDEN HALIBUT CASSEROLE
Number of Servings — 8

1 lb. halibut
2 bay leaves
4 slices onion
4 T. butter
4 T. flour
2 c. milk
Salt and pepper
½ lb. nippy cheese

Steam halibut, bay leaves and onion for 30 minutes. Prepare white sauce of butter, flour, milk, salt and pepper. Grate cheese. Break fish into medium sized pieces. Layer fish with cheese and white sauce. Cover with ½ cup buttered bread crumbs. Bake at 350°F. for 35 minutes.

Margaret P. Jensen, Bountiful H. S.
Bountiful, Utah

OYSTER CASSEROLE
Number of Servings — 6

1 c. chopped mushrooms
8 to 10 small whole mushrooms
½ c. butter
1 c. fine cracker crumbs
1½ pts. oysters
1 c. milk
½ c. light cream
Paprika

Saute all mushrooms in 2 tablespoons butter. Line bottom of greased casserole with ⅓ of crumbs; add a layer of chopped mushrooms and dot with 1 tablespoon butter; add another layer of crumbs, then oysters, remaining chopped mushrooms and a final layer of crumbs. Pour milk, cream and remaining butter, melted, over top. Bake in moderate oven (350°F.) 25 minutes. Stand whole mushrooms upright on top, sprinkle with paprika and place under moderate broiler for about 5 minutes.

Lorene H. English, West Gwinnett H. S.
Norcross, Georgia

CASSEROLE OF OYSTERS
Number of Servings — 6

1 pt. fresh oysters and liquid
1 12-oz. can cream of celery soup
1 t. grated onion
½ c. milk
⅛ t. black pepper, if desired
1½ c. cracker crumbs
3 T. butter or margarine

Oil the bottom of a 1 quart casserole. Alternately arrange layers of oysters, soup, crumbs, onion and pepper, beginning and ending with crumbs. Pour over milk and oyster liquid. Dot with butter and bake in 350°F. oven for 20 minutes or until oysters begin to curl at edges.

Mrs. Verna I. Boyd, Pisgah H. S.
Sand Hill, Mississippi

OYSTER CASSEROLE
Number of Servings — 10

1 pt. oysters
1 c. cubed celery, cooked 20 minutes
1 can cream of chicken soup
1 bouillon cube chicken, melt in cup of hot water
Dash of onion salt
Cracker crumbs
2 eggs
1 T. butter

Sprinkle layer of cracker crumbs in bottom of casserole dish, then a layer of oysters, layer of cooked celery. Continue until all is used. Pour liquid over mixture and let soak for 20 minutes. Cook in a moderate oven (400°F.) for 30 or 40 minutes. Take two beaten eggs and now pour over casserole. Return to oven until brown.

Ruth Groover, Cleburne Co. H. S.
Heflin, Alabama

SALMON CASSEROLE
Number of Servings — 6-8

1 6-oz. can salmon
1 can mushroom soup
½ c. grated cheese
1 c. cooked rice
1 c. medium white sauce
¼ c. chopped celery
½ c. chopped onion
1 T. butter
¾ c. soft bread crumbs

Cook celery and onions in water for 5 minutes. Flake salmon. Grate cheese. Make white sauce. Add salmon, rice, cheese and soup, celery, onion to white sauce and pour into greased casserole. Melt butter and mix with bread crumbs, and spread on top. Bake at 350°F. for 20 minutes.

Mrs. Grace Hollen, Turner Ashby H. S.
Dayton, Virginia

MOTHER'S SHRIMP A LA KAISER
Number of Servings — 6-8

5 T. corn oil margarine
3 c. milk
5 T. flour
1 t. salt
¼ t. pepper
2 lbs. raw shrimp, cook and de-vein
6 hard cooked eggs
1 can well-drained asparagus pieces
Paprika

Melt margarine in a saucepan. Add flour and blend thoroughly. Remove pan from flame and add milk gradually, stirring constantly. Return to flame and cook, stirring constantly, until sauce thickens and bubbles. Add seasonings. In a 2 quart casserole, place half of the asparagus, then half the hard cooked eggs which have been cut into eighths, then half the cooked shrimp which have been slivered in half, lengthwise. Repeat, ending with shrimp. Pour white sauce over all. Sprinkle with paprika. Bake in a moderate (350°F.) oven for 30 minutes. Serve in patty shells or on toast points.

Ellen Donahay, Edison H. S.
Edison, New Jersey

SHRIMP CASSEROLE A LA SHRODER
Number of Servings — 6-8

3 lbs. shrimp
1 lb. mushrooms
1 wine glass of cherry wine
1 T. butter
2 T. catsup
3 T. flour (or more to thickness)
1 pt. cream
1 T. Worcestershire sauce
1 clove garlic

Parboil shrimp. Saute the mushrooms in butter. Make cream sauce, add seasonings, salt and pepper to taste, add mushrooms and main ingredients. Put in buttered casserole. Cover with buttered crumbs. Bake for 45 minutes in 350°F. oven or until the crumbs are browned.

Elizabeth Gibson, St. Peter Claver Com. House
Detroit, Michigan

SHRIMP CASSEROLE
Number of Servings — 12

Two pounds shrimp, shelled and cleaned. Brown together ⅓ cup finely chopped onion, 2 tablespoons butter and 1 clove garlic. Put into a casserole with the shrimp 1 cup raw rice, 1 No. 2½ can tomatoes and 2 cups chicken bouillon. Add 1 small piece bay leaf, ½ teaspoon marjoram, 3 tablespoons chopped parsley, 1 teaspoon chili powder, ½ teaspoon cloves, 1 tablespoon salt, ⅛ teaspoon pepper and dash of cayenne. Cover tightly and bake 1½ hours at 350°F.

Betty Huey, Marysville H. S.
Marysville, Kansas

SEAFOOD CASSEROLE
Number of Servings — 8-12

1 c. thick white sauce
2 cans cream of mushroom soup
1 can mushrooms
2 lbs. frozen shrimp
1 pt. oysters
2 c. cracker crumbs
½ c. slivered almonds

To 1 cup of thick white sauce add the soup, mushrooms, shrimp and oysters. Season with salt and pepper (to taste). Arrange in casserole with layers of cracker crumbs. Spread crumbs on top, dot with butter, and sprinkle with almonds. Bake at 350°F. for 30 minutes, or until crust is brown and casserole is "bubbling."

Mrs. Jacqueline T. Thurmon, Castor H. S.
Castor, Louisiana

SHRIMP CASSEROLE SUPREME
Number of Servings — 4-6

1 lb. cooked, cleaned shrimp
1 c. mushrooms
1 c. blanched almonds
Grated Parmesan cheese
3 c. medium thick cream sauce to which ½ c. of sherry wine has been added
Cracker crumbs

Grease a casserole or a baking dish. Fill in layers by putting shrimp first, then mushrooms, almonds and last, the cream sauce. Repeat until ingredients have all been used. Cover top with cracker crumbs and grated cheese. Bake in a 350°F. oven for 30 minutes. Serve very hot. Note: Omit salt in sauce if sherry wine is used, but use a little pepper.

Shirley Ann Murray, Suffolk H. S.
Suffolk, Virginia

SHRIMP AU GRATIN
Number of Servings — 6-8

2-3 lbs. shrimp
½ c. butter
1 c. flour
4 c. liquid from shrimp
1 t. salt
¼ t. pepper
3 egg yolks
2 T. sherry wine
2 T. grated cheese
Bread crumbs

Clean and wash shrimp. Place in saucepan with a quart of water and a dash of lemon juice, then bring to a boil for 10 minutes. In another pan melt butter, then add flour and stir to a smooth cream. Add shrimp stock a little at a time, stirring constantly. Add seasonings, egg yolk, wine and cheese. Add shrimp and bake in a buttered casserole. Top with crumbs and cheese. Bake in 350°-375°F. oven about 15 minutes.

Ouida T. Hicks, Sidney Lanier H. S.
Montgomery, Alabama

SPAGHETTI WITH SHRIMP, CREOLE-STYLE
Number of Servings — 6

¼ c. butter or margarine
½ c. finely chopped onion
¼ c. finely chopped green pepper
1 clove garlic, minced
¼ c. enriched flour
1 t. salt
½ t. chili powder
⅛ t. pepper
4½ c. tomatoes (2 1-lb., 4-oz. cans)
¾ c. water
1 T. Worcestershire sauce
1 lb. shrimp, cooked, shell removed and
   de-veined
8 ozs. long spaghetti

Melt butter or margarine in large, heavy skillet or sauce pot. Add onion, green pepper and garlic and cook over low heat, about 5 minutes. Stir in flour, salt, chili powder and pepper. Stir in tomatoes, water and Worcestershire sauce. Cook mixture until thickened, stirring constantly. Cook slowly about 15 minutes longer. Cut shrimp into pieces and add to tomato sauce. Simmer uncovered about 20 minutes. While shrimp mixture is cooking, cook spaghetti in boiling salted water until tender (about 7 minutes). Drain. Serve sauce over spaghetti.

Mrs. Mildred I. Green, Hartsell H. S.
Concord, North Carolina

CREOLE SHRIMP IN RICE RING
Number of Servings — 6

2 lbs. fresh shrimp
1 large onion, chopped
1 clove garlic, minced
4 stalks celery, chopped
2 T. salad oil
1 No. 2½ can tomatoes
Dash of salt and pepper
Dash tabasco sauce
Dash Worcestershire sauce
2 c. rice

Cook shrimp until they turn pink. Clean, removing black line. Brown onion, garlic, and celery in hot salad oil; add tomatoes, seasonings, tabasco and Worcestershire sauce. Cook 40 minutes. Add shrimp; cook 10 minutes. Cook rice according to directions on box. Add ¼ cup melted butter, salt and pepper. Pack in 10 inch greased ring mold. Let stand 30 minutes in pan of hot water. Unmold on hot platter; fill center with creole shrimp.

Joan W. Harmon, Robert L. Osborne H. S.
Marietta, Georgia

TUNA SUPREME
Number of Servings — 6

2 c. tuna, left in large pieces
2 c. crushed potato chips
3 c. medium white sauce
¾ c. sliced ripe olives

Arrange in alternate layers in a buttered casserole. Finish with a sprinkle of crushed potato chips. Bake at 350°F. for 35 minutes. Variations: May add 2 sliced hard-boiled eggs.

Mrs. Louis King, Jefferson H. S.
Jefferson, Texas

TUNA CASSEROLE
Number of Servings — 6

½ package spaghetti (7-oz.)
½ c. chopped onion
¼ c. chopped green pepper
3 T. fat
2 T. flour
1 can tuna
¼ c. pimento or pickle relish
1¼ c. milk
1 can (10-oz.) cream of chicken soup

Cook spaghetti in salt water until tender; drain. Saute onions and pepper in fat until tender. Blend in flour slowly and add milk. Cook over low heat until thick, stirring constantly. Add soup, pimento and tuna. Place in layers with spaghetti in greased casserole. Garnish with paprika or cracker crumbs, and bake at 350°F. for 30 minutes.

Mrs. Wilma Tucker, Marion H. S.
Marion, Louisiana

TUNA CASSEROLE
Number of Servings — 6-8

1 can (No. ½ flat) white tuna meat
1 can (No. 303) chow mein noodles
1 can (10½-oz.) mushroom or other cream soup
½ c. chopped cashew nuts
1 medium onion, chopped
1 c. celery, chopped or diced
¼ c. water

Cook onion and celery in water until just slightly crunchy. Combine remainder of ingredients, saving noodles for top. Bake in a casserole 35 minutes at 375°F. Place casserole in a pan of water during baking period.

Mrs. Jeanette Weiss, Ovid H. S.
Ovid, Colorado

TUNA FISH CASSEROLE
Number of Servings — 6

1 box potato chips, crushed (25c)
1 can tuna fish, flaked
1 can drained peas
1 can mushroom soup
1 can cream of chicken soup
1 c. thin cream

Arrange potato chips, tuna, and peas in layers. Heat cream of mushroom and cream of chicken soup and cream until boiling and pour over all. Sprinkle a few potato chips on top and bake in a moderate oven 30 to 40 minutes. Whole kernel corn may be substituted for the peas.

Mrs. Evelith Kuecker, Seward H. S.
Seward, Nebraska

SCALLOPED TUNA AND CHIPS
Number of Servings — 6

¼ c. shortening
¼ c. flour
1 t. salt
⅛ t. pepper
2 6-oz. cans tuna fish
2 c. milk (or liquid from 4-oz. can of mushrooms, and milk to make 2 cups)
1 T. grated onion
1 T. chopped parsley
1 7-oz. pkg. potato chips, finely crushed
1 4-oz. can mushrooms, drained

Melt shortening in a saucepan on medium heat; add flour, salt and pepper and blend well. Add milk, stirring constantly, and continue cooking until sauce begins to thicken. Remove from the heat. Add onion and parsley. Mix well. Place 1 cup of the potato chips in a greased 1½-quart casserole. Cover with a layer of tuna fish, mushrooms (saving a few slices for the top) and sauce; repeat. Place remaining potato chips in a 1 inch border around casserole; the mushroom slices in the center, of the top. Bake in oven at 350°F. for 1 hour.

Mrs. Winifred Iverson, Riggs H. S.
Pierre, South Dakota

CRUNCHY TUNA AND POTATO CHIP CASSEROLE
Number of Servings — 6

1 7-oz. can tuna
1 can cream of mushroom soup
¼ t. pepper
1 c. grated cheese
2 c. potato chips (broken into small pieces)
2 T. grated onion

Heat oven to 375°F. Grease a 1½ quart casserole. Flake the tuna and place in casserole. Add onion and pepper. Gently stir ingredients together. Pour condensed mushroom soup over ingredients in casserole. Sprinkle with potato chip pieces and grated cheese. Bake 20 to 25 minutes in preheated oven.

June Elizabeth Rector, Abingdon H. S.
Abingdon, Virginia

TUNA CRISP CASSEROLE
Number of Servings — 8-10

1 No. 6½ oz. can flaked tuna fish
1 No. 3 can peas
1 can cream of mushroom soup, undiluted
1 c. crackers, crumbled
2 T. pimento
½ c. evaporated milk

Mix lightly all ingredients in mixing bowl. Place in greased 1 quart casserole. Bake in 425°F. oven for 20 to 25 minutes or until top of mixture is golden brown and mixture bubbles.

Mrs. Erma Jean Hamby, Eminence H. S.
Eminence, Kentucky

TUNA TOUCHDOWN
Number of Servings — 4

1 can (1¼ c.) condensed cream of mushroom soup
1 c. (7-oz. can) drained flaked tuna
½ c. milk
1 c. unsalted cooked green peas, drained
1¼ c. crushed potato chips

Preheat oven (375°F). Empty soup into 1-quart casserole. Add milk and mix thoroughly. Add tuna (or salmon), 1 cup potato chips, and peas to soup; stir well. Sprinkle top with remaining ¼ cup potato chips. Bake for 25 minutes or until heated through.

Joyce Thornton, Rosebud H. S.
Rosebud, Texas

TUNA CASSEROLE
Number of Servings — 6-8

1 can tuna, drained, rinsed under cold water
1 can cream of chicken soup, undiluted
1 medium onion, chopped fine
1 c. celery, chopped
2 c. cooked rice (1 c. minute pre-cooked white rice)
½ t. salt
¾ c. mayonnaise
1 T. lemon juice
3 hard cooked eggs, cooled and diced
½ lb. grated or chopped fine mild cheddar or process American cheese

Preparation time 30-45 minutes. Bake in 2 quart pyrex casserole dish at 350°F. for 30 minutes. Assemble, prepare all ingredients as listed above, mix thoroughly, pour into casserole, and bake. Better served hot, but still very delicious when cold.

Mrs. Mary Geiger Matreyek, Montebello Jr. H. S.
Montebello, California

TUNA CASSEROLE
Number of Servings — 4

1 c. noodles
1 t. salt
1 qt. boiling water
1 can flaked tuna (7 oz.)
1 can mushroom soup, undiluted
2 T. butter
2 hard-cooked eggs, sliced
8 stuffed olives, sliced
4 ozs. grated American cheese

Cook noodles. Butter the casserole dish lightly. Place ½ of the noodles on the bottom. Place the tuna on the noodles and pour on ½ the soup. Add the remaining noodles and soup; the olives and the egg. Place the cheese on the top of the casserole. Dot with butter. Place the casserole in preheated oven of 350°F. Bake for 15 minutes with lid on and then for 15 minutes with lid off to brown.

Catherine B. Anthony, Courtney H. S.
Yadkinville, North Carolina

TUNA CASSEROLE
Number of Servings — 4

1 can cream of mushroom soup
½ c. evaporated milk or cream
1 6-oz. can tuna
1 c. drained green peas
2 T. chopped pimento
1⅓ c. crushed potato chips

Mix soup until smooth; add evaporated milk. Add tuna, peas, and pimento; blend together thoroughly. In baking dish place half the potato chips, pour in tuna mixture; top with potato chips. Bake at 350°F. for 25 minutes. Variations: Use chow mein noodles instead of potato chips or add 2 sliced hard cooked eggs or 1 cup chopped chicken instead of tuna.

Mrs. William Creekmur, Litchfield Jr.-Sr. H. S.
Litchfield, Illinois

TUNA SUPREME
Number of Servings — 6

2 c. tuna, in large pieces
2 c. crushed cheese crackers
3 c. medium white sauce
¾ c. sliced ripe olives

Arrange in alternate layers in buttered 1½-quart baking dish. Finish with a sprinkling of the crushed cheese crackers. Bake in moderate oven (350°F.) 35 minutes. Serve hot.

Selma Sailors, Diller Community Schools
Diller, Nebraska

TUNA CASSEROLE
Number of Servings — 6

1 medium can tuna
1 can mushroom soup
1 large bag potato chips

Heat mushroom soup until it begins to boil. (Do not add water). Place ⅓ of tuna in casserole dish, cover with potato chips and add ⅓ heated mushroom soup. Repeat process three times. Place in 350°F. oven for 5 minutes.

Margaret Walker, Greensboro H. S.
Greensboro, Georgia

TUNA CASSEROLE
Number of Servings — 6

1 can tuna
2 c. potato chips
1 can mushroom soup (10½-oz.)

Flake tuna and put half of it in a layer in casserole. Spread on layer of soup, undiluted. Cover with 1 cup of potato chips. Repeat with another layer of tuna, soup and potato chips. Do not crush potato chips too fine. No salt is needed as chips furnish the right amount. Bake in oven at 350°F. for 30 minutes. Serve hot.

Mrs. Pauline S. Slate, Greensville County H. S.
Emporia, Virginia

TUNA CASSEROLE
Number of Servings — 6

1 c. biscuit mix
¼ c. soft butter
3 T. boiling water

Make a short pie dough from biscuit mix. Divide into 6 parts. Flatten each part into 3 inch round, place on baking sheet. Sprinkle with paprika. Bake 8 minutes at 450°F.

1 package frozen peas, lima beans, broccoli or
    corn
1 can cream of mushroom soup
½ c. milk
Salt to taste

Heat oven to 450°F. Cook vegetables (cut broccoli into bite size pieces). Place in 11 x 7 inch baking dish, cover with tuna. Place vegetables. Mix milk and soup, and pour over all. Arrange baked pie rounds on top. Bake 8 to 10 minutes, until heated through.

Ruth J. Adams, Murphysboro Twp. H. S.
Murphysboro, Illinois

CHIPPER TUNA CASSEROLE
Number of Servings — 4

1 can condensed cream of mushroom soup
⅓ c. milk
1 6½- or 7-oz. can tuna
1 c. crushed potato chips
1 c. cooked or canned peas
6 whole potato chips

Empty soup into casserole. Add milk and stir until its mixed. Add tuna, ¾ cup crushed potato chips and the 1 cup drained peas. Mix lightly with a fork. Sprinkle on ¼ cup potato chips and stick the whole chips into the mixture just far enough to make them stand up or at an angle. Bake 25 minutes at 350°F.

Opal Carpenter, Mentone H. S.
Mentone, Indiana

FISH
Number of Servings — 6

¼ lb. noodles
1 qt. water, boiling
½ t. salt
1 small can mushrooms
2 T. table fat
1 can (7 oz.) tuna fish
2 c. thin white sauce
½ c. grated cheese

Add noodles to boiling salted water. Cook until tender (15 minutes). Drain. Heat fat in frying pan and add mushrooms. Stir and cook until browned. Drain oil from tuna, break with fork. Combine noodles, tuna, mushrooms and white sauce. Pour in baking dish. Sprinkle cheese on top and bake at 350°F. for 20 minutes.

Margaret Douglas, Pueblo H. S.
Tucson, Arizona

A CANNED CASSEROLE (Mock Chicken Pie)
Number of Servings — 4

1 6½-oz. can tuna
1 No. 303 can mixed vegetables
1 10-oz. can cream of mushroom soup
¼ t. nutmeg
Salt and pepper
1 recipe drop biscuits or 1 package instant
　mashed potatoes

Combine ingredients and heat at 350°F. for 15 minutes. Drop biscuits on top and bake at 350°F. until biscuits are browned or top with mashed potatoes and brown.

Ann E. Macpherson, James Monroe H. S.
Sepulveda, California

TUNA FISH CASSEROLE
Number of Servings — 4

1 can tuna fish
1 can cream of mushroom soup
½ can water
1 bag potato chips (20c)
1 grated boiled egg

In a baking dish, place a layer of tuna fish, then a layer of potato chips, a layer of egg. Repeat the layers, until all have been used. Pour the cream of mushroom soup which has been thinned with the water over the mixture. Bake at 350°F. until heated through.

Annette Braswell, Monroe Area H. S.
Monroe, Georgia

TUNA CASSEROLE
Number of Servings — 6

1 can mushroom soup
½ c. milk
1 7-oz. can tuna
1½ c. potato chips
1 c. cooked green peas

Add milk to soup and mix in small saucepan. Add tuna and 1 cup potato chips and peas to soup. Put in baking dish that has been buttered. Sprinkle top with rest of chips and bake 20 minutes at 350°F.

Ema Joe Thomas, Burkeville H. S.
Burkeville, Texas

TUNA-SPAGHETTI CASSEROLE
Number of Servings — 6

In a 1½ quart casserole, blend 1 can cream of mushroom soup, ⅔ cup milk, 2 tablespoons finely minced onion. Stir in a 7 ounce can tuna (drained and flaked), 1½ cups cooked spaghetti (about 3 ounces uncooked), 1 cup cooked cut green beans. Circle top with 2 tablespoons buttered bread crumbs. Bake in moderate oven (350°F.) for 30 minutes.

Mrs. Helen T. Pietsch, Lyford H. S.
Lyford, Texas

TUNA CASSEROLE
Number of Servings — 8-10

1 can tuna, chunk (7-oz.)
1 can mushroom soup
1 package egg noodles
½ c. bread crumbs
2 hard cooked eggs, chopped
1 c. grated cheese
1 c. milk

Cook noodles in salt water until tender; rinse. Combine soup, cheese, and milk. Heat until cheese melts. Fold in chopped eggs and tuna. Put in greased baking dish. Top with bread crumbs. Bake at 325°F. until brown.

Romanza Wiphant Johnson, Scottsville H. S.
Scottsville, Kentucky

TUNA CASSEROLE
Number of Servings — 4

1 c. noodles
1 t. salt
1 qt. boiling water
1 c. flaked tuna (7-oz. can)
1 can mushroom soup, undiluted
2 T. butter or substitute
2 hard-cooked eggs, sliced (optional)
8 stuffed olives, sliced (optional)
4 ozs. grated American cheese (optional)

Cook noodles. Butter the casserole dish lightly. Place ½ the noodles on the bottom. Place all the flaked tuna on the noodles and pour on ½ the soup. Add the remaining noodles, the remaining soup, the olives, and the eggs. Set the oven for 350°F. Place the cheese on the top of the casserole. Dot lightly with butter. Put the casserole in the oven for a 30 minute baking. Remove the cover the last 15 minutes so that the top will brown.

Mrs. Mary F. Raman, Chase H. S.
Forest City, North Carolina

TUNA AND NOODLES
Number of Servings — 8

1 box coarse noodles, boiled
1 can mushroom soup
1 large can evaporated milk
1 pimento, chopped fine
1 jar pimento cheese
½ jar old English cheese (or snappy)
⅛ t. salt

Combine and cook for 15 minutes the last 6 ingredients. After cheese melts, add small can of tuna, broken up. Saute ¼ pound mushrooms and add to above mixture. Add noodles and 2 hard cooked eggs, chopped fine. Put mixture in casserole, bake in hot oven (325°F.) about 20 to 30 minutes until top is slightly brown. This casserole, covered, holds well in the oven.

Mrs. Leora G. Essig
Mission Central Catholic H. S.
San Luis Obispo, California

TUNA NOODLE CASSEROLE
Number of Servings — 8

1 8-oz. package noodles
4 T. flour
4 T. butter
2 c. milk
2 hard cooked eggs
1 small can mushrooms (stems and pieces)
½ t. iodized salt
1 package pimento cream cheese
1 pimento, chopped
1 onion, minced
1 green pepper, chopped
8 stuffed olives, chopped
1 can tuna, in pieces

Cook noodles in salted water; drain and rinse. Melt fat in pan; add flour, blend. Add milk and juice from mushrooms. Cook over low heat until thick, stirring constantly. Brown the pimento, onion, green pepper and olives in butter. Add seasonings and cheese. Mix well. Add all ingredients; mix carefully. Place in greased casserole. Spread with buttered crumbs. Bake in medium oven (325°F.) 30 minutes.

Mrs. Naomi A. Hines, Rochelle Twp. H. S.
Rochelle, Illinois

TUNA AND NOODLE CASSEROLE
Number of Servings — 10

1 7-oz. can tuna, drained
2 c. egg noodles, cooked
3 eggs, hard cooked, sliced
⅓ c. ripe olives, chopped
2 pimentos, chopped
2 c. medium cheese sauce
½ c. sliced mushrooms
Salt and pepper
Bread crumbs

Combine ingredients. Season rather highly. Pour into oiled casserole. Cover with bread crumbs. Bake at 375°F. until sauce bubbles and crumbs are brown. Make cheese sauce by melting 2 cups cheese over boiling water.

Mrs. Loretta Sykes, Montgomery Co. H. S.
Ramer, Alabama

TUNA CASSEROLE
Number of Servings — 6

1 can family size tuna fish
1 can cream of mushroom soup
1 package egg noodles
1 can pimento (optional)
⅓ c. milk
½ c. grated cheese

Cook noodles in salted water. Add milk to cream of mushroom soup. Mix all ingredients in a mixing bowl then put in a greased casserole dish and top with grated cheese. Bake in 350°F. oven for 30 to 40 minutes.

Evelyn B. McDonald, Coosa County H. S.
Rockford, Alabama

TUNA FISH-NOODLE CASSEROLE
Number of Servings — 4

1 7-oz. can tuna fish, flaked
1 c. cooked egg noodles
½ can chopped pimento
1 can condensed celery soup
½ c. milk
½ c. English peas
½ c. grated cheese
Salt and pepper to taste

Heat celery soup, peas, pimento and milk together. When hot remove from heat and add tuna fish, cooked noodles and salt and pepper. Pour into a 1½ quart casserole. Bake in a moderate oven (350°F.) for 25 minutes. Then sprinkle the top with grated cheese and continue cooking 10 minutes or until browned.

Emily J. Bonds, Hillcrest H. S.
Simpsonville, South Carolina

TUNA NOODLE CASSEROLE
Number of Servings — 4-6

3 t. chili powder
3 T. cream
2 c. cooked noodles
1½ c. medium white sauce
1 c. grated American cheese
¼ c. chopped parsley (or ½ t. dehydrated)
3 T. chopped onion
1 t. salt
¼ t. pepper
1 7-oz. can tuna (grated tuna is better)

Blend chili powder with cream and stir to dissolve. Prepare the white sauce, then add the grated cheese and stir to melt in the hot sauce. Combine the remaining ingredients, then add the chili mixture and white sauce. Pour into greased casserole and bake at 350°F. for 30 minutes.

Mrs. Katy Jo Powers, Haysi H. S.
Haysi, Virginia

NOODLE-TUNA CASSEROLE
Number of Servings — 15

12 ozs. large or wide egg noodles
2 cans condensed cream of mushroom soup, undiluted
2 cans tuna, chunk style (6½-oz. size)
¼ lb. margarine (less if desired)
Any leftover vegetables can be added to this like peas, corn, carrots

Boil noodles in 3 quarts salted water, using 1 tablespoon of salt, for 10 to 12 minutes. Add butter to hot noodles. Warm 2 cans of cream of mushroom soup and add to the noodles. Flake the tuna chunks and mix with the noodle mixture. Add pepper, salt and a touch of garlic. Put in casserole and bake 20 to 30 minutes in a 325°F. to 350°F. oven.

Mrs. Emily Bierschwale, Junction H. S.
Junction, Texas

TUNA FISH CASSEROLE
Number of Servings — 6

1 can tuna
1 can mushroom soup
2 c. cooked noodles
2 T. chopped onions
½ c. chopped celery
⅓ c. cheese bits

Mix all ingredients together. Pour into greased baking dish. Dot with butter and top with crushed potato chips. Bake in moderate oven 45 minutes.

Marilyn Mills, Georgetown H. S.
Georgetown, Illinois

TUNA CASSEROLE
Number of Servings — 4 large

1 can (large) Chinese noodles
1 can tuna
1 can mushroom soup
1 can milk (use mushroom soup can)
1 medium onion
Salt and pepper
Grated cheese
Pimento and/or green pepper

Combine first 6 ingredients. Place in casserole dish. Bake in slow oven (325°F) for 2 hours. Top with cheese and green pepper during last few minutes of baking.

Marjorie J. Hubert, Norfolk Sr. H. S.
Norfolk, Nebraska

TUNA-NOODLE CASSEROLE
Number of Servings — 6-8

1 package noodles
1-2 cans flaked tuna
Salt and pepper to taste
1 can cream of mushroom soup
1 c. milk

Cook noodles in salted water until tender. Drain. Add 1 or 2 cans of flaked tuna, cream of mushroom soup and milk. Salt and pepper to taste. Bake in moderate oven 30 to 45 minutes.

Mrs. Wilborn N. Day, Lincoln Rural H. S.
Lincoln, Kansas

ASPARAGUS-TUNA CASSEROLE
Number of Servings — 8

1 5-oz. package fine egg noodles
1 6½-oz. can white chunk style tuna
1 14½-oz. can whole green asparagus spears
1 can undiluted cream of mushroom soup
½ c. grated cheese
¼ c. bread crumbs
Dots of butter

Line a 8 x 10 inch casserole dish with the cooked drained noodles. Top the noodles with the ingredients following the order given above. Place in a 375°F. oven for 30 minutes or until bubbly and cheese is melted.

Mrs. Ray White, Hillsboro H. S.
Nashville, Tennessee

TUNA ASPARAGUS BAKE
Number of Servings — 4

2 T. flour
1 T. parsley
1½ t. grated onion
½ t. dry mustard
1 t. salt
Dash pepper
1 c. liquefied nonfat dry milk or skim milk
1 package frozen asparagus spears, cooked, drained
2 hard-cooked eggs, sliced
1 7-oz. can tuna, drained

Start heating oven to 350°F. In small saucepan, combine flour, parsley, onion, mustard, salt and pepper; very gradually stir in milk. Cook over low heat, stirring constantly, until smooth and thickened. In a 1 quart casserole, arrange asparagus, eggs, and tuna. Pour sauce over all in casserole. Bake, covered about 30 minutes. To serve, sprinkle with lemon juice and parsley.

Jo Dunn, Arab H. S.
Arab, Alabama

TUNA-VEGETABLE CASSEROLE
Number of Servings — 8

1 can tuna
1 c. carrots
1 c. English peas
1 can cream of mushroom soup
1 T. tomato catsup
1 t. celery seed
½ t. black pepper
1 c. grated cheese

Combine tuna, peas, and carrots (canned); add pepper, celery seed, and place in a greased casserole. Pour soup over the top, rinsing can with ½ cup milk and use over the mixture. Place dashes of pimento on this; add cheese and bake in hot oven (425°F.) for 20 minutes.

Mable E. Allen, Joppa Com. H. S.
Joppa, Illinois

QUICK RICE AND TUNA DISH
Number of Servings — 6

1 can (13-oz.) light chunk tuna (without oil is better)
1 can cream of mushroom soup
2 T. margarine
1 t. minced onion
Dash black pepper
Few drops Worcestershire sauce
⅓ c. evaporated milk

Put mushroom soup in saucepan; stir in evaporated milk until smooth. Add flaked tuna, then remaining ingredients. Cover and simmer for 10 to 15 minutes. Stir occasionally. Serve over cooked rice.

Martha Ann Langford, Jenkins H. S.
Savannah, Georgia

SEVEN SEAS CASSEROLE
Number of Servings — 6

1 can condensed cream of mushroom soup or condensed cream of celery soup
¼ to ⅓ c. finely chopped onion
1⅓ c. water
¼ t. salt
1 t. lemon juice
⅛ t. pepper
1⅓ c. minute rice
1 box (10 oz.) green peas, partially thawed
1 can tuna, drained and flaked
½ c. grated cheddar cheese
Paprika

Combine soup, onion, lemon juice, salt, and pepper in a saucepan. Bring to a boil over medium heat, stirring occasionally. Pour about half the soup mixture into a greased 1½ quart casserole. Then in layers add minute rice (right from the box), peas, and tuna fish. Add remaining soup. Sprinkle with cheese and paprika. Cover and bake in moderate oven (375°F.) 15 to 20 minutes. Cut through mixtures with knife or fork after 10 minutes of baking to help distribute soup mixture.

Mrs. Rosemary Coopwood, Collierville H. S.
Collierville, Tennessee

CHOW MEIN NOODLE-TUNA CASSEROLE
Number of Servings — 5

1 can chow mein noodles
1 can (7-oz.) tuna
1 can mushroom soup
2 boiled eggs
Pimento
Bay leaves

Sprinkle half of noodles in bottom of casserole. Add mushroom soup to tuna. Add chopped pimento. Spread on top of noodles. Slice egg on top of tuna mixture. Add more noodles on top. Insert bay leaves. Bake at 375°F. until heated through.

Mrs. Dale Findley, Williamsburg Com. H. S.
Williamsburg, Iowa

CHOPSTICK TUNA
Number of Servings — 4-5

1 can mushroom soup
¼ c. water
1 3-oz. can chow mein noodles
1 c. chopped celery
½ c. salted, toasted cashews
¼ c. chopped onion
Dash of pepper
1 7-oz. can tuna

Combine soup and water. Add 1 cup of the noodles, the tuna, celery, cashews, onion, and pepper. Toss lightly. Place in an ungreased baking dish, 10 x 6 x 1½. Sprinkle remaining noodles over top. Bake at 375°F. for 15 minutes or until thoroughly heated.

Alice L. Steinfort, Farmington H. S.
Farmington, New Mexico

TUNA LUNCHEON DISH
Number of Servings — 6

1 4-oz. can chow mein noodles
1 can mushroom soup
1 c. finely cut celery
Dash of pepper
1 can chunk tuna
¼ lb. cashew nuts
¼ c. minced onion

Set aside ½ cup of the noodles. Combine the remaining noodles with the rest of the ingredients. Pour into greased baking dish. Sprinkle with the ½ cup noodles and bake 40 minutes in a 350°F. oven.

Thelma Bryning, Monte Vista H. S.
Monte Vista, Colorado

BAKED TUNA CHOW MEIN CASSEROLE
Number of Servings — 4-6

1 c. cut-up celery
¼ c. chopped onion
2 T. chopped green pepper
1 T. butter
1 7-oz. can tuna
3 ozs. chow mein noodles (save out ¼ c. for topping)
1 can (10½-oz.) cream of mushroom soup, thinned with ¼ c. milk and ¼ c. water
⅛ t. pepper
¼ t. flavor extender
¼ lb. (¾ c.) salted cashew nuts

Heat oven to 350°F. (moderate). Saute celery, onion and green pepper slowly in butter. Mix in rest of ingredients and pour into buttered 1½ quart baking dish. Sprinkle with ¼ cup chow mein noodles. Bake 30 minutes.

Mrs. Beverly Brine, Waterville H. S.
Waterville, Minnesota

TUNA-CASHEW CASSEROLE
Number of Servings — 6

1 3-oz. jar chow mein noodles
1 can condensed cream of mushroom soup, undiluted
¼ c. water
1 can (1 c.) chunk style tuna
¼ lb. cashew nuts, salted or unsalted
1 c. finely diced celery
¼ c. minced onions
Salt to taste
Dash of pepper

Heat oven to 325°F. Set aside ½ cup of chow mein noodles. In 1½ quart casserole combine rest of noodles with next 7 ingredients. Taste; add salt if nuts were unsalted. Sprinkle reserved noodles over top. Bake 40 minutes. If preferred, bake in 6 individual casseroles or scallop shells for 25 minutes.

Mrs. Verna Wright, Russellville Sr. H. S.
Russellville, Arkansas

TUNA BAKE
Number of Servings — 4

⅓ c. chopped green pepper
2 T. chopped onion
1 c. medium white sauce
1 t. salt
black pepper
1 7-oz. can tuna
1 T. lemon juice (fresh, frozen, or canned)
⅓ c. cracker crumbs

Add flaked tuna to white sauce. Add chopped green pepper, chopped onion, salt and pepper, and lemon juice. Pour mixture into buttered one-quart baking dish. Sprinkle with cracker crumbs. Bake in 375°F. oven about 30 minutes. Serve hot.

Mrs. Truman M. Thornton, Runnelstown H. S.
Hattiesburg, Mississippi

TUNA BAKE CHEESE SWIRLS
Number of Servings — 8

⅓ c. chopped green pepper
3 T. chopped onion
3 T. fat
1 t. salt
6 T. enriched flour
1 10½-oz. can condensed chicken soup with rice
1½ c. milk
1 T. lemon juice
1 7-oz. can tuna

Cook pepper and onion in hot fat until golden; add salt and flour; blend. Add soup and milk; cook until sauce is thick, stirring constantly. Add flaked tuna and lemon juice. Pour mixture into greased 10 x 6 x 1½-inch baking dish and top with cheese swirls. Bake in hot oven (425°F.) 30 minutes.

Bettye J. Gaffney, L'Ouverture H. S.
McAlester, Oklahoma

TUNA FISH PIE WITH CHEESE ROLL CRUST
Number of Servings — 8

½ c. chopped green peppers
¼ c. chopped onion
3 T. butter
6 T. flour
1 T. lemon juice
3 c. milk
½ t. salt
1 large can tuna fish, drained

Melt butter, add green peppers and onion and cook until soft. Add flour and stir until well blended. Add salt and milk slowly, stirring constantly until thick and smooth. Bring to boil and boil 2 minutes. Add remaining ingredients. Pour into large baking dish and cover with cheese rolls.

CHEESE ROLLS

1½ c. flour
3 t. baking powder
½ t. salt
few grains cayenne
3 T. shortening
½ c. milk

¾ c. grated cheese
2 pimentos, chopped

Sift together the first 4 ingredients. Add shortening, mix with fork, add milk to make soft dough. Turn out on floured board and toss lightly until outside looks smooth. Roll out ½ inch thick and sprinkle with grated cheese and chopped pimento. Roll up like a jelly roll. With a sharp knife cut into slices about ½ inch thick. Place o ntop of tuna fish pie. Bake in hot oven at 450°F. for 30 minutes.

Mrs. Jo Nell Babst, Fairland H. S.
Fairland, Oklahoma

SAVORY SCALLOPED FISH
Number of Servings — 4-5

1½ c. milk
1 slice onion
1 small blade mace
1 sprig parsley
2 T. butter or margarine
2 T. flour
½ t. salt
⅛ t. pepper
2 egg yolks
2½ c. flaked, cooked fish
1 T. lemon juice
⅔ c. buttered crumbs

Scald the milk with the onion, mace and parsley; strain. Melt the butter; stir in the flour; add the seasoned milk gradually and cook until it boils, stirring constantly. Stir in the salt and pepper; stir in the egg yolks. Place a layer of fish in a shallow, greased baking dish; sprinkle with lemon juice; cover with sauce. Repeat the layers until all the ingredients are used. Top the dish with the buttered crumbs and bake in a hot oven (400° F.) until the food is hot and the crumbs brown.

Patricia Morse, Bellows Falls H. S.
Bellows Falls, Vermont

FISH
Number of Servings — 6

1 6-oz. can tuna or salmon
1 can mushroom soup
½ c. American cheese, grated
1 c. cooked rice
1 c. medium white sauce
¼ c. celery
½ c. chopped onion
1 T. butter or margarine
¾ c. soft bread crumbs

Cook celery and onions in boiling water for 5 minutes. Grease casserole and turn oven to 350°F. Flake tuna or salmon, grate cheese. Make 1 cup medium white sauce. Add salmon or tuna, rice, cheese, soup, celery, and onion to white sauce, mix gently and pour into casserole. Melt butter, mix with crumbs and sprinkle on top. Bake in moderate oven for 20 minutes.

Joyce Gandy Garrison, Chesnee H. S.
Chesnee, South Carolina

Miscellaneous Casseroles

CREAMY MEAT PIE
Number of Servings — 4-5

English pastry:
1½ c. flour
½ c. lard
1½ t. baking powder
¾ t. salt
1 egg yolk
2 t. lemon juice
6 T. hot water
Filling:
1½ c. boned turkey, chicken or pork
1 c. cold chicken dressing
2 to 2½ c. left-over gravy
1 c. mushrooms (or 1 c. shredded celery)
2 T. butter

Line sides of baking dish with pastry. Put in layer of dressing, chicken, mushrooms, dressing, and gravy; top with pastry. Brush pastry with slightly beaten egg white. Bake 30 minutes at 425°F. If it browns quickly, cover with paper to avoid burning.

Roxie J. Simcoe, Declo H. S.
Declo, Idaho

SHEPHERD'S PIE
Number of Servings — 4

2 T. minced onion
2 T. butter
1½ c. diced cooked meat (left-overs)
1 c. condensed tomato soup
½ c. diced, cooked carrots
¼ t. salt
Dash of pepper
1 c. hot, mashed potatoes
Dash of paprika

Saute onion in hot fat until golden brown. Add meat, carrots, tomato soup and seasonings. Mix well and transfer to a greased 9 inch pie plate. Cover with a thin layer of mashed potatoes. Swirl potatoes with back of spoon to make attractive design. Dust with paprika. Bake 400°F. for 20 minutes, or until golden brown.

Mrs. Linda S. Holloway, Reidsville H. S.
Reidsville, Georgia

MONDAY'S MAGIC MEAL
Number of Servings — 6

1 10½-oz. can onion soup
2 T. chopped green pepper
4 ozs. noodles
1 T. fat
¼ c. chopped celery
½ c. water
¾ c. left-over chicken, beef, or pork roast

Add 2 teaspoons salt and noodles to 2 cups boiling water. Boil rapidly, stirring constantly for 2 minutes. Cover, remove from heat and let stand 10 minutes. Melt fat in saucepan; add celery and green pepper and saute for 2 minutes. Add onion soup and ½ cup water. Blanch and drain noodles. Add meat to soup mixture and stir. Add noodles to soup mixture and mix thoroughly. Bake in 1½ quart casserole for 20 to 25 minutes at 350°F.

Jean Passino, Nashwauk H. S.
Nashwauk, Minnesota

CASSEROLE MEAL
Number of Servings — 12

1 lb. veal, small chunks
1 lb. pork, small chunks
1 can pimentos
1 can mushrooms
1 can whole kernel corn
1 large package noodles
1 pt. milk
4 T. flour
4 T. butter
½ lb. cream or processed cheese
Salt to season

Cook veal and pork. To broth add package of noodles and partly cook. Make a white sauce with milk, butter, flour; add cheese. Blend meat, noodles, pimentos, mushrooms, corn and sauce. Bake in large casserole at 325°F. for 1 hour.

Mrs. Pauline Quillin, Pymatuning Joint School
Jamestown, Pennsylvania

WIENER SALAD BAKE
Number of Servings—5-6

3 T. butter or margarine
3 T. flour
1 t. salt
¾ t. dry mustard
¼ t. black pepper
1 medium size onion, chopped
6 wieners, cut in diagonal slices
1½ c. sweet milk
¾ c. mayonnaise or salad dressing
4 potatoes (medium) cooked, peeled and diced
1 can cut green beans, drained (grade A)
Buttered bread crumbs for topping

Melt butter or margarine in saucepan; remove from heat; blend in flour, salt, mustard and pepper; slowly stir in milk. Cook over medium heat, stirring constantly, until mixture thickens and boils 1 minute; remove from heat; blend in mayonnaise or salad dressing; save ¾ cup of sauce. Fold potatoes, green beans, onion and ¾ of the wiener slices into remaining sauce; spoon into baking dish. Arrange remaining wieners in a ring on top; spoon reserved sauce over wieners; sprinkle with buttered bread crumbs. Bake in moderate oven (350°F.) 45 minutes or until bubbly hot.

Mrs. Mildred H. Reid, Chase H. S.
Forest City, North Carolina

Salads

Salads Featuring Meats

VEAL "SYLTA" — SALAD MOLD*
Number of Servings — 8

2 lbs. cubed veal meat
1 small shank or other bone pieces
1 t. salt
6 to 8 peppercorns
1 medium bay leaf
½ c. diced celery
Water to cover meat and bones

Cook until meat is tender. Lift meat and bones from broth. Remove any meat on bones; discard bones. Coarsely grind meat. Strain broth. Add cut meat; season with salt and white pepper to taste. Simmer until broth just covers meat. Pour into pyrex loaf pan or any desired mold. Chill. When congealed, ease sides loose and remove to serving plate. Garnish with parsley, olives, carrot curls, etc. Serve with vinegar or other meat seasoning sauces.
*Swedish Smorgasbord serving.

Edith M. Anderson, Stephen F. Austin H. S.
Austin, Texas

QUICK HAM SALAD
Number of Servings — 4

1 c. cubed, cooked ham
4 hard cooked eggs, chopped
½ c. diced celery
½ c. diced cucumber pickle (either sweet or sour)
Lettuce
Mayonnaise to mix

Combine ham, eggs, celery, pickles and mayonnaise. Serve in lettuce cups. Garnish with paprika.

Mrs. Stella Forrest, Wake Forest H. S.
Wake Forest, North Carolina

HAM SALAD MOLD
Number of Servings — 6-8

2 t. sugar
1 package lemon gelatin (3 oz. size)
3 T. lemon juice
1 c. hot water
2 T. chopped sweet pickle
1 c. chopped ham or tuna
1 c. chopped celery
2 T. diced pimento
1 c. small peas (canned)
1 T. grated onion
½ c. heavy cream, whipped
1 c. mayonnaise
¼ t. salt

Stir gelatin, water, juice and sugar to dissolve. Cool. Add the chopped ham, sweet pickle, celery, pimento, peas, and onion. Lastly, fold in whipped cream mayonnaise and salt. Mold in 8 x 8 inch pan or individual molds. Serve on lettuce.

Mrs. Jean Cummings, Kingsford H. S.
Kingsford, Michigan

PATIO SALAD WITH HAM
Number of Servings — 6

1 package frozen green peas
½ t. salt
1½ c. water
1⅓ c. minute rice
¾ c. mayonnaise
½ c. chopped dill pickles
1 t. grated onion
1 c. cooked ham strips
1 c. Swiss cheese strips
¼ t. pepper

Add frozen peas and salt to boiling water. Boil 2 minutes. Add rice; mix to moisten rice. Cover and remove from heat. Let stand 5 minutes. Stir in mayonnaise, pickle, onion, and pepper. Mix lightly with fork. Chill. Before serving, add ham and cheese. Mix lightly, serve on crisp salad greens and garnish with tomato wedges. Fried bacon, Spam, Treat, or canned ham may also be used.

Betty McDonald, Marion H. S.
Marion, South Carolina

MAIN DISH KIDNEY BEAN SALAD
Number of Servings — 6

1 can kidney beans, drained
½ c. celery, chopped
½ c. green pepper, diced
1 onion, cut in circles
½ c. pickles, chopped
½ lb. cheese, chopped
1 lb. ham, cut in strips
2 eggs, sliced
Mayonnaise

Combine and toss all ingredients except mayonnaise. Chill. Just before serving, add mayonnaise and mix carefully. Place in lettuce cups and serve with hot bread or crackers.

Mrs. Mary Ann Lea, Vilonia H. S.
Vilonia, Arkansas

EASY LUNCHEON SALAD
Number of Servings — 10

1 package lemon jello
1 c. mayonnaise
1 canned corned beef
½ t. salt
1 T. chopped green pepper
1 c. chopped celery
1 T. chopped onion
2 hard cooked eggs, chopped

Prepare jello according to package directions. Let set in refrigerator until thick and syrupy. Beat until light. Fold in mayonnaise. Add to this, the corned beef which has been separated into small bits and all fibres removed, the chopped ingredients, salt. Let congeal and serve on lettuce cups.

Mrs. Mildred E. Ready, Hartington H. S.
Hartington, Nebraska

CORN BEEF SALAD
Number of Servings — 6

Peel 4 medium potatoes and place in saucepan. Cover with water and add ½ teaspoon salt. Simmer until tender. Chill potatoes for 1 hour, then cut into ½ inch cubes. Chill one 12 ounce can of corn beef. Dice the corn beef and chop 4 medium dill pickles into small pieces. Combine potatoes, corn beef and pickle with ½ cup celery and ¼ cup minced onions. *Dressing:* 1 cup salad dressing, 2 tablespoons lemon juice, 2 teaspoons prepared mustard, 1 tablespoon Worcestershire sauce and 1 teaspoon salt and pepper. Mix all together and chill for 1 hour.

Nell P. Stevens, Isola H. S.
Isola, Mississippi

VIENNA'D MACARONI SALAD
Number of Servings — 6

1 8-oz. package elbow macaroni
1 c. chopped celery
1 c. chopped sweet pickles
2 T. grated onion
1 can Vienna sausage
1 c. mayonnaise
2 T. pickle juice
1 t. salt
¼ t. pepper

Cook macaroni just until tender. Drain, blanch in cold water, drain thoroughly. Combine with celery, sweet pickles, onions and Vienna sausage cut in thin slices (save a few slices to decorate top). Blend 1 cup mayonnaise with juice from pickles, salt and pepper. Add to macaroni mixture. Arrange on salad plate. Decorate top with Vienna slices and surround with deviled egg halves.

Ernestine Gresham, Bullard H. S.
Bullard, Texas

CHICKEN SALAD
Number of Servings — 8-10

1 chicken
3 oranges
4 slices pineapple
½ lb. white grapes
Salad Dressing:
½ c. sugar
1 T. flour
½ c. pineapple juice
½ c. water
2 T. lemon juice
1 T. butter
2 eggs
Salt to taste

Cook dressing; cool, and pour over fruit and chicken. Chill. Serve on lettuce.

Mrs. Retta K. Geiger, Ligonier H. S.
Ligonier, Indiana

CHICKEN SALAD
Number of Servings — 4

1 c. fresh cooked chicken, diced
1 c. celery, minced very fine
¼ c. mayonnaise
5 large eggs, hard-cooked
Juice of 2 lemons, or to taste
1 t. salt

Add minced or chopped celery, diced chicken, grated eggs, salt and lemon juice. Stir lightly. Add mayonnaise and stir lightly until well blended. Serve as salad or sandwich spread.

Mexie Lee Chism, McComb H. S.
McComb, Mississippi

CHICKEN SALAD PLATE
Number of Servings — 4-6

3 c. coarsely diced cooked chicken
2 c. diced celery
½ c. mayonnaise
3 T. lemon juice
1 t. seasoned salt
¼ t. pepper

Combine chicken and celery. To mayonnaise, add remaining ingredients, and blend. Pour mayonnaise mixture over chicken and let chill 1 hour before serving. Serve in lettuce cups. Garnish with tomato and hard-cooked egg wedges, ripe olives.

Rachael S. Goodman, Monticello H. S.
Browns Summit, North Carolina

CHICKEN SALAD
Number of Servings — 4-5

1 c. cooked chicken
1 apple
½ c. sweet pickles
¼ c. mayonnaise
Salt, pepper and paprika to taste

Chop chicken, pickles and apple together. Mix with mayonnaise. Serve on lettuce leaves with crackers.

Mrs. Joyce Green Harrison, Sebastopol H. S.
Sebastopol, Mississippi

CHICKEN SALAD
Number of Servings — 6

1 chicken, cooked and diced
1 c. celery, diced
3 hard boiled eggs, chopped
1 large pimento
½ c. pecans
2 pickles (medium)
Juice of ½ lemon
Salt and pepper to taste

Mix well with salad dressing and serve on crisp lettuce.

Myrtle P. Teer, Hutto H. S.
Hutto, Texas

CHICKEN SALAD
Number of Servings — 4-5

2 c. coarsely diced chicken
2 T. lemon juice
½ t. salt
1 c. diced celery
1 c. seedless white grapes
2 hard cooked eggs, chilled and cut
½ c. mayonnaise
¼ c. slivered, blanched and toasted almonds

Sprinkle chicken with lemon juice and salt. Chill several hours. Add celery, grapes, chopped eggs, mayonnaise and almonds. Toss lightly. Season with salt to taste. Serve on lettuce cups.

Patricia McGee, Conrad Sr. H. S.
Conrad, Montana

CHICKEN SALAD
Number of Servings — 6

2 c. diced chicken
1 c. diced celery
3 hard boiled eggs, diced
1 c. broken pecans
1 c. salad dressing
½ c. seeded Tokay grapes
¼ c. drained crushed pineapple
¾ t. salt
⅛ t. pepper

Mix all ingredients together. Add the salad dressing last. Serve very cold on salad greens. Salad dressing may be combined with ½ cup whipped cream, if preferred.

Harriet W. Smythe, Northridge Local H. S.
Homer, Ohio

FROZEN CHICKEN SALAD
Number of Servings — 6

1½ c. diced cooked chicken
¾ c. drained crushed pineapple
½ c. chopped pecans
1 c. heavy cream, whipped
1 c. mayonnaise

Toss chicken, pineapple and nuts together; fold cream into mayonnaise; add to chicken mixture and freeze 2 to 3 hours, or until firm.

Mrs. Luella Robb, Round Valley Union H. S.
Covelo, California

FRUIT AND CHICKEN SALAD SUPREME
Number of Servings — 8

2 c. cubed, cooked chicken
2 T. chopped green olives
¾ c. chopped celery
½ c. toasted almonds
1 c. chopped raw apple
2 T. chopped ripe olives
2 T. chopped sweet pickle
2 hard-cooked eggs, diced
1 c. diced pineapple

½ c. raisins
¾ c. mayonnaise

Combine ingredients; toss lightly. Serve on lettuce and garnish with spiced apple rings, ripe olives and watercress. Just before serving, crush 1 cup of potato chips over the top.

Betty Ann Augustad, Orland H. S.
Madison, South Dakota

CONGEALED CHICKEN SALAD
Number of Servings — 8

1 T. plain gelatin
1¾ c. chicken stock
1 T. lemon juice
1¼ c. diced cooked chicken
½ c. diced celery
½ t. salt
2 T. chopped green peppers

Soften gelatin in ½ cup cold chicken stock. Heat remainder of chicken stock, add salt and stir until dissolved. Pour over gelatin mixture. Add lemon juice. Chill until consistency of unbeaten egg whites. Then fold in chicken, celery and pepper. Chill until firm; unmold and garnish with salad greens, tomato wedges and stuffed olives.

Elsie Snellgrove, Corner H. S.
Warrior, Alabama

CHICKEN MOUSSE
Number of Servings — 8

2 c. cooked chicken, cut up
4 hard cooked eggs, mashed
½ c. celery
8 pickle chips, cut fine
Salt and pepper to taste
Dash Lee & Perrin sauce
Dash of Red pepper
1 small pimento, cut up
2 T. gelatin, soaked in ¼ c. cold water
1 c. mayonnaise
Juice of ½ lemon

Dissolve gelatin in cold water; then add ½ cup boiling water. Stir until gelatin is melted. Let cool and add mayonnaise, and the rest of the ingredients. Congeal in loaf pan and serve in slices.

Elizabeth Heard, Central H. S.
Jackson, Mississippi

CHICKEN SALAD GEL
Number of Servings — 6

1 envelope unflavored gelatin
¼ c. water
1 c. hot chicken broth
1 T. salt
1 T. chopped onion
¼ c. lemon juice
¼ T. paprika
1 c. cold broth or water
¾ c. mayonnaise or salad dressing
1 c. diced chicken
¼ c. sliced stuffed olives
2 T. chopped green pepper
¼ c. chopped celery

Soften gelatin in the ¼ cup water and add to the hot broth. Add salt, paprika, onion, lemon juice and the remaining broth. Cool until it begins to thicken and beat in mayonnaise. Fold in chicken, celery, olives and green pepper. Chill in a shallow container (about 7 x 9 inches rectangular). Cut and unmold on salad plate. Garnish with deviled eggs, radish roses or parsley.

Pauline Waggener, DuQuoin Twp. H. S.
DuQuoin, Illinois

CONGEALED CHICKEN OR TURKEY SALAD
Number of Servings — 8

2 c. diced chicken or turkey
1 c. brown rice
2 hard cooked eggs, diced
2 T. gelatin
½ medium green pepper, sliced thin
2 ribs green celery, sliced diagonally
3 pods pimento, diced
1½ t. salt

Cook the rice in 2½ cups chicken stock (or use bouillon cube). Dissolve gelatin in ½ cup chicken stock until soft. Add diced vegetables and cover with a dressing of ⅓ cup commercial salad dressing, ⅓ cup creamy French dressing, and ⅓ cup chicken stock. Add hard cooked eggs that have been diced, chicken or turkey that has been diced, and the cooked rice. Mix thoroughly and put in a 6 cup ring mold. Chill 4 hours or over night before serving. Can be frozen and thawed before serving.

Mary Jane Wilson, Woodland Jr. H. S.
Fayetteville, Arkansas

HOT CHICKEN SALAD
Number of Servings — 6

6 slices bread
2 c. chicken
½ c. chopped onion
½ c. chopped green pepper
2 eggs, beaten
½ c. chopped celery
½ c. mayonnaise
¾ t. salt
Dash of pepper
1½ c. milk

1 can mushroom soup
½ c. shredded cheese
2 slices bread on bottom of pan

Combine chicken, vegetables, mayonnaise and seasoning. Spoon over cubed bread. Trim crusts off 6 slices and lay on top of mixture. Combine the eggs and milk, and spoon over bread and mixture. Spoon soup over top and bake 1 hour at 325°F. Sprinkle cheese over about 10 minutes before serving. Cut in squares and serve at once. You could cover and chill 1 hour or over night.

Lacquita Olson, Colman Independent School
Colman, South Dakota

HOT BAKED CHICKEN SALAD
Number of Servings — 8-10

2⅝ c. cooked chicken
1½ c. diced celery
½ c. chopped almonds
⅞ t. salt
⅛ t. pepper
1⅛ T. minced onion
3/16 c. lemon juice
⅞ c. mayonnaise
1½ c. crushed potato chips

Mix first 8 ingredients. Pour into greased casserole. Top with potato chips. Bake in 450°F. oven 15 to 20 minutes.

Mrs. Agnes Foster, Hartford H. S.
Hartford, Kentucky

HOT CHICKEN SALAD
Number of Servings — 8

3 c. cooked, diced chicken
1½ c. diced celery
½ c. chopped almonds
1 T. minced onion
1½ c. grated cheddar cheese
1½ t. grated lemon rind
1½ T. lemon juice
⅛ t. black pepper
¾ c. mayonnaise
1½ c. crushed potato chips

Mix all ingredients except cheese and potato chips. Put in baking dish, cover with cheese, then potato chips. Bake 30 minutes in 350°F. oven.

Mrs. Thelma Land, Hickory H. S.
Hickory, Mississippi

HOT CHICKEN SALAD
Number of Servings — 8

3 c. cooked chicken
½ c. chopped almonds
1 T. minced onion
1½ T. lemon juice
⅛ t. pepper
1 c. mayonnaise
1½ c. grated cheddar cheese
1½ c. crushed potato chips
1½ c. diced celery

(Continued on Next Page)

Combine chicken, celery, almonds, onion, lemon juice and pepper in mixing bowl. Add mayonnaise and toss. Divide into individual casseroles. Sprinkle top generously with grated cheese and finish with potato chips. Bake in pre-heated oven (375°F.)for 25 minutes. This casserole may be baked in one dish also. It can be frozen successfully.

Mrs. Wilma Adams, Lockney H. S.
Lockney, Texas

HOT CHICKEN SALAD
Number of Servings — 6

2½ c. chopped, cooked chicken
2 c. chopped celery
½ c. blanched, chopped, salted almonds
¼ c. chopped green pepper
2 T. minced onion
2 T. chopped pimento
¾ t. salt
2 T. lemon juice
½ c. mayonnaise
⅓ c. grated Swiss cheese
3 c. crushed potato chips

Blend chicken, celery, almonds, onion, green pepper, pimento, salt, lemon juice and mayonnaise. Turn into a buttered 1½ quart casserole. Top with grated cheese and crushed potato chips. Bake in moderate oven (350°F.) 25 minutes, or until cheese is melted.

Betty Trout, Ames H. S.
Ames, Iowa

CHICKEN MAYONNAISE
Number of Servings — 12

1 cooked chicken, cut finely
1 c. nuts, chopped
1 No. 2 can English peas, drained
1 pt. salad dressing
2 c. diced celery
3 hard cooked eggs, sliced
2 envelopes gelatin
Salt and pepper to taste

Dissolve gelatin in ½ cup of cold water; add 2 cups hot chicken broth. Let cool, then add other ingredients to gelatin mixture. Let stand over night in refrigerator. Cut in squares and serve on lettuce leaves. Pimentos, garlic salt, red pepper and paprika may be added to suit taste.

Essie L. Stanley, Saltillo Rural H. S.
Saltillo, Texas

CHICKEN MAYONNAISE
Number of Servings — 12-15

1 fat hen, cooked
1 large bunch celery, diced
1 small can pimentos, diced
1 small can tiny green peas
1½ c. mayonnaise
2 envelopes gelatin

Mix in a bowl the chicken, cut in small pieces, diced celery, diced pimentos and the peas that have been drained. Season with a dash of cayenne pepper. Place a cup of stock in a pan and heat it. Dissolve gelatin in ½ cup cold water, then in hot stock. Let cool. Add mayonnaise to the cut ingredients and then the cooled stock and gelatin mixture. Mix well and place in molds. Chill. Serve on lettuce leaf.

Mrs. Obera B. Pruitt, Belton H. S.
Belton, South Carolina

CHICKEN MAYONNAISE
Number of Servings — 20

1 hen (boiled and cut fine)
2 envelopes gelatin
1 c. hot stock
1 t. prepared mustard
Salt and pepper
2 c. diced celery
2 t. chopped olives
2 t. chow-chow
3 sour pickles, chopped
1 can English peas, drained
1 c. pecans
1 pt. salad dressing

Dissolve gelatin in 1 cup hot stock. Cool and add remaining ingredients. Mix well, chill and put in a 9 x 13 x 2 inch pyrex dish. When set, cut in squares and serve on lettuce leaf.

Mrs. Chloe Thorp, Lincoln Jr. H. S.
Abilene, Texas

PARTY SALAD
Number of Servings — 5-6

2 c. cubed turkey or chicken
2 c. sliced celery
½ c. chopped, toasted almonds
½ t. salt
2 t. salt
2 T. lemon juice
1 c. mayonnaise
½ c. grated American cheese
1 c. crushed potato chips

Combine ingredients, except cheese and potato chips. Toss lightly. Pile into individual bakers or custard cups. Sprinkle with grated cheese and potato chips. Bake at 450°F. for 10 minutes.

Dorothy Maxfield, Alton Sr. H. S.
Alton, Illinois

SEAFOOD COCKTAIL
Number of Servings — 8

Any combination of seafood may be used
1 boiled lobster (1 lb. substituted)
1 lb. shrimp, cooked shelled, de-veined
¼ lb. crab meat

May substitute canned seafood. Arrange on bed of greens in individual cocktail glasses. Serve with

Continued on Next Page)

spoonful of this sauce. *Cocktail Sauce:* To ½ cup mayonnaise add ¼ teaspoon salt, a little pepper, ⅛ teaspoon paprika, ⅛ cup India relish, 1 small hard cooked egg (chopped fine), ½ cup chili sauce, ⅛ teaspoon minced chives, ⅛ teaspoon green peppers, chopped, 1 teaspoon minced celery, ¾ teaspoon prepared mustard, dash tabasco. Mix well, chill. Makes 1¼ cups.

Leola M. DuBois, Grafton Central H. S.
Grafton, North Dakota

SEAFOOD SALAD
Number of Servings — 8

Heat 1 can tomato soup. Soak 1 tablespoon gelatin 5 minutes in ¼ cup cold water. While soup is hot add gelatin and water; 3 small cream cheese, or 1 large; 1 can crabmeat; 1 can shrimp; 1 small onion, chopped; 1 green pepper, chopped; ¾ cup celery, chopped; 1 cup salad dressing or mayonnaise. Mold and serve very cold on any salad greens. Three medium sized lobsters may be substituted for the crabmeat and shrimp.

Dorothy B. Tobey, Hampton Jr. H. S.
Hampton, New Hampshire

KING CRAB SALAD
Number of Servings — 6-8

1 can tomato soup
2 packages cream cheese
1 package lemon jello
1 can crab meat
½ c. celery
1 T. green peppers
1 T. minced onion
1 c. canned peas
1 c. mayonnaise
1 T. vinegar
½ t. salt

Dissolve jello in ¾ cup boiling water. Melt cheese in double boiler with tomato soup; cool. Mix crab, diced celery, diced green pepper, onion, peas, mayonnaise, vinegar and salt. Add all ingredients together. Pour in buttered greased mold.

Ruth I. Lamb, Central Kitsap Jr. H. S.
Silverdale, Washington

MIXED HERRING SALAD
Number of Servings — 4-6

1 small cooked beetroot
2 cooking apples
Pickled onions and gherkins
8 cold cooked potatoes
3 fresh salted herring
2 hard cooked eggs
Lettuce or curly endive
2 T. salad oil
2 T. vinegar
Mayonnaise
Salt

Soak the herring 24 hours in a small amount of milk or water. Cut the herring in small pieces and keep a few for decorating. Cut the peeled beetroot and apples in pieces. Chop the onions, gherkins, potatoes and 1 egg. Wash the lettuce or endive and shred it very finely. Put all these ingredients in a big bowl. Mix it well with salad oil, vinegar and salt. Put the salad on a flat dish and smooth the top with a wet spoon. Coat the salad with mayonnaise and decorate with quarters of egg, pieces of herring and surround with lettuce. Serve with toast and butter.

Mrs. Gail van den Doel, East Troy H. S.
East Troy, Wisconsin

SALMON SALAD
Number of Servings — 4

½ lb. red salmon
1 T. granulated gelatin
2 T. cold water
½ c. tomato soup
⅛ t. paprika
¼ t. Worcestershire sauce
Salt and pepper to taste
1 c. whipped cream (measure after whipped)
½ c. mayonnaise
1 t. lemon juice
2 drops red food coloring
⅓ c. minced celery
Dash of soy sauce
2 T. minced green pepper

Bring soup to boiling point. Add gelatin, which has been softened in cold water. Add other ingredients. Fold in mayonnaise and whipped cream, and lastly the flaked salmon. Pile into individual molds, and serve on lettuce leaves.

Nancy Euren, Hope H. S.
Hope, North Dakota

SALMON SALAD
Number of Servings — 6

2 c. salmon
3 hard cooked eggs
½ c. diced cheese
3 medium tomatoes, diced
1½ c. macaroni
¼ c. diced sweet pickles
2 T. sweet pickle juice
½ c. diced celery
Salt to taste
¾ c. mayonnaise

Mix thoroughly and chill.

Frances M. Watson, Lake H. S.
Millbury, Ohio

MOLDED SALMON SALAD
Number of Servings — 6

1 package lime or lemon jello
1 t. sugar
1¾ c. boiling water
3 T. vinegar
¼ t. salt
¼ t. dry mustard

(Continued on Next Page)

½ c. mayonnaise
1 c. chopped celery
1 c. diced cucumber
1 tall can salmon, flaked

Dissolve jello in boiling water and add vinegar. Chill. Combine salt, sugar, mustard, and mayonnaise. When jello is partially thickened, fold in this mixture, then rest of ingredients. Turn into molds rinsed in cold water. Chill until firm. Serve on lettuce.

Dorothy Rae Percival, Riverton H. S.
Riverton, Wyoming

SHRIMP SALAD BOWL
Number of Servings — 4-6

1 lb. cooked shrimp, peeled
1 head lettuce
¼ head curly lettuce
12 stuffed olives, sliced
2 hard-cooked eggs, sliced

Chill shrimp. At serving time, combine well-chilled greens, shrimp and olives in a salad bowl. Toss lightly with Piquant Mustard Dressing. Garnish with eggs.

PIQUANT MUSTARD DRESSING:

1 c. cold evaporated milk
3 T. lemon juice
1 T. chopped chives
3 T. prepared mustard
½ t. salt
¼ t. cayenne pepper

Blend evaporated milk and lemon juice in mixing bowl. Stir in remaining ingredients. Chill. Serve with Shrimp Salad Bowl.

Mrs. Nina T. Smith, Picayune Mem. H. S.
Picayune, Mississippi

MOLDED TUNA SALAD
Number of Servings — 8

2 T. unflavored gelatin
½ c. cold water
1 can cream of chicken soup
¼ c. lemon juice
1 T. prepared mustard
½ c. grated cucumber
¼ c. chopped bell pepper
1 c. mayonnaise
1 c. coarsely chopped celery
1 t. salt
2 6½-oz. cans tuna, drained and flaked

Soften gelatin in cold water. Heat soup until boiling. Remove from heat and add softened gelatin, stirring to dissolve. Blend in lemon juice, mustard and salt. Chill until partially set. Add mayonnaise, then fold in the other ingredients. Pour into oiled 8½ x 4½ x 2½ inch loaf pan or into individual molds and chill until firm. Unmold and serve on bed of salad greens.

Hazel Bussey, William Adams H. S.
Alice, Texas

MOLDED TUNA LOAF
Number of Servings — 10

3 7-oz. cans grated tuna
4 hard cooked eggs, chopped
¼ c. stuffed olives, chopped
2 T. minced onion
2 T. gelatin
½ c. cold water
2 c. mayonnaise
Parsley
Celery curls
1 c. diced celery

Combine first 5 ingredients. Sprinkle gelatin on cold water, using small bowl. Set bowl over hot water, stir gelatin until dissolved. Stir into mayonnaise. Add to tuna mixture and blend well. Turn into 9 x 5 x 3 inch loaf pan. Chill. Unmold and garnish with parsley and celery curls.

Mrs. Betty Temple, Fairfield Com. H. S.
Fairfield, Illinois

DEEP SEA DELIGHT
Number of Servings — 6-10

1 can tuna fish
1 can mushrooms
1 can green asparagus
1 c. grated cheese
1 c. thick white sauce
1 small package noodles
½ green pepper
4 hard cooked eggs, chopped
Salt and pepper

Add cheese to white sauce, and blend. Add cooked noodles, tuna fish, eggs, mushrooms, chopped green pepper and asparagus. (Save a few stalks of asparagus for garnish). Place in a buttered casserole. Bake. Serve on platter garnished with stalks of asparagus and grated cheese. Time—45 minutes. Temperature—350°F.

Mrs. Louise Kregel
Nebraska State Teachers College
Peru, Nebraska

LEMON SALAD SUPREME
Number of Servings — 8

2 packages lime gelatin
3 c. boiling water
¼ c. lemon juice
1 c. mayonnaise
2 c. cut cooked chicken or flaked tuna
1 can (1 lb., 3 ozs.) pineapple chunks, drained
½ c. toasted almonds

Dissolve gelatin in water. Add lemon juice and salad dressing and mix well. Chill in refrigerator until mixture begins to congeal. Beat well, add remaining ingredients and mix. Pour into lightly oiled 2 quart mold. Chill until set. Unmold on salad greens and garnish as desired.

Vicki Lancaster, Putnam County H. S.
Eatonton, Georgia

Sandwiches

Sandwiches Featuring Meats

BARBECUE
Number of Servings — 16

1 qt. cooked lean pork
1 medium onion
2 T. butter
1 T. salad mustard
2 T. cider vinegar
2 T. brown sugar
4 T. lemon juice
1 pt. sieved tomatoes
1 T. Worcestershire sauce
½ c. water
Dash of salt and pepper
1½ c. chopped celery

Brown onions in butter. Add vinegar, brown sugar, lemon juice, tomatoes, Worcestershire sauce, mustard, celery and water. Cook slowly for 20 minutes until flavors are blended. Pour over meat and cook in a moderate oven (350°F.) 20 minutes or longer (or simmer). Serve on medium sized barbecue buns. The sauce may be made a week ahead of time and stored in the refrigerator. 2 pounds of raw ground beef may be added to the sauce and cooked slowly about 15 minutes, stirring constantly to blend.

Mrs. Dorothy Maxwell, Westville Twp. H. S.
Westville, Illinois

BARBECUED HAMBURGERS
Number of Servings — 6

1½ lbs. ground beef
1 medium onion, chopped
1 green pepper, chopped
Salt and pepper
1 T. vinegar
1 T. sugar
2 T. mustard
1 c. catsup

Combine ground beef, onion, pepper, salt and pepper and brown until crumbly. Add remaining ingredients and simmer 30 minutes. Serve on toasted buns.

Mrs. Vicky Sullivan, Ellsworth H. S.
Ellsworth, Wisconsin

BAR-B-CUES
Number of Servings — 6

2 T. fat
1 lb. hamburger
⅔ c. chopped onion
½ t. salt
½ t. pepper
¼ c. water
1 can chicken gumbo soup
1 T. catsup
1 T. mustard

Brown meat in fat with onion, salt and pepper. Add water, soup, catsup and mustard. Simmer 30 minutes. Serve on buns.

Mrs. Kenny Handel, Freeman H. S.
Freeman, South Dakota

BARBECUE SANDWICHES
Number of Servings — 8-10

1 c. celery, cut fine
1 carrot
1 green pepper
1 onion
1½ lbs. ground beef
1 T. brown sugar
3 T. Worcestershire sauce
2 T. vinegar
1¼ c. catsup

Grind carrot, pepper and onion with food grinder. Chop celery fine. Cook the 4 vegetables together for about 10 minutes. Brown 1½ pounds ground beef. Add remaining ingredients to meat and the cooked vegetables. Simmer for 1½ hours. Note: Pork loin may be substituted for the ground beef.

Mrs. Judy Herbig, Timber Twp. H. S.
Glasford, Illinois

MY FAVORITE BARBECUE SANDWICHES
Number of Servings — 10-15

¾ lb. hamburger
½ lb. ground pork
½ bunch celery, cut fine
1 c. tomato juice
1 c. milk
2 medium onions, cut fine
1 c. soft bread crumbs
2 eggs, beaten
1½ t. salt
½ t. pepper

Brown meat and onions to delicate brown. Add other ingredients. Mix well. Bake in oven for 1 hour or simmer on top burner. Stir frequently for top of stove cooking, occasionally in oven. Add more tomato juice if necessary.

Mrs. Anna Newell,
New Knoxville, Ohio

SLOPPY JOES—HOT SUPPER SANDWICHES
Number of Servings — 8

½ c. diced onion
¼ c. finely cut celery
1 lb. ground beef
¼ c. fat
½ c. diced green pepper
1½ c. diced mushrooms
2 c. tomato sauce or tomato soup
½ t. pepper
½ t. paprika
1½ t. salt
1 t. mustard
1 t. Worcestershire sauce

Brown onion, celery and ground beef in fat. Add other ingredients, simmer (the longer the better). Serve in warm buns.

Mrs. Sandra Focht, Stanhope H. S.
Stanhope, Iowa

BAR X SANDWICH
Number of Servings — 12-16

1 loaf (1 lb.) French or Vienna bread
¼ c. sliced ripe olives
⅛ t. pepper
½ t. ground oregano
⅛ t. garlic salt
1 t. salt
⅓ c. minced onion
¾ lb. ground beef
¼ c. grated Parmesan cheese
1 can (6 oz.) tomato paste
1 c. drained tomatoes
6 slices processed American cheese

Cut loaf of bread in half lengthwise. Mix the next 9 ingredients and spread on cut side of the bread. Spread the tomatoes over the tops. Place loaf of bread on a baking sheet and bake in a moderate oven (350°F.) for 20 minutes. Remove and top with cheese slices. Bake 5 minutes longer. Cut and serve at once.

Irene E. Krause, Shawano Sr. H. S.
Shawano, Wisconsin

BEEFWICHES
Number of Servings — 8

1½ lbs. ground beef
1 small onion, chopped
1 t. salt
¼ t. pepper
½ t. sage
1 beaten egg
½ c. milk
1 c. bread crumbs
8 slices onion
8 slices tomato
1½ c. grated cheese (American or cheddar, try
   Blue or Roquefort)

Combine meat, chopped onion, salt, pepper, sage, egg, milk, and bread crumbs thoroughly. Shape into 16 thin patties. On 8 of the patties place 1 slice of onion, 1 slice of tomato and ⅛ of the grated cheese. Top with the remaining 8 patties. Broil 3 to 4 minutes, 3 inches from the heat. Turn quickly, but carefully. Broil 3 to 4 minutes more. Place between warm buns and serve.

Mrs. Mary P. Blackman, Blacklick Twp. H. S.
Twin Rocks, Pennsylvania

BROILED SANDWICHES
Number of Servings — 6

1 c. American cheese, cut in ¼ inch cubes
3 hard cooked eggs, chopped
1 can flaked tuna fish
2 T. chopped onion
2 T. pickle relish
½ c. salad dressing
6 buns

Combine ingredients. Spread on split buns. Broil in pre-heated broiler approximately 10 minutes, or until cheese has melted. May be spread on bottoms of buns only, and covered with toasted tops.

Mrs. Emily Santee, West Greene H. S.
Rogersville, Pennsylvania

CAMP STEW
Number of Servings — 6

1 lb. ground beef
Salt and pepper
½ c. chopped onion
¼ c. chopped green pepper
6 strips bacon
1 can tomato soup, undiluted
½ c. barbecue sauce
1 T. chili powder
12 strips cheese
6 hamburger buns

Fry bacon until crisp, add onions and green peppers, cook until brown; add ground beef, cook until it turns in color. Add remaining ingredients except cheese. Simmer for ½ hour. Serve on hamburger buns, top with cheese strips.

Mrs. Dolores Q. Parks, R. B. Worthy H. S.
Saltville, Virginia

CAROLINA CORN DOG SURPRISE
Number of Servings — 10

¾ c. self rising flour
¼ c. self rising cornmeal
1 T. sugar
1 t. dry mustard
2 T. dry onion soup
1 egg
½ c. milk
1 lb. frankfurters

Mix dry ingredients. Beat egg and milk together and add to dry ingredients; stir until blended. Insert popsicle sticks into franks, which have been wiped with dry cloth and dusted with flour. Dip into batter and drop in corn oil 375°F. Fry until brown and drain on paper towels. Serve piping hot; catsup and mustard may be brushed on before eating.

Harriette McDowell Holton, Shelby Sr. H. S.
Shelby, North Carolina

CHICKEN SALAD BUNS
Number of Servings — 8

2 c. diced cooked chicken
1 c. chopped celery
⅓ c. chopped sweet pickles
¼ t. salt
Chili sauce
Dash of pepper
Dash of onion powder
⅔ c. mayonnaise
4 buns, cut in halves
½ c. shredded American cheese

Combine chicken, celery, pickles, salt, pepper,

(Continued on Next Page)

and onion powder. Moisten with mayonnaise. Spread on bun halves (buns may be toasted first). Spread with chicken mixture; sprinkle with cheese, dot center with chili sauce. Place in broiler or oven to melt cheese and heat buns.

Mrs. Effie Rishoi, Axtell Park Jr. H. S.
Sioux Falls, South Dakota

CHUCK WAGON SPAM SANDWICHES
Number of Servings — 6

1 T. butter
½ c. minced onions
¼ t. pepper
1 t. paprika
1 t. mustard (dry)
1 t. Worcestershire sauce
¼ c. chili sauce
3 T. vinegar
4 t. sugar
1 can Spam (or any canned meat)

Melt butter. Add minced onions and remaining ingredients. Slice Spam, arrange as single layer in baking pan. Pour sauce over Spam and heat in oven (350°F.) for 1 hour. Serve on heated hamburger rolls. May be prepared the day before.

Mrs. Helen L. Eddy, Haverford Twp. Sr. H. S.
Havertown, Pennsylvania

CORNED BEEF CHEESEBURGER
Number of Servings — 9

12 oz. can corned beef, chopped
3 T. finely chopped onion
1 T. prepared mustard
3 T. mayonnaise
1½ t. horseradish
3 T. butter or margarine
9 hamburger buns, split
9 slices American cheese

Combine corned beef and 4 seasonings. Mix well. Spread bun with butter. Spread corned beef mixture on bottom halves of bun, top with slice of cheese. Toast under broiler until cheese melts. Cover with toasted tops of buns.

Mrs. William H. Buxton, Cowden H. S.
Cowden, Illinois

BROILED HAM 'N CHEESE BUNS
Number of Servings — 8

4 hamburger buns
¼ lb. spiced ham luncheon meat (left over ham may be used)
¼ lb. American cheese
1 T. salad dressing or mayonnaise

Grind in food chopper the spiced ham and cheese. Mix in salad dressing. Spread liberally on 8 bun halves. Place under broiler until heated and delicately browned. Serve with a toss salad on a plate. Eat with fork.

Mrs. Cleo Riley, Burlington H. S.
Burlington, Wyoming

HAM AND CHEESE ROLLS
Number of Servings — 8

¼ c. butter and oleo
2 t. mustard
2 t. poppy seed
¼ c. grated onion, or ⅛ t. onion powder
8 slices thin cut ham
8 slices processed cheese
8 hard rolls

Mix butter, oleo, mustard, poppy seed and grated onion (or onion powder). Spread on hard rolls. Place ham and cheese on rolls. Wrap in aluminum foil and place on cookie sheet. Bake 20 minutes in 325°F. oven.

Mrs. Charles Wheeler, Jr., Lebanon Jr. H. S.
Lebanon, Indiana

SWISS HAM SANDWICH
Number of Servings — 8

⅓ c. prepared mustard
⅓ c. mayonnaise
2 T. finely chopped onion
½ t. salt
Dash of Pepper
8 slices ham
8 slices Swiss cheese
8 buns

In a bowl mix the mustard, mayonnaise, onion, salt and pepper. Spread buns with this mixture. In each bun place 1 slice of ham and cheese. Close bun. Wrap bun in foil. Bake at 350°F. for 20 minutes.

Mrs. Robert Tuttle, DePue H. S.
DePue, Illinois

CLUB SANDWICH LOAFER

1 can (12 ozs.) corned beef
1 can cream of mushroom soup
¼ c. pickle relish
3 hard cooked eggs
Pepper to taste
1 loaf French bread

Mash corned beef with a fork. Mix in sufficient soup to hold it together. (Usually ¾ to 1 cup is sufficient). Add relish, chopped egg and pepper. No salt is necessary. Slice the bread; butter 1 slice of each pair. (Use garlic butter if you wish). Spread other slice generously with meat mixture. Cut sandwiches in half, then skewer 3 or 4 pairs together. Wrap loosely in foil. Place in large utility pan. Before serving bake and serve hot. Makes 10 to 12 full sized sandwiches or 20 to 24 after cutting in half. This filling is equally good to use in regular sandwiches or hollowed out rolls for the lunch box. *Garlic Butter:* Soften 1 stick butter or margarine. Either use fresh garlic which has been grated very fine, or garlic powder. Suit your own taste as to amount to use.

Mrs. Ardery Peery, Keota H. S.
Keota, Oklahoma

FRANKFURTERS WITH HAMBURGER SAUCE
Number of Servings — 4-5

1 T. fat
3 or 4 small onions, chopped
½ lb. hamburger
1 No. 2 can tomatoes
1 t. chili powder
1 t. sugar
1 t. salt
1 lb. frankfurters
Long rolls

Brown onions in fat, add hamburger and cook for a few minutes, tossing with fork. Add remaining ingredients and simmer gently for 45 minutes. Heat franks by either boiling, steam or broil. Remove casings, then place franks in the center of rolls and fill center cavity of rolls with the hamburger sauce. Serve very hot. This sauce is good on spaghetti.

Ruth Bosley, Leavenworth H. S.
Leavenworth, Indiana

JUMBO PIZZA SANDWICH

1 loaf French bread (1 lb.)
¼ c. chopped ripe olives
⅛ t. pepper
¼ t. ground oregano
¾ t. salt
2 T. finely chopped green onions
1 c. ground beef
¼ c. grated Parmesan cheese
1 can (6 oz.) tomato paste
8 (1 oz.) slices of processed American cheese
Tomato slices for garnish

Cut loaf of French bread in half horizontally. Combine olives, pepper, salt, onions, beef, Parmesan cheese and tomato paste. Spread this mixture over cut sides of the bread. Place on cooky sheet and bake in 400°F. oven 15 minutes. Remove from oven. Place cheese slices, which have been cut in half diagonally, alternately with tomato slices on top of the loaf. Return to oven for 8 minutes. Remove from oven, cut in sections. Serve hot.

Echo P. Schepman, North Bend H. S.
North Bend, Oregon

SANDWICH STROGANOFF
Number of Servings — 6

1 t. salt
1 lb. ground beef
¼ c. choped onion
¼ t. garlic juice
¼ t. pepper
½ t. Worcestershire sauce
2 T. flour
¼ c. chili sauce
¾ c. dairy sour cream
½ loaf French bread, sliced lengthwise
Grated or sliced cheese, as desired
Tomato slices
Green pepper rings

Add salt to preheated skillet. Brown ground beef and chopped onion. Add garlic juice, pepper and Worcestershire sauce. When meat is cooked stir in flour, then chili sauce. Reduce heat and blend in sour cream. Spoon onto bread. Garnish with tomato slices or pepper rings and cheese. Broil until cheese is melted. Serve immediately. (Slice into six servings).

Martha Wreath Streeter, Wamego Rural H. S.
Wamego, Kansas

TONGUE SANDWICH FILLING
Number of Servings — 8

1 fresh tongue
1 large apple (sweet)
2 sweet pickles (medium)
Mayonnaise as needed
Salt to season

Cover tongue with cold water. Add salt and boil until tender. Cool and remove tissue, bones and skin. Grind with medium fine blade. Wash apple and chop fine. Chop pickles. Mix with ground tongue. Mix with enough salad dressing to make moist. A bit of finely chopped onion and celery may be added if desired.

Mrs. R. E. Bradfield, Lometa H. S.
Lometa, Texas

BROILER BEAN-ER WIENER LOAF
Number of Servings — 5

½ loaf French bread (cut lengthwise)
1 T. prepared mustard
2 T. soft butter
2 c. pork and beans, drained
¼ c. chopped onion
2 T. brown sugar
½ c. shredded sharp process American cheese
5 frankfurters
5 small sweet pickles, cut in fans

Blend mustard and butter; spread on bread. Mix beans, onion and brown sugar; spoon on the buttered bread. Sprinkle with cheese. Broil 7 inches from heat for 5 minutes. Split frankfurters lengthwise without cutting clear through along one side. Place split side up on beans, crosswise of loaf; broil 5 minutes longer. Add pickle fans; drizzle mustard or catsup down center of franks. Cut loaf in 5 slices so each serving has a frank and a pickle fan.

Mrs. Garth Waller, Littlefork-Big Falls H. S.
Littlefork, Minnesota

SUPPER SANDWICH
Number of Servings — 6

1 lb. ground beef
1 c. chopped onions
1 egg, beaten
1 c. sour cream (cottage cheese may be substituted)
¾ t. salt
¼ t. pepper
1 recipe buttermilk biscuits
1 c. grated cheese

Heat oven to 400°F. Grease the bottom of a 9 inch square baking dish. Slowly fry ground beef until done. Remove ground beef and cook onions till tender, not brown. Combine egg, sour cream, salt, pepper and add ground beef. Divide biscuit dough into two equal parts. Roll each part out about the size of the baking dish. Fit one part of the dough in the bottom of the baking dish. Top with ground beef mixture, then onions, then cheese. Fit the other part of the dough over the top. Bake 30 minutes. Cut in squares and serve hot. Spoon tomato sauce over squares if desired.

Buttermilk Biscuits:
2 c. self-rising flour
¼ c. shortening
¼ t. soda
¾ c. buttermilk

Cut shortening into flour until particles are as fine as coarse cornmeal. Add soda to buttermilk and quickly stir into flour mixture. Turn dough out on lightly floured board.

Peggy Stewart, Gordon H. S.
Decatur, Georgia

SALMONBURGERS
Number of Servings — 6

2 c. canned salmon
¾ c. cracker crumbs
1 egg, slightly beaten
1 small onion
2 T. butter
3 large buns

Drain and flake salmon; mix with cracker crumbs and eggs. Mince onion and fry lightly in half of butter; add to salmon mixture and season to taste. Shape into 6 thin cakes and brown quickly in remaining butter. Split and toast buns and place hot salmon cake on each half. Garnish with pickles and onion rings, and serve with chili sauce.

Carol M. Lea, Halls H. S.
Halls, Tennessee

TURKEY AND RELISH SANDWICH FILLING
Number of Servings — 6

1 c. diced cooked turkey or chicken
¾ c. diced celery
3 T. pickle relish
1 hard-cooked egg, chopped
¾ t. salt

Dash of pepper
¼ c. salad dressing or mayonnaise

Combine ingredients and mix well. Makes about 1½ cups filling, or enough for 6 sandwiches.

Mary Murl Moses, Waelder H. S.
Waelder, Texas

TUNA-CHEESE SANDWICH SPREAD
Number of Servings — 10-12

½ lb. processed cheese
1 small can pimento, chopped
1 can (1 c.) tuna fish, flaked and drained of oil
Juice of ½ lemon
Salt to taste
Mayonnaise

Grate or shred cheese. Add chopped pimento, tuna, lemon juice and salt. Add enough mayonnaise to give good spreading consistency. Mix well and spread sandwiches or serve with assorted crackers or potato chips.

Elizabeth S. Thornton, Sparkman H. S.
Toney, Alabama

HOT TUNA SANDWICH
Number of Servings — 4-5

1 can tuna
¼ c. mayonnaise
1 medium tomato
1 small onion
Cheese—type and amount to suit taste
1 loaf French bread

Combine tuna and mayonnaise. Slice loaf into thirds, lengthwise and butter all inside areas. Spread tuna and mayonnaise mixture on bottom layer, topping with diced or sliced onion. Place middle layer of bread on top of bottom layer. Slice tomatoes and top them with cheese. Put on top layer. Bake in 450°F. oven for 30-45 minutes.

Karen I. Perreten, Mitchell H. S.
Mitchell, Nebraska

HOT TUNA SANDWICH LOAF
Number of Servings — 10

1 6-oz. can tuna
4 chopped hard boiled eggs
1 T. grated onion
1 T. mayonnaise
¼ c. cream mushroom soup
⅓ c. chopped stuffed olives

Remove crusts from one pullman loaf of bread and slice lengthwise twice. Butter slices and spread on filling. Brush sides with ⅓ cup melted butter. Wrap in foil and refrigerate overnight. Remove from refrigerator at least 2 hours before baking. Brown on cookie sheet, after removing foil, for 20 minutes at 375°F. Serve with a cream mushroom soup sauce made by adding ⅓ cup milk to the remaining soup.

Mrs. Kay Nelson, Barnesville H. S.
Barnesville, Minnesota

Soups

Soups-Using A Meat Base

BORDER STYLE BEAN SOUP
Number of Servings — 12

3 c. pinto beans
8 c. water
1 lb. ground beef
1 T. cooking oil
1 medium onion
1 large clove garlic
1 T. chili powder
1 T. dried parsley
1 T. dried celery
1 can tomatoes
2 carrots

Wash beans; cover with water and bring to boil. Cut heat to low and allow beans to simmer about an hour. Saute onions and garlic in oil and add ground meat. When brown, add chili powder. Add meat, parsley, celery and tomatoes to beans. Return to boil; cut heat again to low. Cook about 2 hours longer. Add sliced carrots during last hour of cooking time. Salt and pepper to taste. Serve with jalepena peppers. This is my husband's recipe.

Mrs. Kathryn Patrick, Cummings Jr. H. S.
Brownsville, Texas

BEEF ROAST SOUP
Number of Servings — 4

1 c. cold roast (cubed)
1 can tomatoes or juice
1 medium size cooked potato (cubed)
1 can vegetable soup
Salt to desired taste
Pepper to desired taste

Combine soup, tomatoes, juice, potatoes and cold roast. Salt and pepper to desired taste. Dilute tomato juice to directions on can. Add juice from roast. This is a yum-yum concoction. Serve with crackers.

Mrs. Aleta Thompson, Hart H. S.
Hart, Texas

QUICK GROUND BEEF SOUP
Number of Servings — 6

1 lb. good ground beef (lean)
2 qts. cold water
2 c. cabbage (cut medium)
½ c. carrots, cut small
1 medium onion, cut small
½ c. chopped celery
2 T. chopped green pepper
1 c. chopped raw potatoes

Add cold water to ground beef and break into pieces and simmer for 15 minutes (covered). Add above vegetables, salt and pepper to taste and boil low for 15 minutes and serve. This is our favorite quick soup. It is not too expensive and nutritious as well.

Idella I. Alfson, Woonsocket H. S.
Woonsocket, South Dakota

CHICKEN GUMBO AVOYELIES
Number of Servings — 8

1 young hen or large fryer (3-4 lbs.)
1 lb. fresh link pork sausage (optional)
3 qts. water
4 T. lard or bacon drippings
5 T. flour
¼ c. chopped fresh parsley
Salt and black pepper to taste
1 large onion, chopped
1 or 2 cloves garlic, cut very fine
5 shallots (use tops and bottoms)
¼ t. red cayenne pepper
1 T. file

Cut up chicken as for frying. Heat 2 tablespoons fat in a deep Dutch oven, preferably the black cast iron type. Brown chicken lightly about 20 minutes. Remove excess fat, add hot water and set on low heat to simmer. In skillet melt remaining 2 tablespoons fat, when hot, add flour stirring constantly until flour is golden brown. This is the roux. To roux add chopped onion and garlic. Cook on low heat until onions wilt (5 minutes). Add this mixture slowly to chicken. Add salt, black and cayenne pepper. Chicken should be semi-tender. Then add sausage which has been browned lightly, chopped green onions, and parsley. Simmer 45 minutes or until chicken is done (very tender). Turn off heat, add the file. Stir well and let stand covered for 10 minutes before serving. This is served in soup bowls, accompanied by steamed rice, added by each person according to the liking. Baked sweet potatoes in the skin is usually served with this.

Mrs. Odessa N. Smith
Area Supervisor of Home Economics
State Department of Education
Baton Rouge, Louisiana

BRUNSWICK STEW
Number of Servings — 12

5 lb. hen
3 No. 2 cans tomatoes
1 8-oz. can tomato paste
2 No. 2 cans okra
2 No. 2 cans corn
3 lbs. potatoes
3 large onions
1 stick oleo
Red pepper and salt to taste

Stew hen until meat falls from bones; tear meat from bones and place in large heavy boiler along with all broth. Add tomatoes, tomato paste, okra, onions cut fine, and salt and pepper. Cook slowly for about 2 hours. Cook and mash potatoes (instant potatoes may be used). Add mashed potatoes and corn to the chicken mixture and cook longer, stirring occasionally to prevent sticking. Taste for seasoning, add butter or oleo. Longer it is cooked the better it is, but may be eaten about 15 minutes after adding potatoes. Freezes well.

Mrs. E. C. Henry, Madison-Ridgeland H. S.
Canton, Mississippi

SUPER BEEF SUPPER
Number of Servings — 6

3 lbs. beef brisket, neck, chuck or shank
8 c. cold water
3 cabbage leaves, chopped fine
Salt to taste
1 can tomato paste
1 c. chopped celery
1 large marrow bone
5 carrots, diced fine
1 medium onion, chopped
1/8 t. pepper
1/2 c. pearl barley
1/4 c. chopped parsley

Simmer all ingredients 4 to 5 hours. Place thick slice of hot buttered French bread in bowl and pour soup over it. If desired, bread may be sprinkled with grated cheese before adding soup. Lower grades of beef are suitable for this recipe.

Evangeline LaBarre, Belt Valley H. S.
Belt, Montana

PALATINATE CHICKEN CORN SOUP
Number of Servings — 6

1 4-lb. chicken
3 qts. water
2 t. salt
1/4 t. saffron
2 c. noodles
2 c. corn
1 t. chopped parsley
1/8 t. pepper
2 hard-cooked eggs, chopped

Cut up chicken and cover with water. Add salt and saffron. Stew until tender. Remove chicken from stock and cut into small pieces (breast and legs of chicken may be reserved for other cooking uses). Return small chicken to stock. Add noodles and corn to broth and boil 15 minutes. Add parsley, pepper and eggs to broth and serve.

Lucy M. Bamberger, Schaefferstown H. S.
Schaefferstown, Pennsylvania

CHICKEN RICE SOUP
(Kota Soupa Avegolemeno)
A favorite of many of Greek nationality
Number of Servings — 6

6 c. stock from stewing chicken
1 c. rice
1 t. salt
1/4 t. pepper
3 eggs
Juice of 1 lemon

Bring chicken stock to a boil; add rice, salt, and pepper and cook till rice is done. Remove 1 1/2 cups stock to cool. Beat eggs just until foamy. Slowly stir in lemon juice and cooled stock. Add pieces of stewing chicken as desired. Serve at once.

Phyllis Schuelke, Bremen H. S.
Midlothian, Illinois

CHICKEN GUMBO
Number of Servings — 12

2 1/2 c. fresh okra
3 T. fat
1 large onion, chopped
1 green pepper, chopped
2 cloves garlic, chopped
1 8-oz. can tomato juice
2 T. flour
4 c. chopped chicken
2 qts. hot water
3 slices bacon, chopped
1 t. salt
Dash black pepper

Fry okra slowly in fat until soft, add onion, garlic and green pepper; fry until onion is soft. Add flour and blend. Add tomato juice and mix well. Add remaining ingredients. Cook slowly 1 hour. Serve over rice.

Nelda Roark, LaSalle H. S.
Olla, Louisiana

CREOLE CHICKEN GUMBO
Number of Servings — 6

1/2 c. shortening
3/4 c. flour
1 onion, minced
1/2 c. parsley
1/2 c. onion tops, chopped
2 t. salt
2 t. black pepper
1 chicken, cut in serving pieces
1/2 t. gumbo file

Heat fat on high heat. Add flour to hot fat and stir constantly until flour is dark brown. This brown flour-fat mixture is a roux. Add onions and stir until they are slightly wilted. Add 8 cups of cold water, chicken to the roux and let boil until chicken is tender (about 1 1/2 to 2 hours). Add gumbo file just before serving. Serve hot with fluffy rice.

Mrs. Elden Brunet, Oakdale H. S.
Oakdale, Louisiana

CHILI
Number of Servings — 6

1 lb. ground beef
1 small onion, chopped fine
1 No. 2 can red kidney beans
1 can tomato soup
1/2 t. salt
1/2 t. chili powder

Cook ground beef in a greaseless skillet with the chopped up onion until the meat is gray in color. Add the can of beans, plus the juice, tomato soup, salt, and chili powder to the meat and onion. Simmer for 30 minutes. (One may add water or tomato juice to thin it down and use a potato masher to break up the beans to add flavor).

Wilma Gehrke, Mazon Twp. H. S.
Mazon, Illinois

CHILI
Number of Servings — 12

2 lbs. ground beef
1 medium onion, chopped
1 lb. stick chili
2 t. chili powder
2 No. 303 cans chili beans
4 c. tomato juice
2 t. salt
¼ c. water

Place water, ground beef and onion in a large pan and cook until the onion is tender. Add salt, chili powder, stick chili, chili beans and tomato juice and cook slowly about 45 minutes. Serve hot.

Janet Oyler, Glasco Public School
Glasco, Kansas

CHILI
Number of Servings — 6

1 lb. ground beef
1 c. chili beans (dried)
1 T. osago leaves
1 T. cumin seed
2 t. salt
1 T. chili relish
2 c. tomato juice
1 pepper pod (if desired)
4 small onions, ground

Soak beans overnight and cook with diced bacon until tender. Remove bacon. Brown beef and onions. Add tea made from steeping osago leaves and cumin seed for 10 minutes. Add tomato juice and cook until meat is tender. Simmer with beans and other seasonings until well seasoned.

Mrs. Ralph Leach, Bird City Rural H. S.
Bird City, Kansas

CHILI
Number of Servings — 12

2 large onions
2 garlic cloves
1 small green pepper
2 stalks celery
3 cans kidney beans, with chili sauce
1 qt. water
2 lbs. ground beef
½ can paprika
1 bottle chili powder

Chop and simmer onions, garlic and pepper; add meat and brown; add paprika, chili powder and water; add beans and let simmer for 1½ hours.

Rosemary C. Patout, Jeanerette H. S.
Jeanerette, Louisiana

DELICIOUS CHILI
Number of Servings — 6-8

1 lb. ground beef
1 medium onion, chopped
2 qts. water
2 t. salt

½ c. flour, browned
3 T. paprika
1 T. chili powder
¼ t. red pepper or few drops tabasco

Break ground meat in small pieces. Combine with onion, salt, water and simmer 15 minutes. Meantime brown flour in heavy skillet over medium heat, stirring often. When medium to dark brown, sprinkle slowly by spoonsful into rapidly boiling meat-water combination. Add paprika, chili powder and red pepper. Simmer 5-10 minutes longer. Serve in soup bowls with crackers.

Lora Lynn Adams, Vilas H. S.
Alstead, New Hampshire

CHILI
Number of Servings — 8

2 lbs. chili meat
1 medium-size onion, chopped
6 sections garlic
2 T. comino seed
1 can (6 oz.) tomato paste
2 t. salt
1 T. chili powder
2 T. flour
2 T. sugar

Combine meat, onion, garlic, comino seed and salt in skillet. Cook until tender. Blend sugar, flour and chili powder; add to meat mixture. Cook for 5 minutes over low heat. Add tomato paste. Heat. Mixture will be thick. Before serving, add water to desired consistency. Bring to boiling point and serve.

Mrs. Juanita S. Cushman, Morro Bay H. S.
Morro Bay, California

CHILI CON CARNE
Number of Servings — 4-6

2½ lbs. ground beef
1 c. chopped onion
2 t. chili powder
1 t. mustard
½ c. catsup
1 t. salt
½ t. oregano
1 c. water
1 can pinto beans
1 can red kidney beans
½ t. black pepper

Brown hamburger in heavy skillet. Place hamburger and all other ingredients in pot with a tight fitting cover and cook over low heat for about 2 hours.

Lorna Hinson, Hickory Grove H. S.
Hickory Grove, South Carolina

HEARTY SOUP
Number of Servings — 8

1½ lbs. ground beef
3 T. butter
1 medium onion

(Continued on Next Page)

3 cans consomme
2 c. water
1 t. salt
2 c. tomatoes
3 carrots
2 bay leaves
3 stocks celery
1 T. chopped parsley
½ t. thyme
8 peppercorns

Melt butter in kettle; add coarsely chopped onion. Cook onion until limp but not brown. Add ground beef and stir it around in the fat until it loses the red look. Pour in tomatoes, consomme and water; add scraped quartered carrots, bay leaves, chopped celery, parsley, thyme, peppercorn and salt. Cover and simmer for 30 minutes.

Betty MacSpadden, Salinas H. S.
Salinas, California

POLKA DOT SOUP
Number of Servings — 4-5

3 T. butter
¼ c. flour
1 medium onion, finely chopped
4 c. milk
1 c. corn, whole kernel
3 hot dogs sliced crosswise (may be leftovers)
Salt and pepper to taste

Melt butter in large enough saucepan to make soup. Add the onions and brown them. Then add the flour to thicken the mixture. Add milk slowly so it will not become lumpy. Use enough milk so each person will be able to have at least one cup of soup. Add the corn and sliced hotdogs. Salt and pepper to taste. Serve steaming hot. Ideal recipe to use leftovers.

Mrs. Margaret Rettke
Mason County Central Sr. H. S.
Scottville, Michigan

OXTAIL SOUP
Number of Servings — 6

2 oxtails
2 qts. cold water
1 T. salt
1 c. chopped onion
1 can (6 oz.) tomato paste
3 sticks celery, cut
2 c. chopped cabbage (or 1 c. turnips)
¼ lb. noodles
½ t. sugar
2 bouillon cubes

Combine first 3 ingredients, bring to boil, skim froth, add all other ingredients, simmer 2 hours, serve hot. Noodles are less flabby if added in the last hour. This is my father's recipe, and makes a hearty whole-meal soup.

Mrs. June Jaeger Patchett, Young America H. S.
Metcalf, Illinois

MEAT BALL BEEF SOUP
Number of Servings — 8-10

1 lb. piece of beef
3 qts. water
2 sticks celery
1 carrot
1 whole small onion
1 t. parsley flakes
Salt and pepper to taste
½ lb. ground beef
½ c. bread crumbs
1 t. salt
¼ t. pepper
1 egg
1 t. parsley flakes
¼ t. garlic salt

Place 1 pound beef in 3 quarts boiling water and add celery, carrot, onion, parsley flakes, salt and pepper. Cook slowly, for approximately 3 hours, or until meat is done. Meantime, mix well the ground beef, crumbs, salt, pepper, egg, parsley flakes and garlic salt. Roll as large as marbles. After soup is cooked, strain, reboil soup and add meat balls. Cook another ½ hour and add cooked rice or noodles to soup when ready to serve.

Martha DeLuca, West Forest Joint School
Tionesta, Pennsylvania

SEAFOOD CHOWDER
Number of Servings — 4

¼ c. finely cut salt pork
¼ c. finely cut onion
2 cans (7 oz. each) clams and lobster
2 c. cooked diced potatoes
2 c. milk
1 t. salt
⅛ t. pepper

Cook pork in large frying pan for 1 to 2 minutes. Add onion; cook until golden, stirring 2 or 3 times. Drain seafood in sieve; save liquid. Add seafood liquid and potatoes to pork mixture; cook covered until potatoes are thoroughly heated. Mince seafood with knife and add milk and seasonings to pork mixture. Heat slowly to serving temperature.

Mrs. Jo Anne Davis, Ceres H. S.
Ceres, California

VEGETABLE SOUP (HAMBURGER BASE)
Number of Servings — 4-6

1 lb. ground beef
2 T. butter
1 t. salt
½ c. chopped onions
1 c. diced carrots
1 c. diced potatoes
1 c. minced celery
1 c. chopped cabbage
1 c. canned tomatoes or frozen string beans,
　　lima beans, and corn
2 T. rice

Brown meat in butter in heavy stew pan. Add onions and cook with meat for a minute. Add salt. Add tomatoes and simmer while preparing remaining vegetables. Add raw vegetables, except rice. Allow to simmer until tender (about 20 minutes). Use liquor drained from canned vegetables or water to cover these vegetables while simmering. Add remaining cooked vegetables and enough liquor (vegetable) or water as desired for a soup and simmer another 5 minutes. Allow 15 minutes for the rice. This should be added before cooked vegetables. This is delicious served rather thick, something like a chowder. Taste and add more salt if necessary.

Martha J. Barocco, Elkland Joint School District
Elkland, Pennsylvania

FRENCH ONION SOUP
Serve with Duckling or Fowl
Number of Servings — 4-6

2½ c. thinly sliced onions
2½ T. butter or margarine
3 cans condensed beef broth (or use 6 bouillon
　　cubes or 6 t. instant bouillon dissolved in 4
　　c. hot water)
1 t. Worcestershire sauce
2 French rolls or toast (sliced and toasted)
Grated Parmesan cheese

Cook onions in butter until lightly browned. Add broth and Worcestershire sauce. Bring to boil; season with salt and pepper. Sprinkle toast with Parmesan cheese. Pour soup into bowls. Float toast. For a gourmet touch, place in pre-heated broiler a few seconds till cheese is lightly browned.

Naomi P. Schumacher, Maplewood Jr. H. S.
Maplewood Louisiana

BRUNSWICK STEW
Three, 3 to 4 lb. hens
12 lbs. fresh pork ham
4½ lbs. lean beef (ground)
12 cans (No. 2) tomatoes
8 cans (No. 2) cream style corn
3 lbs. onions
1½ pts. tomato catsup
½ c. Worcestershire sauce
1 t. black pepper
¼ c. liquid smoke
2 c. vinegar
½ c. salt
5 pods hot pepper or hot sauce to taste

Cook meats and save broth. Cook onions and pepper together and save broth. Grind meats after they cool (hot meat will not grind easily). Mix all ingredients together. Cook at *low heat*, stirring frequently as this burns easily. Cool before putting in freezer cartons.

Mrs. Theresa H. Smith, Warner Robins H. S.
Warner Robins, Georgia

OLD FASHIONED STEW
Number of Servings — 4

1 lb. stew meat (beef)
2 c. (chunked) carrots
2 c. (chunked) potatoes
1 small (chunked) onion
1 bay leaf
⅛ t. pepper
1 t. salt
2 c. water

Brown meat, add water, simmer for 2 hours. Add carrots, potatoes, onion and seasoning and simmer an additional 1 hour. Add additional water if necessary. (Liquid may be thickened as a gravy).

Mrs. Hazel Johnson, Pavillion H. S.
Pavillion, Wyoming

Out-of-Door Cooking &
Meats for Large Groups

BARBECUED CHICKEN
Number of Servings — ½ chicken per person

Barbecue Sauce: Measure ½ cup cooking oil, ¾ cup lemon juice or vinegar, ¼ cup water, 1½ tablespoons salt, 3 tablespoons sugar and 1½ teaspoons tabasco sauce into saucepan. Heat to boiling and use for basting chicken. Keep hot.

To Barbecue Chicken: Have chickens split lengthwise, quartered, or breast and leg parts. Brush with barbecue sauce. Place on grate set 12 inches or more from heat—skin side away from heat. Cook slowly until tender, turning frequently and basting each time. Allow 1 to 1¼ hours for total cooking time.

Mrs. Rosetta Haire, Wellington H. S.
Wellington, Illinois

BARBECUED CHICKEN
Number of Servings — 8

Sauce:

2½ c. water
1 T. sugar
2½ t. black pepper
2 T. butter
¼ c. vinegar
2½ t. salt
2 T. Worcestershire sauce
¼ onion
1 t. powdered mustard
2 t. chili powder
½ t. tabasco sauce
1 bud garlic

Bring sauce to a rolling boil to mix this; let stand over night to blend flavors. Select oven ready broilers of 2 to 3 pound weights. One half chicken should be provided per person. The chickens should be split in half with the back bone and breast bone removed. The broilers may be marinated in the sauce for some time before cooking. Most people prefer to baste them during cooking with a dish mop dipped in the sauce. This should be done just before the birds are turned, or approximately every 5 to 10 minutes. Cooking time over charcoal, 2 hours.

Requa K. Spears, Mullins H. S.
Pikeville, Kentucky

MARINADE STEAK FOR BARBECUE
Number of Servings — 4

½ c. chopped onion
½ c. lemon juice
¼ c. salad oil
½ t. salt
½ t. celery salt
2½ lbs., ½ inch thick chuck, round or flank steak
½ t. pepper
½ t. thyme
½ t. oregano
½ t. rosemary
1 clove garlic

Combine all ingredients except steak. Marinate steak 4 to 5 hours, turning several times. Cook on grill over hot coals to doneness you like best. Baste with marinade during broiling.

Mrs. Mina Robinson, Perry H. S.
Perry, Kansas

SOUTHERN BARBECUED SPARERIBS

¼ c. cooking oil
¼ c. vinegar
½ c. canned peach juice
½ c. catsup
2 T. brown sugar
2 T. onion juice
1½ t. Worcestershire sauce
2 t. salt
¼ t. oregano
Dash cayenne pepper
Dash tabasco sauce
3-4 lbs. spareribs

Combine all of the sauce ingredients; bring to a boil and simmer 5 minutes. To barbecue on a grill: Brush barbecue sauce over spareribs and arrange on a greased grill. Grill slowly until well done, turning frequenty, and brushing generously with barbecue sauce. To barbecue in oven: Brush the barbecue sauce over the spareribs and arrange on a rack in a pan. Place in a hot oven (450°F.) for 30 minutes. Continue baking in a moderate oven (350°F.), until cooked and well browned, 45 to 60 minutes, turning frequently and brushing with barbecue sauce. This sauce is excellent on hamburgers, frankfurters, chicken, steak, leg of lamb, seafood and other meats.

Lillie Mae Holmes, Danville H. S.
Danville, Alabama

BEEF KA-BOBS
Number of Servings — 6

4 lbs. chuck roast, cubed
⅔ c. oil
½ c. wine or wine vinegar
1 clove garlic, crushed
1 t. salt
¼ t. pepper
¼ c. soy sauce
1 T. Worcestershire sauce
1 T. dry mustard

Bone and cube chuck roast into 2 inch squares. Combine all other ingredients; mix well. Pour the marinate over meat. Refrigerate 24 hours. Barbecue meat on skewers or separately.

Mrs. Creswell, Courtland H. S.
Courtland, California

SHISH KABOB
Number of Servings — 6

2 lbs. boneless lamb
¼ c. salad oil
¼ c. wine vinegar
2 t. salt
2 t. crushed rosemary
½ t. pepper (black)
½ c. sliced onion

Cut lamb into 1½ inch cubes. Make marinade as follows: Combine salad oil, wine vinegar, salt, rosemary, pepper, and onion. Add lamb cubes to marinade and stir to coat. Let refrigerate over night or stand at room temperature 2 or 3 hours, turning meat occasionally. Fill skewers, alternating meat cubes with vegetables (onion, green pepper and tomatoes). Broil over hot coals to medium rare, brushing frequently with melted butter or margarine. Turn often on grill. Serve immediately.

Elaine Reisner, Narbonne H. S.
Harbor City, California

HAMBURGER SKISH KEBABS
Number of Servings — About 8

1 lb. ground beef
1 egg
⅓ c. evaporated milk
½ c. fine bread crumbs
1 t. salt
¼ t. pepper
¼ c. finely chopped onion
2 T. finely chopped green pepper

Mix above ingedients and shape into 16 balls. Alternate on long skewers with onion and tomato slices. Broil over coals, put between long pieces of split French bread.

Mrs. Gerald Banks, Nettleton H. S.
Amory, Mississippi

SMOKED FISH

Select whole fish (striped bass, mullet, brook trout, snappers, flounder or porgies) weighing no more than 2½ pounds each. Allow about 1 pound of fish per serving. Have fish cleaned with heads and tails removed if desired. Brush fish with cooking oil. Place a few smoke chips on the hot briquets. Barbecue the fish 10 to 15 minutes, depending on thinness or until fish flakes with a fork. As smoke chips burn, remove them and replace with more soaked chips. Serve with lime butter or your favorite tartar sauce.

Lime Butter: In a small bowl, cream ¼ cup butter or margarine. Gradually add and beat in 1 tablespoon fresh, frozen or canned lime juice, ¼ teaspoon salt and a dash of pepper. Delicious served with smoked fish.

Mrs. Mary Frances B. Wilson
Cherokee County H. S.
Centre, Alabama

OUTDOOR FISH COOKERY
Number of Servings — 1 or 100

1 fish—trout
4 slices raw potato
2 slices onion
2 or 3 slices tomato
Salt and pepper to taste

After cleaning trout, salt and pepper inside; fill with above raw ingredients, wrap in foil, place in hot coals of the camp fire and cook until done. (A strip of bacon may also be added). Good, served under the pine trees, or the stars, and especially good beside a lake.

Eva M. Grabow, Snowflake Union H. S.
Snowflake, Arizona

GYPSY GUMBO
Number of Servings — 8-10

1 lb. ground beef
Salt and pepper
1 medium bell pepper, chopped
1 medium onion, chopped
3 carrots, sliced
2 can (No. 303) whole kernel corn
1 can tomato sauce
Small amount fat to brown onion

Brown onion and bell pepper in small amount of fat. Combine salt, pepper and ground beef. Add to onion and brown. Add carrots, corn, tomato sauce. Add a little bit of water if too dry. Cook until carrots are well done. Cook this in a cast iron Dutch oven over a low fire out of doors.

Patricia Sladecek, Trenton H. S.
Trenton, Texas

Large Group Recipes

BRUNSWICK STEW
Number of Servings — 50

3 hens
3 lbs. pork
3 lbs. ground beef
3 cans English peas (Size 303)
3 cans tomatoes (Size 303)
3 cans corn (Size 303)
3 cans butter beans (Size 303)
1½ doz. onions
1 doz. hot peppers
1 package garlic
4 T. Worcestershire sauce
3 T. salt

Cook hens and remove meat from bone. Chop pork into small pieces. Add all ingredients together and cook until very thick; about 6 to 8 hours. Serves 50.

Maxine Fowler, Phil Campbell H. S.
Phil Campbell, Alabama

BAKED MEAT SANDWICH
Number of Servings — 52 sandwiches

1½ lbs. ground pork
1½ lbs. ground beef
2 eggs
½ c. prepared mustard
2 c. cracker crumbs

Cook ground beef and pork and then combine with the other ingredients. When combining the beef and pork with the other ingredients, use enough of the broth to make the mixture moist. Bake 1½ hours at 350°F.

Jo Kreidler, Fort Frye H. S.
Beverly, Ohio

MULTI-PURPOSE BARBECUED HAMBURGER MIX
Number of Servings — 40

4 lbs. hamburger
4 medium onions, chopped
3 cloves garlic, chopped
2 c. celery tops, chopped
4 t. salt
½ t. pepper
3 T. Worcestershire sauce
2 bottles (12-ozs. each) catsup

Pan-fry hamburger until all redness of meat disappears, stirring to mix well, put in electric roaster. Saute onions, garlic and celery in fat. Add salt, pepper, Worcestershire sauce and catsup. Simmer 20 minutes. Skim off excess fat. Use as filling for hot buns (¼ cup). This freezes well.

Mrs. Vivian B. Barnes, Argyle H. S.
Argyle, Wisconsin

MEAT LOAF
Number of Servings — 40

6 lbs. hamburger
2 c. rolled oats
3 T. salt
1 t. pepper
1 c. chopped or shredded round cheese
1½ c. milk
1 small onion, chopped finely
1 large can (3 c.) tomatoes
1 c. cooked rice (optional)
⅛ t. nutmeg (optional)

Mix together all ingredients. Place in 2 loaf pans. Bake for 1 hour at 350°F.

Vanora A. Fry, Little River H. S.
Little River, Kansas

MEAT LOAF
Number of Servings — 100

12 lbs. ground beef
5 small onions, chopped fine
8 eggs, beaten
3 qts. tomatoes
8 T. salt
3 green peppers, chopped

7 c. bread crumbs
2 t. black pepper

Mix all ingredients and place in greased baking pans. Bake in oven pre-heated to 350°F. Serve with tomato sauce.

Jewell West, Crowder H. S.
Crowder, Oklahoma

CHILI
Number of Servings — 50

15 lbs. of meat
¾ lbs. chili powder
3 ozs. powdered garlic
½ lb. flour
¼ oz. red pepper
Salt to taste

Mix all dry ingredients in a large mixing bowl. Place meat without water in heavy pan and cook over a low flame, stirring frequently. Cook until juice on meat is clear. Add dry ingredients, stir well and cook approximately 10 minutes. May be used immediately or poured in pans to cool, then cut in blocks and stored in refrigerator or freezer.

Rachel Brewster, Petrolia H. S.
Petrolia, Texas

CHILIBURGER FILLING
Number of Servings — 150-200

15 lbs. ground beef
Salt and pepper to taste
4 lbs. onions
4 bottles catsup (16 oz.)
3 bottles Heinz "57" sauce
1 lb. sugar
1 lb. shortening
1 T. chili powder

Cook the meat until thoroughly browned; stir frequently. Heat the shortening and add the onions, chopped fine, cook until done. They will be clear or translucent in appearance. Add the onions to the meat and blend thoroughly. Add all other ingredients. Simmer for 3 hours. This will serve 200 hot dog buns or 150 hamburger buns.

Mrs. LaRue S. Carter, Lund H. S.
Lund, Nevada

COCKTAIL MEATBALLS
Number of Servings — 36 small meat balls

1 lb. ground beef round
1 T. grated onion
1 clove garlic, finely minced
2 t. salt
½ t. pepper
4 T. heavy cream
½ c. ground walnuts

Finely mince garlic clove. Grind the walnuts. Combine all ingredients in the order given. Shape into small meatballs about 1 inch in diameter. Fry in a skillet until golden brown. Serve hot on toothpicks. Yield: 36 small cocktail meatballs.

Clara M. Dayton, Cokeville H. S.
Cokeville, Wyoming

MEAT SAUCE FOR SPAGHETTI
Number of Servings — 200

100 medium sized onions, chopped
8 garlic bulbs (or 1 oz. garlic powder)
25 lbs. ground beef
2 lbs. butter
1 pt. cooking oil

Brown above ingredients separately and then combine. Add to combined meat and onion mixture: 40 cans, 10 ounce size, tomato soup; 20 cans, 8 ounce size, tomato paste; 20 cans, 6 ounce size, tomato sauce; ½ bottle Worcestershire sauce; 3 tablespoons oregano; 1 can parsley flakes and salt and pepper to taste. Cook slowly for several hours. (The longer the better). Use 25 pounds spaghetti.

Mrs. Sue T. Glovier, Old Fort H. S.
Old Fort, North Carolina

ITALIAN SPAGHETTI AND MEAT BALLS
Number of Servings — 25

Meat Balls:

3 lbs. ground beef
1 qt. minced onions
6 cloves garlic, minced
1 c. chopped parsley
3 c. grated Parmesan cheese
3 c. bread crumbs
6 eggs
3 T. salt
3 t. black pepper

Sauce and Spaghetti:

5 c. chopped onion
10 cloves garlic, minced
½ c. oil
5 cans tomatoes (28-oz.)
5 c. water
1 c. chopped parsley
½ t. dried basil
2½ t. dried thyme
3 T. salt
1 t. black pepper
1 t. crushed red pepper
5 cans tomato paste (6-oz.)
4 lbs. spaghetti
Grated cheese

Mix all ingredients for meat balls, adding a little water, if too dry. Shape in 50 balls. Put balls one layer deep in a baking pan and bake at 450°F. for 30 minutes. Put balls and drippings in a roasting pan. *Sauce:* Cook onion and garlic in oil for 5 minutes. Add all ingredients except spaghetti and cheese and cook on simmer for 30 minutes. Pour over balls and bake covered for 1½ hours at 350°F. Serve over the cooked spaghetti. Top with grated cheese.

Mrs. Annie G. Childress, Mangham H. S.
Mangham, Louisiana

STUFFED PORK CHOPS
Number of Servings — 1-50

Instruct your butcher to cut chops double for stuffing. Stuff each with your favorite bread dressing. Dip each chop into melted butter and roll in corn flake crumbs. Lay carefully on foil on the broiler pan. Season by sprinkling with Accent. Broil 40 minutes at 400°F. Turn only once. Garnish with parsley and serve with tart applesauce. This is an excellent quantity recipe as 1 or 50 are equally easy to prepare.

Avys B. McCadden, Salmon River H. S.
Riggins, Idaho

PORK PILAF
Number of Servings — 50

50 pork chops
¼ c. salt
2 t. pepper
1 c. shortening
2 qts. rice
7 qts. chicken stock
2 t. thyme
1 qt. green pepper, diced
1 qt. onion, diced

Season chops with salt and pepper and brown in shortening. Remove chops and brown uncooked rice in 1 cup of the drippings. Add remaining ingredients to rice; place chops over rice. Cover and bake at 350°F. for 1 hour.

Mrs. Mary Jo Abernathy, Oden H. S.
Oden, Arkansas

CURRIED HAM ROLLS
Number of Servings — 50

1 gal. cooked rice
2 c. minced onion
2 c. finely chopped parsley
½ c. melted butter or margarine
4 t. salt
1 T. curry powder
50 slices boiled ham (not too thin)
50 hard-cooked eggs

Mix cooked rice, onion, parsley, melted butter or margarine, salt, and curry powder together. Place about ⅓ cup (No. 16 dipper) of the cooked rice mixture on each slice of ham. Roll up and place, seam side down, in baking dish. You may cut hard-cooked eggs in half lengthwise and place ½ egg, cut side down, on ham roll. Pour curry sauce over rolls. Bake at 375°F. for 30 to 35 minutes. May be served on thin wedges of toast, if desired.

Curry Sauce:

2 c. butter or margarine or butter-margarine
  mixture
1 T. curry powder
1 T. monosodium glutamate
1 c. cornstarch
4 t. salt
1 gal. milk

Melt butter or margarine in saucepan. Add curry powder, monosodium glutamate, corn starch, and salt. Blend well. Add milk. Cook over medium heat until thick.

Mrs. Maxine Miller, University H. S.
Iowa City, Iowa

HAM LOAF
Number of Servings — 20

1½ lbs. ham
1½ lbs. pork
2 lbs. hamburger
3 eggs
¾ c. milk
3 c. bread crumbs

Sauce:

½ c. vinegar
½ c. brown sugar
½ c. milk
1 t. dry mustard
1 t. salt
⅛ t. pepper

Form into individual ham loaves—top each with a slice of pineapple and a cherry. Bake at 325°F. oven for 2 hours. Simmer sauce for 10 minutes. After ham is in the oven 45 minutes, baste with sauce.

Mrs. Duane Torguson, Bristol H. S.
South Dakota

HAM LOAF
Number of Servings — 48

4 lbs. or 2 qts. smoked ham
4 lbs. or 2 qts. fresh ham
6 or 7 eggs or 12 ozs.
1 lb. or 1¼ qts. dry bread crumbs
1⅓ c. milk

Combine smoked ham and fresh ham. Beat eggs slightly. Combine with meat. Add bread crumbs and milk. Fill 4 loaf pans ⅔ full. Bake in moderate oven (350°F.) about an hour. Pan size 9½ x 5¼ x 2¾ inches. Slice and serve hot or cold.

Glaze for Ham Loaf (Serves 48)

1½ lbs. or 1 qt. brown sugar
1 c. vinegar
1½ T. dry mustard

Blend ingredients until smooth and boil 1 minute. Remove loaves from oven after about 30 minutes. Pour some of this syrup over each meat loaf. Return to oven and bake 25-30 minutes longer.

Janice Benda, Espanola H. S.
Espanola, New Mexico

GLAZED HAM LOAF
Number of Servings — 16

2½ lbs. ham ground with 1½ lbs. fresh pork
3 eggs
1½ c. bread crumbs
1½ c. milk

Combine bread crumbs and milk. Allow to stand until bread crumbs are softened. Combine ground ham and pork with eggs and crumb-milk mixture. Form into 2 loaves. Bake at 325°F. for 2 hours. Baste frequently with a glaze made by mixing 1 cup brown sugar, ½ cup vinegar and ½ cup water.

Mrs. Jean H. Teale
Bentleyville-Ellsworth Area Joint H. S.
Ellsworth, Pennsylvania

DUTCH SAUCIJSES ("PIGS IN BLANKET")
Number of Servings — 20 rolls

Crust:

4 c. flour
3 t. baking powder
1 c. butter, or substitute
1 t. salt
¾ c. milk

Meat:

2 lbs. ground pork, with a little fat
½ lb. ground beef
¼ c. bread crumbs
⅛ t. nutmeg
Salt and pepper to taste

Mix meat and seasonings. Roll meat into 3-inch long sausages, ¾ inch in diameter. Sift dry crust ingredients, blend in shortening to very coarse meal stage, and add milk to soft dough. Divide dough into 2 parts. Roll each part to ⅛ inch crust, cut into 3 x 4 inch squares, moisten one edge of each. Roll a sausage in each square, by folding dough over ends of sausage, then sealing. Place rolls on gresed cooky sheet, brush tops with beaten egg, or cream. Bake in 350°F. oven 40 minutes.

Mrs. Darlene R. Mouw, Community H. S.
Sioux Center, Iowa

PIZZA PIE
Number of Servings — 20

1½ lbs. sausage
1 medium onion
3 wieners
1 large can tomato sauce
1 t. oregano
1 small can mushrooms in steak sauce
½ lb. mild cheese

Combine sausage, onion, wieners and cook. Drain fat. Add cooked meat to tomato sauce. Combine oregano and mushrooms in steak sauce. Simmer 5 minutes. Spread over pizza crusts. Top with grated cheese. Bake in hot oven (400°F.) for 15 to 20 minutes.

Pizza Dough:

1 c. milk
2 T. butter or shortening
2 T. sugar
1 cake yeast softened in ¼ c. water
1 egg
3½-4 c. flour
1 t. salt

Scald milk; melt shortening in milk; add sugar and salt and cool. When lukewarm, add 1 cup flour to form batter. Add egg and beat well. Add yeast. Stir in well. Next add remaining flour and form soft dough. Knead slightly. Let rise till double. Knead and roll each crust to about ⅛ inch. Put in ungreased pizza pans. Top with pizza mixture and grated cheese. Bake in hot (400°-425°F.) oven for 15 to 20 minutes.

Maxine Burgess, Parma H. S.
Parma, Idaho

CHICKEN BOUDINE
Number of Servings — 16

2 5-lb. hens
2 onions
4 carrots
4 ribs celery
Parsley
Bay leaf
Salt and pepper to taste

Cream Sauce No. 1:

1¾ c. stock
6 T. butter
6 T. flour
⅓ c. cooking sherry
½ c. cream
Salt and pepper to taste
Dash of Worcestershire sauce

Cream Sauce No. 2:

1 can mushrooms
½ c. mushroom liquid
1 c. stock
½ c. cooking sherry
½ c. cream
6 T. butter
6 T. flour
Salt and pepper to taste

Make a rich stock from two 5 pound hens, using parsley, onions, carrots, bay leaf, and celery to season. Cook hens until tender. Cut meat in large size pieces. Make a rich cream sauce using the ingredients for sauce No. 1. Fold in chicken. Fold in 12 well-beaten eggs. Place mixture into 2 greased loaf pans. Let mixture stand overnight in refrigerator. Cover loosely with aluminum foil and set in pan of water. Cook in moderate oven (350°F.) for 1 hour. Remove from pans. Make cream sauce No. 2. Serve over loaf.

Jane Johnston, Southwest Dekalb H. S.
Decatur, Georgia

CHICKEN MOUSSE
Number of Servings — 20

2½ pts. finely diced cooked chicken
1 c. chopped olives
1 c. chopped celery
½ c. chopped green pepper
½ c. chopped pimento
½ c. chopped pecans
2 packages (2 T.) unflavored gelatin, softened
   in ½ c. water
2 c. hot chicken stock
1 c. mayonnaise
1 c. whipped cream

Combine first 6 ingredients. Dissolve gelatin in chicken stock; to this add mayonnaise and whipped cream. Add to chicken mixture. Mix well. Pour into two loaf pans. Chill until firm. Unmold and garnish as desired.

Nelle M. Dotson, West Henderson H. S.
Hendersonville, North Carolina

SCALLOPED CHICKEN SUPREME
Number of Servings — 12-16

6 c. cooked chicken
4 c. chicken broth
6 c. cooked rice
3 c. milk
1 T. butter
¾ c. flour
1 T. salt
⅛ t. pepper
1 c. blanched almonds
1 small can pimento
2 c. mushrooms
Buttered bread or cracker crumbs
Paprika

Cover 5 pounds chicken with boiling water. Add 1 teaspoon salt, 3 or 4 stalks celery and 2 small onions. Simmer gently until tender (2 to 3 hours). Let cool in broth. Cut chicken into small pieces and measure. Pour 1 cup chicken broth over cooked rice. Make rich gravy by adding milk to remaining broth and thickening it with butter melted and blended with the flour. Add salt and pepper. Cut almonds in slices and cut pimentos very fine. Slice mushrooms and fry in a little butter until slightly browned. Butter large casserole and cover bottom with rice. Place layer of chicken over rice and add generous amount of gravy. Dot with almonds, mushrooms, pimentos. Repeat with second layer of each ingredient. Sprinkle with buttered crumbs and paprika. Bake at 350°F. for 45 minutes. Use two 8 inch casseroles or one very large one.

Annette Richmire, Rogue River H. S.
Rogue River, Oregon

CREAMED CHICKEN
Number of Servings — 65

7 chickens
16 c. meat stock
4 c. milk
1⅓ c. thin cream
3 c. flour
3 c. water
1 medium green pepper
1 medium onion
1 small jar pimento

Season with salt or pepper as desired. Cook chickens until tender, bone and cut in pieces. Grind skin and giblets, and put in measured meat stock. Cook finely cut pepper and onion in a small amount of water for 5 minutes. Add finely cut pimentos. Heat the measured meat stock and ground mixture to a boil, add scalded milk and cream, then pepper, onion and pimento. Add the smooth flour, water mixture and seasoning. Boil for 10 minutes, stirring constantly. Add chicken, bring to a boil and serve.

Genevieve Overvaag, Public School
Mountain Lake, Minnesota

333

SCALLOPED CHICKEN

Number of Servings — 50

5 lbs. cooked chicken, cubed
2 c. melted chicken fat
8 ozs. flour
4 qts. hot chicken broth
1 oz. salt
Baked sage dressing
Buttered bread crumbs

Combine chicken fat, broth, flour, salt and make as white sauce. Put a layer of sage dressing in baking pan 9 x 12 inches, a layer of sauce, a layer of chicken, then another layer of sauce. Cover with buttered crumbs and bake in a moderate oven (350°F.) until crumbs are toasted (20 to 30 minutes).

Minnie Lou Huneycutt, Piedmont H. S.
Monroe, North Carolina

CHICKEN LEGS

Number of Servings — 100, 3 pieces each

6 lbs. onions, thinly sliced
150 chicken legs (drumsticks and thighs cut apart)
3 c. flour
3 T. salt
1 T. pepper
3 T. paprika
3 lbs. butter or margarine, melted

Arrange half of the onion slices on bottom of shallow baking pans. Add chicken pieces (do not pile on top of one another). Top with remaining onions. Combine flour, salt, pepper, and paprika. Sift together over the chicken and onions. Pour on butter or margarine. Bake in moderate oven (350°F.) 1 hour, or until chicken is brown and tender. Serve with onions and pan juice.

Diane M. Brown, Grayville H. S.
Grayville, Illinois

TURKEY TETRAZZINI

Number of Servings — 25

1 lb. spaghetti, uncooked
½ c. chopped onion
1 clove garlic
2 T. butter
4 cans mushroom soup
2 c. water
1 lb. shredded cheese
2 lbs. diced cooked turkey
¼ c. chopped pimento

Cook spaghetti in boiling salted water until just tender but not soft. Drain. Cook onion and garlic in butter until tender. Blend in soup and water; stir until smooth. Add half of cheese. Cook over low heat until cheese is melted, stirring occasionally. Fold in turkey and pimento. Put spaghetti into greased baking pans and pour turkey mixture over it. Sprinkle on remaining cheese. Bake in 450°F. oven until sauce bubbles and browns.

Mrs. Mary E. McCollum, Haskell H. S.
Haskell, Texas

EMPANADITAS DE CARNE (Meat Turnovers)

Number of Servings — 8 dozen

1 lb. boiling meat
1½ c. raisins
2 c. applesauce or jam
1 c. sugar
1 t. coriander seed
½ t. cloves
1 t. cinnamon
½ c. shelled pinon nuts
1 t. salt
1 cake yeast
1½ c. water or milk
3 T. fat
1½ t. salt
2 T. sugar
4-5 c. sifted flour (all-purpose)

Grind meat and add the next 8 ingredients making a paste. If paste is too dry add a little meat stock; paste should be moist. Heat ½ cup of the liquid to lukewarm; add fat, salt and sugar. Cool to lukewarm and add yeast. Add enough flour to make a medium dough. Roll out pastry ⅛ inch thick and about 4 inches in diameter. Place 1½ teaspoon meat paste one ½ of the pastry; fold the other half over and pinch edges together; then make a turn back in the dough by taking edges between thumb and forefinger, pressing together and turning back in ridges. Let turnovers stand for 5 minutes then deep fat fry.

Marie R. Pompeo, Espanola H. S.
Espanola, New Mexico

STEAK WITH SAUCE

Number of Servings — 300

Ingredients to make sauce:
1 can (No. 10) tomato catsup
2 cans (No. 10) tomato puree
20 large green peppers, chopped
7 lbs. onions, chopped
3 c. apple vinegar
½ c. salt
½ c. sugar
4 T. garlic paste
1 can (No. 10) water

Cook onions and peppers in small amount of fat. Add other ingredients. At the butcher shop, have the meat cut into serving-size pieces (4 ounce cuts). Season meat with salt and roll in flour. Brown meat in fat. Arrange a layer of steak in 2 cups of sauce, followed with another layer of steak in sauce. Use a large electric cooker. Set cooker at 200 to 225°F. Cook for 3 hours.

Frances Moore, Kingfisher H. S.
Kingfisher, Oklahoma

Ready Prepared & Convenience Foods

& Meat Substitutes

Also

Recipes for Dressings, Fillings, Stuffings

Garnishes & Accompaniments

Sauces & Gravies

Ready Prepared & Convenience Foods

BARBECUED BOLOGNA
Number of Servings — 8

4 lbs. bologna, 4-5 inches in diameter, not sliced
Whole cloves
1 c. firmly packed light brown sugar
2 T. prepared mustard
3 T. vinegar
1 t. grated orange rind

Remove plastic casing from bologna. Score meat in diamond shapes. Stick whole cloves in meat at intervals. Place on spit and cook on rotisserie, 350°F. for 30 minutes. Combine sugar, mustard, vinegar, and orange rind. At end of 30 minute cooking period, baste bologna, then again every 10-15 minutes for 30 minutes more, using up all the sauce.

Mrs. Reba Wilson, Brainerd H. S.
Chattanooga, Tennessee

BOLOGNA HOT DISH
Number of Servings — 6-8

1 medium ring of bologna
1 onion
½ green pepper
½ t. salt
1 T. flour
2 c. milk
¼ t. pepper
1 No. 2 can cream style corn
1 can cream of mushroom soup
8 ozs. egg noodles
2 T. butter

Put the bologna, onion and green pepper thru a food chopper. Brown in butter. Then combine all ingredients in a 3 quart casserole and bake 1 hour at 350°F.

Carol Perso, Alexander H. S.
Nekoosa, Wisconsin

CORNED BEEF
Number of Servings — 8

Filling:

1 onion, chopped
2 T. butter or margarine
1 T. flour
1 can corned beef, cut up
Salt and pepper
1 small can tomatoes

Crust:

2 c. flour
1 t. baking powder
½ t. salt
⅓ c. milk
⅓ c. shortening
1 egg yolk

Crust—Sift flour with baking powder and salt. Cut in shortening. Stir in milk mixed with egg yolk. Divide dough in half; roll and cut each half into 4 pieces. Place in muffin tins. Fill with corned

beef filling. Bake at 350°F. until crust is light brown and done. *Filling*—Saute onion in butter or margarine. Add flour, beef, tomatoes, salt and pepper. Simmer 15 to 20 minutes.

Barbara Weiss, Huntley H. S.
Huntley, Wyoming

CORNED BEEF CASSEROLE
Number of Servings — 6

1 can corned beef
1 c. medium white sauce
½ c. chopped celery
¼ c. diced onion
¼ t. salt
½ c. crushed crackers
⅛ t. pepper

Place corned beef in a buttered casserole. Prepare white sauce. Add onion and celery. Cook 5 minutes. Pour over beef in casserole. Crush crackers and sprinkle over top, dot with butter and sprinkle with paprika or pepper.

Gwen Morgenstern, Hamden H. S.
Hamden, Ohio

CORNED BEEF CASSEROLE
Number of Servings — 6-8

1 12-oz. can corned beef
1 8-oz. package macaroni
1 package dry onion soup mix
1 t. Worcestershire sauce
1½ c. cheese, grated or cut into small pieces
2 T. shortening
3 T. flour
2 c. milk
¼ t. salt
Dash of pepper
Bread crumbs

Cook macaroni according to directions on package. Drain. Make cream sauce using fat, flour, milk, salt and pepper. Cook until thick. Combine macaroni, corned beef (broken into small pieces), 1 cup cheese, dry onion soup mix, and Worcestershire sauce. Add cream sauce and mix thoroughly. Pour into large casserole, cover top with bread crumbs and sprinkle on remaining ½ cup cheese. Bake in 400°F. oven for 20 minutes to allow cheese to melt. Serve as one-dish meal or as main dish. (Original Recipe).

Loreen Mowery, Ash Fork H. S.
Ash Fork, Arizona

SPICY CORNED BEEF
Number of Servings — 6-8

3 to 4 lbs. corned beef brisket
1 orange, sliced
1 large onion, quartered
2 stalks celery, cut in half
1 bay leaf
2 cloves garlic, quartered
1 t. dill seed
½ t. rosemary

(Continued on Next Page)

6 whole cloves
3 inches stick cinnamon

Cover corned beef with water. Add remaining ingredients. Cover and simmer (do not boil) 1 hour per pound of meat, or till tender. Remove meat from liquid; while hot, brush with light corn syrup to glaze. Serve at once or chill.

Marlene Cloud, North Whitfield H. S.
Dalton, Georgia

CORN BEEF SALAD MOLD
Number of Servings — 16

1 T. gelatin
¼ c. cold water
1½ c. tomato juice
1 t. lemon juice
½ t. salt
1 c. mayonnaise
1 12-oz. can corn beef
3 hard cooked eggs, sliced
2 c. finely chopped celery
1 T. onion juice
1 cucumber, diced fine

Soak gelatin in the ¼ cup cold water. Heat tomato and add gelatin mixture. When cool add remaining ingredients. Mold in individual molds or in large pyrex pan. Serve on salad greens.

Mrs. Ben H. Varnau, Dulles H. S.
Sugar Land, Texas

HAMBURGER PIE
Number of Servings — 5-6

1 lb. ground beef
⅓ c. tomato sauce
½ c. fine bread crumbs
1 t. powdered onion
1 t. salt
¼ t. pepper
1 can vegetable soup, undiluted
1 package instant mashed potatoes

Combine first 6 ingredients, mix well. Pat into deep 9 or 10 inch pie tin, shaping it like pie crust. Bake at 350°F. for 20 minutes. Drain off accumulated juices or fat. Fill center of "pie crust" with vegetable soup. Prepare envelope of instant mashed potatoes according to directions on the package. (Regular home prepared mashed potatoes may also be used). Pile potatoes on pie like meringue. Sprinkle with cheese if desired. Return to oven for 20 minutes.

Mrs. Roderick Starz, Harmony Area Schools
Harmony, Minnesota

QUICKIE-CHICKEN A LA KING

1 large package cream cheese
1 can cream of mushroom soup
2 cans boned chicken

Melt cheese in top of double boiler. Add soup and stir until smooth. Then add chicken. Serve hot over toast or use as a dip.

Nanci Carolyn White, Lepanto H. S.
Lepanto, Arkansas

QUICK-CHICKEN CASSEROLE
Number of Servings — 6-8

2 small cans chicken
1 can cream of celery soup
1 can cream of mushroom soup
1 can Chinese vegetables
1 can Chinese noodles

Mix all together in casserole dish and top with crushed potato chips and sprinkle grated cheese over the top, if desired. Bake in a moderate oven 20 to 30 minutes. Tuna fish and cream of chicken soup may be substituted for the chicken and celery soup.

Geneva Bird, Laramie Sr. H. S.
Laramie, Wyoming

QUICK SHRIMP DINNER
Number of Servings — 4

1 can frozen shrimp soup
1 can shrimp
½ c. milk
1 c. minute rice

Add milk to soup. Heat on low until thawed and at serving temperature. Prepare rice according to package directions. Drain shrimp, rinse with cold water, drain again. (Sauce will be too salty if this is not done). Add shrimp to sauce and serve over rice.

Laurette Anderson, West H. S.
Bremerton, Washington

GLORIFIED "ROUND STEAK"

4 wieners
4 strips bacon
4 slices cheese, cut into strips
4 wiener buns (optional)

Cook the wieners, partially fry the bacon. Slit the wieners down the middle, placing a slice of cheese in the slit. Wrap bacon around the cheese and wiener. Secure with a toothpick. Place on the griddle and cook until the cheese melts and the bacon is done. Serve in a bun or eat it with a fork.

Dorothy Elson, Hampton Com. H. S.
Hampton, Iowa

CORN DOGS
Number of Servings — 10

1 package cornbread mix
1 package wieners
Catsup
Mustard
Hot dog relish

Make cornbread batter, then roll cooked wieners in batter until thoroughly coated. Deep fat fry. When golden brown, drain on paper towel. Brush with catsup, mustard or any other desired hot dog condiment. Put on a stick and ready to eat.

Mariann Hofstetter, United Twp. H. S.
East Moline, Illinois

GWENDOLYN'S LAST-MINUTE SLUMGULLION
Number of Servings — 6

1½ c. dry elbow macaroni
6 wieners
¾ c. dry skim milk solids
¾ c. whole milk
1 c. diced celery
1½ c. grated cheddar cheese
8 sliced pitted ripe olives
Few basil leaves (crushed type)
Salt, pepper, onion salt to taste

Cook macaroni according to package directions. Meantime, heat wieners, drain, and cut into bite-sized pieces. Place drained macaroni and wieners in top of double boiler; heat over boiling water. Add remaining ingredients, heat through. Serve with some grated cheese sprinkled over top of each serving. (Variations: May substitute for wieners one of following meats—1 family-size can tuna; 1 pound browned ground beef, or cut-up left-over meats).

Mrs. Gwen Bayer, Summerville Union H. S.
Tuolumne, California

PRONTO PUPS
Number of Servings — 8-10

1 lb. frankfurters
Batter mix:
½ c. meal
1½ c. flour
¼ c. sugar
2 t. salt
4 t. baking powder
1 c. milk
1 egg, beaten

Mix all dry ingredients together. Add egg and milk and beat with a rotary egg beater until smooth. Dip franks in batter and fry in hot deep fat until brown on one side. Turn and brown the other side. Drain on paper toweling. Serve hot.

Mrs. Billie Nowlin, Rising Star H. S.
Rising Star, Texas

DEVIL'S DOGS
Number of Servings — 8

1 lb. wieners
⅔ c. cornmeal
1 c. flour
½ t. baking powder
1 t. salt
2 T. sugar
2 T. fat (cut in)
1 egg, slightly beaten
¾ c. milk

Boil wieners, and place part of flour in separate container. Combine ingredients to form paste mixture. Roll wieners in flour and dip in mixture, then fry in deep fat until brown. Leftover batter may be refrigerated for later use.

Mrs. Lera Auberry, East Fannin H. S.
Morganton, Georgia

CROWN ROAST OF WIENERS
Number of Servings — 8

16 wieners
2 T. chopped onion
4 slices bacon, diced
1 can (No. 2½) sauerkraut
1 can (No. 2½) cooked potatoes
¼ c. melted butter or margarine
¼ c. chopped parsley

Run a string through wieners 1 inch from top and another 1 inch from bottom. Tie together forming a circle and stand up on heat-resistant platter. Saute onion and diced bacon together in skillet on SECOND. Place sauerkraut inside of wiener ring and top with onion and bacon mixture. Dip potatoes in melted butter; roll in parsley and place around wieners. Cover entire platter with aluminum foil. Bake in 350°F. oven for 45 minutes. Hot potato salad is very good, placed inside of crown roast instead of potatoes and sauerkraut.

Clara E. Dalton, Piute H. S.
Junction, Utah

WIENER STEW
Number of Servings — 6

1 T. fat
2 pieces bacon, cubed
1 medium onion, diced
1 lb. wieners
1 T. vinegar
½ c. water
3 diced cooked potatoes
Dash of tabasco
Salt and pepper to taste

Put fat in pan, add cubed bacon and fry out; add onion and fry until brown. Cut wieners in quarters and fry until brown. Add diced potatoes, water, tabasco, salt and pepper and simmer for 15 minutes. Add vinegar and simmer for 15 minutes more. Serve.

Elsie E. Eckhoff, Viborg H. S.
Viborg, South Dakota

POTATO CAPPED FRANKS
Number of Servings — 4

8 frankfurters
1 c. dairy sour cream
2 c. seasoned mashed potatoes
¼ c. chopped green onion
¼ t. salt
Paprika

Cut franks lengthwise but not all the way through. Place them with cut side up in an 8 x 12 inch baking dish. Spread each one with ¼ cup mashed potatoes. Combine sour cream, salt and onion and spread over potatoes. Bake uncovered in 450°F. oven for 12 to 15 minutes. Sprinkle with paprika.

Mrs. W. O. Baird, Mayewood H. S.
Sumter, South Carolina

HOT DOG — SWEET 'N SOUR!
Number of Servings — 6

6 frankfurters
¼ c. butter
1 medium onion, diced vertically
1 c. green pepper strips
1 c. bias-sliced celery
2 T. cornstarch
¼ c. pineapple juice
¾ c. water
1 t. soy sauce
1 bouillon cube
¼ t. horseradish
4 slices pineapple, quartered
1 large tomato, cut in eighths
Minute rice

Cut frankfurters in narrow strips, 2 inches in length. Brown in melted butter. Stir in onions, green pepper and celery. Cook 2 minutes. Mix cornstarch with pineapple juice, add water and bouillon cube. Add to frankfurter mixture and stir gently until bouillon cube is dissolved. Add soy sauce, horseradish, pineapple and tomato. Cook slowly for 10 minutes, stirring occasionally. Do not overcook. Add additional water if mixture is too thick. Serve over minute rice.

Marcelle T. Montminy, Manchester Mem. H. S.
Manchester, New Hampshire

TANGERINE-GLAZED FRANKFURTERS
Number of Servings — 6

1 can water
1 can (6 oz.) concentrated tangerine juice
4 t. cornstarch
⅓ c. firmly packed light brown sugar
⅓ t. dry mustard
1 T. Worcestershire sauce
⅓ c. pickle relish
2 lbs. frankfurters

Add 1 can water to the concentrated tangerine juice. Mix cornstarch and sugar together. Then combine all ingredients except frankfurters in a skillet. Cook until mixture thickens, about 5 to 10 minutes. Add frankfurters and cook 10 minutes longer, or until frankfurters are glazed with sauce. Here are frankfurters-with-company manners that the teen-age cook may enjoy fixing. Serve with winter squash, coleslaw, and a savory vegetable.

Martha Tate, Stigler H. S.
Stigler, Oklahoma

STUFFED FRANKFURTERS
Number of Servings — 4

4 slices bacon (optional)
½ c. onions, chopped
½ c. green pepper, chopped
¼ c. parsley, chopped
¼ t. rosemary, if desired
1 10½-oz. can condensed cream of mushroom
   soup, undiluted
1½ c. cracker crumbs
8 skinless frankfurters

Turn on oven and set at 425°F. Cook bacon until crisp, remove from skillet, and drain. Saute chopped onions, pepper, and parsley in the remaining fat until tender and lightly browned. Add the herb, soup, and 1¼ cups crumbs; mix well. Split frankfurters lengthwise in center but not quite all the way through. Fill with stuffing and sprinkle remaining ¼ cup crumbs and crumbled bacon on top. Bake for about 20 minutes or until well-browned.

Teresa V. Holguin, Tularosa H. S.
Tularosa, New Mexico

LUNCHEON MEAT CASSEROLE — (BAKED)
Number of Servings — 4-6

4 ozs. macaroni (bow, elbow or such)
1¼ c. condensed cream of chicken or mushroom soup
⅔ c. milk
2 c. diced luncheon meat
Thyme or such seasoning, to taste if desired
1 T. butter or margarine
2 T. finely chopped parsley
¼ c. fine dry bread crumbs
1 T. butter or margarine, melted

Cook macaroni in boiling salted water until tender (about 8 minutes). Drain and rinse. While macaroni is cooking, empty soup into mixing bowl and stir until smooth. Blend in milk. Add meat. Mix macaroni lightly with butter or margarine and parsley. Turn into greased 1 quart casserole. Pour meat mixture over macaroni and mix lightly. Mix crumbs with melted butter or margarine. Sprinkle over top of casserole. Bake in moderate oven (375°F.) until mixture is bubbly and crumbs are lightly browned (about 25 minutes).

Leora Sayre, Buckskin Valley H. S.
South Salem, Ohio

LUNCHEON MEAT BARBECUE
Number of Servings — 4

1 can luncheon meat
1 can (303) sliced peaches
1 can (8 oz.) tomato sauce
¼ c. brown sugar
3 T. vinegar
½ t. salt
½ t. Worcestershire sauce
1 t. dry mustard
1 t. onion flakes
1 t. chili powder

Combine in large frying pan, tomato sauce, sugar, vinegar and seasonings. Simmer 5 minutes. Add 1 can luncheon meat cut in 9 slices. Insert 1 peach slice into each cut. Add remaining peaches to sauce. Simmer covered 10 minutes. Serve with the extra peach barbecue sauce. (Note: Any favorite barbecue sauce may be used).

Mrs. Lillian Whaley, New Community H. S.
Monroe, Iowa

SPAM HOT DISH
Number of Servings — 8-10

2 c. ground cooked macaroni
1 small onion
1 green pepper
¼ lb. American cheese
1 can Spam
1½ c. hot milk
½ c. butter
1½ c. bread crumbs
4 eggs, separated

Mix milk, butter, beaten egg yolks and pour over crumbs. Add this to mixture of macaroni, onion, pepper, cheese and Spam. Fold in beaten egg whites last. Pour into buttered casserole and bake at 325°F. for 1½ hours. Pour 1 can cream of mushroom soup over for last 20 minutes of baking. This recipe may be prepared and kept in refrigerator until ready to bake.

Mrs. Lois Lovas, Mayville H. S.
Mayville, North Dakota

SPAM STROGANOFF
Number of Servings — 4

1½ T. butter
1 can (7 oz.) mushroom slices with liquid
2 T. minced onion
1 can mushroom soup
½ c. milk
Salt and pepper
¼ t. dry mustard
1 can Spam, sliced and diced
1 c. sour cream

Melt butter in skillet; add mushroom slices and liquid. Cook until liquid has evaporated. Add minced onion and cook until yellow; add mushroom soup and milk. Stir until blended. Stir in salt, pepper, dry mustard and diced Spam. Blend in sour cream just before serving. Serve in toast cup, or over wide egg noodles or rice.

Mrs. Freda Montgomery, Central Union H. S.
Fresno, California

TAMALE-BEAN CASSEROLE
Number of Servings — 12

1 can (28-ozs.) pork and beans
1 can (15½-ozs.) chili, without beans
1 T. prepared mustard
1 T. chopped onion, sauteed
3 slices crumbled fried bacon
2 cans (15½-ozs.) tamales
1 c. grated cheddar cheese
1 c. grated Romano cheese

Combine beans, chili, mustard, onion, and bacon in bowl. Place layer of broken tamales in oiled casserole. Spread with layer of above mixture and sprinkle with cheese. Repeat, making two layers. Bake at 350°F. for 15 minutes.

Mrs. Frances C. Patin, Poydras H. S.
New Roads, Louisiana

TEMT SPECIAL
Number of Servings — 4

1 12-oz. Dubuque's Temt
¼ c. brown sugar
1 8-oz. can tomato sauce
1 c. fruit cocktail (optional)

Slice Temt, making 8 crosswise slices; arrange in electric fry pan. Sprinkle with brown sugar; pour on the tomato sauce. Allow to simmer slowly for 15 minutes. Just before serving, top each slice with 1 tablespoon fruit cocktail.

Mrs. Ethel Parsons, Marysville H. S.
Marysville, California

FIVE CAN CASSEROLE
Number of Servings — 6

1 pt. chicken with broth
1 can cream of chicken soup
1 can cream of celery or mushroom soup
1 small can evaporated milk
1 can chow mein noodles (reserve ¼ can for topping)

Mix all in a buttered casserole. Bake at 350°F. for 25 to 30 minutes.

Lucy White, Wethersfield H. S.
Kewanee, Illinois

Meat Substitutes

MACARONI AND CHEESE
Number of Servings — 6

1 7-oz. package macaroni
½ lb. American cheese, grated
1½ c. milk
1 t. minced onion
1 t. salt
2 T. chopped mango
1 T. chopped pimento

Cook macaroni according to directions on package. Grease a 2-quart casserole. Place ½ of macaroni in casserole. Add ½ of other ingredients. Add another ½ of macaroni and top with remaining ingredients. Bake at 350°F. for 1 hour.

Elaine Buerkel, Three Rivers H. S.
Coshocton, Ohio

MACARONI AND CHEESE DINNER

Eight ounces cooked macaroni. Make a sauce of 3 tablespoons butter, 1 onion, sauted and ¼ cup chopped, green pepper. Add 1½ teaspoons garlic salt, 1 tablespoon flour, dash of cayenne pepper and 1 cup milk. Add 1 beaten egg, ½ pound grated cheese and ¼ cup chopped olives. Alternate macaroni and sauce in casserole. Bake 35 to 40 minutes at 350°F. Garnish with potato chips.

Barbara Pou, Wade Hampton H. S.
Greenville, South Carolina

MACARONI AND CHEESE
Number of Servings — 20

1 c. uncooked macaroni
1 c. bread crumbs
3 eggs, beaten
2 c. grated cheese
2 c. milk
4 T. margarine
1 pod pimento (optional)
1 t. grated onion (optional)

Cook macaroni in 1 quart boiling salted water until almost tender. Drain. Pour 1 cup milk over bread crumbs and let stand a few minutes. Combine all ingredients and mix with macaroni. Pour into a greased casserole. Bake at 350°F. until set.

Mrs. Delma Hunt, Yazoo City H. S.
Yazoo City, Mississippi

MACARONI AND CHEESE
Number of Servings — 6

1 package elbow macaroni (7 oz.)
2 c. milk
3 eggs, beaten
4 T. butter
⅔ lb. cheese, grated
½ t. salt
Dash of pepper

Cook macaroni as directed on package. Combine milk, eggs, salt and pepper. Alternate layers of macaroni, cheese, and butter in a buttered casserole. Pour over milk and egg mixture. Bake at 350°F. about 45 minutes or until firm on outer edges.

Ettie Belle Robinson, Dawson H. S.
Dawson, Texas

DANISH CHEESE SOUFFLE
Number of Servings — 3-4

¾ c. milk
1 c. bread cubes
⅛ t. dry mustard
1 t. melted butter
½ t. salt
⅛ t. pepper
½ t. poppy seed
½ t. grated onion
Dash tabasco
2 small eggs or 1 very large
1 c. grated cheese

Combine milk and onion. Heat to scalding. Add bread cubes, but save a few for top. Add salt, pepper, and cheese. Stir until dissolved. Beat egg yolks; stir in a little of the cheese mixture, then stir egg mixture into cheese. Cool slightly. Beat egg whites stiff and fold in. Turn into casserole. Toss remaining bread cubes with butter and poppy seed. Scatter over top. Bake at 350°F. for 45 to 45 minutes.

Melba Smith, Grandview H. S.
Grandview, Texas

BREAD AND CHEESE CASSEROLE
Number of Servings — 4

6 or 7 slices white bread
1 c. sharp cheddar cheese, grated
2 well beaten eggs
1 c. milk
1 t. salt
¼ t. paprika
¼ t. dry mustard

Spread the bread lightly with butter, cut into 1 inch cubes. There should be 4 cups of diced bread. Place layers of bread and cheese in greased baking dish. Mix the remaining ingredients and pour over the bread and cheese. Bake at 350°F. about 25 minutes. Serve immediately. One cup of finely chopped left over ham or cooked shrimp may be added with the cheese. This, served with a crisp green salad, makes a delicious and economical meal.

Edna Osborne, Jacksonville H. S.
Jacksonville, Illinois

CHEESE AND RICE SOUFFLE
Number of Servings — 8

1 c. cooked rice
2 T. butter
3 T. flour
¾ c. milk
½ lb. cheese
4 eggs
½ t. salt

Melt butter in double boiler, stir in flour. When smooth, stir in milk and cook until thickened. Slice cheese into sauce and cook until cheese is melted. Separate eggs. To egg yolks, add salt and beat with fork, then add slowly to cheese mixture, stirring constantly. Remove from heat. Fold rice into cheese mixture. Beat egg whites until stiff. Gently fold in cheese and rice mixture. Bake in greased casserole 40 minutes at 325°F.

Argent Thomas, East Limestone H. S.
Athens, Alabama

CHEESE PIMENTO CASSEROLE
Number of Servings — 6

1 c. soda cracker crumbs
2 c. medium white sauce (4 T. butter, 4 T. flour
    and 2 c. milk)
7 ozs. pimento grated
½ lb. grated American cheese
4 hard cooked eggs, grated
Buttered crumbs

In a greased 8 x 8 x 2 inch baking dish, place a layer of cracker crumbs and moisten with sauce (½). Next sprinkle ½ of cheese. Now a layer of grated pimento topped with a layer of hard boiled grated eggs. Repeat these layers and again be sure the crumbs are well moistened. Top with buttered crumbs and bake 350°F. about 25 minutes.

Mrs. Chelsea A. Merritt, Tollesboro H. S.
Tollesboro, Kentucky

CHEESE FONDUE
Number of Servings — 8

12 slices white bread, trimmed
½ c. grated American cheese
½ c. grated cheddar cheese
6 slices sandwich cheese
2 eggs
1 qt. sweet milk
1 t. Worcestershire sauce
Paprika
½ t. salt

Make 6 sandwiches with bread and slices of cheese. Cut each sandwich into 1 inch cubes. Place half the cheese and sandwich cubes in buttered casserole, 2 quart size. Continue adding cheese and cubes until dish is filled. Beat eggs, mix with other ingredients and pour over cubes and cheese. Sprinkle top with paprika. Let stand ½ hour in refrigerator, or may stand up to 24 hours. Bake for 30 minutes at 350°F. For added flavor, may add left over ham, chicken or tuna fish to give variety.

Ruth P. Groover, Cleburne County H. S.
Heflin, Alabama

SPAGHETTI FOR "STORMY"
Number of Servings — 8

1 10-oz. package spaghetti
1 can (No. 2) chili
1 bell pepper, chopped
1 onion, chopped
½ c. catsup
2 T. cooking oil
1 c. shredded cheddar cheese

Cook onion and bell pepper in cooking oil in large skillet until limp and slightly brown. Add chili, catsup; cook until well blended (2 to 3 minutes). Cook spaghetti until tender, drain. Cover bottom of well oiled casserole with spaghetti, add layer of meat; repeat. Bake in 400°F. oven for 1 hour. Add cheese during last 10 minutes.

Mrs. Justine H. Black, Cayuga H. S.
Cayuga, Texas

RICE AND CHEESE CASSEROLE
Number of Servings — 6

2 c. cooked rice
2 c. grated cheese
¼ t. salt
1 c. milk
Bread crumbs
2½ T. butter
1 pinch cayenne

In a greased casserole put a layer of rice, then a layer of cheese and sprinkle with seasoning. Continue adding layers until the dish is almost full. Add enough milk to come half way to the top of bowl. Cover with crumbs. Dot with butter and bake in moderate oven (350°F.) 30 minutes.

Louise Adon Hall, Mulvane H. S.
Mulvane, Kansas

RICE CASSEROLE
Number of Servings — 6

1 c. raw rice
1 c. grated American cheese
1 c. chopped black olives
½ c. chopped onion
1 c. stewed tomatoes
½ c. cooking oil
½ c. water
Salt and pepper

Combine the above in order given and place in a greased 1½ quart casserole. Cover and bake 1 hour at 350°F.

Mrs. Leona E. Brt, Wakefield H. S.
Wakefield, Nebraska

SAVORY SNACKS
Number of Servings — 12

½ lb. sharp American cheese
¼ lb. bacon
1 medium onion
2 T. chili sauce
1 loaf French bread

Put cheese, bacon and onion through food grinder together. Add chili sauce; blend thoroughly. Cut bread in ¼ inch slices. Spread each slice with about 1½ tablespoons mixture. Broil until browned. Serve hot.

Pauline Kirby, Marcellus H. S.
Marcellus, Michigan

SUPREME CHEESE SCALLOPED POTATOES
Number of Servings — 6-8

6 medium size Irish potatoes
3 medium size onions
1 large can pimento
¾ lb. processed cheese
¼-½ c. milk
Salt
Pepper

Boil potatoes in skins, cool and peel. Chop onions and pimento; combine. Combine milk and cheese and melt in top of double boiler or over low heat until smooth and of pouring consistency. Slice potatoes very thin and line bottom of greased 1½ or 2 quart casserole dish. Sprinkle layer of onion-pimento mixture over layer of potatoes. Salt and pepper. Continue layers until casserole dish is full, ending with layer of potatoes. Pour melted cheese over mixture. Insert knife and allow to surround mixture. Bake in moderate oven (350° F.) 15 to 20 minutes, or until mixture is hot. Serve. Very good with a hearty combination salad.

Jean Higginbotham Smith, Richardson H. S.
Richardson, Texas

MACARONI PEANUT RING
Number of Servings — 6

1 c. elbow macaroni
1 can cream of mushroom soup

(Continued on Next Page)

2 eggs, well beaten
1 c. finely chopped salted peanuts
½ c. finely chopped celery
⅓ c. bread crumbs

Cook macaroni in about 2 quarts boiling salted water, 10 to 12 minutes, or until almost tender. Drain. Rinse with cold water. Drain well. Blend together soup and egg. Add cooked macaroni and remaining ingredients. Turn into well greased 1 quart ring mold or 8 x 4 x 3 inch loaf pan. Bake in moderate oven (350°F.). Serve with curried egg sauce. *Curried Egg Sauce:* Blend together 1 can condensed cream of mushroom soup, ½ cup milk and 1 teaspoon curry powder in saucepan. Add 2 hard cooked eggs, diced. Heat thoroughly.

Cynthia Nanninga, Lamphere H. S.
Madison Heights, Michigan

GREEN TAMALE PIE
Number of Servings — 6

1 package corn tortillos
1 lb. grated cheese
1 can cream of mushroom soup
3 T. chopped green chile
1 c. minced onion
1 tall can evaporated milk

Simmer soup and milk until it thickens. Fry tortillos as for tacos. Oil casserole and place layers of tortillos, onions, cheese, chile and soup mixture until all ingredients are used. Bake in 350°F. oven for 30 minutes.

Ruth M. Bearup, Silver H. S.
Silver City, New Mexico

WESTERN CASSEROLE
Number of Servings — 6-8

1 large onion
1 large green pepper
½ c. celery, small stalks and leaves
¼ c. oleo or bacon fat
1 can tomato puree or sauce
1 c. water or tomato juice
2 heaping c. uncooked noodles
1 large can whole grain yellow corn
Salt and chili pepper to taste
1 can medium or large ripe olives
1 c. grated cheese

Chop onion, pepper, and celery; saute in fat until tender only (never brown). Add meat and cook until almost done (red gone). Add tomato puree or sauce and water. (A can of tomatoes or diluted tomato soup may be substituted). Add broken up noodles, stir and cook until noodles are tender—adding more water or tomato juice if needed. Add corn, chili or red pepper to taste, then olives. Pour into large buttered casserole or Pyrex long utility pan. Add grated cheese over and stir or rather press into top of mixture to moisten. Cook 30 to 45 minutes at 350°F. (do not brown cheese). Let stand for about 15 minutes and serve in baking dish.

Mrs. Julian A. Raburn, Telfair County H. S.
McRae, Georgia

BAKED LIMA BEANS
Number of Servings — 6

2 c. dry lima beans
6 c. water
1 t. salt
1½ T. catsup
1½ T. vinegar
2 T. molasses
1 T. granulated or brown sugar
Pepper to taste
2 slices bacon, cut up or ham hock

Wash beans. Boil 1½ hours slowly or soak several hours and boil about 1 hour or cook in pressure saucepan according to directions. Then add catsup, vinegar, molasses, sugar, pepper and bacon or ham hock. Put into baking dish and bake ½ to ¾ hours at 325°F.

Mrs. Ruth S. Park, Bend Sr. H. S.
Bend, Oregon

"TOMALLIE" PIE
Number of Servings — 6

4 oz. bag Fritos
1 can (No. 2) chili
½ c. chopped onion
1 c. grated cheese

Place layer of Fritos in bottom of buttered casserole. Spread ½ the chili, onion and cheese over Fritos. Repeat. Bake at 375°F. for 25 minutes.

Bessie Boyd, Huntsville H. S.
Huntsville, Texas

EGG SALAD CASSEROLE
Number of Servings — 8-10

8 hard boiled eggs, chopped
¼ t. salt
¼ t. pepper
¼ c. chopped nuts
1 c. crushed potato chips
1 t. diced onions
⅔ c. mayonnaise
2 T. parsley
1½ c. diced celery
¼ c. grated cheese

Mix and serve cold as a salad or place in baking dish, heat slowly and serve as a casserole.

Rachel Brewster, Petrolia H. S.
Petrolia, Texas

ASPARAGUS AND EGG BAKE
Number of Servings — 4-6

2 T. butter
2 T. flour
¼ t. salt
¼ t. pepper
2 c. cooked asparagus cuts
1⅔ c. milk
3 sliced hard-cooked eggs
8 thin slices cheese
¼ c. chopped toasted almonds

(Continued on Next Page)

Melt butter in saucepan over medium heat. Add flour, salt and pepper; mix till smooth. Gradually add milk; stir until thick and smooth. Arrange half of asparagus, eggs, cheese and almonds in alternate layers in buttered 1-quart casserole. Repeat layers, pour sauce over mixture. Garnish with almonds and grated cheese if desired. Bake at 350°F. for about 20 minutes.

Mrs. Lucille Marker, Robertsdale H. S.
Robertsdale, Alabama

BACON 'N EGG LUNCHEON PIE
Number of Servings — 5

1 9-inch pie shell
16 slices bacon, cooked and drained
5 eggs, beaten
¼ t. pepper
1 t. salt
2½ c. light cream
1 c. Swiss cheese, diced
1 c. frozen peas

Crumble bacon into pie shell. Beat eggs, cream, salt and pepper together. Mix in Swiss cheese and frozen peas. Pour into pie shell. Bake in preheated oven at 375°F. for 40 minutes.

Bernice Bammann, Beecher H. S.
Beecher, Illinois

BAR B Q BAKED BEANS

1 large can pork and beans
2 T. brown sugar
1 T. prepared mustard
¼ bottle catsup
1 large onion
1 c. bar-b-q sauce
1 bell pepper
1 c. bar-b-q meat (which has previously been prepared). Chop this meat. Season lightly with salt and pepper.

Put all ingredients in a deep baking dish, cover and bake at 375°F. for 1½ to 2 hours.

Mrs. Vivian J. Ryland, Lefargue H. S.
Effie, Louisiana

BAKED BEANS
Number of Servings — 10

1 lb. dried navy beans
3 T. chopped onions
3 T. molasses
2 T. brown sugar
¼ t. dry mustard
¼ lb. bacon, cubed
½ c. catsup
1 t. vinegar

Cook dried beans until slightly tender. Season with salt. Add the other above ingredients. Bake in a 2½ to 3 quart casserole in a 325°F. oven for 2½ hours.

Mrs. Pauline M. Wattner, Seagoville H. S.
Seagoville, Texas

BOSTON BAKED BEANS
Number of Servings — 12-15

4 c. navy beans
8 c. water
2 t. salt
⅓ c. molasses
⅔ c. brown sugar
2 t. dry mustard
1 c. catsup
½ lb. salt pork (cut in cubes)
2 medium onions

Wash and soak beans in hot water 1 or more hours. Drain and place in a deep well cooker. Combine water and seasonings; pour over beans; add onions and salt pork. Cover and turn deep well unit to low heat. Cook 8 hours or overnight. Add extra water if needed. If you do not have a deep well cooker, use a bean pot or roaster and cook in oven. Be sure to cook long and slowly.

Ruby C. Irvine, Coalton H. S.
Coalton, West Virginia

CAN CAN BAKED BEANS
Number of Servings — 6-8

3 1-lb. cans baked beans (6 cups)
1 8-oz. can seasoned tomato sauce
1 c. chopped onion
¼ c. brown sugar
½ c. catsup
2 T. prepared mustard
½ t. salt
4 drops tabasco sauce
6 strips bacon (Canadian style)

Combine in 2 quart casserole, beans, tomato sauce, onion, brown sugar, catsup and seasoning. Bury bacon in the beans. Bake uncovered in slow oven (300°F.) 3½ to 4 hours. Near the end of the baking period, fork the bacon to the top.

Beverly M. Anderson, South H. S.
Bakersfield, California

HOME BAKED BEANS
Number of Servings — 8

2 c. navy beans
¼ lb. fat salt pork, sliced
½ t. salt
¼ c. brown sugar
½ t. dry mustard
2 T. molasses
1 small onion, quartered

Wash beans, cover with water and soak overnight. Cook slowly until skins burst or until just tender. Drain, reserving liquor. Place half the beans in bean pot or casserole. Bury part of pork in beans and add half of combine remaining ingredients. Add remaining beans and seasonings. Place remaining salt pork over top. Cover with bean liquor. Cover and bake in slow oven (250°-300° F.) 6 to 8 hours, if necessary add more liquid.

Jessie H. Reynolds, Checotah H. S.
Checotah, Oklahoma

"DOCTORED UP" BEANS
Number of Servings — 8

4 strips bacon
1 large onion, minced
2 large size (2½ or 3) cans baked beans (with pork)
1 t. prepared mustard
¼ c. chili sauce
½ c. brown sugar
1 "drizzle" of molasses

Saute bacon until crisp and onion is yellow. Stir in beans, mustard, chili sauce, brown sugar and molasses. Pour into greased 3 quart baking dish. Bake uncovered in 300°F. oven for 2 to 3 hours or until beans are brown and bubbly. Serve hot.

Mrs. Janice M. Kennedy, Troy Comm. Joint H. S.
Troy, Pennsylvania

SAVORY BAKED BEANS
Number of Servings — 8 large

1 large can (28 ozs.) pork and beans
4 T. brown sugar
½ c. catsup
4 slices bacon
1 very small onion
½ t. dry mustard

Combine ingredients. Bake covered in a casserole in a moderate oven with casserole covered with a lid 20 minutes at 400°F. Reduce temperature to 350°F. and continue baking until done.

Florence O. Wood, Fairmount H. S.
Fairmount, Indiana

Dressings, Fillings & Stuffings

DRESSING FOR 12-14 POUND TURKEY
Number of Servings — 16

1¾ loaf bread (3 qts.) cubed
1½ t. poultry seasoning
1 T. salt
¾ t. pepper
1 large onion
1½ c. celery, diced
1½ c. pecan pieces
2-3 eggs
1½ c. melted butter
1 c. giblet stock, to moisten

Bread for dressing should be at least 1 day old. Combine ingredients. I like this baked separate. Makes crisp dressing.

Marjorie Scott, Bethany H. S.
Bethany, Illinois

TOASTED RICE TURKEY DRESSING
Makes 12 cups or enough for 12 to 15 pound bird

2 c. uncooked converted rice
2 c. chopped onion
2 c. chopped celery
2 c. chopped green pepper
2 t. salt
10 chicken bouillon cubes, dissolved in 5 sups boiling water (or use 5 cups stock, if on hand)
2 eggs, well beaten
1 T. poultry seasoning
½ c. minced parsley or celery tops
If desired, 1 cup mushrooms or toasted almonds, chopped pecans, diced crisp bacon, or chopped hard cooked eggs.

Spread uncooked rice in shallow pan. Toast in moderate oven (350°F.) for 15 or 20 minutes or until kernels are golden brown. Stir occasionally for even browning. Place onion, celery, green pepper, and salt in bouillon or stock. Bring to boil. Stir in toasted rice. Turn heat on low and cover. Cook about 25 minutes or until liquid is absorbed and rice tender. Remove from heat. Fold in eggs, poultry seasoning, and minced parsley or celery tops. Add mushrooms or other special ingredients desired. Taste and add more seasoning if needed.

Mrs. Jennette F. Buhler, Oakley H. S.
Oakley, Idaho

HERB STUFFING FOR TURKEY, CHICKEN OR BEEF STEAK
Makes enough stuffing for one 10 pound turkey

6 qts. stale bread bits (torn rather than cut)
2 eggs
1 T. salt
1½ t. pepper
¼ c. minced celery
2 T. minced parsley (fresh or frozen)
2 T. dried basil leaves or ¾ t. powdered basil
1 T. dried sage leaves or ½ t. rubbed sage
¼ c. minced onion
Enough giblet broth or milk to moisten

Tear bread into bits. Chop parsley, celery and onion; add to bread. Put salt, pepper, basil leaves, sage leaves in a mortar and grind with a pestle; add to bread. Toss lightly until seasonings is well mixed with the bread. Add egg and enough broth or milk to moisten the bread so it will cling together. Press the stuffing gently into the chicken or turkey which has been rubbed with the same herb mixture used to season the stuffing. Place stuffing on ½ of a piece of round steak, cover with second half. Bake in covered pan 325°F.

Ora Goodrich, Coudersport Area Schools
Coudersport, Pennsylvania

SAVORY STUFFING
Number of Servings — 6

½ c. butter
½ c. diced celery
½ c. minced onion
4 c. bread (day-old), cubed
1 package poultry stuffing
1 t. sage
Giblets
Salt and pepper to taste

Melt 4 tablespoons butter. Saute onion and add celery. Cook until clear. Add bread and stir to prevent excessive browning. Cook giblets in enough water to cover. Chop very fine. Add to bread mixture with rest of ingredients. Use water remaining from giblets to moisten. Stir lightly. Add more boiling water until desired consistency is reached. Pack into buttered casserole and top with bits of butter, remaining ¼ cup.

Mary A. Damasevitz, Union H. S.
Union, New Jersey

RICE DRESSING
Number of Servings — 8

2 c. cooked rice
1 stalk celery, chopped
Margarine
½ t. salt
½ t. poultry seasoning
½ t. curry powder
1 can cream of mushroom soup
Turkey or chicken (giblet) broth, chopped
    giblets (optional)

Cook enough rice to make 2 cups. Saute chopped celery in small amount of margarine. Add rest of ingredients. Add enough broth to make the mixture moist. Place in a casserole or around the bird. Bake for 1 hour at 325°F. Sprinkle with paprika.

Veva Ramsey N. Gallatin Comm. Unit
Ridgway, Illinois

DEEP SOUTH RICE DRESSING
Number of Servings — 6-8

4 T. cooking oil
¾ c. celery, minced fine
1 onion, minced fine
½ c. green pepper, chopped
1 lb. ground meat
1½ c. water
2½ c. cooked rice
1½ t. salt
¼ t. red pepper
¼ t. poultry seasoning
2 T. minced onion tops
2 T. minced parsley
1 clove garlic, minced

Saute onion, garlic, and celery slowly in oil until limp, then add ground meat. Cook until slighty brown. Add bell pepper, salt, red pepper, poultry seasoning, onion tops and parsley. Add water. Cook slowly for 30 minutes. Add rice; mix well. 1 eggplant (chopped) may be added after browning meat, for eggplant dressing. This dressing may

be used for stuffing bell peppers, tomatoes, cabbage or baked chicken.

Mrs. Iris H. Mier, Rayne H. S.
Rayne, Louisiana

PENNSYLVANIA DUTCH FILLING
(Use as accompaniment to Meat or Poultry)
Number of Servings — 6

6 medium potatoes
2 T. butter, melted
1 medium size onion, chopped
½ c. diced celery
3 slices bread, cubed
1½ c. warm milk
2 t. salt
⅛ t. pepper
2 T. minced parsley
¼ t. saffron (if desired)
2 eggs, well beaten

Pare potatoes and boil in water until soft. Meanwhile, saute onion, celery, and bread cubes in melted butter. Drain potatoes and mash them. Add onion, celery, bread cubes, warm milk, and seasonings. Beat well. Add eggs and blend well. Turn into a greased casserole and bake 1 hour at 350°F.

Lucy M. Bamberger, Schaefferstown H. S.
Schaefferstown, Pennsylvania

FARM-STYLE CHICKEN STUFFING
Makes enough stuffing for 3-4 pound chicken

Combine 2 cups biscuit or bread crumbs and 2 cups cornbread crumbs. Add ¼ cup chopped onion, ½ cup diced celery, ½ teaspoon salt, ¼ teaspoon black pepper, ⅛ teaspoon sage (or more, if desired), and 4 tablespoons butter, diced. Add 1 slightly beaten egg and mix lightly. Pack tightly into the cavity of the chicken.

Mrs. Dorothy W. Burd, Oldham County H. S.
LaGrange, Kentucky

SAUSAGE DRESSING
Number of Servings — 8

2 c. dry bread crumbs
1 c. cornbread crumbs
½ c. fine sausage meat
1 T. chopped parsley
1 T. chopped onion
1 T. chopped celery
¼ c. butter
1 t. salt
½ t. pepper
Few grains nutmeg
2 eggs, beaten

Soak the bread in cold water until soft; press out all the water; add the sausage meat, seasonings, melted butter and well beaten eggs. If the sausage meat is quite fat, the butter may be omitted.

Mrs. Fern Ruck, Rangely H. S.
Rangely, Colorado

APPLE AND ONION — DUCK STUFFING
Number of Servings — 8

6 medium sized apples
¼ c. spearmint
6 small onions
Salt and pepper to season

Prepare a 4-6 pound duck for roasting. Stuff with the following: core and quarter 6 medium sized apples; quarter 6 small onions; sprinkle ¼ cup of spearmint over the apples and onions. Season with salt and pepper. Place any excess stuffing in the pan around the duck. Sprinkle duck with salt and pepper. Place breast side up on rack in an open roasting pan. Roast 325°F. until tender. Allow 20 minutes per pound. Drain off excess fat. Use brown residue and a small amount of fat to make gravy.

Carol M. Oberle, Silver Lake H. S.
Silver Lake, Kansas

CORN STUFFING (FOR CROWN ROAST OF PORK)
Number of Servings — 10-12

1 lb. can (2 c.) cream style corn
1 12-oz. can (1½ c.) whole kernel corn, drained
1 beaten egg
1 c. soft bread crumbs
¼ c. chopped onion
¼ c. chopped green pepper
2 T. chopped pimento
1½ t. salt

Combine all ingredients. Fill center of Crown Roast of Pork about 1 hour before meat is done.

Evelyn B. Willey, Gatesville H. S.
Gatesville, North Carolina

RICE AND OLIVE STUFFING
Number of Servings — 4-6

3 T. butter
1 c. diced celery
½ c. minced onion
1 c. cooked rice
½ c. chopped, stuffed olives
¼ t. salt
¼ t. pepper
¼ t. sage
¼ t. thyme

Melt butter in skillet; add celery, onion and saute until tender, about 3-5 minutes. Add rice, chopped olives, and seasonings. Toss together to mix. Use to stuff a whole fish or between halibut steaks, then bake.

Bertha C. Stefan, Prophetstown H. S.
Prophetstown, Illinois

SOUTHERN CORNBREAD DRESSING
Number of Servings — 6

1 8-inch pan buttermilk cornbread
3 sticks chopped celery
⅛ c. chopped bell pepper
¼ c. chopped onions, in cornbread

½ c. almond halves
⅛ t. poultry dressing
½ t. salt
½ t. pepper

Crumble cornbread cooked with buttermilk and chopped onions. Add celery, poultry dressing, almond halves, and bell pepper. Mix together thoroughly. Add 1 cup milk. Keep adding remaining milk while baking at 325°F. Bake until browned and solid.

Lila Lee Nosser, Mineral County H. S.
Hawthorne, Nevada

SOUTHERN SPOON BREAD
(So tender it has to be served with a spoon)
Number of Servings — 6

1 c. cornmeal
2 T. all-purpose flour
1 t. salt
2½ c. milk
2 T. melted shortening (butter or margarine)
2 eggs
2 t. baking powder

Combine cornmeal, flour and salt in a large bowl. Scald milk; stir slowly into cornmeal mixture. Beat well to prevent lumping. Add butter or margarine and eggs; beat until smooth. Sprinkle baking powder over surface; beat in quickly. Pour into greased 1½ quart casserole. Bake in 350°F. oven 30 to 35 minutes. Serve at once. (221 calories per serving).

Mrs. Chelsea A. Merritt, Tollesboro H. S.
Tollesboro, Kentucky

Garnishes and Accompaniments

LIME-PINEAPPLE SALAD
Number of Servings — 10-12

1 can crushed pineapple (approx. 2 cups)
1 package lime gelatin
1 T. lemon juice (optional)
1 c. whipping cream
1 c. American cheese, grated
½ c. chopped pecans (optional)

Empty entire can of pineapple into saucepan and bring to boiling point. Stir well so entire amount is hot. Add package of lime gelatin and remove from heat. Stir until dissolved. Lemon juice may be added if desired. Pour into bowl and let chill in refrigerator until partially set. Fold in 1 cup of cream which has been whipped and 1 cup of grated cheese. Pecans may be added. Pour into serving bowl and let chill in refrigerator several hours or overnight.

Mrs. Doris Hutchison, Burkburnett H. S.
Burkburnett, Texas

APRICOT BREAD
(Tart bread for use with ham and other pork)

Soak for 30 minutes in warm water to cover 1 cup dried apricots. Drain and cut with scissors (in eights). Mix together 1 cup sugar, 2 tablespoons soft butter and 1 egg. Stir in ¼ cup water and ½ cup orange juice. Sift together and stir in 2 cups sifted flour, 2 teaspoons baking powder, ¼ teaspoon soda and 1 teaspoon salt. Blend in ½ cup chopped nuts and cut up apricots. Pour into greased pan and let stand 20 minutes. Bake 55 to 65 minutes at 350°F. Fills 2 pans 7½ x 3½ x 2½ inches or 3 number 2 cans if you want round shape.

R. K. Geiger,
Ligonier, Indiana

MUSTARD RELISH
Number of Servings 3 Pints

1 pt. onions, chopped
1 pt. cabbage, chopped
1 pt. green tomatoes, chopped
1 pt. cucumbers, chopped
2 hot peppers, chopped
3 sweet peppers, chopped
½ c. pickling salt
6 c. boiling water
¼ c. dry mustard
¼ c. flour
1 c. sugar
½ T. tumeric
1 T. celery seed
½ T. white mustard seed
1 pt. vinegar

Combine vegetables and salt; cover with boiling water and let stand overnight. Place in cloth bag and squeeze dry. Make a dressing of remaining ingredients; heat to boiling; add vegetables; boil until thick, stirring constantly to prevent scorching. Seal in sterile jars while hot. Note: Delicious on hamburgers and hot dogs.

Mrs. Dimple W. Williams, Independence H. S.
Independence, Mississippi

RAW CRANBERRY RELISH
Number of Servings — 12

1 qt. cranberries
1 apple
2 pears
2½ c. sugar
2 oranges

Put cranberries, apple, pears, and oranges through the food chopper, peelings included. Add the sugar and allow to set for 3 hours. This relish is delicious with chicken or turkey. (This recipe can be used for jellied cranberry salad with the addition of ½ cup of chopped celery and one recipe of strawberry flavored gelatin. 2 cups of the relish should then be added to the gelatin and celery, when cool.

Lena W. Hollifield, Drexel H. S.
Drexel, North Carolina

YORKSHIRE PUDDING WITH ROAST BEEF
Number of Servings — 6

3-4 lb. roast beef or 1 lb. pork sausage links
1 c. flour
1 t. salt
1 c. milk
3 well beaten eggs

Sift flour and salt. Mix milk and eggs. Add to dry ingredients. Beat until smooth. ½ hour before serving, pour ¼ cup drippings in 8-in. square pan. Add Yorkshire; bake 30 minutes at 400°F. Pudding may be poured around the roast beef. Save some drippings for gravy. Cooked sausage may be added to the pudding and baked in the pudding.

Mrs. Glays Severance, Huron Jr. H. S.
Huron, South Dakota

GRITS (A LA SOUTHERN COOKIN')

One-half cup grits, washed in clear water twice. Add to boiling 2½ cups water in which has been placed 1 teaspoon salt. Boil 2 to 3 minutes. (Place in top of double-boiler and cook until done). If remains over direct heat, stir often. Eat with butter or milk.

Mrs. Marolyn K. Whitehead
Miami, Florida

SNAPPY COCKTAIL SAUCE
Number of Servings — 1⅓ cups

½ c. catsup
¼ c. finely chopped celery
½ T. finely chopped onion
2 T. prepared horseradish
¼ c. lemon juice
⅛ t. tabasco sauce

Combine all ingredients and chill. Serve with chilled cooked shrimp or cooked flaked fish.

Mrs. Robert Sampson, Sulphur Springs H. S.
Jonesboro, Tennessee

HUSH-PUPPY
(Accompaniment for Seafoods)
Number of Servings — 4

1 c. cornmeal
½ c. flour (all-purpose)
1½ t. baking powder
1 t. garlic salt
½ t. salt
1 egg
1 c. milk

Sift meal, flour, baking powder, salt and garlic salt together in bowl. Beat egg, add egg and milk to meal mixture and stir until well mixed. Let stand for 5 minutes, add more milk if needed. (Mixture should be thin enough to drop from spoon.) Drop by small spoonfuls in hot corn oil (375°F.). Fry until golden brown. Drain on paper towels.

Margaret Hefner Peden, Hoke County H. S.
Raeford, North Carolina

TUNA DIP
Number of Servings — 8

2 T. butter
2 T. flour
½ t. salt
½ t. dry mustard
¾ c. milk
1 8-oz. jar cheeze-whiz
1 can flaked tuna
3 T. chopped pimento
3 T. chopped fresh parsley
Assorted crackers

Melt margarine, add flour, salt and dry mustard; stir until blended. Add milk and cook over medium flame, stirring constantly, until thickened. Add cheese and tuna; mix well. Add pimento and chopped parsley; mix lightly. Serve hot or cold with crackers.

Mrs. Dwaine Underwood, Bramon H. S.
Bramon, Oklahoma

TARTAR SAUCE

1 c. mayonnaise
1 t. onion, scraped
1 T. dill pickle, minced
1 t. parsley, chopped
1 t. pimento, chopped

Combine the ingredients. Permit to stand in the refrigerator in covered container long enough for the flavors to mingle. Serve with fish or other seafood.

Mrs. Marolyn K. Whitehead
Miami, Florida

Sauces and Gravies

BAR B Q SAUCE
Number of Servings — 3 cups

¼ c. chopped onion
¼ c. chopped celery
2 T. shortening
½ t. paprika
Salt
Juice ½ lemon
¼ c. brown sugar
¼ c. vinegar
1 green pepper, chopped
12 ozs. chili sauce
1 T. Worcestershire sauce
Few dashes tabasco
¼ c. water
1 T. dry mustard

Saute onions and celery in fat. Add rest of ingredients in order indicated. Simmer 30 minutes. Especially good on thinly sliced roasted beef.

Nadine Simmons, Riverview Com. H. S.
Riverview, Michigan

BARBECUE SAUCE

1 c. strong black coffee
2 c. Worcestershire sauce
1 c. tomato catsup
¼ lb. butter
2 T. black pepper
1 T. sugar
1 T. salt

Combine. Simmer over slow flame 30 minutes; stirring to mix thoroughly. This is a "sopping sauce" so brush on the meat or chicken.

Billye Hartman, Princeton H. S.
Princeton, Texas

BARBECUE SAUCE

1 c. catsup
1 t. salt
1 t. celery seed
¼ c. brown sugar
¼ c. Worcestershire sauce
2 c. water
1 onion, chopped
¼ c. vinegar

Boil ingredients together 15 minutes. Pour over browned chicken, pork chops, or parboiled spare-ribs. Put in oven until meat is tender—about 1 hour—300°-325°F.

Louise Green, Cedar Bluff H. S.
Cedar Bluff, Alabama

BARBECUE SAUCE
Number of Servings — Approximately 1 cup

4 t. catsup
2 t. butter
2 t. Worcestershire sauce
4 t. water
4 t. vinegar
½ t. red pepper
1 t. prepared mustard
1 t. paprika
1 t. chili powder

Melt butter. Add all remaining ingredients slowly and heat over low flame for 15 minutes.

Mrs. Jane L. Jones, Summerville H. S.
Summerville, South Carolina

BARBECUE SAUCE
Number of Servings — 6

3 T. margarine or bacon drippings
1 medium onion, chopped
2 T. vinegar
1 c. catsup
3 T. Worcestershire sauce
1 T. prepared mustard
1 c. water
⅛ t. salt
Dash of pepper
½ c. chopped celery (optional)
2 or 3 dashes tabasco sauce (optional)

Melt fat in saucepan, add onion and brown lightly.

(Continued on Next Page)

Add remaining ingredients and cook slowly until flavors are blended (about 15 minutes). Use over browned hamburger meat, pork, lamb, beef, veal or however else desired. Unused sauce may be stored in the refrigerator.

Mrs. Cynthia S. Picha, Wheaton H. S.
Wheaton, Maryland

BAR-B-CUE SAUCE

1 c. catsup
⅓ c. Worcestershire sauce
2 t. chili powder
2 t. salt
2 T. lemon juice
1 T. brown sugar
¼ c. chopped onion
2 cloves garlic
2 c. water

Combine ingredients and bring to boiling point. This sauce may be used for outdoor and indoor meat cookery. Examples: Chicken, spareribs, meat loaf, etc.

Barbara Grover, Whitehall H. S.
Whitehall, Wisconsin

TEXAS BARBECUE SAUCE
Number of Servings — 5

2 T. brown sugar
1 T. paprika
1 t. salt
1 t. dry mustard
¼ t. chili powder
⅛ t. cayenne pepper
2 T. Worcestershire sauce
¼ c. vinegar
½ c. water
1 c. tomato juice
¼ c. catsup

Mix ingredients in a saucepan. Simmer 15 minutes or until slightly thickened.

Mrs. Joyce Boatwright, Ervinton H. S.
Nora, Virginia

TEXAS BARBECUE SAUCE
Number of Servings — Makes 2½ cups

1 small onion, minced
1 clove garlic, minced
½ c. margarine
1½ t. dry mustard
2 T. chili powder
1 c. catsup
½ c. vinegar or lemon juice
½ c. water
1 T. sugar
1 T. Worcestershire sauce

Saute the onion and garlic in the ½ cup butter. Add the remaining ingredients. Simmer for 5 minutes or until thick. This sauce is very good in making oven barbecue from roast beef.

Mrs. Marshall J. King, Gatesville H. S.
Gatesville, Texas

TEXAS BARBECUE SAUCE
Number of Servings — 5

½ c. finely chopped onion
2 T. brown sugar
1 T. paprika
1 t. salt
¼ c. catsup
½ c. water
1 t. dry mustard
¼ t. chili powder
⅛ t. cayenne powder
2 T. Worcestershire sauce
¼ c. vinegar
1 c. tomato sauce

Mix together and simmer 15 minutes. The amount is sufficient for 3 pounds ribs cut in chunks and browned.

Eleanor Tedford, Wiggins H. S.
Wiggins, Colorado

SAUCE FOR BARBECUED CHUCK ROAST
Number of Servings — 8

4-5 lb. chuck roast
Barbecue Sauce:
½ envelope (3 T.) onion soup mix
2 T. sugar
½ t. salt
Dash of pepper
1 T. prepared mustard
¾ c. water
½ c. catsup
¼ c. vinegar
1 T. lemon juice

Sprinkle roast with meat tenderizer, let stand at least 1 hour. Combine all ingredients. Bring to boiling; reduce heat and simmer uncovered 10 minutes, stirring occasionally. Baste chuck roast frequently after chuck is placed on spit, on outdoor barbecue.

Eunice S. Marshall, Spaulding H. S.
Barre, Vermont

SAUCE FOR BARBECUED HAM STEAKS
Number of Servings — 10

5 lbs. sliced tenderized ham, ¾ inch thick or Bar-S ¾ inches thick

Sauce:
1 c. brown sugar
½ c. cider vinegar
2-3 whole cloves
2 T. prepared mustard
1 c. pineapple juice

Simmer together the ingredients of the sauce for 5 minutes. Marinate the ham slices for 30 minutes. Grill over low charcoal fire for 6 to 8 minutes, turn, brush with more sauce, grill another 6 to 8 minutes. Serve hot.

Mrs. John Robson, Flora H. S.
Flora, Louisiana

HAMBURGER SAUCE FOR HOT DOGS, HAMBURGERS (OR ON VEGETABLES)

1 lb. ground beef
½ c. water
½ c. vinegar
1 bottle catsup, regular or hot
1 t. prepared mustard
2 T. sugar
1 t. salt
Pepper, hot sauce, chopped onion, bell pepper or chili (if desired)

Simmer ground meat, water and vinegar for 30 minutes. Add remaining ingredients and cook on low heat for 30 minutes. Serve hot on hot dogs, hamburger, hamburger buns, or over green beans.

Mrs. Nella Watson, Grays H. S.
Early Branch, South Carolina

MEAT LOAF TOPPING

Number of Servings — 1 Meat Loaf 3 x 5 x 8

3 T. brown sugar
¼ c. catsup
¼ t. nutmeg
1 t. dry mustard

Combine and spread over top of meat loaf before baking.

Mrs. Mary K. Erickson, Braham H. S.
Braham, Minnesota

ORANGE SAUCE FOR PORK CHOPS

Number of Servings — 6

5 T. sugar
1½ t. cornstarch
¼ t. salt
¼ t. cinnamon
10 whole cloves
2 t. grated orange rind
½ c. orange juice
4 halved orange slices

Cook sugar, cornstarch, salt, cinnamon, cloves, orange rind and juice (first 7 ingredients), while stirring constantly, until thickened and clear. Add orange slices, cover pan and remove from heat. Pour over pork chops just before serving.

Mrs. Ruth M. Carpenter, Hopkins Academy
Hadley, Massachusetts

MUSTARD SAUCE

Number of Servings — 8-10

¼ c. brown sugar
2 T. prepared mustard
2 T. vinegar
Dash of horseradish (if desired)

Mix together thoroughly ½ hour before serving. Serve with pork roast or baked ham.

June Hastings, Kittitas H. S.
Kittitas, Washington

MUSTARD SAUCE

Number of Servings — 2 slices center cut ham

⅓ c. brown mustard
⅓ c. cola

Stir mustard and beverage until smooth, spoon onto cured ham slices that have been scored and prepared for broiling. When brown turn ham slices, spoon on sauce and brown. Serve while hot.

Glenda Sue Smith, Sardis H. S.
Boaz, Alabama

MEAT SAUCE FOR MEAT BALLS

Number of Servings — 6-8

½ lb. ground beef
1 small onion, chopped
1 bud garlic
1 can (4-oz.) mushroom pieces
½ green pepper, chopped
1 can (8-oz.) tomato paste
1 can tomatoes
2 t. salt
½ t. pepper
1 T. chopped parsley
⅛ t. basil
⅛ t. oregano
2 c. water

Combine ingredients. Cover and simmer 1 to 1½ hours, with your favorite meat balls. This sauce can be frozen for future use.

Esther L. Moorhead, Chattanooga H. S.
Chattanooga, Oklahoma

SPAGHETTI SAUCE

Number of Servings — 4-6

2 cloves garlic
1 T. butter
½ lb. hamburger
1 can tomato sauce
1 can tomato paste
1 or 2 ripe tomatoes
¼ t. or so oregano
Rosemary
Bay leaf
Salt and pepper
¼-⅛ cup grated cheese
Mushrooms, desired amount

Saute garlic in butter until light brown. Add hamburger and cook until red color disappears. Add tomato sauce, tomato paste and tomatoes. Let simmer about 10 minutes. Crush herbs by rolling between palms of hands. Add seasonings and cheese. Simmer about 5 minutes. Add enough water to thin the sauce. Cook slowly on low heat 2 to 3 hours. Before serving, heat mushrooms with sauce about 10 minutes. Pour over hot cooked spaghetti, sprinkle with grated cheese.

Mary Jane Niboli, Tranquillity Union H. S.
Tranquillity, California

MEAT SAUCE FOR SPAGHETTI
Number of Servings — 6 generous

2 T. fat
¼ c. finely chopped onion
2 T. chopped green pepper
1½ lbs. lean ground beef
1 t. garlic salt
2 t. chili powder, or more
Salt and pepper
1 can (8-oz.) tomato sauce
1 can (8-oz.) water

Saute onions and green peppers until tender (onions will be transparent). Add ground beef and cook until well browned and crisp. Add garlic salt, chili powder, salt and pepper. Combine tomato sauce plus 1 can of water with meat mixture. Simmer 20 minutes. Serve over spaghetti and top with grated cheese.

Sonnie Hallerman, Milan Local H. S.
Milan, Ohio

SPAGHETTI SAUCE OR PIZZA SAUCE
Number of Servings — 6-8

1 lb. hot sausage
2 cans (8-oz.) tomato sauce
1 can (7-oz.) tomato paste
1 can (2-lb., 3-ozs.) plumb tomatoes
1 small onion, diced
2-5 whole garlic cloves
1 crumbled bay leaf
½ t. oregano (heaping)
3 t. sugar
Dash salt and pepper
Few Italian herbs (optional)

Brown sausage; strain plum tomatoes and add to sausage together with pulp left in the sieve. Add all other ingredients. Place in glass dish or bowl and allow to stand overnight. Simmer 6 to 8 hours with lid tilted.

Mrs. Helen M. Colony, Jewell H. S.
Jewell, Iowa

QUICK SPAGHETTI AND MEAT BALL SAUCE
Number of Servings — 4-6

1½ lbs. ground beef
1½ t. monosodium glutamate
1½ slices day old bread
Milk
Pepper to taste
1 package spaghetti sauce mix
1 can (No. 2) tomato juice
1 can tomato paste or sauce

Soak bread in small amount milk—drain excess liquid, add ground beef, monosodium glutamate and pepper; mix well. Form into 2 inch meat balls and brown in small amount cooking oil. Drain off all oil; add tomato juice, paste and spaghetti mix. Simmer in covered container 1 hour.

Helen Bolton, Bixby H. S.
Bixby, Oklahoma

GRAVY

BROWN or PAN GRAVY for roasts, panfried or broiled meat or poultry.
¼ c. pan fat
¼ c. flour
2 c. boiling water
¼ t. salt

Pour off all but ¼ cup of the pan fat. Put roaster, broiler or frying pan on stove over low heat. Add flour. Stir and blend until flour is brown—about 2 minutes. Add the boiling water slowly, stirring all the time. Bring mixture to the simmering point. Add salt. Cook 5 minutes.

GRAVY FOR STEWS AND POT ROASTS— made in the pan with the meat and vegetables.

Allow 1-2 tablespoons flour for every cup of liquid. Blend the flour with ½ cup cold water. Be sure the paste is very smooth. A fork works well for this, or shake together in covered jar. Stir the flour mixture slowly into the hot liquid stirring constantly. Simmer 5 minutes. Variations: Cook 1 slice onion with gravy. Add 1 tablespoon sour cream just before serving. This gives the gravy a golden color.

Frances Ford, West H. S.
Minneapolis, Minnesota

FOR ADDITIONAL RECIPES PERTAINING TO THIS SECTION, SEE BEEF, SEAFOOD, POULTRY AND FOREIGN DISH SECTIONS

Foreign Meat Dishes

Beef Foreign Meat Dishes

BEEF CHATEAUBRIAND
Number of Servings — 6

3 to 4 lbs. beef tenderloin (whole)
1½ t. salt
½ t. pepper
1 t. garlic salt
1 t. monosodium glutamate
1 package French salad dressing herbs (dry)
1 c. corn oil
½ c. wine vinegar

Strip membranes from outside of tenderloin. Rub tenderloin with salt, pepper, garlic salt, monosodium glutamate and salad herbs. Place in a shallow baking dish. Mix oil and vinegar, brush over tenderloin. Marinate meat from 4 to 6 hours, turning several times in marinate. Pour off marinate in small pan, place tenderloin under broiler to brown on both sides. Baste meat with marinate. When brown, insert meat thermometer and cook in oven (325°F.) until the desired temperature is reached. When served, slice about ¾ inch thick on the diagonal.

Mrs. Elizabeth F. Smith, Area Supervisor
Home and Family Life Education
Big Spring, Texas

BIEROCKS
Number of Servings — 4

½ lb. hamburger
1 onion, chopped
2 c. cabbage, shredded
2 T. butter
Salt to taste
Pepper to taste
Dash of monosodium glutamate
1 box hot roll mix

Brown onion and hamburger. Wilt cabbage in the butter. Add cabbage to hamburger mixture; salt and pepper to taste. Add monosodium glutamate. Cool. Roll dough in long roll about 2 inches in diameter. Cut and shape into balls; roll out very thin. Fill with meat mixture and pinch opposite sides together. Place upside down on greased cookie sheet. Bake in 350°F .oven.

Mrs. Phyllis Barton, Lee H. S.
Springfield, Virginia

BEUROC
Number of Servings — 8

1 lb. ground beef
¼ t. pepper
½ t. salt
3 c. cabbage
2 c. onion
1 package hot roll mix (or your favorite hot roll recipe)

Brown ground beef and chopped onions in skillet. Boil cabbage until tender; add to beef mixture and cook about 5 minutes. Let cool. Roll out dough. Cut in 9 inch squares; place 3 tablespoons of meat mixture in center. Fold corners together.

Place in warm place to rise. Bake until brown. Place folded side down. Top will look like hamburger bun.

Maurita Taylor, Claude H. S.
Claude, Texas

BEEF MEXICANA
Number of Servings — 4

1 large onion, sliced
2 T. fat
½ lb. ground beef
2 cans tomato sauce
1 can (No. 2) whole kernel corn, drained (2 c.)
¾ t. salt
⅛ t. pepper
Pinch of chili powder, if desired

Saute onion in hot fat until tender. Add beef and brown lightly, stirring to break it up. Add remaining ingredients; cover and let simmer 20 minutes. Serve on beds of hot rice.

Patricia Ann Champion, Chilton County H. S.
Clanton, Alabama

BEEF STROGANOFF (RUSSIAN)
Number of Servings — 6

3 lbs. sweet onions
2 lbs. sirloin steak
1 lb. mushrooms
1 c. butter
2 cans tomato sauce
1 c. sour cream
1 t. salt
Dash of pepper
1 t. Worcestershire sauce

Chop onions, cut meat in very thin slices; trim off excess fat. Slice mushrooms and brown with meat in butter. Add onions; remove from heat. Combine tomato sauce, sour cream and seasonings; add to meat mixture. Cover and simmer for 1 hour.

Phyllis J. Hill, Paradise Valley H. S.
Phoenix, Arizona

CARACUS
Number of Servings — 6-8

1 T. butter
1 package dried beef
1 lb. cheese
1 T. chili powder
1 can (No. 2) tomatoes
1 T. Worcestershire sauce
3 eggs

Cook beef in butter until it curls up. Add tomatoes, chili powder, Worcestershire sauce and chipped cheese. Last add slightly beaten eggs and cook until well blended. Serve on hot water corn cakes.

Mildred Mason, Cherokee Vocational H. S.
Cherokee, Alabama

CAJUN CHOW MEIN
Number of Servings — 6-8

1 lb. ground beef
2 T. fat
1 c. chopped onion
1 c. chopped celery
1 c. diced bell pepper
1 can (4 oz.) mushrooms
1 can (No. 2) tomatoes
4 t. salt
½ t. pepper
1 c. raw rice
Few drops tabasco sauce

Brown ground beef in fat. Add remaining ingredients. Cover and bring to boil. Reduce flame to simmer. Cook 30 to 40 minutes.

Mrs. Myrtle D. Deranger, Sunset H. S.
Sunset, Louisiana

DUTCH OVEN ROAST
Number of Servings — 4-6

3-4 lbs. top round beef
2 T. cooking oil
4 medium onions
4 medium carrots
4 medium potatoes
2 celery stalks
½ c. tomato puree
½ c. red wine
4 c. water or soup stock

Brown beef in Dutch oven in cooking oil. Pour in tomato puree, wine and stock. Cook slowly 1½ hours. Add onions, celery, carrots and potatoes. Continue cooking ½ hour.

Dorothy Maltby, Hanover-Horton H. S.
Horton, Michigan

EMPANDAS (MEAT PIES)
Number of Servings — 20 pies

1 c. cooked beef, seasoned
1 hard-boiled egg
1 thin slice onion
2 green olives
2 T. seedless raisins
2 T. tomato

Make your favorite pie dough, roll thin, cut in 4-inch squares or circles. Place a teaspoon of filling on each piece of dough, fold dough diagonally and press together with the tines of a fork. Bake on a cookie sheet at 400°F. until delicately browned, about 10 minutes. The proportions for the filling and a recipe for a covered 9-inch pie should make 20 empandas. Empandas may also be filled with canned salmon, tuna, diced cooked chicken or hamburger fried with onion and seasoned with a sprinkling of chili powder, salt and pepper.

Elsie Keller, Cordova H. S.
Cordova, Alaska

ENGLISH PASTY PIE
Number of Servings — 4

¾ lb. round steak, ½ inch thick
4 medium size potatoes
1 small onion
Salt and pepper
Pastry for 1 pie shell and top

Remove fat from round steak and cut in ¼ inch squares. Peel potatoes and wipe off any moisture. Place round steak squares in bottom of unbaked pie shell. Sprinkle with a little salt. Slice layers of raw potato on top of meat. Sice onions on top of potatoes. Season with salt and pepper. Cover with top shell and bake at 350°F. for 1 hour. This is not intended to be a wet meat pie. The Welsh people usually bake the meat in turnovers.

Mrs. Ruth B. Marsh, Penn Manor H. S.
Millersville, Pennsylvania

GARANCHES
Number of Servings — 6

One cup cornmeal and 1 teaspoon salt cooked in boiling water to make a mush. Cool slightly. Keeping the hands wet with cold water shape 6 cases 3 inches in diameter and ⅜ inch thick. Bake on a well-greased griddle. Turn only once and do not get too brown. Split cases, scoop out insides and fill. For filling combine ¾ cup ground cooked beef (left-overs as roast are very acceptable), 2 tablespoons chopped onion and 6 tablespoons chili sauce. Season to taste with salt and pepper. Fill cases, place lids on, heat again on griddle and serve with Parmesan cheese.

Rita Dickinson, Melrose H. S.
Melrose, New Mexico

ROAST BEEF — ITALIANO
Number of Servings — 6-8

4-5 lb. beef chuck roast
1 garlic bud
1 c. diced sweet green mango
1 c. diced onion
½ c. tomato catsup
1 T. horseradish
1 c. water
1 T. oregano
½ t. chili powder
⅛ t. marjoram
½ t. celery salt
½ t. salt
Dash of pepper

Roll beef chuck in flour. Brown in hot fat. Place in heavy roaster pan. Add all dry seasonings. Top roast with sliced garlic bud, diced onion, mango, horseradish and catsup, then add 1 cup of water around meat. Cover roaster. Place in 350°F. oven for 3 to 4 hours until very tender. Garnish with ripe olives, tomato wedges and parsley.

Mrs. Arthur Enoch, Shelby City H. S.
Shelby, Ohio

ITALIAN DINNER (A meal in one dish)
Number of Servings — 12

1 lb. ground beef
2 t. salt
½ t. pepper
½ t. paprika
1 can (No. 2) tomatoes
1 can (No. 2) cream style corn
1 medium size package egg noodles
¼ lb. grated cheese
1 large green pepper, chopped
1 large onion, chopped
3 T. salad oil

Fry the chopped green pepper and chopped onion until it begins to brown. Add the ground beef and cook until it loses it's red color. Add the noodles which have been cooked according to directions on the package, drained; add the tomatoes and corn; mix well and pour into a large roasting pan or pyrex baking dish and bake 1 hour in a moderate oven, 300°F. When ready to serve, sprinkle grated cheese over the top, if served in the baking dish, or if baked in a roaster, pour into a large platter, then sprinkle with grated cheese. Excellent for buffet service, or for a large group.

Mrs. Vada Belle Zellner
South San Antonio Sr. H. S.
San Antonio, Texas

JAMAICAN MEAT PATTIES
Number of Servings — 10 patties

3 T. salad oil
⅔ c. chopped onions
1 lb. ground lean beef
1 c. chopped fresh tomatoes
1½ t. salt
½ t. black pepper
¼ t. ground red pepper
1½ t. garlic powder
1½ t. powdered dry mustard
1 t. red hot sauce
2 eggs, slightly beaten
1 box pastry mix

Saute onions in hot salad oil. Add beef and cook until brown. Add tomatoes and seasonings and cook until tender. Remove from heat and stir in eggs. Cook until slightly thickened. Cool. Mix pastry as directed. Roll 1/16 inch thick. Cut into 6 inch circles, using saucer as a pattern. Spread one side of each with ½ cup meat mixture. Fold over remaining half of pastry. Crimp edges. Prick top with fork. Bake on ungreased cooky sheet in 425°F. oven for 20 minutes. Makes 10 patties.

Vesta Glessner, Shanksville-Stonycreek H. S.
Shanksville, Pennsylvania

KOEFTASI (Beef Balls in Tomato Sauce)
A dish from Turkey
Number of Servings — 6

2 slices dry white bread with crusts removed
1 lb. ground beef
½ t. salt
¼ t. pepper
3 T. fat
2½ c. tomato sauce (puree)
½ t. garlic salt

Crumble bread and combine with meat, salt and pepper. Form into 1½-inch balls and brown in fat. Place balls in shallow baking dish. Add garlic salt to tomato sauce and pour over meat balls. Cover. Bake for 5 minutes in a moderate oven (350°F.).

Shirley Ramseyer, Jefferson Township H. S.
Kempton, Indiana

KEEMA (India and Palestine)

1½ lbs. hamburger
¼ onion

Saute onions in large kettle; fry hamburger in saucepan. When hamburger is half browned, add ¼ cup water, ½ cup catsup, sprinkle of onion salt, garlic salt, turmeric, curry powder and lots of salt. After onions are browned add 3 cups of rice. Add 4 whole cloves to hamburger mixture. Add 4 bay leaves to rice. Add 1 can peas and juice to hamburger mixture. Add 1 quart or more water to rice mixture; boil; add water if it becomes thick. Simmer hamburger mixture with lid. When rice is ¾ done put it in heated oven 450°F., not more than an hour. Serve the hamburger mixture over the rice mixture. Be sure to take out the bay leaves before serving (or warn the guests).

Sharon Kinsey, Hot Springs County H. S.
Thermopolis, Wyoming

PURI (like bread) Indian Pancake

Melt 3 inches of fat in 1½ quart size sauce pan. Whole wheat flour and water to make a dough. Kned for 5 minutes; put in cylinder shape. Pull off balls the size of an egg. Roll out small rounds, dipping in flour about twice as you go. Roll from center to side with a rocking motion, until thin (⅛ to ¼ inch).Slap circle of dough from one hand to the next (on flat of fingers). Cook in deep fat pressing down with pancake turner. Turn over and press down under the fat until the center rises (air inside the shell). Place on absorbent paper. Tear of pieces of Puri to eat the Keema by holding the pieces of Puri in the fingers, pushing the Keema on to the Puri with the thumb.

Sharon Kinsey, Hot Springs County H. S.
Thermopolis, Wyoming

MACARONI BAKE FROM MEXICAN BORDER
Number of Servings — 16

8 ozs. macaroni
1 lb. ground, lean beef
¼ c. oil
1 c. chopped onion
1 c. chopped green pepper
1 clove garlic, minced
1 can (8 oz.) mushroom pieces
1 can (No. 2½) tomatoes

(Continued on Next Page)

1 can (No. 2) creamed corn
1 T. salt
1 t. Worcestershire sauce
¼ t. pepper
2 t. chili powder
1 can (tall) pitted olives

Heat oil in large heavy skillet or small roaster. Add ground beef and cook till partially browned. Stir in chopped onions, pepper and minced garlic. Add canned tomatoes, corn, pepper, chili powder and Worcestershire sauce. Turn down heat and cook slowly till vegetables are soft and brown. Break macaroni into mixture. Slice and add ripe olives. Mix thoroughly. Add can of mushroom pieces. Add water to keep moist. Turn into 2½ quart casserole and bake in oven for at least 1½ hours at 325°F. Take off cover last half hour.

Mrs. Elizabeth W. Knape, Douglas Sr. H. S.
Douglas, Arizona

MEXICAN MAIN DISH
Number of Servings — 8

2 T. shortening
½ lb. vermicelli, broken into small pieces, ¼-inch long
1 lb. beef, ground
3 garlic cloves, minced
2 onions, medium size, chopped
1 can (No. 2½) whole tomatoes, including juice
½ c. boiling water
1 green pepper, chopped
4 celery stalks, chopped
½ c. whole kernel corn, drained
1 T. salt
1-3 t. chili powder, as desired
1 t. black pepper
½ clb. sharp cheese, sliced

Preheat skillet to 325°F. Melt shortening and brown vermicelli to a medium color. Add meat and cook. Stir occasionally. Add remaining ingredients, except cheese, and press into liquid. Reduce temperature to 200°F. Cover with vent closed and cook 20 minutes. Place a layer of sharp cheese on top of meat mixture. Cover and continue cooking 5 minutes until cheese melts.

Mrs. Edith Marshall, Cambridge H. S.
Cambridge, Maryland

MALFOOF MAHSHI
(Stuffed Cabbage Leaves)
Number of Servings — 6

1 c. raw rice
½ lb. ground meat
½ c. butter
1 t. salt
½ t. pepper
½ t. cinnamon
1 small head cabbage
2 c. tomato juice

Cook rice until tender (30 minutes). Drain and add meat, butter and seasonings. Form into small rolls. Cook individual cabbage leaves in a small

amount of water until wilted (about 5 minutes). Wrap around meat rolls and place in heavy skillet. Add tomato juice, cover, and cook for 30 minutes. This recipe comes from Saudi Arabia.

Mrs. Carrie Hoffman, Hamilton H. S.
Hamilton, Texas

ITALIAN LASAGNE
Number of Servings — 4-6

¼ lb. lasagne
2 T. butter or margarine
½ c. finely chopped onion
1 clove garlic, chopped
½ lb. ground beef
¾ c. (6 oz. can) tomato paste
2½ c. (1 lb., 4 oz. can) tomatoes
1 t. salt
⅛ t. pepper
¼ t. dried basil, crumbled
¼ t. dried oregano, crumbled
½ lb. Ricatta or cottage cheese
½ lb. natural or process Swiss cheese, sliced
¼ c. grated Parmesan cheese

Cook lasagne in 4 quarts boiling, salted water until tender (about 15 minutes). Stir occasionally with wooden spoon while cooking. Drain and rinse with hot water. Separate lasagne and hang over edge of colander or pan to allow for easier handling later. While lasagne is cooking, melt butter or margarine in large skillet. Add onion and garlic and cook gently about 5 minutes. Add ground beef and cook slowly, stirring frequently, until all red color disappears from meat. Stir in tomato paste, tomatoes, salt and pepper, basil and oregno. Continue cooking, stirring occasionally, about 30 minutes. Grease on 8 inch square baking dish and in it make layers of meat sauce, lasagne and Ricatta, Swiss and Parmesan cheese, using about ⅓ of each. Repeat layers twice to use all ingredients, topping with the last of the Parmesan cheese. Bake in moderate oven (350°F.) until mixture is bubbly and cheese is lightly browned, about 35 to 40 minutes.

Mildred Williams, Austin H. S.
El Paso, Texas

ORIENTAL RICE
Number of Servings — 8

1½ lbs. round steak, cubed
1 c. diced celery
¼ c. onions (if preferred)
1 can cream of mushroom soup
1 can cream of chicken soup
1 c. rice
2 c. cold water
2 T. soy sauce

Salt and dredge in flour the cubed meat. Brown in very small quantity of shortening. Add celery and onions with soy sauce to the meat. Cook 5 minutes. Add to the meat mixture the soup, rice and water. Stir well. Pour into casserole. Bake 1 hour and 15 minutes at 350°F.

Ruth I. Schwarz, Galesburg Sr. H. S.
Galesburg, Illinois

ORIENTAL SUPPER
Number of Servings — 8-10

2 beaten eggs
½ c. water
1 c. flour
1 t. salt
1 t. ginger
¾ lb. lean round steak, 1 inch cubes
¾ lb. lean pork shoulder, 1 inch cubes
1 lb. 14 oz. can pineapple cubes
2 chicken bouillon cubes
½ c. brown sugar
¼ c. molasses
⅓ c. vinegar
⅓ c. cornstarch

Combine eggs, water, flour, salt and ginger to make a smooth batter. Dip meat in batter and brown. Drain. Drain syrup from pineapple and add water to make 2 cups; heat to boiling. Add bouillon cubes, brown sugar, molasses and vinegar. Stir in cornstarch smoothed to a paste with ¼ cup water. Cook, stirring constantly until sauce thickens. Arrange in sauce in skillet fried beef and pork, pineapple cubes, 2 cups sliced cooked carrots, 2 green peppers diced, 2 tomatoes cut in wedges, 1 can green beans drained. Cover, simmer 20 minutes. Serve on hot cooked rice.

Harriet R. Peck, Lakers H. S.
Pigeon, Michigan

MANZO ALLA PARMIGIANA
(Ground Beef Parmesan)
Number of Servings — 6

1½ lbs. ground beef
1 egg, well beaten
1 medium-size onion, chopped
1 t. salt
½ t. monosodium glutamate
⅛ t. pepper

Mix above ingredients together thoroughly. The method of cooking may be either baking or broiling. For broiling, shape meat mixture into a large square about inch thick. Cut into 6 equal portions. Arrange portions on a broiler rack. Set temperature control of range at broil. Place in boiler with top of meat 2 inches from heat source. Broil on first side 10 minutes, turn, and broil 5 minutes on other side. Then spread with a mixture of ¾ cup (6 ounce can) tomato paste, 1 tablespoon grated Parmesan cheese. Top portions with 6 slices (3 ounces) Mozarella cheese (1 slice per portion). Broil until cheese is lightly browned. For baking, follow the same general directions, placing meat in large baking pan. Bake 30 minutes at 350°F. Then spread with paste and cheese, and bake until cheese melts.

Mrs. Dorothy F. Bent, Whitcomb H. S.
Bethel, Vermont

DANISH MEAT LOAF
Number of Servings — 6

1 medium onion, chopped
¼ c. chopped green pepper
2 T. butter
½ c. chili sauce
2 T. water
1½ lbs. ground beef
¼ lb. sausage meat
½ t. salt
⅛ t. pepper
½ t. dry mustard
¼ t. sage
2 c. fine dry bread crumbs
1 c. milk
2 eggs, slightly beaten
¾ c. (4 ozs.) bland cheese, crumbled

Cook onion and green pepper in butter 5 minutes; add ¼ cup chili sauce and the water, and cook 3 minutes longer. Put this into a 9 x 5 x 3 inch loaf pan. Mix remaining ¼ cup chili sauce and all other ingredients. Press into pan on top of first mixture. Bake in moderate oven (375°F.), about 1½ hours. Turn out on platter.

Mrs. Mary Pinkston Whaley
Tuscaloosa County H. S.
Northport, Alabama

DUTCH MEAT LOAF
Number of Servings — 6

1 medium onion
3 slices bread
1 egg
1½ lbs. ground beef
1½ t. salt
¼ t. pepper
1 t. Worcestershire sauce
1 t. dry mustard
1 can (8 ozs.) tomato sauce
½ c. water
2 T. vinegar
1 T. dry mustard
2 T. brown sugar

Set oven at 350°F. Peel and chop onion fine. Pull bread into crumbs with a fork (makes about 1 cup crumbs). Beat egg until bubbly. Add onion, bread crumbs, egg, salt, pepper, Worcestershire sauce, 1 teaspoon dry mustard and ½ cup tomato sauce to the ground meat. Mix together lightly but thoroughly with a fork. Pack meat mixture lightly in a 9 x 5 x 3 inch loaf pan. Mix the remaining tomato sauce, water, vinegar, dry mustard and brown sugar together and pour over the meat loaf. Bake uncovered 1½ hours. Slice and serve.

Mrs. Kathryn Whitten, Hanford Union H. S.
Hanford, California

POLINESSIAN BEEF LIVER
Number of Servings — 4-6

1 lb. beef liver
1 c. soy sauce
3 small garlic cloves
4-6 bacon strips
½ c. chopped parsley
1 t. salt
½ c. shortening (use bacon drippings, if preferred)
½ c. flour

(Continued on Next Page)

Marinate liver with garlic cloves in soy sauce for 4-6 hours. Mix flour and salt; cover outside of liver with it. Fry liver in fat or drippings of bacon at medium temperature for 25 minutes; remove from skillet; garnish with parsley and bacon strips. Serve immediately.

Helen Henson, So. Kitsap H. S.
Port Orchard, Washington

RAVIOLI
Number of Servings — 11

½ lb. pork, ground
½ lb. beef, ground
1 can tomatoes
1 can tomato soup (optional)
1 clove garlic
1 onion
4 sticks celery
1 green pepper
1 package wide noodles

Brown onion in fat; mix in other vegetables and cook until celery is done. Fry meat; mix it in the vegetables. Cook noodles separately; mix in with the vegetables shortly before serving.

Madge L, Capel, Woden H. S.
Woden, Texas

ROLLADEN (German Beef Rolls)
Number of Servings — 4

4 ½-inch slices of flank steak or less tender cut
    of beef
3 small onions
4 slices bacon
½ t. pepper
½ c. water
1 dill pickle
1 t. salt
2 t. mustard (prepared)
Gravy:
½ c. water
2 T. flour

Pound beef with edge of saucer to tenderize meat tissue. Spread mustard thinly over meat. Sprinkle with pepper and salt. Place ¼ dill pickle and ½ onion and 1 strip of bacon on meat. Roll up tightly and tie with thread or hold together using toothpicks. Place meat in a Dutch oven with a small amount of fat and brown slowly on all sides to a rich color. Add 1 onion, cut in quarters while meat is browning. When brown, slip trivit under meat, add ½ cup water, cover tightly and cook over very low heat until tender, about 1½ hours. More water may be needed if pot becomes dry or for a greater amount of gravy. When meat is tender place in bowl. Measure water and flour into a glass and stir into a smooth paste. Stir into liquid in Dutch oven and cook until smooth and thickened. Pour gravy over meat and serve with boiled potatoes and red cabbage.

Mrs. Evelyn Fay Grabowski, Hillsborough H. S.
Tampa, Florida

SAUERBRATEN (German)
Number of Servings — 6

3 lbs. beef shoulder
2 t. salt, pepper, garlic
2 c. vinegar
2 c. water
½ c. sliced onion
2 bay leaves
1 t. peppercorns
¼ c. sugar
Fat
Flour
1 c. sweet or sour cream

Rub meat with a cut surface of garlic, salt and pepper and place in bowl. Heat vinegar, water, onion, bay leaves, peppercorns and sugar together, but do not boil. Pour hot mixture over meat, cover bowl, and let stand in cool place 4 to 8 days, turning meat each day. Drain, saving vinegar mixture. Brown meat in fat, add half of the strained vinegar, cover pan and simmer until tender, 2 to 3 hours, adding more vinegar as required to keep liquid about ½ inch deep in pan. Strain liquid and thicken with 2 tablespoons flour for each cup of liquid. Cook until thickened and add cream.

Margaret S. Yoder, Upper Perkiomen H. S.
East Greenville, Pennsylvania

ITALIAN SPAGHETTI MEAT SAUCE
Number of Servings — 4-6

1 lb. ground beef
2 large onions, chopped
3 cloves garlic
2 cans tomato paste
⅓ t. cayenne pepper
1 can pimentos, chopped
1 small can mushrooms
1 t. Worcestershire sauce

Brown together the ground beef, onions and garlic. Remove garlic clove. Add the other ingredients and simmer for 2 or 3 hours. Serve over the long Italian style spaghetti.

Mrs. Florence Wiest, Wishek H. S.
Wishek, North Dakota

MEXICAN SPAGHETTI
Number of Servings — 4-6

1 lb. ground beef
⅓ c. chopped onion
⅓ c. diced pepper
⅓ c. olives or sweet pickles
½ c. celery
1 c. frozen corn
1 c. cheese
1 can tomato soup
Salt and pepper
1 T. Worcestershire sauce
1 t. A-1 sauce
1 c. spaghetti

Combine onion, pepper, ground beef and celery; brown in electric skillet. Combine pickles, corn, soup, seasonings and simmer 20 minutes. Pour this over spaghetti and top with shredded cheese. Cook in electric skillet, over low heat.

Donna Stockdale, Waynetown H. S.
Waynetown, Indiana

SPANISH DELIGHT
Number of Servings — 12

1 lb. ground meat
4 buttons garlic
6 T. garlic
½ can chili powder
1 No. 2 can tomatoes
1 pkg. noodles
1 can (No. 2) tomatoes
1 can (No. 2) corn
2 t. salt
Pinch sugar
6 slices cheese
2 bell peppers, chipped

Sear garlic in fat, add meat and flour and sear a few minutes. Add chili powder, tomatoes, sugar, corn, salt and bell peppers and cook 30-40 minutes. Add noodles and cook about 15 minutes. If mixture gets thick while cooking add water. Pour in greased baking dish and place cheese on top. Bake 10-15 minutes in moderate oven. Makes 2 medium size dishes. The dish may be made one day and placed in refrigerator and baked just before serving the next day.

Mrs. Lucille H. Stewart, Farmerville H. S.
Farmerville, Louisiana

SUKI YAKI
Number of Servings — 4

1 lb. lean round steak, slivered
2 t. butter or margarine
½ lb. sliced mushrooms
3 large stalks celery, thinly sliced
2 medium size onions, thinly sliced
1 can (5 oz.) bamboo shoots, drained
2 T. sugar
1 chicken bouillon cube
¼ c. soy sauce
¼ c. water
½ t. salt

3 c. spinach leaves, washed and broken into bite-size pieces
4 c. hot cooked rice

Heat butter or margarine until sizzling hot in electric fryer or blazer pan of chafing dish. Add meat, cook 10-15 minutes, or until well-browned. Add remaining ingredients except spinach; cook slowly, stirring occasionally for 20-40 minutes, or until vegetables are crisply tender. Add spinach leaves, and cook 5 to 10 minutes or until spinach is lightly cooked. Mixture may or may not be thickened. Serve over hot cooked rice.

Mrs. Carol Stephenson, Springport H. S.
Springport, Michigan

SALLY'S SWEDISH MEAT BALLS
Number of Servings — 6

1 lb. ground beef
¼ c. minced onion
¼ c. minced celery
1 egg, slightly beaten
¼ c. mushroom soup
¼ c. milk
¾ c. fine bread crumbs
¼ c. oats
1½ t. salt
⅛ t. pepper
½ t. nutmeg
¼ c. parsley
¼ c. applesauce

Soak bread crumbs and oats in milk. Add onion, celery, egg, meat and seasonings; mix thoroughly. Shape into 1 inch balls. Saute in skillet until lightly browned on all sides. Add remaining mushroom soup and equal amount of water and pour over meat balls and simmer on top of stove for 15 minutes or until meat balls are done.

Sara Rhoads Parks, Audubon H. S.
Audubon, New Jersey

TERIYAKI STICKS
(Broiled Tenderloin on Skewers—Japanese Style)
Number of Servings — 6

2 lbs. beef tenderloin
1 c. soy sauce
2 cloves garlic, chopped
1 T. chopped fresh ginger
1 small onion, chopped fine
½ c. sugar
½ c. sherry

Cut beef tenderloin in strips approximately 1 x 2 inches. Spear 3 pieces on each bamboo skewer stick or metal skewer. Combine remaining ingredients in bowl. Marinate tenderloin on skewer in sauce for about 1 hour. Then drain meat slightly and broil over charcoal or in the broiler until both sides are well cooked.

Ann Yamasaki, Highland Jr. H. S.
Battle Creek, Michigan

Pork

AFRICAN CHOP SUEY
Number of Servings — 8-10

1 lb. veal, cubed
1 lb. pork, cubed
1 c. chopped onion
1 can cream of chicken soup
1 c. water
4 T. soy sauce
2 c. celery, cut up
1 c. cream of mushroom soup
1 c. uncooked rice

Brown meat, remove from pan and brown onions and celery. Put meat, onions, celery, soup and water in fry pan. Cook until tender (1 hour). Add rice which has been soaked 1 hour or more. Add soy sauce. Put in greased casserole and bake 1 hour. Cover part of baking time. Mushrooms may be added if desired.

Mrs. Joan Marotzke, Kennedy H. S.
Kennedy, Minnesota

BALKEN BRIJ (Dutch Breakfast Mush)

2 lbs. pork liver
1 lb. fat pork
1 T. salt
2 c. buckwheat flour
1 c. graham flour or oatmeal

Put the pork, liver, and salt in a pan, cover with water, and cook slowly until well done (about 1½ hours). Grind meat rather finely. Put meat mixture back on stove, add 6 pints of water, mix and heat. Mix the flours and add slowly to the meat mixture, stirring constantly. Cook and stir until thick. Add salt and pepper to taste. Put in loaf pans and chill in refrigerator. Slice loaves as needed and fry slices brown on both sides, with very little shortening.

Ethel Timkovich, Marion H. S.
Marion, Michigan

CHINESE ALMOND RICE
Number of Servings — 6

1 lb. sausage
⅓ c. chopped onion
⅓ c. chopped green pepper
⅔ c. chopped celery
1 package chicken-noodle soup
3 c. hot water
¼ c. sliced almonds
¾ c. rice, raw

Brown sausage in skillet, add chopped vegetables and cook until clear. Simmer packaged soup in water for 10 minutes. Brown rice with the meat and vegetables. Combine soup mixture with meat and vegetable mixture. Add almonds and mix. Place in casserole and bake at 350°F. for 1 hour.

Mrs. Irma Haley, Castleford H. S.
Castleford, Idaho

CHINESE PORK SECT GUM
Number of Servings — 6

1 lb. lean pork, cubed
¼ c. butter
½ c. chopped green onion
1 green pepper, cut in thin strips
½ lb. sliced mushroooms
1 can (No. 303) chop suey vegetables, drained
½ c. water chestnuts, sliced
1½ c .chicken stock
2 T. cornstarch
1 T. soy sauce
Salt and pepper
Chow mein noodles

Brown pork in butter; cover and cook 15 minutes. Add onions, green pepper, and mushrooms; cook until tender. Add chop suey, vegetables, water chestnuts, chicken stock and pork. Combine cornstarch and soy sauce; stir until smooth. Add to meat mixture, season to taste. Bring to a boil reduce to simmer for 10-15 minutes, stirring occasionally. Serve over chow mein noodles.

Rosalie Osowski, Buffalo H. S.
Buffalo, Minnesota

CHOP SUEY
Number of Servings — 6

1½ lbs. pork tenderloin, cut in small cubes
1 bunch celery
1 lb. onions
1 can bean sprouts
Soy sauce

Fry pork until brown on all sides. Add soy sauce to taste; add celery and onions chopped fine. Add 1 cup water and let simmer until tender. (Should cook 30 to 45 minutes). Add more soy sauce to taste. Add bean sprouts about 10 minutes before serving. Serve on bed of rice (1 cup rice—before cooked). Top with toasted noodles. Mushrooms may be added.

Glaray Sue Lacy, Kermit H. S.
Kermit, West Virginia

HAMALAYA CASSEROLE
Number of Servings — 4-6

1 can condensed cream of mushroom soup
1 c. water or milk
¼ t. salt
1 c. cooked rice or minute rice
¼ c. chopped onion
Dash of pepper
1½ c. diced cooked ham
1 c. cooked green beans

Combine soup, water or milk, salt, onion and pepper in saucepan. Mix well. Bring to a boil, stirring occasionally. Pour about ½ of soup mix-

(Continued on Next Page)

ture into a greased casserole baking dish. Then pour rice into casserole. Combine ham and beans; pour into casserole. Top with remaining soup. Sprinkle with grated cheese and paprika, if desired. Cover and bake in a moderate oven (350° F.) for 20 minutes.

Voncile M. Kight, Effingham County H. S.
Springfield, Georgia

JAMBALAYA
Number of Servings — 4

8 oz. can Brown 'N Serve Sausage
¼ c. butter
½ lb. fresh mushrooms, sliced
1 lb. can French-style green beans, drained
½ c. quick-cooking rice
1 lb. can stewed tomatoes
¼ t. salt
½ c. shredded medium sharp cheddar cheese

Saute sliced mushrooms in butter, in a skillet. Add green beans. Sprinkle rice over beans and cover with tomatoes and salt. Cover and simmer for about 20 minutes, or until rice is tender. Drain juice from sausages. Place sausages on top of tomatoes and sprinkle cheese over meat. Heat for 5 minutes or until sausages are hot and cheese has melted. Serve hot.

Mrs. Bette Jenness
Linesville-Conneaut-Summit H. S.
Linesville, Pennsylvania

JAPANESE FRIED RICE
Number of Servings — About 8

2 c. grated carrots
2 c. chopped celery
1 c. chopped onion
½ t. salt
½ lb. bacon, cut in small pieces
½ lb. pork steak, cut in small pieces
½ lb. beef steak, cut in small pieces
3 c. rice

Fry bacon but not crisp. Remove from pan and brown beef and pork in fat. Remove meat. Steam vegetables in the fat and ½ cup water until vegetables are soft. Add bacon, meat, 2 tablespoons soy sauce, 3 cups rice, and enough water to cover. Cover and steam until rice is soft.

Mrs. Evelyn Hansen, Buffalo H. S.
Buffalo, Minnesota

MEXICAN LUNCH
Number of Servings — 6

1 lb. bulk pork sausage
1 c. diced onions
1 c. diced green pepper
2 c. canned tomatoes
1¾ c. buttermilk
2 c. uncooked macaroni, shell or elbow
1 T. sugar
1 T. chili powder
1 t. salt

Brown sausage, onion and green pepper in large skillet. Add tomatoes, buttermilk, macaroni and seasonings. Stir. Cover. Use high heat until steaming. Turn to low or simmer for 25 minutes.

Mrs. Ila S. Williams, New Kent H. S.
New Kent, Virginia

CHINESE PORK CHOPS
Number of Servings — 6

6 pork chops
1 t. salt
¼ c. water
1 chicken bouillon cube
1 c. hot water
½ t. Worcestershire sauce
1 t. soy sauce
⅓ c. pineapple juice
1 T. vinegar
¼ t. mustard
2 T. cornstarch
2 T. cold water
1 can (9 oz.) sliced pineapple (cut in cubes)
½ green pepper, sliced thin
1 tomato, cubed
½ c. chopped celery
4 c. cooked rice

Brown chops thoroughly without fat, salt. Add ¼ cup water, cover and simmer 30 minutes. Remove chops and pour off fat. In the skillet dissolve bouillon cube in 1 cup hot water, add Worcestershire and soy sauces, pineapple juice, vinegar and mustard. Combine cornstarch and cold water, stir into skillet, simmer until thick, stirring constantly. Add chops and remaining ingredients, except rice. Simmer 10 minutes. Serve over hot rice.

Mildred Elliott, Sparks H. S.
Sparks, Nevada

CHOP CHOP
Number of Servings — 4

4 pork chops
½ t. sugar
1½ c. hot water
1 large onion, sliced
½ c. celery, sliced
½ lb. whole green beans
2 c. sliced cabbage
1 T. cornstarch
2 T. cold water
3 T. soy sauce

Sprinkle sugar over bottom of skillet. As soon as sugar has browned, place chops in skillet and brown on both sides. Add onions and hot water, cover and simmer for 30 minutes. Add celery and beans; cook for 5 minutes. Then add cabbage and cook for 5 more minutes. Thicken with cornstarch, water, and soy sauce mixture. Serve with additional soy sauce. 350 calories per serving. Preparation time, 45 minutes.

Mrs. Faith Wilde, Arbor Vitae-Woodruff Jr. H. S.
Woodruff, Wisconsin

FRENCH PORK CHOPS WITH ONION SAUCE
Number of Servings — 6

6 center-cut pork chops, ¾ inch thick
2 T. fat
1 large onion, chopped
1 T. fat
1 t. flour
Salt and pepper
1 t. prepared mustard
1 c. beef stock or canned bouillon
2 T. chopped sweet pickles

Saute chops in 2 tablspoons fat. Brown on both sides. Cook onion in 1 tablespoon fat until golden in color and add flour, salt, pepper, and mustard; stir until well blended. Add stock and cook 5 minutes. Add sweet pickles and more seasoning if necessary, to give well-seasoned sauce. Pour over meat and cook 50 minutes, or until well done and stock is reduced. Serve on platter garnished with parsley and strips of pimento.

Mrs. Sanders McWhorter, Roxboro H. S.
Roxboro, North Carolina

PORK CHOPS ORIENTAL
Number of Servings — 4

2 T. shortening (or salad oil)
4 large shoulder pork chops
½ t. salt
Dash of pepper
¼ c. honey
½ c. chicken consomme
¼ c. soy sauce
2 T. catsup
Dash of ground ginger
½ clove crushed garlic

Melt shortening in skillet. Season chops with salt and pepper and fry until nicely browned. Mix remaining ingredients. Pour over chops, cover and cook over a low heat for 1 to 1½ hours.

Kirsten G. Giving, Climax Jr. H. S.
Climax, Minnesota

SPANISH PORK CHOPS
Number of Servings — 6

6 pork chops
1 package frozen peas
2 t. salt
1 pt. whole tomatoes
2 small onions
Pepper

Flour pork chops. Place in hot skillet with 1 tablespoon shortening. Season with salt and pepper. Brown both sides of pork chops. Add 1 pint of tomatoes, 1 package of frozen peas, and 2 small onions, chopped fine. Cover skillet with lid. Put in oven and bake at 350°F. for 1½ hours. Serve with French bread.

Genevieve Williams, Asst. State Supvr. H. E.
Bridgeport, West Virginia

SPANISH PORK CHOPS

Select pork chops of uniform size according to the number of persons to be served. Arrange them close together in bottom of roasting pan. Place a slice of Spanish onion about ¼ thick on each chop. Place 1 tablespoon of dry rice on onion. Place a whole canned tomato, carefully on the rice. Add salt and sugar to taste. Pour remaining tomato juice at side of arranged individual servings. Bake for 1½ hours in a covered roasting pan. Remove lid only when rice is tender. Lift each individual serving carefully to dinner plate or serving tray. Garnish with fresh parsley.

Jean Main, Casey Com. Unit C-1
Casey, Illinois

HAWAIIAN PORK
Number of Servings — 4

1 lb. boneless pork, cut in 1 inch cubes
1 egg
2 T. flour
⅛ t. pepper
½ T. flour
3 T. lard or drippings
3 green peppers
Chinese noodles or cooked rice
½ c. pineapple chunks
2½ T. cornstarch
2½ T. soy sauce
¼ c. sugar
¼ c. vinegar
½ c. pineapple juice

Beat together egg, flour, salt and pepper. Thoroughly coat cubes of pork in egg-flour batter. Brown on all sides in hot lard or drippings in frying pan. Cover and cook slowly for about 30 minutes. Remove stems and seeds from green peppers. Cut into 1 inch squares. Boil 10 minutes, drain. Add green peppers and pineapple to meat. Cover and simmer 10 minutes. Stir and cook together cornstarch, soy sauce, sugar, vinegar and pineapple juice until clear, about 2 minutes. Pour over meat mixture and simmer 5 minutes. Serve over Chinese noodles or cooked rice.

Mrs. Wilda Jean Davis, Lumpkin County H. S.
Dahlonega, Georgia

CHINESE CHOP SUEY
Number of Servings — 6

½ lb. lean pork
2 T. fat
1 c. sliced onions
1 c. chicken bouillon
¼ lb. mushrooms, sliced
1 T. cornstarch
2 T. water
1 can (No. 2½) bean sprouts, drained
1 t. salt
Dash of pepper
Dash of paprika
¼ t. sugar
3 c. boiled rice

(Continued on Next Page)

Cut pork in small pieces and brown in fat; add celery, onions and bouillon, cover and simmer 20 minutes; add mushrooms and paste made of cornstarch and water, and cook 10 minutes, stirring until thickened. Add bean sprouts and seasonings, and heat thoroughly; serve hot with boiled or steamed rice. If desired, 2 tablespoons soy sauce may be added to chop suey for additional flavoring. Sprinkle with Chinese noodles.

Mrs. Mabel Jones, Eden H. S.
Eden, Texas

BOHEMIAN SPARERIBS
Number of Servings — 4

2 lbs. spareribs
1 t. salt
¼ t. pepper
1 T. caraway seed
1 can (No. 2(sauerkraut
1 medium onion, sliced
1 can (No. 2) tomatoes

Cut spareribs into individual servings. Season with salt and pepper. Mix caraway seeds with sauerkraut and place in 8 x 12 inch baking pan. Arrange onion slices on sauerkraut and pour tomatoes over mixture. Place spareribs on top. Bake in moderate oven (350°F.) for 2 hours.

Mrs. Ardyce Gilbert, Scotland H. S.
Scotland, South Dakota

CHINESE SPARERIBS
Number of Servings — 4-6

4 lbs. pork spareribs
1½ c. wine vinegar
1½ c. light brown sugar
1-1½ t. powdered ginger
1½ t. salt

Rub ribs with salt and ginger. Add ribs to vinegar and sugar mixture. Cover and cook at low temperature until done. Let set overnight in liquid. Just before serving heat in oven at 450°F. until brown.

Mrs. Myrtice Edenfield, Metter H. S.
Metter, Georgia

ITALIAN STYLE RIBS
Number of Servings — 6-8

1 c. vinegar
1 c. water
2 c. catsup (about 1 bottle)
1 T. salt
1 T. black pepper
2 t. chili powder
1 t. red pepper (very scant)
½ to 1 c. dark brown sugar

Trim fat from ribs; place in roaster, pour sauce over them and cover. Bake in slow oven (325°F.) for about 3 hours, or until ribs are tender and sauce is thickened. Spoon fat off surface as it accumulates and baste ribs frequently after first 2 hours of baking.

Laura F. Magro, Three Oaks Township School
Three Oaks, Michigan

SWEET-SOUR SPARERIBS
(Hawaiian Version)
Number of Servings — 4

1½ lbs. pork spareribs (2 inch lengths)
1 c. vinegar
1 c. water
½ t. salt
½ c. brown sugar (more optional)
1 T. soy sauce
1 T. flour
Chunk pineapple

Roll cut spareribs in flour, soy sauce and salt. Let them stand several minutes. Fry in well-heated oil until brown. Drain excess fat leaving 2 tablespoons in pan. Add vinegar, water and sugar. Simmer until tender on low heat. Add chunk pineapple before serving. (Pineapple juice may be substituted for part of the water).

Mrs. Theda Ashley, Roosevelt H. S.
Emporia, Kansas

SWEET AND SOUR SPARERIBS
Number of Servings — 6

2½ to 3 lbs. meaty spareribs
Salt and pepper
2 T. oil
1 small onion, chopped
½ green pepper, cut in strips
¼ c. diagonally cut celery
1 can (No. 2) pineapple tidbits
1 T. cornstarch
¼ c. vinegar
1 T. soy sauce

Have spareribs cut into finger size pieces. Sprinkle with salt and pepper. Arrange in roasting pan. Roast at 300°F. for 1½ hours. Turn pieces and pour off fat often. Heat oil in saucepan. Add onion, green pepper and celery. Cook 3 to 4 minutes. Drain syrup from pineapple into cup. Stir cornstarch into syrup. Add tidbits, cornstarch syrup, vinegar and soy sauce to vegetables. Cook, stirring, until slightly thickened. Drain spareribs. Pour sauce over them. Bake and baste 45 minutes longer. Serve.

Mrs. Georgia Balls, Alameda Jr. H. S.
Pocatello, Idaho

PIZZA
Number of Servings — 4-6

1 package dry yeast or 1 cake compressed yeast
1 c. lukewarm water
2 t. sugar
1¾ t. salt
1 lb. ground pork sausage or link sausage, half-cooked
1 T. shortening
3½ to 3¾ c. flour
1 egg white, beaten
2 cans (6 oz.) tomato sauce
½ lb. cheese, Mozzarella or cheddar
½ c. chopped onion
Sweet basil, oregano, salt, pepper

(Continued on Next Page)

Soften yeast in ¼ cup water. Let stand 10 minutes. Add sugar, salt, shortening and 1 cup flour to remaining water. Beat until smooth. Add yeast mixture and stir well. Fold in egg white, then add flour to make a stiff dough. Knead until smooth. Place in greased bowl and cover. Let rise in warm place, 85°F., until double in bulk. Knead down. Cut into 4 portions, cover, let rest 10 minutes. Roll out into very thin circles. Lift into pie pans. Brush dough with salad oil. Spread tomato sauce over bottom. Sprinkle with ⅛ teaspoon sweet basil. Add ¾ grated cheese, then the half-cooked sausage, onion, and remaining cheese. Sprinkle with salt, pepper and ¾ teaspoon crumbled oregano. Bake at 450°F. for about 20 minutes. Cut in wedges and serve immediately.

Maicille Carr, Big Piney H. S.
Big Piney, Wyoming

SAUSAGE PIZZA
Number of Servings — 4-6

½ t. dry yeast
¾ c. and 2 T. warm water
3-3¼ c. sifted flour
1 can (No. 2½) tomatoes, sieved
2 cans tomato paste
½ t. oregano
½ t. rosemary
½ t. salt
¼ t. pepper
2 T. olive oil
⅔ c. chopped mushrooms
1 T. butter
¼ c. grated Parmesan cheese
1 lb. Italian sausage (or use hot pork sausage)
6 to 12 ozs. Mozzarella cheese, sliced thin

Dissolve yeast in water. Blend in flour to make stiff dough. Knead lightly on floured surface. Place in greased bowl; turn to grease top. Cover and let rise in warm place until doubled (1½ to 2 hours). Divide into 2 parts. Roll each part into a 14 x 10 inch rectangle (or to fit a large pizza pan). Place on pizza pan or on oblong pan with shallow sides on baking sheets. Roll edge to make stand-up ridge. Combine tomatoes, tomato paste and seasonings. Spread over each piece. Sprinkle with oil. Saute mushrooms in butter and spread over top of pizza. Over each piece sprinkle Parmesan cheese, spread browned and drained sausage and top with cheese. Bake at 425°F. for 25 to 30 minutes.

Merle Garrett, Kodiak H. S.
Kodiak, Alaska

SWISS ALPINE PIE
Number of Servings — 4-6

1 10 inch pastry shell (unbaked)
1 package frozen broccoli (cooked)
2 c. (½ lb.) pre-cooked ham cubes
2 c. shredded Swiss cheese
3 T. chopped onion
1½ c. milk (scalded)
3 eggs, slightly beaten

⅛ t. salt
⅛ t. pepper

Preheat oven to 450°F. Drain and chop broccoli. Layer half of broccoli, ham, and cheese in pastry shell. Repeat. Sprinkle onion over top and set aside. Gradually stir milk into eggs; add seasonings. Pour into pastry shell. Bake 10 minutes. Reduce heat to 325°F.; continue to bake additional 30 to 35 minutes. Remove from oven; let stand a few minutes before serving.

Wanda Judson, South Jr. H. S.
Rapid City, South Dakota

SWEDISH HAMBURGERS
Number of Servnigs — 4

⅓ c. fine bread crumbs
¾ t. salt
½ t. paprika
¼ t. pepper
½ c. water
1½ c. cream
1 lb. ground pork
1 egg
2 T. chopped parsley
¼ c. (½ stick) margarine
3 c. sliced onions (3 medium onions)
1 T. flour

Combine bread crumbs, salt, paprika and pepper. Stir in water and ½ cup cream. Let stand 10 minutes. Mix in ground pork, egg and parsley. Shape into 8 round flat patties. Melt margarine in skillet. Fry patties about 4 to 5 minutes on each side at medium heat. Place on warm serving platter and keep warm. Saute onions in margarine and drippings remaining in skillet. When onions are tender sprinkle with flour. Stir in remaining cream. Cook mixture a few minutes longer until thickened, stirring constantly. Spoon over meat. Serve hot.

Mrs. Ruth Ogden, Melvin-Sibley H. S.
Melvin, Illinois

SWEDISH HAM BALLS
Number of Servings — 6

1 lb. smoked ham, uncooked preferred
1½ lbs. ground pork (or 1 lb. ground pork and ½ lb. ground beef)
2 c. bread crumbs
2 eggs, well beaten
1 c. milk
1½ c. brown sugar
1 t. dry mustard
½ c. vinegar
½ c. water

Combine brown sugar, vinegar, mustard and water. Stir until sugar is dissolved. Combine meats, crumbs, eggs and milk. Mix thoroughly. Place in casserole. Pour brown sugar mixture over meat balls. Bake in slow oven (275°F.) for 1½ hours. Baste frequently with sauce.

Mrs. Loretta C. Bennett,
Edgar Allen Poe Inter. School
Annandale, Virginia

Poultry

ARROZ CON POLLO
Number of Servings — 4-6

1 ready to cook fryer chicken (disjointed)
¼ c. oil
1 medium onion, chopped
1 medium green pepper, chopped
1 clove garlic, minced
1 c. uncooked rice
1 can (8 oz.) tomato sauce
1 c. water
2 t. salt
¼ t. pepper
1 can (8½ ozs.) peas, drained saving liquid

Coat the chicken with oil to keep moist. Brown in heavy skillet over medium heat. Remove chicken and add green pepper, onion, garlic and rice. Stir occasionally to distribute the heat evenly while rice browns. Blend in tomato sauce, water, salt, pepper and liquid from peas. Add the browned chicken. Cover and cook over low heat 30 minutes. Remove cover; lift rice with a fork to fluff. Add peas and cook over low heat about 5 minutes longer.

Mrs. Wynne Hromanik, Freedom Area H. S.
Freedom, Pennsylvania

ARROZ CON POLLO (CHICKEN WITH RICE)
Number of Servings — 4-6

2 to 3 lb. fryer chicken, cut in pieces
1 t. salt
¼ t. pepper
¼ c. salad oil
1 medium size onion, chopped
1 or 2 cloves garlic, minced
2 T. paprika
1 bay leaf
5 whole cloves
½ t. oregano
Boiling water
Salt and pepper to taste
1½ c. uncooked rice
½ c. sliced pimento
6 green olives, cut in half
1 package (10 oz.) frozen peas

Sprinkle chicken with salt and pepper and brown in hot oil. Remove chicken and brown rice in remaining oil. Return chicken to frying pan with rice. Add onion, garlic, paprika, bay leaf, cloves and oregano. Pour over just enough boiling water to cover chicken. Add salt and pepper to taste. Cover and simmer slowly for 30 minutes. Add pimentos, olives and peas; cover and simmer 15 minutes more, or until all liquid is absorbed.

Mrs. Janette M. Dillavou, Kofa H. S.
Yuma, Arizona

ARROZ CON POLLO (CHICKEN WITH RICE)
Number of Servings — 4-6

1-3 lb. chicken, cut up into pieces
¼ c. cooking oil
1 clove garlic, minced
½ c. chopped onion
1 green pepper, chopped
3 tomatoes, diced (may use canned tomatoes)
2 c. chicken broth
1 c. uncooked rice
¼ t. cayenne pepper
2 t. salt

In a heavy skillet or Dutch oven, heat the oil and brown the chicken, remove. Add onion, garlic and green pepper and saute until golden. Return chicken to skillet, add tomatoes and broth and bring to boil. Stir in the rice, cayenne pepper and salt. Cover and simmer over low heat until chicken and rice are tender and liquid is absorbed, about 30 to 40 minutes. Serve garnished with pimento strips or chopped ripe olives.

Mrs. Stenson Terry, San Perlita H. S.
San Perlita, Texas

CHICKEN CACCIATORA
Number of Servings — 4

¼ c. flour
1½ t. salt
1 t. paprika
½ t. pepper
1 3-lb. chicken, cut up into pieces
⅓ c. butter
½ c. minced onion
½ c. minced green pepper
½ lb. mushrooms, cut up
1 can tomatoes
1 can (6 oz.) tomato paste
1 clove garlic, minced
⅛ t. red pepper
1 t. oregano
¾ c. sherry

Flour, salt, pepper and paprika chicken. Brown in ⅓ cup butter. Add onion, green pepper, mushrooms and cook 5 minutes. Add tomatoes, tomato paste, garlic, red pepper and oregano and cook until tender (about 30 minutes). Add sherry, mix well, and bring to a boil. Serve hot with cooked spaghetti.

Marcella Stone, Robert E. Lee H. S.
Montgomery, Alabama

CHICKEN CHOW MEIN
Number of Servings — 6

2 c. cubed cooked chicken
2 T. butter

(Continued on Next Page)

2 c. thinly sliced celery
1½ c. sliced onions
⅛ t. pepper
1 t. salt
2 c. chicken broth
1 can (1 lb.) mixed Chinese vegetables, drained
1 can (4 oz.) mushrooms, drained
2 T. cornstarch
3 T. soy sauce

Brown chicken lightly in butter. Add next 5 ingredients. Cook covered about 15 minutes or until vegetables are just tender. Add drained Chinese vegetables and mushrooms. Heat to boiling. Add cornstarch mixed with soy sauce. Simmer 2 minutes.

Mrs. Ray Davis, Trumann H. S.
Trumann, Arkansas

CHICKEN AND PORK ADOBO (Filipino)
Number of Servings — 6-8

2 lbs. lean pork, cut into pieces 2 inches long
    and 1½ inches thick
1 medium-sized chicken (lean), cut up
1 head garlic, crushed
½ c. soy sauce
1 t. black pepper
1 T. lard
3 c. water
1 c. vinegar
1 onion, quartered
2 bay leaves

Place cut pork and chicken in a large saucepan. Add vinegar, garlic. pepper, soy sauce, onion, bay leaves and water. Cover and cook slowly until most of the sauce has evaporated. Drain (save). Separate the pieces of onion from the pork and chicken and saute in lard until brown. Add the pork and chicken and fry until brown. Add the sauce and let simmer for 5 minutes longer. Serve hot.

Mrs. Larry Colgrove
Fort Lupton Consolidated Jr.-Sr. H. S.
Fort Lupton, Colorado

CHOP SUEY
Number of Servings — 10-12

Saute ¾ cup onions and 1 cup celery in 3 tablespoons butter until brown. Add 4 tablespoons flour and while stirring add 1 can mushroom soup, diluted with 1 can water. Stir until smooth and then add 1 teaspoon each of salt and pepper, ¼ teaspoon mustard, ⅛ teaspoon paprika, 1 tablespoon brown sauce and 2 teaspoons soy sauce. Cook until smooth and then add diced chicken from a 4 or 5 pound cooked hen, and 1 can mushrooms. Just before serving add 1 can bean sprouts. Serve over cooked vermicilla noodles.

Mrs. R. A. Moore, Breckenridge H. S.
Breckenridge, Texas

CHOP SUEY
Number of Servings — 16-18

3 lb. hen, stewed and boned (reserve broth if
    needed)
2 T. fat
1 c. chopped celery
1 can bean sprouts
1 green pepper, chopped
2 c. tomato juice
1 can (4 oz.) mushrooms
1 can (5 oz.) bamboo shoots
1 can (5 oz.) water chestnuts
2 T. soy sauce
Salt and pepper

Melt fat in large frying pan. Lightly brown celery and green pepper. Add chicken, bean sprouts, tomato juice, mushrooms, bamboo shoots and water chestnuts. Simmer 30 minutes. Add chicken broth if needed. Add soy sauce, salt and pepper. Serve on mound of rice. Garnish with chop suey noodles.

Lora Ella Pierce, Wister Public H. S.
Wister, Oklahoma

CHOW MEIN
Number of Servings — 4-6

1 lb. chopped chicken
2 T. fat
1 t. salt
¼ t. pepper
1½ c. chopped onion
1½ c. chopped celery
½ c. chopped green pepper
1½ c. water
¼ c. soy sauce
1 can (No. 2) bean sprouts

Brown chicken in melted fat. Add all ingredients except soy sauce and bean sprouts. Cover and simmer for 40 minutes. Add soy sauce and bean sprouts and heat thoroughly. Thicken with 4 tablespoons of cornstarch mixed in ½ cup cold water. Stir this into hot mixture until smooth and thickened. Serve over noodles.

Lillian B. Cockran, Floyd H. S.
Floyd, Virginia

CHINESE HOT DISH
Number of Servings — 18

1 can chow mein vegetables, drained
1 can chow mein noodles
2 c. boned chicken, turkey or tuna
1 can cream of chicken soup
1 can cream of mushroom soup
1 c. milk
1 c. cracker crumbs

Mix all ingredients except the cracker crumbs and bake in a greased baking dish. Bake 1 hour then sprinkle the top with the cracker crumbs and continue baking for ½ hour more or longer. Bake in 250°F. oven, 1½ hours or longer.

Mrs. Frances E. Smith, Alpena H. S.
Alpena, South Dakota

COG AU VIN

Number of Servings — 4

1 fryer (2½ lbs.)
1 t. salt and pepper
3 T. cooking oil
6 small whole onions
3 green onions, sliced
2 T. flour
1 clove garlic, minced
1 can (4 oz.) sliced mushrooms
1½ c. red wine
1 large bay leaf
¼ c. minced parsley

Coat chicken with seasoned flour. Brown in heavy skillet in hot cooking oil. Remove from heat. Add onions and garlic. Cook until tender. Add remaining ingredients and cover. Simmer 1 hour until tender.

Sue Sorrell, Fayette County School System
Lexington, Kentucky

CHICKEN ORIENTAL

Number of Servings — 6

1 can mushroom soup
1 can water
1 can chicken, cut in small pieces
1 can cashew nuts
1½ cans Chinese noodles
1 can chopped celery
1 can chopped onion

Note: The mushroom soup can is used for all measuring. If less onion is desired, substitute more celery. Mix and top with crushed potato chips and grated cheese. Bake 1 hour in covered dish. Cover may be removed the last 15 minutes to assure browning.

Mildred Weigley Wood
State Department of Vocational Education
Phoenix, Arizona

CHICKEN ORIENTAL

Number of Servings — 4-5

1 3-lb. frying chicken (2 to 2½ cups bite size chunks)
1 t. salt
1 t. pepper
1 c. flour
¼ c. butter or shortening
1 c. pineapple chunks
1 T. cornstarch
½ c. pineapple juice
2 T. soy sauce

Cut chicken from the bones into bite size chunks. Dredge chicken in flour mixed with salt and pepper. Melt butter in automatic electric skillet. Brown chicken at 350°F. to 360°F. Add pineapple chunks. Mix cornstarch, juice and soy sauce. Pour over chicken, cover and cook at 220°F. for 30 minutes. Serve with rice. Sprinkle with salted almonds, if desired.

Helen M. McKinley, Oxnard H. S.
Oxnard, California

SINGAPORE CURRY

Number of Servings — 8

1 medium fryer
1 c. water
¾ t. salt
Sauce Measurements:
1½ t. curry powder
5 T. flour
½ t. salt
3 c. liquid (broth and milk)
6 T. margarine
1 T. finely chopped onion

Cook fryer whole in water which has been salted, until tender (about 30 minutes). Remove from broth, cool and cut into bite size pieces. *For Sauce:* Melt margarine, add onions and cook 3-4 minutes. Mix salt, flour, and curry powder. Add to margarine and stir until smooth. Add liquid and cook, stirring constantly until thick. Add chicken and cook about 5 minutes longer until chicken is thoroughly heated. Serve buffet style with cooked rice in center of plate, then dip chicken mixture over that, top with sliced tomatoes, sliced bananas, pineapple chunks, coconut, salted peanuts and last French fried onion rings.

Measurements for Topping:

1 c. rice (measured uncooked)
1 can (No. 2) pineapple chunks
1 can coconut
1 can (8 oz.) peanuts
3 to 4 bananas
3 to 4 tomatoes
4 onions

This is a complete meal. Not even a dessert is needed.

Mrs. T. W. Colby, Abilene Christian H. S.
Abilene, Texas

CHINESE CHICKEN

Number of Servings — 8

6 chicken breasts
¼ c. butter
1 c. diced water chestnuts
1 c. bamboo shoots
2 c. diced celery
2 c. cut green beans
3 c. chicken broth
¼ c. soy sauce
2½ t. salt
2 t. monosodium glutamate
1 t. sugar
1 t. pepper

Skin and slice chicken. Saute in butter in large pan. Add water chestnuts, bamboo shoots, celery and green beans. Pour chicken broth over mixture. Add soy sauce and seasonings. Cover and steam 5 minutes. Blend 2 tablespoons cornstarch with small amount of water. Add to chicken and cook until broth is thick and transparent. Add 1 cup slivered almonds. Serve over cooked rice.

Mrs. Mary Katherine Hammer, West End H. S.
Nashville, Tennessee

CUBAN CHICKEN OREGANO
Number of Servings — 4-6

1 ready to cook fryer chicken (2½ to 3 lbs.),
   disjointed
¼ c. fat
1 medium onion, chopped
1 clove garlic, minced
1 t. salt
¼ t. pepper
1 T. oregano
2 fresh tomatoes, diced
1 can (4 oz.) mushrooms, chopped

Coat pieces of chicken with melted fat. Brown in
heavy skillet over medium heat. Add onion and
garlic; cook several minutes. Sprinkle with salt,
pepper and oregano. Add tomatoes and mushrooms with juice. Cover and cook over low heat
30 minutes, until tender. A parsley garnish adds
to this.

Mary L. Robison, Nappanee H. S.
Nappanee, Indiana

QUICK CURRIED CHICKEN HAWAIIAN
Number of Servings — 6

1 3 to 3½ lb. fryer
1 clove garlic, sliced
3 T. fat or salad oil
6 to 8 scallions, top and all cut in 1 inch pieces
1½ t. salt
½ t. pepper
½ c. hot water
1½ c. top milk
3 T. flour
1 to 2 T. curry powder

Have chicken legs, thighs, wings, breast, back,
chopped crosswise, through bone and meat into
pieces 1 inch long. Saute peeled garlic in fat in
2 skillets 5 minutes; discard garlic; saute chicken
in fat 15 minutes or until lightly browned, turning occasionally. Place all chicken in skillet; add
next 4 ingredients; cover; simmer 45 minutes or
until chicken is very tender. Put next 3 ingredients
in pint jar; cover; shake until smooth. Add all at
once to chicken. Cook stirring gently until thickened. Serve with or on steamed rice.

Laura F. Margo, Three Oaks Township H. S.
Three Oaks, Michigan

HAWAIIAN CHICKEN
Number of Servings — 6

Flour cut pieces of frying chicken and brown in
fat. Remove from fat and place in baking dish, 1
layer deep. Drain 1, No. 1 can of crushed pineapple and spread over chicken. Place in hot oven
and bake at 350°F. until golden brown. Sprinkle
top with Angel flake coconut and brown the last
few minutes. Serve hot. (A good way to use left
over chicken).

Vada C. Turnham, Senior H. S.
Arlington, Texas

HAWAIIAN CHICKEN
Number of Servings — 8-10

2 3 to 3½ lb. chickens, cut up
⅓ c. cornstarch
½ c. salad oil
1 can (No. 2½) pineapple chunks, drained
3 large white onions, cut in thick slices
3 green peppers, seeded and cubed
1 c. celery, cut in medium chunks
¼ c. dark brown sugar
¼ c. soy sauce
2 T. sliced, fresh ginger (powdered can be used)

Coat chicken with cornstarch; fry in oil until
medium brown. Place in bottom of roaster pan.
Add brown sugar, ginger and soy sauce to frying
oil (after removing chicken) with pineapple,
onions, celery and peppers. Cover and cook over
low heat until tender (30 minutes). Mix with
chicken and simmer until sauce has been absorbed
by chicken and chicken is tender.

Mrs. Betty R. Dyer, Windthorst H. S.
Windthorst, Texas

HUNGARIAN CHICKEN
Number of Servings — 16

Cut 2 chickens as for frying; salt, and let stand
2 hours. Slice 2 large onions and fry in hot fat
until light brown. Dredge each piece of chicken
in flour and brown in the fat. Remove chicken
from pan and pour off all but 2 tablespoons fat.
Add the yolks of 2 eggs mixed with 1 cup sour
cream; sprinkle with 1 tablespoon paprika, a little
salt and pepper. Return chicken to pan and simmer until tender.

Florence Tustison, Sentinel H. S.
Sentinel, Oklahoma

ITALIAN CHICKEN
Number of Servings — 12-14

2 T. fat
1 clove garlic
2 c. tomato sauce
1 T. Worcestershire sauce
1 can cream of mushroom soup or cream of
   chicken soup
2 bell peppers, chopped
1 c. midget English peas
1 t. tabasco sauce (optional)
1 box (12 oz.) wide noodles
1 qt. chicken stock
1 fat hen

Place in large skillet, fat, peppers, garlic and sauce
and brown. Add all other ingredients except the
noodles and turn heat very low at once. All meat
from hen which has been steamed until tender.
Add noodles that have been cooked as directed on
the package. This will serve 12 to 14 people. It is
even better the second day.

Pat McDonald, Borden H. S.
Borden, Indiana

CHICKEN ITALIAN
Number of Servings — 6

1 hen (or large fryer)
2 large onions, thinly sliced
2 green peppers, sliced
2 cloves garlic, finely chopped
2 can tomato sauce (1⅓ c.)
1 large package (14 oz.) noodles or two small packages)
2 cans mushrooms, cut in pieces

Put chicken in large saucepan with enough salted water to barely cover and boil until tender. Remove chicken from saucepan and cut from bones. Saute together the onions, green pepper and garlic. Add tomato sauce and simmer very slowly for 1 hour. Add noodles, and simmer until noodles are partly softened. Add sauce and pieces of chicken. Add mushrooms, and simmer very slowly until noodles are soft. Serve hot.

Frances Champion, State FHA Adviser
State Department of Education
Tallahassee, Florida

MEXICAN CHICKEN
Number of Servings — 4

4½ to 5 lb. chicken
1 t. salt
⅛ t. pepper
½ c. flour
2 T. chili powder
¼ t. oregano
¼ c. margarine
¼ c. cooking fat
½ c. stuffed olives, sliced
1 c. mild onion, sliced
1 c. water

Shake cut-up chicken in salt, pepper, flour, chili powder and oregano. Pack in a casserole and pour margarine and cooking fat over chicken. Cover and bake 1 hour at 350°F. Add stuffed olives, onions and water and bake 1 more hour, covered. Serve over rice. Optional: ½ cup broken nutmeats may be added to gravy made from the liquid in the casserole.

Mrs. Alice Requa Smith, Sunrise Park Jr. H. S.
White Bear Lake, Minnesota

POULET A' LA KISMIS
Number of Servings — 4-5

1 large frying chicken
1 T. flour
¾ t. seasoned salt
½ t. paprika
2 or 3 T. cooking oil (half butter, if desired)
⅓ c. chicken broth or water
2 T. vinegar
1 can (11 oz.) mandarin oranges
1 bottle (4 oz.) maraschino cherries
1 T. cornstarch
1 T. cold water
½ c. seedless raisins

Have chicken cut for frying. Rinse, dry and toss pieces with flour mixed with salt and paprika. Richly brown chicken in oil over moderate heat. Add broth, vinegar and syrups drained from oranges and cherries. Cover and cook slowly until tender, 25 to 30 minutes. Remove chicken pieces and keep hot. Skim excess fat from pan liquid; stir in cornstarch mixed with water. Add raisins and cook until liquid thickens, about 5 minutes. Add cherries and orange segments. Pour over chicken and serve hot.

Sarah Ivey Twilley, A. L. Miller Jr. H. S.
Macon, Georgia

SPANISH FRIED CHICKEN
Number of Servings — 4

1 frying chicken
4 T. butter
1 medium onion
2 tomatoes
1 c. rice
1-2 T. chili powder
2½ c. water

Have chicken cut up. Brown in butter with the onion you have chopped. Chop peppers and tomatoes. Place all in casserole, adding rice and water. Season with salt and bake in moderate oven until meat is tender, and rice is done, about 40 minutes.

Rosemary Kutchie
Champion-Humboldt Community School
Champion, Michigan

CHICKEN TACOS
Number of Servings — 8

1 fryer, cut up
3 T. salad oil
½ c. water
32 corn tortillas (approximate)
½ c. salad oil
1 lettuce, shredded
6 tomatoes, cubed
3 avocadoes, sliced
3 jalapenos peppers, sliced thinly

Brown fryer lightly in salad oil. Add water, cook 45 minutes. Cool, strip meat thinly from bones. Salt and pepper to taste. Heat rest of salad oil. Place tortillas in oil, one at a time, to soften for 1 minute. Fill center of tortilla with meat, roll, secure with toothpick. Brown to desired crispness. Serve 4 per person with salad and jalapenos sprinkled over the tacos.

Jilma G. Vidaurri, Cunningham Jr. H. S.
Corpus Christi, Texas

CHICKEN TERIYAKI
Number of Servings — 4

2 small frying chickens
½ c. imported soy sauce
5 T. sugar
1 t. sodium glutamate
2 c. steamed rice

(Continued on Next Page)

Cut fryers in bite-size pieces. Fry chicken pieces in deep fat at a medium temperature until done. Be careful not to let chicken get brown or crusty. Mix sugar, sodium glutamate, with soy sauce and stir until dissolved. Pour sauce in frying pan and add chicken; turn burner to medium and cover. In 3-4 minutes when boils, remove cover and stir chicken until a glaze forms on meat pieces. Keep burner low so sauce won't burn. Serve with hot rice and pour left-over sauce over it.

Mrs. May Round, Jones Jr. H. S.
Laurel, Mississippi

CHICKEN TETRAZINNI
Number of Servings — 8-10 with "seconds"

1 hen
Salt and pepper
1 package spaghetti
4 cans cream of mushroom soup
2 medium sized bell peppers, chopped
1 c. chopped celery
4 small garlic cloves
4 medium onions, chopped
½ c. chopped almonds

Boil hen until completely tender. Cut into chunks. Cook spaghetti in the boiling chicken broth until tender. Chop together celery, peppers, onions and minced garlic. Tenderize in little oil or fat. Add to the spaghetti. Add the chopped chicken and mushroom soup. Add chopped almonds, salt and pepper. Pour into casserole. Cover with grated cheese. Bake in moderate oven 30-40 minutes.

Mrs. Mary L. Whitley, Caledonia H. S.
Caledonia, Mississippi

TURKEY BOMBAY
Number of Servings — 4

2 T. curry powder
4 T. butter
3 medium onions (1½ c.)
2 T. flour
2 chicken bouillon cubes
2 c. water
1 c. (about 9 oz.) crushed pineapple
3 c. diced turkey, cooked
2 T. lemon juice
½ t. ground ginger

Heat curry powder in butter in large frying pan, stirring often, 2 or 3 minutes. Stir in onions and cook until softened. Blend in flour and ginger, then add bouillon cubes, water and pineapple and syrup. Heat to boiling, stirring until cubes are dissolved; simmer, uncovered, 5 minutes. Stir in turkey, cover, simmer 10 minutes more. Stir in lemon juice. Serve with Rice Mingle.

RICE MINGLE

½ c. brown rice
1 t. salt
3 c. boiling water
½ c. white rice
1 pimento, diced

¼ c. chopped pecans or pistachio nuts

Stir in brown rice and salt into boiling water in large heavy saucepan, cover, simmer 20 minutes. Stir in white rice; cover again; simmer, stirring once or twice with a fork, 15 to 20 minutes, or until rices are tender and water is absorbed. Stir in pimento and nuts; heat, shaking pan gently, 1 to 2 minutes to dry and fluff rice. Serves 4.

Mary K. Albrittain, Glasva H. S.
Faulkner, Maryland

SOPA ELEGANTE
Number of Servings — 8

1½ c. turkey, diced
¼ c. minced onion
¼ lb. cashew nuts
¼ c. sherry
1 c. celery, diced
1 can mushroom soup
1 can Chinese noodles
Peas and mushrooms to taste

Combine all ingredients but keep half of noodles for top. Toss all ingredients lightly together. Bake 30 minutes at 325°F.

Leda Callahan, Ysleta H. S.
El Paso, Texas

Wild Game

CABRITO CASSEROLE
Number of Servings — 6-8

¼ cabrito (billy goat)
1 can (No. 303) whole tomatoes
½ can tomato sauce
1 t. pepper
3 T. salad oil
1 T. salt
½ t. oregano
½ t. garlic salt
1 T. Worcestershire sauce

Cut cabrito in small pieces. Cook over medium heat until brown in salad oil. Combine all other ingredients and add to cabrito. Add about ¼ cup water and let it simmer for about 15 minutes.

Estela Carrera, Roma H. S.
Roma, Texas

CURRY AND RICE (NEW ZEALAND)
Number of Servings — 4

1 lb. mutton
1 oz. drippings
1 onion
1 apple
1 oz. flour
2 t. curry powder
2 t. chutney

(Continued on Next Page)

1 t. salt
¾ pt. stock or water

Melt drippings, lightly fry the onion; add cut up apple and cubes of meat (fat removed) coated with flour. Add curry and seasonings, then add stock or water. Bring to simmering point and cook gently for 2 hours. Coconut or raisins may be added. Serve with a border or boiled rice.

Mary Jane McMillion, South Lebanon H. S.
Lebanon, Pennsylvania

ORIENTAL PHEASANT
Number of Servings — 8-10

½ c. butter
½ c. flour
1 T. salt
1 c. cream
3 c. milk
2 c. pheasant stock

Melt butter in top of double boiler, add flour and salt and cook until bubbly; add cream, milk, and stock, stirring until smooth. Cook over hot water for 30 minutes. Just before serving add and heat thoroughly 2 cups diced pheasant, ½ cup sauteed mushrooms, ½ cup blanched almonds, 1 cup sliced water chestnuts and ¼ cup pimento, cut in strips. Serve over cheese souffle, or in a pastry shell; over rice, or what have you.

Mrs. Frances B. Baker, Senior H. S.
Denton, Texas

CARNE DE VENADO AL ESTILO NUEVO MEXICAN (Venison, New Mexico Style)
Number of Servings — 6

1 lb. lean, twice ground venison
Salt and pepper to taste
½ c. cooking wine (home made Mission Grape or commercial)
4 T. salad oil
1 large clove garlic, chopped
¼ c. wine (cooking type)
¼ c. tomato sauce
½ t. sugar
¼ t. sweet basil leaves, ground between fingers
¼ t. oregano leaves, ground between fingers
3 T. red chili (enchilida sauce) from hot red large chili pepper

Combine meat, salt, pepper and cooking wine; mix well and form into 6 patties. Pan broil or oven broil. Baste frequently before turning and after turning with the following sauce prepared from the remaining ingredients. Brown garlic in salad oil and add remaining ingredients in order named above; simmer a few minutes before basting meat patties. NOTE: Antelope, ground, or any wild meat may be substituted as well as beef or lamb. A venison or antelope roast marinated in cooking wine for 24 hours before placing in roaster and basted frequently with sauce of the above ingredients is very tasty.

Lelia Cook Greenwald, Socorro H. S.
Socorro, New Mexico

REHKOTELETT (VENISON STEAK)
Number of Servings — 6

2 lbs. venison
1 stick celery
2 carrots
1 onion
1 leek
4 slices white crustless bread
3 oz. butter
1 oz. flour
½ bottle white wine
1 oz. truffle
Sugar, salt and pepper
½ t. meat extract

Hammer the meat lightly, skin and wash it. Cut into thick steaks. Fry the onion in butter, add the other vegetables, and about one pint of boiling water. Bring to the boil, add the meat extract, and cook until you have a well-flavored stock. Thicken with flour, add the wine, sugar, salt and pepper, then rub through a fine wire sieve. Dip the steaks into this sauce, then fry on both sides in fat until tender, adding the truffle. Cut the bread into triangles and fry until crisp. Arrange the steaks on a hot plate, cover with the sauce, and garnish with the bread. Serve with chestnuts, glazed or mashed, and sauteed small potato balls.

Christine Knutson, Perham Public H. S.
Perham, Minnesota

DANISH RULLEPOLSE (ROLLED MEAT FOR SANDWICHES)
Number of Servings — 100 thin slices

1 double breast of venison (beef or a combination of both)
1 T. salt
½ t. allspice or cloves
½ t. pepper
1 T. grated onion
1 t. (scant) saltpeter

Remove bones and sinews from meat and wash thoroughly. Sew pieces together to form large square or rectangle. Flatten out and sprinkle on whole surface: salt, pepper, allspice, onion, and saltpeter. Roll very tightly and hold with meat fork while sewing ends and sides. Tie around with cord and place in brine. Make brine by dissolving 1 pound un-iodized salt, ½ teaspoon saltpeter, and ¼ cup sugar in 2½ quarts boiling water. Chill thoroughly before using. After 10 days remove meat from brine and cover with boiling water. Boil slowly 2 hours. Drain. Place in a clean cloth, roll up and place between 2 boards or platters and press by placing a weight over platter. When cool remove, slice thin for open face sandwiches. Note: If beef or veal is used, use flanks, remove sinews and tough portions. Place strips of fat inside in order that the pressed meat should not be too dry. To sew this meat thread a darning needle with white greased cord or dental floss. The venison is best also if you trim off as much fat as possible.

Mrs. Edith Jorgensen, Emery H. S.
Emery, South Dakota

Miscellaneous

LUTE FISH UND POTATOES
Number of Servings — 6-8

2 or 3 lbs. lute fish
4 c. medium white sauce
8 medium potatoes
8 T. horseradish
¼ lb. margarine

Cook lute fish until skin and bones loosen. Drain. Save 1 cup broth. Remove all bones and skin. Make 4 cups medium white sauce with 3 cups milk and 1 cup broth. Cook potatoes in jackets until tender, peel. Warm horseradish and butter. Serve potatoes topped by fish, white sauce and horseradish sauce.

Ruth E. Carlson, Donovan H. S.
Donovan, Illinois

INDIAN SHRIMP CURRY
Number of Servings — 6-8

Simmer until tender 5 tablespoons butter and ½ cup minced onions. Put into top of double boiler, then add 6 tablespoons flour, 2½ teaspoons curry powder, 1¼ teaspoons salt, 1¼ teaspoons sugar and ¼ teaspoon ground ginger. Gradually add 1 chicken bouillon cube dissolved in 1 cup boiling water. Add 2 cups milk. Cook over boiling water, stirring until thickened. Add 3 pounds shrimp, cooked and cleaned and 1 teaspoon lemon juice. Serve hot with hot rice ring. 1 to 1½ cups white rice, cooked. Serve with curry in center of rice ring. Serve with curry accompaniments: chutney, tomato wedges, raisins, salted peanuts, snipped parsley, sauted onion rings, crisp bacon bits, chopped egg.

Phayee Mizell, Riverdale H. S.
Riverdale, California

CHINESE TUNA
Number of Servings — 6-8

2 cans tuna
2 cans chow mein noodles
2 cans mushroom soup
¼ c. diced green pepper
¼ c. diced onion
1 39c package cashew nuts
1 T. margarine

Saute green pepper and onion in 1 tablespoon margarine. In 9 x 9 casserole dish place layers of ingredients in this order: 1 can tuna, 1 can mushroom soup, ½ of onion and green pepper mixture, ½ of nuts, and 1 can chow mein noodles. Repeat second layer in same order, topping with chow mein noodles. Bake in 350°F. oven 30 minutes. Serve with fresh vegetables, salad and tea.

Guy'lene Stover, Canyon H. S.
Canyon, Texas

MEXICAN TOSTADOS
Number of Servings — 6

6 tortillas
1 lb. uncooked pinto beans, or 2 cans refried beans
1 head lettuce, cut in bite size pieces
3 medium size tomatoes, cut in bite size pieces
1 lb. grated cheddar cheese
12 radish roses, for garnish
12 ripe olives, for garnish

Pinto beans should be cooked with seasoning until done, then put in skillet with ⅓ cup oil and cooked until a paste. Fry tortillas in skillet to which ½ cup oil has been added until lightly crisp on each side. On each tortilla place a layer of fried beans, lettuce, tomato, grated cheese and top with 2 olives on each and 2 radish roses. Serves 6.

Mrs. Marjorie L. Burke, Cherryvale H. S.
Cherryvale, Kansas

SOUR CREAM ENCHILADAS
Number of Servings — 6

1 10-oz. can enchilada sauce
1 1-lb. can tomatoes
1 small onion, chopped
½ t. salt
½ lb. grated cheese
1 dozen corn tortillas
1 c. sour cream
Cooking oil

In saucepan, combine tomatoes, enchilada sauce, onion and salt. Heat to boiling point. Dip tortillas in hot cooking oil for several seconds to soften, then drain. Make enchiladas this way: On each tortilla place a generous tablespoon of sauce and some grated cheese. Roll up and place in casserole. Pour remaining sauce over the enchiladas and heat in 450°F. oven for five minutes. Serve individually or in casserole with sour cream (at room temperature) spooned on top of enchiladas. Garnish, if desired, with strips of green peeled chili. Makes 12 enchiladas (6 servings).

Gloria R. McHenry, East Jr. H. S.
Mesa, Arizona

ADDITIONAL FOREIGN RECIPES MAY BE FOUND IN MANY OTHER SECTIONS OF THE BOOK

We wish to gratefully acknowledge those teachers whose recipes were received by the publisher too late for publication. The teachers listed below sent their recipes which were of top quality and which would have been included in the book had they been received sooner.

Mrs. Joyce Alverson, Gordon H. S.
Decatur, Georgia

Glida J. Alexander, Carroll H. S.
Ozark, Alabama

Audrey H. Anderson, Martin Behrman H. S.
New Orleans, Louisiana

Mrs. Shirley A. Anderson, Rock Falls Twp. H. S.
Rock Falls, Illinois

Mrs. Jean Applegarth, Smith Center H. S.
Smith Center, Kansas

Mrs. Nell M. Arnold, Russellville H. S.
Russellville, Alabama

Mrs. Henrietta C. Auman, Hillsboro H. S.
Hillsboro, North Carolina

Edna Axt, Gackle Special H. S.
Gackle, North Dakota

Mrs. J. T. Barnett, Tulia H. S.
Tulia, Texas

Mrs. Edna Earle Beck, Anson H. S.
Anson, Texas

Ella Sue Beck, Lanark H. S.
Lanark, Illinois

Mrs. Carol Bedsole, Santo H. S.
Santo, Texas

Mrs. Ira Black, Sulphur Springs H. S.
Sulphur Springs, Texas

Mrs. Lois Borba, Gustine Union H S.
Gustine, California

Mrs. Pearl D. Bowman, Atascadero Union H. S.
Atascadero, California

Virginia Boxley, Tyronza H. S.
Tyronza, Arkansas

Mrs. Helen W. Brink,
South Williamsport Area H. S.
South Williamsport, Pennsylvania

Mrs. Bernice Britt, West Hardin County H. S.
Saratoga, Texas

Mrs. Lorajane Bolli, Burwell Public School
Burwell, Nebraska

Mrs. Louise Bush, Shady Grove H. S.
Laurel, Mississippi

Mrs. Margaret Campbell, Chumuckla H. S.
Milton, Florida

Mrs. Mary Beth Carruthers, Buna H. S.
Buna, Texas

Mrs. Barbara B. Cavin, Fort Payne H. S.
Fort Payne, Alabama

Mrs. Louise Chambers, Weinert Rural H. S.
Weinert, Texas

Marjorie Chaney, Zachary H. S.
Zachary, Louisiana

Mrs. Mary Jo Clapp, Jamaica Con. H. S.
Sidell, Illinois

Mrs. Jack Clinton, Limestone H. S.
Peoria, Illinois

Betty Clyburn, Man H. S.
Man, West Virginia

Bernice M. Cobb, Westminster H. S.
Westminster, Colorado

Eileen Collins, Church Hill H. S.
Church Hill, Tennessee

Mrs. Frances Conway, Walla Walla H. S.
Walla Walla, Washington

Mary Alice Covelli, Weldon Valley H. S.
Weldona, Colorado

Mrs. Gloria Costello, Coulterville H. S.
Coulterville, Illinois

Mrs. Effie Crawford, Clarke Com. H. S.
Osceola, Iowa

Mrs. Mary Criss, Stranahan H. S.
Fort Lauderdale, Florida

Pat Crouch, Aiken H. S.
Aiken, South Carolina

Mrs. Estella Crowell, Whitmore Lake H. S.
Whitmore Lake, Michigan

Thrath C. Curry, Carrollton H. S.
Carrollton, Alabama

Mrs. Christine Dale, Toccopola H. S.
University, Mississippi

Helen Danaher, Ida Grove H. S.
Ida Grove, Iowa

Mrs. Frances D. Daniel, Central Gwinnett H. S.
Lawrenceville, Georgia

Jean Darnell, Brookport H. S.
Brookport, Illinois

Mrs. Runette Davis, Glynn Co. Jr. H. S.
Brunswick, Georgia

Mrs. Delores Dexter, Spearfish H. S.
Spearfish, South Dakota

Joyce Ann Dixon, Plano H. S.
Plano, Illinois

Mildred H. Dodge, Wyalusing Valley Jt. H. S.
Wyalusing, Pennsylvania

Lorena G. Donsted, San Simon H. S.
San Simon, Arizona

Mrs. Peggy Draughn, Benton H. S.
Benton, Mississippi

Mrs. Audrey Eckert, Dakota Lutheran Academy
Minot, North Dakota

Vivian Eggers, Chester H. S.
Chester, Illinois

Mrs. Harold England, Owen County H. S.
Owenton, Kentucky

Margaret Fagot, Fairbury-Cropsey H. S.
Fairbury, Illinois

Freda Ferguson, Prague H. S.
Prague, Oklahoma

Dorothea C. Ferrill, Pueblo County H. S.
Pueblo, Colorado

(Continued on Next Page)

Mrs. Joel Ferrell, Brinkley H. S.
Brinkley, Arkansas

Dora Helen Caldwell Fields
Pendleton Memorial H. S.
Falmouth, Kentucky

Nadine Flippo, Biggers-Reyno H. S.
Biggers, Arkansas

Mrs. Louise Frame, Coraopolis Jr. H. S.
Coraopolis, Pennsylvania

Mrs. Harriet Frederick, Guernsey H. S.
Guernsey, Wyoming

Cecilia Gallegos, West Las Vegas H. S.
Las Vegas, New Mexico

Sarah Beth Galloway, Rigby H. S.
Rigby, Idaho

Lois S. Gass, Mahanoy Joint H. S.
Herndon, Pennsylvania

Gladys Glendenning, Grand Junction H. S.
Grand Junction, Colorado

Mildred B. Goe, Wy'east H. S.
Hood River, Oregon

Mrs. L. E. Golding, Elk Creek H. S.
Elk Creek, California

Mrs. Viola Gracey, Hermleigh H. S.
Hermleigh, Texas

Mary Jane Greer, Livingston Central H. S.
Burna, Kentucky

Eloise W. Hadden, Auburn H. S.
Auburn, Kentucky

Mrs. Tommy Lee Hailey, Marfa H. S.
Marfa, Texas

Mrs. Betty Hall, Crossville H. S.
Crossville, Illinois

Carrie L. Haney, Saltillo H. S.
Saltillo, Tennessee

Mrs. Clara Handley, La Cygne Rural H. S.
La Cygne, Kansas

Mrs. L. E. Hansberger, Canton Sr. H. S.
Canton, Illinois

Mrs. Mary C. Harbour, Philadelphia H. S.
Philadelphia, Mississippi

Carol Hedges, Fort Recovery H. S.
Fort Recovery, Ohio

Louise Herrin, Three Forks H. S.
Three Forks, Montana

Carole Hillen, Ganesha H. S.
Pomona, California

Carrie E. Hinton, Morton Attendance Center
Morton, Mississippi

Mrs. H. H. Hitchcock, Healdton H. S.
Healdton, Oklahoma

Mrs. Peggy Hogan, Fannindel H. S.
Ladonia, Texas

Beda Sue Hogue, Green Forest H. S.
Green Forest, Arkansas

Frances Holben, Stonington H. S.
Stonington, Illinois

Mary Ellen Hoyt, Eaton Rapids H. S.
Eaton Rapids, Michigan

Mrs. June Hubbard, Louisville H. S.
Louisville, Colorado

Mrs. Ruth C. Humphrey, Wheeler County H. S.
Alamo, Georgia

Sally F. Humphries, Driftwood Jr. H. S.
Hollywood, Florida

Mrs. Clifford Irwin, Shawnee H. S.
Wolf Lake, Illinois

Mrs. Gaynelle James, Gardner H. S.
Gardner, Illinois

Nana E. James, Southeastern H. S.
Hammond, Louisiana

Mrs. Jane P. Janey, Giles H. S.
Pearisburg, Virginia

Wilmetta I. Jessick, Harbor Springs H. S.
Harbor Springs, Michigan

Mrs. Charles E. Johnson, Southeast H. S.
Bradenton, Florida

Mrs. Gladys Johnston, Clear Lake H. S.
Clear Lake, South Dakota

Mrs. Carol Jones, Prospect H. S.
Mt. Prospect, Illinois

Mrs. Shirley Jones, Dunlap H. S.
Dunlap, Illinois

Eleanor Johnson, Chetek H. S.
Chetek, Wisconsin

Madeline Johnson, Pinehurst Jr. H. S.
Pinehurst, Idaho

Ann Kathman, Fairfield H. S.
Fairfield, Montana

Eleanor Jane Keim, Winola H. S.
Viola, Illinois

Sarah P. Kenamond, Lewisburg Joint H. S.
Lewisburg, Pennsylvania

Mrs. Sylvia O. Kinder, Briarcliff H. S.
Atlanta, Georgia

Flora A. Koetsier, Berrien Springs Sr. H. S.
Berrien Springs, Michigan

Dianne Kroeger, Wilton Junction H. S.
Wilton Junction, Iowa

Mrs. Violet Kueker, Community Unit Dist. No. 5
Waterloo, Illinois

Mrs. Agnes R. LaFleur, Lawtell H. S.
Lawtell, Louisiana

DeWayne Law, Valley H. S.
Hot Springs, Virginia

Mrs. Carrie Lou Limb, Chetopa H. S.
Chetopa, Kansas

Hazel I. Lindquist, Highland Park H. S.
Topeka, Kansas

Mrs. Grace B. Loos, Marion H. S.
Marion, Illinois

Mrs. Lorena Maddox, Garden Grove Union H. S.
Garden Grove, California

Mrs. Jennie June Magnuson, Woodburn H. S.
Woodburn, Oregon

Mrs. Mildred Mahan, Sheridan Rural Agr. School
Sheridan, Michigan

(Continued on Next Page)

Shirley M. Markham, Lewes Special School
Lewes, Delaware

Mrs. Joyce H. Marks, Escambia H. S.
Pensacola, Florida

Mrs. Boone Martin, Panhandle H. S.
Panhandle, Texas

Mrs. Ruth Martin, Senior H. S.
Weatherford, Texas

Mrs. Dorothy Martinson, Prospect H. S.
Mt. Prospect, Illinois

Mrs. Lynda K. Mayfield, Azle H. S.
Azle, Texas

Amelean Maud, Adena H. S.
Adena, Ohio

Mrs. Helen Ruth McElwee, Veedersburg H. S.
Veedersburg, Indiana

Mrs. Rebecca McGaughy, Montevallo H. S.
Montevallo, Alabama

Lucile B. McGehee, Southwest DeKalb H. S.
South Decatur, Georgia

Regene McNair, Bullock Co. H. S.
Union Springs, Alabama

Mildred McNutt, Lodi H. S.
Lodi, Wisconsin

Ruth L. Meis, Mt. Pleasant H. S.
Mt. Pleasant, Michigan

Sue C. Melton, Alwood H. S.
Woodhull, Illinois

Mrs. Myrtle Menefee, Clint H. S.
Clint, Texas

Barbara Miller, New London H. S.
New London, Minnesota

Mrs. Katie Moon, Senior H. S.
Jonesboro, Arkansas

Della Jean Morris, Central H. S.
Florence, Alabama

Mildred H. Morris, Reeltown H. S.
Notasulga, Alabama

Mrs. E. G. Mosley
Batesville, Arkansas

Mrs. Elizabeth Moss, Home Economics Supvr.
Memphis City Schools
Memphis, Tennessee

Mrs. Beverly Murphy, Middleton H. S.
Middleton, Wisconsin

Mrs. Faye L. Murphy, Azle H. S.
Azle, Texas

Mary Nell Noble, Delaplaine H. S.
Delaplaine, Arkansas

Maribeth Page, Conecut Co. H. S.
Castleberry, Alabama

Gladys Parry, Two Harbors H. S.
Two Harbors, Minnesota

Gregorita Pera, Arroyo Grande Union H. S.
Arroyo Grande, California

Mrs. Marie Della-Penna, Jefferson Union H. S.
Richmond, Ohio

Ramona Sue Perkins
Howard, Kansas

Mrs. Clemit Phillips, Star City H. S.
Star City, Arkansas

Elizabeth Phillips, Asheboro H. S.
Asheboro, North Carolina

Lodi M. Pierce, Block H. S.
Jonesville, Louisiana

Mrs. Eunice A. Pretila, Naperville Com. H. S.
Naperville, Illinois

Dorotha Prowell, Hereford Sr. H. S.
Hereford, Texas

Mrs. Ruth Radcliffe, Litchville H. S.
Litchville, North Dakota

Frances Rademacher, Calipatria H. S.
Calipatria, California

Louise Rasmussen, Owen-Withee Jr. H. S.
Withee, Wisconsin

Mrs. Barbara Rawdon, Grants Sr. H. S.
Grants, New Mexico

Mrs. Jane Recktenwald, Coats H. S.
Coats, North Carolina

Mrs. Mary Reece, Warsaw H. S.
Warsaw, Indiana

Violet Rhodes, Odin Community H. S.
Odin, Illinois

Mrs. Ruth Riffe, Hobart H. S.
Hobart, Oklahoma

Mrs. Fred Roberson, Central H. S.
Cookeville, Tennessee

Mrs. Norma Jean Rogers
Thoreau Intermediate School
Vienna, Virginia

Josephine Rummler, Belding Area Schools
Belding, Michigan

Mrs. Mary Sallee, Pocahontas H. S.
Pocahontas, Arkansas

Mrs. Marguerite Samples, Ballard Mem. H. S.
Barlow, Kentucky

Mrs. Delores Sandbeck, Dilworth H. S.
Dilworth, Minnesota

Grace A. Schmidt, Hippner H. S.
Hippner, Oregon

Nevaleen Joy Selmat, Covington H. S.
Covington, Oklahoma

Mrs. Laura D. Selph, Cotton Valley H. S.
Cotton Valley, Louisiana

Mrs. Lois Simmonds, DeSoto H. S.
DeSoto, Wisconsin

Mrs. Gloria Smith, Valders H. S.
Valders, Wisconsin

Grace L. Smith, North Whitfield H. S.
Dalton, Georgia

Joyce F. Smith, Carl Hayden H. S.
Phoenix, Arizona

Mrs. Phyllis Smith, Brownstown Com. H. S.
Brownstown, Illinois

Mrs. Mae R. Smythe, East Lynn H. S.
East Lynn, Illinois

Margaret Q. Snelgrove, Baron DeKalb H. S.
Westville, South Carolina

(Continued on Next Page)

Mrs. Eunie V. C. Stacy, Marthaville H. S.
Marthaville, Louisiana

Bonnie Lu Standaert, Cashton Public H. S.
Cashton, Wisconsin

Donnalie Stratton, Johns Creek H. S.
Pikeville, Kentucky

Wanda Sullivan, Gillham H. S.
Gillham, Arkansas

Nina Swindler, Newbern H. S.
Newbern, Tennessee

Mrs. Momoyo Tada, Airport Jr. H. S.
Los Angeles, California

Bernice Tanner, Columbus H. S.
Columbus, Indiana

Mrs. Virginia N. Tandy, F. H. A. Advisor
Lexington H. S., Lexington, Virginia

Mrs. Melvin Tavares, Kempton Cabery H. S.
Kempton, Illinois

Mrs. Audra Taylor, Triopia Sr. H. S.
Chapin, Illinois

Margaret Sue Thomas, Atoka H. S.
Atoka, Oklahoma

Deanna Thompson, Linden H. S.
Linden, Indiana

Joyce Thompson, Wilson H. S.
Wilson, Oklahoma

Dimple F. Turner, Christian County H. S.
Hopkinsville, Kentucky

Earle H. Vallentine, Edisto H. S.
Cordova, South Carolina

Mavis W. Van Beek, Central H. S.
Aberdeen, South Dakota

Mary Fern Vanpool, Berryhill H. S.
Tulsa, Oklahoma

Leona Curtis Vaughn, Ferndale Sr. H. S.
Ferndale, Washington

Mrs. Emagene Veal, Dallas H. S.
Dallas, Oregon

Doris S. Vicars, J. J. Kelly H. S.
Wise, Virginia

Mrs. Alice M. Waldron, Klamath Union H. S.
Klamath Falls, Oregon

Mrs. Willene Walsh, Union City H. S.
Union City, Oklahoma

Mrs. Marie K. Webster, Sugar-Salem H. S.
Sugar City, Idaho

Mrs. Frances M. Whited, Toledo H. S.
Toledo, Oregon

Annie Lou Wigley, Buckhorn H. S.
Huntsville, Alabama

Lucinda B. Wild, South Emery H. S.
Ferron, Utah

Mrs. Doris T. Wildes, Surrency H. S.
Surrency, Georgia

Mrs. Edna K. Wilk, Pine H. S.
Franklinton, Louisiana

LaVergne Wilken, Burlington H. S.
Burlington, Colorado

Mrs. Juanita Willis, Carlsbad Sr. H. S.
Carlsbad, New Mexico

Mrs. Nancy Williston, Lakers H. S.
Pigeon, Michigan

Naomia Wilson, Auburn H. S.
Auburn, Alabama

Mrs. Helen H. Wise, Manheim Twp. Sr. H. S.
Neffsville, Pennsylvania

Patricia Woller, Villa Grove H. S.
Villa Grove, Illinois

Jessie B. Wood, Addison H. S.
Addison, Alabama

Nannie Lou Wulff, Hot Springs Sr. H. S.
Hot Springs, Arkansas

Mrs. Martha Zimmorman, Taylorsville H. S.
Taylorsville, Illinois

INDEX

The recipes are indexed according to the following sections:

Many of the recipes with a basic title, such as Meat Loaf, can be found in two or more sections since these recipes can be prepared by using various types of meats. Therefore, by referring to more than one section, you may find alternate methods of preparing recipes of this type.

(Continued on Next Page)

INDEX (Continued)

(Continued on Next Page)

(Continued on Next Page)

INDEX (Continued)

(Continued on Next Page)

INDEX (Continued)

Order Blanks Over

Share These Favorite Recipes

ORDER A BOOK FOR A FRIEND

- *Nearly 2,000 Favorite Meat Recipes*
  - *Spiral Bound — Plastic Coated Cover*
    - *Meat Cut Photographs*
  - *Meat, Herb & Spice Charts*
- *Many other popular features*

Perfect Gift Idea

PUBLISHERS NOTE

You can obtain copies of this book from the F.H.A. Chapter in your community that sold the book. Only F.H.A. Chapters can offer this book for the low price of $2.95. If ordered from the publisher, the price is $3.95 which includes all mailing cost. Fifty-cents from every sale made by the publisher direct goes into a scholarship fund of which all will go to the F.H.A. Chapters who participate in future sales of Favorite Recipes of American Home Economics Teachers.

Order Blanks

Price $3.95 — (includes all mailing cost)

- - - - - - - - - - - - - - - - - - - Cut along line - - - - - - - - - - - - - - - - - - -

ORDER BLANK

Send_____copies of MEATS EDITION

TO:_____

_____

_____

☐ $3.95 per book —
enclosed (check or money order)

☐ Bill me at $4.25 per book
(extra added for billing)
Home-Ec Press

Box 7803   Washington 4, D. C.

ORDER BLANK

Send_____copies of MEATS EDITION

TO:_____

_____

_____

☐ $3.95 per book —
enclosed (check or money order)

☐ Bill me at $4.25 per book
(extra added for billing)
Home-Ec Press

Box 7803   Washington 4, D. C.

- - - - - - - - - - - - - - - - - - - Cut along line - - - - - - - - - - - - - - - - - - -

ORDER BLANK

Send_____copies of MEATS EDITION

TO:_____

_____

_____

☐ $3.95 per book —
enclosed (check or money order)

☐ Bill me at $4.25 per book
(extra added for billing)
Home-Ec Press

Box 7803   Washington 4, D. C.

ORDER BLANK

Send_____copies of MEATS EDITION

TO:_____

_____

_____

☐ $3.95 per book —
enclosed (check or money order)

☐ Bill me at $4.25 per book
(extra added for billing)
Home-Ec Press

Box 7803   Washington 4, D. C.

- - - - - - - - - - - - - - - - - - - Cut along line - - - - - - - - - - - - - - - - - - -

Gift Order

Send one copy of
MEATS EDITION

TO:_____
              Name

_____
              Address

_____
City   State

☐ $3.95 Enclosed
☐ Bill me at $4.25

_____
              My Name

_____
              Address

_____
City   State